Acronyms, Initialisms & Abbreviations Dictionary

Supplement

DSC

Acronyms, Initialisms & Abbreviations Dictionary

Supplement

VOLUME 2 of
Acronyms, Initialisms & Abbreviations Dictionary
Twenty-Fourth Edition

*A Guide to Acronyms, Abbreviations,
Contractions, Alphabetic Symbols, and Similar Condensed Appellations*

Covering: Aerospace, Associations, Banking, Biochemistry, Business, Data Processing,
Domestic and International Affairs, Economics, Education, Electronics, Genetics,
Government, Information Technology, Internet, Investment, Labor, Law, Medicine, Military Affairs,
Periodicals, Pharmacy, Physiology, Politics, Religion, Science, Societies, Sports, Technical
Drawings and Specifications, Telecommunications, Trade, Transportation, and Other Fields

Mary Rose Bonk
Editor

Pamela Dear
Associate Editor

Phyllis Spinelli
Assistant Editor

GALE

DETROIT · NEW YORK · LONDON

Editor: Mary Rose Bonk

Associate Editor: Pamela Dear
Assistant Editor: Phyllis Spinelli

Contributing Editors: Mildred Hunt, Miriam M. Steinert

Data Entry Manager: Eleanor M. Allison
Data Entry Coordinator: Kenneth Benson
Data Entry Associates: Arlene Kevonian, Constance Wells

Production Director: Mary Beth Trimper
Production Assistant: Shanna Heilveil

Graphic Services Manager: Barbara J. Yarrow
Desktop Publisher: Gary Leach

Manager, Technical Support Services: Theresa A. Rocklin
Programmer: Charles Beaumont

Library of Congress Catalog Number 84-643188
ISBN 0-7876-2142-0
ISSN 0270-4404

Printed in the United States of America

Contents

Gale's publications in the acronyms and abbreviations field include:

***Acronyms, Initialisms & Abbreviations Dictionary* series:**

Acronyms, Initialisms & Abbreviations Dictionary (Volume 1). A guide to acronyms, initialisms, abbreviations, and similar contractions, arranged alphabetically by abbreviation.

Acronyms, Initialisms & Abbreviations Supplement (Volume 2). An interedition supplement in which terms are arranged alphabetically both by abbreviation and by meaning.

Reverse Acronyms, Initialisms & Abbreviations Dictionary (Volume 3). A companion to Volume 1 in which terms are arranged alphabetically by meaning of the acronym, initialism, or abbreviation.

***Acronyms, Initialisms & Abbreviations Dictionary* Subject Guide series:**

Computer & Telecommunications Acronyms (Volume 1). A guide to acronyms, initialisms, abbreviations, and similar contractions used in the field of computers and telecommunications in which terms are arranged alphabetically both by abbreviation and by meaning.

Business Acronyms (Volume 2). A guide to business-oriented acronyms, initialisms, abbreviations, and similar contractions in which terms are arranged alphabetically both by abbreviation and by meaning.

***International Acronyms, Initialisms & Abbreviations Dictionary* series:**

International Acronyms, Initialisms & Abbreviations Dictionary (Volume 1). A guide to foreign and international acronyms, initialisms, abbreviations, and similar contractions, arranged alphabetically by abbreviation.

Reverse International Acronyms, Initialisms & Abbreviations Dictionary (Volume 2). A companion to Volume 1, in which terms are arranged alphabetically by meaning of the acronym, initialism, or abbreviation.

***Periodical Title Abbreviations* series:**

Periodical Title Abbreviations: By Abbreviation (Volume 1). A guide to abbreviations commonly used for periodical titles, arranged alphabetically by abbreviation.

Periodical Title Abbreviations: By Title (Volume 2). A guide to abbreviations commonly used for periodical titles, arranged alphabetically by title.

New Periodical Title Abbreviations (Volume 3). An interedition supplement in which terms are arranged alphabetically both by abbreviation and by title.

A Word about
Acronyms, Initialisms & Abbreviations
Dictionary Supplement

> Contains nearly 10,000 newly coined or newly found terms

As acronyms continue to simplify and accelerate modern communication, the need for timely access remains essential. Publication of this supplement to the twenty-fourth edition of *Acronyms, Initialisms & Abbreviations Dictionary (AIAD)* makes terms available while their currency is at a peak, keeping you informed and up to date in a constantly expanding field.

Timely Coverage

The more dynamic fields of endeavor tend to generate the largest number of acronyms. *Acronyms, Initialisms & Abbreviations Dictionary Supplement (AIAD-S)* reflects this trend by providing increased coverage in:

- the Arts

- Education

- the Internet

- Finance

- Periodicals

Current events and new technology often produce abbreviated designations intended as time and space savers. Colorful examples in this supplement include:

- ALPHA...................Alternative Learning Program for High School Age

- BEARS...................Bond Enabling Annual Retirement Savings

- BLAM.....................Barrel-Launched Adaptive Munitions

- DEWKS..................Dual Employed with Kids

Major Sources Cited

AIAD-S, like *AIAD*, contains entries from a wide variety of sources. Although many terms are from published sources, the majority of entries are sent by outside contributors, are uncovered through independent research by the editorial staff, or are located in miscellaneous broadcast or print media references. Therefore, it is impossible to cite a source on every entry in *AIAD-S*. It was felt, however, that the citation of selected sources would assist the user in his or her research.

A code for the source of the entry (represented in small capital letters within parentheses) is given only for those print sources that provided at least 50 items. Complete bibliographical information about the publications cited can be found in the List of Selected Sources following the User's Guide. The editor will provide further information upon request.

Acknowledgments

In addition to the inhouse staff, other people have contributed significantly to the compilation of this supplement. The editor wishes to thank Mildred Hunt, Monica Langley, James U. Rose, Janet I. Rose, Miriam M. Steinert, and Tracey Head Turbett for their contributions.

Available in Electronic Format

AIAD and *AIAD-S* are available for licensing on magnetic tape or diskette in a fielded format. Either the complete database or a custom selection of entries may be ordered. The database is available for internal data processing and nonpublishing purposes only. For more information, call 800-877-GALE.

Comments and Suggestions Are Welcome

Users can make unique and important contributions to future supplements and new editions by notifying the editor of subject fields that are not adequately covered, by suggesting sources for covering such fields, and even by sending individual terms they feel should be included.

User's Guide

Acronyms, Initialisms & Abbreviations Dictionary Supplement comprises two sections, providing numeric and alphabetic access to entries either by acronym or by meaning.

By Acronym Section

Acronyms are arranged alphabetically in letter-by-letter sequence, regardless of spacing, punctuation, or capitalization. If the same abbreviation has more than one meaning, the various meanings are then subarranged alphabetically in word-by-word sequence. Entries may contain some of the elements noted in the example below:

Abbreviation or acronym ─

Location ─

English Translation─

Sponsoring Organization ─

AP	Absolute Pardon
A/P	Account-Purchase Phrase
A & P	Agricultural and Pastoral
ap	Antiperiplanar [*Chemistry*]
AP	Appendectomy
APA	Automobile Protection Association [*Canada*]
APB	All Points Bulletin
APC	Anno post Christum Natum [*Latin*]
APC	Archives Publiques du Canada [*Public Archives of Canada*]
APC	Area Planning Council [*Department of Education*]
APCA	Aft Power Controller Assembly (MCD)

─ Meaning or Phrase

─ Subject area

─ Language

─ Source code (Decoded in the List of Selected Sources)

By Meaning Section

Terms are arranged in word-by-word sequence according to the explanation of the acronym. Minor parts of speech (articles, conjunctions, prepositions) are generally not considered in the alphabetizing. If a particular explanation of the acronym has more than one initialism representing it, the various choices are then subarranged alphabetically, letter-by-letter, as they are in the *By Acronym* section.

Meaning or Phrase ─

Second Audio Program	SAP
Second Audio Program	SAPRO
Second Audio Program	SECAP
Second Base [*Baseball*]	2B
Secondary School Admission Test Board [*Princeton, NJ*]	SSATB
Secretariat for Catholic-Jewish Relations	CJR
Secretariat Europeen des Fabricants d'Emballages Metalliques Legers [*European Secretariat of Manufacturers of Light Metal Packages*]	SEFEL
Secretariat for Hispanic Affairs [*National Conference of Catholic Bishops*]	SHA
Secundum [*Latin*]	SEC
Secure Acoustic Data Relay	SADR

─ Abbreviation or Acronym

List of Selected Sources

Each of the print sources included in the following list contributed at least 50 terms. It would be impossible to cite a source for every entry because the majority of terms are sent by outside contributors, are uncovered through independent research by the editorial staff, or are located in miscellaneous broadcast or print media references.

Unless further described in an annotation, the publications listed here contain no additional information about the acronym, initialism, or abbreviation. The editor will provide further information about these sources upon request.

(AD)   *Abbreviations Dictionary.* 8th ed. By Ralph De Sola. Boca Raton, FL: CRC Press, 1992.

(AIE)   *Acronyms and Initialisms in Education.* 6th ed. Compiled by John Hutchins. Norwich, England: Librarians of Institutes and Schools of Education, 1995.

(BRI)   *Book Review Index. 1997 Cumulation.* Edited by Beverly Baer. Detroit, MI: Gale Research, 1998.

(NGC)   *Catalogue of the National Gallery of Canada.* Compiled by National Gallery of Canada. Ottawa, Canada: National Gallery of Canada, 1988.

(DFIT)   *Dictionary of Finance and Investment Terms.* 4th ed. Edited by John Downes and Jordan Elliot Goodman. Hauppauge, NY: Barron's Educational Series, 1995.

(DOM)   *The Dictionary of Multimedia: Terms & Acronyms.* By Brad Hansen. Wilsonville, OR: Franklin, Beedle & Associates, 1997.

(DD)   *The Financial Post Directory of Directors 1997.* Toronto, Canada: The Financial Post, 1996.

(WYGK)   *HR Words You Gotta Know!* By William R. Tracey. New York, NY: AMACOM, 1994.

(VRA)   *VRA Special Bulletin. No. 2, 1987: Standard Abbreviations for Image Descriptions for Use in Fine Arts Visual Resources Collections.* Compiled by Nancy S. Schuller. Austin, TX: Visual Resources Association, 1987.

(WDMC)   *Webster's New World Dictionary of Media and Communications.* Revised and updated ed. By Richard Weiner. New York, NY: Webster's New World, 1996.

Numerics
By Acronym

A
By Acronym

A .... Advanced-Level Examination [*Education*] (AIE)
A .... Includes Extra [*Investment term*] (DFIT)
AAA .... Alberta Association of Architects [*1906*] [*Canada*] (NGC)
AAAGA .... Association of American Geographers Annals [*A publication*] (BRI)
AAE .... African-American English [*A dialect*]
AAE .... Association for Adult Education (AIE)
AAFRC .... American Association of Fund-Raising Counsel, Inc.
AAH .... Apache Attack Helicopter [*Military*] (RDA)
AAMA .... American Automobile Manufacturers Association
A & S Sm .... Air & Space/Smithsonian [*A publication*] (BRI)
AANFM .... Association des Artistes Non Figuratifs de Montreal [*1956-61*] [*Canada*] (NGC)
A Anth .... American Anthropologist [*A publication*] (BRI)
AAP .... Association des Arts Plastiques, Montreal [*1955*] [*Canada*] (NGC)
AAPSS-A ..... American Academy of Political and Social Science. Annals [*A publication*] (BRI)
A Arch .... American Archivist Quarterly [*A publication*] (BRI)
A Art .... American Artist [*A publication*] (BRI)
AATEM .... Association for the Advancement of Teacher Education in Music (AIE)
AAU .... Arua [*Uganda*] [*Airport symbol*] (AD)
AAY .... Al Ghaydah [*Aden*] [*Airport symbol*] (AD)
AB .... AB Bookman's Weekly [*A publication*] (BRI)
AB .... Aharonov-Bohm [*Physics*]
AB .... Falcon Airlines [*ICAO designator*] (AD)
ABA .... Ababa [*Ethiopia*] [*Airport symbol*] (AD)
ABA .... Architectural Barriers Act of 1968 (WYGK)
ABA Jour ..... ABA Journal [*A publication*] (BRI)
abal .... Abalone (VRA)
ABC .... Administrative, Business, and Commercial (AIE)
ABC .... [*Secretary of State Madeleine*] Albright, [*National-Security Adviser Sandy*] Berger, [*and Defense Secretary William*] Cohen [*A troika known in Washington*]
ABCTG .... Administrative, Business, and Commercial Training Group (AIE)
ABE .... Autonomous Benthic Explorer [*Oceanography*]
ABH .... Association of Hispanists of Great Britain and Ireland (AIE)
ABIOS .... Advanced Basic Input/Output System [*Computer science*] (DOM)
ABP .... Account Balance Pension (WYGK)
ABR .... American Book Review [*A publication*] (BRI)
ABRE .... Adoptive Bit Rate Encoding [*Computer science*]
ABS .... Automated Bond System [*Investment term*] (DFIT)
ABSCT .... Autologous Peripheral Blood Stem Cell Transplantation [*Medicine*]
abu .... Aburra (VRA)
ABW .... Abau [*Papua*] [*Airport symbol*] (AD)
ABX .... Albury [*New South Wales*] [*Airport symbol*] (AD)
AC .... Accredited Center [*Youth Training Scheme*] [*British*] (AIE)
AC .... Annotated Card Program
ACA .... Anti-Corruption Agency
ACAA .... Association of Canadian Alumni Administrators
acad .... Academy (VRA)
acad bd .... Academy Board (VRA)
ACAL .... Association for Computer Assisted Learning (AIE)
acant .... Acanthus (VRA)
ACATS .... Advanced Digital Television Service
ACBA .... Associate of the Canadian Bankers Association (DD)
ac/c .... Acrylic on Canvas (VRA)
ACCEPT ...... Addictions Community Centres for Education, Prevention, Treatment, and Research [*British*] (AIE)
ACCO .... Aminocyclopropanecarboxylicacid Oxidase [*An enzyme*]
acctg .... Accounting (DD)
ACE .... Advanced Certificate of Education (AIE)
ACE .... Aids to Communication in Education (AIE)
ACE .... World Association of Commercial and Special Vehicle Editors
ACER .... Afro-Caribbean Educational Resource Project (AIE)
acet .... Acetate (VRA)
ACET .... Advisory Council on Education and Training (AIE)
ACF .... Acquisition Career Field [*Army*] (RDA)
ACF .... Advanced Collaborative Filtering [*Firefly Network*] [*Computer science*]
ACFRE .... Advanced Certified Fund Raising Executive [*National Society of Fund Raising Executives*]
ACG .... Annual Capital Grant [*Education*] (AIE)
ACI .... Alderney [*United Kingdom*] [*Airport symbol*] (AD)
ACIB .... Associate of the Corporation of Insurance Brokers [*Canada*] (DD)
ACIBM .... American Center for Immuno-Biology and Metabolism
ACID test ..... Atomicity, Consistency, Isolation, and Durability Test (DOM)

ACIP .... Advisory Committee on Immunization Practices
ACITT .... Association for Computers and Information Technology in Teaching (AIE)
ACM .... Another Chicago Magazine [*A publication*] (BRI)
ACMA .... Acquisition Career Management Advocate [*Army*] (RDA)
ACN .... Mbala [*Zambia*] [*Airport symbol*] (AD)
ACO .... African Curriculum Organisation (AIE)
ACORDD ..... Advisory Committee for the Research and Development Department [*British Library*] (AIE)
ACQDA .... Arkansas County Quality Deer Association
ACR .... Annual Curriculum Review [*Education*] (AIE)
acrpl .... Acropolis (VRA)
acrt .... Acroteria (VRA)
ACS .... Aerial Common Sensor [*Military*] (RDA)
ACS .... Alternative Curriculum Strategies [*Education*] (AIE)
ACS .... Associate in Customer Service [*Canada*] (DD)
ACSET(FE) ... Advisory Committee for the Supply and Education of Teachers, Further Education Sub-Committee (AIE)
act .... Active (VRA)
ACTEMS .... Advisory Committee for Teacher Education in the Mid-South (AIE)
ActSc .... Actuarial Science (DD)
ACUR .... Ambulatory Care Utilization Review [*Insurance*] (WYGK)
ACV .... Arcata-Eureka [*California*] [*Airport symbol*] (AD)
ACVT .... Advisory Committee for Vocational Training (AIE)
AD .... Exec Express [*ICAO designator*] (AD)
ADAF .... Advection-Dominated Accretion Flow [*Planetary science*]
adb .... Adobe (VRA)
ADC .... Advisory Defense Committee
ADCM .... Art Directors Club of Montreal [*1950*] [*Canada*] (NGC)
A/D converter... Analog-to-Digital Converter [*Computer science*] (DOM)
ADCT .... Art Directors Club of Toronto [*1947*] [*Canada*] (NGC)
ADE .... Association of Directors of Education (AIE)
ADH .... Ada [*Oklahoma*] [*Airport symbol*] (AD)
ADL .... Activities of Daily Living (WYGK)
ADL .... Aerobic Dive Limit [*Pysiology*]
AdmA .... Administrateur Agree [*Canada*] (DD)
admin .... Administration (DD)
AdminSc ...... Administrative Science (DD)
ADN .... Aydin [*Turkey*] [*Airport symbol*] (AD)
Adoles .... Adolescence [*A publication*] (BRI)
ADONIS .... Acoustic-Daylight, Ambient-Noise Imaging System
ADP .... Anuradhapura [*Ceylon*] [*Airport symbol*] (AD)
ADR .... Alternative Dispute Resolution (WYGK)
ADRS .... Automatic Document Request (AIE)
ADS .... Astrophysics Data System
ADT .... Antigen Detection Test [*Clinical chemistry*]
Adult L .... Adult Learning [*A publication*] (BRI)
adv .... Advisory (DD)
advt .... Advertisement (VRA)
advtg .... Advertising (DD)
AE .... Adult Education Quarterly [*A publication*] (BRI)
AE .... Air Europe [*ICAO designator*] (AD)
AECAL .... Audio Enhanced Computer Aided Learning (AIE)
aed .... Aedicula (VRA)
AEH .... Abecher [*Chad*] [*Airport symbol*] (AD)
AEI .... Adult Education Institute (AIE)
AEMS .... Arts Education for a Multicultural Society (AIE)
AEPE .... Association Europea de Profesores de Espanol (AIE)
AEPS .... Aminoethylaminopropylsilane
AERA .... Ancient Egypt Research Associates
Aero .... Aeronautics (DD)
AES/EBU ..... Audio Engineering Society/European Broadcast Union (DOM)
AESOP .... Automated Endoscopic System for Optimal Positioning [*Medicine*]
AF .... American Forests [*A publication*] (BRI)
AFC .... Association for Colleges (AIE)
AFCASI .... Associate Fellow of the Canadian Aeronautic and Space Institute (DD)
AFFOR .... All Faiths for One Race (AIE)
Afgh .... Afghanistan (VRA)
AFI .... Amalfi [*Colombia*] [*Airport symbol*] (AD)
AFLO .... Advocates for Library Outreach [*Office for Literacy and Outreach*] [*American Library Association*]
AFLRT .... Armed Forces Librarians Round Table [*American Library Association*]
AFP .... Acute Flaccid Paralysis [*Medicine*]
Afr .... Africa (VRA)
Afr Am R ..... African American Review [*A publication*] (BRI)

Africa T .... Africa Today [*A publication*] (BRI)
AFRP BC ...... Association of Fund Raising Professionals of British Columbia [*Canada*]
Afr Rep .... Africa Report [*A publication*] (BRI)
AFT .... Adapter Fault Tolerance [*Intel*] [*Computer science*]
aft .... After (VRA)
AFT .... Automated Flow Technology
AFY .... Afyon [*Turkey*] [*Airport symbol*] (AD)
ag .... Agate (VRA)
AG .... Air Bridge Carriers [*ICAO designator*] (AD)
AG .... Andean Group
AGF .... Assurances Generales de France
AGHWG .... Arctic Goose Habitat Working Group
AGILE .... Aspects of Gymnastics and Independent Learning Experience (AIE)
AGP .... Accelerated Graphics Port [*Computer science*]
AGP .... Advanced Graphics Port [*Intel*] [*Computer science*]
AGQ .... Agrinion [*Greece*] [*Airport symbol*] (AD)
AGQ .... Association des Graveurs du Quebec [*1971, CGQ from 1978, CQE from 1984*] [*Canada*] (NGC)
agr .... Aggregate (VRA)
Agr .... Agricultural (DD)
Agr .... Agriculture (DD)
AgrEng .... Agricultural Engineering (DD)
AGTI .... Association of Geography Teachers of Ireland (AIE)
agwr .... Agateware (VRA)
AGX .... Araguacema [*Brazil*] [*Airport symbol*] (AD)
AGZ .... Agri [*Turkey*] [*Airport symbol*] (AD)
AH .... Air Algerie [*ICAO designator*] (AD)
AH .... American Heritage [*A publication*] (BRI)
AHF .... Anhydrous Hydrogen Fluoride [*Inorganic chemistry*]
AHNC .... Anisotropic Hypernetted Chain [*Chemical physics*]
AHOPSS ...... Association of Heads of Polytechnic Student Services [*British*] (AIE)
AHP .... Association for Healthcare Philanthropy
AHR .... American Historical Review [*A publication*] (BRI)
AI .... Air India [*ICAO designator*] (AD)
AIA .... Air Intelligence Agency [*Air Force*]
AIA .... American Institute of Architects, Washington, D.C. [*1867*] (NGC)
AIA .... Anti-Injunction Act of 1932 (WYGK)
AIAD .... Academic Individual Advanced Development [*Military*] (RDA)
AIB .... Associate Insurance Broker (DD)
AIBC .... Architectural Institute of British Columbia [*1914*] [*Canada*] (NGC)
AICB .... Associate of the Institute of Canadian Bankers (DD)
AIDR .... International Association for Rural Development Overseas (AIE)
AIEE .... Associate of the Institute of Electrical Engineers of Canada (DD)
AIESEC .... Association Internationale des Etudiants en Sciences Economiques et Commerciales (AIE)
AIF .... Apoptosis-Inducing Factor [*Cytology*]
AIF .... Apoptosis-Inducing Factor [*Biochemistry*]
AIM .... Automated Interactive Microscope
AIM .... Salima [*Malawi*] [*Airport symbol*] (AD)
AIMER .... Access to Information on Multicultural Educational Resources (AIE)
AIMS .... Activities Integrating Math and Science
AIN .... Army Interoperability Network (RDA)
airbr .... Airbrush (VRA)
AIRPAC .... Air Pacific [*ICAO designator*] (AD)
airpt .... Airport (VRA)
AIRS .... Access to Information and Reading Service (AIE)
Air UK .... United Kingdom Airlines [*ICAO designator*] (AD)
AITP .... Association of Information Technology Professionals
AJ .... All Island Air [*ICAO designator*] (AD)
AJA .... American Journal of Archaeology [*A publication*] (BRI)
AJE .... American Journal of Education [*A publication*] (BRI)
AJJ .... Akjoujt [*Mauritania*] [*Airport symbol*] (AD)
AJMR .... American Journal on Mental Retardation [*A publication*] (BRI)
AJP .... American Journal of Philology [*A publication*] (BRI)
A J Psy .... American Journal of Psychology [*A publication*] (BRI)
AJPsych ...... American Journal of Psychiatry [*A publication*] (BRI)
AJR .... AJR: American Journalism Review [*A publication*] (BRI)
AJS .... American Journal of Sociology [*A publication*] (BRI)
AKH .... Akhisar [*Turkey*] [*Airport symbol*] (AD)
AKN .... King Salmon-Naknek [*Alaska*] [*Airport symbol*] (AD)
AKY .... Akyab [*Burma*] [*Airport symbol*] (AD)
AL .... Allegheny Airlines [*ICAO designator*] (AD)
AL .... American Literature [*A publication*] (BRI)
ALACE .... Autonomous Lagrangian Circulation Explorer [*Oceanography*]
Alaska .... Alaska Airlines [*ICAO designator*] (AD)
Alb .... Albania (VRA)
alb .... Album (VRA)
ALBR .... Academic Library Book Review [*A publication*] (BRI)
ALBTCX .... Airborne Lidar Bathymetry Technical Center of Expertise [*US Army Corps of Engineers*]
alch .... Alchemy (VRA)
ALCT .... Arts and Letters Club, Toronto [*1908*] [*Canada*] (NGC)
ALCU .... Agricultural Librarians in Colleges and Universities (AIE)
ALD .... Assistive Listening Device (WYGK)
ALFA .... Access to Learning for Adults (AIE)
ALFLEX .... Automatic Landing Flight Experiment [*Japan*]
Alg .... Algeria (VRA)
A Lib .... American Libraries [*A publication*] (BRI)
ALL .... Albenga [*Italy*] [*Airport symbol*] (AD)
alleg .... Allegory (VRA)
ALO .... Accredited Leasing Officer [*Canada*] (DD)
ALPAG .... All London Parents' Action Group [*British*] (AIE)
ALPHA .... Alternative Learning Program for High School Age
ALPT .... Albumen (VRA)

ALR .... Augmentor of Liver Regeneration [*Biochemistry*]
ALSCI .... Association of Lecturers in Scottish Central Institutions (AIE)
ALSSF .... Adult Literacy Support Services Fund (AIE)
alt .... Alternate (VRA)
ALT .... Alternative Lengthening of Telomeres [*Genetics*]
Alta .... Alberta [*Canada*] (DD)
ALTARF .... All London Teachers Against Racism and Fascism [*British*] (AIE)
altpc .... Altarpiece (VRA)
Alt Pr R .... Alternative Press Review [*A publication*] (BRI)
alum .... Aluminum (VRA)
ALUS .... Adult Language Use Survey (AIE)
aly .... Alloy (VRA)
AM .... Alberta Medal [*Canada*] (DD)
Am .... America [*A publication*] (BRI)
Am Ant .... American Antiquity [*A publication*] (BRI)
amb .... Amber (VRA)
AMBE .... Association of Management and Business Education (AIE)
ambul .... Ambulatory (VRA)
AMC .... Am-Timan [*Chad*] [*Airport symbol*] (AD)
AMC .... ATI Multimedia Channel [*Computer science*]
Am Craft ..... American Craft [*A publication*] (BRI)
AMDUCA ...... Animal Medicinal Drug Use Clarification Act of 1994
Amer .... America (VRA)
Amerasia J. .. Amerasia Journal [*A publication*] (BRI)
Amer R .... Americas Review: A Review of Hispanic Literature and Art of the USA [*A publication*] (BRI)
Am Ethnol ... American Ethnologist [*A publication*] (BRI)
AMF .... Amparafaravola [*Malagasy*] [*Airport symbol*] (AD)
Am Geneal ... American Genealogist [*A publication*] (BRI)
AMGS .... Association for Maintained Girls' Schools (AIE)
AMH .... Arba Mintch [*Ethiopia*] [*Airport symbol*] (AD)
Am Hist ...... American History [*A publication*] (BRI)
AMI .... Ampenan [*Indonesia*] [*Airport symbol*] (AD)
Am Ind CRJ .. American Indian Culture and Research Journal [*A publication*] (BRI)
AML .... Puerto Armuellas [*Panama*] [*Airport symbol*] (AD)
Am M .... American Music [*A publication*] (BRI)
Am MT .... American Music Teacher [*A publication*] (BRI)
AMO .... Mao [*Chad*] [*Airport symbol*] (AD)
AMP .... Army Modernization Plan (RDA)
Am Phil .... American Philatelist [*A publication*] (BRI)
AMPS .... Advanced Mobile-Phone System
ampth .... Amphitheater (VRA)
Am Q .... American Quarterly [*A publication*] (BRI)
Ams .... Americas: A Quarterly Review of Inter-American Cultural History [*A publication*] (BRI)
Am Sci .... American Scientist [*A publication*] (BRI)
Am Spect .... American Spectator [*A publication*] (BRI)
Am Theat .... American Theatre [*A publication*] (BRI)
AMTIS .... Arts Management Training Initiative, Scotland (AIE)
Am Vis .... American Visions [*A publication*] (BRI)
AN .... Ansett Airlines of Australia [*ICAO designator*] (AD)
ANA .... Associate of the National Academy of Design, New York (NGC)
Analog .... Analog Science Fiction and Fact [*A publication*] (BRI)
anc .... Ancient (VRA)
And .... Andorra (VRA)
Ang .... Angola (VRA)
ANGV .... Advanced Natural Gas Vehicle
ANH .... Nhill [*Victoria, Australia*] [*Airport symbol*] (AD)
ANO .... Antonio Enes [*Mozambique*] [*Airport symbol*] (AD)
anod alum ... Anodized Aluminum (VRA)
anon .... Anonymous (VRA)
ANQ:QJ .... ANQ: A Quarterly Journal of Short Articles, Notes, and Reviews [*A publication*] (BRI)
ANSTO .... Australian Nuclear Science and Technology Organisation
Ant & CM .... Antiques & Collecting Magazine [*A publication*] (BRI)
Antar .... Antarctica (VRA)
Anthro .... Anthropology (DD)
anthrop .... Anthropology (VRA)
Antiq J .... Antiquaries Journal [*A publication*] (BRI)
antq .... Antique (VRA)
Ant R .... Antioch Review [*A publication*] (BRI)
ANV .... Angle Neovascularization [*Opthalmology*]
AO .... Avisco [*ICAO designator*] (AD)
AOA .... Accident Officers Association (AIE)
AOC .... Advice of Charge [*Telecommunications*] (DOM)
AOD .... Abou Deia [*Chad*] [*Airport symbol*] (AD)
AON .... Arona [*New Guinea*] [*Airport symbol*] (AD)
AOO .... Altoona-Martinsburg [*Pennsylvania*] [*Airport symbol*] (AD)
AOP .... Association of Online Professionals
AOS .... Average Oxidation State [*Physical chemistry*]
AOT .... Abbottabad [*Pakistan*] [*Airport symbol*] (AD)
ap .... Apostle (VRA)
AP .... Apprenticeship Program (DD)
AP .... Aspen Airways [*ICAO designator*] (AD)
APA .... Accreditation of Prior Achievement [*Education*] (AIE)
APA .... Amapa [*Brazil*] [*Airport symbol*] (AD)
APA .... Member of the Institute of Accredited Public Accountants [*Canada*] (DD)
APALS .... Autonomous Precision Approach and Landing System [*Lockheed-Martin's radical landing-guidance system*]
apcys .... Apocalypse (VRA)
APDA .... Apple Programmers and Developers Association (DOM)
APE .... Adaptation to Premises and Equipment Scheme [*Education*] (AIE)
APEAL .... Automotive Performance Execution and Layout

By Acronym

APEGGA.......	Association of Professional Engineers, Geologists, and Geophysicists of Alberta [*Canada*] (DD)
APEL...........	Advanced Product Evaluation Laboratory
APEO	Professional Engineers Ontario [*Canada*] (DD)
APEX...........	Association of Professional, Executive, Clerical, and Computer Staff (AIE)
APFIM.........	Atom-Probe Field-Ion Microscopy
APL.............	Accreditation of Prior Learning (AIE)
apliq...........	Applique (VRA)
APMLTU	Association of Professors of Modern Languages in Technological Universities (AIE)
Apo.............	Apollo [*A publication*] (BRI)
apocph........	Apocrypha (VRA)
app.............	Application [*Computer science*]
appl	Applied (VRA)
Apple PIE....	Parental Involvement in Education
AppMinSci ...	Applied Mineral Sciences (DD)
APPT...........	Assessment of the Provision of Part Time Training [*Education*] (AIE)
appx...........	Approximate (VRA)
APR.............	Accredited in Public Relations [*Canadian Public Relations Society, Inc.*] (DD)
APR	American Poetry Review [*A publication*] (BRI)
APS.............	Advanced Photo System
APS.............	Anapolis [*Brazil*] [*Airport symbol*] (AD)
APS.............	Assisted Places Scheme (AIE)
APS.............	Auction Preferred Stock [*Investment term*] (DFIT)
Apsac.........	American Professional Society on the Abuse of Children
APSR	American Political Science Review [*A publication*] (BRI)
apt.............	Apartment (VRA)
APT&C........	Administrative, Professional, Technical, and Clerical Grades [*Education*] (AIE)
APTV..........	Associated Press Television
APWA	Association of Principals, Wardens, and Advisers of University Women Students [*British*] (AIE)
APXS	Alpha Proton X-Ray Spectrometer
APY.............	Alto Parnaiba [*Brazil*] [*Airport symbol*] (AD)
AQ..............	Air Anglia [*ICAO designator*] (AD)
AQ..............	Aloha Airlines [*ICAO designator*] (AD)
aqdt	Aqueduct (VRA)
AQR	Alenquer [*Brazil*] [*Airport symbol*] (AD)
AQU	Aquidauana [*Brazil*] [*Airport symbol*] (AD)
aqut............	Aquatint (VRA)
AR..............	Accounting Review [*A publication*] (BRI)
Arab...........	Arabia (VRA)
ARAC	Avis Rent a Car
ar/arm	Arms & Armor (VRA)
ARBA	American Reference Books Annual [*A publication*] (BRI)
arbsq..........	Arabesque (VRA)
ARC	Archival Research Catalog
ARC	Army Research Consortium (RDA)
ARCA	Associate of the Royal Canadian Academy of Arts (NGC)
arch	Architecture (VRA)
archeo	Archaeology (VRA)
Archiv	Archivaria [*A publication*] (BRI)
archt	Architect (VRA)
archtr.........	Architrave (VRA)
archv	Archive (VRA)
ARCnet	Attached Resource Computer Network
ARD............	Andradina [*Brazil*] [*Airport symbol*] (AD)
AREIAC	Association of Inspectors, Advisers, and Consultants for Religious Education (AIE)
Arena..........	Arena Magazine [*A publication*] (BRI)
ARF.............	Auxin Response Factor [*Biochemistry*]
Arg.............	Argentina (VRA)
argil...........	Argillite (VRA)
arh.............	Arch (VRA)
ARH	Atharan Hazari [*Pakistan*] [*Airport symbol*] (AD)
ARICS	Professional Associate of the Royal Institution of Chartered Surveyors [*Canada*] (DD)
arl vw	Aerial View (VRA)
Arm............	Armenia (VRA)
ARM............	Associate in Risk Management [*Canada*] (DD)
ARMALCOLITE...	Armstrong Aldren Collins [*Lunar mineral named after three astronauts*]
Arm Det.......	Armchair Detective [*A publication*] (BRI)
Arm F & S...	Armed Forces and Society [*A publication*] (BRI)
armt...........	Armature (VRA)
ARNT	Arylhydrocarbon-Receptor Nuclear Translocator [*Genetics*]
AROPS	Association of Representatives of Old Pupils' Societies (AIE)
ARP	Agree en Relations Publiques [*Canada*] (DD)
ARP	Ammunition Resupply Projectile [*Military*] (RDA)
ARQ	Automatic Request [*Computer science*] (DOM)
arric...........	Arricaccato (VRA)
ART	Advanced Reproductive Technology [*Medicine*]
Art Am........	Art in America [*A publication*] (BRI)
Art Bull.......	Art Bulletin [*A publication*] (BRI)
Art Dir	Art Direction [*A publication*] (BRI)
ARTEN	Anti Racist Teacher Education Network (AIE)
artif...........	Artificial (VRA)
artist coll....	Artist's Collection (VRA)
Art J...........	Art Journal [*A publication*] (BRI)
Art N...........	ARTnews [*A publication*] (BRI)
arvlt...........	Archivolt (VRA)
ARW	Air Reserve Wing [*Canada*] (DD)
ARY	Arusha [*Tanzania*] [*Airport symbol*] (AD)

AS...............	American Scholar [*A publication*] (BRI)
AS...............	Anthranilate Synthase [*An enzyme*]
As...............	Asia (VRA)
ASA............	Alberta Society of Artists [*1931*] [*Canada*] (NGC)
ASA............	American Sportfishing Association
ASAAA	Alliance of State Aftermarket Associations
ASAP	Academic Strategic Alliances Program
ASAS/SFT ...	All Source Analysis System/Software [*Military*] (RDA)
ASB............	Aggregated School Budget (AIE)
asb.............	Asbestos (VRA)
ASBYP	Appraisal: Science Books for Young People [*A publication*] (BRI)
ASC............	Agreed Syllabus Conference [*Education*] (AIE)
ASC............	Association for Student Counsellors (AIE)
ASEO	Army System Engineering Office (RDA)
ASF.............	Active Streaming Format [*Computer science*]
ASH	Achaete-Scute Homologue [*Genetics*]
ASH	Average Student Hours [*Education*] (AIE)
ASI.............	Armored Systems Integration [*Army*] (RDA)
ASInt..........	American Studies International [*A publication*] (BRI)
ASLIB..........	Association of Special Libraries and Information Bureaux [*Association for Information Management*] [*British*] (AIE)
ASM............	Asmara [*Ethiopia*] [*Airport symbol*] (AD)
asmblg........	Assemblage (VRA)
As Min	Asia Minor (VRA)
ASPE...........	Association for the Study of Primary Education (AIE)
ASQ	Association des Sculpteurs du Quebec [*1961, CSQ from 1978*] [*Canada*] (NGC)
Assn...........	Association (DD)
assoc	Associates (VRA)
asst............	Assistant (DD)
ASTAMIDS...	Airborne Standoff Minefield Detection System [*Military*] (RDA)
ASTDP	Academic Staff Training and Development Programme [*British*] (AIE)
Astro	Astronautics (DD)
Astron	Astronomy [*A publication*] (BRI)
AT..............	Attainment Target (AIE)
AT..............	Royal Air Maroc [*ICAO designator*] (AD)
ATA	Alternative Technologies and Approaches [*Military*] (RDA)
ATA	Army Technical Architecture [*Military*]
ATACC	Absolute Total and Complete Camouflage [*Hunting*]
ATACMS-BAT...	Army Tactical Missile System-Brilliant Anti-Armor Submunition (RDA)
ATACMS BLK II...	Army Tactical Missile System Block II (RDA)
ATAMS........	Automated Tracking and Monitoring System
AT&T GIS....	AT&T Global Information Solutions [*Computer science*]
ATC............	Accredited Training Centre [*Education*] [*British*] (AIE)
ATCH	Autochrome (VRA)
ATCODE.......	Association of Teachers in Colleges and Departments of Education (AIE)
ATDT...........	Attention Dial Tone [*Computer science*] (DOM)
ATE............	Assessment and Training for Employment (AIE)
ATF.............	Association of Teachers of French (AIE)
ATL.............	Association of Teachers and Lecturers (AIE)
Atl..............	Atlantic Monthly [*A publication*] (BRI)
Atl BT	Atlantic Books Today [*A publication*] (BRI)
atlr.............	Antler (VRA)
atmos	Atmosphere (VRA)
ATO............	Approved Training Organisation [*Manpower Services Commission*] (AIE)
ATOC	Acoustic Thermometry of Ocean Climate
ATOFMS	Aerosol Time-of-Flight Mass Spectrometer
ATP	Adult Employment Training Programme [*British*] (AIE)
ATR.............	Star [*Mauritania*] [*Airport symbol*] (AD)
ATS.............	Adult Training Strategy (AIE)
ATS.............	Applicant Tracking System [*Human resources*] (WYGK)
attr............	Attributed (VRA)
ATV.............	Ati [*Chad*] [*Airport symbol*] (AD)
ATVIC..........	Association of Teachers in Sixth Form and Tertiary Colleges [*British*] (AIE)
ATYP...........	Ambrotype (VRA)
ATZ.............	Assiut [*Egypt*] [*Airport symbol*] (AD)
AU..............	Austral Lineas Aereas [*ICAO designator*] (AD)
AUCF	Average Unit of Council Funding [*Higher Education Funding Council*] (AIE)
Aud............	Audubon [*A publication*] (BRI)
AUD............	Augustus Downs [*Queensland*] [*Airport symbol*] (AD)
audit...........	Auditorium (VRA)
AUJ.............	Active Universal Joints
AUM............	Austin [*Minnesota*] [*Airport symbol*] (AD)
AUP	Adult Unemployed Project [*Department of Education and Science*] [*British*] (AIE)
AUP	American University of Paris
Aurig..........	Aurignacian (VRA)
AURIS	Aberdeen University Research and Industrial Services (AIE)
Aust	Austria (VRA)
Aust Bk R	Australian Book Review [*A publication*] (BRI)
Austr..........	Australia (VRA)
aut	Autoroute (DD)
auth	Author (VRA)
authn..........	Authentic (VRA)
av..............	Avenue (DD)
AV..............	Avianca [*ICAO designator*] (AD)
AVA............	Authorized Validating Agency (AIE)
ave.............	Avenue (VRA)
Ave	Avenue (DD)
AVERT	Anti-Virus Emergency Response Team [*McAfee*] [*Computer science*]

av-gd .... Avant-Garde (VRA)
AVI .... Audio Video Interleave [*Computer science*]
AVI .... Audio-Video Interleaved [*Computer science*]
AVL .... Asheville-Henderson [*North Carolina*] [*Airport symbol*] (AD)
AVLDS .... American Veterinary Lyme Disease Society
AVP .... Scranton-Wilkes-Barre [*Pennsylvania*] [*Airport symbol*] (AD)
AVT .... Advanced Vehicle Technologies [*Military*] (RDA)
AVX .... Avalon Bay [*Santa Catalina, California*] [*Airport symbol*] (AD)
AW .... Aeroquetzal [*ICAO designator*] (AD)
AWCP .... Associated Water Colour Painters, Toronto [*1912*] [*Canada*] (NGC)
AWCS .... American Water Color Society, New York [*1878, founded 1866 as American Society of Painters in Water Colors*] (NGC)

AWE .... Advanced Wave Effects [*Sound synthesis*] (DOM)
AWHMT .... Association of Waste Hazardous Materials Transporters
AWIPS .... Automated Weather Information Processing System
AWK .... Wake [*Wake Island, Pacific Ocean*] [*Airport symbol*] (AD)
AWPU .... Age Weighted Pupil Unit [*Education*] (AIE)
AWT .... Abstract Windowing Toolkit [*Computer science*]
AX .... Connectair [*ICAO designator*] (AD)
AXA .... Anguilla [*Leeward Islands*] [*Airport symbol*] (AD)
axon .... Axonometric (VRA)
AY .... Finnair [*ICAO designator*] (AD)
AYCF .... Association of Young Computer Enthusiasts (AIE)
Azo .... Azores (VRA)

B	Annual Rate Plus Stock Dividend [*Investment term*] (DFIT)
b	Birthdate (DD)
b	Black (VRA)
b	Born (VRA)
BAA	Baccalaureat en Administration des Affaires [*Canada*] (DD)
BA/BMgmt	Bachelor of Arts/Bachelor of Management Combines (DD)
BA/BS	Bachelor of Arts/Bachelor of Science Combined (DD)
BAC	British Action for Children's Television (AIE)
BACH	British Association for Construction Heads (AIE)
BACODINE	Batse Coordinates Distribution Network
Bactr	Bactrian (VRA)
BActSci	Bachelor of Actuarial Sciences (DD)
Baha	Bahamas (VRA)
Bahr	Bahrain (VRA)
baldc	Baldachino (VRA)
BALEAP	British Association of Lecturers in English for Academic Purposes (AIE)
balstr	Balustrade (VRA)
bal wd	Balsa Wood (VRA)
b&w	Black & White (VRA)
Bangl	Bangladesh [*E. Pakistan*] (VRA)
BAPed	Bachelor of Arts in Pedagogy (DD)
bapt	Baptist (VRA)
Barb	Barbados (VRA)
BARC	Budget Analysis and Review Committee [*American Library Association*]
barlf	Bas Relief (VRA)
Barq	Baroque (VRA)
bar vlt	Barrel Vault (VRA)
BAS	Baccalaureat en Sciences Administratives [*Canada*] (DD)
BAS	Bachelor of Science in Agriculture (DD)
BAS	Bulletin of the Atomic Scientists [*A publication*] (BRI)
basl	Basilica (VRA)
baswd	Basswood (VRA)
BATD	British Association of Teachers of the Deaf (AIE)
bathrm	Bathroom (VRA)
BATS	Bradford Action on Teacher Shortages (AIE)
BAX	Burlington Air Express [*ICAO designator*] (AD)
BB	Air Great Lakes [*ICAO designator*] (AD)
BBIC	Behavior-Based Incentive Compensation [*Human resources*] (WYGK)
BBS	Blind Bronchial Sampling [*Clinical chemistry*]
BBW	Bath & Body Works
BC	BC (VRA)
BC	Biogenic Carbon [*Chemistry*]
BC	Book Collector [*A publication*] (BRI)
BC	Brymon Airways [*ICAO designator*] (AD)
BCAL	British Caledonian Airways [*ICAO designator*] (AD)
BCES	British Comparative Education Society (AIE)
BCh	Bachelor in Surgery (DD)
BChemEng	Bachelor of Chemical Engineering (DD)
BChir	Bachelor in Surgery (DD)
bcksk	Buckskin (VRA)
BCM	Bachelor of Computer Management (DD)
BCM	Boots Contract Manufacturing
BCNU	Be Seein' You [*Computer science*] (DOM)
BCP	Biology, Chemistry, Physics (DD)
BCP	Block Copolymer [*Organic chemistry*]
BCSA	British Columbia Society of Artists [*1949-68, founded 1908 as BCSFA*] [*Canada*] (NGC)
BCSFA	British Columbia Society of Fine Arts [*1908, BCSA from 1949*] [*Canada*] (NGC)
BCSSC	British Computer Society Schools Committee (AIE)
BCUL	Buildings for College and University Libraries Committee [*Library Administration and Management Association*] [*American Library Association*]
bd	Board (VRA)
BD	British Midland Airways [*ICAO designator*] (AD)
BD	Broker-Dealer (DFIT)
bdrm	Board Room (VRA)
BDT	Bradley Desktop Trainer [*Military*]
bdyco	Bodycolor (VRA)
BE	Bachelor of Engineering Science (DD)
BE	Bachelor of Science in Engineering (DD)
BE	Enterprise Airlines [*ICAO designator*] (AD)
bea	Beads (VRA)
BEACON	Boston Exchange Automated Communication Order-Routing Network (DFIT)
BEARS	Bond Enabling Annual Retirement Savings (DFIT)
Beav	Beaver [*A publication*] (BRI)
beawk	Beadwork (VRA)
BECG	British Educational Contractors Group (AIE)
BE CLEAR	Bradford Community Learning and Education Resource (AIE)
becwd	Beech (VRA)
bedrm	Bedroom (VRA)
bef	Before (VRA)
BEFMC	British Educational Furniture Manufacturers Council (AIE)
beg	Beginning (VRA)
BEL	Bell [*Computer science*] (DOM)
Belg	Belgium (VRA)
Belles Let	Belles Lettres [*A publication*] (BRI)
B Ent	Black Enterprise [*A publication*] (BRI)
BESA	British Educational Suppliers Association (AIE)
bet	Between (VRA)
BETA	Balanced Extravehicular Training Aircraft [*NASA*]
bev	Bevel (VRA)
BF	Iowa Airlines and Horizon Airways [*ICAO designator*] (AD)
BFSS	British and Foreign Schools Society (AIE)
BFYC	Books for Your Children [*A publication*] (BRI)
BG	Bangladesh Biman [*ICAO designator*] (AD)
BGen	Business Education Council General Award (AIE)
BGNS	Background Natural Sound
BH	Augusta Airways [*ICAO designator*] (AD)
BHR	Business History Review [*A publication*] (BRI)
BHRB	British Humanities Research Board (AIE)
BI	Business Intelligence
BI	Royal Brunei Airlines [*ICAO designator*] (AD)
BIAM	Bank of Ireland Asset Management
BIB	British Interactive Broadcasting
BIBCO	Bibliographic Cooperative Program [*American Library Association*]
BIBE	International Bulletin of Bibliography on Education [*A publication*] (AIE)
bibl	Bibliotheque (VRA)
BIC	Books in Canada [*A publication*] (BRI)
BICH	Bichromate (VRA)
BIE	Books in English (AIE)
bilbd	Billboard (VRA)
BIMBO	Blacks in Media Broadcasting Organization
Bing	Baccalaureat en Ingenierie [*Canada*] (DD)
Bio	Biology (DD)
Biochem	Biochemistry (DD)
Biography	Biography: An Interdisciplinary Quarterly [*A publication*] (BRI)
BiomedEng	Biomedical Engineering (DD)
BioSci	BioScience [*A publication*] (BRI)
BIPP	British Institute of Professional Photography (AIE)
BIR	Bachelor of Industrial Relations (DD)
bir	Birch (VRA)
BIRD	Bird Investigation, Review, and Deterrent [*NASA*]
BIS	Business Improvement Services (AIE)
bist	Bistre (VRA)
BJ	Bakhtar Afghan Airlines [*ICAO designator*] (AD)
bk	Book (VRA)
BK	Chalk's International Airline [*ICAO designator*] (AD)
Bkbird	Bookbird [*A publication*] (BRI)
bkgr	Background (VRA)
Bks & Cult	Books & Culture [*A publication*] (BRI)
Bks Keeps	Books for Keeps [*A publication*] (BRI)
BL	Air BVI [*ICAO designator*] (AD)
BL	Baccalaureat en Loisirs [*Canada*] (DD)
BL	Bachelor in Law (DD)
bl	Blue (VRA)
BL	Booklist [*A publication*] (BRI)
BLAM	Barrel-Launched Adaptive Munitions
bldg	Building (DD)
bldr	Builder (VRA)
bldst	Bloodstone (VRA)
BLIS	British Library Information Skills (AIE)
blk	Block (VRA)
blkpr	Block Print (VRA)
Bloom Rev	Bloomsbury Review [*A publication*] (BRI)
BLRDD	British Library Research and Development Division (AIE)
Bl S	Black Scholar [*A publication*] (BRI)

BLSR	Bi-Directional Line-Switched Rings		**BSH**	Brighton [*England*] [*Airport symbol*] (AD)
blts	Bit-Block Transfers [*Computer science*]		**bskt**	Basket (VRA)
Blvd	Boulevard (DD)		**BSN**	Bossangoa [*Central African Republic*] [*Airport symbol*] (AD)
blvd	Boulevard (VRA)		**B-spline**	Basic Spline (DOM)
BM	Aero Transporti Italiani [*ICAO designator*] (AD)		**BSR**	Basra [*Iraq*] [*Airport symbol*] (AD)
BM	Burlington Magazine [*A publication*] (BRI)		**BSS**	Balsas [*Brazil*] [*Airport symbol*] (AD)
BMA	Bachelor of Management Arts (DD)		**BSS**	Broadcasting Support Services (AIE)
BMgmt	Bachelor of Management (DD)		**bst**	Basalt (VRA)
BMIT	Behaviour Modification Information Test (AIE)		**BSTF**	British Science and Technology in Education (AIE)
BMP	Bit-Mapped Graphics [*Computer science*]		**BT**	Air Martinique (Satair) [*ICAO designator*] (AD)
BMTP	Blagden Management Training Programme [*British*] (AIE)		**BTB**	Biblical Theology Bulletin [*A publication*] (BRI)
bndr	Binder (VRA)		**BTC**	Batticaloa [*Ceylon*] [*Airport symbol*] (AD)
BNP	Bangladesh Nationalist Party [*Political party*]		**BTD**	Brunett Downs [*Northern Territory, Australia*] [*Airport symbol*] (AD)
BNST	Bed Nucleus of the Stria Terminalis [*Brain anatomy*]		**BTECNC**	Business and Technology Education Council National Certificate
bntwd	Bentwood (VRA)			(AIE)
BO	Bouraq Indonesia Airlines [*ICAO designator*] (AD)		**btga**	Bottega (VRA)
BOAS	British Quality Awards Scheme (AIE)		**BTH**	Bathurst [*Gambia*] [*Airport symbol*] (AD)
BOATS	Boat Owners Association of the United States		**BTI**	British Technology Index (AIE)
BOB	Bora-Bora [*Society Islands*] [*Airport symbol*] (AD)		**BTJ**	Banda Atjeh [*Indonesia*] [*Airport symbol*] (AD)
BODAS	Brigade Operations Display and After Action Review System [*Army*]		**btk**	Batik (VRA)
	(RDA)		**BTN**	Brunei Town [*Brunei*] [*Airport symbol*] (AD)
bodh	Bodhisattva (VRA)		**BTO**	Build-to-Order [*Compaq Computer Corp.*] [*Computer science*]
BOE	Board of Education (AIE)		**BTO**	St. Barthelemy [*Leeward Islands, West Indies*] [*Airport symbol*] (AD)
BOHICA	Bend Over, Here It Comes Again [*Business term*]		**BTX**	Betoota [*Queensland*] [*Airport symbol*] (AD)
BOJ	Burgas [*Bulgaria*] [*Airport symbol*] (AD)		**BU**	Braathens SAFE Airtransport [*ICAO designator*] (AD)
Bokh	Bokhara (VRA)		**BUCS**	Bath University Computing Services [*British*] (AIE)
Bol	Bolivia (VRA)		**BUL**	Bulolo [*New Guinea*] [*Airport symbol*] (AD)
Books	Books Magazine [*A publication*] (BRI)		**Bulg**	Bulgaria (VRA)
BOP	Bouar [*Central African Republic*] [*Airport symbol*] (AD)		**BUN**	Buenaventura [*Colombia*] [*Airport symbol*] (AD)
Boro	Borobudur (VRA)		**bur**	Burlap (VRA)
Boston R	Boston Review [*A publication*] (BRI)		**burn**	Burnished (VRA)
bot	Bottom (VRA)		**Buru**	Burundi (VRA)
Botsw	Botswana (VRA)		**bus**	Business (DD)
boul	Boulevard (DD)		**Bus Bk R**	Business Book Review [*A publication*] (BRI)
BOY	Bobo Dioulass [*Volta*] [*Airport symbol*] (AD)		**BusLR**	Business Library Review [*A publication*] (BRI)
boz	Bozzetto (VRA)		**BusMgmt**	Business Management (DD)
BP	Air Botswana [*ICAO designator*] (AD)		**Bus Soc**	Business and Society [*A publication*] (BRI)
BPh	Bachelor of Pharmacy (DD)		**BusStudies**	Business Studies (DD)
BPOA	Business Professionals of America		**Bus W**	Business Week [*A publication*] (BRI)
BPTO	Blind Persons Technical Officer [*British*] (AIE)		**BUTEC**	British Universities Transatlantic Exchange Committee (AIE)
BQ	Business Jets [*ICAO designator*] (AD)		**butr**	Buttress (VRA)
BQR	Butare [*Rwanda*] [*Airport symbol*] (AD)		**BUX**	Bunia [*Zaire*] [*Airport symbol*] (AD)
br	Burl (VRA)		**BUZ**	Bushire [*Iran*] [*Airport symbol*] (AD)
braz	Brazed (VRA)		**bv**	Cover (VRA)
Braz	Brazil (VRA)		**bv**	Covered (VRA)
BRC	Before Rotary Cutting [*Quilting*]		**BV**	Northwest Skyways [*ICAO designator*] (AD)
brcd	Brocade (VRA)		**BVA**	Beauvais [*France*] [*Airport symbol*] (AD)
BRESCU	Bachelor of Recreation Education (DD)		**BVH**	Vilhena [*Brazil*] [*Airport symbol*] (AD)
BRESCU	Building Research Energy Conservation Support Unit (AIE)		**BVO**	Bartlesville [*Oklahoma*] [*Airport symbol*] (AD)
brev	Breviary (VRA)		**BVS**	Bela Vista [*Brazil*] [*Airport symbol*] (AD)
BRF	Bradford [*England*] [*Airport symbol*] (AD)		**BW**	Book World [*A publication*] (BRI)
bri	Brick (VRA)		**BW**	Business Week [*A publication*]
briq	Briquettes (VRA)		**BW**	BWIA International [*ICAO designator*] (AD)
Brit	Britain (VRA)		**BWatch**	Bookwatch [*A publication*] (BRI)
brk	Bark (VRA)		**BWB**	Blended Wing Body [*Megaplane*]
brkcth	Barkcloth (VRA)		**BWBA**	Blue Water Bridge Authority
brn	Brown (VRA)		**BWF**	Breit-Wigner-Fano [*Spectra interference*]
B Rpt	Book Report [*A publication*] (BRI)		**BWG**	Bowling Green [*Kentucky*] [*Airport symbol*] (AD)
BRPT	Bromoil Print (VRA)		**BWP**	Bahawalpur [*Pakistan*] [*Airport symbol*] (AD)
bru	Brush (VRA)		**bwr**	Blackware (VRA)
BRUFS	British Council Undergraduate Fellowship Scheme (AIE)		**bx**	Box (VRA)
BRZ	Bruzual [*Venezuela*] [*Airport symbol*] (AD)		**bxwd**	Boxwood (VRA)
BS	Auxaire-Bretagne [*ICAO designator*] (AD)		**BYI**	Burley-Rupert [*Idaho*] [*Airport symbol*] (AD)
bs	Brass (VRA)		**byte**	Binary Term [*Computer science*]
BSA	Baccalaureat en Sciences Administratives [*Canada*] (DD)		**BYV**	Baiyer River [*New Guinea*] [*Airport symbol*] (AD)
BSA	Boarding Schools Association (AIE)		**Byz**	Byzantine (VRA)
BSA-P	Bibliographical Society of America Papers [*A publication*] (BRI)		**bz**	Bronze (VRA)
BSc	Bachelor of Science [*Academic degree*] (AIE)		**BZ**	Capital Airlines [*ICAO designator*] (AD)
BScComm	Bachelor of Commercial Science (DD)		**BZ**	Skyfreighters [*ICAO designator*] (AD)
BScE	Bachelor of Science, Engineering (DD)		**BZI**	Balikesir [*Turkey*] [*Airport symbol*] (AD)
BSc(Eng)	Bachelor of Science in Engineering (DD)		**BZL**	Barisal [*Bangladesh*] [*Airport symbol*] (AD)
BSE	Sematan [*Sarawak, Malaysia*] [*Airport symbol*] (AD)		**BZO**	Bolzano [*Italy*] [*Airport symbol*] (AD)
BSG	Bata [*Spanish Guinea*] [*Airport symbol*] (AD)		**BZY**	Brasileia [*Brazil*] [*Airport symbol*] (AD)

C
By Acronym

c .... Canvas (VRA)
c .... Century (VRA)
C .... Liquidating Dividend [*Investment term*] (DFIT)
C200 .... Committee of 200 [*An association*]
CA .... Curriculum Association (AIE)
CABE .... Computers and Adult Basic Education [*Liverpool Institute of Higher Education*] [*British*] (AIE)
CABN .... Cabinet Card (VRA)
cabo .... Cabochon (VRA)
CAC .... Canadian Art Club, Toronto [*1907-15*] (NGC)
CAC .... Cultural Action Committee
CACGS .... Computer Assisted Careers Guidance System (AIE)
CADA .... Confederation of Art and Design Associations (AIE)
CADCA .... Community Anti-Drug Coalitions of America
CAdm .... Chartered Administrator (DD)
CAEDO .... Canadian Association of Education Development Officers
CAETR .... Center for Acquisition Education, Training, and Research [*Military*] (RDA)
CAF .... Carauari [*Brazil*] [*Airport symbol*] (AD)
CAF .... College of Agriculture and Forestry (AIE)
CAFCAL .... Contact a Family Computer Assisted Learning (AIE)
CAGP .... Canadian Association of Gift Planners
CAHP .... Certified Member of AHP [*Association of Healthcare Philanthropy*]
CAI .... Computer Assisted Instruction (AIE)
CAIB .... Canadian Accredited Insurance Broker (DD)
CAIB .... Certified Associate of the Institute of Bankers [*Canada*] (DD)
CAJE .... Computer-Assisted Job Evaluation [*Human resources*] (WYGK)
cal .... Calendar (VRA)
CAL .... Computer Assisted Learning (AIE)
caldm .... Caldarium (VRA)
calig .... Calligraphy (VRA)
CALIM .... Consortium of Academic Libraries in Manchester [*British*] (AIE)
calit .... Callitype (VRA)
CALM .... Computer Aided Learning in Mathematics (AIE)
CALOT .... Calotype (VRA)
CALS .... Continuous Acquisition and Life-Cycle Support [*Military*] (RDA)
CALT .... Computer Assisted Language Teaching (AIE)
cam .... Camera (VRA)
Camb .... Cambodia (VRA)
CAMF .... Course Approval and Monitoring Form [*Inner London Education Authority*] [*British*] (AIE)
cam obs ...... Camera Obscura (VRA)
CAN .... Calculator-Aware Number [*Project*] (AIE)
Can .... Canada (VRA)
CAN .... Canton [*China*] [*Airport symbol*] (AD)
Can CL .... Canadian Children's Literature [*A publication*] (BRI)
C & A .... Configuration and Administration
C&F .... Cost and Freight (DFIT)
C & U .... College and University [*A publication*] (BRI)
Can Hist R ... Canadian Historical Review [*A publication*] (BRI)
Can Lit .... Canadian Literature [*A publication*] (BRI)
Can Mat ...... CM: A Reviewing Journal of Canadian Materials for Young People [*A publication*] (BRI)
cap .... Capital (VRA)
CAP .... Closing Agreement Program (WYGK)
CAP .... Community-Acquired Pneumonia
CAPA .... Creative and Performing Arts
CAPITB .... Clothing and Allied Products Industry Training Board (AIE)
CAPL .... Civilian Acquisition Position List [*Army*] (RDA)
CAPQ .... Conseil des Artistes Peintres du Quebec [*1982, founded 1966 as SAPQ*] [*Canada*] (NGC)
CAPRT .... Center for Aquatic Plant Research and Technology [*Army*]
CAPS .... Convertible Adjustable Preferred Stock [*Investment term*] (DFIT)
Capt .... Captain (DD)
CAPTIVE ..... Collaborative Authoring Production and Transmission of Interactive Video for Education (AIE)
car .... Carre (DD)
CAR .... Certificate for Automobile Receivables [*Investment term*] (DFIT)
CArb .... Certified Arbitrator [*Canada*] (DD)
CARB .... Consortium for Advanced Residential Buildings
carbor .... Carborondum (VRA)
CARD .... Canadian Advertising Rates and Data
CARDS .... Certificates for Amortizing Revolving Debts [*Finance*] (DFIT)
CARE .... Cooperative Alliance for Refuge Enhancement
CARGO .... Careers Guidance Observed (AIE)
carnl .... Carnelian (VRA)

CARP .... Cast Arrested Repeating Persons [*Fictitious fishing term*]
CARSE .... Centre for Alcohol and Road Safety Education [*British*] (AIE)
Carth .... Carthage (VRA)
cas .... Casein (VRA)
CASE .... Cognitive Acceleration through Science Education (AIE)
CASE .... Complete Affinity Server Enclosure [*Computer science*]
CASE .... Council for the Advancement and Support of Education
CASEP .... Cognitive Acceleration through Science Education Project (AIE)
cashm .... Cashmere (VRA)
CASI .... Cognitive Abilities Screening Instrument
CASROS ...... Campaign Against Secret Records on Schoolchildren (AIE)
CASSC .... Clinical Academic Staff Salaries Committee [*Committee of Vice Chancellors and Principals*] (AIE)
cat .... Catalog (VRA)
CAT .... Cat Island [*Bahamas*] [*Airport symbol*] (AD)
CAT .... College of Art and Technology (AIE)
CAT .... Curriculum Analysis Taxonomy [*Education*] (AIE)
CATE .... Council for the Accreditation of Teacher Education (AIE)
Cat Fan .... Cat Fancy [*A publication*] (BRI)
cath .... Cathedral (VRA)
Cath W .... Catholic World [*A publication*] (BRI)
CATS .... Consortium for Assessment and Testing in Schools (AIE)
CATS .... Criteria of Teacher Selection [*Project*] (AIE)
CAVE .... Computer Assisted Virtual Environment
CAY .... Come-All-Ye [*A publication*] (BRI)
CB .... Coulomb Blockade [*Physics*]
CBA .... Certificate in Business Administration [*Academic degree*] (AIE)
CBDCOM ...... Chemical and Biological Defense Command [*Army*] (RDA)
CBELT .... Computer Based English Language Testing (AIE)
CBH .... Colomb Bechar [*Algeria*] [*Airport symbol*] (AD)
CBIRF .... Chemical/Biological Incident Response Force [*Marine Corps*]
CBM .... Commemorative Bucks of Michigan
CBN .... Cabarien [*Cuba*] [*Airport symbol*] (AD)
CBO .... Collateralized Bond Obligation [*Investment term*] (DFIT)
CBPT .... Carbonprint (VRA)
CBQ .... Competence-Based Qualification [*Education*] (AIE)
CBRA .... Canadian Book Review Annual [*A publication*] (BRI)
CBRS .... Children's Book Review Service [*A publication*] (BRI)
CBS .... Certified Business Solutions
CBSE .... Certified Building Society Executive [*Canada*] (DD)
CBT .... Competency Based Teaching (AIE)
CBV .... Chartered Business Valuator [*Canada*] (DD)
CBZ .... Cucui [*Brazil*] [*Airport symbol*] (AD)
CC .... Christian Century [*A publication*] (BRI)
CC .... College of Commerce (AIE)
CC .... Companion of the Order of Canada (DD)
CC .... Crown Aviation [*ICAO designator*] (AD)
CCAE .... Canadian Council for the Advancement of Education
CCAT .... Cambridgeshire College of Arts and Technology [*British*] (AIE)
CCB-B .... Center for Children's Books. Bulletin [*A publication*] (BRI)
CCBOM .... Certificant, Canadian Board of Occupational Medicine (DD)
CCBS .... Completion of Calls to Busy Subscriber [*Telecommunications*] (DOM)
CCD .... Cleidocranial Dysplasia [*Medicine*]
CCDQ .... Counselling and Career Development Organisation [*British*] (AIE)
CCE .... Centre for Environmental Education [*British*] (AIE)
CCEA .... Commonwealth Council for Educational Administration [*British*] (AIE)
CCEM .... Consulting Committee on Educational Matters (AIE)
CCF .... Conservative Collegiate Forum (AIE)
CCFP .... Certificate of the College of Family Physicians of Canada (DD)
CCH .... Chile Chico [*Chile*] [*Airport symbol*] (AD)
CCH .... Commerce Clearing House (DFIT)
CCHL .... China Container Holdings
CCK .... Cocos Island [*Keeling Islands, Australia*] [*Airport symbol*] (AD)
CCO .... Contingency Contracting Officers [*Military*] (RDA)
CCol .... Chartered Colorist (DD)
CCP .... Cooperative Cardiovascular Project
CCPF .... Combined Cooling Performance Factor
CCQ .... Cachoeira do Sul [*Brazil*] [*Airport symbol*] (AD)
CCR&R .... Child Care Resource and Referral Program (WYGK)
CCRC .... Continuing-Care Retirement Communities
CCS .... Corporation of Certified Secretaries (AIE)
CCSS .... Comanche Crew Support System [*Army*] (RDA)
CCT .... College of Commerce and Technology (AIE)
CCTM .... Communication Connect Time Monitor [*Computer science*]
CCTV .... Closed Circuit Television (AIE)
CCW .... Curriculum Council for Wales (AIE)

CD.............. Call Deflection [Telecommunications] (DOM)
cd .... Card (VRA)
CD.............. Career Development (WYGK)
CD.............. Trans-Provincial Airlines [ICAO designator] (AD)
CDA............ Communications Decency Act
CDAD......... Clostridium Difficile-Associated Diarrhea [Medicine]
cdbd........... Cardboard (VRA)
CDC............ Centers for Disease Control and Prevention
CDC............ Council for Disabled Children (AIE)
CDEV .... Control Panel Device [Computer science] (DOM)
CDF............ Channel Definition Format [Microsoft Corp.] [Computer science]
CDF............ Confined Disposal Facilities
CDF............ Cortina d'Ampezzo [Italy] [Airport symbol] (AD)
CDG............ Competitive Development Group [Army] (RDA)
CD-I........... Compact Disc-Interactive [Computer science]
CDMS......... Cryogenic Dark Matter Search [Astrophysics]
Cdn .... Canadian (DD)
CDP............ Certified Data Processor (DD)
CDP .... Chandpur [Bangladesh] [Airport symbol] (AD)
CDR .... Clinical Dementia Rating
CDS .... Center for Development Studies
CD-SEM ..... Critical Dimension Scanning Electron Microscopes
cdst .... Card Stock (VRA)
CDT............ Community Development Trust (AIE)
CDU .... Christian Democratic Union [Germany] [Political party]
CDVT .... Carte-de-Visite (VRA)
CD-WO....... Compact Disc-Write Once [Computer science] (DOM)
CE .... Air Virginia [ICAO designator] (AD)
CE.............. Childhood Education [A publication] (BRI)
CE.............. Corps Eligible [Army] (RDA)
CEA............ Conductive Education Association (AIE)
CEAM-TU .... Advanced Materials at Tuskegee University (RDA)
CEAS.......... Composite Educational Abilites Scale (AIE)
CECS.......... Center for Evaluative Clinical Sciences
CEDAR .... Centre for Educational Development, Appraisal and Research
              [University of Warwick] [British] (AIE)
CEDP .... Committee for the Employment of Disabled People (AIE)
CEG............ Careers Education and Guidance (AIE)
CEG............ Chester [England] [Airport symbol] (AD)
CEH............ Central European History [A publication] (BRI)
ceil .... Ceiling (VRA)
cel .... Celadon (VRA)
CELIA......... Computer Enhanced Language Instruction Archive (AIE)
CELP .... College Employers Links Project (AIE)
celph .... Cellophane (VRA)
celtx........... Celotex (VRA)
cem .... Cement (VRA)
cemet .... Cemetery (VRA)
CE/MHE....... Construction Equipment and Materials Handling Equipment
              [Military] (RDA)
CENESC ...... Committee for Exchange with Non-English Speaking Countries (AIE)
Cent Afr Rep... Central African Republic (VRA)
Cent Am ...... Central American (VRA)
CEO............ Chief Education Officer (AIE)
CEO............ Collective-Electronic Oscillator [Physics]
CEPEP........ Centre Europeen des Parents de l'Ecole Publique (AIE)
CEQ............ Cannes [France] [Airport symbol] (AD)
cer .... Ceramics (VRA)
CERAD .... Consortium to Establish a Registry for Alzheimer's Disease
Ceram Mo ... Ceramics Monthly [A publication] (BRI)
CEREQ .... Centre d'Etudes et de Recherches sur les Qualifications (AIE)
CERN .... European Laboratory for Particle Physics
CERnet........ China Education and Research Network [Computer science]
Cert............ Certificate (DD)
CertHSM..... Certificate in Health Services Management [Academic degree] (AIE)
CESC........... Continuing Education for Senior Citizens
CESC........... Continuing Education Standing Committee (AIE)
CET............. Community Enterprise Trust (AIE)
CETYCW ..... Council for Education and Training in Youth and Community Work
              (AIE)
Ceyl .... Ceylon (VRA)
CF.............. Canadian Forum [A publication] (BRI)
CF.............. Carried Forward [Finance] (DFIT)
CF.............. Faucett [ICAO designator] (AD)
CFAR .... Collaborative Forecasting and Replenishment [Computer science]
CFB............. Call Forwarding Busy [Telecommunications] (DOM)
CFC............ Chartered Financial Counselor (DFIT)
CFD............ Bryan [Texas] [Airport symbol] (AD)
CFE............ Carbon-Fibre Electrode
CFE............ Certified Fraud Examiner [Canada] (DD)
CFE............ College of Further Education (AIE)
CFHE.......... College of Further and Higher Education (AIE)
CFI............. Closed-Fist Injury
CFNR .... Call Forwarding No Reply [Telecommunications] (DOM)
CFQ............ Cognitive Failure Questionnaire [Education] (AIE)
CFS............. Commercial Financial Services Inc.
C/FSE......... Customer/Field Support Elements (RDA)
CFU............ Call Forwarding Unconditional [Telecommunications] (DOM)
CG............. Canadian Geographic [A publication] (BRI)
CG............. Clubair [ICAO designator] (AD)
CGAP........ Cancer Genome Anatomy Project [A Cooperative database]
CGH........... Congenital Generalized Hypertrichosis [Werewolf syndrome]
              [Medicine]
CGLI........... City and Guilds of London Institute [British] (AIE)
CGNG.......... Collodion Glass Negative (VRA)

CGO............ Chengchow [China] [Airport symbol] (AD)
CGP .... Canadian Group of Painters [1933-69] (NGC)
CGQ .... Conseil de la Gravure du Quebec [1978, founded 1971 as AGQ,
              CQE from 1984] [Canada] (NGC)
CGSC .... Cancer Genetics Studies Consortium
ch .... Chemin (DD)
ch .... Church (VRA)
CH.............. Church History [A publication] (BRI)
CH.............. Express Airways [ICAO designator] (AD)
cha............. Chasing (VRA)
Cha Men ..... Changing Men [A publication] (BRI)
champ........ Champleve (VRA)
CHARISMA... Chicago-Argonne Resonant Ionization Spectrometer for Microanalysis
              [Astronomy]
CHART .... Continuous Hormones as Replacement Therapy [Medicine]
CHASSIS...... Cheshire Achievement of Scientific Skills in Schools [British] (AIE)
ChB............. Bachelor of Surgery (DD)
Ch Bk News... Children's Book News [A publication] (BRI)
chbr .... Chamber (VRA)
CHBR .... Chlorobromide Print Process (VRA)
Ch BWatch... Children's Bookwatch [A publication] (BRI)
CHDDS......... Committee of Heads of Drama Departments in Scotland (AIE)
che............. Cherry (VRA)
CHE............ Chronicle of Higher Education [A publication] (BRI)
CHEESE...... Cheshire Experiment in Educational Software [British] (AIE)
Chel .... Chelsea [A publication] (BRI)
Chem .... Chemistry (DD)
CHEM DEMIL... Chemical Demilitarization [Military] (RDA)
Chem/PetEng... Chemical/Petroleum Engineering (DD)
CHEPS .... Centre for Higher Education Policy Studies [British] (AIE)
CHEST .... Combined Higher Education Software Team (AIE)
Chev .... Chevalier (DD)
CHFC .... Certified Financial Consultant [Canada] (DD)
CHGR.......... Chemogram (VRA)
chiaro .... Chiaroscuro (VRA)
Child Lit ...... Children's Literature [A publication] (BRI)
Chino .... Chinoiserie (VRA)
CHL............. Chalna [Bangladesh] [Airport symbol] (AD)
chl .... Charcoal (VRA)
ChLAQ........ Children's Literature Association Quarterly [A publication] (BRI)
chldy........... Chalcedony (VRA)
Ch Lit Ed .... Children's Literature in Education [A publication] (BRI)
chlith .... Chromolithograph (VRA)
chlr .... Chlorite (VRA)
ChM............ Master of Surgery (DD)
CHPF .... Combined Heating Performance Factor
chpt .... Chapter (VRA)
chpt hs .... Chapter House (VRA)
CHR .... Catholic Historical Review [A publication] (BRI)
chr .... Chair of the Board (DD)
chr .... Chrome (VRA)
Ch Rev Int ... China Review International [A publication] (BRI)
CHRM .... Certificate in Human Resources Management (DD)
CHRP .... Certified Human Resources Professional [Canada] (DD)
chr scrn ...... Choir Screen (VRA)
chsbl........... Chasuble (VRA)
CHSC .... Central Health Services Council (AIE)
CHSR .... Child Health Services Research
chstnt.......... Chestnut (VRA)
CHT............. Chita [USSR] [Airport symbol] (AD)
Ch Today .... Christianity Today [A publication] (BRI)
CHU .... Chabua [India] [Airport symbol] (AD)
chvt............ Chevet (VRA)
CHW .... Charleston [West Virginia] [Airport symbol] (AD)
chya........... Chaitya (VRA)
CI................ Central Institution [Scotland] (AIE)
CI................ China Airlines [ICAO designator] (AD)
Cia .... Compania [Company] [Spanish] (DFIT)
Ciao .... Columbia International Affairs Online [Computer science]
CIBCH .... Cibachrome (VRA)
cibr .... Ciborium (VRA)
CIC............. Chartered Investment Counsellor [Canada] (DD)
CIC............. Completely in-the-Canal [Audiology]
CIC............. Computers in the Curriculum [Education] (AIE)
CIC............. Creative Incentive Coalition
CICATS........ Computer Industry Coalition for Advanced Television Service
CID............. Commander's Integrated Display [Military] (RDA)
CIDD........... Confederation of Institute Directors (AIE)
CIDE........... Cambridge International Dictionary of English [A publication]
CIHE........... Council for Industry and Higher Education (AIE)
CII.............. Chitipa [Malawi] [Airport symbol] (AD)
CILT........... Centre for Information on Language Teaching and Research
              [British] (AIE)
CIN............. Council of Indian Nations
CIP............. Canadian Insolvency Practitioner (DD)
CIP............. Cash Index Participation [Investment term] (DFIT)
CIR............. Cairo [Illinois] [Airport symbol] (AD)
Cir.............. Circle (DD)
Circt........... Circuit (DD)
CIRIS .... Computerised Information Retrieval in Schools [Project] (AIE)
CIS............. Canton Island [Phoenix Islands] [Airport symbol] (AD)
CISE........... Colleges, Institutes, and Schools in Education (AIE)
CITAR .... Computers in Training as a Resource (AIE)
CITO........... Ceramics Industry Training Organisation [British] (AIE)
CIY............. Comiso [Italy] [Airport symbol] (AD)

CJ .... Classical Journal [*A publication*] (BRI)
CJ .... Colgan Airways [*ICAO designator*] (AD)
CJR .... Columbia Journalism Review [*A publication*] (BRI)
CJZ .... Cajazeiras [*Brazil*] [*Airport symbol*] (AD)
ck .... Chalk (VRA)
CK .... Connair [*ICAO designator*] (AD)
ckcl .... Crackle (VRA)
CKE .... Carl Karcher Enterprises
CKG .... Chungking [*China*] [*Airport symbol*] (AD)
CL .... Capitol International Airways [*ICAO designator*] (AD)
cl .... Clay (VRA)
CLA .... Chartered Loss Adjuster (DD)
CLA .... Comilla [*Bangladesh*] [*Airport symbol*] (AD)
CLAIRE .... County Links Access to Information about Resources and Expertise [*Education*] (AIE)
CLASS .... Computer Literacy and Studies in Schools (AIE)
Class Out..... Classical Outlook [*A publication*] (BRI)
Class R .... Classical Review [*A publication*] (BRI)
CLD .... Centre for Learning and Development [*British*] (AIE)
CLEA/ST ..... Council of Local Education Authorities/School Teacher Committee (AIE)
CLF .... Clear [*Alaska*] [*Airport symbol*] (AD)
clg .... College (VRA)
CLH .... Coolah [*New South Wales*] [*Airport symbol*] (AD)
CLID .... Curriculum Led Institutional Development (AIE)
Clio .... Clio: A Journal of Literature, History and the Philosophy of History [*A publication*] (BRI)
CLIP .... Calling Line Identification Presentation [*Telecommunications*] (DOM)
CLIPS .... Careers Literature and Information Prescription Service (AIE)
CLIR .... Calling Line Identification Restriction [*Telecommunications*] (DOM)
clm .... Column (VRA)
CLN .... Carolina [*Brazil*] [*Airport symbol*] (AD)
CLO .... Copyright Licensing Organisation [*British*] (AIE)
CLOC .... Comparative Library Organization Committee [*American Library Association*]
clois........... Cloisonne (VRA)
CLPT .... Collodion Print (VRA)
clr .... Color (VRA)
CLR .... Columbia Law Review [*A publication*] (BRI)
CLRP .... Color Prints [*Not tinted*] (VRA)
CLS .... Comparative Literature Studies [*A publication*] (BRI)
CLSC .... Community Language in the Secondary Curriculum [*Project*] (AIE)
clst .... Clerestory (VRA)
clstr .... Cloister (VRA)
CLT .... Charitable Lead Trust
CLVR .... Cliche Verre (VRA)
CLW .... Catholic Library World [*A publication*] (BRI)
CLZ .... Cristalandia [*Brazil*] [*Airport symbol*] (AD)
CM .... Mariana Islands (VRA)
CM .... Master of Surgery (DD)
CMA .... Certified Management Accountant (DD)
CMAP .... Compound Muscle Action Potential [*Neurophysiology*]
CMAQ .... Congestion Mitigation & Air Quality [*An association*]
CM-ARI .... Contrast Media-Induced Acute Renal Insufficiency [*Medicine*]
CMC .... Correlation Metric Construction [*Analysis of chemical reaction*]
CMC .... Customized Multimedia Connection
CMED .... Council for Management Education and Development (AIE)
CMgE .... Certified Manufacturing Engineer (DD)
CMI .... Component Management Interface [*Computer science*]
CML .... Cammooweal [*Queensland*] [*Airport symbol*] (AD)
CML .... Classical and Modern Literature [*A publication*] (BRI)
CMLS .... Cellular and Molecular Life Sciences [*A publication*] [*Formerly Experientia*]
CMM .... Commander of the Order of Military Merit [*Canada*] (DD)
cmo .... Cameo (VRA)
CMO .... Case Management Organization (WYGK)
cmpnl .... Campanile (VRA)
CMR .... Capture-Mark-Recapture [*Demography*]
CMS .... Charlotte-Mecklenburg School District
CMT .... Cataloging Management Team [*American Library Association*]
CMT .... Certified Market Technician (DD)
CMT .... Class Music Teaching (AIE)
CMU .... Cheyenne Mountain Upgrade
CMV .... Cayo Mambi [*Cuba*] [*Airport symbol*] (AD)
CMX .... Hancock-Houghton [*Michigan*] [*Airport symbol*] (AD)
CN .... Tropic Air [*ICAO designator*] (AD)
CNA .... Cananea [*Mexico*] [*Airport symbol*] (AD)
CNB .... Cyclic-Nucleotide-Binding [*Neurobiology*]
CN/CMS ...... Counternarcotics Command Management System [*Army*] (RDA)
CNF .... Cytotoxic Necrotizing Factor [*Immunology*]
Cng .... Change [*A publication*] (BRI)
CNOM .... Conseil National de l'Ordre des Medecins [*France*]
CNP .... Customized Networking Platform
CNR .... Chanaral [*Chile*] [*Airport symbol*] (AD)
CNST .... Consiglio Nazionale Scienza Tecnologia [*Italy*]
cnte .... Conte (VRA)
cnte .... Conte Crayon (VRA)
cntr .... Central (VRA)
cntrps .... Contrapposto (VRA)
CNV .... Choroidal Neovascularization [*Opthalmology*]
CO .... Certificate of Origin [*Investment term*] (DFIT)
Co .... Company (DD)
CO .... Continental Airlines [*ICAO designator*] (AD)
co .... County (VRA)
Coast .... Cambridge Optical Aperture Synthesis Telescope

COCH .... Concorde out, Concorde Home
cochr .... Co-Chair of the Board (DD)
cod .... Codex (VRA)
cod .... Codices (VRA)
COD .... Collect on Delivery (DFIT)
COE .... Committee on Education [*American Library Association*]
CoEd .... Co-Educational (AIE)
COFCO .... China National Cereals Oils & Foodstuffs Import & Export Corp.
COH .... Cooch Behar [*India*] [*Airport symbol*] (AD)
COIU .... Careers and Occupational Information Unit (AIE)
col .... Collage (VRA)
Col .... Colonel (DD)
COL .... Committee on Legislation [*American Library Association*]
colab .... Collaboration (VRA)
Col Comp..... College Composition and Communication [*A publication*] (BRI)
COLI .... Corporate-Owned Life Insurance (WYGK)
coll .... Collection (VRA)
Col Lit .... College Literature [*A publication*] (BRI)
colnd .... Colonnade (VRA)
colo .... Colony (VRA)
COLOR .... Corporation for Laser Optics Research
COLTY .... Collotype (VRA)
COM........... Catalogues on Microfiche (AIE)
COM........... Center for Optics Manufacturing (RDA)
comb .... Combination (VRA)
COMBSE ...... Confidential Measurement-Based Self-Evaluation [*Project*] (AIE)
comm .... Commission (DD)
COMM MGT SYS... Communications Management Systems [*Military*] (RDA)
commr......... Commissioner (DD)
commun....... Communications (DD)
comp .... Comparison (VRA)
Comp .... Computer (DD)
COMPAS ...... Careers Office Management and Public Appraisal System (AIE)
compbd........ Composition Board (VRA)
compd .... Compound (VRA)
Comp Dr...... Comparative Drama [*A publication*] (BRI)
CompEng ..... Computer Engineering (DD)
Comp L........ Comparative Literature [*A publication*] (BRI)
compl .... Completed (VRA)
compr.......... Computer (VRA)
comps......... Composition (VRA)
CompSc .... Computer Science (DD)
compt .... Comptroller (DD)
Compt & H... Computers and the Humanities [*A publication*] (BRI)
CompuServe... CompuServe Information Service
COMSAT ...... Communications Satellite Corp. (DFIT)
Comt .... Commentary [*A publication*] (BRI)
Comw .... Commonweal [*A publication*] (BRI)
CON .... Concord [*New Hampshire*] [*Airport symbol*] (AD)
Conc .... Concession (DD)
concep......... Conceptual (VRA)
concr .... Concrete (VRA)
condo......... Condominium (VRA)
CONF .... Add-On Conference Call [*Telecommunications*] (DOM)
CONFU........ Conference on Fair Use
conj .... Conjunction (VRA)
CONPR........ Contact Print (VRA)
cons .... Consulting (DD)
consol .... Consolidated (DD)
consr .... Consecrated (VRA)
const .... Construction (DD)
ConstEng ..... Construction Engineering (DD)
ConstMgmt... Construction Management (DD)
constr .... Construction (VRA)
cont .... Contemporary (VRA)
cont .... Controller (DD)
Cont Ed....... Contemporary Education [*A publication*] (BRI)
Cont Pac..... Contemporary Pacific [*A publication*] (BRI)
COO .... Cotonou [*Dahomey*] [*Airport symbol*] (AD)
COP .... Coat Protein
COPADOCI ... Committee on Principals and Directors of Central Institutions (AIE)
COPIOR........ Committee of Professors in Operational Research (AIE)
Copt .... Coptic (VRA)
CORAD........ Committee on Restrictions Against Disabled People (AIE)
CORBA........ Common Object Request Broker Architecture [*Computer science*]
Corin........... Corinthian (VRA)
corp .... Corporate (VRA)
Corp .... Corporation (DD)
corr............. Corresponding (VRA)
Cors .... Corsica (VRA)
COS .... Certificate of Office Studies [*Academic degree*] (AIE)
COSHEP ...... Committee of Scottish Higher Education Principals (AIE)
COSPEN ...... Committee on Special Educational Needs [*Scotland*] (AIE)
COSSEC ...... Cambridge, Oxford & Southern Secondary Examinations Council [*British*] (AIE)
COSTA .... Council of Subject Teaching Associations (AIE)
cot .... Cotton (VRA)
COTCH .... Concorde out, Tourist Class Home
COTFMA ...... Chippewa-Ottawa Treaty Fishery Management Authority
COUP .... Conference on University Purchasing (AIE)
CoVRT .... Commander and Staff Visualization Research Tool [*Army*] (RDA)
COW .... Corowa [*New South Wales*] [*Airport symbol*] (AD)
CP .... Case Postale (DD)
CP .... Contemporary Psychology [*A publication*] (BRI)
CP .... Council of Principals (AIE)

CPA............ Commission on Preservation and Access
CP Air......... Canadian Pacific Airlines [*ICAO designator*] (AD)
CPE............. Campeche [*Mexico*] [*Airport symbol*] (AD)
CPE............. Certificate of Proficiency in English [*Cambridge*] [*British*] (AIE)
CPE............. Society of Canadian Painter-Etchers and Engravers [*1916-76*] (NGC)
CPFF.......... Cost Plus Fixed Fee [*Investment term*] (DFIT)
CPG............ Carmen de Patagones [*Argentina*] [*Airport symbol*] (AD)
CPIW......... Certified Professional Insurance Women's Association [*Canada*] (DD)
CPL............ Chaparral [*Colombia*] [*Airport symbol*] (AD)
cpl............. Chapel (VRA)
CP/M.......... Control Program for Microcomputers (DOM)
CP/M.......... Control Program for Microprocessors [*Computer science*]
CPO............ Central Pay Office (AIE)
CPO............ Copaipo [*Chile*] [*Airport symbol*] (AD)
CPP............ Certified Professional Purchaser [*Canada*] (DD)
CPQ............ Conseil de la Peinture du Quebec [*1978, founded 1966 as SAPQ, SAVVQ from 1980, CAPQ from 1982*] [*Canada*] (NGC)
CPR .... Canadian Philosophical Reviews [*A publication*] (BRI)
CPR .... Circular Polarization Ratio [*Physics*]
CPRS.......... Canadian Public Relations Society
CPRX.......... CompScript
cps............. Characters per Second [*Computer science*]
CPsych....... Certified Psychologist [*Canada*] (DD)
cpt............. Carpet (VRA)
CPT............ Common Procedural Terminology [*Human resources*] (WYGK)
CPVE.......... Certificate of Pre-Vocational Education [*Academic degree*] (AIE)
CQ.............. Aero-Chaco [*ICAO designator*] (AD)
CQ.............. Aerolinea Federal Argentina [*ICAO designator*] (AD)
CQ.............. Carolina Quarterly [*A publication*] (BRI)
CQE............ Conseil Quebecois de l'Estampe [*1984, founded 1971 as AGQ, CGQ from 1978*] [*Canada*] (NGC)
CQF............ Calais [*France*] [*Airport symbol*] (AD)
CQQ........... Crato [*Brazil*] [*Airport symbol*] (AD)
CR.............. Conseil de la Reine [*Canada*] (DD)
CR.............. Contemporary Review [*A publication*] (BRI)
CR ARM...... Crusader Armaments [*Army*] (RDA)
cray .... Crayon (VRA)
CRB .... Course Record Book [*Education*] (AIE)
CRE............ Conference Permanente des Recteurs, Presidents et Vice Chancellors (AIE)
CREG .... Centre for Research and Education on Gender [*University of London*] [*British*] (AIE)
Cres........... Crescent (DD)
Cres........... Cressent [*A publication*] (BRI)
CRESST ...... Cryogenic Rare Event Search with Superconducting Thermometers [*Astrophysics*]
CRF............ Carnot [*Central African Republic*] [*Airport symbol*] (AD)
C Rica .... Costa Rica (VRA)
Crim J & B.. Criminal Justice and Behavior [*A publication*] (BRI)
CRIS .... Curriculum and Resource Information Service (AIE)
CRITE......... Committee for Research into Teacher Education (AIE)
Critiq .... Critique [*A publication*] (BRI)
Critm .... Criticism [*A publication*] (BRI)
Crit Q .... Critical Quarterly [*A publication*] (BRI)
Crit R .... Critical Review [*A publication*] (BRI)
CRL............ College & Research Libraries [*A publication*] (BRI)
CRM........... Canadian Risk Manager (DD)
CrMg.......... Cro-Magnon (VRA)
CR MOB...... Crusader Mobility [*Army*] (RDA)
CR MUN/RES... Crusader Munitions/Resupply [*Army*] (RDA)
crmwr .... Creamware (VRA)
crnhs .... Cornhusks (VRA)
crnltn .... Crenellation (VRA)
crnr .... Corner (VRA)
crois .... Croissant (DD)
CROSH........ Changing Role of the Secondary Head [*Project*] (AIE)
CRS .... Contingency Remoting System [*Military*] (RDA)
crsg .... Crossing (VRA)
CRT............ Charitable Remainder Trust
Crt.............. Court (DD)
crtch .... Cartouche (VRA)
crtn .... Cartoon (VRA)
crtnstl .... Corten Steel (VRA)
CRU .... Consultancy and Research Unit [*Department of Information Studies, University of Sheffield*] [*British*] (AIE)
CRV .... Caravelas [*Brazil*] [*Airport symbol*] (AD)
crv .... Carved (VRA)
crys........... Crystal (VRA)
crytd .... Caryatid (VRA)
CS.............. Air Toronto [*ICAO designator*] (AD)
CS.............. Communication Studies (AIE)
CS.............. Contemporary Sociology [*A publication*] (BRI)
CSA............ Catalysed Signal Amplification [*Analytical biochemistry*]
CSAE.......... Canadian Society of Association Executives
CSAM/MEADS... Corps Surface-to-Air Missile/Medium Extended Air Defense System [*Military*] (RDA)
CSAP .... Canadian Society of Applied Art [*1905, founded 1903 as Society of Arts and Crafts of Canada*] (NGC)
CSB............ Careers Service Branch [*Department of Employment*] [*British*] (AIE)
CSCFC .... Conference of Scottish Centrally Funded Colleges (AIE)
CSD............ Chemical Stockpile Disposal [*Military*] (RDA)
CSEA.......... Canadian Society for Education through Art [*1951*] (NGC)
CSEP.......... Chemical Stockpile Emergency Preparedness [*Military*] (RDA)
CSFRE .... Canadian Society of Fund Raising Executives

CSGA .... Canadian Society of Graphic Art [*1923-76, founded c.1903 as GAC, SGA from 1912*] (NGC)
CSI .... Cable Systems International
CSJ............. Cape St. Jacques [*South Vietnam*] [*Airport symbol*] (AD)
CSM........... Christian Science Monitor [*A publication*] (BRI)
CSME......... Centre for Science and Mathematics Education [*British*] (AIE)
CSN............ Contract Student Numbers (AIE)
CSO............ Carrasco [*Montevideo, Uruguay*] [*Airport symbol*] (AD)
CSP............ Conspecific Sperm Precedence [*Entomology*]
CSPG.......... Canadian Society of Petroleum Geologists (DD)
CSPWC........ Canadian Society of Painters in Water Colour [*1925*] (NGC)
CSQ........... Conseil de la Sculpture du Quebec [*1978, founded 1961 as ASQ*] [*Canada*] (NGC)
CSRA .... Compound-Specific Radiocarbon Analyses
CSS............ Cascading Style Sheets [*Computer science*]
CSSAS........ Campaign for State-Supported Alternative Schools (AIE)
cst............. Cast (VRA)
CSTA.......... Council of Subject Teaching Associations (AIE)
cstu........... Costume (VRA)
CSU............ Community Skills Unit (AIE)
CT.............. Children Today [*A publication*] (BRI)
CT.............. Command Airways [*ICAO designator*] (AD)
ct.............. Court (VRA)
CTA............ Canadian Trucking Association
CTA............ College of Technology and Art (AIE)
CTA............ Cyanoacrylate Tissue Adhesive [*Medicine*]
CTAD .... Cambridge Training and Development [*British*] (AIE)
CTE............ Constitutive Transport Element [*Biochemistry*]
CTEA.......... Canadian Transportation Equipment Association
CTES.......... Council for Tertiary Education in Scotland (AIE)
CTGF.......... Connective-Tissue Growth Factor [*Biochemistry*]
cth .... Cloth (VRA)
CTH............ Crateus [*Brazil*] [*Airport symbol*] (AD)
cths........... Courthouse (VRA)
CTI .... Computers in Teaching Initiative (AIE)
CTISS......... Computers in Teaching Initiative Support Service (AIE)
ctmb .... Catacomb (VRA)
CTP............ Critical Technical Parameters (RDA)
CTQ............ Santa Vitoria [*Brazil*] [*Airport symbol*] (AD)
CTR............ Cooperative Threat Reduction [*Military*] (RDA)
ctry .... Country (VRA)
CTTS .... Classical T Tauri Stars [*Astronomy*]
CTUT.......... Committee on the Training of University Teachers (AIE)
CTW........... Crotone [*Italy*] [*Airport symbol*] (AD)
ctyd........... Courtyard (VRA)
CTYP.......... Cyanotype (VRA)
cu .... Copper (VRA)
CU............. Cubana Airlines [*ICAO designator*] (AD)
CUA Architecture... Common User Access Architecture [*Computer science*] (DOM)
CUB .... Citizens United for Bear
CUB .... Coalition United for Bear
cub............. Cubicle (VRA)
CUBS.......... Calls Underwritten by Swanbrook [*Investment term*] (DFIT)
CUCD .... Council for University Classics Departments (AIE)
CUDE .... Cambridge University Department of Education [*British*] (AIE)
CUEFL........ Communicative Use of English as a Foreign Language (AIE)
Cu H .... Current History [*A publication*] (BRI)
CUJ............ Canutama [*Brazil*] [*Airport symbol*] (AD)
CUK............ Combika [*Sao Paulo, Brazil*] [*Airport symbol*] (AD)
CUL............ Communist University of London [*England*] (AIE)
CUL8R......... See You Later [*Computer science*] (DOM)
cunif .... Cuneiform (VRA)
cuplt .... Copperplate (VRA)
Cur R .... Curriculum Review [*A publication*] (BRI)
CUV............ Casigua [*Venezuela*] [*Airport symbol*] (AD)
CUWU......... Claimants and Unemployed Workers' Union (AIE)
CV.............. Associated Airlines [*ICAO designator*] (AD)
CV.............. Convertible Security [*Investment term*] (DFIT)
CVA............ Cumulative Volcano Amplitude [*Volcanology*]
CVI............. Counterflow Virtual Impactor [*Instrumentation*]
CVO............ Albany-Corvallis [*Oregon*] [*Airport symbol*] (AD)
CVPT.......... Certificate for Vocational Preparation Tutors (AIE)
CVQ............ Carnarvon [*Western Australia*] [*Airport symbol*] (AD)
CVRD.......... Companhia Vale do Rio Doce
CVSMP........ Combat Vehicle Signature Management Plan [*Army*] (RDA)
CVST.......... Cerebral Venous Sinus Thrombosis [*Medicine*]
CVU............ Calibration Validation Unit [*Instrumentation*]
CVYS.......... Council for Voluntary Youth Service (AIE)
CW............. Classical World [*A publication*] (BRI)
CW............. St. Andrews Airways [*ICAO designator*] (AD)
CWE........... Cromwell [*New Zealand*] [*Airport symbol*] (AD)
CWID.......... Call-Waiting Identification [*Telecommunications service*]
CWP........... Campbellpore [*Pakistan*] [*Airport symbol*] (AD)
CX............. Cathay Pacific Airways [*ICAO designator*] (AD)
CXA............ Caicara de Orinoco [*Venezuela*] [*Airport symbol*] (AD)
CXE............ Charge Exchange Excitations [*Physics*]
CXJ............ Caxias do Sul [*Brazil*] [*Airport symbol*] (AD)
CXS............ Caxias [*Brazil*] [*Airport symbol*] (AD)
CY............. Cyprus Airways [*ICAO designator*] (AD)
cyl............. Cylindrical (VRA)
cyp............. Cypress (VRA)
Cyp........... Cyprus (VRA)
CYSA.......... Community and Youth Service Association (AIE)
CZ.............. Cascade Airways [*ICAO designator*] (AD)
CZA............ Coari [*Brazil*] [*Airport symbol*] (AD)

CZT .... Cadmium, Zinc, and Telluride
CZU .... Corozal [*Colombia*] [*Airport symbol*] (AD)
CZY .... Cluny [*Queensland*] [*Airport symbol*] (AD)

D

By Acronym

d .... Died (VRA)
DA .... Dan-Air Services [*ICAO designator*] (AD)
DA .... Distribution-Abundance [*Ecology*]
DA .... Documents against Acceptance [*Investment term*] (DFIT)
DAA .... Deposit Administration Arrangement (WYGK)
DACA .... Design Accreditation and Certification Advisers (AIE)
DAD .... Danang [*South Vietnam*] [*Airport symbol*] (AD)
DADS .... Dads Advising Dads
Dah .... Dahomy (VRA)
DAH .... Dathina [*Yemen*] [*Airport symbol*] (AD)
DAI .... Development Alternatives, Inc.
DAISEY .... Development Assessment and Instruction for Success in the Early Years [*Education*] (AIE)
DALI .... Digitally Archived Library Images
Dal R .... Dalhousie Review [*A publication*] (BRI)
Dance .... Dance Magazine [*A publication*] (BRI)
Dance RJ .... Dance Research Journal [*A publication*] (BRI)
DAPP .... Defense Acquisition Pilot Program [*Army*] (RDA)
DARO .... Defense Airborne Reconnaissance Office
DARS .... Digital Audio Radio Service
DASI .... Developing Anti-Sexist Innovations (AIE)
DASP .... Defense Acquisition Scholarship Program [*DoD*] (RDA)
DATA .... Design and Technology Association (AIE)
DATEC .... Design and Art Technician Education Council (AIE)
DAVIC .... Digital Audio Visual Council (DOM)
DB .... Brittany Air International [*ICAO designator*] (AD)
DBA .... Dynamic Bandwidth Allocation [*Computer science*]
dbl .... Double (VRA)
DBM .... Debra Markos [*Ethiopia*] [*Airport symbol*] (AD)
DBO .... Dubbo [*New South Wales*] [*Airport symbol*] (AD)
DBP .... Defined Benefit Plan [*Human resources*] (WYGK)
dbrs .... Debris (VRA)
DBT .... Debra Tabor [*Ethiopia*] [*Airport symbol*] (AD)
Dbt .... Downbeat [*A publication*] (BRI)
dc .... Duck (VRA)
DC .... Trans Catalina Airlines [*ICAO designator*] (AD)
DCA .... Detrended Correspondence Analysis [*Mathematics*]
DCAP .... Dependent Care Assistance Plan [*Insurance*] (WYGK)
DCC .... Data Communication Channel (DOM)
DCE .... Data Communications Equipment (DOM)
DCE .... Department of Continuing Education (AIE)
D-channel .... Delta Channel [*Used for communicating between the phone company switch and an ISDN adapter*] [*Computer science*]
DCI .... Disseminated Cryptococcus Neoformans Infection [*Medicine*]
DCM .... Disability Case Management [*Insurance*] (WYGK)
DCOM .... Distributed Component Object Model [*Computer science*]
DCP .... Defined Contribution Plan [*Insurance*] (WYGK)
DCP .... Dental Capitation Plan [*Insurance*] (WYGK)
DCP .... Dental Care Plan [*Insurance*] (WYGK)
DCP .... Dependent Care Program [*Insurance*] (WYGK)
DCR .... Dependent-Care Reimbursement [*Insurance*] (WYGK)
DCRB .... Descriptive Cataloging of Rare Books [*American Library Association*]
DCU .... Data Capture Unit (AIE)
DCW .... Dependent Coverage Waiver [*Insurance*] (WYGK)
DD .... Command Airways [*ICAO designator*] (AD)
DD .... Doctor of Divinity (DD)
DDACM .... Deputy Director for Acquisition Career Management [*Army*] (RDA)
DDAR .... Department of Disarmament and Arms Regulation [*United Nations*]
DDB .... Double-Declining-Balance Depreciation Method [*Finance*] (DFIT)
DDL .... Dodollo [*Ethiopia*] [*Airport symbol*] (AD)
DDMAC .... Division of Drug Marketing, Advertising, and Communications [*Food and Drug Administration*]
DDN .... Devis Directeurs Nationaux [*Canada*] (DD)
DDN .... Diploma de Droit Notarial [*Canada*] (DD)
DDPLO .... Designated Disabled Persons Liaison Officer (AIE)
DDR .... Digital Disk Recorder (DOM)
DDS .... Digital Dataphone Service [*Telecommunications*] (DOM)
DDU .... Dadu [*Pakistan*] [*Airport symbol*] (AD)
DDZ .... Dedza [*Malawi*] [*Airport symbol*] (AD)
DE .... Downeast Airlines [*ICAO designator*] (AD)
DEAPSIE .... Department of Economic, Administrative, and Policy Studies (AIE)
dec .... Decorative (VRA)
ded .... Dedicated (VRA)
DEd .... Doctor of Education (AIE)
delfwr .... Delftware (VRA)
DELTA .... Dedication and Everlasting Love to Animals [*An association*]

DELTA .... Development of Learning and Teaching in the Arts (AIE)
Den .... Denmark (VRA)
DEP .... Double-Exposure Prevention [*Advanced photo system*]
depict .... Depicting (VRA)
dept .... Department (DD)
DEQ .... Daydream Island [*Queensland*] [*Airport symbol*] (AD)
des .... Design (VRA)
DES .... Diplome d'Etudes Superieures [*Canada*] (DD)
DESc .... Doctor of Environmental Studies (DD)
DESc .... Doctor of Economic Science (DD)
DesScEco .... Docteur es Sciences Economiques (DD)
DESTECH .... Design and Technology in Education (AIE)
destr .... Destroyed (VRA)
det .... Detail (VRA)
detch .... Detached (VRA)
DEUCE .... Deployable Universal Combat Earthmover (RDA)
DEurL .... Doctor of European Law (DD)
devel .... Development (DD)
DEWKS .... Dual Employed With Kids (DFIT)
DF .... Air Nebraska [*ICAO designator*] (AD)
DFC .... Digital Future Coalition
DFI .... Differential Fluorescence Induction [*Analytic biochemistry*]
DFWA .... Drug-Free Workplace Act of 1988 (WYGK)
DG .... Darien Airlines [*ICAO designator*] (AD)
DGU .... Dedougu [*Upper Volta*] [*Airport symbol*] (AD)
DGVT .... Director General for Vocational Training (AIE)
DH .... Discovery Airlines [*ICAO designator*] (AD)
DH .... Double Homology [*Biochemistry*]
DH .... Tonga Air Service [*ICAO designator*] (AD)
DHC .... Doctorat Honoris Causa [*Canada*] (DD)
DHL .... Dhala [*Aden*] [*Airport symbol*] (AD)
dHTML .... Dynamic HTML [*HyperText Markup Language*] [*Computer science*]
DI .... Delta Air [*ICAO designator*] (AD)
DI .... Divisional Inspector [*Education*] (AIE)
dia .... Diameter (VRA)
diag .... Diagram (VRA)
Dialogue .... Dialogue: Canadian Philosophical Review [*A publication*] (BRI)
DIBBL .... Dismounted Infantry Battle Space Battle Lab [*Army*] (RDA)
DIBOA .... Dihydroxy Benoxazin One [*Organic chemistry*]
DIC .... Dili [*Zaire*] [*Airport symbol*] (AD)
DIC .... Diploma of the Imperial College of Science, Technology, and Medicine [*Canada*] (DD)
did .... Didactic (VRA)
DID .... Drivers Integrated Display [*Military*] (RDA)
DIF .... Dakota Indian Foundation
dif .... Different (VRA)
DIG .... Diffuse Ionized Gas [*Astrophysics*]
DIGITALIS .... Discussion Group on Information Technology in Library and Information Studies Schools (AIE)
DII .... Defense Information Infrastructure [*Military*]
DIJ .... Dijon [*France*] [*Airport symbol*] (AD)
DIL .... Dilly [*Portuguese Timor*] [*Airport symbol*] (AD)
dim .... Dimension (VRA)
DIMM .... Dual In-Line Memory Module [*Computer science*] (DOM)
DINKS .... Dual-Income, No Kids (DFIT)
DIP .... Diapaga [*Upper Volta*] [*Airport symbol*] (AD)
Dip .... Diploma (DD)
DIPC .... Diisopropyl Carbodiimide [*Organic chemistry*]
DipDN .... Diplome en Droit Civil (DD)
DIP switch .... Dual In-Line Package Switch [*Electronics*] (DOM)
dir .... Director (DD)
DIS .... Deep Inelastic Scattering [*Particle physics*]
Dis .... Dissent [*A publication*] (BRI)
DISA .... Data Interchange Standards Association
DISC .... Drop-In Skills Centre [*British*] (AIE)
disp .... Dispersion (VRA)
dist .... Distant (VRA)
DISTAR .... Direct Instructional Systems to Arithmetic and Reading (AIE)
distr .... District (VRA)
distrb .... Distribute (VRA)
DITTO .... Directory of Independent Training and Tutorial Organisations (AIE)
DIV .... Days in Vitro [*Cell culture*]
div .... Division (DD)
divers .... Diversion (VRA)
DJ .... Air Djibouti [*ICAO designator*] (AD)
DJB .... Djambi [*Indonesia*] [*Airport symbol*] (AD)

DJJ	Djajapura [*West Irian, Indonesia*] [*Airport symbol*] (AD)
DJM	Djambala [*Congo*] [*Airport symbol*] (AD)
DJR	Dajarra [*Queensland*] [*Airport symbol*] (AD)
DJV	Dabajuro [*Venezuela*] [*Airport symbol*] (AD)
dk	Dark (VRA)
DK	Decatur [*ICAO designator*] (AD)
DLB	d'Albertis [*Australia*] [*Airport symbol*] (AD)
DLB	Dementia with Lewy Bodies [*Nerve cell pathology*]
DLH	Duluth [*Minnesota-Superior, Wisconsin*] [*Airport symbol*] (AD)
DLI	Dalat [*South Vietnam*] [*Airport symbol*] (AD)
DLP	Digital Light Processing
DLPFC	Dorsolateral Prefrontal Cortex [*Brain anatomy*]
DLS	[*The*] Dalles [*Oregon*] [*Airport symbol*] (AD)
DM	DodecylMaltoside [*Organic chemistry*]
D/M	Dr. & Mrs. (VRA)
DM	Meersk Air [*ICAO designator*] (AD)
DMC	Destination Digital Media Computers [*Computer science*]
dmd	Diamond (VRA)
DME	Designated Mechanic Examiners
DMG	Deterministic Microgrinding [*Optics manufacturing*] (RDA)
DMil Sc	Doctorate of Military Science (DD)
DMJM	Daniel, Mann, Johnson, & Mendenhall [*A major contributor to architecture in Jakarta, Sidney, Manila, and Seoul*]
DMS	Desktop Management Suite [*Computer science*]
DMS	Dynamic Modelling System (AIE)
dmsk	Damask (VRA)
DMT	Diamantina [*Brazil*] [*Airport symbol*] (AD)
DMV	Doctorat en Medecin Veterinaire (DD)
DMV	Dolphin Morbillivirus
DN	Directory Number [*Computer science*]
DN	Skystream Airlines [*ICAO designator*] (AD)
DNG	Danghila [*Ethiopia*] [*Airport symbol*] (AD)
DNI	Wad Medani [*Sudan*] [*Airport symbol*] (AD)
DNT	Dermonecrotic Toxin [*Immunology*]
DNT	Natitingou [*Dahomey*] [*Airport symbol*] (AD)
D/O	Delivery Order (DFIT)
DO	Dominicana de Aviacion [*ICAO designator*] (AD)
DoE	Department of Energy
DoEd	Department of Education
DOER	Dredging Operations and Environmental Research [*US Army Corps of Engineers*]
DOG	Difference of Gaussians [*Image processing*]
Dog Fan	Dog Fancy [*A publication*] (BRI)
DoH	Department of Health (AIE)
DoI	Department of the Interior
DOL	Deauville [*France*] [*Airport symbol*] (AD)
DOM	Dominica [*Leeward Islands*] [*Airport symbol*] (AD)
DOMES	Digest of Middle East Studies [*A publication*] (BRI)
Dom Rep	Dominican Republic (VRA)
DOPS	Dioleoylphosphatidylserine [*Biochemistry*]
DOR	Dori [*Upper Volta*] [*Airport symbol*] (AD)
dorm	Dormitory (VRA)
DOTAP	Dioleoyl Trimethylammonium Propane [*Organic chemistry*]
DOTS	Directly Observed Treatment Short-Course [*Therapy regime*]
DOV	Dover [*Delaware*] [*Airport symbol*] (AD)
DOY	Deboyne [*Louisiade Archipelago, Papua*] [*Airport symbol*] (AD)
DP	Cochise Airlines [*ICAO designator*] (AD)
dp	Depth (VRA)
DP	Documents against Payment (DFIT)
DPI	Dry Powder Inhaler [*Pharmacy*]
DPO	Data Processing Officer (AIE)
DPPO	Dental Preferred Provider Organization [*Insurance*] (WYGK)
DPTS	Dimethylamino Pyridiniumtoluenesulfonic Acid [*Organic chemistry*]
dpty	Diptych (VRA)
DPU	Dumpu [*New Guinea*] [*Airport symbol*] (AD)
DQ	Coastal Air Transport [*ICAO designator*] (AD)

DQF	Division of Quality Enhancement (AIE)
DR	Advance Airlines [*ICAO designator*] (AD)
Dr	Doctor (DD)
dr	Door (VRA)
Dr	Drive (DD)
DRE	Direct-Recording Electronic [*Technology*]
DREN	Defense Research and Engineering Network [*DoD*]
DRF	Direct Radiative Forcing [*Atmospheric science*]
DRG	Diagnosis-Related Group [*Insurance*] (WYGK)
DRGN	Distributed Real-Time Groove Network [*Computer science*]
DRI	Dietary Reference Intakes
DRM	Drama [*Greece*] [*Airport symbol*] (AD)
DRUV	Diffuse-Reflectance Ultraviolet-Visible [*Spectra*]
dryp	Drypoint (VRA)
DS	Air Senegal [*ICAO designator*] (AD)
DSA	Dell SCSI Array [*Computer science*]
DSA	Diplome en Sciences Administratives (DD)
DSA	Docteur es Sciences Agricole [*Doctor of Agricultural Sciences*] (DD)
DSA	Doctor of Agricultural Sciences (DD)
DSig	Digital Signature Initiative [*Computer science*]
DSL	Daru [*Sierra Leone*] [*Airport symbol*] (AD)
DSO	Companion of the Distinguished Service Order [*Canada*] (DD)
DSPS	Digital Signal Processors [*Computer science*]
DSR	Departmental Staff Records (AIE)
DSS	Desktop Security Suite [*McAfee Associates, Inc.*] [*Computer science*]
DSS	Direct Satellite System
DT	TAAG-Angola Airlines [*ICAO designator*] (AD)
DTA	Dance Teachers' Association (AIE)
DTN	Digital Television Network
DTT	Detroit [*Michigan*] [*Airport symbol*] (AD)
DTTP	Documents to the People [*Government Documents Round Table*] [*American Library Association*]
DTYP	Daguerreotype (VRA)
DU	Diploma in Urology (DD)
DU	Docteur d'Universite [*Doctor of the University*] [*Canada*] (DD)
DU	Roland Air [*ICAO designator*] (AD)
DUEG	Development Unit Executive Group [*Scotland*] (AIE)
DUI	Duisburg [*Germany*] [*Airport symbol*] (AD)
DUN	Dial-Up Networking [*Microsoft Windows 95*] [*Computer science*]
dup	Duplicate (VRA)
DUTN	Duotone (VRA)
DV	Nantucket Airlines [*ICAO designator*] (AD)
DVC	Digital Video Cassette (DOM)
DVD	Digital Versatile Disc
DVD	Digital Versatile Disk
DVE	Driver's Vision Enhancer [*Military*]
DVM	Discrete Variation Method
DVP	Davenport Downs [*Queensland*] [*Airport symbol*] (AD)
DW	DLT Deutsche Regional [*ICAO designator*] (AD)
Dwango	Dial-Up Wide Area Network Gaming Operation [*Computer science*]
dwg	Drawing (VRA)
dwl	Dwelling (VRA)
DWP	Dalbandin [*Pakistan*] [*Airport symbol*] (AD)
DWT	Discrete Wavelet Transformation (DOM)
DX	Danair [*ICAO designator*] (AD)
DXA	Dual Energy X-Ray Absorptiometry [*Painless bone mass test*] [*Medicine*]
DXB	Dubai [*Trucial Oman*] [*Airport symbol*] (AD)
DXF	Data Exchange File [*Computer science*]
DXT	Dhoxaton [*Greece*] [*Airport symbol*] (AD)
DXY	Derby [*England*] [*Airport symbol*] (AD)
DY	Alyemda Democratic Yemen [*ICAO designator*] (AD)
DYM	Diamantina Lakes [*Queensland*] [*Airport symbol*] (AD)
DYTRPT	Dye Transfer Print (VRA)
DYW	Daly Waters [*Northern Territory, Australia*] [*Airport symbol*] (AD)
DYW	Detached Youth Worker (AIE)
DZ	Douglas Airways [*ICAO designator*] (AD)

E
By Acronym

E .... Declared or Paid in the Preceding 12 Months [*Investment term*] (DFIT)
ea .... Early (VRA)
EA .... Education Association (AIE)
EA .... Evaluation Agree [*Canada*] (DD)
EACPD .... Emergency Advisory Committee for Political Defense
EAEB .... East Anglian Examinations Board (AIE)
EAH .... El Arish [*Egypt*] [*Airport symbol*] (AD)
EALS .... English & American Literature Section [*Association of College and Research Libraries*] [*American Library Association*]
EAMM .... Electronic Access to Medieval Manuscripts
EAP .... Electronic Access Project
EARAC .... East Anglian Regional Advisory Council for Further Education (AIE)
EAS .... Electronic Actuation System
EASP .... Educational Advice Service Project (AIE)
EBD .... Emotional and Behavioural Difficulties (AIE)
EBITA .... Earnings before Interest, Taxes, Depreciation, and Amortization [*Investment term*] (DFIT)
EBLIDA .... European Bureau of Library Information and Documentation Associations (AIE)
EBMT .... European Bone Marrow Transplantation
ebn .... Ebonized (VRA)
ebn .... Ebony (VRA)
EBST .... Educational Broadcasting Services Trust (AIE)
EBW .... Ebolowa [*Cameroon*] [*Airport symbol*] (AD)
EC .... Air Ecosse [*ICAO designator*] (AD)
ECaP .... Exceptional Cancer Patients [*Therapy program*]
EcATT .... Economic Awareness Teacher Training (AIE)
ECB .... Enhanced Cubic Grain [*Photography*]
ECC .... Error Correction and Control
eccles .... Ecclesiastical (VRA)
ECEJ .... Early Childhood Education Journal [*A publication*] (BRI)
ECF .... Extended Care Facility (WYGK)
ECG .... Elizabeth City [*North Carolina*] [*Airport symbol*] (AD)
ECG .... Epicatechin Gallate [*Biochemistry*]
ECHO .... Environment, Conservation, and Hunting Outreach [*An association*]
ECIS .... Engineering Careers Information Service (AIE)
ECM .... Emerging Company Marketplace (DFIT)
Econ .... Economics (DD)
Econ .... Economist [*A publication*] (BRI)
Econ J .... Economic Journal [*A publication*] (BRI)
ECP .... Electronic Check Presentment [*Finance*]
ECPH .... [*The*] Electronic Communications Privacy Act
ECRE .... European Council on Refugees and Exiles
ECS .... Educational Counselling Service [*British Council*] (AIE)
ECT .... Explicit Call Transfer [*Telecommunications*] (DOM)
Ecu .... Ecuador (VRA)
ECYEB .... European Community Youth Exchange Bureau (AIE)
ED .... Canadian Efficiency Decoration [*Military*] (DD)
ed .... Edition (VRA)
Ed .... Education (DD)
ED .... Sunbird [*ICAO designator*] (AD)
EDAP .... Employee Development and Assistance Programme (AIE)
EDDIS .... Electronic Document Delivery: Integrated Solutions [*Project*] (AIE)
Ed F .... Educational Forum [*A publication*] (BRI)
EDO DRAM... Enhanced Data Output Dynamic Access Random [*Computer science*]
EDP .... Enterprise Development Programme [*University of Glasgow*] (AIE)
EDR .... Electromagnetic Dent Removal [*Aviation*]
Ed Theory ... Educational Theory [*A publication*] (BRI)
EDU .... Enterprise and Deregulation Unit (AIE)
educ .... Education (VRA)
EDWAAA ...... Economic Dislocation and Worker Adjustment Assistance Act of 1988 (WYGK)
EE .... Eagle Commuter Airlines [*ICAO designator*] (AD)
EEAA .... Employee Educational Assistance Act of 1978 (WYGK)
EEB .... Ecology and Evolutionary Biology [*A discipline division*]
EEG .... Employment and Enterprise Group (AIE)
EEN .... Brattleboro, Vermont-Keene, New Hampshire [*Airport symbol*] (AD)
EEN .... Education for Enterprise Network (AIE)
EEng .... Electrical Engineering (DD)
EEP .... Education Excellence Partnership
EF .... Far Eastern Air Transport [*ICAO designator*] (AD)
efg .... Effigy (VRA)
EFK .... Newport [*Vermont*] [*Airport symbol*] (AD)
EG .... Economic Geography [*A publication*] (BRI)

EG .... Roederer Aviation [*ICAO designator*] (AD)
EGAS .... Educational Grants Advisory Service (AIE)
EGC .... Epigallocathechin [*Biochemistry*]
EGL .... Neghelli [*Ethiopia*] [*Airport symbol*] (AD)
EGP .... Eastern Group of Painters, Montreal [*1938*] [*Canada*] (NGC)
Egy .... Egypt (VRA)
EHA .... Education for All Handicapped Children Act (AIE)
EHC .... Electrohydrodynamic Convection [*Physics*]
EHD .... Extended-Height-to-Diameter [*Aviation*]
EHOP .... Employee Home Ownership Plan [*Human resources*] (WYGK)
EHR .... English Historical Review [*A publication*] (BRI)
EI .... Air Lingus [*ICAO designator*] (AD)
EI .... Educational Insights
EI .... Employee Involvement [*Human resources*] (WYGK)
EIC .... European Information Centre (AIE)
EIDE .... Enhanced Integral Drive Electronics (DOM)
EIESP .... European Institute of Education and Social Policy (AIE)
Eight-C St ... Eighteenth-Century Studies [*A publication*] (BRI)
EIS .... Beef Island [*British Virgin Islands*] [*Airport symbol*] (AD)
EIS .... Education in Science (AIE)
EIT .... Eilat [*Israel*] [*Airport symbol*] (AD)
EJ .... English Journal [*A publication*] (BRI)
EJ .... New England Airlines [*ICAO designator*] (AD)
EJO .... Nejo [*Ethiopia*] [*Airport symbol*] (AD)
EK .... Masling Commuter Services [*ICAO designator*] (AD)
EKIP .... Eastman Kodak Inst. Print Film (VRA)
EKT .... Ektachrome (VRA)
EL .... Educational Leadership [*A publication*] (BRI)
EL .... Nihon Kinkyori Airways [*ICAO designator*] (AD)
ELAB .... Environmental Laboratory Advisory Board [*Environmental Protection Agency*]
ELAS .... Education Law Advisers Service (AIE)
elctr .... Electronic (VRA)
elctrpl .... Electroplate (VRA)
eld .... Elder (VRA)
ELE .... El Adem [*Libya*] [*Airport symbol*] (AD)
elem .... Element (VRA)
ElEng .... Electronic Engineering (DD)
ELG .... El Golea [*Algeria*] [*Airport symbol*] (AD)
ELID .... Electrolytic-in-Process-Dressing [*Optics manufacturing*] (RDA)
ELITE .... Enterprise Learning through Information Technology [*University of Durham*] (AIE)
ELM .... Corning-Elmira [*New York*] [*Airport symbol*] (AD)
ELMSS .... Educators of Library Media Specialists Section [*American Association of School Librarians*] [*American Library Association*]
elmwd .... Elmwood (VRA)
ELRF .... Eyesafe LASER Rangefinder (RDA)
ELS .... Education Learning Services (AIE)
ELST .... Endolymphatic Sac Tumors [*Oncology*]
ELSTPT .... Electrostatic Print (VRA)
ELT .... English Literature in Transition 1880-1920 [*A publication*] (BRI)
ELTA .... European Learning Technology Association (AIE)
elv .... Elevation (VRA)
ELW .... Enhanced Land Warrior [*Military*] (RDA)
EM .... Empire Airlines [*ICAO designator*] (AD)
EM .... Extra-Mural (AIE)
EM .... Hammond's Air Service [*ICAO designator*] (AD)
E Mag .... E Magazine [*A publication*] (BRI)
e-mail .... Electronic Mail [*Computer science*]
EMASHE ...... Establishing Multimedia Authoring Skills in Higher Education (AIE)
embr .... Embroidery (VRA)
embrs .... Embrasure (VRA)
embs .... Embossed (VRA)
EMC .... Every Member Canvas [*Fundraising*]
Emerg Lib.... Emergency Librarian [*A publication*] (BRI)
EMEU .... East Midlands Education Union [*British*] (AIE)
EMF .... Enhanced Metafile [*Computer science*]
EMHT .... Early to Mid-Holocene Transition
eml .... Emulsion (VRA)
emp .... Emperor (VRA)
EMP .... Executive Management Program (DD)
EMRACSE ..... East Midland Regional Advisory Committee on Special Education [*British*] (AIE)
emrl .... Emerald (VRA)
EMRU .... Employment Market Research Unit (AIE)
EMV .... Equine Morbillivirus

EMV	Every Member Visit [*Fundraising*]
EN	Air Caravane [*ICAO designator*] (AD)
enc	Encaustic (VRA)
ENED	Education Network for Environment and Development (AIE)
eng	Engineering (DD)
Eng	England (VRA)
Eng&Bus	Engineering & Business (DD)
Engl	English (DD)
engr	Engraving (VRA)
EngSc	Engineering Science (DD)
EngTech	Engineering Technology (DD)
En Jnl	Energy Journal [*A publication*] (BRI)
ENK	Enniskillen [*Northern Ireland*] [*Airport symbol*] (AD)
enl	Enamel (VRA)
enlgmnt	Enlargement (VRA)
ENQ?	Are You There? [*Computer science*] (DOM)
ensb	Ensemble (VRA)
entbl	Entablature (VRA)
entr	Entrance (VRA)
Ent W	Entertainment Weekly [*A publication*] (BRI)
Env	Environment [*A publication*] (BRI)
envir	Environment (VRA)
envirl	Environmental (DD)
EO	Aeroamerica [*ICAO designator*] (AD)
EO	Air Nordic Sweden [*ICAO designator*] (AD)
EOF mark	End-of-File Mark [*Computer science*]
EO/IR	Electro-Optic/Infrared (RDA)
EOP	English for Occupational Purposes (AIE)
EOR	El Dorado [*Venezuela*] [*Airport symbol*] (AD)
EOS	Exodus Online Services [*Computer science*]
EP	Epileptic (AIE)
EP	Tropic Air Services [*ICAO designator*] (AD)
EPA	European Parent Association (AIE)
EPE	Elvis Presley Enterprises
EPEB	Ecosystem Processes and Effects Branch [*Army*]
EPED	Environmental Processes and Effects Division [*Army*]
EPI	Educational Priority Indices (AIE)
EPOC	Employers' Perceptions of Colleges (AIE)
EPR	Education in Personal Relationships (AIE)
equip	Equipment (DD)
ER	Ecumenical Review [*A publication*] (BRI)
ERA	Education Reform Act [*1988*] (AIE)
ERA	Erigavo [*Somalia*] [*Airport symbol*] (AD)
ERB	Education Research Branch (AIE)
ERC	Erzincan [*Turkey*] [*Airport symbol*] (AD)
ERCS	Elective Repeat Cesarean Section [*Obstetrics*]
ERDM	Employment Rehabilitation Divisional Manager (AIE)
ERG	Eromanga [*New Hebrides*] [*Airport symbol*] (AD)
ERID	Emerging and Reemerging Infectious Diseases [*Medicine*]
ERM	Environmental Resources Management
EROS	Event-Related Optical Signal [*Imaging science*]
ERRC	Employment Relations Resource Centre [*British*] (AIE)
ERTEC	Eastern Region Teacher Education Consortium (AIE)
erthwk	Earthwork (VRA)
erthwr	Earthenware (VRA)
ERV	Endogenous Retrovirus
ES	Air Atlantique [*ICAO designator*] (AD)
ES	Educational Studies [*A publication*] (BRI)
ESAC	Education Service Advisory Committee (AIE)
E Sal	El Salvador (VRA)

ESE	Environmental Science Education (AIE)
ESITC	Electrical Supply Industry Training Committee (AIE)
ESN	Easton [*Maryland*] [*Airport symbol*] (AD)
ESnet	Energy Sciences Network [*Department of Energy*]
esp	Especially (VRA)
ESPI	Education Service of the Plastics Industry (AIE)
Espl	Esplanade (DD)
ESRB	Entertainment Software Rating Board
ESS	Education Support Staff (AIE)
Essays CW	Essays on Canadian Writing [*A publication*] (BRI)
EST	Energy Saving Trust (AIE)
est	Established (VRA)
ESTEAM	Enrichment Science and Technology for Exceptionally Able and Motivated Pupils (AIE)
Esto	Estonia (VRA)
ET	Ethiopian Airlines [*ICAO designator*] (AD)
ETAP	Extended Task Analysis Procedure [*Education*] (AIE)
etch	Etching (VRA)
ETEMA	Education Technology and Equipment Manufacturing Association (AIE)
Eth	Ethiopia (VRA)
ETLL	Educational Technology and Language Learning (AIE)
ETR	End-of-Treatment Response [*Medicine*]
Etru	Etruria (VRA)
ETSP	Evaluation of Testing in Schools Project (AIE)
ETUDE	English Teachers in University Departments of Education (AIE)
EUI	European University Institute [*Florence, Italy*] (AIE)
EUN	El Aaiun [*Morocco*] [*Airport symbol*] (AD)
EUP	Eastern Upper Peninsula [*Michigan*]
Eur	Europe (VRA)
EURED	European Unified Research on Educational Development (AIE)
EUROSTEP	European Association of Users of Satellites in Training and Education Programmes (AIE)
EUS	Endoscopic Ultrasonography [*Medicine*]
EV	Atlantic Southeast [*ICAO designator*] (AD)
evang	Evangelist (VRA)
EVB	Examining and Validating Body (AIE)
EVS	Event Verification System [*Technology that encripts time and location on video recordings*]
EW	East-West Airlines [*ICAO designator*] (AD)
EWB	Fall River-New Bedford [*Massachusetts*] [*Airport symbol*] (AD)
EWI	Educational Workers' International (AIE)
EWR	Newark [*New Jersey*] [*Airport symbol*] (AD)
EX	Eagle Aviation [*ICAO designator*] (AD)
EX	Emirates Airlines [*ICAO designator*] (AD)
ex	Example (VRA)
Ex Child	Exceptional Children [*A publication*] (BRI)
exec	Executive (DD)
exh	Exhibit (VRA)
ExMBA	Executive Master's of Business Administration (RDA)
ExMSE	Executive Master's of Science in Science and Technology Commercialization (RDA)
exp	Exposure (VRA)
explor	Exploration (DD)
expo	Exposition (DD)
Expy	Expressway (DD)
ext	Exterior (VRA)
Ext	Extrapolation [*A publication*] (BRI)
extns	Extension (VRA)
EY	Europe Aero Service [*ICAO designator*] (AD)
EZ	Sun-Air of Scandinavia [*ICAO designator*] (AD)

F
By Acronym

F .... Dealt in Flat [*Investment term*] (DFIT)
f .... Female (DD)
F2F .... Face-to-Face [*Fundraising*]
FaAA .... Failure Analysis and Associates (RDA)
fab .... Fabric (VRA)
FAB .... Firecracker Alternative Book [*Award Program*]
fac .... Facade (VRA)
FACADE .... Further and Adult Council for Art and Design Education (AIE)
FACLS .... Federation of the Association of College Lecturers in Scotland (AIE)
fact .... Factory (VRA)
FACT .... Focused Appendix Computed Tomography [*Medicine*]
FACTL .... Fellow of the American College of Trial Lawyers (DD)
FAdmA .... Fellow of the Administration Association (DD)
FAE .... Follicle-Associated Epithelium [*Immunology*]
FAET .... Forum for the Advancement of Educational Therapy (AIE)
FAG .... Fagurholsmyri [*Iceland*] [*Airport symbol*] (AD)
FAHP .... Fellow Association for Healthcare Philanthropy
fai .... Faience (VRA)
Fam in Soc... Families in Society [*A publication*] (BRI)
Fam Relat ... Family Relations [*A publication*] (BRI)
F&F .... Furniture and Fixtures (DFIT)
FAS .... Functional Acquisition Specialist [*Army*] (RDA)
FASB .... Financial Accounting Standards Board
FASB .... Financial and Accounting Services Branch (AIE)
fasc .... Fascimile (VRA)
FASEM .... Fabrication and Architecture of Single-Electron Memories [*Computer Science*]
FBA .... Fellow of Business Administration (DD)
FBA .... Fonte Boa [*Brazil*] [*Airport symbol*] (AD)
FBF .... Female Bowhunter Fingers [*International Bowhunting Organization*] [*Class equipment*]
FBP .... Flexible Benefits Program [*Human resources*] (WYGK)
fbr .... Fiber (VRA)
FBU .... Oslo [*Norway*] [*Airport symbol*] (AD)
FC .... Chaparral Airlines [*ICAO designator*] (AD)
FC .... Film Comment [*A publication*] (BRI)
FCAE .... Fellow of the Canadian Academy of Engineering (DD)
FCAM .... Fellow of the Institute of Certified Administrative Managers (DD)
FCAS .... Fellow of the Casualty Actuarial Science (DD)
FCCA .... Fellow of the Association of Certified Accountants (DD)
FCCP .... Fellow of the Canadian College of Physicians (DD)
FCCUI .... Fellow of the Canadian Credit Union Institute (DD)
FCE .... First Certificate in English [*Cambridge University*] [*British*] (AIE)
FCEU .... Fire Control Electronics Unit [*Military*] (RDA)
FCFP .... Fellow of the College of Family Physicians (DD)
FCGA .... Fellow of the Canadian Certified General Accountants Association (DD)
FCIB .... Fellow of the Chartered Institute of Bankers (DD)
FCIC .... Fellow of the Canadian Institute of Chemistry (DD)
FCIM .... Fellow of the Chartered Institute of Marketing (DD)
FCIS .... Fellow of the Institute of Chartered Secretaries and Administrators (DD)
FCMA .... Fellow of the Society of Management Accountants of Canada (DD)
FCMC .... Fellow of the Institute of Certified Management Consultants (DD)
FCommA ...... Fellow of Commercial Actuaries (DD)
FCP .... Family Care Program [*Insurance*] (WYGK)
FCP .... Fellow of the College of Physicians (DD)
FCSCE .... Fellow of the Canadian Society of Civil Engineers (DD)
FCSI .... Fellow of the Canadian Securities Institute (DD)
FD .... Wiscair [*ICAO designator*] (AD)
FDA .... Fundacion [*Colombia*] [*Airport symbol*] (AD)
FDB .... Forte Princip [*Brazil*] [*Airport symbol*] (AD)
FDDI .... Fiber-Optic Digital Device Interface [*Computer science*]
FDHD .... Floppy Drive High Density [*Computer science*]
FDIS .... Fault Detection and Isolation Subsystem (RDA)
FDLDP .... Federal Defense Laboratory Diversification Program (RDA)
FDP .... Faridpur [*Bangladesh*] [*Airport symbol*] (AD)
FDT .... Flourescent Discharge Tube [*Technology*]
FDT .... Fluorescent Discharge Tube [*Panasonic*]
fdtn .... Foundation (VRA)
FE .... Florida Airlines and Air South [*ICAO designator*] (AD)
fe .... Iron (VRA)
FEAA .... Fellow of the English Association of Accountants and Auditors (DD)
FEAS .... Fellow of the English Association of Corporate Secretaries (DD)
FEBP .... Foundation for Education Business Partnerships (AIE)
FED .... Field Emission Display

FEDORA....... Forum Europeen de l'Orientation Academique (AIE)
Fed Prob...... Federal Probation [*A publication*] (BRI)
FEER .... Far Eastern Economic Review [*A publication*] (BRI)
FEI .... Financial Executives Institute of Canada (DD)
FEIS .... Further Education Information Service (AIE)
FEMU .... Further Education Marketing Unit (AIE)
FEN .... Family Education Network [*Computer science*]
FERAS .... Further Education Revenue Account Survey (AIE)
FESC .... Further Education Staff College
FESWG .... Fuze Engineering Standardization Working Group [*Military*] (RDA)
fewd........... Ironwood (VRA)
FEWEC........ Further Education Work Experience Co-Ordinator (AIE)
FEZ .... Fez [*Morocco*] [*Airport symbol*] (AD)
FF .... Air Link [*ICAO designator*] (AD)
FF .... Fanfare [*A publication*] (BRI)
FFF .... Federation of Fly Fishers
FFG .... Functional Feeding Groups [*Ecology*]
FFT .... Frankfurt [*Kentucky*] [*Airport symbol*] (AD)
FFT .... Free-Floating Thrombus [*Medicine*]
FF-TEM .... Freeze-Fracture Transmission Electron Microscopy
FFU .... Futaleufu [*Chile*] [*Airport symbol*] (AD)
FG .... Ariana Afghan Airlines [*ICAO designator*] (AD)
f/g .... Form/Genre
FGD .... Ft. Derik [*Mauritania*] [*Airport symbol*] (AD)
FGFR .... Fibroblast Growth-Factor Receptor [*Biochemistry*]
FGL .... Fox Glacier [*New Zealand*] [*Airport symbol*] (AD)
FH .... Mall Airways [*ICAO designator*] (AD)
FHB .... Fine Homebuilding [*A publication*] (BRI)
FHI .... Fellow of the Ontario Hostelry Institute [*Canada*] (DD)
FHIMA .... Fellow of the Hotel and Catering International Management Association (DD)
FI .... Flugfelag-Icelandair [*ICAO designator*] (AD)
FIAL .... Fellow of the International Institute of Arts and Letters, Zurich [*1931*] (NGC)
fibd .... Fiberboard (VRA)
fibgl .... Fiberglass (VRA)
FICB .... Fellow of the Institute of Canadian Bankers (DD)
FICIA .... Fellow of the Guild of Industrial, Commercial, & Institutional Accounts (DD)
Fic Int......... Fiction International [*A publication*] (BRI)
FIEE .... Fellow of the Institution of Electrical Engineers (DD)
fig .... Figure (VRA)
FIG .... Fria [*Guinea*] [*Airport symbol*] (AD)
Film Cr .... Film Criticism [*A publication*] (BRI)
FIM .... Fellow of the Institute of Materials (DD)
FIMgt .... Fellow of the Institute of Management (DD)
fin .... Finance (DD)
fin .... Finish (VRA)
fin .... Finished (VRA)
Fine Gard .... Fine Gardening [*A publication*] (BRI)
finl .... Financial (DD)
Finl .... Finland (VRA)
FinlMgmt...... Financial Management (DD)
FInstP......... Fellow of the Institute of Physics (DD)
FIR .... Films in Review [*A publication*] (BRI)
FIRST........ Far Infrared and Submillimeter Space Telescope [*Proposed European*]
FIRST.......... Far Infrared Space Telescope
firwd.......... Firwood (VRA)
FISH.......... Friends Involved in Sportfishing Heritage
FISTA II .... Flying Infrared Signature Technology Aircraft [*Air Force*]
FIT .... Fitchburg [*Massachusetts*] [*Airport symbol*] (AD)
FITLOG .... Foundation for Information Technology in Local Government (AIE)
FIU .... Fingerprint Identification Unit [*Sony Corp.*]
FIX .... Ferndale Internet Experiment [*Computer science*]
FJ .... Air Pacific [*ICAO designator*] (AD)
FJO .... Ft. Johnson [*Malawi*] [*Airport symbol*] (AD)
FK .... Flamenco Airlines [*ICAO designator*] (AD)
FK .... Geelong Air Travel [*ICAO designator*] (AD)
fl .... Floor (DD)
fl .... Flourished (VRA)
flamby .... Flamboyant (VRA)
flan .... Flannel (VRA)
Fland .... Flanders (VRA)
FLAW......... Foreign Languages at Work (AIE)
FLB .... Floriano [*Brazil*] [*Airport symbol*] (AD)

FLE .... Forward Logistical Element [*Military*]
Flem .... Flemish (VRA)
FLLAP .... Foreign Languages for Lower Attaining Pupils [*Project*] (AIE)
FLMI .... Fellow of the Life Management Institute (DD)
flok .... Flocked (VRA)
flour .... Flourescent (VRA)
flr .... Floor (VRA)
flt .... Felt (VRA)
FLUNCI .... Foreign Language Use in Northern Commerce and Industry (AIE)
Fly .... Flying [*A publication*] (BRI)
fly butr......... Flying Buttress (VRA)
Fly Needle... Flying Needle [*A publication*] (BRI)
fm .... Foam (VRA)
FMA .... Fabricators and Manufacturers Association
FMC .... Fellow of the Institute of Management Consultants (DD)
FMC .... Forces Mobile Command [*Canada*] (DD)
FMLA .... Family and Medical Leave Act of 1993 (WYGK)
FMMS .... Functionalized Monolayers on Mesoporous Supports [*Organic chemistry*]
FN .... Air Carolina [*ICAO designator*] (AD)
fndobj .... Found Object (VRA)
FNE .... Finnsnes [*Norway*] [*Airport symbol*] (AD)
FNI .... Nimes [*Frances*] [*Airport symbol*] (AD)
FNJ .... Feng Yang-Pyongyang [*North Korea*] [*Airport symbol*] (AD)
fnstr .... Fenestration (VRA)
fnt .... Front (VRA)
fntpc .... Frontispiece (VRA)
FO .... Southern Nevada [*ICAO designator*] (AD)
FOAF........... Friend of a Friend
FOCAL .... Foundations of Communication and Language (AIE)
FOG .... Foggia [*Italy*] [*Airport symbol*] (AD)
Folkl .... Folklore [*A publication*] (BRI)
FOLUSA .... Friends of Libraries USA [*American Library Association*]
FOM .... Foumban [*Cameroon*] [*Airport symbol*] (AD)
FON .... Federation of Ontario Naturalists [*Canada*]
FOO .... Field Ordering Officer [*Army*] (RDA)
FOO .... Noemfoor [*New Guinea*] [*Airport symbol*] (AD)
FoodSc .... Food Science (DD)
For Aff .... Foreign Affairs [*A publication*] (BRI)
foresh .... Foreshorten (VRA)
forg.............. Forged (VRA)
forgr............ Foreground (VRA)
form .... Form (VRA)
ForServ....... Foreign Service (DD)
FOTF........... Fellow of the Ontario Teachers' Federation [*Canada*] (DD)
fount .... Fountain (VRA)
FP .... Simmons [*ICAO designator*] (AD)
FPD............. Flat-Panel Display [*Instrumentation*]
FPDD .... Familial Pure Depressive Disease
FPDL........... Flashlamp-Pumped Dye LASER
FPES .... Femtosecond Photoelectron Spectroscopy
FPH............. Freephone Supplementary Service [*Telecommunications*] (DOM)
FPM .... Fixed-Payment Mortgage (DFIT)
FPOA .... Federation of Professional Officers Association (AIE)
FPP............. Fetal Protection Policy [*Insurance*] (WYGK)
fps .... Frames Per Second [*Electronics*]
FQ .... Air Aruba [*ICAO designator*] (AD)
FQ............... Compagnie Aerienne du Languedoc [*ICAO designator*] (AD)
FQ............... Film Quarterly [*A publication*] (BRI)
Fr .... France (VRA)

FR................ French Review [*A publication*] (BRI)
fr.................. From (VRA)
FR................ Susquehanna [*ICAO designator*] (AD)
fra............... Frame (VRA)
frag............. Fragment (VRA)
FRCGS........ Fellow of the Royal Canadian Geographical Society (DD)
FRCM.......... Fellow of the Royal College of Medicine [*Canada*] (DD)
FRCPC .... Fellow of the Royal College of Physicians of Canada (DD)
FRCSC .... Fellow of the Royal College of Surgeons of Canada (DD)
frd............... Fired (VRA)
FRFV........... Four by Five Inches (VRA)
FRG .... Faculty Review Group [*Education*] (AIE)
FRI.............. Fellow of the Real Estate Institute (DD)
FRICS .... Fellow of the Royal Institute of Chartered Surveyors [*Canada*] (DD)
FRJ.............. Frejus [*France*] [*Airport symbol*] (AD)
FRL............. Forli [*Italy*] [*Airport symbol*] (AD)
FRS............. Family Radio Service
FRS............. Fellow of the Royal Society of London [*1660*] (NGC)
FRSA .... Fellow of the Royal Society of Arts, London [*1909, founded 1754 as Society of Arts*] (NGC)
frsc .... Fresco (VRA)
Fr Soma ..... French Somaliland (VRA)
frutwd .... Fruitwood (VRA)
frz .... Frieze (VRA)
fs .... Filmstrip (VRA)
FS .... Key Airlines [*ICAO designator*] (AD)
FSA............. Family Support Act of 1988 (WYGK)
FSA............. Forward Sortation Area [*Mailing technique*]
FSAA........... Fellow of the Society of Accountants and Auditors (DD)
FSI.............. Fellow of the Surveyors' Institution (DD)
fsl .... Fossil (VRA)
FSMAC........ Fellow of the Society of Management Accountants of Canada (DD)
FSR............. Female Seniors [*International Bowhunting Organization*] [*Class Equipment*]
FSTC .... Financial Services Technical Consortium
ft .... Fortification (VRA)
FTase.......... Farnesyltransferase [*An enzyme*]
FTC .... Forestry Training Council (AIE)
fthrs .... Feathers (VRA)
FTI .... Fellow of Trust Institute (DD)
FTPM .... Fixed Time Printing Mode [*Photography*]
FTX .... Ft. Rousset [*Congo*] [*Airport symbol*] (AD)
FU .... Air Littoral [*ICAO designator*] (AD)
FUM............ Familial Uveal Melanoma [*Oncology*]
FUN............ Funafuti Atoll [*Ellice Islands*] [*Airport symbol*] (AD)
furn .... Furniture (VRA)
fus .... Fuse (VRA)
Fut .... Futurist [*A publication*] (BRI)
futr.............. Futurism (VRA)
FV .... Frisia Luftverkehr [*ICAO designator*] (AD)
fvrl gls......... Favrile Glass (VRA)
FW .... Isles of Scilly Skybus [*ICAO designator*] (AD)
Fwy............. Freeway (VRA)
FX .... Express Air [*ICAO designator*] (AD)
FX .... Mountain West Airlines [*ICAO designator*] (AD)
FXO............ Nova Freixo [*Mozambique*] [*Airport symbol*] (AD)
fxt .... Fixative (VRA)
FY .... Metroflight Airlines and Great Plains Airline [*ICAO designator*] (AD)
FYA............. Faya Largeau [*Chad*] [*Airport symbol*] (AD)
FZ .... Air Chico [*ICAO designator*] (AD)
FZB .... Mansa [*Zambia*] [*Airport symbol*] (AD)

G
By Acronym

G .... Dividends and Earnings in Canadian Dollars [*Investment term*] (DFIT)
GA .... Gage
Ga .... Galatians [*New Testament book*]
GA .... Garuda Indonesian Airways [*ICAO designator*] (AD)
GAASD .... Gallium Arsenide [*Phosphide Semiconductor*]
GAC .... General Areas of Competence [*Education*] (AIE)
GAC .... Graphic Art Club, Toronto [*c.1903, SGA from 1912, CSGA from 1923*] [*Canada*] (NGC)
GADT .... Graded Assessment in Design and Technology (AIE)
GAL .... Get a Life
GALA .... Guidance and Learner Autonomy [*Project*] (AIE)
GALIC .... General American Life Insurance Co.
gall .... Gallery (VRA)
galv .... Galvanized (VRA)
GAMM .... German Association for Applied Mathematics and Mechanics
GAMO .... German Army Material Office
GAO .... German Army Office
GAP .... Gadolinium Aluminium Perovskite [*Inorganic chemistry*]
GAPE .... Geographical Association Package Exchange (AIE)
Ga R .... Georgia Review [*A publication*] (BRI)
GAR .... Guided Aerial Rocket
Garbage ...... Garbage: The Independent Environmental Quarterly [*A publication*] (BRI)
gard .... Garden (VRA)
GARP .... Growth at the Right Price
GAS .... Gach Saran [*Iran*] [*Airport symbol*] (AD)
GAS .... Gas Anti-Solvent [*Chemical engineering*]
GASP .... Graded Assessment in Science Project (AIE)
GB .... Air Inter Gabon [*ICAO designator*] (AD)
GB .... Gould Belt [*Galactic science*]
GBCS .... Ground-Based Common Sensor
GBI .... Governesses Benevolent Institute [*British*] (AIE)
GBM .... Gesellschaft Fuer Biochemie Und Molekularbiologie [*Germany*]
GBO .... Gissel Bargaining Order [*Labor relations*] (WYGK)
GBU .... Khasm el Girba [*Sudan*] [*Airport symbol*] (AD)
GC .... Lina-Congo [*ICAO designator*] (AD)
GCCS .... Global Command and Control System
GCDP .... Gunner's Control and Display Panel [*Military*] (RDA)
GCLJ .... Grand Cross, St. Lazarus of Jerusalem (DD)
GCM .... Geriatric-Care Manager
GCMS .... Gas Chromatography and Mass Spectroscopy
GCN .... Government Computer News
GCO .... GC Optronics, Inc.
GCO .... Government Concept of Operations (RDA)
GCP .... Gross Criminal Product
GCT .... Glasgow College of Technology (AIE)
GD .... Air North [*ICAO designator*] (AD)
GD .... General Delivery (DD)
GDA .... General Dynamics Astronautics
GDAM .... Graduate Division of Applied Mathematics
GDC .... General Dynamics, Convair
GDH .... Sargodha [*Pakistan*] [*Airport symbol*] (AD)
GDip .... Graduate Diploma (DD)
GDMS .... Global Data Management System
Gdns .... Gardens (DD)
GDPA .... Graduate Diploma in Public Accountancy (DD)
GDPA .... Graduate Diploma in Public Accounting (DD)
GDS .... Global Distribution Systems
GE .... Guernsey Airlines [*ICAO designator*] (AD)
GED .... Gas-Phase Electron Diffraction [*Physics*]
GED .... Georgetown [*Delaware*] [*Airport symbol*] (AD)
GEE .... General Estimating Equation [*Mathematics*]
gel .... Gelatin (VRA)
GEM .... Gateway to Educational Materials
GEMSAT ...... Girls' Education in Mathematics, Science, and Technology (AIE)
gen .... General (VRA)
Generation... Generations [*A publication*] (BRI)
GEO-EAS ..... Geostatistical Environmental Assessment Software [*US Environmental Protection Agency*]
Geog .... Geographical [*A publication*] (BRI)
Geog .... Geography (DD)
Geol .... Geology (DD)
GeolSci .... Geological Science (DD)
Geoph .... Geophysics (DD)
GER .... Geomagnetic Electrorinetograph
Ger .... Germany (VRA)

GERIACT ...... Great Education Reform Act [*1988*] (AIE)
Ger Q .... German Quarterly [*A publication*] (BRI)
ges .... Gesso (VRA)
GET .... Graduate Employment and Training Survey (AIE)
GETAC .... General Electric Telemetering and Control
GF .... Gulf Air [*ICAO designator*] (AD)
GFL .... Glens Falls [*New York*] [*Airport symbol*] (AD)
GFR .... Granville [*France*] [*Airport symbol*] (AD)
GFRP .... Gap Filler/Reporting Post
GFRP .... Government Furnished Repair Parts
GFX .... Ghuraf [*South Arabia*] [*Airport symbol*] (AD)
GG .... Gem State Airlines [*ICAO designator*] (AD)
GGDF .... Gas Gathering Data File [*Phillips Petroleum*]
GGG .... Gladewater-Kilgore-Longview [*Texas*] [*Airport symbol*] (AD)
GGNG .... Gelatin Glass Negative (VRA)
GGP .... GPS [*Global Positioning System*] Guidance Package
GGPP .... Giant Gaseous Protoplanet [*Planetary science*]
GGQ .... Gagnoa [*Ivory Coast*] [*Airport symbol*] (AD)
GH .... Ghana Airways [*ICAO designator*] (AD)
GHCP .... Georgia Hospital Computer Group
GH-MATRIX ... Generalized Hadamand Matrix
GHO .... Grahamstown [*South Africa*] [*Airport symbol*] (AD)
GHQS .... General Headquarters Exercise
GI .... Air Guinee [*ICAO designator*] (AD)
GI .... Genetics Institute, Inc.
GII .... Siguiri [*Guinea*] [*Airport symbol*] (AD)
GIL .... Gilgit [*Pakistan*] [*Airport symbol*] (AD)
GIM .... Miele Mimbale [*Gabon*] [*Airport symbol*] (AD)
GINLC .... Grosse Ile Nature and Land Conservancy
GIREP .... International Group for the Advancement of Physics Teaching (AIE)
GIS .... Government Information Subcommittee [*American Library Association*]
GJ .... Ansett Airlines of South Australia [*ICAO designator*] (AD)
GJ .... Geographical Journal [*A publication*] (BRI)
GJB .... Marie-Galante Island [*Guadeloupe*] [*Airport symbol*] (AD)
GJM .... Guajara Mirim [*Brazil*] [*Airport symbol*] (AD)
GK .... Laker Airways [*ICAO designator*] (AD)
GKO .... Kongo Boumba [*Gabon*] [*Airport symbol*] (AD)
GL .... Gronlandsfly [*ICAO designator*] (AD)
GLAFLI .... Graded Levels of Achievement in Foreign Language Learning (AIE)
GLB .... Gilbues [*Brazil*] [*Airport symbol*] (AD)
glit .... Glitter (VRA)
GLL .... Galileo [*NASA*]
GLO .... Cheltenham-Gloucester [*England*] [*Airport symbol*] (AD)
glo .... Gloss (VRA)
GL RADAR ... Gun Laying RADAR
gls .... Glass (VRA)
glsn .... Glassine (VRA)
glt .... Gilding (VRA)
glt .... Gilt (VRA)
GLTB .... Greater London Training Board [*British*] (AIE)
gly .... Glyph (VRA)
glypto .... Glypotheca (VRA)
glz .... Glaze (VRA)
glz .... Glazed (VRA)
GM .... Air America [*ICAO designator*] (AD)
G-MEM .... GPC [*General Purpose Computer*] Memory
GMM .... Gamboma [*Congo*] [*Airport symbol*] (AD)
GMML .... Ground Master Measurements List
GMPT........... Gum Print [*Gum bichromates*] (VRA)
GMS............. Grant Maintained School (AIE)
GMU .... Goose Management Unit
GN .... Air Gabon [*ICAO designator*] (AD)
GNL .... Greenwood [*Mississippi*] [*Airport symbol*] (AD)
GNN .... Ghinnir [*Ethiopia*] [*Airport symbol*] (AD)
GNZ .... Ghanzi [*Botswana*] [*Airport symbol*] (AD)
GO .... Gambia Air Shuttle [*ICAO designator*] (AD)
go .... Gold (VRA)
GOAL .... Game Oriented Activities for Learning (AIE)
GOALI .... Grant Opportunities for Academic Liaison with Industry [*National Science Foundation*]
GOALS .... Greater Orlando Area Legal Services [*Florida*]
GOB .... General Obligation Bonds [*Finance*]
GOB .... Goba [*Ehtiopia*] [*Airport symbol*] (AD)
GOD .... Guaranteed Overnight Delivery
GOE .... Gore [*New Zealand*] [*Airport symbol*] (AD)

go lf .... Gold Leaf (VRA)
GOONQ .... Grand Officier de l'Ordre National du Quebec [Canada] (DD)
GOP .... Group of Pictures [Computer science]
GOSG .... General Officer Steering Group
GOT .... Government of Tunisia
Goth .... Gothic (VRA)
gou .... Gouache (VRA)
gov .... Government (VRA)
gov .... Governor (DD)
govt .... Government (DD)
GOY .... Gal Oya [Ceylon] [Airport symbol] (AD)
gp .... Group (VRA)
GP .... Hadag Air Seebaederflug [ICAO designator] (AD)
GPA .... Georgians for Preservation Action [An association]
GPADS .... Guided Parafoil Aerial Delivery System
GPAVTS .... Great Planes Area Vocational Technical School [Oklahoma]
GPC .... Great Plains Coliseum [Lawton, OK]
GPCR .... G-Protein-Coupled Receptor [Biochemistry]
GPHMO .... Group Practice Health Maintenance Organization [Insurance]
               (WYGK)
GPP .... Guarapuava [Brazil] [Airport symbol] (AD)
GPS/INS .... Global Positioning System/Inertial Navigation System [Air Force]
GQ .... Big Sky Airlines [ICAO designator] (AD)
GR .... Aurigny Air Services [ICAO designator] (AD)
gra .... Graphics (VRA)
GRACE .... Grass Roots Art and Community Effort [Vermont]
GRADSCOPE... Graduate Search by Computer after Personal Evaluation (AIE)
GRAIN .... Genetic Resources Action International [Spain]
gran .... Granite (VRA)
GRAPE-4 ...... GRAvity PipE no. 4 [Computer science]
grd .... Ground (VRA)
Gre .... Greece (VRA)
GRG .... Georgetown [Guyana] [Airport symbol] (AD)
GRIC .... Global Roaming Internet Connection [Computer science]
GRIDS .... Guidelines for Review and Internal Development in Schools (AIE)
GRIP .... Glutamate Receptor Interacting Protein [Neurochemistry]
gris .... Grisaille (VRA)
Grld .... Greenland (VRA)
grmt .... Garment (VRA)
grn .... Green (VRA)
Grnds .... Grounds (DD)
grnln .... Granulation (VRA)
GRP .... General Receptor for Phosphoinositide [Biochemistry]
grp .... Group (DD)
grph .... Graphite (VRA)
GRS .... Grosseto [Italy] [Airport symbol] (AD)
GRT .... Gujrat [Pakistan] [Airport symbol] (AD)

GRTA .... Group Relations Training Association (AIE)
GRU .... Grajau [Brazil] [Airport symbol] (AD)
grv .... Gravure (VRA)
GS .... BAS Airlines [ICAO designator] (AD)
GS .... General Secretariat
GSA .... Geinsheim Staging Activity
GSA .... Gusau [Nigeria] [Airport symbol] (AD)
GSB .... General School Budget (AIE)
GSCC .... Global Simulation Control Center
GSMB .... Graphic Standards Management Board
GSR .... Gunshot Residue [Forensics]
GSS .... Gerstmann-Straussler-Sheinker [Disease]
GSTAMIDS... Ground Standoff Minefield Detection System [Military] (RDA)
GSU .... Gedaref [Sudan] [Airport symbol] (AD)
GSW .... Greater Southwest [Ft. Worth and Dallas, Texas] [Airport symbol]
             (AD)
GTASFA .... Grand Traverse Area Sportfishing Association [Michigan]
GTBWI .... Grand Traverse Bay Watershed Initiative
GTC .... Gateway to Care
GTL .... Glass Training Ltd. (AIE)
GTR .... Great Barrier Island [New Zealand] [Airport symbol] (AD)
GTS .... General Technical Services, Inc.
gtwy .... Gateway (VRA)
GU .... Aviateca [ICAO designator] (AD)
Guat .... Guatemala (VRA)
GUF .... Grand Unified Force
GUG .... N'Guigmi [Niger] [Airport symbol] (AD)
Guin .... Guinea (VRA)
GULP .... Group Universal Life Policy [Insurance] (DFIT)
GUM .... Guam [Marianas] [Airport symbol] (AD)
GURC .... Gulf Universities Research Corp.
GUU .... Gulu [Uganda] [Airport symbol] (AD)
GUZ .... Guiratinga [Brazil] [Airport symbol] (AD)
GV .... Talair [ICAO designator] (AD)
GVD .... Gravdal [Norway] [Airport symbol] (AD)
GvHD .... Graft-Versus Host Disease [Immunology]
GVL .... Gainesville [Georgia] [Airport symbol] (AD)
GvL .... Graft-Versus-Leukemia [Medicine]
G/VLL-D .... Ground Vehicular LASER Locator Designator [Military]
GW .... Golden West Airlines [ICAO designator] (AD)
GW .... Guardian Weekly [A publication] (BRI)
GX .... Great Lakes Airlines [ICAO designator] (AD)
GXI .... Global Exchange, Inc.
GXQ .... Coyhaique [Chile] [Airport symbol] (AD)
GY .... Guyana Airways [ICAO designator] (AD)
gym .... Gymnasium (VRA)
GZ .... Air Rarotonga [ICAO designator] (AD)

H
By Acronym

H................. Declared or Paid after Stock Dividend or Split-Up [*Investment term*] (DFIT)
H................. Momentum [*Measurement*]
HAAP .... High Air Pollution Potential
HAART........ Highly Active Antiretroviral Therapy [*Medicine*]
HAC .... Human Artificial Chromosome [*Genetics*]
HAE............. Hatia [*Bangladesh*] [*Airport symbol*] (AD)
HAG .... [*The*] Hague [*Netherlands*] [*Airport symbol*] (AD)
HAHR.......... Hispanic American Historical Review [*A publication*] (BRI)
HAL............. Home Automated Living
HALCA .... Highly Advanced Laboratory for Communications and Astronomy [*Japanese satellite*]
HALF........... Half-plate (VRA)
halftmb....... Half-timber (VRA)
HALO .... High Arcal Learning Objectives (AIE)
ham .... Hammered (VRA)
handmd ...... Handmade (VRA)
handscr....... Handscroll (VRA)
HAR .... Harrisburg-New Cumberland [*Pennsylvania*] [*Airport symbol*] (AD)
Har Bus R... Harvard Business Review [*A publication*] (BRI)
hardbd........ Hardboard (VRA)
haSH........... Human Achaete-Scute Homologue [*Genetics*]
HASTAM ..... Health and Safety Technology Management (AIE)
Hast Cen R.. Hastings Center Report [*A publication*] (BRI)
HATS .... Huntsville Association of Technical Societies
HAWK .... Hunting and Angling With Kids
HB............... Air Melanesiae [*ICAO designator*] (AD)
HB............... Horn Book Magazine [*A publication*] (BRI)
HBA .... Honours Bachelor of Arts in Business Administration (DD)
HBDE .... Huntington Beach Development Engineering [*McDonnell Douglas Aircraft Corp.*]
HBG .... Hattiesburg [*Mississippi*] [*Airport symbol*] (AD)
HB Guide..... Horn Book Guide [*A publication*] (BRI)
HBI.............. Horizontal Blanking Interval (DOM)
HBLR .... Hidden Broad-Line Region [*Spectra*]
HC............... Haiti Air International [*ICAO designator*] (AD)
HC............... Hand Carry
HC............... Higher Certificate [*Academic degree*] (AIE)
HCA .... Big Spring [*Texas*] [*Airport symbol*] (AD)
HCCM .... Hadley Centre Climate Model
HCE............. Highly Compensated Employee [*Human resources*] (WYGK)
HCF............. High Circle Fatique
HCFA .... [*United States*] Health Care Financing Administration
HCIS .... Hospital Communication and Information System [*McDonnell Douglas Automation Co.*]
HCTC .... Hotel and Catering Training Co. (AIE)
HD.............. Histone Deacetylase [*An enzyme*]
HD .... Holddown
HD .... New York Helicopter [*ICAO designator*] (AD)
HDA .... Honda [*Colombia*] [*Airport symbol*] (AD)
HDCOL........ Hand Colored (VRA)
HDipEd .... Higher Diploma in Education [*Academic degree*] (AIE)
HDM .... Hamadan [*Iran*] [*Airport symbol*] (AD)
HDSL .... High-Data-Rate Digital Subscriber Line [*Telecommunications*] (DOM)
hdwe........... Hardware (VRA)
HDWY......... Headway Corporate Resources
HE............... Green Bay Aviation [*ICAO designator*] (AD)
HE............... Human Events [*A publication*] (BRI)
HEA............. Higher Education Authority [*Ireland*] (AIE)
HEART .... Higher Education Action Research Team (AIE)
Heartsong R.. Heartsong Review [*A publication*] (BRI)
HEBE .... Higher Education Business Enterprises Ltd. (AIE)
HEC............. Hautes Etudes Commerciales (DD)
HECSU .... Higher Education Careers Service Unit (AIE)
HED .... Hidrotic Ectodermal Dysplasia [*Dermatology*]
HED .... Howardite, Eucrite, Diogenite [*Meteorite composition*]
HEERA .... Higher Education External Relations Association (AIE)
HEFC........... Higher Education Funding Council (AIE)
HEI.............. Hall-Effect Imaging [*Medical imaging*]
HEIS .... Higher Education Information Service (AIE)
HEL............. Hardware Emulation [*Computer science*]
HEL............. Hardware Emulation Layer [*Computer science*]
HELPIS .... Higher Education Learning Programmes Information Service (AIE)
HEM............ Heavy Equipment Maintenance
HEPP .... Human Engineering Program Plan
HER .... Harvard Educational Review [*A publication*] (BRI)

her .... Heraldry (VRA)
HERATES .... Hourly Earnings Rate
HERBB .... Hanscom Electronic Request [*for Proposals*] Bulletin Board [*Air Force*]
HERS .... Heart and Estrogen/Progestin Replacement Study [*Medicine*]
HESES .... Higher Education Students Early Statistics (AIE)
HET............. Hall Effect Transducer
HETE........... High Energy Transient Explorer
HETE........... Higher Education Teachers of English (AIE)
HEU .... Hull Electronics Unit [*Military*] (RDA)
HF............... First Air [*ICAO designator*] (AD)
H/F.............. Held For [*Investment term*] (DFIT)
HFC............. Hospital Financial Control [*McDonnell Douglas Automation Co.*]
HFC............. Hybrid Fiber-Coax [*Telecommunications*]
HFM............ Hand, Foot, and Mouth [*Disease*]
HFPT........... Held for Perishable Tools
HFTL .... Held for Tool Liaison
HFW .... Haverfordwest [*Wales*] [*Airport symbol*] (AD)
HG.............. Harbor Airlines [*ICAO designator*] (AD)
HGA .... Hammel Green and Abrahamson, Inc. [*A national leader in innovative design*]
H G & L Rev... Harvard Gay & Lesbian Review [*A publication*] (BRI)
HGED .... High-Gain Emissive Display [*Technology*]
HGH............ Hangchow [*China*] [*Airport symbol*] (AD)
Hghlds .... Highlands (DD)
HGS .... Human Genome Sciences
HGTV .... Home & Garden Television
HH.............. Somali Airlines [*ICAO designator*] (AD)
HHGCB........ Household Goods Carriers Bureau
HI............... Papillon Airways [*ICAO designator*] (AD)
HIBOR......... Hong Kong Interbank Offered Rate (DFIT)
hick............. Hickory (VRA)
HID .... High-Intensity Discharge
hiergl........... Hieroglyph (VRA)
HIF.............. Hypoxia-Inducible Factor [*Physiology*]
HIFI............. Hawaii Imaging Fabry-Perot Interferometer
HIPC .... High Pressure Chamber
Hipparcos.... High-Precision Parallax Collecting Satellite [*European Space Agency*]
Hisp............ Hispania [*A publication*] (BRI)
hist............. History (VRA)
Hist&PolSc... History & Political Science (DD)
Hist & T....... History and Theory [*A publication*] (BRI)
HIT.............. High Interest Tracks
HIU .... Higuerote [*Venezuela*] [*Airport symbol*] (AD)
HJAS........... Harvard Journal of Asiatic Studies [*A publication*] (BRI)
HK.............. South Pacific Island Airways [*ICAO designator*] (AD)
HKG .... Hong Kong [*British Crown Colony*] [*Airport symbol*] (AD)
HKR .... Hydrolytic Kinetic Resolution
HLD .... Hold
HLDLC .... High-Level Data Link Control [*Computer science*] (DOM)
HLFTN .... Halftone (VRA)
HLG .... Wheeling [*West Virginia*] [*Airport symbol*] (AD)
HLR .... Harvard Law Review [*A publication*] (BRI)
HLS .... St. Helens [*Tasmania*] [*Airport symbol*] (AD)
HM.............. Air Mahe [*ICAO designator*] (AD)
HM.............. Harper's Magazine [*A publication*] (BRI)
HMA ..... Head Masters' Association (AIE)
HMML......... Hill Monastic Manuscript Library [*Saint John's University, Collegeville, MN*]
HMMP .... HyperMedia Management Protocol [*Computer science*]
HMMS .... Hyper-Media Management Schema [*Computer science*]
HMOA .... Health Maintenance Organization Acts of 1973 and 1988 (WYGK)
HMOM .... HyperMedia Object Manager [*Computer science*]
HMPD .... Hoffman Military Products Division
HMPT.......... Human Factors, Manpower, Personnel, and Training [*Military*] (RDA)
HMR .... Hoechst Marion Roussel
HMR .... Hungry Mind Review [*A publication*] (BRI)
HMS .... Hemin Storage
HMT............ High Mobility Trailer
HMXB .... High-Mass X-Ray Binary [*Star system*]
HN.............. NLM-Dutch Airlines [*ICAO designator*] (AD)
hng .... Hanging (VRA)
hngscr .... Hanging Scroll (VRA)
HNO .... Hercegnovi [*Yugoslavia*] [*Airport symbol*] (AD)
HNS .... Hughes Network Systems
HO .... Airways International [*ICAO designator*] (AD)

HO .... Charterair [*ICAO designator*] (AD)
H/O .... Handover
HOB .... Home-on-Burn
HOF .... Head of Faculty [*Education*] (AIE)
HOGE .... Hover out of Ground Effect
HOLD .... Call Hold [*Telecommunications*] (DOM)
holgr........... Hologram (VRA)
Holl .... Holland (VRA)
Hon............. Honorable (DD)
Hond .... Honduras (VRA)
honry .... Honorary (DD)
Hons .... Honors (DD)
HOO .... Quang Duc [*South Vietnam*] [*Airport symbol*] (AD)
HOPE .... Hackers on Planet Earth [*An association*]
HOPS .... Host Proximity Service [*Computer science*]
Hort .... Horticulture [*A publication*] (BRI)
HOS .... Health Online Service [*Computer science*] [*Medicine*]
HOS .... Hosana [*Ethiopia*] [*Airport symbol*] (AD)
hosp........... Hospital (VRA)
HOTT .... Hands-on Turret Trainer [*Military*]
HP............... Air Hawaii [*ICAO designator*] (AD)
HP............... America West Airlines [*ICAO designator*] (AD)
HPC .... Handheld PC [*Personal Computer*]
HPHC.......... Harvard Pilgrim Health Care
HPnP .... Home Plug and Play [*Technology*]
HPO .... Health Care Purchasing Organization [*Insurance*] (WYGK)
HPO .... Hippo Valley [*Zimbabwe*] [*Airport symbol*] (AD)
HPR .... Halden Reactor Project [*Norway*]
HPRP .... Human Potential Research Project [*University of Surrey*] [*British*] (AIE)
HQ .... Business Express [*ICAO designator*] (AD)
HQ .... Heussler Air Service [*ICAO designator*] (AD)
HQ .... New York Helicopter [*ICAO designator*] (AD)
HR .... Air Bremen [*ICAO designator*] (AD)
hr............... Hair (VRA)
HR .... Hudson Review [*A publication*] (BRI)
HRA .... Haura [*South Arabia (Yemen)*] [*Airport symbol*] (AD)
HRD .... Harstad [*Norway*] [*Airport symbol*] (AD)
HRDP.......... Human Resources [*Research*] and Development Program
HRDS.......... Human Resource Development Staff
HRIS .... Human Resources Information System (WYGK)
HR Mag ...... HR Magazine [*A publication*] (BRI)
HRNB.......... History: Reviews of New Books [*A publication*] (BRI)
hs .... House (VRA)
HS............... Marshall's Air [*ICAO designator*] (AD)

HSA .... Hollandse Signaalapparaten [*Dutch*]
H Sch M ...... High School Magazine [*A publication*] (BRI)
HSCP .... Historical Sources Collection Program
HSD .... Harnosand [*Sweden*] [*Airport symbol*] (AD)
HSGMOC..... Honorary Sergeant Major of the Corps [*Marine Corps*]
HSIL............ High-Grade Squamous Intraepithelial Lesions [*OCLC symbol*]
HSL............. Home-School Liaison (AIE)
HSOT .... Howitzer Strap-On Trainer [*Military*] (RDA)
HSP .... Hot Springs [*Virginia*] [*Airport symbol*] (AD)
HSPF .... Heating Seasonal Performance Factor
HSR .... Hot Springs [*South Dakota*] [*Airport symbol*] (AD)
HSSW .... High Salinity Shelf Water [*Oceanography*]
HSTAMIDS... Handheld Standoff Minefield Detection System [*Military*] (RDA)
HT............... Air Tchad [*ICAO designator*] (AD)
ht................ Height (VRA)
HT............... History Today [*A publication*] (BRI)
HT............... Horizontal Tab [*Computer science*] (DOM)
HTB............. Hairdressing Training Board (AIE)
HTI.............. Hamilton Technology, Inc.
HTI.............. Horizons Technology, Inc.
htnd............ Heightened (VRA)
HTNT .... High Technology National Training (AIE)
HTPS .... Hull-Turret Position Sensor [*Military*] (RDA)
Hts .... Heights (DD)
HTYP .... Heliotype [*Modified collotype*] (VRA)
HU .... Trinidad and Tobago Air Services [*ICAO designator*] (AD)
Hughes .... Hughes Air West [*ICAO designator*] (AD)
HUI .... Hue [*South Vietnam*] [*Airport symbol*] (AD)
Hum............ Humanist [*A publication*] (BRI)
HumRRO...... Human Resources Research Office [*George Washington University*]
Hung........... Hungary (VRA)
HUR .... Hurn [*England*] [*Airport symbol*] (AD)
HUY .... Hull [*England*] [*Airport symbol*] (AD)
HV .... Air Central [*ICAO designator*] (AD)
hv .... Heavy (VRA)
HW.............. Havasu Airlines [*ICAO designator*] (AD)
HW.............. North-Wright Air Ltd. [*ICAO designator*] (AD)
HWMA .... Hazardous Waste Management Association
HWN .... Haldwani [*India*] [*Airport symbol*] (AD)
Hwy .... Highway (DD)
HX............... Hamburg Airlines [*ICAO designator*] (AD)
HY............... Metro Airlines [*ICAO designator*] (AD)
hypst........... Hypostyle (VRA)
HYT............. Humaita [*Brazil*] [*Airport symbol*] (AD)
HYTIWYG.... How You Test is What You Get [*Education*] (AIE)
HZ................ Henebery Aviation [*ICAO designator*] (AD)

I

By Acronym

i .... Ink (VRA)
I .... Paid This Year, Dividend Omitted, Deferred, or No Action Taken at Last Dividend Meeting [*Investment term*] (DFIT)
IA .... Intelligent Agent
IAASE .... Independent Appeals Authority for School Examinations (AIE)
IACC .... Island Arts and Crafts Club, Victoria [*1910, IACS from 1922*] (NGC)
IACD .... Irish Association for Curriculum Development (AIE)
IACESC .... Inter-American Council for Education, Science, and Culture
IACPR .... Inter-American Committee of Presidential Representatives
IACS .... Island Arts and Crafts Society, Victoria [*1922, founded 1910 as IACC*] (NGC)
IACST .... Inter-American Committee for Science and Technology
IANA .... Intermodal Association of North America
IARD .... International Association for Rural Development (AIE)
IAS .... Inter-American System
IASC .... Inter-American Statistical Teaching Center
IASI .... Inter-American Statistical Institute
IAT .... Institute for Academic Technology
IATC .... Inter-American Telecommunications Commission
IB .... Iberia Air Lines of Spain [*ICAO designator*] (AD)
IBACOS .... Integrated Building and Construction Solutions
IBIS .... Inspectors Based in Schools [*British*] (AIE)
IBM .... Inclusion Body Myositis
IBO .... International Bowhunting Organization
IBS .... Integrated Booking System [*Army*] (RDA)
IBT .... International Brotherhood of Teamsters [*Union*]
IBU .... Itambacuri [*Brazil*] [*Airport symbol*] (AD)
IC .... Indian Airlines [*ICAO designator*] (AD)
ICA .... Icabaru [*Venezuela*] [*Airport symbol*] (AD)
ICAL .... Initiative on Communication Arts for Children (AIE)
ICAN .... Interlibrary Cooperation & Networking [*Association of Specialized and Cooperative Library Agencies*] [*American Library Association*]
ICAS .... Institute of Chartered Accountants of Scotland (AIE)
ICC .... Inter-American Cultural Council
ICCB .... International Center for Cooperation in BioInformatics [*UNESCO*]
ICCD .... Intensified Charge-Coupled Device [*Electronics*]
ICE .... Institute for Continuing Education (AIE)
ICE .... Intelligent Concept Extraction [*Technology*] [*Computer science*]
Icel .... Iceland (VRA)
ICGS .... Interactive Careers Guidance System (AIE)
ICIA .... Industrial, Commercial, and Institutional Accountant (DD)
ICM .... Individual Case Management (WYGK)
ICME .... International Congress on Mathematical Education (AIE)
icn .... Icon (VRA)
ICO .... Identified Camouflaged Objects [*Hunting*]
iconst .... Iconostasis (VRA)
ICP .... International Comfort Products
ICP .... Internet Content Provider [*Computer science*]
ICR .... Individually Carried Records [*Military*]
ICS .... Ion-Channel Switch [*Biochemistry*]
ICSA .... Institute of Chartered Secretaries and Administrators (AIE)
ICSI .... Intracytoplasmic Sperm Injection
ICT .... Intramolecular Charge Transfer [*Physical chemistry*]
ID .... Apollo Airlines [*ICAO designator*] (AD)
IDE .... Interdisciplinary Enquiry [*Education*] (AIE)
IDEA .... Interactive Digital Electronic Appliance [*Computer science*]
IDIQ .... Indefinite Delivery/Indefinite Quantity [*Military*] (RDA)
I-DMV .... Internet Department of Motor Vehicles
IDP .... Independence [*Kansas*] [*Airport symbol*] (AD)
IDPAR .... Institute of Donations and Public Affairs Research [*Canada*]
IDR .... Indore [*India*] [*Airport symbol*] (AD)
IDS .... Inter-Disciplinary Studies [*Education*] (AIE)
idv .... Individuals
IE .... Solomon Islands Airways [*ICAO designator*] (AD)
IEEE Exp ...... IEEE Expert: Intelligent Systems and Their Applications [*A publication*] (BRI)
IEG .... Internet Entertainment Group, Inc.
IEL .... Improved Efficiency of Learning [*Project*] (AIE)
IF .... Interflug [*ICAO designator*] (AD)
IFC .... Istituto di Fisica Cosmica [*Italy*]
IFCS .... Intergovernmental Forum on Chemical Safety
IFPO .... International Freelance Photographers Organization
IFRRO .... International Federation of Reproductive Rights Organisations (AIE)
IFSAR .... Interferometric Synthetic Aperture RADAR (RDA)
IG .... Alisarda [*ICAO designator*] (AD)
IG .... [*Office of the*] Inspector General

IGA .... Great Inagua Island [*Bahamas*] [*Airport symbol*] (AD)
IGCSE .... International General Certificate of Secondary Education (AIE)
IGERT .... Integrating Graduate Education and Research Training [*National Science Foundation*]
IGH .... Icy Grain Halo [*Model of comet structure*]
IGI .... Investigative Group International
IGP .... International Garment Processors
IGS .... Interchromatin Granular Cluster [*Cytology*]
IGZ .... Iguatu [*Brazil*] [*Airport symbol*] (AD)
IH .... Channel Flying [*ICAO designator*] (AD)
IH .... Itavia [*ICAO designator*] (AD)
IHDP .... Infant Health and Development Program
II .... Illegal Immigrant
II .... Imperial Airlines [*ICAO designator*] (AD)
II .... Independent Inspector (AIE)
II .... London City Airways [*ICAO designator*] (AD)
IILA .... Institute for the Integration of Latin America
IIOP .... Internet Inter-ORG [*Object Request Broker*] Protocol [*Computer science*]
IITPW .... Inertial Interchange True Polar Wander [*Geophysics*]
IJ .... Touraine Air Transport [*ICAO designator*] (AD)
IJFRS .... Irish Joint Fiction Reserve Scheme (AIE)
IJIR .... International Journal of Impotence Research [*A publication*]
IK .... Eureka Aero Industries [*ICAO designator*] (AD)
IK .... Inverse Kinematics [*Computer science*]
IKL .... Ikela [*Zaire*] [*Airport symbol*] (AD)
IL .... Island Air [*ICAO designator*] (AD)
ILEx .... Institute of Legal Executives (AIE)
ILF .... Milford Haven [*Wales*] [*Airport symbol*] (AD)
ILINC .... Interactive Learning International Corp.
illum .... Illuminated (VRA)
illus .... Illustration (VRA)
illus mat ...... Illustrative Material (VRA)
ILN .... Illustrated London News [*A publication*] (BRI)
ILP .... Individual Learning Programme (AIE)
ILP .... Isle des Pins [*New Caledonia*] [*Airport symbol*] (AD)
ILR .... International Labour Review [*A publication*] (BRI)
ILRR .... Industrial and Labor Relations Review [*A publication*] (BRI)
ILS .... Integrated Learning System (AIE)
ILS .... Irish Literary Supplement [*A publication*] (BRI)
ILTEB .... Inner London Tertiary Education Board [*British*] (AIE)
IM .... Inoffizielle Mitarbeiter [*Unofficial Collaborators*] [*German*]
IM .... Instant Messaging [*Computer science*]
IM .... Jamaire [*ICAO designator*] (AD)
IMAC 90 ...... Immigration Act of 1990 (WYGK)
IMHE .... Institutional Management in Higher Education (AIE)
imp .... Impasse (DD)
IMP .... Integrated Mathematics Project (AIE)
IMPAC .... International Merchant Purchases Authorization Care [*Visa*] (RDA)
Impr .... Impressionism (VRA)
imprm .... Imprimatura (VRA)
impst .... Impasto (VRA)
IMTC .... International Multimedia Teleconferencing Consortium
IN .... East Hampton Air [*ICAO designator*] (AD)
in .... Inch (VRA)
in .... Inches (VRA)
INA .... Icana [*Brazil*] [*Airport symbol*] (AD)
inc .... Incised (VRA)
ind .... Industrial (DD)
IndAdmin ..... Industrial Administration (DD)
INDEL .... Industry Education Liaison (AIE)
IndEng .... Industrial Engineering (DD)
IndHealth .... Industrial Health (DD)
ind i .... India Ink (VRA)
INDTEL .... Industry and Teacher Education Liaison (AIE)
info .... Information (DD)
infra .... Infrared (VRA)
ing .... Ingenieur (DD)
INH .... Inhambane [*Mozambique*] [*Airport symbol*] (AD)
inl .... Inlay (VRA)
INLOGOV ..... Institute of Local Government [*University of Birmingham*] [*British*] (AIE)
INM .... Innamincka [*South Australia*] [*Airport symbol*] (AD)
INOS .... Isoform of Nitric Oxide Synthase [*An enzyme*]
ins .... Instant (VRA)
inscr .... Inscription (VRA)

25

inst .... Institution (VRA)
Inst .... Instructor [*A publication*] (BRI)
INSTEP .... In-Service Training and Education Panel (AIE)
instl .... Installation (VRA)
instr .... Instrument (VRA)
int .... Interior (VRA)
INT .... Winston-Salem [*North Carolina*] [*Airport symbol*] (AD)
INTENT .... Initial Teacher Education and New Technology [*Project*] (AIE)
InterNIC .... Internet Network Information Center [*Computer science*]
intg .... Intaglio (VRA)
intl .... International (VRA)
IntlAffairs .... International Affairs (DD)
Intpr .... Interpretation: A Journal of Bible and Theology [*A publication*] (BRI)
intr .... Intarsia (VRA)
intr-md .... Inter-media (VRA)
INV .... Iris Neovascularization [*Opthalmology*]
invest .... Investment (DD)
INVOG .... Information Officers Working in Voluntary Organisations (AIE)
INX .... Inanwatan [*West Irian, Indonesia*] [*Airport symbol*] (AD)
IO .... Air Paris [*ICAO designator*] (AD)
I/O .... Input/Output [*Computer science*]
IOK .... Industrial and Occupational Knowledge (AIE)
IoM .... Institute of Medicine
IOSTE .... International Organisation for Science and Technology Education (AIE)
IOW .... Iowa City [*Iowa*] [*Airport symbol*] (AD)
IP .... Airlines of Tasmania [*ICAO designator*] (AD)
IPG .... Phoolbagh [*India*] [*Airport symbol*] (AD)
IPO .... Initial Public Offering [*Stock exchange term*]
IPO .... Ipora [*Brazil*] [*Airport symbol*] (AD)
IPPDT .... Integrated Product and Process Development Team [*Military*] (RDA)
IPQ .... International Philosophical Quarterly [*A publication*] (BRI)
I/Pro .... Interactive Profiles [*Computer science*]
ips .... Inches per Second (DOM)
IPS .... Internet Printing System [*Computer science*]
IPSE .... Implementing Primary Science Education (AIE)
IPW .... Ipswich [*England*] [*Airport symbol*] (AD)
IPWSOM ...... Institute of Practitioners in Work Study, Organisation, and Management (AIE)
IQ .... Caribbean Airways [*ICAO designator*] (AD)
IQCODE .... Informant Questionnaire on Cognitive Decline in the Elderly
IR .... Iran Air [*ICAO designator*] (AD)
IR .... Iran National Airlines [*ICAO designator*] (AD)
IRBT .... Infrared Brightness Temperature
IRDAC .... Industrial Research and Development Advisory Committee [*European Union*]
Ire .... Ireland (VRA)
IREF .... Ischemia Research and Education Foundation
IRG .... Iron Range [*Queensland*] [*Airport symbol*] (AD)
irid .... Irridescent (VRA)
IRL .... Immigration Restriction League
IRLA .... Information Retrieval & Library Automation [*A publication*] (BRI)
IRO .... Birao [*Central African Republic*] [*Airport symbol*] (AD)
IRP .... Iron Regulatory Protein [*Biochemistry*]
IRQ .... Interrupt Request Line [*Computer science*]
IS .... Eagle Air [*ICAO designator*] (AD)
IS .... Image Stabilization [*Technology from Canon*]
IS .... Industrial Society (AIE)
IS .... Instruction Section [*Association of College and Research Libraries*] [*American Library Association*]
ISA .... Index of Spouse Abuse
ISAI .... Independent Schools Association Inc. (AIE)
ISAPI .... Internet Server API [*All-Purpose Interface*] [*Microsoft and Process Software Corp.*] [*Computer science*]
ISAPI .... Internet Services API [*Computer science*]
ISB .... Internet3D Space Builder
ISB .... Nisab [*South Arabia*] [*Airport symbol*] (AD)
ISC .... Information Systems Committee [*Universities Funding Council*] (AIE)
ISC .... Intuit Services Corp.
ISCHE .... International Standing Conference for the History of Education (AIE)
ISD .... Instructional Systems Design (DOM)

ISE .... Interactive Software Engineering
ISE .... International Stock Exchange of the United Kingdom and the Republic of Ireland (DFIT)
ISEA .... Inland Seas Education Association
ISFC .... International Symposium on Fluorine Chemistry
ISG .... Insurance Services Group
ISII .... International Society for Individualized Instruction (AIE)
ISIS .... Intermarket Surveillance Information System (DFIT)
ISJAC .... Independent Schools Joint Action Committee (AIE)
ISK .... Iskenderon [*Turkey*] [*Airport symbol*] (AD)
iso .... Isometric (VRA)
ISP .... Image Synthesis Processor [*Computer science*]
ISP .... Information Systems Professional (DD)
ISPEC .... Independent Schools Physical Education Conference (AIE)
ISQL .... Interactive SQL [*Computer science*]
ISR .... Ice Sounding RADAR
ISR .... Incoherent Scatter RADAR [*Instrumentation*]
Isr .... Israel (VRA)
ISRC .... International Survey Research Corp.
ISS .... Independent Schools Section [*American Association of School Libraries*] [*American Library Association*]
IST .... Instrumented Sensor Technologies
ISVR3 .... Intel Smart Video Recorder III
ISW .... Integrated Sachs-Wolfe [*Effect in cosmic microwave background*]
ISWG .... Independent Schools Working Group (AIE)
IT .... Air Inter [*ICAO designator*] (AD)
It .... Italy (VRA)
ITA .... Interstate Truckers Association
ITA .... Itacoatiara [*Brazil*] [*Airport symbol*] (AD)
ITCCU .... Information Technology Centre Consultancy Unit [*British*] (AIE)
ITeMS .... Ideas in the Teaching of Mathematics and Science (AIE)
ITI .... Itapetinga [*Brazil*] [*Airport symbol*] (AD)
ITJ .... Itajai [*Brazil*] [*Airport symbol*] (AD)
ITOO .... Independent Truck Owner-Operators Association
ITQ .... Itaqui [*Brazil*] [*Airport symbol*] (AD)
ITS .... AmericaIntelligent Transportation Society of America [*Formerly, IVHS America*]
ITS .... Industrial Training Service (AIE)
ITT .... Initial Teacher Training (AIE)
ITT .... Wittenoom Gorge [*Western Australia*] [*Airport symbol*] (AD)
IU .... Midstate Airlines [*ICAO designator*] (AD)
IUBS-CBE ..... IUBS Commission on Biological Education (AIE)
IUR .... Inventory Update Rule [*Environmental Protection Agency*]
IUSC .... Inter-University Software Committee [*Inter-University Committee on Computing*] (AIE)
IV .... British Island Airways [*ICAO designator*] (AD)
iv .... Ivory (VRA)
Iv Co .... Ivory Coast (VRA)
IVEC .... In Vitro Expression Cloning [*Analytical biochemistry*]
IVI .... Indeo Video Interactive [*Computer science*]
IVIE .... Interactive Video in Education [*National Interactive Video Centre*] (AIE)
IVS .... Interactive Voice System [*Electronics*]
IVUS .... Intravascular Ultrasound [*Medicine*]
IW .... International Air Bahama [*ICAO designator*] (AD)
IWA .... Iwakuni [*Japan*] [*Airport symbol*] (AD)
IWS .... Information Warfare Squadron [*Air Force*]
IX .... Flandre Air [*ICAO designator*] (AD)
IX .... Information Exchange [*Advanced photo system*]
IXH .... Kailashahar [*India*] [*Airport symbol*] (AD)
IXN .... Khowai [*India*] [*Airport symbol*] (AD)
IXP .... Pathankot [*India*] [*Airport symbol*] (AD)
IXQ .... Kamalpur [*India*] [*Airport symbol*] (AD)
IXT .... Pasighat [*India*] [*Airport symbol*] (AD)
IXV .... Along [*India*] [*Airport symbol*] (AD)
IXW .... Jamshedpur [*India*] [*Airport symbol*] (AD)
IXY .... Kandla [*India*] [*Airport symbol*] (AD)
IY .... Yemen Airways [*ICAO designator*] (AD)
IYY .... International Youth Year [*1985*] (AIE)
IZ .... Arkia-Israel Inland Airlines [*ICAO designator*] (AD)
IZT .... Ixtepec [*Mexico*] [*Airport symbol*] (AD)

J
By Acronym

JA .... Bankair [*ICAO designator*] (AD)
ja .... Jade (VRA)
JAAC .... Journal of Aesthetics and Art Criticism [*A publication*] (BRI)
JAAL .... Journal of Adolescent & Adult Literacy [*A publication*] (BRI)
JAAR .... Journal of the American Academy of Religion [*A publication*] (BRI)
Jacbn .... Jacobean (VRA)
J Account .... Journal of Accountancy [*A publication*] (BRI)
jadt .... Jadeite (VRA)
JAE .... Jacksonville [*Illinois*] [*Airport symbol*] (AD)
J Aes Ed ..... Journal of Aesthetic Education [*A publication*] (BRI)
JAF .... Jaffna [*Ceylon*] [*Airport symbol*] (AD)
JAF .... Journal of American Folklore [*A publication*] (BRI)
JAH .... Journal of American History [*A publication*] (BRI)
JAHWGS ...... Joint Ad Hoc Working Group on Shipping [*ASEAN*]
JAL .... Journal of Academic Librarianship [*A publication*] (BRI)
Jama .... Jamaica (VRA)
J Am Cult .... Journal of American Culture [*A publication*] (BRI)
JAML .... Journal of Arts Management, Law & Society [*A publication*] (BRI)
J Am St ...... Journal of American Studies [*A publication*] (BRI)
Jap .... Japan (VRA)
JAR .... JavaSoft Java Archive [*Computer science*]
JAS .... Journal of Asian Studies [*A publication*] (BRI)
JASPER .... Joint Academic Services Providers to Education and Research (AIE)
JB .... Junior Bookshelf [*A publication*] (BRI)
JB .... Pioneer Airways [*ICAO designator*] (AD)
JBIC .... Journal of Biological Inorganic Chemistry [*A publication*]
JBL .... Journal of Biblical Literature [*A publication*] (BRI)
J Bl St .... Journal of Black Studies [*A publication*] (BRI)
J Broadcst ... Journal of Broadcasting and Electronic Media [*A publication*] (BRI)
JC .... Journal of Communication [*A publication*] (BRI)
JC .... Rocky Mountain Airways [*ICAO designator*] (AD)
J Car P & E .. Journal of Career Planning and Employment [*A publication*] (BRI)
JCB .... Joacaba [*Brazil*] [*Airport symbol*] (AD)
J Chem Ed ... Journal of Chemical Education [*A publication*] (BRI)
J Ch St .... Journal of Church and State [*A publication*] (BRI)
J ClinPsyc ... Journal of Clinical Psychiatry [*A publication*] (BRI)
JCMT .... Joint Collection Management Tools [*Army*] (RDA)
J Con A .... Journal of Consumer Affairs [*A publication*] (BRI)
JCP .... Job Creation Programme [*Manpower Services Commission*] (AIE)
JCS .... Jaicos [*Brazil*] [*Airport symbol*] (AD)
JD .... Doctor of Jurisprudence (DD)
JD .... Toa Domestic Airlines [*ICAO designator*] (AD)
JE .... Journal of Education [*A publication*] (BRI)
JE .... Yosemite Airlines [*ICAO designator*] (AD)
Jeep .... Graduated Payment Mortgage (DFIT)
JEGP .... Journal of English and Germanic Philology [*A publication*] (BRI)
JEH .... Journal of Economic History [*A publication*] (BRI)
JEL .... Journal of Economic Literature [*A publication*] (BRI)
JES .... Joint Efficiency Study (AIE)
JF .... LAB Flying Service [*ICAO designator*] (AD)
JFA .... Jaffa [*Israel*] [*Airport symbol*] (AD)
J Film & Vid... Journal of Film & Video [*A publication*] (BRI)
JG .... Swedair [*ICAO designator*] (AD)
J Gov Info.... Journal of Government Information [*A publication*] (BRI)
JH .... Nordeste-Lineas Aereas Regionais [*ICAO designator*] (AD)
JHI .... Journal of the History of Ideas [*A publication*] (BRI)
J Hi E .... Journal of Higher Education [*A publication*] (BRI)
J Hist G ...... Journal of Historical Geography [*A publication*] (BRI)
J Homosex ... Journal of Homosexuality [*A publication*] (BRI)
JI .... Gull Air [*ICAO designator*] (AD)
JI .... Jet Express [*ICAO designator*] (AD)
JIB .... Journal of International Business Studies [*A publication*] (BRI)
JIH .... Journal of Interdisciplinary History [*A publication*] (BRI)
JIIG-CAL ...... Job Ideas and Information Generator - Computer Assisted Learning (AIE)
JIN .... Jinja [*Uganda*] [*Airport symbol*] (AD)
JIP .... Jipijapa [*Ecuador*] [*Airport symbol*] (AD)
JJ .... Coddair Air East [*ICAO designator*] (AD)

JJU .... Julienhaab [*Greenland*] [*Airport symbol*] (AD)
JK .... Sun World [*ICAO designator*] (AD)
JKT .... Djakarta [*Java, Indonesia*] [*Airport symbol*] (AD)
JLO .... Jesolo [*Italy*] [*Airport symbol*] (AD)
JLP .... Juan-les-Pins [*France*] [*Airport symbol*] (AD)
jlry .... Jewelry (VRA)
JLW-155 ...... Joint Lightweight 155mm Howitzer (RDA)
JM .... Journal of Marketing [*A publication*] (BRI)
JMCQ .... Journalism & Mass Communication Quarterly [*A publication*] (BRI)
JMF .... Journal of Marriage and the Family [*A publication*] (BRI)
JMH .... Journal of Modern History [*A publication*] (BRI)
J Mil H .... Journal of Military History [*A publication*] (BRI)
JMM .... Journal of Molecular Medicine [*A publication*]
JMSW .... Journal of Multicultural Social Work [*A publication*] (BRI)
JNA .... Januaria [*Brazil*] [*Airport symbol*] (AD)
JNC .... Joint National Council (AIE)
JNE .... Journal of Negro Education [*A publication*] (BRI)
JNP .... Jasper National Park [*Alberta*] [*Airport symbol*] (AD)
JNX .... Jackson [*Michigan*] [*Airport symbol*] (AD)
JO .... Holiday Airlines [*ICAO designator*] (AD)
JOM .... Njombe [*Tanzania*] [*Airport symbol*] (AD)
Jor .... Jordan (VRA)
Journ .... Journalism (DD)
JOYS .... Journal of Youth Services in Libraries [*American Library Association*]
JP .... Indo-Pacific International [*ICAO designator*] (AD)
JP .... Journal of Parapsychology [*A publication*] (BRI)
JPC .... Journal of Popular Culture [*A publication*] (BRI)
JPC .... Judgement Purchase Corp.
JPE .... Journal of Political Economy [*A publication*] (BRI)
J Phil .... Journal of Philosophy [*A publication*] (BRI)
JPO .... Pomona [*California*] [*Airport symbol*] (AD)
J Pol .... Journal of Politics [*A publication*] (BRI)
J Pop F&TV... Journal of Popular Film and Television [*A publication*] (BRI)
JPR .... Journal of Peace Research [*A publication*] (BRI)
JQ .... Journalism Quarterly [*A publication*] (BRI)
JQ .... Trans-Jamaican Airlines [*ICAO designator*] (AD)
JR .... Journal of Religion [*A publication*] (BRI)
Jr .... Junior (DD)
J Rehab RD... Journal of Rehabilitation Research and Development [*A publication*] (BRI)
JRS .... Job Rehearsal Scheme (AIE)
JS .... Korean Airways [*ICAO designator*] (AD)
JSCAACR ..... Joint Steering Committee for Revision of AACR [*Anglo-American Cataloging Rules*]
JSF .... Joint Strike Fighter
JSH .... Journal of Southern History [*A publication*] (BRI)
J Soc H .... Journal of Social History [*A publication*] (BRI)
jsp .... Jasper (VRA)
JSS .... Jewish Social Studies [*A publication*] (BRI)
JSU .... Sukkertoppen [*Greenland*] [*Airport symbol*] (AD)
JT .... Iowa Airways [*ICAO designator*] (AD)
J Teach Ed ... Journal of Teacher Education [*A publication*] (BRI)
JTI .... Jatai [*Brazil*] [*Airport symbol*] (AD)
JTR .... Thira [*Greece*] [*Airport symbol*] (AD)
JTS .... Joint Training Scheme (AIE)
JTT/CIBSM ... Joint Tactical Terminal/Common Integrated Broadcast System Module [*Military*] (RDA)
JU .... Yugoslav Airlines [*ICAO designator*] (AD)
JUD .... Juris Utrisuque Doctor (DD)
JUN .... Jundah [*Queensland*] [*Airport symbol*] (AD)
J Urban H ... Journal of Urban History [*A publication*] (BRI)
JV .... Bearskin Lake [*ICAO designator*] (AD)
JV .... Jersey European Airways [*ICAO designator*] (AD)
JVM .... Java Virtual Machine [*Computer science*]
JW .... Polar Avia [*ICAO designator*] (AD)
JW .... Royal American [*ICAO designator*] (AD)
JX .... Bougair [*ICAO designator*] (AD)
JY .... Jersey European [*ICAO designator*] (AD)
JZ .... Alamo Commuter Airlines [*ICAO designator*] (AD)

K
By Acronym

K .... Declared or Paid This Year on a Cumulative Issue with Dividends in Arrears [*Investment term*] (DFIT)
KA .... Coastal Plains Commuter [*ICAO designator*] (AD)
KAC .... Kamishli [*Syria*] [*Airport symbol*] (AD)
kakm .... Kakemono (VRA)
KAL .... Keywords and Learning (AIE)
KAM .... Kamaran Island [*South Arabia (Yemen)*] [*Airport symbol*] (AD)
KAPS .... Kawasaki Automatic Power-Drive System [*Kawasaki Motors Corp.*]
KAR .... Kars [*Turkey*] [*Airport symbol*] (AD)
Kash .... Kashmir (VRA)
KATYP .... Kallitype (VRA)
KAU .... Kauhava [*Finland*] [*Airport symbol*] (AD)
KB .... Burnthills [*ICAO designator*] (AD)
KBA .... Beni Abbes [*Algeria*] [*Airport symbol*] (AD)
KBK .... Kirkjubaejar [*Iceland*] [*Airport symbol*] (AD)
KBO .... Kabalo [*Zaire*] [*Airport symbol*] (AD)
KBO .... Kuiper Belt Objects [*Planetary science*]
KBP .... Koala Bear Park [*Adelaide*] [*Airport symbol*] (AD)
Kbps .... Kilobits per Second [*Computer science*]
KBps .... Kilobytes per Second [*Computer science*] (DOM)
KBU .... Kotabaru [*West Irian, Indonesia*] [*Airport symbol*] (AD)
KC .... Cook Islands International [*ICAO designator*] (AD)
KCLJ .... Knight Commander of the Order of St. Lazarus of Jerusalem (DD)
KCN .... Kids' Clubs Network (AIE)
KD .... Kendell Airlines [*ICAO designator*] (AD)
KDA .... Kolda [*Senegal*] [*Airport symbol*] (AD)
KDI .... Knowledge and Distributed Intelligence
KDJ .... Njdole [*Gabon*] [*Airport symbol*] (AD)
KDL .... Koronadal [*Mindanao, Philippines*] [*Airport symbol*] (AD)
kdlth .... Kodalith (VRA)
KDU .... Skardu [*Pakistan*] [*Airport symbol*] (AD)
KE .... Korean Air Lines [*ICAO designator*] (AD)
KEF .... Keflavik [*Iceland*] [*Airport symbol*] (AD)
Ken .... Kenya (VRA)
Ken R .... Kenyon Review [*A publication*] (BRI)
KERA .... Kentucky Education Reform Act
KF .... Catskill Airways [*ICAO designator*] (AD)
KG .... Catalina Airlines [*ICAO designator*] (AD)
KGO .... Kasongo [*Zaire*] [*Airport symbol*] (AD)
KH .... Cook Islandair [*ICAO designator*] (AD)
KHE .... Kherson [*USSR*] [*Airport symbol*] (AD)
KHL .... Khulna [*Bangladesh*] [*Airport symbol*] (AD)
KHS .... Knight of the Holy Sepulchre of Jerusalem (DD)
KHS .... Kushtia [*Bangladesh*] [*Airport symbol*] (AD)
KIA .... Kaiapit [*New Guinea*] [*Airport symbol*] (AD)
KIK .... Kirkuk [*Iraq*] [*Airport symbol*] (AD)
kin .... Kinetic (VRA)
Kiplinger ..... Kiplinger's Personal Finance Magazine [*A publication*] (BRI)
KIR .... Killer-Cell Inhibitory Receptor [*Immunology*]
KISC .... Knowledge Information Skills and Curriculum [*Project*] (AIE)
KIU .... Kainantu [*New Guinea*] [*Airport symbol*] (AD)
KJ .... Air Guyane [*ICAO designator*] (AD)
KL .... Air Atlantique [*ICAO designator*] (AD)
KLA .... Kampala [*Uganda*] [*Airport symbol*] (AD)
KLC .... Kaolack [*Senegal*] [*Airport symbol*] (AD)
KLE .... Kaele [*Cameroon*] [*Airport symbol*] (AD)
KLH .... Knight of the Legion of Honour (DD)
KLH .... Long Akha [*Malaysia*] [*Airport symbol*] (AD)

Kliatt .... Kliatt Young Adult Paperback Book Guide [*A publication*] (BRI)
KLJ .... Knight of the Military and Hospitalier Order of St. Lazarus (DD)
KLY .... Kalima [*Zaire*] [*Airport symbol*] (AD)
KM .... Air Malta [*ICAO designator*] (AD)
KM .... Knight of the Sovereign and Military Order of Malta (DD)
KMK .... Makabana [*Congo*] [*Airport symbol*] (AD)
KMP .... Kent Mathematics Project [*British*] (AIE)
KN .... Air Kentucky [*ICAO designator*] (AD)
kn .... Known (VRA)
KN .... Temsco Airlines [*ICAO designator*] (AD)
KNN .... Kankan [*Guinea*] [*Airport symbol*] (AD)
KNT .... Sanandaj [*Iran*] [*Airport symbol*] (AD)
KODCH .... Kodachrome (VRA)
KON .... Kontum [*South Vietnam*] [*Airport symbol*] (AD)
Kor .... Korea (VRA)
KOX .... Kokonao [*West Irian, Indonesia*] [*Airport symbol*] (AD)
KP .... Safair [*ICAO designator*] (AD)
KPT3 .... Kai's Power Tools [*Computer science*]
KPU .... Khapalu [*Pakistan*] [*Airport symbol*] (AD)
KQ .... Kenya Airways [*ICAO designator*] (AD)
KR .... Kar-Air [*ICAO designator*] (AD)
KR .... Kirkus Review [*A publication*] (BRI)
KR .... Knight-Ridder
KRA .... Kerang [*Victoria, Australia*] [*Airport symbol*] (AD)
KRII .... Knight-Ridder Information Inc.
KS .... Key Stage [*Of National Curriculum*] [*British*] (AIE)
KS .... Peninsula Airways [*ICAO designator*] (AD)
KSH .... Kermanshah [*Iran*] [*Airport symbol*] (AD)
KSI .... Kissidougou [*Guinea*] [*Airport symbol*] (AD)
KSN .... Sam Neua [*Laos*] [*Airport symbol*] (AD)
KST .... Kosti [*Sudan*] [*Airport symbol*] (AD)
KStJ .... Knight of the Order of St. John of Jerusalem (DD)
KT .... Turtle Airways [*ICAO designator*] (AD)
KTI .... Kratie [*Cambodia*] [*Airport symbol*] (AD)
KTL .... Kitale [*Kenya*] [*Airport symbol*] (AD)
KTR .... Katherine [*Northern Territory, Australia*] [*Airport symbol*] (AD)
KTU .... Kutaisi [*USSR*] [*Airport symbol*] (AD)
KU .... Kuwait Airways [*ICAO designator*] (AD)
KUS .... Kulusuk Island [*Greenland*] [*Airport symbol*] (AD)
Kush .... Kushan (VRA)
KUT .... Kutahya [*Turkey*] [*Airport symbol*] (AD)
KUU .... Kulu [*India*] [*Airport symbol*] (AD)
Kuw .... Kuwait (VRA)
KV .... Transkei Airways [*ICAO designator*] (AD)
KVG .... Kavieng [*New Ireland*] [*Airport symbol*] (AD)
KW .... Kilowatt (DFIT)
KWE .... Kweiyang [*China*] [*Airport symbol*] (AD)
KWH .... Kilowatt-Hour (DFIT)
KWU .... Kawau Island [*New Zealand*] [*Airport symbol*] (AD)
KWZ .... Kolwezi [*Zaire*] [*Airport symbol*] (AD)
KX .... Cayman Airways [*ICAO designator*] (AD)
KXU .... Kastamonu [*Turkey*] [*Airport symbol*] (AD)
KY .... Sun West [*ICAO designator*] (AD)
KYA .... Konya [*Turkey*] [*Airport symbol*] (AD)
KYC .... Know Your Customer [*Investment term*] (DFIT)
kyst .... Keystone (VRA)
KYZ .... Kayseri [*Turkey*] [*Airport symbol*] (AD)
KZ .... Oriens & King [*ICAO designator*] (AD)
KZR .... Khuzdar [*Pakistan*] [*Airport symbol*] (AD)

L

By Acronym

LA .... Language Arts [*A publication*] (BRI)
la .... Late (VRA)
LAAGOWRNAFE... Local Authority Associations Group of Work Related Non-Advanced Further Education (AIE)
LA Ant .... Latin American Antiquity [*A publication*] (BRI)
lac .... Lacquer (VRA)
LACAS .... Local Authority Catering Advisory Service (AIE)
LAD.............. Logistics Anchor Desk [*Army*] (RDA)
LAERF.......... Lewisville Aquatic Ecosystem Research Facility [*Army*]
LAFIS.......... Local Authority Financial Institution System (AIE)
LAG.............. La Guaira [*Venzuela*] [*Airport symbol*] (AD)
LAITG.......... Library Association Information Technology Group (AIE)
LAL.............. Lakeland [*Florida*] [*Airport symbol*] (AD)
lam .... Laminated (VRA)
Lam Bk Rpt... Lambda Book Report [*A publication*] (BRI)
LAN.............. Library Advocacy Now [*American Library Association*]
LANC .... Local Application Numerical Control [*Sony Corp.*] (DOM)
Lang Soc .... Language in Society [*A publication*] (BRI)
L Anti.......... Antilles (VRA)
L Anti.......... Lesser Antilles (VRA)
LAP.............. Low Achievers Project [*Education*] (AIE)
LAPD .... Link Access Procedure-D [*Telecommunications*] (DOM)
LAPS.......... Low Attaining Pupils in Secondary Schools (AIE)
LAQ............. Al Bayda [*Libya*] [*Airport symbol*] (AD)
LAR............. Library Association Record [*A publication*] (BRI)
LASS.......... Library Access and Sixth-Form Studies [*British*] (AIE)
lat .... Lateral (VRA)
LATBR .... Los Angeles Times Book Review [*A publication*] (BRI)
LATE .... London Association for the Teaching of English [*British*] (AIE)
Latv .... Latvia (VRA)
Law Q Rev... Law Quarterly Review [*A publication*] (BRI)
LB .... Lloyd Aereo Boliviano [*ICAO designator*] (AD)
LBR............. Labrea [*Brazil*] [*Airport symbol*] (AD)
LBR............. Living Benefits Rider [*Insurance*] (WYGK)
LBY............. La Baule [*France*] [*Airport symbol*] (AD)
L/C............. Letter of Credit (DFIT)
LC .... Loganair [*ICAO designator*] (AD)
LCCEB........ London Chamber of Commerce Examinations Board [*British*] (AIE)
LCCM.......... LanClient Control Manager [*Computer science*]
LCD............. Letter Carrier Depot (DD)
LCDS .... Liquid-Crystal Displays [*Computer science*]
LCHE .... Luton College of Higher Education (AIE)
LCL............. Less-than-Carload Lot (DFIT)
LCM............. La Cumbre [*Argentina*] [*Airport symbol*] (AD)
LCMO.......... Lanthanum/Calcium/Manganese/Oxygen [*Inorganic chemistry*]
LCS............. Last Cast Syndrome [*Fictitious fishing malady*]
LC/TC......... Livonia Career/Technical Center
LCV............. Llymphocryptovirus
LDAP .... Lightweight Directory Access Protocol [*Computer science*]
LDCM.......... LANDesk Client Manager Technology [*Intel*] [*Computer science*]
LDOCE .... Longman's Dictionary of Contemporary English [*A publication*]
LDR .... Lodar [*South Arabia*] [*Airport symbol*] (AD)
ldscp.......... Landscape (VRA)
LDZ............. Lodz [*Poland*] [*Airport symbol*] (AD)
LE .... Magnum Airlines [*ICAO designator*] (AD)
lea .... Leather (VRA)
LEAP.......... Local Education Authorities Project for School Management Training (AIE)
LEAP.......... Lower-Extremity Amputation Protocol [*Orthopedics*]
LEAPS........ Long-Term Equity Anticipation Securities [*Investment term*] (DFIT)
LEASIB....... Local Education Authorities and Schools Item Banking [*Project*] (AIE)
LEATGS....... Local Education Authority Training Grants Scheme (AIE)
Leb .... Lebanon (VRA)
LEconSc..... License Economic Sciences [*Canada*] (DD)
lectn .... Lectionary (VRA)
LEDO .... Long-Term Effects of Dredging Operations [*Coastal Engineering Research Center*]
LEG............. Aleg [*Mauritania*] [*Airport symbol*] (AD)
LEG............. Language of Functions and Graphs (AIE)
Legacy........ Legacy: A Journal of American Women Writers [*A publication*] (BRI)
LEK............. Labe [*Guinea*] [*Airport symbol*] (AD)
lekyt.......... Lekythos (VRA)
LEN.............. Local Employment Network (AIE)
LENS.......... LASER-Engineered Net Shaping
L'Esprit........ L'Esprit Createur [*A publication*] (BRI)
LETEC .... London East Training and Enterprise Council [*British*] (AIE)

LEW .... Auburn-Lewiston [*Maine*] [*Airport symbol*] (AD)
lf .... Leaf (VRA)
LF .... Line Feed [*Computer science*] (DOM)
LF .... Linjeflyg [*ICAO designator*] (AD)
LFRC.......... Library Fundraising Resource Center [*American Library Association*]
lf sz .... Life Size (VRA)
lft............... Left (VRA)
lgd .... Legend (VRA)
LGL............. La Gloria [*Colombia*] [*Airport symbol*] (AD)
LGMB.......... Local Government Management Board (AIE)
lgth .... Length (VRA)
LGY............. Lagunillas [*Venezuela*] [*Airport symbol*] (AD)
LH .... Lufthansa German Airlines [*ICAO designator*] (AD)
LHD .... Doctor of Humane Letters (DD)
LHD .... Doctor of Literature (DD)
LHD .... Doctor of the Humanities (DD)
LHV............. Lock Haven [*Pennsylvania*] [*Airport symbol*] (AD)
LHX............. La Junta [*Colorado*] [*Airport symbol*] (AD)
L/I .... Letter of Intent (DFIT)
LIA .... Licentiate in Accountancy (DD)
LIASE.......... Linking Industry and School Education (AIE)
Lib .... Library [*A publication*] (BRI)
Lib & Cult.... Libraries & Culture [*A publication*] (BRI)
Liber........... Liberia (VRA)
libr............. Library (VRA)
LICO........... Low Income Cut-Off [*Canada*]
lin .... Linen (VRA)
LINC .... Language Information Network Coordination [*Education*] (AIE)
lindwd .... Lindenwood (VRA)
lino .... Linocut (VRA)
Lino .... Linotronic [*Computer science*]
LIP .... Library Information Plan (AIE)
LISU........... Library and Information Statistics Unit (AIE)
litg............. Liturgy (VRA)
Lith .... Lithuania (VRA)
litho .... Lithograph (VRA)
LJ .... Library Journal [*A publication*] (BRI)
LJ .... Sierra Leone Airways [*ICAO designator*] (AD)
LJZ............. Lajes [*Brazil*] [*Airport symbol*] (AD)
LK .... Letaba Airways [*ICAO designator*] (AD)
LKM............. Nekempt [*Ethiopia*] [*Airport symbol*] (AD)
LKW............. Larkana [*Pakistan*] [*Airport symbol*] (AD)
LL .... Bell-Air [*ICAO designator*] (AD)
ll .... Lapis Lazuli (VRA)
LLB .... Bachelor of Laws (DD)
LLB .... Luluabourg [*Zaire*] [*Airport symbol*] (AD)
LLD .... Doctor of Laws (DD)
LLJ............. Lalmonirhat [*Bangladesh*] [*Airport symbol*] (AD)
LLM............. Long Lama [*Malaysia*] [*Airport symbol*] (AD)
LLMI........... Local Labour Market Information/Intelligence [*British*] (AIE)
LM .... Lentigo Maligna [*Oncology*]
LMC............. London Montessori Centre [*British*] (AIE)
LMC............. Loss of Mesodermal Competence [*Developmental biology*]
LMCC.......... Licentiate of the Medical College of Canada (DD)
LMDS.......... Local Multipoint Distribution Systems [*Broadcasting term*]
LMP............. Linguistic Minorities Project [*Education*] (AIE)
LMQ............. Marsa Brega [*Libya*] [*Airport symbol*] (AD)
LMR............. Literary Magazine Review [*A publication*] (BRI)
lmst .... Limestone (VRA)
lmwd .... Limewood (VRA)
LN .... Libyan Arab Airlines [*ICAO designator*] (AD)
ln .... Line (VRA)
LNH............. Lengeh [*Iran*] [*Airport symbol*] (AD)
LNL............. Land O'Lakes [*Wisconsin*] [*Airport symbol*] (AD)
lnsd .... Linseed Oil (VRA)
LOB............. Lobito [*Angola*] [*Airport symbol*] (AD)
loc .... Location (VRA)
LOCATE....... List of Common Abbreviations in Training and Education (AIE)
log .... Loggia (VRA)
LOI............. Laredo [*Texas*] [*Airport symbol*] (AD)
longit.......... Longitudinal (VRA)
Lon R Bks.... London Review of Books [*A publication*] (BRI)
LOO............. Laghouat [*Algeria*] [*Airport symbol*] (AD)
LOP............. Loanda [*Brazil*] [*Airport symbol*] (AD)
LOQ............. Lobatsi [*Botswana*] [*Airport symbol*] (AD)
LOV............. Monclova [*Mexico*] [*Airport symbol*] (AD)

low.............. Lower (VRA)
LP................ Air Alpes [*ICAO designator*] (AD)
LPA.............. Local Pay Authority (AIE)
LPO.............. Late Pleistocene Origins [*Ecology*]
LPQ............. Luang Prabang [*Laos*] [*Airport symbol*] (AD)
LPS.............. Lightning Protection System [*Boating*]
LPT.............. Line Printer [*Computer science*] (DOM)
LQ............... Inland Empire Airlines [*ICAO designator*] (AD)
LQ............... Library Quarterly [*A publication*] (BRI)
lqtx .... Liquitex (VRA)
LR................ Library Review [*A publication*] (BRI)
LREB........... London Regional Examining Board [*British*] (AIE)
LRI.............. Lorica [*Colombia*] [*Airport symbol*] (AD)
LRTS........... Library Resources & Technical Services [*Association for Library Collections and Technical Services*] [*American Library Association*]
LS .... Marco Island Airways [*ICAO designator*] (AD)
LSAB........... Learning Systems and Access Branch [*Education*] (AIE)
LSC.............. La Serena [*Chile*] [*Airport symbol*] (AD)
LSc .... Licentiate in Science (DD)
LScAdmin .... Licence in Administration [*Canada*] (DD)
LScC........... Licentiate in Commercial Science (DD)
LScComm .... Licentiate in Commercial Science (DD)
LScCompt .... Licencie en Sciences Comptables [*Licentiate of Accounting*] (DD)
LScEco........ Licence in Economics [*Canada*] (DD)
LScO........... Licence in the Science of Optometry [*Canada*] (DD)
LScRel........ Licentiate in Religion (DD)
LSP............. Land Surface Parmeterization [*Environmental science*]
LSPT........... London School of Polymer Technology [*British*] (AIE)
LSPVPD ...... Library Service to People with Visual or Physical Disabilities Forum [*Association of Specialized and Cooperative Library Agencies*] [*American Library Association*]
lsr .... Laser (VRA)
LSSDDPMAG... Library Service to Developmentally Disabled Persons Membership Activity Group [*Association of Specialized and Cooperative Library Agencies*] [*American Library Association*]
LSSDPF .... Library Service to the Developmentally Disabled Persons Forum [*Association of Specialized and Cooperative Library Agencies*] [*American Library Association*]

LSSE........... Licentiate in Social, Economic, & Political Sciences (DD)
LSSU .... Lake Superior State University [*Michigan*]
lstwx........... Lost Wax (VRA)
LT .... Great Sierra [*ICAO designator*] (AD)
LT .... Library Talk [*A publication*] (BRI)
lt .... Light (VRA)
LT .... Long Throw [*Speaker system*]
LTC .... Lai [*Chad*] [*Airport symbol*] (AD)
Ltd .... Limited (DD)
LTDI........... Learning Technology Dissemination Initiative (AIE)
LTMFM .... Low-Temperature Magnetic Force Microscope
LTNS.......... Long Time, No See [*Computer science*] (DOM)
LTR............ Library Technology Reports [*American Library Association*]
LTRN .... Lantern Slide (VRA)
LTT .... Lithium Thallium Tartrate [*Inorganic chemistry*]
ltx .... Latex (VRA)
LU............... Theron Airways [*ICAO designator*] (AD)
LUIE............ Leeds University Institute of Education [*British*] (AIE)
lun .... Lunette (VRA)
LUS............ Laparoscopic Ultrasonography [*Medicine*]
lus .... Lustre (VRA)
LUT............. Miri [*Malaysia*] [*Airport symbol*] (AD)
Lux............. Luxembourg (VRA)
LUY............ Lushoto [*Tanzania*] [*Airport symbol*] (AD)
lvl .... Level (VRA)
LVO............. Lieutenant of the Victorian Order [*Canada*] (DD)
LW.............. Air Nevada [*ICAO designator*] (AD)
LWM........... Lawrence [*Massachusetts*] [*Airport symbol*] (AD)
LWULT........ Least Widely Used and Least Taught Languages (AIE)
LX .... Crossair [*ICAO designator*] (AD)
LXG............. Luong Namtha [*Laos*] [*Airport symbol*] (AD)
LXU............. Lukulu [*Zambia*] [*Airport symbol*] (AD)
LY............... El Al Israel Airlines [*ICAO designator*] (AD)
LYBNT .... Last Year but Not This [*Fundraising*]
LYM............ Lympne [*England*] [*Airport symbol*] (AD)
lyot .... Layout (VRA)
LYP............. Lyallpur [*Pakistan*] [*Airport symbol*] (AD)
LZ .... Balkan [*ICAO designator*] (AD)

M
By Acronym

m .... Male (DD)
M .... Matured Bonds [*Investment term*] (DFIT)
M .... Milli (DFIT)
MA .... Modern Age [*A publication*] (BRI)
MAA .... Manitoba Association of Architects [*1914*] [*Canada*] (NGC)
Mac .... Maclean's [*A publication*] (BRI)
MAccSc .... Master in Accounting Science (DD)
MACE .... Metropolitan Architectural Consortium for Education (AIE)
Madag .... Madagascar [*Malagasy Republic*] (VRA)
Madag .... Malagasy Republic (VRA)
MAE .... Medium Altitude Endurance (RDA)
mag .... Magazine (VRA)
Mag Antiq ... Magazine Antiques [*A publication*] (BRI)
Mag Bl .... Magical Blend [*A publication*] (BRI)
Magdl .... Magdalenian (VRA)
magns .... Magnesium (VRA)
mah .... Mahogany (VRA)
MAI .... Marianna [*Florida*] [*Airport symbol*] (AD)
MAIBC .... Member of the Architectural Institute of British Columbia [*Canada*] (DD)
MAITA .... Marine and Allied Industries Training Association (AIE)
maj .... Majolica (VRA)
makm .... Makimono (VRA)
MAL .... Malone [*New York*] [*Airport symbol*] (AD)
Malay .... Malaysia (VRA)
MALLS .... Multiangle LASER Light-Scattering [*Instrumentation*]
MAMB .... Military Acquisition Management Branch [*Army*] (RDA)
man .... Managing (DD)
Man .... Manitoba [*Canada*] (DD)
mandl .... Mandorla (VRA)
M&L .... Matched and Lost [*Investment term*] (DFIT)
m & o .... Maintenance and Overhaul (AD)
m & o .... Management and Organization (AD)
M & O .... Muscat and Oran (AD)
m & p .... Materials and Processes (AD)
M&Q .... Mines and Quarries (AD)
m & r .... Maintainability and Reliability (AD)
m & r .... Maintainability and Repairs (AD)
M&R .... Martini & Rossi
M & S .... Maintenance and Supply (AD)
M&S .... Maternity and Surgical (AD)
M&S .... Medical and Surgical (AD)
M & S .... Medicine and Surgery (AD)
m & s .... Model and Series (AD)
m & s .... Mud and Snow (AD)
manif .... Manifesto (VRA)
MAP .... Microelectronics Application Programme (AIE)
MAP .... Microwave Anisotropy Probe [*NASA*]
maq .... Maquette (VRA)
MAQ .... Sena Madureira [*Brazil*] [*Airport symbol*] (AD)
marb .... Marble (VRA)
Mar Crp G ... Marine Corps Gazette [*A publication*] (BRI)
mark .... Market (VRA)
marq .... Marquetry (VRA)
MAS .... Manus Island [*Bismarck Archipelago*] [*Airport symbol*] (AD)
mas .... Masonry (VRA)
MASc .... Master of Agricultural Science (DD)
masl .... Meters above Sea Level
masn .... Masonite (VRA)
MASN .... Maximum Aggregate Student Number [*Higher Education Funding Council*] (AIE)
MAST-E .... Multicenter Acute Stroke Trial-Europe [*Neurology*]
mat .... Material (VRA)
MAT .... Multimedia Access Terminals [*Philips*] [*Electronics*]
MATCH .... Matching Alcoholism Treatments to Client Heterogeneity
Math .... Mathematics (DD)
Math T .... Mathematics Teacher [*A publication*] (BRI)
MATMO .... Military Advanced Technology Management Office (RDA)
MAU .... Mastung [*Pakistan*] [*Airport symbol*] (AD)
Maurti .... Mauritania (VRA)
mauso .... Mausoleum (VRA)
MB .... Countrywide [*ICAO designator*] (AD)
MB .... Western Airlines [*ICAO designator*] (AD)
MBA .... Male Bowhunter Aided [*International Bowhunting Organization*] [*Class equipment*]
MBARI .... Monterey Bay Aquarium Research Institute [*California*]

MBL .... Mannan-Binding Lectin [*Immunology*]
MBM .... Mambone [*Mozambique*] [*Airport symbol*] (AD)
MBMI .... Mind/Body Medical Institute
MBN .... Mombo [*Tanzania*] [*Airport symbol*] (AD)
M-bone .... Multicast Backbone [*Computer science*] (DOM)
MBR .... Mbout [*Mauritania*] [*Airport symbol*] (AD)
mbr .... Member (DD)
MBS .... Bay City-Midland-Saginaw [*Michigan*] [*Airport symbol*] (AD)
MBS .... Mortgage-Backed Security (DFIT)
MBT .... Mid-Blastula Transition [*Developmental biology*]
MBTT .... Marine Builders Training Trust (AIE)
MBZ .... Maues [*Brazil*] [*Airport symbol*] (AD)
MC .... Managed Care [*Insurance*] (WYGK)
MC .... Marginal Credit (DFIT)
MC .... Rapidair [*ICAO designator*] (AD)
MCA .... Macenta [*Guinea*] [*Airport symbol*] (AD)
MCA .... Magnetocrystalline Anisotropy [*Physics*]
M-CATS ...... Municipal Certificates of Accrual on Tax-Exempt Securities [*Investment term*] (DFIT)
McCall Nee... McCall's Needlework [*A publication*] (BRI)
MCCRA .... Medicare Catastrophic Coverage Repeal Act of 1989 (WYGK)
MCDB .... Molecular Cellular, and Developmental Biology [*A discipline division*]
MCE .... Merced [*California*] [*Airport symbol*] (AD)
MCF .... Meta Content File [*Netscape*] [*Computer science*]
MCFF .... Moving Call for Fire [*Military*]
MCGA .... Memory Controller Gate Array [*Computer science*]
MCGA .... Multicolor /Graphics Array [*Computer science*]
MCID .... Malicious Call Identification [*Telecommunications*] (DOM)
MCIM .... Member Canadian Institute of Mining and Metallurgy (DD)
MCMFA .... Meeting of Consultation of Ministers of Foreign Affairs
MCN .... Molecular and Cellular Neuroscience [*A publication*]
MCO .... Medicare Carve-Out [*Insurance*] (WYGK)
MCommSc... Master in Commercial Science (DD)
MCommun... Master in Communication (DD)
MCRA .... Mitomycin C Resistance Protein A
MCS .... Monte Caseros [*Argentina*] [*Airport symbol*] (AD)
McSPI .... Multicenter Study of Perioperative Ischemia
MCV .... Measles-Containing Vaccine
MD .... Air Madagascar [*ICAO designator*] (AD)
MDA .... Management Development Adviser (AIE)
MDCM .... Doctor of Medicine and Master of Surgery (DD)
MDD .... Puerto Maldonado [*Peru*] [*Airport symbol*] (AD)
MDL .... Mandalay [*Burma*] [*Airport symbol*] (AD)
MDOT .... Michigan Department of Transportation
MDP .... Multidomain Polymer [*Biology*]
MDRAM ...... Multibank DRAM [*Computer science*]
mdse .... Merchandise (DD)
mdsg .... Merchandising (DD)
mdvl .... Medieval (VRA)
ME .... Middle East Airlines [*ICAO designator*] (AD)
MEARS .... Multi-User Engineering Change Proposal Automated Review System (RDA)
MECC.......... Muslim Education Co-Ordinating Council (AIE)
mech .... Mechanical (DD)
med .... Medal (VRA)
MEDes .... Master of Environmental Design (DD)
medi .... Media (VRA)
Media M ...... Media and Methods [*A publication*] (BRI)
MEDICS ...... Majors Electronic Data Interchange Communications System [*Computer science*]
medi gen..... Media Generated (VRA)
M Ed J........ Music Educators Journal [*A publication*] (BRI)
medln .... Medallion (VRA)
MEF .... Melfi [*Chad*] [*Airport symbol*] (AD)
meg .... Megaron (VRA)
MEG .... Midlands Examining Group [*British*] (AIE)
MEGA .... Molecular Evolutionary Genetics Analysis [*Computer software*]
MEI .... [*The*] Ministry of Electronics Industry [*China*]
MEJ .... Middle East Journal [*A publication*] (BRI)
MEK .... Meknes [*Morocco*] [*Airport symbol*] (AD)
MELB .... Mission Enhancement-Little Bird [*Military*] (RDA)
memrl.......... Memorial (VRA)
Men's J .... Men's Journal [*A publication*] (BRI)
MEnv .... Master of Environmental Studies (DD)
MEP .... Middle East Policy [*A publication*] (BRI)
MEQ .... Middle East Quarterly [*A publication*] (BRI)

MERC............ Multi-Racial Education Resources Centre [*British*] (AIE)
MES............ Master of Environmental Science (DD)
MesoAm...... Meso American (VRA)
Mesol......... Mesolithic (VRA)
Mesop........ Mesopotamia (VRA)
METD......... Management Education Training and Development (AIE)
MetEng........ Metallurgical Engineering (DD)
METI........... Medical Education Technologies, Inc.
metpt.......... Metalpoint (VRA)
METRO....... Messenger Transport Organizer [*Developmental biology*]
metwk........ Metalwork (VRA)
MEU........... Marromeu [*Mozambique*] [*Airport symbol*] (AD)
MEWA......... Multiple-Employer Welfare Association (WYGK)
Mex .... Mexico (VRA)
MEZ............ Merces [*Brazil*] [*Airport symbol*] (AD)
mez............ Mezzotint (VRA)
mezn........... Mezzanine (VRA)
MF .... Red Carpet Flying Service [*ICAO designator*] (AD)
mfg............. Manufacturing (DD)
MFH........... Master of the Fox Hunt (DD)
MFisc......... Maitrise en Fiscalite (DD)
MFISH........ Multiplex Fluorescence in Situ Hybridization
MFLOP........ Mega Floating-Point Operations per Second [*Computer science*]
MFPT.......... Machinery Failure Prevention Technology (RDA)
mfr............. Manufacture (DD)
MFS .... Modern Fiction Studies [*A publication*] (BRI)
MFSF.......... Magazine of Fantasy and Science Fiction [*A publication*] (BRI)
MG............. Matrix Glass [*Geology*]
MG............. MGM Grand Air [*ICAO designator*] (AD)
MG............. Pompano Airways [*ICAO designator*] (AD)
MGM........... Milligram (DFIT)
mgmt.......... Management (DD)
MGN.......... Magangue [*Colombia*] [*Airport symbol*] (AD)
MGO .... Mato Grosso [*Brazil*] [*Airport symbol*] (AD)
mgr............. Manager (DD)
mgrd.......... Middleground (VRA)
MGS............ Mars Global Surveyor [*NASA*]
MH............. Malaysian Airline System [*ICAO designator*] (AD)
MH............. Mentally Handicapped (AIE)
MHD .... Meshed [*Iran*] [*Airport symbol*] (AD)
MHLA......... McGraw-Hill Learning Architecture
MHO .... Mohanbari [*India*] [*Airport symbol*] (AD)
MHR .... Medical Humanities Review [*A publication*] (BRI)
MHSA .... Master of Health Services Administration (DD)
MI.............. Mackey International Airlines [*ICAO designator*] (AD)
MI.. .... Melt Inclusions [*Geology*]
MIBs .... Management Information Bases [*Compaq*] [*Computer science*]
mid............. Middle (VRA)
Mid-Am....... Mid-America: An Historical Review [*A publication*] (BRI)
MIDAS .... Multitier Distributed Application Services [*Computer science*]
MIDS .... Matrix Information and Directory Services, Inc.
MIEC .... Mixed Ionic and Electronic Conducting [*Polymers*]
MIESR .... Matrix Isolation and Electron Spin Resonance [*Analytical chemistry*]
MIG-1 .... Moody's Investment Grade (DFIT)
Mil Rev....... Military Review [*A publication*] (BRI)
MIM .... Master of International Management (DD)
MIM........... Member of the Institute of Management (DD)
MIM........... Minorities in Medicine [*Eastern Michigan University Macy Scholarship*]
MIM........... Multilateral Initiative in Malaria
MIME .... Microcomputers in Mathematics Education (AIE)
MIMM......... Master of Mining and Metallurgy (DD)
Min............. Minimum (DFIT)
min............. Mining (DD)
minat.......... Miniature (VRA)
miner.......... Minerology (DD)
Ming .... Maitrise en Ingenierie [*Master of Engineering*] (DD)
MIPD .... Manpower Intelligence and Planning Division (AIE)
MIQ............ Maiquetia [*Venezuela*] [*Airport symbol*] (AD)
MIR .... Monastir [*Tunisia*] [*Airport symbol*] (AD)
mirr .... Mirror (VRA)
Misc........... Miscellaneous (DFIT)
MISP .... Mathematics in Society Project (AIE)
MISR .... Mars In-situ-utilization Sample Return [*Computer science*]
MITO.......... Meat Industry Training Organisation (AIE)
MITS .... Michigan Travel System
MITTINS ..... Michigan Travel Trade Information Service
MIX............ Mores Island [*Bahamas*] [*Airport symbol*] (AD)
MJ............. Lineas Aereas Privadas Argentinas [*ICAO designator*] (AD)
MJG........... Mayajigua [*Cuba*] [*Airport symbol*] (AD)
MJH........... Majma [*Saudi Arabia*] [*Airport symbol*] (AD)
MJI .... Maji [*Ethiopia*] [*Airport symbol*] (AD)
MJP .... Mastuj [*Pakistan*] [*Airport symbol*] (AD)
MJX .... Masjed Soleyman [*Iran*] [*Airport symbol*] (AD)
MJZ .... Mahfid [*South Arabia*] [*Airport symbol*] (AD)
MK .... Air Mauritius [*ICAO designator*] (AD)
mkr............ Maker (VRA)
mktg .... Marketing (DD)
MKX........... Mukalla [*South Arabia*] [*Airport symbol*] (AD)
ML .... Aviation Services [*ICAO designator*] (AD)
ML .... Modern Languages (AIE)
MLA........... Valetta [*Malta*] [*Airport symbol*] (AD)
M Lab R ..... Monthly Labor Review [*A publication*] (BRI)
MLandArch.. Master of Landscape Architecture [*Canada*] (DD)
MLD........... Moderate Learning Difficulties (AIE)

mld .... Mold (VRA)
MLE .... Mariner-Like Elements [*Genetics*]
MLFA.......... Merrill Lynch Financial Advantage
MLJ .... Modern Language Journal [*A publication*] (BRI)
MLK .... Martin Luther King, Jr.
MLN .... MLN (Modern Language Notes) [*A publication*] (BRI)
MLR .... Modern Language Review [*A publication*] (BRI)
MLWG .... Modern Languages Working Group (AIE)
MM............. Millimeter (DFIT)
mm............. Mixed Media (VRA)
M/M........... Mr. & Mrs. (VRA)
MM............. Sociedad Aeronautica Medellin [*ICAO designator*] (AD)
MMAR .... Money Management Analytical Research Group
MMC........... Ciudad Mante [*Mexico*] [*Airport symbol*] (AD)
MMC........... Meet Me Conference [*Telecommunications*] (DOM)
MMC........... Multimedia Marketing Council (DOM)
MMCD .... Multimedia Compact Disc
MME .... Middlesborough [*England*] [*Airport symbol*] (AD)
MMM .... Member of the Order of Military Merit [*Canada*] (DD)
MMMA .... Music Masters and Mistresses Association (AIE)
MMO .... Intel Mobile Module [*Computer science*]
MMO .... Mobile Module [*Computer science*]
MMR .... Multi-Market Radio
MMTO .... Missiles Made to Order [*Military*] (RDA)
MMU .... Manchester Metropolitan University [*British*] (AIE)
MMX .... Micron's Millenia XKU [*Computer science*]
MMX .... Miracema do Norte [*Brazil*] [*Airport symbol*] (AD)
MNC........... Nacala [*Mozambique*] [*Airport symbol*] (AD)
MNE .... Mentone [*France*] [*Airport symbol*] (AD)
MNK .... Mankoya [*Zambia*] [*Airport symbol*] (AD)
mnm .... Minimum (AD)
mnm .... Mnemonic (AD)
MNNP .... Malawi Nyika National Park (AD)
mnos .... Metallic Nitrogen-Oxide Semiconductor (AD)
MNP........... Malay National Party [*Political party*] (AD)
MNP........... Marsabit National Park [*Kenya*] (AD)
MNP........... Meru National Park [*Equatorial Kenya*] (AD)
MNP........... Mikumi National Park [*Tanzania*] (AD)
MNP........... Mushandike National Park [*Rhodesia*] (AD)
mnpo .... Main Port (AD)
mnpz .... Monopolize (AD)
mnpzd .... Monopolized (AD)
mnpzg .... Monopolizing (AD)
mnpzn......... Monopolization (AD)
mnr............ Massive Nuclear Retaliation (AD)
mnr............ Mean Neap Rise (AD)
Mnr............ Mijnheer [*Mr.*] [*Dutch*] (AD)
MNR .... Mozambique National Resistance [*Political party*] (AD)
MNRJ.......... Museo Nacional de Rio de Janeiro [*National Museum of Rio de Janeiro*] [*Portugal*] (AD)
mnrl........... Mineral (VRA)
Mnrsm........ Mannerism (VRA)
mnrt........... Minaret (VRA)
MNRU .... Medical Neuropsychiatric Research Unit (AD)
Mns .... Manaus (AD)
mns .... Metal-Nitride-Semiconductor (AD)
Mns .... Mines (AD)
Mnstr .... Munster (AD)
mnt............ Mean Neap Tide (AD)
MNT .... Minnesota and Ontario Paper [*Stock exchange symbol*] (AD)
mntmp .... Minimum Temperature (AD)
mntn .... Maintain (AD)
mntnc .... Maintenance (AD)
mntnd .... Maintained (AD)
mntng .... Maintaining (AD)
MNTO .... Moroccan National Tourist Office (AD)
mntr .... Monitor (AD)
MNU .... Maniti Sugar [*Stock exchange symbol*] (AD)
MNV .... Marion Power Shovel [*Stock exchange symbol*] (AD)
MNWEB ...... Merseyside and North Wales Electricity Board [*British*] (AD)
MNWR .... Malheur National Wildlife Refuge [*Oregon*] (AD)
MNWR .... Mattamuskeet National Wildlife Refuge [*North Carolina*] (AD)
MNWR .... Merced National Wildlife Refuge [*California*] (AD)
MNWR .... Mingo National Wildlife Refuge [*Missouri*] (AD)
MNWR .... Minidoka National Wildlife Refuge [*Idaho*] (AD)
MNWR .... Mississiquoi National Wildlife Refuge [*Vermont*] (AD)
MNWR .... Modoc National Wildlife Refuge [*California*] (AD)
MNWR .... Montezuma National Wildlife Refuge [*New York*] (AD)
MNWR .... Moosehorn National Wildlife Refuge [*Maine*] (AD)
Mnx .... Manx Gaelic (AD)
Mnzlo......... Manzanillo (AD)
MO............. Calm Air International [*ICAO designator*] (AD)
Mo............. Maestro GG1MasterGG2 [*Italian*] (AD)
mo............. Mail Order (AD)
m/o........... Maintenance-to-Operation (AD)
m/O........... Male Oriental (AD)
mo............. Manual Operation (AD)
MO............. Marketing Organization (AD)
mo............. Masonry Opening (AD)
mo............. Mass Observation (AD)
mo............. Master Oscillator (AD)
mo............. Method of Operation (AD)
m/o........... Mi Orden [*My Order*] [*Spanish*] (AD)
Mo............. Missourian (AD)
mo............. Molecular Orbital (AD)

mo	Moment (AD)
m-o	Months Old (AD)
M-O	Morris-Oxford (AD)
mo	Moth Eaten (AD)
mo	Motor Operated (AD)
mo	Mustered Out (AD)
MOA	Marine Office of America (AD)
moa	Medium Observation Aircraft (AD)
M o A	Memorandum of Agreement (AD)
MOA	Metropolitan Opera Association (AD)
MOA	Metropolitan Opera Auditions (AD)
MOA	Military Operations Area (AD)
MoA	Ministry of Agriculture [British] (AD)
MOA	Minnesota Orchestral Association (AD)
moa	Minute of Angle (AD)
moa	Missile Optical Alignment (AD)
moa	Mud on Airstrip (AD)
moAt	Mainstream of American Thought (AD)
moat	Missile-on-Aircraft Testing [Military] (AD)
mob	Make or Buy (AD)
mob	Mobile (AD)
Mob	Mobile, Alabama [Maritime abbreviation] (AD)
mob	Mobile Vulgus [Disorderly Group of People] [Latin] (AD)
MOB	Montreux-Oberland-Bernois [Railway] [Canada] (AD)
Mo' Bay	Mobile Bay, Alabama [Montego Bay, Jamaica] (AD)
MOBCOM	Mobile Command [Canada] (AD)
mobcom	Mobile Communications (AD)
mobeu	Mobile Emergency Unit (AD)
MOBIDACS	Mobile Data Acquisition System (AD)
mobidic	Mobile Digital Computer (AD)
mobil	Mobility (AD)
Mobilarian	Mobile Branch Librarian (AD)
mobilary	Mobile Library (AD)
mobl	Macro-Oriented Business Language [Computer science] (AD)
mobl	Mopliert [Furnished] [German] (AD)
moblas	Mobile LASER Satellite Tracking Station (AD)
mob lib	Mobile Librarian (AD)
mob lt	Man Overboard and Breakdown Light (AD)
mobot	Mobile Robot (AD)
MOBTA	Mobilization Table of Distribution and Allowances (AD)
mobula	Model-Building Language (AD)
MOC	Makapuu Oceanic Center [Hawaii] (AD)
moc	Manufacturing Other Charges (AD)
moc	Master Operation Control (AD)
MOC	Mauna Olu College [Maui] (AD)
moc	Mission Operations Computer (AD)
moc	Mocassin (AD)
moca	Minimum Obstruction Clearance Altitude (AD)
mocamp	Motor Camp (AD)
MOCCC	Massachusetts Organized Crime Control Council (AD)
MOCF	Manchester Open College Federation [British] (AIE)
mochwr	Mochaware (VRA)
MOCI	Ministry of Commerce and Industry [British] (AD)
MoCom	Mobile Command (AD)
mocp	Missile Out of Commission for Parts [Military] (AD)
mocr	Mission Operation Control Room (AD)
mod	Magneto-Optical Disc (AD)
m-o-d	Mesial-Occlusal-Distal [Dentistry] (AD)
M o D	Ministry of Defence [British] (AD)
mod	Model (AD)
mod	Moderate (AD)
Mod	Modern (AD)
mod	Modern (AD)
mod	Modification (AD)
mod	Modular (AD)
modasm	Modular Air-to-Surface Missile [Military] (AD)
m-o-d-b	Mesial-Occlusal-Distal-Buccal [Dentistry] (AD)
modcom	Modernity Commercialized (AD)
mod-cons	Modern-Construction Houses (AD)
mod cons	Modern Conveniences (AD)
moddem	Modulator-Demodulator (AD)
mod/demod	Modulate-Demodulate (AD)
ModE	Modern English (AD)
modem	Modulating-Demodulating (AD)
Modern Lib	Modern Library (AD)
modf	Modification (AD)
ModHeb	Modern Hebrew (AD)
mod/iran	Modification, Inspection, and Repair as Necessary (AD)
modo	Moderato [Moderately] [Italian] (AD)
mod pres	Modo Prescripto [In the Manner Prescribed] [Latin] (AD)
mod pst	Modeling Paste (VRA)
modr	Moderate Room Rate Desired (AD)
mods	Mesial-Occlusal-Distal [Dentistry] (AD)
MODS	Multiple Organ Dysfunction Syndrome [Medicine]
modto	Moderato [Moderately] [Italian] (AD)
moe	Measure of Effectiveness (AD)
MoE	Ministry of Education [British] (AD)
M o E	Ministry of Energy [British] (AD)
MOEA	Ministry of Economic Affairs [British] (AD)
mof	Maximum Observed Frequency (AD)
mof	Member of the Police Force (AD)
mof	Metal Oxide Film (AD)
MoF	Ministry of Finance [British] (AD)
M of Hist	Magazine of History [A publication] (BRI)
M of R	Minister of Reconstruction [British] (AD)
Mog	Margaret (AD)
MOG	Master of Obstetrics and Gynecology (AD)
mogas	Motor Gasoline (AD)
moh	Material Overhead (AD)
moh	Maximum Operating Hours (AD)
M o H	Ministry of Health [British] (AD)
Moham	Mohammedan (AD)
MOHLG	Ministry of Housing and Local Government [British] (AD)
mohms	Milliohms (AD)
moho	Mohorovicic Discontinuity [Geology] (AD)
mohs	Mud, Oil, Hooks, Slings [Insurance] (AD)
moi	Maximum Obtainable Irradiance (AD)
moi	Military Occupational Information (AD)
MoI	Ministry of the Interior [British] (AD)
moi	Multiplicity of Infection (AD)
MOIC	Medical Officer in Command (AD)
moip	Missile on Internal Power [Military] (AD)
MOIS	Minnesota Occupational Information System (AD)
Moish	Moishe (AD)
moiv	Mechanically Operated Inlet Valve (AD)
MOJ	Muong Sing [Laos] [Airport symbol] (AD)
MOK	Mohawk Carpet Mills [Stock exchange symbol] (AD)
Mok	Mokpo (AD)
mol	Machine-Oriented Language (AD)
mol	Maximum Output Level (AD)
M o L	Minister of Labour [British] (AD)
mol	Molecular (AD)
Mol	Mollendo (AD)
mol	Mollis [Soft] [Latin] (AD)
molab	Mobile Laboratory (AD)
MOLAB	Mobile Lunar Laboratory (AD)
Mol Crys Liq Crys	Molecular Crystals and Liquid Crystals (AD)
Moldv	Moldavia (AD)
mole	Molecular (AD)
molecom	Molecularized Computer (AD)
Molink	Moscow Link (AD)
moll	Metallo-Organic Liquid LASER (AD)
mollie	Mollienisia (AD)
Mollus	Mollusca (AD)
MOLLUSA	Military Order of the Loyal Legion of the USA (AD)
Mol Phys	Molecular Physics (AD)
molt	Molten (AD)
mol wt	Molecular Weight (AD)
moly	Molybdenum (AD)
m/ o m/	Mas o Menos [More or Less] [Spanish] (AD)
mom	Micromation Online Microfilmer [Computer science] (AD)
m-o-m	Middle of Month (AD)
mom	Military Ordinary Mail (AD)
mom	Milk of Magnesia (AD)
Mom	Momma (AD)
MOM	Musee Oceanographique Monaco [Monaco Oceanographic Museum] [France] (AD)
MoMA	Museum of Modern Art [New York] (AD)
momar	Modern Mobile Army (AD)
momau	Mobile Mine Assembly Unit (AD)
m-o-m in am if no bm by pm	Milk-of-Magnesia in the Morning if No Bowel Movement by Evening [Medicine] (AD)
Moml	Moslem Meal (AD)
MOMR	Mayor's Office of Manpower Resources (AD)
MOMS	Manganese Oxide Mesoporous Structure [Inorganic Chemistry]
moms	Mervaerdiomsaetningsskat [Value-Added Tax] [Danish] (AD)
MOMS	Micro-Opto-Mechanical Systems
moms	Missile Operate Mode Simulator (AD)
mon	Maison [House] [French] (AD)
Mon	Monaco (AD)
Mon	Monday (AD)
Mon	Monegasque (AD)
mon	Monetary (AD)
Mon	Mongol (AD)
Mon	Monitor (AD)
Mon	Monmouthshire (AD)
Mon	Monongahela (AD)
mon	Monsoon (AD)
Mon	Montag [Monday] [German] (AD)
Mon	Monument (AD)
mon	Monument (AD)
mon	Motor Octane Number (AD)
Mona	Madonna [Our Lady] [Italian] (AD)
Mona	Monaco (VRA)
Monag	Monaghan (AD)
Monas	Monastic (AD)
monbas	Monobasic (AD)
monch	Monochrome (VRA)
mon/dir	Monitoring Direction (AD)
monex	Monsoon Experiment (AD)
Mong	Mongol (AD)
mong	Mongolisch [Mongolian] [German] (AD)
Mongo	Mongolia (VRA)
mon-H	Monohydrogen (AD)
monik	Moniker (AD)
mono	Mononucleosis [Medicine] (AD)
mono	Monophonic (AD)
mono	Monopoly (AD)
mono	Monopropellant (AD)
mono	Monorail (AD)

mono	Monotype (AD)
monob	Mobile Noise Barge (AD)
monocl	Monoclinic (AD)
Monod	Monon Railroad (AD)
monog	Monogram (AD)
monog	Monograph (AD)
monos	Monitor Out of Service (AD)
monot	Monotonous (AD)
monot	Monotype (AD)
monpl	Monopoly (AD)
monpr	Monoprint (VRA)
Mon River ...	Monongahela River (AD)
Mons	Monsieur [*Mister*] [*French*] (AD)
Mons Cur.....	Monsoon Current (AD)
Monsig	Monseigneur [*My Lord*] [*French*] (AD)
monstro	Monstrosity (AD)
Mont	Montana (AD)
Mont	Monterrey (AD)
Mont	Montevideo (AD)
Mont	Montgomery (AD)
Mont	Montpelier (AD)
Mont	Montreal (AD)
mont	Monument (VRA)
Monte	Montebianco (AD)
Monte	Monte Carlo (AD)
Monte	Montefiore (AD)
Monte	Montevideo (AD)
Monte	Montgomery (AD)
montg	Montage (VRA)
Montgom	Montgomeryshire [*England*] (AD)
montp	Monotype (VRA)
Montparno ...	Montparnasse (AD)
Montr	Montreal [*Canada*] (AD)
montrg	Monitoring (AD)
Mont S	Montreal Star [*A publication*] (AD)
Monty	Montgomery (AD)
Monty	Montmorency (AD)
Mony	Monastery (AD)
MONY	Music Operators of New York (AD)
MOO	MUD [*Multi-User Dungeon*] Object-Oriented [*Computer science*] (DOM)
moop	Mechlorethamine, Vincristine, Procarbazine, Prednisone [*Medicine*] (AD)
Moor...........	Dartmoor Prison [*Devon, England*] (AD)
Moore's Adj...	Moore's International Adjudications [*Legal term*] (AD)
Moore's Arb...	Moore's International Arbitrations [*Legal term*] (AD)
Moore's Dig...	Moore's Digest [*Legal term*] (AD)
moot	Moved Out of Town (AD)
MOOTW	Military Operations Other than War (RDA)
mop	Medical Outpatient (AD)
M o P	Member of Parliament [*British*] (AD)
MOP............	Ministerio de Obras Publicas [*Ministry of Public Works*] [*Spanish*] (AD)
M o P	Minister of Pensions [*British*] (AD)
M o P	Minister of Power [*British*] (AD)
M o P	Minister of Production [*British*] (AD)
mop	Mother of Pearl (AD)
mop	Mustering-Out Pay (AD)
mopa	Master Oscilator Power Amplifier (AD)
MOPA	Museum of Photographic Arts [*San Diego*] (AD)
MoPac	Missouri Pacific - Texas & Pacific (AD)
mopar..........	Master Oscillator-Power Amplifier RADAR (AD)
mopb	Manually Operated Plotting Board (AD)
mopeds........	Motorized Pedals (AD)
mopf	Missile Onloading Prism Fixture (AD)
MOPITT.......	Measurements of Pollution in the Troposphere
mopr...........	Manner of Performance Rating (AD)
mopr...........	Mop Rack (AD)
moprl	Mother-of-Pearl (VRA)
MOPS	Merchandise Ordering Processing System (AD)
MOPS	Missile Operations System (AD)
MOPSS	Management & Operation of Public Services Section [*Reference and User Services Association*] [*American Library Association*]
MOPSS	Multispectral Opium Poppy Sensor System (AD)
mor...........	Middle of the Road (AD)
M o R	Ministry of Reconstruction [*British*] (AD)
Mor...........	Morelia (AD)
Mor...........	Morelos (AD)
mor...........	Morendo [*Dying Away*] [*Italian*] (AD)
Mor...........	Morisco (AD)
Mor...........	Moroccan (AD)
mor...........	Morocco (AD)
mor...........	Mortar (AD)
Morav	Moravia (AD)
Morb..........	Morbihan (AD)
Mord..........	Mordehai (AD)
Mordhy	Mordehai (AD)
mor dict	More Dicto [*As Directed*] [*Latin*] (AD)
Mordy	Mordechai (AD)
MORE	Mission for Outreach, Renewal, and Evangelism (AD)
moreps	Monitor Station Reports (AD)
mor fib	Moral Fiber (AD)
MORG	Museo Oceanografico de Rio Grande [*Oceanographic Museum of Rio Grande*] [*Brazil*] (AD)
morg mar	Morganatic Marriage (AD)

moritzer.......	Mortar Howitzer (AD)
Mor Lib........	Morgan Library (AD)
Morm..........	Mormon (AD)
Mor Maj	Moral Majority (AD)
morn...........	Morning (AD)
Moro	Book of Moroni (AD)
Moro	Morocco (VRA)
Moroc	Moroccan (AD)
morph.........	Morphine (AD)
morph.........	Morphology (AD)
morphophysio...	Morphophysiological (AD)
MORS	Midland Operational Research Society (AD)
mor sal.......	More Solito [*In the Usual Manner*] [*Latin*] (AD)
moRt..........	Mainstream of Republican Thought (AD)
mor t	Morse Taper (AD)
mort...........	Mortal (AD)
mort...........	Mortar (AD)
Mort...........	Mortemart (AD)
mort...........	Mortgage (AD)
mort...........	Mortician (AD)
Mort...........	Mortimer (AD)
Mort...........	Morton (AD)
Mos	Book of Mosiah (AD)
MOS...........	Magneto-Optical System (AD)
mos	Metal-Oxide Semiconductor (AD)
mos	Metal-Oxide Silicon (AD)
mos	Military Occupational Specialty (AD)
mos	Missile On Stand (AD)
mos	Mit-Out Sound (AD)
mos	Months (AD)
mos	Mosaic (VRA)
Mos	Mosca [*Moscow*] [*Italian*] (AD)
Mos	Moscou [*Moscow*] [*French*] (AD)
Mos	Moscow (AD)
Mos	Moscu [*Moscow*] [*Spanish*] (AD)
Mos	Moshe (AD)
Mos	Moskau [*Moscow*] [*German*] (AD)
Mos	Moskou [*Moscow*] [*Dutch*] (AD)
Mos	Moslem (AD)
Mosbas.......	Moscow Basin (AD)
mosc...........	Manned Orbital Systems Concept (AD)
MOSC	Midland-Odessa Symphony and Chorale (AD)
MOSCA	McNamara-O'Hara Service Contract Act of 1965 (WYGK)
Mose	Moises (AD)
Mose	Moseley (AD)
Mose	Mosen (AD)
Mose	Moses (AD)
mosfet	Metal-Oxide Semiconductor Field-Effect Transistor (AD)
mosic..........	Metal-Oxide-Semiconductor Integrated Circuit (AD)
MOSID	Ministry of Supply Inspection Department [*British*] (AD)
Mosk..........	Moscovici (AD)
Mosk..........	Moscowitz (AD)
Mosk..........	Moskowitz (AD)
mosm	Milliosmol (AD)
MOSOP.......	Missouri Sexual Offender Program (AD)
MOS Poland...	Ministerstwo Opieki Spotecznes [*Ministry of Social Welfare*] [*Poland*] (AD)
moss...........	Maintenance-Operations Support Set (AD)
MOSS	Management and Organisation in Secondary Schools (AIE)
MOSS	Market Opening Sector Specific (AD)
most...........	Metal-Oxide Semiconductor Transistor (AD)
MOST..........	Michigan Opportunities and Skills Training (AD)
mostl	Metal-Oxide Semiconductor Transistor Logic (AD)
mot............	Mean Operating Time (AD)
mot............	Mechanical Operability Test (AD)
mot............	Member of Our Tribe (AD)
mot............	Middle of Target (AD)
M o T..........	Minister of Transport [*British*] (AD)
mot............	Motor (AD)
MOTAT.......	Museum of Transport and Technology (AD)
MOTC.........	Ministry of Transit and Communications [*Philippines*] (AD)
M o TCP	Ministry of Town and Country Planning [*British*] (AD)
MOTET........	Mother Tongue and English Teaching (AIE)
moth	Mother (AD)
moth-in-law...	Mother-in-Law (AD)
Moth Jones...	Mother Jones [*A publication*] (BRI)
motoboard ...	Motorized Skateboard (AD)
motocross.....	Motorcycle Cross Country Race (AD)
mot op	Motor Operated (AD)
motorcade ...	Motorized-Vehicle Parade (AD)
motorcross....	Motorcycle Cross (AD)
mots	Minitrack Optical Tracking System (AD)
MoU	Memorandum of Understanding (AD)
mou	Memorandum of Understanding (AD)
MOUSE	Minimum Orbital Unmanned Satellite (AD)
MOUSS	Management and Operation of User Services Section
mov	Movable (AD)
mov	Movimento [*Movement*] [*Italian*] (AD)
mov	Multiple-Orifice Valve (AD)
movem	Movement Overseas Verification of Enlisted Members (AD)
moverep	Movement Report (AD)
Move Short Soc...	Movement Shorthand Society (AD)
movi	Movie (AD)
movord	Movement Order (AD)
M o W	Minister of Works [*British*] (AD)

mowasp......	Mechanization of Warehousing and Shipment Processing (AD)
MoWD........	Ministry of Works and Development [*British*] (AD)
M o WT	Minister of War Transport [*British*] (AD)
mox...........	Mixed Oxides (AD)
mox	Oxidized Metal Explosive (AD)
moy...........	Money (AD)
MOY...........	Monterrey [*Colombia*] [*Airport symbol*] (AD)
MOZ...........	Mezhdunarodnaya Organizacia Zhurnalistov [*International Organization of Journalists*] [*Russian*] (AD)
Moz............	Mozambique (AD)
Mozam.......	Mozambique (AD)
Moz Cur......	Mozambique Current (AD)
mozza	Mozzarella (AD)
MP..............	Atlantis Airlines [*ICAO designator*] (AD)
mp.............	Mail Payment (AD)
mp.............	Maintenance Part (AD)
mp.............	Manifold Pressure (AD)
MP..............	Maschinenpistole [*Submachine Gun*] [*German*] (AD)
mp.............	Medium Pressure (AD)
mp.............	Meeting Point (AD)
mp.............	Melting Point (AD)
m-p............	Metal-Point (AD)
MP..............	Methylphenidate [*Central Nervous system stimulant*]
mp.............	Mezzo-Piano [*Moderately Soft*] [*Italian*] (AD)
mp.............	Milepost (AD)
m/p............	Milk Powder (AD)
mp.............	Mille Pasuum [*Thousand Paces*] [*Latin*] (AD)
MP..............	Mining Permit (AD)
MP..............	Minister Provincial (AD)
MP..............	Miscellaneous Proposal (AD)
MP..............	Modern Philology [*A publication*] (BRI)
mp.............	Motion Picture (AD)
mp.............	Multipole (AD)
mp.............	Multipurpose (AD)
MPA............	Marine Physician Assistant (AD)
mpa	Maritime Patrol Aircraft (AD)
mpa	Maryland Port Authority (AD)
MPA............	Master Photographers Association (AD)
MPA............	Medroxyprogesterone [*Medicine*] (AD)
mpa	Megapascal (AD)
MPA............	Metropolitan Pensions Associations (AD)
mpa	Multiple Product Announcement (AD)
MPAC..........	Master Plan for Academic Computing (AD)
mpad	Maximum Permissible Annual Dose (AD)
mpai	Maximum Permissible Annual Intake (AD)
mpam	Maritime Polar Air Mass (AD)
mp & rs......	Motive Power and Rolling Stock (AD)
m part	Movable Partition (AD)
mpas	Millipascal Second (AD)
m payl	Maximum Payload (AD)
mpb	Male Pattern Baldness (AD)
MPB............	Miniature Precision Bearings (AD)
mpbb	Maximum Permissible Body Burden [*of Radiation*] (AD)
MPBC..........	Memphis Power Boat Club [*Tennessee*] (AD)
mp br..........	Multipunch Bar (AD)
MPBS..........	Mutual Permanent Building Society (AD)
mpc	Marginal Propensity to Consume (AD)
mpc	Marine Protein Concentrate (AD)
mpc	Materials Program Code (AD)
mpc	Mathematics, Physics, Chemistry (AD)
mpc	Maximum Permissible Concentration (AD)
MPC............	Metropolitan Police College (AD)
MPC............	Metropolitan Police Commissioner (AD)
mpc	Military Payment Certificate (AD)
MPC............	Military Police Force (AD)
mpc	Minimum Planning Chart (AD)
MPC............	Model Penal Code (AD)
mpc	Multipurpose Carrier (AD)
MPCA..........	Marine and Ports Council of Australia (AD)
MPCA..........	Master Pastry Cooks Association (AD)
MPCB..........	Manufacturing Plan Control Board (AD)
mpc black....	Medium-Processing Channel Black (AD)
MPCC..........	Minnesota Private College Council (AD)
MPCL..........	Movimiento Patriotico Cuba Libre [*Free Cuba Patriotic Movement*] [*Political party*] (AD)
mpcp	Missile Power Control Panel (AD)
MPCS..........	Master Plan for Computing Services (AD)
mpcur	Maximum Permissible Concentration of Unidentified Radionuclides (AD)
mpd	Magnetoplasmadynamics (AD)
mpd	Maximum Permissible Dose (AD)
MPD............	Metropolitan Park District (AD)
MPD............	Metropolitan Police Department (AD)
MPD............	Military Pay Division (AD)
mpd	Missile Purchase Description (AD)
MPD............	Mpanda [*Tanzania*] [*Airport symbol*] (AD)
mpd	Multiple Personality Disorder (AD)
MPDA..........	Motion Picture Distributors Association (AD)
mp di	Multipunch Die (AD)
MPDPIS.......	Master Plan for Data Processing and Information Systems (AD)
MPDSA........	Master Painters, Decorators, and Signwriters Association (AD)
MPDT..........	Minnesota Perception Diagnostic Test (AD)
mpe	Maximum Permissible Exposure [*to Radiation*] (AD)
MPEA..........	Motion Picture Exhibitors Association (AD)
MPEAUS......	Master Printers and Engravers Association of the United States (AD)
MPEG..........	Motion Picture Experts Group
M Pen.........	Minister of Pensions [*British*] (AD)
M Pen.........	Ministry of Pensions [*British*] (AD)
MPers.........	Middle Persian (AD)
MPES..........	Mathematical, Physical, and Engineering Science (AD)
MPF............	Malaysian Peasants Front [*Political party*] (AD)
MPF............	Metallurgical Plantmakers Federation (AD)
mpf............	Motion-Picture Film (AD)
mpf............	Multi-Purpose Food (AD)
MPG...........	Magnetic Porous Glass [*Materials science*]
MPGA..........	Maine Personnel and Guidance Association (AD)
MPGA..........	Maryland Personnel and Guidance Association (AD)
MPGA..........	Michigan Personnel and Guidance Association (AD)
MPGA..........	Minnesota Personnel and Guidance Association (AD)
MPGA..........	Missouri Personnel and Guidance Association (AD)
mpgn..........	Membrano Proliferative Glomerulonephritis [*Medicine*] (AD)
MPGR..........	Mana Pools Game Reserve [*Rhodesia*] (AD)
MPH............	Meat Packing House (AD)
MPHEC........	Maritime Provinces Higher Education Commission (AD)
mphps........	Miles Per Hour Per Second (AD)
MPhysics.....	Master of Physics (DD)
mpi............	Magnetic Particle Inspection (AD)
mpi............	Marginal Propensity to Invest (AD)
MPI............	Material Process Instruction (AD)
mpi............	Maximum Point of Impulse (AD)
MPI............	Max Planck Institute (AD)
mpi............	Mean Point of Impact (AD)
MPI............	Medicine in the Public Interest (AD)
MPI............	Mitsui Petrochemical Industries (AD)
mpi............	Multiphasic Personality Inventory (AD)
mpi............	Multiphoton Ionization (AD)
MPI............	Museum of the Plains Indians (AD)
M-pill.........	Menstruation Pill [*Medicine*] (AD)
MPIM/SRAW...	Multi-Purpose Individual Munition/Short Range Assault Weapon [*Military*] (RDA)
MPK............	McKinley Park [*Alaska*] [*Airport symbol*] (AD)
mPk	Polar Maritime Air Colder than Underlying Surface (AD)
mpl............	Mathematical Programming Language [*Computer science*] (AD)
mpl............	Maximum Payload (AD)
mpl............	Maximum Permissible Language (AD)
mpl............	Maximum Permissible Level (AD)
MPL............	Memphis Public Library (AD)
mpl............	Message Processing Language [*Computer science*] (AD)
MPL............	Metropolitan Police Laboratory (AD)
MPL............	Miami Public Library (AD)
MPL............	Milwaukee Public Library (AD)
MPL............	Missouri Pacific Lines (AD)
MPL............	Montreal Public Library [*Canada*] (AD)
mpl............	Multiple-Position Lock (AD)
MPLP..........	Marxist Progressive Labor Party [*Political party*] (AD)
Mpls	Minneapolis (AD)
MPM...........	Master of Pest Management (DD)
mpm...........	Meters Per Minute (AD)
MPM...........	Milwaukee Public Museum (AD)
mpm...........	Missile Power Monitor (AD)
MPM...........	Modest Petrovich Mussorgsky [*1839-1881*] (AD)
mpm...........	Mole-Percent Metal (AD)
mpm...........	Multipurpose Meal (AD)
MP-M..........	Museum Plantin Moretus [*Belgium*] (AD)
mpn...........	Most Probable Number (AD)
MPO...........	Management and Personnel Office (AIE)
MPO...........	Memorandum Purchase Order (AD)
mpo...........	Memory Printout (AD)
MPO...........	Miami Philharmonic Orchestra (AD)
MPO...........	Mobile Printing Office (AD)
MPOS	Manportable Office System [*Army*] (RDA)
mpp	Marginal Physical Product (AD)
mpp	Most Probable Position (AD)
MPPCA........	Maryland Probation, Patrol and Corrections Association (AD)
mppcf	Millions of Particles per Cubic Foot of Air (AD)
MPPhS........	Member of the Royal Pharmaceutical Society [*Canada*] (DD)
mp pl	Multipunch Plate (AD)
MPPP..........	Money-Purchase Pension Plan [*Human resources*] (WYGK)
mpps	Million Pulses per Second (AD)
mpq	Manpower-Planning Quota (AD)
MPR...........	Madjelis Permusiawaratan Rakat [*People's Deliberative Assembly*] [*Indonesia*] (AD)
MPR...........	Maintainability Program Requirements (AD)
mpr	Medium-Power RADAR (AD)
mpress	Medium Pressure (AD)
MPRP..........	Muslim Peoples Republican Party [*Political party*] (AD)
mps	Marbled Paper Sides (AD)
mps	Megacycles per Second (AD)
mps	Meters per Second (AD)
MPS............	Milwaukee Public Museum (AD)
mps	Motor Parts Stock (AD)
MPS............	Multiprogramming System (AD)
mpsh	Mean Pressure Suction Head (AD)
MPSS..........	Multiple Protective Structure System (AD)
mpt	Male Pipe Thread (AD)
Mpt............	Maryport (AD)
mpt	Melting Point (AD)
mpt	Microprocessing Programmable Terminal [*Computer science*] (AD)
mpt	Midpoint (AD)
MPT............	Miles per Tankful (AD)

mpt .... Miles per Tankful (AD)
mpt .... Multiple Pure Tone (AD)
mpt .... Multipower Transmission (AD)
MPTA .... Machine Power Transmission Association (AD)
mpta .... Main Propulsion Test Article (AD)
MPU .... Mental Parents Union (AD)
mpu .... Microprocessor Unit (AD)
MPU .... Missing Persons Unit (AD)
mpu .... Monitor Printing Unit (AD)
M-P v .... Mason-Pfizer Virus [Medicine] (AD)
mpv .... Multipurpose Vehicle (AD)
MPW .... Minneapolis-Moline [Stock exchange symbol] (AD)
MPWBS ...... Master Plan Works Breakdown Structure (AD)
mpx .... Multiplex (AD)
mpxr .... Multiplexor (AD)
Mpy .... Maatschappij [Company] [Dutch] (AD)
mpy .... Multiply (AD)
MPZ .... Mid-Continent Petroleum [Stock exchange symbol] (AD)
MQ .... Magnum Airlines [ICAO designator] (AD)
MQ .... Memory Quotient
mq .... Memory Quotient (AD)
mq .... Metol-Quinol [Medicine] (AD)
MQ .... Metol-Quinone [Medicine] (AD)
mq .... Metol-Quinone [Medicine] (AD)
Mq .... Mosque (AD)
mq .... Multiple Quotient (AD)
MQ .... Musical Quarterly [A publication] (BRI)
MQ .... Simmons Airlines [ICAO designator] (AD)
MQA .... Medical Quality Assurance (AD)
MQAB .... Medical Quality Assurance Board (AD)
MQD .... Metallurgical Quenching Dilatometry
Mqe .... Martinique (AD)
mqf .... Mobile Quarantine Facility (AD)
MQG .... Milgarra [Queensland] [Airport symbol] (AD)
MQI .... Maiquetia [Venezuelan airport] (AD)
mqil .... Miniature Quartz Incandescent Lamp (AD)
mql .... Miniature Quartz Lamp (AD)
MQM .... Master of the Queen's Music [British] (AD)
MQQ .... Moundou [Chad] [Airport symbol] (AD)
MQR .... Michigan Quarterly Review [A publication] (BRI)
MQS .... Mobile Quality Services (AD)
MQV .... Ministere de la Qualite de la Vie [Ministry of the Quality of Life] [France] (AD)
mqyco .... Minimum Quantity Yards per Color (AD)
mqyds .... Minimum Quantity Yards per Design (AD)
mr .... Machine Record (AD)
mr .... Machine Rifle (AD)
MR .... Magnetic Resonating (AD)
M/R .... Map Reading (AD)
m/r .... Map Reading (AD)
mr .... Map Reference (AD)
mr .... Marginal Revenue (AD)
MR .... Mark Russell (AD)
Mr .... Master (AD)
M/R .... Mates Receipt (AD)
mr .... Medium Range (AD)
mr .... Meester [Master] [Dutch] (AD)
mr .... Mentally Retarded (AD)
mr .... Metabolic Rate (AD)
mr .... Methyl Red (AD)
MR .... Michigan Reformatory (AD)
m/r .... Middle Right (AD)
MR .... Military Railroad (AD)
mR .... Milliroentgen (AD)
mr .... Mill Run (AD)
mr .... Mineral Rubber (AD)
mr .... Mine Run (AD)
MR .... Minnesota Review [A publication] (BRI)
MR .... Mobilizacion Republicana [Republican Mobilization] [Nicaragua] [Political party] (AD)
MR .... Monon Railroad (AD)
Mr .... Mother (AD)
mr .... Motivational Research (AD)
MR .... Motormannes Riksforbund [Motorists' Association] [Swedish] (AD)
MR .... Multifamily Residential Zone (AD)
MR-13 Movement of 13 NoGuatemala... Movimiento Revolucionario de 13 de Noviembre [Revolutionary Movement of 13 November] [Guatemala] [Political party] (AD)
MRA .... Master Retailers Association (AD)
mra .... Medium-Powered Radio Range (AD)
mra .... Metro Rating Area (AD)
mra .... Minimum Reception Altitude (AD)
mraam .... Medium-Range Air-to-Air Missile [Military] (AD)
mrac .... Manifold-Regulator Accumulator Charging (AD)
mrad .... Megarad (AD)
mrad .... Millirad (AD)
MRAL .... Mandatory Retirement Age Law of 1978 (WYGK)
MR & DC .... Medical Research and Development Command [Army] (AD)
MR&DF .... Malleable Research and Development Foundation (AD)
MR & S ...... Materials Research and Standards (AD)
MRAP .... Management Review and Analysis Program (AD)
mrasm .... Medium-Range Air-to-Surface Missile [Military] (AD)
mrat .... Medium-Range Applied Technology (AD)
MRAUSCAN... Masonic Relief Association of the United States and Canada (AD)
mrb .... Marble Base (AD)

MRBA .... Mississippi River Bridge Authority (AD)
mrbm .... Medium-Range Ballistic Missile [Military] (AD)
mrc .... Magnetic Rectifier Control (AD)
MRC .... Malaria Research Centre [India]
MRC .... Marlin-Rockwell Corp. (AD)
Mrc .... Mauricio [Mauritius] [Spanish] (AD)
MRC .... Men's Republican Club [Political party] (AD)
MRC .... Methods Research Corp. (AD)
MRC .... Mid-Roll Interchange [Advanced photo system]
MRC .... Minnesota Restitution Center (AD)
MRC .... Modern Railroad Club (AD)
MRC .... Motor Racing Club (AD)
MRCA .... Market Research Corp. of America (AD)
mrca .... Multirole Combat Aircraft (AD)
MRCI .... Medical Registration Council of Ireland (AD)
MRCo. .... Malaysian Refrigerator Co. (AD)
MRCP .... Maoist Revolutionary Communist Party [Political party] (AD)
MRCPUK...... Member of the Royal College of Physicians of the United Kingdom [British] (AD)
MRCWA ...... Midland Railway Company of Western Australia (AD)
MRD .... Medical Reference Department (AD)
mrd .... Metal Rolling Door (AD)
mrd .... Metal Roof Deck (AD)
MRD .... Microbiological Research Department (AD)
mrd .... Minimum Reacting Dose (AD)
MRD .... Motorized Rifle Division [Military] (AD)
mrdf .... Machine-Readable Data Files [Computer science] (AD)
mrdhd .... Maximum Recommended Daily Human Dose (AD)
MRDN .... Material Receipt Discrepancy Notice (AD)
MRE .... Manicore [Brazil] [Airport symbol] (AD)
mre .... Meal Ready to Eat (AD)
MRE .... Meals Rejected by Everyone
mre .... Mean Radial Error (AD)
MRELB........ Malaysian Rubber Exchange and Licensing Board (AD)
mrem .... Milliroentgen Equivalent Man (AD)
MRF .... Magnetorheological Finishing [Optics manufacturing] (RDA)
mrf .... Maintenance Replacement Factor (AD)
mrf .... Marble Floor (AD)
MRF .... Mayo Research Foundation (AD)
MRFB.......... Malayan Rubber Fund Board (AD)
mr flight ...... Meteorological Research Flight (AD)
mrg .... Magnetic Radiation Generator (AD)
MRG .... Maintainability Requirements Group (AD)
mrg .... Margin (AD)
mrg .... Marginalia (AD)
MRG .... Mesters Vig [Greenland] [Airport symbol] (AD)
mrg .... Methane-Rich Gas (AD)
MRG .... Minorities Research Group (AD)
MRGO .... Mississippi River Gulf Outflow (AD)
MRH .... Member of the Royal Household [British] (AD)
MRHMC ...... Michael Reese Hospital and Medical Center (AD)
MRI .... Magazine Research, Inc. (AD)
mri .... Magnetic-Resonance Imager (AD)
mri .... Magnetic Rubber Inspection (AD)
mri .... Mean Rise Interval (AD)
MRI .... Medical Records Index (AD)
mri .... Medium-Range Interceptor (AD)
MRI .... Meteorological Research Institute (AD)
MRI .... Military Reform Institute (AD)
mri .... Milstrip Routing Identifier (AD)
mri .... Monopulse Resolution Improvement (AD)
MRI .... Motor Repair Insurance (AD)
MRINZ .... Meat Research Institute of New Zealand (AD)
mrir .... Medium Resolution Infrared (AD)
mrk .... Mark (VRA)
mrkd .... Marked (AD)
mrkg .... Marking (AD)
mrkr .... Marker (AD)
Mrkts .... Markets (AD)
MRL .... Medical Records Library (AD)
mrl .... Medium-Powered Radio Range (AD)
mrl .... Motor Refrigerator Lighter (AD)
mrl .... Multiple Rocket Launcher (AD)
mrm .... Mail Readership Measurement (AD)
mrm .... Mechanically Recovered Meat (AD)
mrm .... Miles of Relative Movement (AD)
MRMVA ...... Master Retail Milk Vendors Association (AD)
MRN .... Material Recorder Notice (AD)
mrng .... Mooring (AD)
mrng .... Morning (AD)
MRNP .... Mount Rainier National Park [Washington] (AD)
MRNP .... Mount Revelstoke National Park [British Columbia] (AD)
Mro .... Maestro (AD)
mro .... Maintenance, Repair, and Operating (AD)
MRO .... Media Resources Officer (AIE)
MROAR........ Modification and Repair Order and Acceptance Record (AD)
mrov .... Moreover (AD)
mrp .... Machine-Readable Passport (AD)
mrp .... Manned Reusable Payload (AD)
mrp .... Manned Reusable Product (AD)
mrp .... Marginal Revenue Product (AD)
MRP .... Master in Regional Planning (DD)
mrp .... Maximum Resolving Power (AD)
mrp .... Maximum Retail Price (AD)
MRPA .... Metropolitan Region Planning Authority (AD)

MRPhS	Member of the Royal Pharmaceutical Society [*Canada*] (DD)
MRPP	Maoist Reorganization Movement of the Party of the Proletariat [*Political party*] (AD)
M rps	Mauritius Rupee [*Monetary unit*] (AD)
MRQ	Marquardt Corp. [*Stock exchange symbol*] (AD)
mrr	Medical Research Reactor (AD)
MRRAS	Murder Release Risk Assessment Scale (AD)
MRRDB	Malaysian Rubber Research and Development Board (AD)
mrs	Marginal Rate of Substitution (AD)
MRS	Ministry of Recreation and Sport [*British*] (AD)
Mrs	Missus (AD)
Mrs	Mistress (AD)
MRS	Mountain Rescue Service (AD)
mrsa	Medium-Range Surveillance Aircraft (AD)
MR San Asn	Member of the Royal Sanitary Association [*British*] (AD)
MRSMGB	Member of the Royal Society of Musicians of Great Britian (AD)
MRSP	Myakka River State Park [*Florida*] (AD)
mrsss	Manned Revolving Space Systems Simulator (AD)
Mrt	Maart [*March*] [*Dutch*] (AD)
Mrt	Martinique (AD)
MRT	Mass Rapid Transit (AD)
mrt	Mean Radiant Temperature (AD)
mrt	Mid-Range Trajectory (AD)
mrt	Mildew-Resistant Thread (AD)
mrt	Military-Rated Thrust (AD)
MRT	Military Review Team (AD)
mrt	Mission Readiness Tester (AD)
MRT	Modulus of Rupture Test (AD)
MRTA	Maintenance Requirements Task Analysis (AD)
mrtm	Maritime (AD)
Mrtnz	Martinez (AD)
mrto	Miscellaneous Reference Tool (AD)
mrts	Marginal Rate of Technical Substitution (AD)
MRTS	Mass Rapid Transit System (AD)
Mrts	Mauritius (AD)
mru	Mass Radiography Unit (AD)
MRU	Medical Rehabilitation Unit (AD)
mru	Minimal Reproductive Unit (AD)
mru	Mobile Radio Unit (AD)
MRU	Most Recently Used [*Computer science*]
mrv	Material Receipt Voucher (AD)
MRV	Missile Recovery Vessel (AD)
mrv	Missile Re-Entry Vehicle (AD)
mrv	Mixed Respiratory Vaccine [*Medicine*] (AD)
mrV-P	Methyl Red Voges-Proskauer [*Bacteriology*] (AD)
MRVT	Miravant [*NASDAQ symbol*]
mrw	Morale, Recreation, and Welfare (AD)
mr/w	Multiple Read/Write (AD)
MRWA	Midland Railway of Western Australia (AD)
mrwc	Multiple Reading, Writing, Compiling (AD)
MRX	Mineiros [*Brazil*] [*Airport symbol*] (AD)
mrytm	Must Have Reply Here by Tomorrow Morning (AD)
mrz	Marzo [*March*] [*Spanish*] (AD)
MS	Egyptair [*ICAO designator*] (AD)
ms	Machine Screw (AD)
ms	Machine Steel (AD)
ms	Main Switch (AD)
ms	Maintenance and Service (AD)
ms	Major Subject (AD)
M/S	Mannlicher-Schoenauer (AD)
ms	Manuscript (VRA)
ms	Margin of Safety (AD)
Ms	Mariners [*Seattle Baseball Team*] (AD)
m/s	Marking and Stenciling (AD)
ms	Mass Spectrometric (AD)
ms	Master Switch (AD)
ms	Matched Set (AD)
MS	Material Standard (AD)
Ms	Mature Motion Pictures (AD)
ms	Maximum Stress (AD)
ms	Mean Square (AD)
ms	Medium Shot (AD)
ms	Medium Steel (AD)
Ms	Mendes (AD)
Ms	Mesothorium (AD)
m/s	Metal Shank (AD)
ms	Meters per Second (AD)
ms	Metric System (AD)
MS	Michigan State University of Agriculture and Applied Sciences (AD)
ms	Microseismic (AD)
ms	Mild Steel (AD)
m/s	Milestone (AD)
m/s	Miniature Sheet of Stamps (AD)
ms	Minimum Stress (AD)
ms	Mint State (AD)
ms	Mitral Stenosis (AD)
M-S	Monday through Saturday (AD)
m/s	Month after Sight (AD)
ms	Months after Sight (AD)
m/s	Motorskib [*Motorship*] [*Norwegian*] (AD)
ms	Multiple Sclerosis (AD)
ms	Multiple Starters (AD)
ms	Muscle Strength (AD)
MSA	Manitoba Society of Artists [*1925*] [*Canada*] (NGC)
MSA	Medical Savings Account
MSA	Medical Service Agency (WYGK)
MSAA	Microsoft Active Accessibility [*Computer science*]
MSAA	Multiple Sclerosis Association of America
MSAWA	Migrant and Seasonal Agricultural Worker Act of 1983 (WYGK)
MSC	Marrow Stromal Cell [*Biochemistry*]
MSc	Master of Science [*Academic degree*] (AIE)
MSC	Master of Science in Commerce (DD)
MSC	Mathematics/Science/Computer
MScA	Master of Applied Science (DD)
MScC	Master of Science in Commerce (DD)
MScComm	Master in Commercial Science (DD)
MSCDEX	Microsoft Compact Disc Extension [*Computer science*] (DOM)
MScE	Master of Science in Engineering (DD)
MScEcon	Master of Science in Economics (DD)
MSD	Mossoro [*Brazil*] [*Airport symbol*] (AD)
MSDN	Microsoft Developer Network [*Computer science*]
MSE	Manston [*England*] [*Airport symbol*] (AD)
MSGI	Marketing Services Group
MSI	Moshi [*Tanzania*] [*Airport symbol*] (AD)
MSIO	Medical Systems Integration Office [*Army*] (RDA)
MSK	Mastic Point [*Andros Islands, Bahamas*] [*Airport symbol*] (AD)
MSL	Microgravity Science Laboratory [*NASA*]
MSMV	Monk Seal Morbillivirus
MSN	Multiple Subscriber Number [*Telecommunications*] (DOM)
MSR	Macrophage Scavenger Receptor [*Immunology*]
MSR	Makassar [*Sulawesi, Indonesia*] [*Airport symbol*] (AD)
MSR	Male Seniors [*International Bowhunting Organization*] [*Class equipment*]
mss	Illuminated Manuscript (VRA)
MS-SPRING	Multiplex-Section, Shared-Protection Rings
MST	Movimento Sem Terra [*Political party*] [*Brazil*]
mstb	Mastaba (VRA)
mstr	Master (VRA)
MSX	Mascota [*Mexico*] [*Airport symbol*] (AD)
MT	Mac Knight Airlines [*ICAO designator*] (AD)
mt	Mountain (VRA)
MTA	Muslim Teachers' Association (AIE)
MTBM	Microtunneling Boring Machine (RDA)
MTCI	Member of the Trust Companies Institute (DD)
mtd	Mounted (VRA)
MTE	Monte Alegre [*Brazil*] [*Airport symbol*] (AD)
MTF	Microsoft Tape Format [*Computer science*]
mtge	Mortgage (DD)
MTI	Member of the Trust Institute (DD)
MTLS-P	Mesial Temporal Lobe Seizure [*Medicine*]
MTP	Mother Tongue Project (AIE)
MTU	Metric Units (DFIT)
mtydm	Martyrdom (VRA)
MU	China Eastern Airlines [*ICAO designator*] (AD)
MU	Misrair [*ICAO designator*] (AD)
MUD	Multi-User Domain [*Computer science*]
MUD	Municipal Utility District [*Investment term*] (DFIT)
MUD	Murchison Falls [*Uganda*] [*Airport symbol*] (AD)
MUE	Microcomputer Users in Education (AIE)
MUH	Mersa Matruh [*Egypt*] [*Airport symbol*] (AD)
MultiCul R	MultiCultural Review [*A publication*] (BRI)
Multilink PPP	Multichannel Connection Protocol Based on the Point-to-Point Protocol [*Computer science*]
mur	Mural (VRA)
mus	Musee (VRA)
mus	Museen (VRA)
mus	Museo (VRA)
mus	Museum (VRA)
musi	Musical (VRA)
musl	Muslin (VRA)
MUST	Malaysian University of Science and Technology
MUW	Mutarara [*Mozambique*] [*Airport symbol*] (AD)
MUZM	Makerere-University Zoology Museum [*Uganda*]
MV	MacRobertson-Miller Airline Service [*ICAO designator*] (AD)
MVA	Market Value Added
MVA	Market Value Appraiser
MVC	Management Verification Consortium (AIE)
MVO	Mongo [*Chad*] [*Airport symbol*] (AD)
MVU	Mulege [*Mexico*] [*Airport symbol*] (AD)
MW	Maya Airways [*ICAO designator*] (AD)
MWHF	Michigan Wildlife Habitat Foundation
MWL	Mineral Wells [*Texas*] [*Airport symbol*] (AD)
MWP	Mangla [*Pakistan*] [*Airport symbol*] (AD)
MWTHA	Michigan Wild Turkey Hunters Association
MX	Mexicana de Aviacion [*ICAO designator*] (AD)
MXD	Marion Downs [*Queensland*] [*Airport symbol*] (AD)
MXK	Metekel [*Ethiopia*] [*Airport symbol*] (AD)
MXR	Moussoro [*Chad*] [*Airport symbol*] (AD)
MY	Air Mali [*ICAO designator*] (AD)
MYC	Massenya [*Chad*] [*Airport symbol*] (AD)
MYH	Rosh-Pina [*Israel*] [*Airport symbol*] (AD)
MYHEC	Michigan Youth Hunter Education Challenge
MYP	Montgomery [*Pakistan*] [*Airport symbol*] (AD)
MYV	Marysville [*California*] [*Airport symbol*] (AD)
MYZ	Mayoko [*Gabon*] [*Airport symbol*] (AD)
MZ	Merpati Nusantara Airlines [*ICAO designator*] (AD)
MZB	Mocimboa da Praia [*Mozambique*] [*Airport symbol*] (AD)
MZN	Minj [*New Guinea*] [*Airport symbol*] (AD)
MZQ	Mozambique [*Mozambique*] [*Airport symbol*] (AD)
MZU	Muzaffarpur [*India*] [*Airport symbol*] (AD)

MZX .... Massio [*Ethiopia*] [*Airport symbol*] (AD)
MZY .... Mzimba [*Malawi*] [*Airport symbol*] (AD)
MZZ .... Marion [*Indiana*] [*Airport symbol*] (AD)

N
By Acronym

N .... New Issue [*Investment term*] (DFIT)
NA .... Academician of the National Academy of Design, New York [*1825*] (NGC)
Na .... Exchangeable Body Sodium (AD)
NAACE .... National Association of Advisers in Computer Education (AIE)
NA & G .... Norgulf Lines (North Atlantic & Gulf) (AD)
NABO .... North Atlantic Biocultural Organization [*A research cooperative*]
NAC .... North Atlantic Current [*Oceanography*]
NACCB .... National Accreditation Council for Certification Bodies (AIE)
NACE .... National Association of Counsellors in Education (AIE)
NACESW ..... National Association of Chief Education Social Workers (AIE)
NACG .... National Association of Conservative Graduates (AIE)
NACP .... National Association of Chiefs of Police (AD)
nacro .... Night-Alarm Cutoff (AD)
NACSW ...... National Action Committee on the Status of Women [*Canada*] (AD)
NACT .... National Association of Careers Teachers (AD)
NACT .... National Association of Cycle Trades (AD)
NACTST ...... National Advisory Council on the Training and Supply of Teachers (AD)
NACUBO ..... National Association of College and University Business Office Associations (AD)
NACW .... National Advisory Committee on Women (AD)
NACWPI ...... National Association of College Wind and Percussion Instruments (AD)
NACYS .... National Advisory Council for Youth Services (AIE)
nad .... Nadir (AD)
NAD .... National Alliance for Democracy [*Political party*] (AD)
Nad .... Nedezhda (AD)
nad .... Networking Addressing Device [*Computer science*] (AD)
nad .... No Apparent Defect (AD)
nad .... No Appreciable Difference (AD)
nad .... No Appreciable Disease (AD)
nad .... Nothing Abnormal Detected (AD)
nad .... Not on Active Duty [*Military*] (AD)
NADA .... National Association of Drug Addiction (AD)
NADABB ...... National Alzheimer's Disease Autopsy and Brain Bank (AD)
NADAC .... National Anti-Drug Abuse Campaign (AD)
NADB .... National Aerometric Data Bank (AD)
NADC .... Northern Agricultural Development Corp. (AD)
NADDIS ...... Narcotics and Dangerous Drugs Intelligence File (AD)
NaDefCo ..... NATO [*North Atlantic Treaty Organization*] Defense College (AD)
NaDevCen.... Naval Air Development Center (AD)
NADF .... National Alzheimer's Disease Foundation (AD)
NADFAS ...... National Association of Design and Fine Art Societies (AD)
NADFS .... National Association of Drop Forgers and Stampers (AD)
NADH .... Dihydronicotinamide Adenine Dinucleotide (AD)
NAD/NADH.. Nicotinamide Adenine Dinucleotide (AD)
NADOW .... National Association for Training the Disabled in Office Work (AD)
nadp .... Nicotinamide Adenine Dinucleotide Phosphate (AD)
NADPH........ Dihydronicotinamide Adenine Dinucleotide Phosphate (AD)
nadph .... Dihydronicotinamide Adenine Dinucleotide Phosphate (AD)
NADWARN .. National Disaster Warning System (AD)
nae .... National Administrative Expenses (AD)
NAE .... Naval Aeronautical Establishment [*Canada*] (AD)
NAE .... Naval Aircraft Establishment (AD)
nAe .... No American Equivalent (AD)
nae .... Not Always Excused (AD)
NAEA .... National Art Education Archive (AIE)
NAEIAC .... National Association of Educational Inspectors, Advisers, and Consultants (AIE)
NAEP .... National Assessment of Educational Progress (AD)
NAEP .... National Association of Educational Programs [*Carnegie Foundation*] (AD)
NAF............. National Abortion Foundation (AD)
naf .... Nonappropriated Funds (AD)
NAF............. Norges Automobil Fornund [*Norway Automobile Association*] (AD)
NAFA .... National Academy of Foreign Affairs (AD)
NAFA .... National Aerobic Fitness Award (AD)
NAFAS .... National Association of Flower Arrangement Societies (AD)
NAFD .... National Air Forwarding Division [*Institute of Freight Forwarders*] (AD)
naff .... Need for Affiliation (AD)
NAFFP .... National Association of Frozen Food Producers (AD)
NAFI............ Naval Avionics Facility (AD)
NAFINSA...... Nacional Financiera [*National Finance Coro.*] [*Spanish*] (AD)
NAFM........... National Armed Forces Museum (AD)

NAFP .... New Armed Forces of the Philippines (AD)
NAFRLG....... National Alliance of Financially-Responsible Local Governments (AD)
NAFS .... National Association of Foot Specialists (AD)
NAFS .... National Association of Forensic Sciences (AD)
NAFSA .... National Association of Foreign Student Advisors (AD)
NAFT........... National Alternative Fuel Test (AD)
NAFTA .... New Zealand-Australia Free Trade Agreement (AD)
NAFWR .... National Association of Furniture Warehousemen and Removers (AD)
Nag .... Nagasaki [*Japan*] (AD)
Nag .... Nagoya [*Japan*] (AD)
NAG .... Neighborhood Action Group (AD)
nag .... Net Annual Gain (AD)
Nagas .... Nagasaki [*Japan*] (AD)
N-age.......... Nuclear Age (AD)
Nagp .... Nagpur, India (AD)
NAGPM .... National Association of Grained Plate Makers (AD)
NAGRA......... Nationalen Genossenschaft fuer die Lagerung Radioaktiver Abfaelle [*National Cooperative Society for the Storage of Radioactive Wastes*] [*Germany*] (AD)
Nah .... [*The Book of*] Nahum (AD)
NAH .... National Association of Homebuilders (AD)
NAHA .... National Association of Health Authorities in England and Wales (AIE)
Nahal.......... Na'or Halutsi Lohem [*Fighting Pioneer Youth*] [*Israel*] (AD)
NAHCAC....... National Ad Hoc Committee Against Censorship (AD)
NAHSC .... National Automated Highway System Consortium
NAHSTA....... National Hiking and Ski Touring Association (AD)
nai .... No Action Indicated (AD)
nai .... No Address Instruction (AD)
NAIC .... Naval Aircraft Investigation Center (AD)
NAIDS .... North Atlantic Institute for Defense Studies [*NATO*] (AD)
NAIL........... Naval Aircraft Inventory Log (AD)
naiop .... Navigational Aids Inoperative for Parts (AD)
Nairns .... Nairnshire, Scotland (AD)
NAISS .... National Association of Iron and Steel Stockholders (AD)
NAJC........... National Assessment of Juvenile Correction [*University of Michigan*] (AD)
NAJC........... Northern Australia Jockey Club (AD)
NAJC........... Northwest Alabama Junior College (AD)
NAJE........... National Association of Jazz Education (AD)
nak .... Negative Acknowledge Character [*Computer science*] (AD)
NAK .... Negative Acknowledgment (DOM)
nak .... Negative Knowledge (AD)
nak .... Nothing Adverse Known (AD)
nakl .... Naklad [*Edition*] [*Polish*] (AD)
nakl .... Nakladatel [*Edition*] [*Czech*] (AD)
NAL............. National Aerospace Laboratory (AD)
NAL............. National Airlines (AD)
NAL............. Nigeria America Line (AD)
NALEAO .... National Association of Latino Elected and Appointed Officials (AD)
NALGG......... National Association for Lesbian and Gay Gerontology (AD)
NALGO......... National Association of Local Government Officers (AIE)
NALSA .... North American Land Sailing Association (AD)
NALSAT .... National Association of Land Settlement Association Tenants (AD)
NAM............ National Aero Manufacturing (AD)
NAM............ Nederlandsche Aluminium Maatschappij [*Netherlands Aluminum Co.*] (AD)
nam .... Network Access Machine [*Computer science*] (AD)
nam .... Non-Aligned Movement (AD)
N Am .... North America (AD)
NAM............ North American Movement (AD)
NAMA .... New Amsterdam Musical Association (AD)
NAMA .... North American Maritime Agencies (AD)
NAMBO .... National Association of Motor Bus Operators (AD)
NAMC .... Nihon Aeroplane Manufacturing Co. (AD)
NAMCO .... Naval and Mechanical Co. (AD)
NAME .... National Association of Marine Engineers (AD)
NAME .... National Association of Metal Name Plate Manufacturers (AD)
NAMEB .... National Association of Marine Engine Builders (AD)
Namib......... Namibia (AD)
NAMilCom ... North Atlantic Military Committee (AD)
naml .... Namligen [*Namely*] [*Swedish*] (AD)
NAMM .... National Association of Music Merchandisers (AD)
NAMMC .... Natural Asphalt Mineowners' and Manufacturers' Council (AD)

NAMMO Development a... NATO [*North Atlantic Treaty Organization*] Multi-Role Combat Aircraft Development a (AD)
NAMP .... National Association of Married Priests (AD)
nampg........ Nautical Air Miles per Gallon (AD)
NAMPMW .... Vietnam Prisoners of War [*An association*] (AD)
namppf....... Nautical Air Miles per Pound of Fuel (AD)
Nan............. Nancy (AD)
Nan............. Nanette (AD)
Nan............. Nanking [*China*] (AD)
nan .... Nisi Aliter Notetur [*Unless It is Otherwise Noted*] [*Latin*] (AD)
nana .... N-Acetylneuraminic Acid (AD)
NANA.......... National Advertising News Association (AD)
NANAC........ National Aviation Noise Abatement Council (AD)
nanova........ Non-Orthogonal Analysis of Variance (AD)
NANTIS .... Nottignham and Nottinghamshire Technical Information Service [*British*] (AD)
NANVH&SWO... National Assembly of National Voluntary Health and Social Welfare Organizations (AD)
NAO .... National Association of Outfitters (AD)
NAO .... Noise Abatement Office (AD)
NAOA .... Navy Officers Accounts Office (AD)
NAOC .... Nigerian Agip Oil Co. (AD)
NaOH .... Sodium Hydroxide (AD)
NAOJ .... National Astronomical Observatory of Japan
nap .... Knapsack (AD)
nap .... Napalm (AD)
nap .... Naphtha (AD)
Nap .... Naples (AD)
Nap .... Napoleon (AD)
NAP .... National Aerospace Plane (AD)
NAP .... National Association for the Paralysed (AD)
nap .... Naval Aviation Pilot (AD)
NAP .... Neighborhood Awareness Program (AD)
nap .... Non-Agency Purchase (AD)
nap .... Not at Present (AD)
napalm .... Naphthene Palmitate (AD)
NAPBC......... National Action Plan on Breast Cancer
napc............ Non-Adherent Peritoneal Cells (AD)
NAPD .... National Association of Police Driving (AD)
NAPE .... National Association of Partners in Education
naph .... Naphtha (AD)
naph .... Naphthyl (AD)
NAPHC......... National Association of Plumbing/Heating/Cooling Contractors (AD)
NAPIA .... National Affiliate of Printing Industries of America (AD)
NAPLP .... National Association of Para-Legal Personnel (AD)
NAPLPS .... North American Presentation Level Protocol Standard (DOM)
NAPO .... National Association of Performing Artists (AD)
NAPO .... National Association of Purchasing Agents (AD)
na pr........... Na Priklad [*For Example*] [*Czech*] (AD)
NAPRC .... National Association for the Prevention of Rape by Castration (AD)
NAPS .... National Alliance of Postal Supervisors (AD)
NAPS .... Nissan Air Pollution System (AD)
NAPSA......... National Association of Pretrial Service Agencies (AD)
Nap's bones... Napier's Bones [*First slide rule*] (AD)
NaPTEC....... National Primary Teacher Education Conference (AIE)
NAPVD .... National Association for the Prevention of Venereal Disease (AD)
NAQI .... National Air Quality Index (AD)
Nar............. Narragansett (AD)
nar............. Narrow (AD)
NAR .... Nelson Aldrich Rockefeller (AD)
nar............. Net Assimilation Rate (AD)
nar............. No Apparent Rate (AD)
NAR .... North American Review [*A publication*] (BRI)
NAR .... North American Royalties (AD)
NARA .... Nippon Australian Relations Agreement (AD)
NARAD........ Navy Research and Development (AD)
narc .... Narcotic (AD)
narc .... Narcotics Agent (AD)
NARC.......... National Archives and Records Service (AD)
NARC.......... National Association of Retired Catholics (AD)
narco .... Narcotic (AD)
NARCO........ Narcotics Commission [*United Nations*] (AD)
narco .... Narcotics Officer (AD)
narcocard..... Narcotic-Addict Registration Card (AD)
narcodollars... Narcotic Traffic Dollars (AD)
Narconon..... Narcotics Anonymous [*An association*] (AD)
narcos .... Narcotics (AD)
narcos .... Narcotics Police Officers (AD)
narcot .... Narcotic (AD)
narcotest ..... Narcotics Test (AD)
narco-traf..... Narcotics Traffick (AD)
narcs .... Narcotics (AD)
narcs .... Narcotics Agents (AD)
narcs .... Narcotics Hospital (AD)
narcs .... Narcotics Officers (AD)
narcs .... Narcotics Treatment Centers (AD)
NARD.......... National Association of Regimental Drummers (AD)
nard .... Spikenard (AD)
Nar Div .... Narodni Divadlo [*National Theater*] [*Czechoslavakia*] (AD)
narec .... Naval Research Electronic Computer (AD)
NARF .... National Association of Retail Furnishers (AD)
narf............ Natural Axial-Resonant Frequency (AD)
NARF .... Nuclear Aircraft Research Facility (AD)
NARGA........ National Association of Retail Grocers of Australia (AD)
NARI........... National Atmospheric Research Institute (AD)

NARIC.......... National Academic Recognition Information Centre (AIE)
Nar Inv .... Narcotics Investigation (AD)
narist.......... Naristillae [*Nasal Drops*] [*Latin*] (AD)
NARK.......... Nikolai Andreyvich Rimsky-Korsakov (AD)
Narkomvneshtorg... Narodny Komissariat Vneshney Torgovli [*People's Commissariate of Foreign Trade*] [*Russian*] (AD)
NARM .... National Association of Retail Merchants (AD)
N-arm .... Nuclear Armament (AD)
NARMCO...... National Research and Manufacturing Co. (AD)
N-armed ..... Nuclear-Armed (AD)
NARO.......... North American Regional Office (AD)
NARP.......... Neurogenic Muscle Weakness, Ataxia, and Retinitis Pigmentosa [*Medicine*]
NARP.......... Nuclear Weapons Accident Report Procedures (AD)
Nar Rep Bul. Narodna Republika Bulgaria [*Bulgarian People's Republic*] [*Political party*] (AD)
NARSIS........ National Association for Road Safety Instruction in Schools (AD)
NARTM .... National Association of Rope and Twine Merchants (AD)
NARU.......... North Australian Research Unit (AD)
NARWACL.... North American Regional World Anti-Communist League (AD)
nas............. Nasal (AD)
NAS .... National Agricultural Society (AD)
NAS .... Native American Studies (AD)
n-a-s .... No Added Salt (AD)
N A S .... Noise Abatement Society (AD)
NASA .... North American Sailing Association (AD)
NASAA......... National Aeronautics and Space Administration Act (AD)
NASA-CF Florida... National Aeronautics and Space Administration - Cocoa Beach, Florida (AD)
NASA-CO ..... National Aeronautics and Space Administration - Cleveland, Ohio (AD)
NASACRE..... National Association for Standing Advisory Councils for Religious Education (AIE)
NASA-EC California... National Aeronautics and Space Administration - Edwards, California (AD)
NASAEN....... National Association for State-Enrolled Assistant Nurses (AD)
NASA-GM Maryland... National Aeronautics and Space Administration - Greenbelt, Maryland (AD)
NASA-HA Alabama... National Aeronautics and Space Administration - Huntsville, Alabama (AD)
NASA-HT...... National Aeronautics and Space Administration - Houston, Texas (AD)
Nasakom ..... Nationalist-Communist (AD)
NASA LST Telescope... National Aeronautics and Space Administration Large Space Telescope (AD)
NASA-LV Virginia... National Aeronautics and Space Administration - Langley Field, Virginia (AD)
NASA-MC California... National Aeronautics and Space Administration - Moffett Field, California (AD)
NAS & FCA... National Automatic Sprinkler and Fire Control Association (AD)
NASA-SC California... National Aeronautics and Space Administration - Santa Monica, California (AD)
NASC .... North American Sporting Clays [*An association*]
NASCAR....... National Association for Stock Car Advancement and Research (AD)
NASCAR....... National Association of Sports Car Racing (AD)
NASCIS .... National Acute Spinal Cord Injury Study
NASCO........ National Automotive Service Co. (AD)
NASCOM...... National Aeronautics and Space Administration Tracking Network (AD)
NASCom ..... Naval Air Systems Command (AD)
NASD .... National Amalgamated Stevedores and Dockers (AD)
NASD .... Naval Aviation Supply Depot (AD)
NASD .... Nippon Advanced Ship Design (AD)
NASDAQS..... National Association of Security Dealers Automated Quotation System (AD)
NASE .... National Association of Stationary Engineers (AD)
nase........... Neutral Atom Space Engine (AD)
NASEN .... National Association for Special Educational Needs (AIE)
NASF .... National Aboriginal Sports Foundation (AD)
NASFO .... National Asset Seizure and Forfeiture Office (AD)
NAS-GB....... Noise Abatement Society of Great Britain (AD)
Nash .... Nashville [*Tennessee*] (AD)
NASH .... National Association of Specimen Hunters (AD)
NASHA......... North American Survival and Homesteading Association (AD)
NASML .... National Air and Space Museum Library [*Smithsonian Institute*] (AD)
NASP .... National Aero-Space Plane (AD)
Nas Par ...... Nasionale Party [*National Party*] [*Political party*] (AD)
Nas Pers..... Nasionale Pers [*National Press*] [*South Africa*] (AD)
Nass .... Nassau, Bahamas (AD)
NASS .... National Association of School Superintendents (AD)
NASSO........ National Association of Socialist Students' Organizations [*Political party*] (AD)
NASSP-B....... National Association of Secondary School Principals. Bulletin [*A publication*] (BRI)
NASSR........ Nahichevan Autonomous Soviet Socialist Republic (AD)
NASSTRAC... National Small Shipments Traffic Council
NASTI .... Naval Air Station, Terminal Island (AD)
NASTL .... National Anti-Steel-Trap League (AD)
Nat............. Natalia (AD)
Nat............. Natalie (AD)
Nat............. Natasha (AD)
Nat............. Nathalie (AD)
Nat............. Nathan (AD)
Nat............. Nathaniel (AD)
nat............. Nation (AD)

Nat............. Nation [*A publication*] (BRI)
Nat............. National (AD)
nat............. National (AD)
nat............. Native (AD)
nat............. Natural (AD)
nat............. Naturalist (AD)
nat............. Naturalization (AD)
nat............. Nature (AD)
nat............. Natuurkunde [*Natural Science*] [*Dutch*] (AD)
NAT............. New Attainment Target (AIE)
nat............. Normal Allowed Time (AD)
NATA .... National Automated Transportation Association (AD)
Nat Absten... National Abstentionalist (AD)
Nat Arc .... National Archives (AD)
Nat Assn...... National Association (AD)
natat........... Natation (AD)
Nat Bur Econ Res... National Bureau of Economic Research (AD)
Nat Bur Stand Circ... National Bureau of Standards Circular [*A publication*] (AD)
NATC .... National Air Traffic Controllers (AD)
Natch .... Natchez (AD)
natch .... Naturally (AD)
NATCO .... National Tank Co. (AD)
natcol .... Natural Color (AD)
natcom .... National Communications (AD)
Nat Dem ...... National Democrats [*Political party*] (AD)
NATE.......... National Association for the Teaching of English (AD)
NATE.......... Native American Teacher Education (AD)
NATELCA .... National Association for Teaching English and other Community Languages to Adults [*Formerly, NATELSA*] (AIE)
Nat Fed....... National Federation (AD)
Nat For .... National Forum [*A publication*] (BRI)
Nat Gal .... National Gallery (AD)
Nat Geog Mag... National Geographic Magazine [*A publication*] (AD)
Nath B .... Nathaniel Bowditch (AD)
nat hist .... Natural History (AD)
Nathl........... Nathaniel (AD)
NATIDC .... Netherlands-Australia Trade and Industrial Development Council (AD)
nation .... Nationality (AD)
Nativ........... Nativity (AD)
NATKE .... National Association of Theatrical and Kine Employees (AD)
natl .... National (AD)
N Atl .... North Atlantic (AD)
N Atl Cur .... North Atlantic Current (AD)
Nat Lib .... National Liberal (AD)
Nat Lib .... National Library of Canada (AD)
NATLIBCAN... National Library of Canada (AD)
NATLIBNZ... National Library of New Zealand (AD)
Natlm.......... Naturalism (VRA)
NATMAP....... National Mapping (AD)
Nat Mon ...... National Monument (AD)
Nat Mus ...... Natal Museum (AD)
Nat Mus ...... National Museum (AD)
Nat Obs ...... National Observer [*A publication*] (AD)
Nat Peop .... Native Peoples [*A publication*] (BRI)
nat phil....... Natural Philosophy (AD)
Nat R .... National Review [*A publication*] (BRI)
natr............ Natrium [*Sodium*] [*Latin*] (AD)
Nats............ Nationalists (AD)
Nats............ Natsionalnyii [*National*] [*Russian*] (AD)
NATS .... Naval Air Test Station (AD)
Nat ScD ...... Doctor of Natural Science (AD)
Nat Sci Fdn.. National Science Foundation (AD)
Nat Sec Soc... National Secular Society (AD)
NATSEMI ..... National Semiconductor Inc. (AD)
Nat Sup ...... National Superannuation (AD)
N Att .... Naval Attache (AD)
N-attack...... Nuclear Attack (AD)
NATTC .... National Tank Truck Carriers (AD)
Nat U .... Nations Unies [*United Nations*] [*French*] (AD)
Nat Uni .... National University (AD)
natur........... Naturalist (AD)
NATUSA...... North African Theater of Operations (AD)
naty .... Naturally (AD)
Nau............. Nauruan (AD)
Nau............. Nauru Island (AD)
nau .... Nautica [*Nautical*] [*Spanish*] (AD)
NAU............ North Arizona University (AD)
NAUA .... National Aircraft Underwriters' Association (AD)
nauga .... Naugahide (AD)
naut .... Nautical (AD)
n aux b .... New Auxiliary Boiler (AD)
NAV............. Natividade [*Brazil*] [*Airport symbol*] (AD)
Nav............. Navaho (AD)
Nav............. Naval (AD)
nav............. Naval (AD)
Nav............. Navarra (AD)
Nav............. Navarre (AD)
Nav............. Navassa Island (AD)
nav............. Navigable (AD)
nav............. Navigation (AD)
n/a/v........... Net Asset Value (AD)
NAVA .... Net Asset Value (AD)
navaco.......... Navigation Action Cutout (AD)
NAVAERORECOVF... Naval Aerospace Recovery Facility (AD)

NAVAIRREWORKF... Naval Air Rework Facility (AD)
NAVAL .... National Audio Visual Aids Library (AIE)
NavAus .... Navigation in Australian Waters (AD)
NAVBALTAP... Naval Forces Baltic Approaches [*NATO*] (AD)
navbm .... Naval Ballistic Missile (AD)
nav brz .... Naval Bronze (AD)
Nav Bs .... Naval Base (AD)
NavCad .... Naval Cadet (AD)
NavCm......... Navigation Countermeasures and Deception (AD)
navcom....... Navigation Communication (AD)
NAVDAC...... Navigation Data Assimilation Center (AD)
navdac....... Navigation Data Assimilation Computer (AD)
Nav Dep ..... Naval Deputy [*NATO*] (AD)
NavEams ..... Navigation in the Eastern Atlantic and the Mediterranean (AD)
NavEast .... Navigation along the East Coast of Asia (AD)
navex .... Navigation Exercise (AD)
NAVFE .... Naval Forces Far East (AD)
NAVFEC ...... Naval Facilites (AD)
NAVFECENGCOM... Naval Facilities Engineering Command (AD)
NAVFOR....... Naval Forces (AD)
NAVFORJAP... Naval Air Forces, Japan (AD)
NAVFORKOR... Naval Air Forces, Korea (AD)
NAVH .... National Aid to Visually Handicapped (AD)
Nav I.......... Navassa Island (AD)
navicert....... Naval Inspection Certificate (AD)
NavInd .... Navigation in the Indian Ocean (AD)
NAVMAR...... Naval Forces, Marianas (AD)
NavMisCen... Naval Missile Center (AD)
NAVNON...... Naval Forces, Northern Norway [*NATO*] (AD)
NavNoPac... Navigation in the North Pacific (AD)
NavNorlant... Navigation in the North Atlantic (AD)
NavOceanO... Naval Oceanographic Officer (AD)
NAVPERS...... Naval Personnel (AD)
NAVPHIL...... Naval Forces - Philippines (AD)
NAVPUB....... Naval Publications (AD)
NAVROM...... Romanian Merchant Marine (AD)
navsat........ Navigational Satellite (AD)
NavSat........ Navigation in the South Atlantic (AD)
NAVSCAP..... Naval Forces, Scandinavian Approaches [*NATO*] (AD)
NAVSEACENTLANT... Naval Sea Support Center - Atlantic (AD)
NAVSEACENTPAC... Naval Sea Support Center - Pacific (AD)
NAVSHIPCOM... Naval Ship Systems Command (AD)
NavShipyd ... Naval Shipyard (AD)
NavSoPac .... Navigation of the South Pacific (AD)
NAVSOUTH... Naval Forces, Southern Europe (AD)
NAVSTAR..... Navigation System Using Time and Ranging (AD)
NAVSUPORANT... Naval Support Forces, Antarctica (AD)
NAVTAC ...... Navigation Tactical (AD)
navtac......... Navigation Tactical (AD)
NAVTIS .... National Vessel Traffic Information System (AD)
NAVUWSEC... Naval Underwater Weapons Systems Engineering Center (AD)
NAWH .... Norwegian-American Historical Museum (AD)
NAYTA .... National Association of Youth Training Agencies (AIE)
NB.............. New Haven Airways [*ICAO designator*] (AD)
NBS............ Nucleotide Binding Site [*Genetics*]
NBTI............ Nitrobenzylthioinosine [*Organic chemistry*]
NC.............. National Curriculum [*Education*] (AIE)
NC.............. Network Computer [*Computer science*]
NC.............. Newair [*ICAO designator*] (AD)
NCAL .... National Centre for Athletics Literature (AIE)
NCCH .... Nurses' Central Clearing House (AIE)
NCE............ National Commission for Education (AIE)
NCES .... National Council for Educational Standards (AIE)
NCF............ NetWare Configuration File [*Computer science*]
NCFEAD ...... National Council for Foundation Education in Art and Design (AIE)
NCG............ Nueva Casas Grandes [*Mexico*] [*Airport symbol*] (AD)
NCGR.......... National Center for Genome Resources
NCHSR......... National Center for Health Services Research
NCI............. Network Computer, Inc.
NCITT.......... National Committee for the In-Service Training of Teachers [*Scotland*] (AIE)
NCM........... New Moon [*Queensland*] [*Airport symbol*] (AD)
NCMTT........ National Council for Mother Tongue Teaching (AIE)
NCPC .... National Cancer Pain Coalition
NCR............ National Civic Review [*A publication*] (BRI)
NCSB .... National Centre for School Biotechnology (AIE)
NCT............ Nicoya [*Costa Rica*] [*Airport symbol*] (AD)
NCT............ Non-Contact Time (AIE)
NCUP .... National Conference of University Professors (AIE)
ND .... National Diploma [*Academic degree*] (AIE)
nd .... No Date (VRA)
ND .... Nordair [*ICAO designator*] (AD)
nd .... Updated (VRA)
NDD .... Novo Redondo [*Angola*] [*Airport symbol*] (AD)
NDE .... Notodden [*Norway*] [*Airport symbol*] (AD)
NDG .... National Distribution Guide [*Mailing technique*] (AD)
NDH .... Delhi [*India*] [*Airport symbol*] (AD)
ndlwk.......... Needlework (VRA)
NDPS........... Novell Distributed Print Services [*Computer science*]
NDR .... Nador [*Morocco*] [*Airport symbol*] (AD)
Ndthl.......... Neanderthal (VRA)
NE .... Air New England [*ICAO designator*] (AD)
ne .... Neon (VRA)
NEAB .... Northern Examinations and Assessment Board (AIE)
NEAT .... Near-Earth Asteroid Tracking

necrp .... Necropolis (VRA)
NEEDIS .... National Enterprise Education Development and Information Service (AIE)
neg .... Negative (VRA)
NEGPT .... Negative Print (VRA)
NEIC........... National Equivalence Information Centre (AIE)
Neol............ Neolithic (VRA)
Nep............. Nepal (VRA)
neph .... Nephrite (VRA)
NEQ .... New England Quarterly [*A publication*] (BRI)
NetBIOS ...... Network Basic Input/Output System [*Computer science*] (DOM)
NETE........... Network of European Teacher Education (AIE)
Nethl........... Netherlands (VRA)
NETSL......... New England Technical Services Librarians
NEV............ Negative Expected Value
NEV............ Neighborhood Electric Vehicle
New Ad....... New Advocate [*A publication*] (BRI)
New Age..... New Age Journal [*A publication*] (BRI)
New ER....... New England Review [*A publication*] (BRI)
NEWPIN...... New Parent-Infant Network (AIE)
New R .... New Republic [*A publication*] (BRI)
New Sci...... New Scientist [*A publication*] (BRI)
New TB....... New Technical Books [*A publication*] (BRI)
New York.... New York Magazine [*A publication*] (BRI)
NExt........... New Experiences in Teaching [*Mathematics*]
NF............... EJA/Newport [*ICAO designator*] (AD)
NFCT .... National Federation of Class Teachers (AIE)
Nfld........... Newfoundland [*Canada*] (DD)
NFMY.......... National Festival of Music for Youth (AIE)
NFWHF .... National Fresh Water Fishing Hall of Fame
NG .... Green Hills Aviation [*ICAO designator*] (AD)
NGI .... Next Generation Internet [*A governmental research initiative*]
NGSQ .... National Genealogical Society Quarterly [*A publication*] (BRI)
NH .... All Nippon [*ICAO designator*] (AD)
NH .... Natural History [*A publication*] (BRI)
NHB .... Kodiak [*Alaska*] [*Airport symbol*] (AD)
NHMF .... National Heritage Memorial Fund (AIE)
NHP .... Nonhuman Primate
NHRP.......... Next Hop Resolution Protocol [*Computer science*]
NHRRC .... National Hybrid Rice Research Center [*China*]
nhx.............. Narthex (VRA)
ni .... Nickel (VRA)
NIAL........... Network for Informal Adult Learning (AIE)
NIC............. Network Interface Card [*Computer science*]
Nic............. Nicaragua (VRA)
NIC............. Nicosia [*Cyprus*] [*Airport symbol*] (AD)
Ni-Cd .... Nickel-Cadmium
NICER .... Northern Ireland Council for Educational Research (AIE)
NICS .... Newly Industrialized Countries (DFIT)
niel............. Niello (VRA)
NIFEGS .... Northern Ireland Further Education Guidance Service (AIE)
NIG&P .... Nanjing Institute of Geology and Paleontology [*China*]
Nigr............ Nigeria (VRA)
NILTC.......... National Industrial Language Training Centre (AIE)
NIM............ Networked Interactive Multimedia
NINDS......... National Institute of Neurological Disorders and Stroke
NINE .... Ninth-Plate (VRA)
Nine-C Lit.... Nineteenth-Century Literature [*A publication*] (BRI)
NINR .... National Institute for Nursing Research
NISEC .... Northern Ireland Schools Examination Council (AIE)
NISS .... National Information of Software and Services (AIE)
NISTA .... Northern Independent Steel Training Association (AIE)
NJ .... Namakwaland Lugdiens [*ICAO designator*] (AD)
NJC .... National Joint Council (AIE)
NK.............. Nielsen-Kellerman
NKL............ Nkolo [*Zaire*] [*Airport symbol*] (AD)
NL.............. Air Liberia [*ICAO designator*] (AD)
NL.............. New Leader [*A publication*] (BRI)
NLA............ New Large Airplane
NLEV........... National Low-Emission Vehicles
NLI............. National Library of Ireland (AIE)
NLI............. New Learning Initiative (AIE)
NLSY .... National Longitudinal Study of Youth
NM............. Mt. Cook Airlines [*ICAO designator*] (AD)
NMD/GBR .... National Missile Defense-Ground Based RADAR [*Army*] (RDA)
NMMHMO.... Network and Mixed Model Health Maintenance Organization [*Insurance*] (WYGK)
NMR .... Nappamerrie [*Queensland*] [*Airport symbol*] (AD)
NN .... Air Trails [*ICAO designator*] (AD)
NNI .... New Nickerie [*Surinam*] [*Airport symbol*] (AD)
NNU .... Nanuque [*Brazil*] [*Airport symbol*] (AD)
NO .... Air North [*ICAO designator*] (AD)
NOAHS........ New Opportunities in Animal Health Sciences
NOCN.......... National Open College Network (AIE)

NOD .... National Organization on Disability
NOG .... Arizona-Nogales [*Mexico*] [*Airport symbol*] (AD)
nonpoly........ Nonpolychrome (VRA)
NOP .... National Oracy Project (AIE)
Nor.............. Norway (VRA)
Nortel .... Northern Telecom [*Canada*]
NOSS .... Navy Ocean Surveillance System
Notes .... Notes (Music Library Association) [*A publication*] (BRI)
NOV .... Nova Lisboa [*Angola*] [*Airport symbol*] (AD)
NP .... Desert Pacific [*ICAO designator*] (AD)
NP .... National Parks [*A publication*] (BRI)
N/P.............. Notes Payable [*Finance*] (DFIT)
NPA .... Napan [*West Irian, Indonesia*] [*Airport symbol*] (AD)
NPDSA......... National Public Domain Software Archive (AIE)
NPF............. National Policy Forum
NPGA .... National Propane Gas Association
NPH .... Natural Protamine Hagadorn [*Insulin*]
NPOI .... Navy Prototype Optical Interferometer
NPP .... New Physics Project (AIE)
NPTC .... National Private Truck Council
NPTC .... National Proficiency Test Council (AIE)
NQ .... Cumberland Airlines [*ICAO designator*] (AD)
NQB .... No Qualified Bidders [*Investment term*] (DFIT)
NQSO .... Nonqualified Stock Options (WYGK)
nr................ Near (VRA)
NRI .... Natural Resources International
NRIC .... Negative Return in Cartridge [*Advanced photo system*]
NRJ............. Natural Resources Journal [*A publication*] (BRI)
NRMI .... National Registry of Myocardial Infarction
NROVA........ National Record of Vocational Achievement (AIE)
NS .... New Statesman [*A publication*] (BRI)
NS .... Nuernberger [*ICAO designator*] (AD)
NS & S .... New Statesman & Society [*A publication*] (BRI)
NSAPI .... Netscape Server API [*All-Purpose Interface*] [*Computer science*]
NSCA .... National Sporting Clays Association
NSCM .... Non-Stockpile Chemical Materiel [*Military*] (RDA)
NSG .... National Steering Group (AIE)
NSI.............. Network Solutions, Inc.
NSREC .... National Society's Religious Education Centre (AIE)
NSSA .... Nova Scotia Society of Artists [*1922-72*] [*Canada*] (NGC)
NSSC .... National Space Science Center [*British*]
NSTX .... National Spherical Torus Experiment [*Plasma physics*]
NT............... Lake State Airways [*ICAO designator*] (AD)
NT............... Neurologically Typical [*Psychology*]
NTAC .... New Technology Access Centre (AIE)
NTCF........... National Telemarketing Fulfillment Center
NTEI........... New Technical Education Initiative (AIE)
NTFC........... National Telemarketing Fulfillment Center
NTFS........... NT File System [*Computer science*]
ntL............. National (DD)
NTMP.......... Nitrate Motion Picture (VRA)
NTNG .... Nitrate Negative (VRA)
NTP .... Neuronal Thread Protein [*Biology*]
NTSC .... National Television Standards Committee
NTVEI.......... New Technical and Vocational Education Initiative (AIE)
NU .... Southwest Airlines [*ICAO designator*] (AD)
NUD .... En Nahud [*Sudan*] [*Airport symbol*] (AD)
NUJMB .... Northern Universities Joint Matriculation Board (AIE)
NURBS........ Nonuniform Rational B-Spline [*A type of spline*] [*Computer science*]
NUTA .... National Used Truck Association
NUWT .... National Union of Women Teachers (AIE)
NV .... Northwest Territorial Airways [*ICAO designator*] (AD)
NVA .... National Vulvodynia Association [*Disseminate information about vulvar pain and establish support networks across the country*] [*Medicine*]
NVFET......... Non-Volatile Field-Effect-Transistor [*Electronics*]
NW .... Newsweek [*A publication*] (BRI)
NWPYVO...... National Working Party of Youth Volunteer Organisers (AIE)
NWS .... New Workers Scheme (AIE)
NWSA Jnl .... NWSA Journal [*A publication*] (BRI)
nwspa......... Newspaper (VRA)
NX............... New Zealand Air Charter [*ICAO designator*] (AD)
NY............... New Yorker [*A publication*] (BRI)
NYCSCE....... New York Coffee, Sugar, and Cocoa Exchange (DFIT)
NYCTN,CA.... New York Cotton Exchange, Citrus Associates (DFIT)
NYDO.......... National Youth Development Officer (AIE)
nymphm ...... Nymphaeum (VRA)
NYRB.......... New York Review of Books [*A publication*] (BRI)
NYSPCC....... New York Society for the Prevention of Cruelty to Children
NYTBR......... New York Times Book Review [*A publication*] (BRI)
NYTLa......... New York Times (Late Edition) [*A publication*] (BRI)
NYWCC....... New York Water Color Club [*1890-1941*] (NGC)
NZE............. Nzerekore [*Guinea*] [*Airport symbol*] (AD)
N Zea......... New Zealand (VRA)

O

By Acronym

o .... Oil (VRA)
OA .... Office for Accreditation [*American Library Association*]
OAA .... Ontario Association of Architects [*1890*] [*Canada*] (NGC)
OAGCM .... Ocean-Atmosphere General Circulation Model [*Oceanography*]
o & c .... Onset and Course [*Medicine*] (AD)
o & cc .... Order and Change Control (AD)
o & d .... Origin and Destination (AD)
o & e .... Operations and Engineering (AD)
o & i .... Organizational and Intermediate (AD)
O & K .... Orenstein & Koppel (AD)
O & M .... Operation and Maintenance (AD)
OAQ .... Order of Architects of Quebec [*1974, founded 1890 as PQAA*] [*Canada*] (NGC)
OAS/EOM .... Organization of American States Electoral Observation Mission
OAS-OGN .... Organization of American States-Observer Group in Nicaragua
OB .... Opal Air [*ICAO designator*] (AD)
OBC .... Order of British Columbia [*Canada*] (DD)
o/bd .... Oil on Board (VRA)
OBE .... Officer of the Order of the British Empire (NGC)
OBI .... Obidos [*Brazil*] [*Airport symbol*] (AD)
OBI .... Operation Blessing International [*An association*]
obj .... Object (VRA)
obp .... Oxygen at High Pressure (AD)
obs .... Obscura (VRA)
Obs .... Observer (London) [*A publication*] (BRI)
obstl .... Obstruction Light (AD)
obstr .... Obstruction (AD)
obsv .... Observation (AD)
obsv .... Observatory (AD)
obsv .... Observer (AD)
ob syn .... Organic Brain Syndrome [*Medicine*] (AD)
obt .... Obedient (AD)
obt .... Obiit [*He Died*] [*Latin*] (AD)
OBT .... Overseas Branch Transfer (AD)
OBTA .... Oak Bark Tanners' Association (AD)
obtd .... Obtained (AD)
obts .... Offender-Based Transaction Statistics (AD)
OBU .... Operative Bootmakers Union (AD)
O Bul .... Old Bulgarian (AD)
o/bur .... Oil on Burlap (VRA)
obv .... Obverse (AD)
obv .... Obvious (AD)
obv .... Ocean Boarding Vessel (AD)
obv .... Octane Blending Value (AD)
obvy .... Obviously (AD)
Obw .... Oberwerk [*Highest Organ Bank*] [*German*] (AD)
obw .... Observation Window (AD)
OC .... Air California [*Air carrier designation symbol*] (AD)
OC .... Oberlin College (AD)
OC .... Oblate College (AD)
oc .... Obstetrical Conjugate [*Medicine*] (AD)
OC .... Occidental College (AD)
Oc .... Ocean (AD)
oc .... Ocean (AD)
OC .... Odessa College (AD)
oc .... Odor Control (AD)
OC .... Office Consultation (AD)
OC .... Officer in Charge (AD)
OC .... Officer of the Order of Canada (DD)
OC .... Ohio College (AD)
o/c .... Oil on Canvas (VRA)
OC .... Okolona College (AD)
OC .... Olivet College (AD)
OC .... Olympic College (AD)
oc .... On Camera (AD)
oc .... On Center (AD)
oc .... Open Charter (AD)
OC .... Open College (AIE)
o/c .... Open Cover (AD)
oc .... Open Cup (AD)
OC .... Opera-Comique [*Comic Opera*] [*French*] (AD)
OC .... Opera Company (AD)
oc .... Opere Citato [*In the Work Cited*] [*Latin*] (AD)
oc .... Optometric Corp. (AD)
oc .... Oral Contraceptive [*Medicine*] (AD)
o/c .... Organized Crime (AD)

OC .... Organo Corale [*Choir Organ*] [*Latin*] (AD)
OC .... Organ of Consultation
OC .... Oriel College (AD)
OC .... Orlando College (AD)
OC .... Otero College (AD)
o/c .... Overcharge (AD)
oc .... Overdraft Charge [*Banking*] (AD)
OC .... Overseas Chinese (AD)
OC-5 .... Organizing Committee for a Fifth Estate (AD)
oca .... Ocarina (AD)
OCA .... Office of the City Attorney (AD)
OCA .... Ohio College Association (AD)
OCA .... Oil Company of Australia (AD)
OCA .... Open Communications Architecture (AD)
OCA .... Oregon Corrections Association (AD)
OCAA .... Organization of Central American Armies (AD)
ocal .... On-Line Cryptanalytic Aid Language [*Computer science*] (AD)
OCAL .... Overseas Containers of Australia, Ltd. (AD)
OC & E .... Oregon, California, and Eastern Railroad (AD)
OCAQ .... Ordre de Comptables Agrees du Quebec [*Canada*] (DD)
OCAS .... Office of Civil Aviation Security (AD)
O Cat .... Old Catalan (AD)
OCAW .... Oil, Chemical, and Atomic Workers (AD)
ocb .... Oil Circuit Breaker (AD)
OCBC .... Overseas Chinese Banking Corp. (AD)
oc b/l .... Ocean Bill of Lading (AD)
occ .... Occasionally (AD)
Occ .... Occulting (AD)
occ .... Occupation (AD)
OCC .... Oklahoma Crime Commission (AD)
OCC .... Olney Communication College (AD)
OCC .... Onondaga Community College (AD)
occas .... Occasional (AD)
OCCC .... Oil Control Coordination Committee (AD)
OCCC .... Orange County Community College (AD)
OCCC .... Organized Crime-Control Commission [*California*] (AD)
Oc C Cm O.. Office of the Chief Chemical Officer (AD)
occd .... Occupied (AD)
OCCDC .... Oregon Coastal Conservation and Development Commission (AD)
OCCF .... Oklahoma City Community Foundation (AD)
occip .... Occipital (AD)
occl .... Occlude (AD)
OCCL .... Ontario Community College Librarians [*Canada*] (AD)
OCCSA .... Ohio Correctional and Court Services Association (AD)
occ th .... Occupational Therapy (AD)
occup .... Occupation (AD)
ocd .... Obsessive Compulsive Disorder [*Medicine*] (AD)
ocd .... On-Line Communications Driver [*Computer science*] (AD)
ocd .... Operational Capability Date (AD)
ocd .... Optical Character Definition [*Computer science*] (AD)
ocd .... Ovarian Cholesterol Depletion [*Medicine*] (AD)
o/cdbd .... Oil on Cardboard (VRA)
O/Cdt .... Officer-Cadet (AD)
oce .... Operational Control Equipment (AD)
Ocean Inst .. Oceanografiska Institute [*Oceanographic Institute*] [*Goeteborg, Sweden*] (AD)
oceano .... Oceanologist (AD)
oceanog ...... Oceanography (AD)
OCEL .... Optical Coating Evaluation Laboratory (AD)
OCEL .... Oxford Companion to English Literature [*A publication*] (AD)
O Celt .... Old Celtic (AD)
ocf .... Originally Cultured Formulation (AD)
OCF .... Ossining Correctional Facility [*Sing Sing*] (AD)
OCFR .... Oxford Committee for Family Relief [*British*] (AD)
OCFT .... Office of Curriculum Frameworks and Textbooks (AD)
OCG .... Oesterreichische Computer Gesellschaft [*Austrian Computer Society*] [*German*] (AD)
ocg .... Omnicardiogram [*Medicine*] (AD)
och .... Ochre (AD)
OCHS .... Old Colony Historical Society (AD)
OCI .... Office of the Coordinator of Information (AD)
OCI .... Operational Checkout Instruction (AD)
oci .... Organization Conflict of Interest (AD)
OCIB .... Organized Crime Intelligence Bureau (AD)
OCJA .... Oklahoma Criminal Justice Association (AD)
OCJP .... Office of Criminal Justice Planning (AD)

OCL.............. Ocean Cargo Line (AD)
ocl .... Operator Control Language (AD)
ocl .... Optical Communications Linkage (AD)
OCL.............. Overseas Container Line (AD)
OCL.............. Overseas Containers Ltd. (AD)
OCL/ACT ...... Overseas Container Lines and Associated Container Transport (AD)
OCLU .... Overseas Container Line Unit (AD)
ocm .... Oil Content Monitor (AD)
OCM.............. Oxford Companion to Music [*A publication*] (AD)
OCN .... Open College Network (AIE)
OCNAUD ...... Oficina del Coordinador de las Naciones Unidas para la Ayuda en los Desastres [*Office of the Coordinator of the United Nations for Help in Disasters*] [*Spanish*] (AD)
Ocn Bch ...... Ocean Beach (AD)
ocnl .... Occasional (AD)
OCNM .... Oregon Caves National Monument (AD)
OCO .... Ontario College of Ophthalmology [*Canada*] (AD)
oco.............. Open-Close-Open (AD)
OCOA .... Organismo Coordinador de Operaciones Antisubversivas [*Coordinating Organism of Antisubversive Operations*] [*Uruguay*] (AD)
OCOM .... Oficina Central de Organizacion y Metodos [*Central Office of Organization and Methods*] [*Spain*] (AD)
OComS .... Office of Community Services (AD)
OConUS ...... Outside Continental Limits of the United States (AD)
O Corn .... Old Cornish (AD)
OCP .... Office of Consumer Protection (AD)
OCP .... Office of Cultural Presentations (AD)
OCP .... Office of the Chief of Protocol [*US Department of State*] (AD)
OCP .... Oficina Central de Personal [*Central Personnel Office*] [*Spain*] (AD)
ocp.............. Output Control Pulses (AD)
ocp.............. Overland Common Points (AD)
OCPCJR ...... Office of Crime Prevention and Criminal Justice Research (AD)
OCPD .... Officer-in-Charge Police District (AD)
OCPL .... Oklahoma City Public Library (AD)
OCQ .... Membre de l'Ordre des Chimistes du Quebec [*Canada*] (DD)
OCR .... Office of the County Recorder (AD)
ocr .... Optical Character Reader [*Computer science*] (AD)
ocr .... Optical Character Recognition [*Computer science*] (AD)
OCR .... Oxidizable Carbon Ratio
OCRA .... Organisation Clandestine de la Revolution Algerienne [*Secret Organization of the Algerian Revolution*] [*France*] (AD)
ocre .... Optical Character Recognition Equipment [*Computer science*] (AD)
OCRE .... Organizations Concerned about Rural Education (AD)
ocrit .... Optical Character-Recognizing Intelligent Terminal [*Computer science*] (AD)
OCRSF .... Organized Crime and Racketeering Strike Force (AD)
OCRU .... Office of Communication and Research Utilization (AD)
ocs.............. Obstacle Clearance Surface (AD)
ocs.............. On Company Service (AD)
OCS .... Organe de Controle des Stupefiants [*Narcotic Drug Control Organization*] [*France*] (AD)
ocs.............. Outler Continental Shelf (AD)
OCS .... Overseas Civil Servants (AD)
OCS .... Overseas Courier Service (AD)
ocsf.............. Office Contents Special Form [*Inventor*] (AD)
ocsn.............. Occasion (AD)
ocsnl.............. Occasional (AD)
ocsnly.............. Occasionally (AD)
OCSPC .... Outer Continental Shelf Policy Committee [*California*] (AD)
ocst.............. Overcast (AD)
oct .... Octagon (AD)
oct .... Octal (AD)
oct .... Octane (AD)
Oct .... Octans (AD)
oct .... Octave (AD)
Oct .... Octavius (AD)
oct .... Octavo (AD)
oct .... Octet (AD)
Oct .... October (AD)
octe .... Optical Component Testing and Evaluation (AD)
oct pars ...... Octava Pars [*Eighth Part*] [*Latin*] (AD)
octr prot ...... Octrooi Protectie [*Patent Protected*] [*Dutch*] (AD)
octupl .... Octuplicate (AD)
octv.............. Open-Circuit Television (AD)
ocu.............. Operational Conversion Unit (AD)
OCUA .... Ontario Council on University Affairs [*Canada*] (AD)
OCUFA .... Ontario Confederation of University Facility Associations [*Canada*] (AD)
ocul .... Oculis [*To the Eyes*] [*Latin*] (AD)
oculent .... Oculentum [*Eye Ointment*] [*Latin*] (AD)
ocv.............. Open-Circuit Voltage (AD)
oc vu .... Ocean View (AD)
OCZ.............. Ocean Container Zebrugge (AD)
OD .... Emerald Airlines [*ICAO designator*] (AD)
od .... Och Dylika [*And the Like*] [*Swedish*] (AD)
od .... Oculus Dexter [*Right Eye*] [*Latin*] (AD)
od .... Odur [*or*] [*German*] (AD)
od .... Olive-Drab (AD)
od .... On Demand (AD)
od .... Optical Density (AD)
od .... Organizational Development (AD)
OD .... Organization Development [*Human resources*] (WYGK)
od .... Original Design (AD)
od .... Outside Diameter (AD)

od .... Outside Dimension (AD)
od .... Oven Dried (AD)
od .... Overdose (AD)
od .... Overdrive (AD)
oda .... Occipito-Dextra Anterior (AD)
Oda .... Odessa (AD)
ODA .... Office of Drug Abuse (AD)
ODA .... Office of the District Administrator (AD)
ODA .... Office of the District Attorney (AD)
ODa .... Old Danish (AD)
ODA .... Ouadda [*Central African Republic*] [*Airport symbol*] (AD)
ODA .... Overseas Development Assistance (AD)
odat .... One Day at a Time (AD)
odb .... Opiate-Directed Behavior (AD)
odb .... Output to Display Buffer [*Computer science*] (AD)
odc.............. Other Direct Costs (AD)
odc.............. Outer Dead Center (AD)
ODC.............. Overseas Development Corp. (AD)
ODCTI .... Old Dominion College Technical Institute (AD)
odd .... Operator Distance Dialing (AD)
ODE .... Oil Drilling and Exploration (AD)
ode .... One-Day Event (AD)
ODEC .... Ocean Design Engineering Corp. (AD)
ODECO .... Ocean Drilling and Exploration Co. (AD)
ODEPLAN .... Oficina de Planificacion Nacional [*Office of National Planning*] [*Spain*] (AD)
ODF .... Old Dominion Foundation (AD)
ODF .... Operational Deployment Force (AD)
odfc .... Outside Diameter of Female Coupling (AD)
ODH .... Ontario Department of Health [*Canada*] (AD)
ODI .... Open-Door International [*An association*] (AD)
ODIL .... Overseas Development Institute Ltd. (AD)
ODJ.............. Ouanda Djalle [*Central African Republic*] [*Airport symbol*] (AD)
ODL .... Cordillo Downs [*South Australia*] [*Airport symbol*] (AD)
ODL .... Object Definition Language [*Computer science*]
ODL .... Open and Distance Learning (AIE)
odlsq .... Odalisque (VRA)
odm .... Ophthalmodynamometry [*Ophthalmology*] (AD)
ODM .... Optimized Delivery Model [*Compaq*] [*Computer science*]
ODM .... Optimized Distribution Model [*Compaq Computer Corp.*] [*Computer science*]
ODM .... Order of De Molay (AD)
ODMA .... Optical Distributors and Manufacturers Association (AD)
odmc .... Outside Diameter of Male Coupling (AD)
Odn .... Odense (AD)
Odn.............. Odin (AD)
odn .... Own Doppler Nullifer (AD)
ODOE .... Oregon Department of Energy (AD)
odom .... Odometer (AD)
odont .... Odontology (AD)
odop .... Offset Doppler (AD)
odorl .... Odorless (AD)
ODOTS........ One-Day One-Trial System (AD)
odp.............. Occipito-Dextra Posterior (AD)
ODP .... Office of Disaster Preparedness (AD)
odp .... Order-Despatched (AD)
odr.............. Order (AD)
ODS .... Office of Defender Services (AD)
ods.............. Oxide Dispersion Strengthened (AD)
odsd.............. Overseas Duty Selection Date (AD)
ODSR .... Office of the Director of Scientific Research (AD)
odt .... Occipito-Dextra Transverse (AD)
odt .... Octal Debugging Technique (AD)
odt .... Odor Detection Threshold (AD)
odt .... One-Day Trials (AD)
odt .... On-Line Debugging Technique [*Computer science*] (AD)
ODT .... Otago Daily Times [*A publication*] (AD)
od units ...... Optical-Density Units (AD)
oe .... Oersted (AD)
oe .... Omissions Expected (AD)
o/e .... On Examination (AD)
oe .... Open End (AD)
oe .... Organizational Effectiveness (AD)
oe .... Organo Espressivo [*Swell Organ*] [*Italian*] (AD)
o/e .... Otitis Externa (AD)
oe .... Outdoor Education (AD)
OE .... Samoan [*ICAO designator*] (AD)
OEA.............. Oahu Education Association [*Hawaii*] (AD)
OEA.............. Office Executives Association (AD)
OEA.............. Office of Environmental Affairs (AD)
OEA.............. Ohio Education Association (AD)
OEA.............. Oregon Education Association (AD)
OEAA .... Oil Engineering Apprentices Association (AD)
OEB.............. Oregon Educational Broadcasting (AD)
OEC.............. Oesterreichischer Aero-Club [*Austrian Aero Club*] [*German*] (AD)
OEC.............. Oil Exporting Countries (AD)
oec.............. Organizational Entity Code (AD)
OECCNU...... Organizacion para la Educacion la Ciencia, y la Cultura [*Organization for Education, Science, and Culture*] [*United Nations*] (AD)
OECF .... Overseas Economic Cooperation Fund (AD)
oeco.............. Outboard Engine Cutoff (AD)
OECQ .... Organisation Europeene pour la Controle de la Qualite GG1European Quality-Control OrganizationGG2 [*France*] (AD)
oecu.............. Outboard Engine Cutoff (AD)
OEDP .... Office of Employment Development Programs (AD)

oee	Outer Enamel Epithelium (AD)
OEF	Osteopathic Educational Foundation (AD)
oegt	Observable Evidence of Good Teaching (AD)
OEHMO	Open-Ended Health Maintenance Organization [*Insurance*] (WYGK)
oei	Organizational Entity Identity (AD)
OEL/MA	Ohio Educational Library/Media Association (AD)
oem	Oil-Emulsion Mud (AD)
oem	Optical Electron Microscope (AD)
OEM	Original Equipment Manufacturer (AD)
oem	Original Equipment Manufacturer (AD)
OEMA	Office Equipment Manufacturers Association (AD)
oemcp	Optical Effects Module Electronic Controller and Processor (AD)
oen	Oenanthic (AD)
oen	Oenanthyl (AD)
oen	oenomancy (AD)
oen	oenomel (AD)
oen	oenometer (AD)
oen	oenophilist (AD)
oen	oenophobist (AD)
oen	oenopoetic (AD)
oeo	Officer's Eyes Only (AD)
OEO	Ordnance Engineer Overseer (AD)
OEP	Office of Emergency Planning (AD)
OEP	Open-Ended Plan [*Human resources*] (WYGK)
OEP	Optional Educational Programs (AD)
OEQC	Office of Environmental Quality Control (AD)
OER	Office of Aerospace Research [*Air Force*] (AD)
OER	Officer Engineering Reserve (AD)
OER	Organization for European Research (AD)
oer	Original Equipment Replacement (AD)
oerc	Optimum Earth-Reentry Corridor (AD)
OERPA	Office of Exploratory Research and Problem Assessment [*National Science Foundation*] (AD)
OES	Open-Ended System [*Computer science*]
OES	Organizacion de Estados Americanos [*Organization of American States*] [*Spain*] (AD)
OES	Organization of European States (AD)
oesbr	Oil-Extended Styrene-Butadiene Rubber (AD)
oesoph	Oesophagus (AD)
OESP	O Estado de Sao Paulo [*State of Sao Paulo*] [*Brazil*] [*A publication*] (AD)
OET	Office of Education and Training (AD)
OET	Overseas Exchange Transactions (AD)
OEVE	Office of Earthquakes, Volcanoes, and Engineering [*US Geological Survey*] (AD)
OEX	Standard & Poor's 100 Stock Index (DFIT)
OEZ	Osteuropaeische Zeit [*East European Time*] [*German*] (AD)
OF	Noosa Air [*ICAO designator*] (AD)
of	Old Face (AD)
of	Optional Form (AD)
of	Outside Face (AD)
0f	Ovenstone Factor (AD)
OF	Oxbow Falls (AD)
OF	Oxenstierna Foundation (AD)
OF	Oxford Foundation (AD)
o/f	Oxidation/Fermentation (AD)
o/f	Oxidizer to Fuel Ratio (AD)
of	Oxidizing Flame (AD)
OFA	Old Folks Association (AD)
ofc	Office (AD)
OFC	Open Financial Connectivity [*Microsoft Computer Software*] [*Computer Science*]
OFC	Overseas Food Corp. (AD)
OFCA	Ontario Federation of Construction Associations [*Canada*] (AD)
ofcl	Official (AD)
ofd	One-Function Diagram (AD)
ofd	Optical Fire Detector (AD)
OFE	Office of Fuels and Engergy (AD)
OFE	Ottawa Fundraising Executives [*Ontario, Canada*]
OFEMA	Office Francais d'Exportation de Materiel Aeronautique [*French Office for theExportation of Aeronautical Materiel*] (AD)
off	Office (DD)
Off	Officer (AD)
offen	Offensive (AD)
offeq	Office Equipment (AD)
offer	Offertories (AD)
offg	Offering (AD)
offic	Official (AD)
Office Pubns	Office Publications (AD)
off-st pkg	Off-Street Parking (AD)
ofhc	Oxygen-Free High-Carbon (AD)
ofhc	Oxygen-Free High Conductivity (AD)
OFI	Office of the Federal Inspector (AD)
ofic	Oficial [*Official*] [*Spanish*] (AD)
OFIC	Ohio Foundation of Independent Colleges (AD)
ofl	Official (AD)
Oflag	Offizierlager [*Officer's Prison Camp*] [*German*] (AD)
Ofly	Offaly (AD)
OFN	Ottawa Fundraisers Network [*Ontario, Canada*]
OFNS	Observer Foreign News Service (AD)
ofr	Off Frequency Rejection (AD)
OfR	Office for Research (AD)
O Fr	Old French (AD)
OFR-ALA	Office of Recruitment-American Library Association (AD)
OFris	Old Frisian (AD)

O Frk	Old Frankish (AD)
ofs	One-Function Sketch (AD)
OFS	Ontario Federation of Students [*Canada*] (AD)
OFST	Office of the Secretary of the Air Force (AD)
ofst	Offset (VRA)
OFSTED	Office for Standards in Education (AIE)
OFT	Ohio Federation of Teachers (AD)
OFTC	Overseas Finance and Trade Corp. (AD)
OFTS	Office of Technical Services (AD)
OFTS	Office of Transportation Security (AD)
OFTS	Officers Training School (AD)
OFTS	Overseas Fixed Telecommunications System (AD)
OFX	Open Financial Exchange [*Computer science*]
OFY	Opportunities for Youth [*Canada*] (AD)
OG	Air Guadeloupe [*ICAO designator*] (AD)
OG	Oesterreichische Galerie [*Austrian Gallery*] (AD)
og	Oh Gee (AD)
og	Oil Gland (AD)
OG	Old Gaelic (AD)
og	Old Girl (AD)
og	On Ground (AD)
og	On Guard (AD)
O/G	Opto/Graphic (AD)
o/g	Opto-Graphic (AD)
o-g	Orange-Green (AD)
og	Original Gum (AD)
o/g	Outgoing (AD)
O Gael	Old Gaelic (AD)
OGB	Oesterreichischer Gewerkschaftsbund [*Austrian Trade Union Federation*] [*German*] (AD)
OGD	Ogden [*Utah*] [*Airport symbol*] (AD)
Ogd	Ogdensburg (AD)
OGDC	Oil and Gas Development Corp. (AD)
oge	Operational Ground Equipment (AD)
OGELS	Observer Group in El Salvador
OGES	Operating Ground Equipment Specification [*Italian*] (AD)
ogf	Option Growth Fund (AD)
ogg	Oggetto [*Object*] [*Italian*] (AD)
OGI	Oesterreichische Gesseleschaft fuer Informatik [*Austrian Society for Information Processing*] [*German*] (AD)
OGI	Opera Guilds International (AD)
OGJ	Oil and Gas Journal [*A publication*] (AD)
ogl	Obscure Glass (AD)
OGNR	Oribi Gorge Nature Reserve [*South Africa*] (AD)
OGPU	Obiedinennoye Gosudartsvennoye Politicheskoye Upravlenie [*United State Political Administration*] [*Russian*] (AD)
OGR	Official Guide of the Railways [*A publication*] (AD)
OGR	Ontario Government Railway [*Canada*] (AD)
ogse	Operational Ground-Support Equipment (AD)
OGSR	Office of Graduate Studies and Research (AD)
o-g stain	Orange-Green Stain (AD)
ogt	On-Going Thing (AD)
ogt	Outlet Gas Temperature (AD)
ogv	Outlet Guide Vane (AD)
OH	Comair [*ICAO designator*] (AD)
OH	Hydroxyl Radical (AD)
OH	Ocular Herpes [*Medicine*] (AD)
oh	Office Hours (AD)
OH	Omega House (AD)
oh	Omni Hora [*Hourly*] [*Latin*] (AD)
oh	On Hand (AD)
o-H	On-Hudson (AD)
oh	Open Hearth (AD)
OH	Opera House (AD)
oh	Out Home (AD)
oh	Oval Head (AD)
o/h	Overhaul (AD)
oh	Overhead (AD)
OHA	Occupational Health Administration (AD)
OHA	Oriental Herb Association (AD)
oha	Outside Helix Angle (AD)
OH-B	Ocean Hill-Brownsville (AD)
OHC	Ocean Heat Convergence
OHC	Office of Humanities Communication (AD)
ohc	Outer Hair Cells (AD)
ohc	Overhead Cam (AD)
OHC	Overseas Hotel Corp. (AD)
OHCS	Office of Home Care Services (AD)
ohd	Organic Hearing Disease [*Medicine*] (AD)
ohd	Organic Heart Disease [*Medicine*] (AD)
OHD & W	Outer Harbor Dock and Wharf (AD)
oheat	Overheat (AD)
ohf	Omsk Hemorrhagic Fever (AD)
ohf	Overhaul Factor (AD)
ohi	Ocular Hypertension Indicator (AD)
OHI	Oil Heat Institute (AD)
Ohio Turn	Ohio Turnpike (AD)
Ohio U Pr	Ohio University Press (AD)
OHIP	Ontario Hospital Insurance Plan [*Canada*] (AD)
OHL	Oberste Herresleitung [*Supreme Headquarters*] [*German*] (AD)
ohm	Ohmmeter (AD)
ohm-cm	Ohm-Centimeter (AD)
OHMS	Onboard Health Monitoring System (AD)
OHNO	Occupational Health Nursing Officer (AD)
OHNS	Occupational Health Nursing Sister (AD)

oho .... Out-of-House Operation (AD)
ohp .... Overhead Projection (AD)
oh Ped .... Ohne Pedale [*Without Pedals*] [*German*] (AD)
ohrf .... Overhaul Replacement Factor (AD)
OHRG .... Official Hotel and Resort Guide [*A publication*] (AD)
OHS .... Ontario Humane Society [*Canada*] (AD)
ohs .... Open-Hearth Steel (AD)
OHS .... Oral Hygiene Service (AD)
OHS .... Organization of Historical Studies (AD)
OHSIP .... Ontario Health-Services Insurances Plan [*Canada*] (AD)
OHSPAC ..... Occupational Health-Safety-Programs Accreditation Commission (AD)
OHT .... Ocean Heat Transport
oht .... Overheating Temperature (AD)
ohv .... Overhead Valve (AD)
oi .... Oil-Immersed (AD)
o/i .... Opsonic Index (AD)
o-i .... Orgasmic Impairment (AD)
OI .... Oriental Institute (AD)
OIA .... Ocean Industries Association (AD)
OIA .... Office of Industrial Associates (AD)
OIA .... Optical Immunoassay [*Clinical chemistry*]
OIAB .... Oil Import Appeals Board (AD)
OIAC .... Organizacion Internacional de la Aviacion Civil [*International Civil Aviation Organization*] [*Spanish*] (AD)
OIAJ .... Office for Improvements in the Administration of Justice (AD)
OIB .... Ohio Inspection Bureau (AD)
OIB .... Oklahoma Inspection Bureau (AD)
OIC .... Office of the Insurance Commissioner (AD)
O-i-C .... Officer-in-Charge (AD)
OIC .... Oh, I See [*Computer science*] (DOM)
OIC .... Oil Industry Commission (AD)
O-I-C .... Organisation Interafricaine du Cafe [*Inter-African Coffee Organization*] [*French*] (AD)
OIC .... Overseas Investment Commission (AD)
OICA .... Ontario Institute of Chartered Accountants [*Canada*] (DD)
OICF .... Oklahoma Independent College Foundation (AD)
OICF .... Oregon Independent College Foundation (AD)
OICI .... Organizacion Interamericana de Cooperacion [*Inter-American Cooperation Organ ization*] [*Spanish*] (AD)
OICJ .... Office of International Criminal Justice (AD)
oid .... Original Issue Discount (AD)
OIE .... Office of International Epizootics (AD)
OIER .... Office of International Economic Research (AD)
OIG .... Organisation Intergouvernementale [*Inter-Governmental Organization*] [*French*] (AD)
OIH .... Ovulation-Producing Hormone [*Medicine*] (AD)
OII .... Office of Invention and Innovation (AD)
oiloff .... Oil Ripoff (AD)
OILSR .... Office of Interstate Land Sales Registration (AD)
OIM .... Oriental Institute Museum [*University of Chicago*] (AD)
OING .... Organisation Internationale Non-Gouvernementale [*Non-Governmental International Organization*] [*French*] (AD)
oint .... Ointment (AD)
OIO .... Oklahomans for Indian Opportunity (AD)
oip .... Oil in Place (AD)
OIP .... Ontario Institute of Painters, Toronto [*1958*] [*Canada*] (NGC)
oip .... Oxford India Paper (AD)
OIPC .... Organisation Internationale de Police Criminelle [*International Criminal Police Organization*] [*French*] (AD)
OIPH .... Office of International Public Health (AD)
OIQ .... Ordre des Ingenieurs du Quebec [*Canada*] (DD)
OIR .... Office of Inter-American Radio (AD)
OIr .... Old Irish (AD)
OIRB .... Oregon Insurance Rating Bureau (AD)
OIRM .... Office and Industrial Records Management (AD)
OIS .... Optical Imaging Systems (RDA)
OIS .... Overseas Investors Services (AD)
OISA .... Office of International Scientific Affairs (AD)
OISS .... Online Information Search Service [*Computer science*] (AD)
OISTV .... Organisation Internationale pour la Science et la Technique du Vide [*International Organization for Vacuum Science and Technology*] [*French*] (AD)
O i T .... Officer in Training (AD)
O lt .... Old Italian (AD)
OITP .... Office for Information Technology Policy [*American Library Association*]
OIVV .... Office Internationale de la Vigne et du Vin [*International Office of Vines and Wines*] [*French*] (AD)
OIW .... Oceanographic Institute Wellington New Zealand (AD)
OIWP .... Oil Industry Working Party (AD)
OJ .... Air Texana [*ICAO designator*] (AD)
oJ .... Ohne Jahr [*Without Year*] [*German*] (AD)
oj .... Open-Joint (AD)
oj .... Orange Juice (AD)
OJapan .... Order of Japan (DD)
OJC .... Organisation Juive de Combat [*Jewish Combat Organization*] [*French*] (AD)
OJEC .... Official Journal of the European Communities [*A publication*] (AD)
oji .... On-the-Job Injuries (AD)
OJJ .... Office of Juvenile Justice (AD)
oJr .... Old Jamaica Rum (AD)
ojt .... On-the-Job Training (AD)
OJW .... Otjiwarongo [*South-West Africa*] [*Airport symbol*] (AD)
OK .... Czechoslovak Airlines [*ICAO designator*] (AD)

ok .... Ohne Kosten [*Without Cost*] [*German*] (AD)
ok .... Ola Kala [*All is Fine*] [*Greek*] (AD)
ok .... Optical Klystron (AD)
ok .... Outer Keel (AD)
oka .... Otherwise Known As (AD)
Okin .... Okinawa (AD)
Okla .... Oklahoma (AD)
OklaC .... Oklahoma City (AD)
OKM .... Oberkommando der Marine [*Naval High Command*] [*Germany*] (AD)
okt .... Oktober [*October*] [*GRM*] (AD)
okt .... Oktyab [*October*] [*Russian*] (AD)
OKT .... Oslo Kommune Tunnelbanekontoret [*Oslo Subway System*] (AD)
Oktronics ..... Oklahoma Electronics (AD)
OKY .... Oakey [*Queensland*] [*Airport symbol*] (AD)
OL .... October League (AD)
ol .... Oculus Laevus [*Left Eye*] [*Latin*] (AD)
ol .... Oil Level (AD)
ol .... Oleum [*Oil*] [*Latin*] (AD)
Ol .... Olive [*Political party*] (AD)
OL .... Olsen Line (AD)
OL .... Open Learning (AIE)
ol .... Operating License (AD)
o/l .... Operations/Logistics (AD)
ol .... Or Less (AD)
o/l .... Outlook (AD)
ola .... Occipito-Laeva Anterior (AD)
OLA .... Ohio Library Association (AD)
OLA .... Oklahoma Library Association (AD)
OLA .... Ontario Library Association [*Canada*] (AD)
OLADE .... Organizacion Latin-Americana de Energia [*Latin American Energy Organization*] [*Spanish*] (AD)
ol & t .... Owners, Landlords, and Tenants (AD)
OLAPEC ...... Organization of Latin American Petroleum Exporting Countries (AD)
OLAS .... Office of Arid Land Studies [*University of Arizona*] (AD)
OLAS .... Organizacion Latino-Americana de Solidaridad [*Latin American Solidarity Organization*] [*Spanish*] (AD)
OLAS .... Organization of Latin American Students (AD)
Olav Tryg .... Olav Trygvason (AD)
olbm .... Orbital Launched Balistic Missile (AD)
OlBr .... Olive Brown (AD)
olc .... On-Line Computer (AD)
olcc .... Optimum Life-Cycle Costing (AD)
O L Cr .... Ordinance Lieutenant-Commander (AD)
OLCS .... On-Line Computer System (AD)
Old Bailey ... London's Central Criminal Court [*England*] (AD)
old-fash ...... Old Fashioned (AD)
Oldfos .... Old Established Forces (AD)
Old Maid's... Old Maid's Day [*June 4*] (AD)
old rep .... Old Repertory (AD)
Olds .... Oldsmobile (AD)
Old Test ...... Old Testament (AD)
OLE .... Olean [*New York*] [*Airport symbol*] (AD)
OLE .... Ontario Land Economist [*Canada*] (DD)
OLE .... Organizational Leadership for Executives [*Military*] (RDA)
OLEA .... Office of Law Enforcement Assistance (AD)
oleo .... Oleoresins (AD)
OLEP .... Office of Law Enforcement and Planning (AD)
olericult ...... Olericulture (AD)
O-levels ...... Ordinary Levels [*of educational tests*] (AD)
OLF .... Ohio Library Foundation (AD)
olf .... On-Line Filing (AD)
OLG .... Nordmaling [*Sweden*] [*Airport symbol*] (AD)
OlG .... Olive Green (AD)
Oli .... Oliver (AD)
O-license .... Operator's License (AD)
Olig .... Oligocene (AD)
Olive .... Olivera (AD)
OLL .... Office of Legislative Liaison (AD)
OLM .... Olympia [*Washington*] [*Airport symbol*] (AD)
OLMR .... Office of Labor Management Relations (AD)
olmr .... Organic Liquid-Moderator Reactor (AD)
OLN .... Colonia Sarmiento [*Argentina*] [*Airport symbol*] (AD)
OLO .... Olomouc [*Czechoslovakia*] [*Airport symbol*] (AD)
ol ol .... Olive Oil (AD)
olos .... Out of Line of Sight (AD)
olow .... Orbiter Liftoff Weight (AD)
olp .... Occipito-Laeva Posterior (AD)
OLP .... Open Learning Programme (AIE)
OLP .... Organizacion para la Liberacion Palestina [*Palestinian Liberation Organization*] [*Spanish*] [*Political party*] (AD)
olp .... Original List Price (AD)
olpar .... Other Large Phased-Array RADAR (AD)
olq .... Officer-Like Qualities (AD)
olr .... Overload Relay (AD)
OLRB .... Ontario Labor Relations Board [*Canada*] (AD)
ol res .... Oleoresin (AD)
olrt .... On-Line Real Time [*Computer science*] (AD)
OLS .... Ontario Land Surveyor [*Canada*] (DD)
olsc .... On-Line Scientific Computer (AD)
olt .... Occipito-Laeva Transverse (AD)
Olt .... Old Italian (AD)
oltt .... On-Line Teller Terminal [*Computer science*] (AD)
olv .... Olivaceous (AD)
olv .... Olive (AD)
olv .... On-Line Validation [*Computer science*] (AD)

OLV	Onze Lieve Vrouw [Our Lady] [Dutch] (AD)
Oly	Olympia (AD)
Oly	Olympic (AD)
Olym	Olympia (AD)
Olympic	Olympic National Park, Washington (AD)
OM	Air Mongol [ICAO designator] (AD)
Om	Book of Omni (AD)
OM	Member of the Order of Merit [Canada] (DD)
om	Old Man (AD)
om	Old Measurement (AD)
Om	Omaha (AD)
Om	Oman (AD)
om	Omni Mane [Every Morning] [Latin] (AD)
om	Operational Monitor (AD)
Om	Ordinance Map (AD)
om	Organic Matter (AD)
om	Our Memo (AD)
om	Outer Marker (AD)
OMA	Ocean Mining Administration (AD)
OMA	Office of Maritime Affairs (AD)
Oma	Omaha, Nebraska (AD)
OMA	Ontario Medical Association [Canada] (AD)
oma	Orderly Marketing Arrangement (AD)
OMA	Overall Manufacturers' Association (AD)
omarb	Omarbetad [Revised] [Swedish] (AD)
OMARS	Outstanding Media Advertising by Restaurants (AD)
Omb	Ombudsman (AD)
OMBAC	Old Mission Beach Athletic Club (AD)
om bid	Omnibus Bidendis [Every Two Days] [Latin] (AD)
omd	Off-Market Date (AD)
omdr	Off-Market Date Received (AD)
OMDR	Optical Memory Disc Recorder (DOM)
OMEGA	Optimal Missile Engagement Guidance Algorithm (AD)
OMEL	Orient Mid-East Lines (AD)
O-Mess	Officer's Mess [Military] (AD)
OMF	Office of Management and Finance (AD)
OMF	Open Media Framework (DOM)
omfp	Obtaining Money by False Pretenses (AD)
OMG	Opthalmology Medical Group (AD)
OMH	Office of Mental Health (AD)
OMI	Olympic Media Information (AD)
OMI	Organizacion Maritima Internacional [International Maritime Organization] [Spanish] (AD)
OMII	Oxy Metal Industries International (AD)
omiom	Original Meaning is the Only Meaning (AD)
omit	Orinthine-Decarboxylase, Motility, Indole, Trytophandeaminase (AD)
omkr	Omdring [About] [Norwegian] (AD)
OML	Ontario Motor League [Canada] (AD)
oml	Outside Mold Line (AD)
OMLAC	Oxfordshire Modern Languages Achievement Certificate [British] (AIE)
OMLJ	Officer of Merit, Order of St. Lazarus of Jerusalem (DD)
OMM	Officer of the Order of Military Merit [Canada] (DD)
omn bih	Omni Bihora [Every Two Hours] [Latin] (AD)
omni	Omnirange (AD)
omni	Omnivisual (AD)
omni	Onmidirectional (AD)
omn man	Omni Mane [Every Morning] [Latin] (AD)
omn noct	Omni Nocte [Every Night] [Latin] (AD)
OMO	Mostar [Yugoslavia] [Airport symbol] (AD)
omor	One Man, One Responsibility (AD)
omp	Organo-Metallic Polymer (AD)
ompa	One-Man Pension Arrangement (AD)
ompf	Omphaloskepsis (AD)
OMPO	Oahu Metropolitan Planning Organization [Hawaii] (AD)
ompr	Optical Mark Page Reader (AD)
OMPRA	Office of Minerals Policy and Research Analysis (AD)
OMPU	Oficina Municipale de Planeamiento Urbano [Municipal Office of Urban Planning] [Spain] (AD)
omr	Office Methods Research (AD)
omr	Optical Mark Reader (AD)
omr	Optical Mark Recognition (AD)
OMRD	Overseas Mineral Resource Development (AD)
oms	Output per Man Shift (AD)
OMSIP	Ontario Medical Surgical Insurance Plan [Canada] (AD)
OMT	Oral Mucosal Transudate [Clinical chemistry]
omt	Orthomode Transducer (AD)
ON	Air Nauru [ICAO designator] (AD)
on	Octane Number (AD)
ON	Ogden Nash (AD)
on	Omni Nocte [Every Night] [Latin] (AD)
on	Onomastikon [Lexicon] [Greek] (AD)
On	Onorevole [Honorable] [Italian] (AD)
On	Onsdag [Wednesday] [Danish] (AD)
ON	Ontario Northland Railway [Canada] (AD)
ON	Opera News [A publication] (BRI)
o/n	Own Name (AD)
ONA	Winona [Minnesota] [Airport symbol] (AD)
ONB	Monkey Bay [Malawi] [Airport symbol] (AD)
ONE	Open Network Environment [Netscape network] [Computer science]
OnIssues	On the Issues [A publication] (BRI)
ONM	Condamine [Queensland] [Airport symbol] (AD)
ONO	Ontario [Oregon] [Airport symbol] (AD)
ONR	Monkira [Queensland] [Airport symbol] (AD)
Ont	Ontario [Canada] (DD)
ONU	Kongoussi [Upper Volta] [Airport symbol] (AD)
onx	Onyx (VRA)
OO	Sunaire Lines [ICAO designator] (AD)
OOB	Off Our Backs [A publication] (BRI)
OOL	Coolangatta [Queensland] [Airport symbol] (AD)
OOnt	Order of Ontario [Canada] (DD)
OOR	Mooraberrie [Queensland] [Airport symbol] (AD)
OP	Air Panama Internacional [ICAO designator] (AD)
o/p	Oil on Panel (VRA)
o/pa	Oil on Paper (VRA)
OPALs	Older People with Active Lifestyles [Lifestyle classification]
OPEN	Online Public Education Network
oper	Operation (DD)
OPK	Operative Personenkontrolle [Operational Person Control] [German]
OPM	Operating Procedure for Ministers
OPM	Owner President Management Program (DD)
OPRI	Office de Protection contre les Rayonnements Ionisants [France]
OPS	Obstacle Planner Software (RDA)
OPS	Occupational Preparation Scheme (AIE)
OPS	Open Profiling Standard [Firefly Network] [Computer science]
Opticam	Optics Automation and Management (RDA)
OPTIS	Oxfordshire Project for the Training of Instructors and Supervisors [British] (AIE)
OPTYP	Opalotype (VRA)
OPUS	Optical Prism Uniformity System
OQ	Ordre du Quebec [Order of Quebec] [Canada] (DD)
OQ	Royale Airlines [ICAO designator] (AD)
OR	Air Comores [ICAO designator] (AD)
ORA	Oran [Argentina] [Airport symbol] (AD)
ORACLE	Observation Research and Classroom Learning Evaluation (AIE)
ORE	Greenfield [Massachusetts] [Airport symbol] (AD)
ORF	Olfactory Research Fund
OrgBehav	Organizational Behaviour (DD)
orig	Origin (VRA)
ORM	Northampton [England] [Airport symbol] (AD)
orm	Ormolu (VRA)
ornam	Ornament (VRA)
ORO	Porto Seguro [Brazil] [Airport symbol] (AD)
ORP	Ormara [Pakistan] [Airport symbol] (AD)
ORS	Office for Research & Statistics [American Library Association]
orthg	Orthogonals (VRA)
ORU	Oruro [Bolivia] [Airport symbol] (AD)
ORW	Orange Walk [British Honduras] [Airport symbol] (AD)
ORX	Oriximina [Brazil] [Airport symbol] (AD)
OS	Austrian Airlines [ICAO designator] (AD)
OS	Other Side [A publication] (BRI)
OSC	Occupational Standards Council (AIE)
OSCAR II	Outside Cable Rehabilitation II [Army] (RDA)
OSM	Mosul [Iraq] [Airport symbol] (AD)
OSM	On-Screen Manager [Computer science]
OSRP	Oil Spill Response Plan [Pollution prevention]
ostk	Oilstick (VRA)
OT	Evergreen Helicopters of Alaska [ICAO designator] (AD)
OT	Occupational Training (AIE)
OT	Open Transport [Computer science]
OTA	Mota [Ethiopia] [Airport symbol] (AD)
OTC	Bol [Chad] [Airport symbol] (AD)
OTD	Optical Transient Detector
oth	Other (VRA)
OTIS	One Term In-Service Course (AIE)
OTL	Boutilimit [Mauritania] [Airport symbol] (AD)
OTTSU	Open Tech Training Support Unit (AIE)
OTV	Otavi [South-West Africa] [Airport symbol] (AD)
OTW	Owning the Weather [Army] (RDA)
OU	City Express [ICAO designator] (AD)
OU	Otonabee Airways [ICAO designator] (AD)
OUDS	Oxford University Dramatic Society [British] (AIE)
OUG	Ouahigouya [Upper Volta] [Airport symbol] (AD)
OUI	Ban Houei Sai [Laos] [Airport symbol] (AD)
OUT	Bousso [Chad] [Airport symbol] (AD)
outl	Outline (VRA)
ov	Over (VRA)
OW	Trans Mountain Airlines [ICAO designator] (AD)
OWB	Owensboro [Kentucky] [Airport symbol] (AD)
OWBPA	Older Workers Benefit Protection Act of 1990 (WYGK)
OWR	Order of the White Rose of Finland (DD)
OX	Air Atlantic Airlines [ICAO designator] (AD)
ox	Oxides (VRA)
OXC	Waterbury [Connecticut] [Airport symbol] (AD)
OXF	Oxford [England] [Airport symbol] (AD)
OXO	Orientos [Queensland] [Airport symbol] (AD)
OY	New Jersey Airways [ICAO designator] (AD)
OYK	Oiapoque [Brazil] [Airport symbol] (AD)

P

By Acronym

p .... Panel (VRA)
P .... Polytechnic (AIE)
pa .... Paper (VRA)
PAB .... Pedro Afonso [*Brazil*] [*Airport symbol*] (AD)
PABA .... Pro-Am Bowfishing Association
PAC .... Planned Amortization Class [*Investment term*] (DFIT)
PAC .... Political Action Committee
PAC .... Pre-Authorized Chequing [*Canada*]
PAC .... Priority Area Children (AIE)
PAC .... Public Awareness Committee [*American Library Association*]
Pac A .... Pacific Affairs [*A publication*] (BRI)
PACE .... Parental Alliance for Choice in Education (AIE)
PACE .... Public Affairs Council for Education [*Canada*]
Pac S .... Pacific Studies [*A publication*] (BRI)
PACT .... Parents, Children, and Teachers (AIE)
PAdm .... Professional Administrator (DD)
PAF .... Paraburdoo [*Western Australia*] [*Airport symbol*] (AD)
PAG .... Panjim [*India*] [*Airport symbol*] (AD)
PAg .... Professional Agrologist (DD)
PAH .... Polycyclic Aromatic Hydrocarbon
PAIRS .... Parent Assisted Instruction in Reading and Spelling (AIE)
Pak .... Pakistan (VRA)
pal .... Palette (VRA)
PAL .... Passive Activity Loss [*Investment term*] (DFIT)
PAL .... Premier Automobiles Ltd. [*India*]
pala .... Palace (VRA)
pala .... Palazzo (VRA)
Pale .... Palestine (VRA)
Paleol .... Paleolithic (VRA)
Pan .... Panama (VRA)
PANA .... Panorama (VRA)
panchr .... Panchromatic (VRA)
P&I .... Principal and Interest [*Finance*] (DFIT)
P&L .... Profit and Loss Statement [*Finance*] (DFIT)
p&m .... Probate and Matrimonial (AD)
P & N .... Piedmont and Northern Railroad (AD)
p & n .... Psychiatry and Neurology (AD)
p & o .... Paints and Oil (AD)
P & O .... Peninsular & Occidental Steamship Co. (AD)
p & o .... Pickled and Oiled (AD)
p & oo .... Pianistic and Orchestral Orgasm [*Music*] (AD)
p & p .... Parsimonious and Penurious (AD)
p&p .... Payments and Progress (AD)
p & pp .... Pull and Push Plate (AD)
P & PU .... Peoria and Pekin Union [*Railroad*] (AD)
p & q .... Peace and Quiet (AD)
p & r .... Parallax and Refraction (AD)
P&R .... Parks & Recreation [*A publication*] (BRI)
PANS .... Priority Admission to Nursery Schools (AIE)
pap .... Papyrus (VRA)
pAP .... Presynaptic Action Potential [*Neurochemistry*]
PAPT .... Palladium Print (VRA)
Par .... Parents Magazine [*A publication*] (BRI)
PAR .... Preadmission Review (WYGK)
PAR .... Public Administration Review [*A publication*] (BRI)
Parameters... Parameters: US Army War College Quarterly [*A publication*] (BRI)
parc .... Parchment (VRA)
Par Ch .... Parents' Choice [*A publication*] (BRI)
PARG .... Polytechnic Academic Registrars' Group (AIE)
PARIS .... Portable Automated Remote Inspection System [*Failure Analysis Associates*] (RDA)
Parnassus.... Parnassus: Poetry in Review [*A publication*] (BRI)
PARS .... Preservation & Reformatting Section [*Association for Library Collections and Technical Services*] [*American Library Association*]
part.............. Partial (VRA)
parti bd........ Particle Board (VRA)
PASB .... Pan American Sanitary Bureau
Pass........... Passage (DD)
PASS .... Professional Accounting System for Schools (AIE)
pat .... Patina (VRA)
pavl .... Pavilion (VRA)
PAYG .... Pay-As-You-Go
PAYSOP....... Payroll-Based Stock Option Plan [*Human resources*] (WYGK)
PB .... Air Burundi [*ICAO designator*] (AD)

PBMS........... Performance-Based Measurement System [*Environmental Protection Agency*]
PBR .... Price-to-Book Value Ratio [*Investment term*] (DFIT)
PBR .... Puerto Barrios [*Guatemala*] [*Airport symbol*] (AD)
PBS .... Plettenberg Bay [*South Africa*] [*Airport symbol*] (AD)
PBS .... Public Broadcasting System
PBY .... Pillars Bay [*Alaska*] [*Airport symbol*] (AD)
PC .... Fiji Air [*ICAO designator*] (AD)
PC .... Parents' Charter (AIE)
pc .... Piece (VRA)
PCA .... Potato Carrot Agar [*Culture Media*]
PCA .... Program Calibration Area [*Computer science*] (DOM)
PCAC .... Professional Classes Aid Council (AIE)
PCC .... Permanent Consultative Committee
PCC .... Program for Cooperative Cataloging [*American Library Association*]
PCC .... Puerto Rico [*Colombia*] [*Airport symbol*] (AD)
PCCC .... Polytechnics and Colleges Computer Committee (AIE)
PC-DOS....... Personal Computer-Disk Operating System (DOM)
PCE .... Palm Island [*Queensland*] [*Airport symbol*] (AD)
PCH .... Pari-Cachoeira [*Brazil*] [*Airport symbol*] (AD)
pch .... Porch (VRA)
PCI .... Press Control, Inc.
PCL .... Printer Command Language [*Hewlett Packard*] [*Computer science*]
PCMCIA ...... Portable Computer Memory Card Industry Association (DOM)
PCN .... PointCast Network [*Computer science*]
PCO .... Principal Careers Officer (AIE)
PCOAS........ Permanent Council of the Organization of American States
PCT .... Private Communications Technology [*Computer science*]
PCZ .... Panama Canal Zone [*Panama*] [*Airport symbol*] (AD)
PD............... Pem Air [*ICAO designator*] (AD)
PDA .... Personal Digital Assistant [*Computer science*]
PDA .... Pregnancy Discrimination Act of 1978 (WYGK)
PDCC .... Print and Drawing Council of Canada [*1976*] (NGC)
PDE .... Professional Development Education [*Military*] (RDA)
PDES .... Phase Image of Poly(diethylsiloxane) [*Organic chemistry*]
PDF .... Platform Independent File Format [*Computer science*]
PDGF .... Platelet-Derived Growth Factor [*Medicine*]
pdm .... Podium (VRA)
PDO .... Prado [*Brazil*] [*Airport symbol*] (AD)
PDP .... Prescription Drug Plan [*Insurance*] (WYGK)
PDS .... Piedras Negras [*Mexico*] [*Airport symbol*] (AD)
pdstl .... Pedestal (VRA)
PDUFA......... Prescription Drug User Fee Act
pe .... Pen (VRA)
PE .... People Express [*ICAO designator*] (AD)
PE .... Price Earnings Ratio [*Investment term*] (DFIT)
PE .... Primary Education (AIE)
PEA .... Pennsylvania Electric Association
pearwd .... Pear Tree Wood (VRA)
PECIACESC.. Permanent Executive Committee of the Inter-American Council for Education, Science, and Culture
PECIAECOSOC... Permanent Executive Committee of the Inter-American Economic and Social Council
pedm .... Pediment (VRA)
PEGS .... Project Engineering System
pe/i .... Pen and Ink (VRA)
PEK............. Peking [*China*] [*Airport symbol*] (AD)
PEL .... Paid Educational Leave (AIE)
PEL .... Personal Effectiveness Inventory (AIE)
PEMN.......... Program Engineering Management Network [*Computer science*] (RDA)
pend .... Pendant (VRA)
PEng .... Registered Professional Engineer (DD)
Pentl........... Pentelic (VRA)
pentu .... Pentateuch (VRA)
PEP .... Prolyl Endopeptidase
PEPES........ People Persecuted by Pablo Escobar
PEPP .... Permanent-Equity Pension Plan [*Human resources*] (WYGK)
per............. Period (VRA)
Per .... Persia (VRA)
Per A J .... Performing Arts Journal [*A publication*] (BRI)
perf............. Performance (VRA)
peric .... Pericope (VRA)
perp .... Perpendicular (VRA)
Per Psy....... Personnel Psychology [*A publication*] (BRI)
pers .... Personnel (DD)
```
```

persp .... Perspective (VRA)
Pers PS ...... Perspectives on Political Science [*A publication*] (BRI)
PERT/CPM ... Program Evaluation and Review Technique/Critical Path Method [*Computer science*] (DOM)
PESD .... Private and Executive Secretary's Diploma (AIE)
Pet .... Petroleum (DD)
PETE .... Portable Educational Tools Environment (AIE)
Pet PM .... Petersen's Photographic Magazine [*A publication*] (BRI)
petrgly .... Petroglyph (VRA)
PEV .... Positive Expected Value
PEVE .... Post Experience Vocational Education (AIE)
pew .... Pewter (VRA)
PF .... Pro Female [*International Bowhunting Organization*] [*Class Equipment*]
PF .... Trans Pennsylvania Airlines [*ICAO designator*] (AD)
PFD .... Preferred Stock [*Investment term*] (DFIT)
PFR .... Port Francqui [*Zaire*] [*Airport symbol*] (AD)
PFS .... Pay for Skills [*Human resources*] (WYGK)
PG .... Florida Commuter [*ICAO designator*] (AD)
pg .... Page (VRA)
PGA .... Pin-Grid Arrays
PGB .... Personal Guidance Base (AIE)
PGeol .... Professional Geologist (DD)
PGeoph .... Professional Geophysicist (DD)
PGH .... Pantnagar [*India*] [*Airport symbol*] (AD)
PGM .... Palenque [*Mexico*] [*Airport symbol*] (AD)
PGRV .... Photogravure (VRA)
PGSS .... Paget-Gorman Sign System (AIE)
PGT .... Porangatu [*Brazil*] [*Airport symbol*] (AD)
PH .... Penthouse (DD)
Pharm .... Pharmacy (DD)
PHENG .... Photoengraving (VRA)
PHET .... Photoetching (VRA)
PHGNDWG .. Photogenic (VRA)
PHGRM .... Photogram (VRA)
PHH .... Phan Thiet [*South Vietnam*] [*Airport symbol*] (AD)
Phil .... Philippines (VRA)
Phil .... Philosophy (DD)
PHIL .... Potential Host Institures List [*European Commission*]
Phil R .... Philosophical Review [*A publication*] (BRI)
PHLITHO ..... Photolithographic (VRA)
PHN .... Port Huron [*Michigan*] [*Airport symbol*] (AD)
photmur ...... Photo Mural (VRA)
photo .... Photograph (VRA)
photomon .... Photomontage (VRA)
PHR .... Pacific Historical Review [*A publication*] (BRI)
PhRMA .... Pharmaceutical Research and Manufacturers of America
PHS .... Physicians' Health Study
PHV .... Pahlavi [*Iran*] [*Airport symbol*] (AD)
Phys .... Physics (DD)
Phys Today... Physics Today [*A publication*] (BRI)
PIC .... Picos [*Brazil*] [*Airport symbol*] (AD)
PICS .... Platform for Internet Content Selection [*Computer science*]
PICS .... Platform for Internet Content Specification [*Computer science*]
pictg .... Pictograph (VRA)
PIE .... Clearwater-St. Petersburg [*Florida*] [*Airport symbol*] (AD)
PIF .... Project in Foreign Language Pedagogy (AIE)
PIK .... Prestwick [*Scotland*] [*Airport symbol*] (AD)
PIK Securities... Payment-in-Kind Securities [*Investment term*] (DFIT)
pil .... Pilaster (VRA)
PIM .... Personal Information Manager [*Computer science*]
PIN .... Parintins [*Brazil*] [*Airport symbol*] (AD)
PIN .... Power Information Network [*Computer science*]
PIP .... Parental Involvement Project (AIE)
PITYP .... Pinatype (VRA)
PIU .... Pathological Internet Use
PJ .... Air St. Pierre [*ICAO designator*] (AD)
pk .... Park (VRA)
Pk .... Park (DD)
PKB .... Protein Kinase B [*An enzyme*]
PKC .... Phuket [*Thailand*] [*Airport symbol*] (AD)
PKY .... Pak Lay [*Laos*] [*Airport symbol*] (AD)
Pky .... Parkway (DD)
PKZ .... Pakse [*Laos*] [*Airport symbol*] (AD)
PL .... Aero Peru [*ICAO designator*] (AD)
pl .... Pencil (VRA)
pl .... Piazza (VRA)
pl .... Place (VRA)
Pl .... Place (DD)
pl .... Platz (VRA)
pl .... Plaza (VRA)
pla .... Plaster (VRA)
PLAB .... Professional and Linguistic Assessment Board (AIE)
PLAD .... Public Lands Appreciation Day
PLand .... Professional Landman [*Canada*] (DD)
PLANET....... Probing Lensing Anomalies Network [*Astronomy*]
plas .... Plastic (VRA)
plat .... Plate (VRA)
platn .... Platinum [*Metal*] (VRA)
PLC .... Planeta Rica [*Colombia*] [*Airport symbol*] (AD)
PLC .... Provisional Legislative Council [*Hong Kong*]
PLC .... Public Liability Company (DFIT)
PLE .... Professional Land Economist [*Canada*] (DD)
plexg .... Plexiglass (VRA)
PLF .... Pala [*Chad*] [*Airport symbol*] (AD)

PLMES......... Planning, Measurements & Evaluation Section [*Public Library Association*] [*American Library Association*]
plr............... Poplar (VRA)
PLR............. Primary Language Record [*Education*] (AIE)
PLRD .... Polaroid (VRA)
Pltrsq......... Plateresque (VRA)
PLTYP......... Plumbeotype (VRA)
ply .... Plywood (VRA)
plyc........... Polychrome (VRA)
plyes.......... Polyester (VRA)
plym .... Polymer (VRA)
plypt .... Polyptic (VRA)
plyst.......... Polystyrene (VRA)
plyur.......... Polyurethane (VRA)
plyvn......... Polyvinyl (VRA)
Plz .... Plaza (AD)
P/M............ Pacific Molasses (AD)
pm .... Papier Mache (VRA)
pm .... Paramilitary (AD)
PM .... Peabody Museum (AD)
p-m............ Permanent Magnet (AD)
PM .... Petroleos Mexicanos [*Spanish*] (AD)
p-m............ Phase Modulation (AD)
PM .... Pilgrim Airlines [*ICAO designator*] (AD)
pm .... Poids Moliculaire [*Molecular Weight*] [*French*] (AD)
pm .... Post Meridiem [*After noon*] [*Latin*] (AD)
pm .... Post Mortem (AD)
pm .... Premium (AD)
pm .... Premolar [*Dentistry*] (AD)
pm .... Presystolic Murmur [*Medicine*] (AD)
pm .... Preventive Maintenance (AD)
pm .... Program Manager (AD)
pm .... Publicity Man (AD)
pm .... Pulse Modulation (AD)
pm .... Pumice (AD)
pma .... Paramethoxyamphetamine (AD)
PMA .... Parts Manufacturing Associates (AD)
PMA .... Philadelphia Museum of Art (AD)
PMA .... Photo Marketing Association (AD)
pma .... Positive Mental Attitude (AD)
PMA .... Programa Mundial de Alimentos [*World Food Program*] [*Spanish*] (AD)
PMAE.......... Peabody Museum of Archeology and Ethnology (AD)
PM & OA .... Printers' Managers and Overseers Association (AD)
pm & r........ Physical Medicine and Rehabilitation (AD)
PM-ASI .... Program Management Office for Armored Systems Integration [*Army*] (RDA)
pmb .... Post-Menopausal Bleeding [*Medicine*] (AD)
PMBC.......... Pacific Motor Boat Club (AD)
PMBC.......... Portland Motor Boat Club [*Oregon*] (AD)
pmbo.......... Participative Management by Objectives (AD)
PMBOK .... Project Management Body of Knowledge
pmbx.......... Private Manual Branch Exchange (AD)
PMC .... Pennsylvania Military Academy (AD)
pmc .... Precision Mirror Calorimeter (AD)
pmc .... Preventive Maintenance Contract (AD)
PMC .... Project Management Committee (AD)
pMc .... Pure Mexican Cocaine (AD)
pmcs .... Process Monitoring and Control Systems (AD)
Pmd .... Portmadoc (AD)
pmd .... Post-Mortem Dumps (AD)
PMD........... Program for Management Development [*Harvard Business School*] (DD)
pmd .... Projected Map Display (AD)
PMD/BMI .... Project Management Division/Batelle Memorial Institute (AD)
PMDC .... Pakistan Minerals Development Corp. (AD)
pmds .... Projected Map Display Set (AD)
pme .... Performance-Measuring Equipment (AD)
PME .... Personnel Management for Executives [*Military*] (RDA)
pme .... Planning, Management, Evaluation (AD)
P Me............ Portland, Maine (AD)
PME .... Portsmouth [*England*] [*Airport symbol*] (AD)
pme .... Protective Multiple Earthing (AD)
PMEL .... Precision Measuring Equipment Laboratory (AD)
pmest .... Personality, Matter, Energy, Space, Time (AD)
pmet .... Painted Metal (AD)
PMF............ Presidential Medal of Freedom (AD)
pmf .... Probable Maximum Flooding (AD)
pmf .... Progressive Massive Fibrosis [*Medicine*] (AD)
PMF............ Pro Male Fingers [*International Bowhunting Organization*] [*Class equipment*]
PmG............ Paymaster General (AD)
PmG............ Postmaster General (AD)
PMgr........... Professional Manager (DD)
pmh .... Past Medical History (AD)
pmh .... Probable Maximum Hurricane (AD)
PMHP .... Primary Mental Health Project (AD)
PMI .... Palma de Mallorca Balearic Islands, Spain (AD)
PMI .... Partai Muslimin Indonesia [*Indonesian Muslim Party*] [*Political party*] (AD)
pmi .... Photographic Micro-Image (AD)
pmi .... Point of Maximum Impulse (AD)
PMI .... Pre-Marital Inventory (AD)
pmi .... Private Mortgage Insurance (AD)
PMIC.......... President's Management Improvement Council (AD)

PMIG .... Political-Military Interdepartmental Group (AD)
PMIS........... Planning Management Information System (AD)
PMIS........... Product Management Information System (AD)
PMJ .... Porto Murtinho [Brazil] [Airport symbol] (AD)
PMJC.......... Pine Manor Junior College (AD)
pmk .... Pitch Mark (AD)
pmk .... Postmark (AD)
PML .... Pacific Micronesian Line (AD)
pml............. Probable Maximum Loss (AD)
pmla .... Parmelia (AD)
PMLA......... Publication of the Modern Language Association of America (AD)
PMLD......... Profound and Multiple Learning Difficulties (AIE)
PMLO......... Principal Military Landing Officer (AD)
pmm .... Pulse Mode Multiplex (AD)
pmma .... Polymethylmethacrylate (AD)
pmmu .... Paged Memory-Management Unit (AD)
pmn .... Polymorphonuclear Neutrophil (AD)
pmn .... Producto Material Neto [Net Material Product] [Spain] (AD)
PMNA .... Pacific Mountain Network Association (AD)
PMNA .... Parkers Marsh Natural Area [Virginia] (AD)
PMNH .... Peabody Museum of Natural History (AD)
pmnl........... Polymorphonuclear Leukocyte (AD)
pmnr.......... Periadenitis Mucosa Necrotica Recurrens (AD)
PM NV/RSTA... Project Manager for Night Vision/Reconnaissance Surveillance and
                    Target Acquisition [Military] (RDA)
pmo .... Palomar Mountain Observatory (AD)
pmo .... Pianissimo [Very Softly] [Italian] [Music] (AD)
pmo .... Printed Matter Only (AD)
P Mor .... Port Moresby (AD)
PMOSC .... Primary Military Occupational Code (AD)
pmp .... Per-Member Payment (AD)
pmp .... Precious Metal Plating (AD)
PMP............ Preliminary Management Plan (AD)
pmp .... Previous Menstrual Period [Medicine] (AD)
PMP............ Procurement Methods and Practices (AD)
PMP............ Project Management Professional
Pmr............. Paymaster (AD)
pmr............. Pressure-Modulated Radiometer (AD)
PMR............ Pro Male Release [International Bowhunting Organization] [Class
                    equipment]
PMS............ Peabody Museum of Salem (AD)
PMS............ Permanent Manual System (AD)
pms .... Phenazine Methosulphate (AD)
pms .... Pollution-Monitoring Satellite (AD)
pms .... Poor Miserable Soul (AD)
PMS............ Popular Music and Society [A publication] (BRI)
pms .... Post-Menopausal Syndrome [Medicine] (AD)
pms .... Pregnant Mare's Serum (AD)
pms .... Pre-Menstrual Syndrome [Medicine] (AD)
p-m-s.......... Processors-Memories-Switches (AD)
PMSA.......... Pacific Merchant Shipping Association (AD)
pmsg .... Pregnant Mare's Serum Gonadotrophin (AD)
pm specialists... Paramilitary Specialists (AD)
PMSSMS .... Planned Maintenance System for Surface Missile Ships (AD)
pmt .... Payment (AD)
pmt .... Photomultiplier Tubes (AD)
pmt .... Positive Matte Technique (AD)
pmt .... Premenstrual Tension [Medicine] (AD)
pmt .... Programs, Materials, Techniques (AD)
PMTB.......... Pacific Motor Tariff Bureau (AD)
PMU .... Pattern Makers Union (AD)
pmu .... Performance Monitor Unit (AD)
pmu .... Physical Mockup (AD)
pmu .... Productive Man Work Unit (AD)
PMUSAOAS... Permanent Mission of the United States of America to the
                    Organization of American States (AD)
PMV............ Private Market Value [Investment term] (DFIT)
PMVB.......... Pocono Mountain Vacation Bureau (AD)
pmvi .... Periodic Motor Vehicle Inspection (AD)
pmvp .... Precio Maximo de Venta al Publico [Maximum Price Charged the
                    Public] [Spanish] (AD)
p mvr.......... Prime Mover (AD)
pmx .... Private Manual Exchange (AD)
pmyob .... Please Mind Your Own Business (AD)
PMZ .... Palmar [Costa Rica] [Airport symbol] (AD)
PN................ Coastal Airways [ICAO designator] (AD)
PN................ Nacionalista [Nationalist Party] [Spain] [Political party] (AD)
Pn................ North Celestial Pole (AD)
PN................ Pacific Northern [Airline] (AD)
PN................ Pan-American World Airways [Stock exchange symbol] (AD)
PN................ Partido Nacional [National Party] [Spain] [Political party] (AD)
pn................ Partition (AD)
P/N............... Part Number (AD)
pn................ Part Number (AD)
pn................ Percussion Note (AD)
Pn................ Perigean Range (AD)
pn................ Pine (VRA)
pn................ Please Note (AD)
PN................ Point of No Return (AD)
pn................ Position (AD)
PN................ Princeton Aviation [ICAO designator] (AD)
pn................ Promissory Note (AD)
pn................ Psychiatry-Neurology (AD)
pn................ Punch-On [Computer science] (AD)
PNA .... Pacific Northern Airlines (AD)

PNA .... Panna [India] [Airport symbol] (AD)
PNA .... Philippines News Agency (AD)
PNAC .... President's National Advisory Committee (AD)
PNAI .... Provincial Newspapers Association of Ireland (AD)
pnavq.......... Positive-Negative Ambivalent Quotient (AD)
PNB .... Philippine National Bank (AD)
PNB .... Porto Nacional [Brazil] [Airport symbol] (AD)
pnb .... Producto Nacional Bruto [Gross National Product] [Spanish] (AD)
PNB .... Produto National Bruto [Gross National Product] [Portugal] (AD)
PNBA .... Pacific Northwest Booksellers Association (AD)
PNBB .... Parc National de la Boucle du Baoule [Baoule River Bend National
                    Park] [French] [Mali] (AD)
PNBP .... Parc National de la Boucle de la Pendjari [Penjari River Bend
                    National Park] [French] [Dahamey] (AD)
PNC .... Parque Nacional Canaima [Canaima National Park] [Venezuela]
                    (AD)
pnc............. Pencillin (AD)
pnc............. Plate Number Coil (AD)
pnc............. Premature Nodal Contraction (AD)
PNCC .... President's National Crime Commission (AD)
pnch........... Punch (AD)
Pncla .... Pensacola, Florida (AD)
Pnd .... Pandjang (AD)
pnd .... Paroxysmal Noctural Dyspnoea (AD)
pnd .... Postnasal Drip [Medicine] (AD)
pndb .... Perceived Noise Decibels (AD)
pndg .... Pending (AD)
P-N-D-L-R.... Park-Neutral-Drive-Low-Reverse (AD)
pndnt .... Pendentive (VRA)
Pndo .... Pinedo (AD)
PNE .... Pacific National Exchange Vancouver [Vancouver] (AD)
PNE .... Pacific National Exhibition [Vancouver] (AD)
pne .... Peaceful Nuclear Explosion (AD)
PNe............. Pointe Noire (AD)
pne .... Practical Nurse's Education (AD)
PNEA .... Parque Nacional El Avila [El Avila National Park] [Spanish] (AD)
Pnes .... Pines (AD)
pneu .... Pneumatic (AD)
pneumoccon... Pneumocconiosis [Medicine] (AD)
pneumog ..... Pneumograph (AD)
pneumonoultra... Pneumonoultra-Microscopicsilicovolcanoconiosis [Medicine] (AD)
pnf .... Proprioceptive Neuromuscular Facilitation (AD)
pnfd .... Present Not for Duty (AD)
PNG .... Papua Nueva Guinea [Papua New Guinea] [Spanish] (AD)
PNG .... Parque Nacional Guatopo [Guatopo National Park] [Venezuela]
                    [Spanish] (AD)
Png .... Penang (AD)
png .... Persona Non Grata [An Unacceptable Person] [Latin] (AD)
PNG .... Popondetta [New Guinea] [Airport symbol] (AD)
PNG .... Portable Network Graphics [Computer science] (DOM)
PNGL .... Papua New Guinea Line (AD)
pnh .... Paroxysmal Nocturnal Hemoglobinuria (AD)
PNHP .... Parque Nacional Henri Pittier [Henri Pittier National Park]
                    [Venezuela] [Spanish] (AD)
PNI............. Parque Nacional Iguazu [Iguazu National Park] [Spanish] (AD)
pni .... Positive Noninterfering (AD)
pni .... Psychoneuroimmunology (AD)
pni .... Pulsed Neutron Interrogation (AD)
P Nic .... Port Nicholson (AD)
PNITC .... Pacific Northwest International Trade Council (AD)
PNJ .... Paterson [New Jersey] [Airport symbol] (AD)
PNL .... Pacific Naval Laboratories (AD)
pnl .... Panel (AD)
PNL .... Philippine National Line (AD)
PNM .... Pinnacles National Monument [California] (AD)
pn nb .... Piano Nobile (VRA)
PNO .... Parque Nacional Ordesa [Ordesa National Park] [Spanish] (AD)
pno .... Pergamino [Parchment] [Spanish] (AD)
pno .... Piano (AD)
PNO .... Port of New Orleans (AD)
PNOC .... Philippine National Oil Co. (AD)
PNP .... Platt National Park [Oklahoma] (AD)
pnp .... Positive Negative Positive (AD)
pnpn .... Positive-Negative Positive-Negative (AD)
pnpr............ Positive-Negative Pressure Respiration (AD)
Pnr............. Pioneer (AD)
PNR .... Pittsburg Naval Reactor (AD)
pnr............. Point of No Return (AD)
pnr............. Prior Notice Required (AD)
PNR .... Pulletop Nature Reserve [New South Wales] (AD)
PNRP .... Philadelphia Pulmonary Neoplasm Research Project (AD)
PNS .... Pacific Navigation Systems (AD)
PNS .... Pakistan Naval Ship (AD)
pns............. Parasympathetic Nervous System (AD)
pns............. Peripheral Nervous System (AD)
PNS .... Philadelphia Naval Shipyard (AD)
PNSN .... Parque Nacional Sierra Nevada [Sierra Nevada National Park]
                    [Venezuela] [Spanish] (AD)
PNSP .... Penicillin-Nonsusceptible S. Pneumoniae [Clinical chemistry]
PNSTDC....... Pakistan National Scientific and Technical Documentation Center
                    (AD)
pnt .... Paint (AD)
PNT .... Parque Nacional Tijuca [Tijuca National Park] [Brazil] [Portuguese]
                    (AD)
Pnt.............. Pentagon (AD)

Pnt Anx	Pentagon Annex (AD)
PNTBT	Partial Nuclear Test Ban Treaty (AD)
pntd	Painted (AD)
pntr	Painter (AD)
PNTYP	Panno Type (VRA)
PNU	Pneumatic Scale Corp. [*Stock exchange symbol*] (AD)
pnutbutsan	Peanut-Butter Sandwich (AD)
p-nut butter	Peanut-Butter Sandwich (AD)
pnutbutwich	Peanut-Butter Sandwich (AD)
PNWD/BMI	Pacific Northwest Division/Battelle Memorial Institute (AD)
PNWR	Piedmont National Wildlife Refuge [*Georgia*] (AD)
PNWR	Presquile National Wildlife Refuge [*Virginia*] (AD)
PNWR	Pungo National Wildlife Refuge [*North Carolina*] (AD)
pnx	Pneumothorax [*Medicine*] (AD)
pnxt	Pinxit [*He or She Painted It*] [*Latin*] (AD)
PNYCTC	Pennsylvania New York Central Transportation Co. (AD)
Pnz	Penzance (AD)
PO	Aeropelican Intercity Commuter Air Services [*ICAO designator*] (AD)
P/O	Parole Officer (AD)
p/o	Part of (AD)
po	Per Os [*By Mouth*] [*Latin*] (AD)
P/O	Pilot Officer (AD)
po	Poetry (AD)
po	Polarity (AD)
PO	Portland Oregonian [*A publication*] (AD)
p-o	Postoperative (AD)
po	Power-Operated (AD)
po	Power Oscillator (AD)
po	Previous Orders (AD)
PO	Principal Only (DFIT)
P/O	Probation Officer (AD)
P-O	Pyrenees-Orientales (AD)
PO 1/C	Petty Office First Class [*Military*] (AD)
PO 2/C	Petty Office Second Class [*Military*] (AD)
PO 3/C	Petty Office Third Class [*Military*] (AD)
poa	Place of Acceptance (AD)
POA	Portland Opera Association [*Oregon*] (AD)
PoA	Power of Attorney (AD)
poa	Primary Optical Area (AD)
POAC	Peace Officers Association of California (AD)
POAC	Post Office Advisory Council (AD)
POAG	Peace Officers Association of Georgia (AD)
pob	Persons on Board (AD)
pob	Pilot on Board (AD)
pob	Poblacion [*Population*] [*Spanish*] (AD)
pob	Point of Beginning (AD)
PoB	Port of Baltimore (AD)
pob	Prevention of Blindness (AD)
pobra	Pony and Zebra (AD)
POC	Pittsburgh Opera Co. (AD)
poc	Point of Contact (AD)
poc	Principal Operating Component (AD)
POC	Prison Officer's Club (AD)
poc	Privately Owned Conveyance (AD)
POC	Public Oil Co. (AD)
pock	Pocket (AD)
Pocket Bks	Pocket Books (AD)
pocul	Poculum [*Cup*] (AD)
pod	Paid on Delivery (AD)
pod	Payable on Death (AD)
pod	Point-of-Origin Device (AD)
pod	Port of Debarkation (AD)
pod	Port of Departure (AD)
pod	Probability of Detection (AD)
pod	Process-Oriented Design (AD)
podex	Photographic Exercise (AD)
podia	Podiatrist (AD)
poe	Polyoxyethylene (AD)
POE	Port of Embarkation (DFIT)
poe buoy	Plank-on-Edge Buoy (AD)
poecrit	Poetry Criticism (AD)
poet	Poetical (AD)
Poet	Poetry [*A publication*] (BRI)
Poetics T	Poetics Today [*A publication*] (BRI)
POF	Philharmonic Orchestra of Florida (AD)
pof	Please Omit Flowers (AD)
POG	Pacific Oceanographic Group [*British Columbia*] (AD)
POGO	Pennzoil Offshore Gas Operators (AD)
Poh	Pohang (AD)
poh	Pull Out of Hole (AD)
POI	Potosi [*Bolivia*] [*Airport symbol*] (AD)
pois	Poison (AD)
POL	Patent Office Library (AD)
pol	Petroleum-Oil-and-Lubricants (AD)
Pol	Poland (VRA)
pol	Polar (AD)
Pol	Polen [*Poland*] [*Norwegian*] (AD)
pol	Polished (VRA)
POL	Polish Ocean Lines (AD)
POL	Porto Amelia [*Mozambique*] [*Airport symbol*] (AD)
pol	Problem-Oriented Language (AD)
p-ola	Payola (AD)
POLA	Prostitutes of Los Angeles [*An association*] (AD)
polad	Political Adviser (AD)
Pol Ad	Political Adviser (AD)
polang	Polarization Angle (AD)
polar	Polarity (AD)
Polar BEAR	Polar Beacon Experiments and Auroral Research (AD)
Pol Col	Police College (AD)
Pol Com	Police Commissaire [*Interpol*] [*British*] (AD)
Pol Com	Police Commissioner (AD)
pol com	Political Committee (AD)
polcrit	Political Critic (AD)
poldamr	Petroleum, Oil, and Lubrication Installation Damage Report (AD)
pol econ	Political Economy (AD)
polem	Polemic (AD)
polf	Parents of Large Families (AD)
Pol Fed	Police Federation [*London*] (AD)
POLFER	Polizia Ferroviaria [*Railroad Police*] [*Italian*] (AD)
Pol Found	Police Foundation [*Washington, D.C.*] (AD)
poli	Politician (AD)
pol ind	Pollen Index (AD)
pol in the pen	Politician in the Penitentiary (AD)
polio	Poliomyelitis [*Medicine*] (AD)
polit	Political (AD)
Politburo	Politicheskoe Byuro [*Political Bureau of the Central Committee*] [*Russian*] (AD)
poll	Pollution (AD)
poln	polnisch [*Polish*] [*German*] (AD)
Polon	Polonais [*Polish*] [*French*] (AD)
Pol Res Q	Political Research Quarterly [*A publication*] (BRI)
Pol Rze Lud	Polaska Rzeczpospolita Ludowa [*Polish People's Republic*] (AD)
pols	Political Prisoners (AD)
pols	Politicians (AD)
PolSc	Political Science (DD)
pol sci	Political Science (AD)
POLSTRADA	Polizia Stradale [*Highway Police*] [*Italian*] (AD)
Pol Stud J	Policy Studies Journal [*A publication*] (BRI)
polwar	Political Warfare (AD)
poly	Polyethylene (AD)
poly	Polymer (AD)
Poly	Polynesia (AD)
Poly	Polytechnic (AD)
poly	Polytechnic (AD)
poly	Polyvinyl (AD)
poly bot	Polyethylene Bottle (AD)
polyg	Polygraph (AD)
polymorph	Polymorphous (AD)
Polyn	Polynesia (VRA)
poly sci	Political Science (AD)
polysex	Polysexual (AD)
polywater	Polymerized Water (AD)
pom	Polycyclic Organic Matter (AD)
pom	Polyoxymethylene (AD)
pom	Pomeranian (AD)
pom	Pomeridiano [*Afternoon*] [*Italian*] (AD)
pom	Pomological (AD)
pom	Pom-Pom (AD)
PoM	Port of Miami (AD)
pom	Preparation for Overseas Movement (AD)
pomato	Potato-Tomato (AD)
pomcus	Prepositioned Material Configured in Unit Sets (AD)
POMFLANT	Polaris Missile Facility, Atlantic (AD)
pomol	Pomologic (AD)
Pomp	Pompey (AD)
POMPAC	Polaris Missile Facility, Pacific (AD)
pomsee	Preparation, Operation, Maintenance, Shipboard Electronics Equipment (AD)
pon	Pontoon (AD)
PON	Program Opportunity Notification (AD)
pona	Paraffin, Olefin, Naphthene, Aromatic (AD)
PonBrg	Pontoon Bridge (AD)
pond	Pondere [*By Weigh*] [*Latin*] (AD)
Pondo	Pondoland (AD)
p-on-n	Positive on Negative (AD)
pons	Profile of Nonverbal Sensitivity (AD)
Pont	Pontevedra (AD)
pont b	Pontoon Bridge (AD)
Ponti	Pontiac (AD)
Pont Max	Pontifex Maximus [*Supreme Pontiff*] [*Latin*] (AD)
POO	Parents Opposed to Opting Out [*An association*] (AIE)
Poo	Poole (AD)
pood	Poodle Dog (AD)
poof	Peripheral On-Line-Oriented Function [*Computer science*] (AD)
poop	Nincompoop (AD)
poosslq	Person of Opposite Sex Sharing Living Quarters (AD)
POoW	Petty Officer on Watch [*Military*] (AD)
POP	Palletizing Optimization Potential (AD)
pop	Perpendicular Ocean Platform (AD)
pop	Persistent Occipito-Posterior (AD)
POP	Persistent Organic Pollutant (AD)
pop	Plasma Osmotic Pressure (AD)
pop	Plaster of Paris (AD)
POP	Point of Presence [*Telecommunications*] (DOM)
pop	Popliteal (AD)
Pop	Poppa (AD)
pop	Poppet (AD)
pop	Popular (AD)
pop	Population (AD)
POP	Portugese Overseas Province (AD)

p-op............	Post-Operative (AD)
POP	Public Offering Price (AD)
Popa	Popayan, Colombia (AD)
pop advertising...	Point-of-Purchase Advertising (AD)
pop art........	Popular Art (AD)
popb	Proposed Operating Plan and Budget (AD)
POPE	Product Oriented Procedures Evaluation (AD)
popex..........	Population Explosion (AD)
popf	Prepared-on-Premises Flavor (AD)
popi	Post Office Position Indicator [British] (AD)
poplit..........	Popliteal (AD)
pop music ..	Popular Music (AD)
pop psych....	Popular Psychiatry (AD)
popr	Pilot Overhaul Provisioning Review (AD)
pops..........	Popular Concerts (AD)
Pop Sci.......	Popular Science [A publication] (AD)
poq	Periodic Order Quantity (AD)
POQ	Public Opinion Quarterly [A publication] (AD)
p-o-r	Pay-on-Receipt (AD)
Por.............	Porifera (AD)
Por.............	Porogi [Waterfall] [Russian] (AD)
por.............	Porosity (AD)
Por.............	Portland (AD)
Por.............	Portugal (AD)
Por.............	Portuguese (AD)
por.............	Public Opinion Research (AD)
PORA..........	Police Officers Research Association (AD)
PORC..........	Peralta Oaks Research Center (AD)
porc	Porcelain (AD)
PORIS	Post Office Radio Interference Station (AD)
porksan.......	Pork Sandwich (AD)
porkwich......	Pork Sandwich (AD)
porm..........	Plus or Minus (AD)
porn...........	Pornographic (AD)
pornette......	Pornographic Cassette (AD)
pornfilm......	Pornographic Motion Picture Film (AD)
porno	Pornofilm (AD)
porno	Pornographer (AD)
pornobio......	Pornographic Biography (AD)
pornofilm.....	Pornographic Motion Picture (AD)
porno mag...	Pornographic Magazine (AD)
pornovel	Pornographic Novel (AD)
pornovelist...	Pornographic Novelist (AD)
Porn Squad...	Pornographic Squad (AD)
pornzines.....	Pornographic Magazines (AD)
PORP..........	Printed on Recycled Paoer (AD)
porph..........	Porphyry (VRA)
PORS	Post Office Research Station (AD)
port	Photo-Optical Recorder Tracker (AD)
port............	Portable (AD)
port............	Portrait (AD)
Port............	Portugal (VRA)
port............	Portugiesisch [Portuguese] [German] (AD)
PORT	Presentation Portfolio (VRA)
Port Ade	Port Adelaide [South Australia] (AD)
Port Ald	Port Alberni [Vancouver Island, British Columbia] (AD)
portalet.......	Portable Toilet (AD)
Port Alex	Port Alexander [Alaska] (AD)
Port Ant......	Port Antonio [Jamaica] (AD)
Port Art......	Port Arthur (AD)
Port Chi......	Port Chicago (AD)
Port Chi......	Portuguese China (AD)
Port Dal	Port Dalhousie [Ontario, Canada] (AD)
Port Ind	Portuguese India (AD)
Port Jack	Port Jackson Sydney [Sydney, New South Wales, Australia] (AD)
Port Liz.......	Port Elizabeth [South Africa] (AD)
Port Liz.......	Port Elizabeth [New Jersey] (AD)
Port Nick	Port Nicholson [Wellington, New Zealand] (AD)
Port Phil	Port Phillip [Melbourne, Victoria, Australia] (AD)
Port Rich	Port Richmond [Staten Island, New York] (AD)
Port Sud	Port Sudan (AD)
Port Swett ...	Port Swettenham [Malaysia] (AD)
Port Talb	Port Talbot [Wales] (AD)
Port Tew.....	Port Tewfik [Egypt] (AD)
Port Tim	Portuguese Timor (AD)
Portug.........	Portugais [Portuguese] [French] (AD)
Port Wash ...	Port Washington [Long Island, New York] (AD)
Port Wel......	Port Wellen [Ontario, CAN] (AD)
pos.............	Point of Sale (AD)
POS	Point-of-Service [Human resources] (WYGK)
POs.............	Police Officers (AD)
PoS.............	Port of Service (AD)
PoS.............	Port of Spain (AD)
pos.............	Position (AD)
pos.............	Positive (AD)
pos.............	Possibility (AD)
POs.............	Postal Orders (AD)
pos.............	Product of Sums (AD)
posa............	Payment Outstanding Suspense Accounts (AD)
posb............	Possibly (VRA)
POSD	Post Office Savings Department (AD)
posdcorb......	Planning-Organization-Staffing-Directing-Coordinating-Reporting-Budgeting g (AD)
posdsplt.......	Port Side Out, Starboard Side Home [British slang] (AD)
posdsplt.......	Positive Displacement (AD)

posh............	Permuted on Subject Headings (AD)
posistor	Positive Resistor (AD)
posit	Position (AD)
posit	Positive (AD)
posit	Positron (AD)
positron.......	Positive Electron (AD)
POSIX.........	Portable Operating Systems for Computer Environments (AD)
posm..........	Patient-Operated Selected Mechanisms (AD)
posn...........	Position (AD)
POSNY........	People of the State of New York (AD)
pos pron......	Possessive Pronoun (AD)
P-O-S S	Point-of-Sale System (AD)
P-O-S S	Point-of-Service System (AD)
poss...........	Possession (AD)
posses........	Possessive (AD)
possIq.........	Person of the Opposite Sex in Same Living Quarters (AD)
POST	Frederick Post Drafting Equipment (AD)
POST	Police Officer Student Training (AD)
post	Postage (AD)
post	Poster (VRA)
post	Posterior [Spanish] (AD)
post	Post Mortem (AD)
POST	Processes of Science Test (AD)
post-Aug.....	Post-Augustan (AD)
post aur......	Post Aurem [Behind the Ear] [Latin] (AD)
post d	Posterior Diameter (AD)
poster	Posterior (AD)
pos terminal...	Point-of-Sale Terminal (AD)
Postgrad Med Inst...	Postgraduate Medical Institute (AD)
posth	Posthumous (AD)
postl	Postlude (AD)
post-mort....	Post Mortem (AD)
post ofc	Post Office (VRA)
post-op.......	Post-Operative (AD)
post part....	Post Partum [Afterbirth] [Latin] (AD)
Post Script..	Post Script: Essays in Film and the Humanities [A publication] (BRI)
post-sync....	Post-Synchronization (AD)
pot	Point of tangency (AD)
pot	Portable Outdoor Toilet (AD)
pot	Potash (AD)
pot	Potential (AD)
pot	Potentiometer (AD)
potash alum...	Potassium Aluminum Sulfate (AD)
potats	Potatoes (AD)
P o TD	Port of The Dalles (AD)
POTIB	Poseidon Technical Information Bulletin [A publication] (AD)
potossIq......	Persons of the Opposite Sex Sharing Living Quarters (AD)
potr	Potrero [Cattle Ranch] [Spanish] (AD)
pots	Plain Old Telephone Service (AD)
pots	Potentiometers (AD)
pott	Pottery (AD)
pot w	Portable Water (AD)
poul	Poultry (AD)
POUR..........	President's Organization for Unemployment Relief (AD)
POV	Pend Oreille Valley Railroad (AD)
p-o-v...........	Point-of-View (AD)
POV	Presov [Czechoslovakia] [Airport symbol] (AD)
pov.............	Privately Owned Vehicle (AD)
pow............	Power (AD)
P o W	Prince of Wales (AD)
pow............	Prisoner of War (AD)
P o W	Prisoner of Watergate (AD)
POW Country...	Potash, Oil, and Wheat Country [Saskatoon, Saskatchewan] (AD)
powd	Powder (AD)
power	Programmed Operational Warshot Evaluation and Review (AD)
POX	Port Alexander [Alaska] [Airport symbol] (AD)
POY	Lovell-Powell [Wyoming] [Airport symbol] (AD)
poy.............	Pre-Oriented Yarn (AD)
Poz.............	Poznan (AD)
PP...............	Pacific Petroleum (AD)
pp...............	Panel Point (AD)
Pp...............	Papa [Father] [Latin] (AD)
pp...............	Parcel Post (AD)
pp...............	Part Paid (AD)
pp...............	Passive Participle (AD)
pp...............	Pellagra Preventive (AD)
P-P.............	Pellagra-Preventive Factor (AD)
pp...............	Perceptual Performance (AD)
pp...............	Permanent Party (AD)
pp...............	Per Person (AD)
PP...............	Phillips Airlines [ICAO designator] (AD)
pp...............	Physical Profile (AD)
pp...............	Physical Properties (AD)
pp...............	Pickpocket (AD)
pp...............	Piena Pelle [Full Leather] [Italian] (AD)
pp...............	Planning Permission (AD)
pp...............	Postage Paid (AD)
pp...............	Post Partum [Afterbirth] [Latin] (AD)
pp...............	Present Position (AD)
PP...............	Present Pupil (AIE)
pp...............	Pressure-Proof (AD)
pp...............	Privately Printed (AD)
pp...............	Private Property (AD)
pp...............	Professional Paper (AD)
pp...............	Purchased Part (AD)

p-p	Push-Pull (AD)
PPA	Pakistan Press Association (AD)
ppa	Palpitation, Percussion, Auscultation (AD)
PPA	Pension Portability Act of 1992 (WYGK)
PPA	People for Prison Alternatives [An association] (AD)
PPA	Personnel Pool of America [An association] (AD)
ppa	Phenylpropanolamine (AD)
ppa	Phiala Prius Agitate [Bottle Having First Been Shaken] [Latin] (AD)
ppa	Photo-Peak Analysis (AD)
PPA	Professional Photographers of America (AD)
PPA	Proletarian Party of America [Political party] (AD)
pp & a	Palpitation, Percussion, and Auscultation (AD)
pp&b	Paper, Printing, and Binding (AD)
PP & E	Program Planning and Evaluation (AD)
PP&L	Pacific Power and Light (AD)
PP&L	Pennsylvania Power and Light (AD)
PPATRA	Printing, Packaging, and Allied Trades Research Association (AD)
Ppb	Pappaband [Hard Cover] [German] (AD)
ppb	Parts per Billion (AD)
PPB	Polybrominated-Biphenyl (AD)
PPB	Presidente Prudente [Brazil] [Airport symbol] (AD)
PPBAS	Planning-Programming-Budgeting-Accounting System (AD)
PPC	Pet Population Control (AD)
ppc	Picture Postcard (AD)
ppc	Plan-Paper Copier (AD)
PPC	Positive Peer Culture (AD)
p p c	Pour Prendre Conge [To Take Leave] [French] (AD)
ppc	Progressive Patient Care (AD)
PPC	Purchase Price Control (AD)
pPc	Pure Peruvian Cocaine (AD)
ppca	Plasma Prothrombin Conversion Accelerator (AD)
PPCD	Plant Pest Control Division (AD)
ppcf	Plasma Prothrombin Conversion Factor (AD)
PPCLI	Princess Patricia's Canadian Light Infantry (AD)
PPCS	Personnel Protection and Communication Services [British] (AD)
PPCS	Primary Producers' Cooperative Society (AD)
PPD	Paranoid Personality Disorder (AD)
PPD	Petroleum Production Division (AD)
PPD	Portland Public Docks (AD)
ppd	Purified Protein Derivative (AD)
PPDA	Produce Packaging Development Association (AD)
PPDC	Polymer Products Development Center (AD)
ppdi	Pilot's Projected-Display Indicator (AD)
ppdo	Per Person, Double Occupancy (AD)
PPDS	Publishers' Parcels Delivery Service (AD)
PPDSE	Plate Printers, Die Stampers, and Engravers [Union] (AD)
ppe	Philosophy, Politics, and Economics (AD)
PPF	Panamanian Public Force (AD)
ppf	Personal Property Floater [Insurance] (AD)
PPF	Plumbers and Pipefitters [Union] (AD)
p-p factor	Pellagra-Preventive Factor (AD)
ppg	Planning and Programming Guidance (AD)
PPGA	Pennsylvania Personnel and Guidance Association (AD)
ppga	Post-Pill Galactorrheamenorrhea [Medicine] (AD)
pph	Pamphlet (AD)
pph	Post-Partum Hemorrhage [Medicine] (AD)
pph	Pounds Per Hour (AD)
pph	Pulses Per Hour (AD)
P Php	Port Phillip (AD)
pphpm	Parts Per Hundred Parts of Mix (AD)
pphpm	Pints Per Hundred Parts of Mix (AD)
pphr	Parts Per Hundred Parts of Rubber (AD)
ppi	Pages Per Inch (AD)
ppi	Parcel Post Insured (AD)
ppi	Plan Position Indicator (AD)
ppi	Policy Proof of Interest (AD)
PPI	Protective Packaging, Inc. (AD)
PPIC	Plumbing and Piping Industry Council (AD)
ppif	Photo-Processing Interpretation Facility (AD)
p-pille	Praeventivpille [Dano-Norwegian] [Contraceptive pill] (AD)
pp/in	Pages Per Inch (AD)
PPIQ	Personality and Personal Illness Questionnaire (AD)
PPK	Palmoplantar Keratoderma [Dermatology]
pPk	Purplish Pink (AD)
PPL	Philadelphia Public Library (AD)
PPL	Phoenix Public Library (AD)
ppl	Pipeline (AD)
PPL	Pittsburgh Public Library (AD)
PPL	Planned Parenthood League (AD)
PPL	Police Protective League (AD)
PPL	Providence Public Library (AD)
P-plane	Pilotless Airplane (AD)
PPLC	Patients Protection Law Commission (AD)
pple	Past Participle (AD)
pplo	Pleuropneumonia-Like Organism (AD)
PPM	Partido Proletario de Mexico [Proletarian Party of Mexico] [Political party] (AD)
ppm	Parts Per Million (AD)
ppm	Peak Program Meter (AD)
PPM	Persutuan Perpustakaan Malaysia [Library Association of the Federation of Malaysia] (AD)
ppm	Pounds Per Minute (AD)
ppm	Pulse Position Modulation (AD)
PPMA	Petroleum Marketers Association of America
ppma	Post-Polio Muscular Atrophy [Medicine] (AD)

ppn	Proportion (AD)
PPNP	Point Pelee National Park [Ontario, Canada] (AD)
PPNW	Physicians for the Prevention of Nuclear War (AD)
ppo	Polyphenylene Oxide (AD)
PPO	Preferred-Provided Organization [Insurance] (AD)
ppo	Prior Permission Only (AD)
PPOG	Polytechnic Personnel Officers Group (AIE)
p-p-ola	Political Plugola (AD)
ppom	Particulate Polycyclic Organic Matter (AD)
P-POP	Plain Paper Optimized Printing [Canon] [Computer science]
PPP	Penultimate Profit [Investment term] (DFIT)
PPP	Peoples Party of Pakistan [Political party] (AD)
PPP	Petroleum Production Pioneers (AD)
ppp	Piu Pianissimo [Very Very Softly] [Italian] [Music] (AD)
PPPLS	Public Policy for Public Libraries Section [Public Library Association] [American Library Association]
pppp	Piu Piu Piu Pianissimo [Very, Very, Very Softly] [Italian] [Music] (AD)
ppq	Polyphenylquinoxaline (AD)
PPR	Pirapora [Brazil] [Airport symbol] (AD)
PPri	Port Pirie (AD)
ppr	Present Participle (AD)
ppr	Printed Paper Rate (AD)
ppr	Prior Permission Required (AD)
PPR	Procurement Problem Report (AD)
pprbd	Paperboard (AD)
PPRICA	Pulp and Paper Research Institute of Canada (AD)
PPS	Pacific Passenger Services (AD)
PPS	Pennsylvania Prison Society (AD)
PPS	Personal Portable Shopper [Computer science]
PPS	Persutuan Perpustakaan Singapura [Library Association of Singapore] (AD)
pps	Pictures Per Second (AD)
p-ps	Post-Polio Syndrome [Medicine] (AD)
pps	Pounds Per Second (AD)
PPS	Primary Protection System [Computer science]
pps	Private Parliamentary Secretary [British] (AD)
pps	Pulses Per Second (AD)
PPSAWA	Pan Pacific and Southeast Asia Women's Association (AD)
PPSB	Periodical Publishers' Service Bureau (AD)
ppsn	Present Position (AD)
ppso	Per Person, Single Occupancy (AD)
PPT	Papeete, Society Islands [Airport] (AD)
PPT	Pericles, Prince of Tyre [A publication] (AD)
ppt	Precipitate (AD)
pptd	Precipitated (AD)
pptn	Precipitation (AD)
PPTP	Point-to-Point Tunneling Protocol [Computer science]
PPTPP	Promulgators of Public Toilets in Public Parks (AD)
ppty	Property (AD)
ppu	Platform Position Unit (AD)
PPU	Primary Producers Union (AD)
ppv	Pay-Per-View (AD)
ppv	People-Powered Vehicle (AD)
PPZ	Puerto Paez [Venezuela] [Airport symbol] (AD)
pq	Peculiar (AD)
pq	Permeability Quotient (AD)
pq	Personality Quotient (AD)
p-q	Phenol-Hydroquinone [Photography] (AD)
PQ	Philological Quarterly [A publication] (BRI)
pq	Previous Question (AD)
pq	Punishment Quarters (AD)
PQ	South Pacific Airlines of New Zealand (AD)
pqa	Procurement Quality Assurance (AD)
PQAA	Province of Quebec Association of Architects [1890, OAQ from 1974] [Canada] (NGC)
PQC	Phuquoc [South Vietnam] [Airport symbol] (AD)
PQD	Plant Quarantine Division (AD)
pqe	Post-Qualification Education (AD)
PQI	Print Quality Improvement [Advanced photo system]
pqi	Professional Qualification Index (AD)
PQIH	Plant Quarantine Inspection House (AD)
PQR	Program Quality Review (AD)
pqrs	Productivity Increases, Quality Control, Robotization, and Savings [Japanese formula for economic success] (AD)
PQS	Percentage Quota System (AD)
PQS	Personnel Qualification Standard (AD)
pr	Pair (AD)
Pr	Panama-Red Marijuana (AD)
PR	Paradise Regained [A publication] (AD)
Pr	Parana (AD)
pr	Parcel Receipt (AD)
PR	Park Ranger (AD)
PR	Partisan Review [A publication] (BRI)
P/R	Payroll (AD)
pr	Payroll (AD)
PR	Peking Review [A publication] (AD)
P-R	Pennsylvania-Reading [Seashore Lines] (AD)
pr	Percentile Rank (AD)
pr	Peripheral Resistance (AD)
pr	Per Rectum [By the Rectum] [Latin] (AD)
PR	Philippine Airlines [ICAO designator] (AD)
PR	Pinar del Rio (AD)
PR	Polskie Radio [Polish Radio] (AD)
Pr	Praca [Plaza] [Portuguese] (AD)
Pr	Prairie (AD)

Pr...............	Presbyopia (AD)		projt............	Projector (VRA)
Pr...............	Presbyter [Elder] [Latin] (AD)		prom............	Promenade (DD)
Pr...............	Press (AD)		ProMED......	Program to Monitor Emerging Diseases
Pr...............	Prince (AD)		prop............	Property (DD)
pr...............	Print (VRA)		PROPH.......	Profile of Phonology (AIE)
Pr...............	Proctoscopy (AD)		proPO	Prophenoloxidase
PR...............	Proctosigmoidoscopy [Medicine] (AD)		prov............	Provenance (VRA)
Pr...............	Promenade (DD)		prpylm.........	Propylaeum (VRA)
PR...............	Psychiatric Record (AD)		PRQ.............	Presidente Roque Saenz Pena [Argentina] [Airport symbol] (AD)
pr...............	Public Relations (AD)		PRS.............	Puerto Lempira [Honduras] [Airport symbol] (AD)
pr...............	Punctum Remotum [Remote Point] [Latin] (AD)		prsmc	Prismacolor (VRA)
pR...............	Purplish Red (AD)		PRSP...........	Penicillin-Resistant S. Pneumoniae [Clinical chemistry]
pra.............	Payroll Audit (AD)		prtd.............	Printed (VRA)
pra.............	Plasma Renin Activity [Medicine] (AD)		PRU.............	Paranagua [Brazil] [Airport symbol] (AD)
PRA	Postal Reorganization Act (AD)		prv	Private (VRA)
pra.............	Print Alphanumerically (AD)		prv coll	Private Collection (VRA)
pra.............	Probation and Rehabilitation of Airmen (AD)		PS...............	Partially Sighted (AIE)
pra.............	Progressive Retinal Atrophy [Medicine] (AD)		ps...............	Pastel (VRA)
PRA	Puerto Rico Association (AD)		PS...............	Prairie Schooner [A publication] (BRI)
prac............	Practice (AD)		PSB.............	Bellefonte-Clearfield-Philipsburg [Pennsylvania] [Airport symbol] (AD)
pracl...........	Page-Replacement Algorithm and Control Logic (AD)		PSB.............	Professional and Statutory Board (AIE)
pract...........	Practical (AD)		PSCACM	Permanent Secretariat of the Central American Common Market
pract...........	Practice (AD)		PSCD..........	Postcard (VRA)
pract...........	Practitioner (AD)		PSD.............	Port Said [Egypt] [Airport symbol] (AD)
Praeger.......	Frederick A. Praeger (AD)		PSDN..........	Packet-Switching Data Network [Computer science] (DOM)
praen..........	Praenomen (AD)		PSE.............	Prison Service Establishment (AIE)
prag...........	Pragmatic (AD)		PSF.............	Pittsfield [Massachusetts] [Airport symbol] (AD)
pragma......	Processing Routines Aided by Graphics for Manipulation of Arrays (AD)		PSI.............	Personalised System of Induction (AIE)
PRAIC	President of the Royal Architectural Institute of Canada (NGC)		PSL.............	Perth [Scotland] [Airport symbol] (AD)
PRAICO......	Puerto Rican American Insurance Co. (AD)		pslt	Psalter (VRA)
prais..........	Passive-Ranging Interferometer Sensor (AD)		PSM.............	Portsmouth [New Hampshire] [Airport symbol] (AD)
PRAISE	Pilot Records of Achievement in Schools Evaluation (AIE)		PSME..........	Personal Social and Moral Education (AIE)
pral............	Principal [Principal] [Spanish] (AD)		PSP.............	Performance Share Plan [Human resources] (WYGK)
pram..........	Perambulator (AD)		PSQ.............	Political Science Quarterly [A publication] (BRI)
Pram..........	Poseidon Random-Access Memory (AD)		PSR.............	Political Science Reviewer [A publication] (BRI)
Pram..........	Prambanam (VRA)		PSR.............	Pro Seniors [International Bowhunting Organization] [Class Equipment]
pram..........	Productivity, Reliability, Availability, and Maintainability (AD)		PSS.............	Performance Support System [Human resources] (WYGK)
prand.........	Prandium [dinner] [Latin] (AD)		PSSR...........	Primary School Staff Relations [Project] (AIE)
PRAT	Prattsburgh Railroad (AD)		pst	Paste (VRA)
p rat aet	Pro Ratione Aetatis [In Proportion to Age] [Latin] (AD)		PST.............	Preston [Cuba] [Airport symbol] (AD)
PRATRA	Philippines Relief and Trade Rebilitation Administration (AD)		pstbd	Pasteboard (VRA)
PRAY	Paul Revere Associated Yeoman (AD)		PSTS...........	Primary School Teachers and Science [Project] (AIE)
PRB	Partido de la Revolucion Boliviana [Bolivian Revolutionary Party] [Political party] (AD)		pstyl...........	Peristyle (VRA)
PRB	Paso Robles [California] [Airport symbol] (AD)		PSUD..........	Psychoactive Substance Use Disorder
PRB	People's Republic of Benin (AD)		Psych..........	Psychology (DD)
PRB	Personnel Review Board (AD)		pt...............	Paint (VRA)
prb	Principal Borehole (AD)		PT...............	Performance Technology [Human resources] (WYGK)
PRC.............	Pain Rehabilitation Center (AD)		PT...............	Permeability Transition [Biochemistry]
PRC.............	Palestine Red Crescent (AD)		Pt...............	Point (DD)
PRC.............	Pay-Raise Commission (AD)		PT...............	Provincetown-Boston Airline [ICAO designator] (AD)
PRC.............	Picatinny Research Center [Picatinny Arsenal] (AD)		PT...............	Psychology Today [A publication] (BRI)
prc	Polysulphide Rubber Compound (AD)		PTC.............	Plugged Telescoping Catheter [Clinical chemistry]
PRCA	Public Relations Club (AD)		PTC.............	Program of Technical Cooperation [Organization of American States]
PRCA	President of the Royal Canadian Academy of Arts (NGC)		PTCD..........	Private Training College for the Disabled (AIE)
prcd	Priced (AD)		ptd	Painted (VRA)
Pr Ch	Parish Church (AD)		PTE.............	Nouadhibou [Mauritania] [Airport symbol] (AD)
prchst	Parachutist (AD)		ptg	Painting (VRA)
prcht	Parachute (AD)		PthG...........	Partially Hearing (AIE)
prcs	Process (AD)		PTK.............	Passport to Knowledge [Children's computer program sponsored by NASA and NSF]
prcst	Precast (AD)		PTL	Pietermaritzburg [South Africa] [Airport symbol] (AD)
prcu	Power Regulation and Control Unit (AD)		ptl	Portal (VRA)
prd	Partial Reaction of Degeneration (AD)		PTMC..........	Photomechanical (VRA)
PRD	Pesticides Regulation Division (AD)		PTPA...........	Portal-to-Portal Act of 1947 (WYGK)
prd	Printer Dump (AD)		PTPT...........	Platinum Print (VRA)
prd	Pro-Rata Distribution (AD)		ptr	Painter (VRA)
prdl	Predella (VRA)		PTR.............	Port Macquarie [New South Wales] [Airport symbol] (AD)
PRE.............	Pre-Retirement Education (AIE)		ptrt.............	Portrait (VRA)
prec............	Precious (VRA)		ptry	Pottery (VRA)
prelm..........	Preliminary (VRA)		ptst	Paintstick (VRA)
prep............	Preparatory (VRA)		Pty	Proprietary (DD)
PRE-RE	Prerefunded Municipal Note [Investment term] (DFIT)		Pub	Public (DD)
pres............	President (DD)		Pub Op Q	Public Opinion Quarterly [A publication] (BRI)
presby.........	Presbytery (VRA)		Pub Rel J	Public Relations Journal [A publication] (BRI)
presen	Presentation (VRA)		PUK.............	Paducah [Kentucky] [Airport symbol] (AD)
Pres SQ	Presidential Studies Quarterly [A publication] (BRI)		pulpbd	Pulpboard (VRA)
PRF.............	Plasmacytoma Repressor Factor [Cytology]		pulpwd.........	Pulpwood (VRA)
prf	Proof (VRA)		PUN.............	Punia [Zaire] [Airport symbol] (AD)
PRIME	Primary Initiatives in Mathematics Education (AIE)		PUP	Po [Upper Volta] [Airport symbol] (AD)
prin............	Principle (VRA)		purch...........	Purchasing (DD)
PRISM	Peace and Reconciliation Inter-Schools Movement (AIE)		PUT.............	Persons Using Television (WDMC)
PRJ.............	Capri [Italy] [Airport symbol] (AD)		PUT.............	Putao [Burma] [Airport symbol] (AD)
prl.............	Pearl (VRA)		PUZ.............	Puerto Cabezas [Nicaragua] [Airport symbol] (AD)
PRM.............	Puerto Lopez [Colombia] [Airport symbol] (AD)		PVI.............	Paranavai [Brazil] [Airport symbol] (AD)
PRMH..........	Profoundly Retarded Multiply Handicapped (AIE)		PVP.............	Plant Variety Protection
PRNG..........	Paper Negative (VRA)		PVS.............	Partner Violence Screen [Health]
prob............	Probably (VRA)		Pvt	Private (DD)
proc............	Process (VRA)		PW.............	Publishers Weekly [A publication] (BRI)
prod............	Production (DD)		PWT.............	Professional Walleye Trail
prof............	Profile (VRA)		PX...............	Air Niugini [Air New Guinea] [ICAO designator] (AD)
PROG...........	Peer Review Oversight Group [National Institutes of Health]		PXA.............	Parana [Brazil] [Airport symbol] (AD)
Prog............	Progressive [A publication] (BRI)		PXU.............	Pleiku [South Vietnam] [Airport symbol] (AD)
Prog Arch ...	Progressive Architecture [A publication] (BRI)		PXX.............	Porto Alfonso [Brazil] [Airport symbol] (AD)
proj............	Project (VRA)		PY...............	Surinam Airways [ICAO designator] (AD)

PYR .... Pyrgos [*Greece*] [*Airport symbol*] (AD)
pyrm .... Pyramid (VRA)
pyrox .... Pyroxiline (VRA)

Q
By Acronym

Q................. Quadrillion (AD)
Q................. Quai [*Embankment*] [*French*] (AD)
Q................. Quaker Line (AD)
q................. Quality Factor (AD)
Q................. Quantity [*Microeconomics*] (AD)
q................. Quaque [*Each*] [*Latin*] (AD)
Q................. Quarantine (AD)
q................. Quart (AD)
q................. Quarter (AD)
q................. Quartile (AD)
Q................. Quartile Variation [*Symbol*] (AD)
q................. Quarto (AD)
Q................. Quebec (AD)
q................. Queer (AD)
q................. Quench (AD)
q................. Question (AD)
q................. Quick (AD)
q................. Quintal (AD)
q................. Quire (AD)
Q................. San Quentin Prison (AD)
Q1................ Quintal [*Hundred-weight*] [*Spanish*] (AD)
QA............... Air Caribe [*ICAO designator*] (AD)
QA............... Quality Acceptance (AD)
qa............... Quality Assurance (AD)
qa............... Quick-Acting (AD)
qa............... Quick Assembly (AD)
qa............... Quiescent Aerial (AD)
Q-A.............. Quint-A (AD)
QA & P........ Quanah, Acme & Pacific Railroad (AD)
QAB............. Quality Assurance Board (AD)
QAB............. Quality Assurance Bulletin (AD)
QAC............. Quality Assurance Check (AD)
QAC............. Quality Assurance Coding (AD)
qac............. Quaternary Ammonium Compound (AD)
QAD............. Quality Assessment Division [*Higher Education Funding Council*] (AIE)
QAD............. Quality Assurance Department (AD)
qad............. Quick-Attach-Detach (AD)
QADI............ Quality Assurance Department Instruction (AD)
qadk............ Quick Attach-Detach-Kit (AD)
QADS........... Quality Assurance Data Summary (AD)
QAF............. Quality Achievement Factor (RDA)
qaf............. Quality-Assurance Firing (AD)
QAFCO......... Quatar Fertilizer Co. (AD)
QAFL............ Queensland Australian Football League (AD)
qafo............ Quality-Assurance Field Operation (AD)
QAG............. Quaker Action Group (AD)
QAGA.......... Queensland Amateur Gymnastic Association [*Australia*] (AD)
qagc........... Quiet Automatic Gain Control (AD)
Qahira......... El Qahira [*Cairo*] [*Egyptian Arabic*] (AD)
QAI............. Queen's Award to Industry [*British*] (AD)
QAICG......... Quality Assurance Interface Coordination Group (AD)
qak............. Quick-Attach Kit (AD)
qal............. Quartz Aircraft Lamp (AD)
qal............. Quaternary Alluvium (AD)
QAL............ Queensland Alumina Ltd. [*Australia*] (AD)
qal............. Quintal [*Hundred-weight*] [*French*] (AD)
QALD.......... Quality-Assurance Liaison Division (AD)
qall............ Quartz Aircraft Landing Lamp (AD)
qam............ Quadrature Amplitude Modulation (AD)
qam............ Queued Access Method (AD)
QAMIS......... Quality Assurance Monitoring Information System (AD)
QAMS.......... Quad-Phase Amplitude Modulation System (AD)
q & d.......... Quick and Dirty (AD)
Q & O......... Quebec and Ontario [*Canada*] (AD)
q & t.......... Quenched and Tempered (AD)
qao............ Quality Assurance Operation (AD)
QAOC.......... Quality Assurance Overview Contractor (AD)
QAOP.......... Quality Assurance Operating Procedure (AD)
QAP............ Quality Assurance Planning (AD)
qap............ Quinine, Atebrin, Plasmoquine [*Medicine*] (AD)
QAPL........... Queensland Airlines Proprietary Ltd. [*Australia*] (AD)
QAPS........... Queensland Association of Personnel Services [*Australia*] (AD)
QAR............ Quality Assurance Report [*A publication*] (AD)
qar............ Quick-Access Recording (AD)
QARAFNS .... Queen Alexandra's Royal Air Force Nursing Service [*British*] (AD)

QARANC ...... Queen Alexandra's Royal Army Nursing Service [*British*] (AD)
QAS............ Quality Answering System (AD)
QAS............ Quality Assurance System (AD)
qas............ Quick-Acting Scuttle (AD)
QASA.......... Queensland Amateur Swimming Association [*Australia*] (AD)
QASAR........ Quality Assurance Systems Analysis Review (AD)
Qat............ Qatar (AD)
QAT............ Quantitative Assessment and Training Center (AD)
QATB.......... Queensland Ambulance Transport Brigade [*Australia*] (AD)
QATP.......... Quality Assurance Test Procedure (AD)
qavc........... Quiet Automatic Volume Control (AD)
QAWA.......... Queensland Amateur Wrestling Association [*Australia*] (AD)
qb............. Qualified Bidders (AD)
qb............. Quarterback (AD)
QB............. Queensboro Bridge [*New York City*] (AD)
qb............. Quick Break (AD)
QBA........... Quebecair (AD)
QBA........... Queensland Bowling Association [*Australia*] (AD)
QBAA.......... Quality Brands Associates of America (AD)
QBB........... Queensland Butter Board [*Australia*] (AD)
Qbc........... Quebec (AD)
QBD........... Queensland Book Depot [*Australia*] (AD)
QBI........... Queen's Bureau of Investigation [*British*] (AD)
qbi........... Quite Bloody Impossible [*Slang*] (AD)
qbop.......... Quality Basic-Oxygen Process (AD)
QBRs.......... Queen's Bench Reports [*A publication*] (AD)
QBSM......... Que Besa su Mano [*Who Kisses Your Hand*] [*Spanish*] (AD)
QBSP......... Que Besa sus Pies [*Who Kisses Your Feet*] [*Spanish*] (AD)
QC............ Quadrantal Correction (AD)
qc............ Qualcosa [*Something*] [*Italian*] (AD)
qc............ Qualification Course (AD)
qc............ Quality Control (AD)
qc............ Quantitative Command (AD)
qc............ Quantum Counter (AD)
qc............ Quartz Crystal (AD)
QC............ Quebec City (AD)
QC............ Quezon City (AD)
q/c........... Quick Change (AD)
qc............ Quick Connect (AD)
QC............ Quincy College (AD)
QC............ Quinnipiac College (AD)
qc............ Quit Claim (AD)
QCA........... Quantum-Dot Cellular Automata [*Microelectronics*]
QCA........... Queensland Coal Associates [*Australia*] (AD)
QCA........... Queensland Cricket Association [*Australia*] (AD)
QCA........... Queensland Croquet Association (AD)
Q-cab......... Quiet Cab (AD)
QC & R....... Quality Control and Reliability (AD)
QC & T....... Quality Control and Test (AD)
Q-card........ Qualification Card (AD)
QCB........... Quality Control Bulletin (AD)
qcb........... Queue Control Block [*Data processing*] (AD)
QCBC......... Queen's Commendation for Brave Conduct [*British*] (AD)
qcbm.......... Quick-Connects Bulkhead Mounting (AD)
qcc........... Qualification Correlation Certification (AD)
QCC........... Queensland Conservation Council [*Australia*] (AD)
qcc........... Quick-Connect Coupling (AD)
QCCA......... Queensland Cleaning Contractors Association [*Australia*] (AD)
qcd........... Quality-Control Data (AD)
qcd........... Quantum Chromodynamics (AD)
qcd........... Quit-Claim Deed (AD)
QCDI.......... Quality Control Departmental Instruction (AD)
QCE........... Quality Control Engineering (AD)
QCEU......... Queensland Colliery Employees Union [*Australia*] (AD)
qcf........... Quartz-Crystal Filter (AD)
qcfo.......... Quartz-Crystal Frequency Oscillator (AD)
QCGC......... Queensland Cane-Growers Council [*Australia*] (AD)
qch........... Quick-Connect Handle (AD)
qci........... Quality-Control Information (AD)
QCI........... Queensland Confederation of Industry [*Australia*] (AD)
Q Cic......... Quintus Tullius Cicero (AD)
QC Isl........ Queen Charlotte Islands (AD)
Q City........ Quezon City [*Philippines*] (AD)
qck........... Quick-Connect Kit (AD)
qcl........... Quality-Control Level (AD)
QCM.......... Quality of Care Measurement [*Insurance*] (WYGK)

QCM	Queensland Coal Mining [Australia] (AD)
QCMA	Queensland Cooperative Milling Association [Australia] (AD)
QCMP	Queens' Council Member of Parliament [British] (AD)
QCNIC	Quad-Cities Nuclear Information Center (AD)
QCO	Quality Completion Order (AD)
qco	Quartz-Crystal Oscillator (AD)
Q Co	Queens County (AD)
QCO	Quick Changeover [Manufacturing]
QCP	Queens College Press [Australia] (AD)
QC/R	Quality Control/Reliability
qcr	Quality Control/Reliability (AD)
qcr	Quick-Change Response (AD)
QCRC	Quebec Central Railway Co. [Canada] (AD)
QC Rep	Quality-Control Representative (AD)
QC Rept	Quality-Control Report (AD)
qcrt	Quick-Change Real Time (AD)
QC Ry	Quebec Central Railway [Canada] (AD)
QCSO	Quality Control Stop Order (AD)
QCSR	Quaker Committee on Social Rehabilitation (AD)
QC Stand	Quality-Control Standard (AD)
qct	Questionable Corrective Task (AD)
qct	Quiescent Carrier Telephony (AD)
qcu	Quartz Crystal Unit (AD)
qcu	Quick-Change Unit (AD)
qcus	Quartz Crystal Unit Set (AD)
qcvc	Quick-Connect Valve Coupler (AD)
qcw	Quadrant Continuous Wave (AD)
QCWA	Queensland Country Women's Association [Australia] (AD)
Qcy	Quincy (AD)
qd	Quarterdeck (AD)
qd	Quartile Deviation (AD)
qd	Quater in Die [Four Times a Day] [Latin] (AD)
qd	Questioned Document (AD)
qd	Quick Delivery (AD)
qd	Quick Detachable [Weapon] (AD)
q-d	Quick-Disconnect (AD)
qda	Quantity Discount Agreement (AD)
qdc	Quick Detachable Communication (AD)
qdc	Quick-Disconnect Cap (AD)
qdcc	Quick-Disconnect Circular Connection (AD)
qdd	Qualified for Deep Diving (AD)
qdd	Quantized Decision Detection (AD)
QD/GD	Quincy Division/General Dynamics (AD)
qdh	Quick-Disconnect Handle (AD)
qdk	Quick-Disconnect Kit (AD)
QDMA	Quality Deer Management Association
qdn	Quick-Disconnect Nipple (AD)
qdo	Quadripartite Development Objective (AD)
Qd'O	Quai d'Orsay (AD)
QDO	Queensland Dairymens Organisation [Australia] (AD)
qdp	Quick-Disconnect Pivot (AD)
QDR	Quadrennial Defense Review [Army]
qdrnt	Quadrant (AD)
QDS	Quantitative Decision System (AD)
qds	Quick-Disconnect Series (AD)
qds	Quick-Disconnect Swivel (AD)
qdta	Quantitative Differential Thermal Analysis (AD)
qdv	Quick Disconnect Valve (AD)
qe	Quadrant Elevation (AD)
QE	Quebec (AD)
qe	Quick Estimate (AD)
qe	Quod Est [Which Is] [Latin] (AD)
qeav	Quick-Exhaust Air Valve (AD)
qec	Quick Engine Change (AD)
QECC	Queen Elizabeth Chemical Center [British] (AD)
qecu	Quick Engine-Change Unit (AD)
QED	Quality, Efficiency, Dependability (AD)
qed	Quantitative Evaluative Device (AD)
qed	Quantum Electrodynamics (AD)
qed	Quick-Reaction Dome (AD)
qed	Quod Erat Demonstrandum [That Which Was to Be Proved] [Latin] (AD)
qee	Quadruple Expansion Engine (AD)
qeev	Quantum Electrodynamics Electron Volts (AD)
QEF	Queensland Employers Federation [Australia] (AD)
qef	Quod Erat Faciendum [That Which Was to Be Done] [Latin] (AD)
QEFD	Queen Elizabeth's Foundation for the Disabled [British] (AD)
qei	Quod Erat Inveniendum [That Which Was to Be Discovered] [Latin] (AD)
qel	Quiet Extended Life (AD)
qem	Quadrant Electrometer (AD)
QEM	Quality Education for Minorities (AD)
QENP	Queen Elizabeth National Park [Uganda] (AD)
qeo	Quality Engineering Operations (AD)
QEP	Queen Elizabeth Park (AD)
QEP	Queen Elizabeth Planetarium (AD)
QEP	Queensland Environmental Program [Australia] (AD)
qer	Qualitative Equipment Requirements (AD)
QER	Quarterly Economic Review [A publication] (AD)
qescp	Quality Engineering Significant Control Points (AD)
QESP	Queen Emma Summer Palace (AD)
QESTS	Query, Update Entry, Search, Time Sharing [Computer science] (AD)
QET	Quality in Education [Project] (AIE)
QET	Queen Elizabeth Theatre [Vancouver] (AD)
qev	Quick Exhaust Valve (AD)

qf	Quality Factor (AD)
qf	Quench Frequency (AD)
qf	Quick Freeze (AD)
qfa	Quality per Final Article (AD)
qfc	Quantitative Flight Characteristics (AD)
qfcc	Quantitative Flight Characteristics Criteria (AD)
qfe	Quartz Fiber Electrometer (AD)
Q-fellows	Quartermaster Fellows (AD)
Q-fellows	Queer Fellows (AD)
Q fever	Query Fever (AD)
qff	Quadruple Flip-Flop (AD)
qfirc	Quick-Fix Interference-Reduction Capability (AD)
qfl	Quasi-Fermi Level (AD)
qfm	Quantized Frequency Modulation (AD)
qfo	Quartz Frequency Oscillator (AD)
qfp	Quartz Fiber Product (AD)
QFRI	Queensland Fisheries Research Institute [Australia] (AD)
QFS	Queensland Fisheries Service [Australia] (AD)
QFSM	Queen's Fire Services Medal [British] (AD)
qft	Quantized Field Theory (AD)
qg	Quadrature Grid (AD)
QG	Quartier General [Headquarters] [French] (AD)
QG	Quartier Generale [Headquarters] [Italian] (AD)
QGGA	Queensland Grain Growers Association [Australia] (AD)
qgm	Quarter-Girth Measure (AD)
QGPO	Qatar General Petroleum Organization (AD)
QGTB	Queensland Government Tourist Bureau [Australia] (AD)
qgv	Quantized Gate Video (AD)
qh	Quaque Hora [Every Hour] [Latin] (AD)
q-h	Quartz-Halogen (AD)
qh	Quartz Helix (AD)
QH	Queen's Hall (AD)
QH	West African Airways [ICAO designator] (AD)
QHV	Queen's Honorary Veterinarian [British] (AD)
QI	Cimber Air [ICAO designator] (AD)
qi	Quality Improvement (AD)
qi	Quality Indices (AD)
QI	Quarterly Index [A publication] (AD)
QI	Queensland Insurance [Australia] (AD)
QIA	Queensland Institute of Architects [Australia] (AD)
qiam	Queued Indexed Access Memory [Computer science] (AD)
qic	Quality Inspection Criteria (AD)
qic	Quartz-Iodine Crystal (AD)
qid	Quater in Die [Four Times a Day] [Latin] (AD)
QIE	Qualified International Executive (AD)
qie	Qunatitative Immuno-Electrophoresis (AD)
QIER	Queensland Institute for Educational Research [Australia] (AD)
QIH	Quality International Hotels (AD)
qil	Quartz Incandescent Lamp (AD)
qil	Quartz Iodine Lamp (AD)
QIMR	Queensland Institute of Medical Research [Australia] (AD)
qip	Quartz Insulation Part (AD)
QIPA	Queensland Institute of Public Affairs [Australia] (AD)
QIPS	Qualitative Incentive Procurement Service (AD)
QIR	Quechan Indian Reservation (AD)
qisam	Queued-Indexed Sequential-Access Method [Computer science] (AD)
qit	Qualification Information and Test (AD)
QIT	Queensland Institute of Technology [Australia] (AD)
QJC	Quincy Junior College (AD)
QJS	Quarterly Journal of Speech [A publication] (BRI)
QJSA	Quarterly Journal of Studies in Alcohol [A publication] (AD)
qjump	Queue Jump (AD)
qk	Quick (AD)
Qk Fl	Quick Flashing (AD)
qkly	Quickly (AD)
qkm	Quadratkilometer [Square Kilometer] [German] (AD)
QL	Lesotho Airways [ICAO designator] (AD)
ql	Quantum Libet [As Much as You Like] [Latin] (AD)
Q/L	Quarantine Launch (AD)
ql	Quarrel (AD)
QL	Queensland [Airline code] (AD)
ql	Query Language (AD)
ql	Quick Look (AD)
ql	Quilate [Carat] [Portuguese] (AD)
ql	Quintal (AD)
Qld	Queensland (AD)
qlfy	Qualify (AD)
qlfyg	Qualifying (AD)
qlfyn	Qualification (AD)
QLGA	Queensland Local Government Association [Australia] (AD)
qli	Quality of Life Index (AD)
qlii	Quais-LASER-Intensity Interferometer (AD)
qlit	Quick-Look Intermediate Tape (AD)
qll	Quartz Landing Lamp (AD)
qlm	Quasi-LASER Machine (AD)
QLOC	Queensland Light Opera Co. [Australia] (AD)
QLPC	Queensland Library Promotion Council [Australia] (AD)
QLS	Quebec Land Surveyor [Canada] (DD)
QLS	Queensland Law Society [Australia] (AD)
QLS	Queensland Littoral Society [Australia] (AD)
QLS	Quick Law Systems (AD)
QLS	Quick Loading System (AD)
qlsm	Quasi-LASER Sequential Machine (AD)
qlt	Quantitative Leak Test (AD)

QLTA	Queensland Lawn Tennis Association [*Australia*] (AD)
qlty	Quality (AD)
QM	Air Malawi [*ICAO designator*] (AD)
qm	Quadratmeter [*Square Meter*] [*German*] (AD)
qm	Quantum Mechanics (AD)
qm	Quaque Mane [*Every Morning*] [*Latin*] (AD)
QM	Queens Museum (AD)
qm	Query Message (AD)
qm	Quintal Metrico [*Metric Quintal*] [*Spain*] (AD)
qm	Quo Modo [*In What Manner*] [*Latin*] (AD)
QMA	Qatar Monetary Agency (AD)
qma	Qualified Military Available (AD)
qma	Quality Material Approach (AD)
qmao	Qualified for Mobilization Ashore Only (AD)
Q-max	Quarantine Maximum (AD)
qmb	Quick Make-and-Break (AD)
QMBA	Queensland Master Builders Association [*Australia*] (AD)
qmdk	Quick Mechanical Disconnect Kit (AD)
QME	Quantock Marine Enterprises (AD)
qme	Queueing Matrix Evaluation (AD)
QMFCI	Quartermaster Food and Container Institute (AD)
QMIA	Queensland Motor Industry Association [*Australia*] (AD)
QMM	Marina di Massa [*Italy*] [*Airport symbol*] (AD)
qmo	Qualitative Material Objective (AD)
QMP	Quezon Memorial Park [*Philippines*] (AD)
QMPA	Queensland Master Painters Association [*Australia*] (AD)
qmqb	Quick-Make Quick-Break (AD)
qmr	Qualitative Material Requirement (AD)
Qmr	Quartermaster [*Military*] (AD)
QMR & E	Quartermaster Research and Engineering [*Military*] (AD)
Qm Sgt	Quartermaster Sergeant [*Military*] (AD)
qmsw	Quartz Metal Sealed Window (AD)
QMT	Queens-Midtown Tunnel (AD)
qmw	Quartz Metal Window (AD)
QN	Bush Pilots Airways [*ICAO designator*] (AD)
qn	Quaque Nocte [*Every Night*] [*Latin*] (AD)
Qn	Queen (AD)
qn	Question (AD)
qn	Quotation (AD)
qna	Quality per Next Assembly (AD)
Qndk	Quensk [*Language of the Quains*] (AD)
QNP	Quezon National Park [*Philippines*] (AD)
qns	Quantity Not Sufficient (AD)
Qns	Queens (AD)
QNS & L	Quebec North Shore and Labrador Railway [*Canada*] (AD)
Qns Coll	Queen's College (AD)
Qnsd	Queensland (AD)
Qns Pk	Queens Park (AD)
qnt	Quantisizer (AD)
qnt	Quintet (AD)
qnty	Quantity (AD)
QNWR	Quivira National Wildlife Refuge [*Kansas*] (AD)
QO	Bar Harbor Airlines [*ICAO designator*] (AD)
qo	Quick Opening (AD)
QOA	Quasi-Official Agencies (AD)
QOD	Quebec Order of Dentists [*Canada*] (AD)
qod	Quick-Opening Device (AD)
QOF	Quaker Oats Foundation (AD)
QOIC	Quarantine Officer in Charge [*Military*] (AD)
qon	Quarter Ocean Net (AD)
qopri	Qualitative Operational Requirements (AD)
qor	Qualitative Operational Requirement (AD)
QOS	Quick on System (AD)
qot	Quote (AD)
qotn	Quotation (AD)
q-P	Quanti-Pirquet (AD)
qp	Quantum Placet [*At Discretion*] [*Latin*] (AD)
qp	Queen Post (AD)
QP	Queen's Printer [*British*] (AD)
qp	Quick Process (AD)
QP	Sunbird [*ICAO designator*] (AD)
qpa	Qualitative Point Average (AD)
qpa	Quantity per Article (AD)
qpa	Quantity per Assembly (AD)
QPA	Queensland Police Academy [*Australia*] (AD)
QPA	Queensland Polynesian Association [*Australia*] (AD)
Q P & S	Quaker Peace and Service (AD)
QPC	Qatar Petroleum Co. (AD)
qpei	Quality per End Item (AD)
qpf	Quantitative Precipitation Forecast (AD)
QPF	Quebec Police Force [*Canada*] (AD)
QPFC	Queen's Park Football Club (AD)
QPFL	Queensland Professional Fishermens League [*Australia*] (AD)
qpi	Quadratic Performance Index (AD)
QPIS	Quality Performance Instruction Sheet (AD)
QPL	Queens Public Library (AD)
qplt	Quiet Propulsion Lift Technology (AD)
QPM	Queen's Polar Medal [*British*] (AD)
QPM	Questions of Procedure for Ministers (AD)
QPP	Quebec Provincial Police [*Canada*] (AD)
QPP	Quetico Provincial Park [*Ontario, Canada*] (AD)
QPR	Quantity Progress Report (AD)
qps	Quantitative Physical Science (AD)
qpsk	Quad-Phase Shift Key [*Computer science*] (AD)
QPTC	Quarry Products Training Council (AIE)
QQ	Michigan Airways [*ICAO designator*] (AD)
QQ	Qara Qash [*Sinkiang province of China*] (AD)
QQ	Qara Qum [*Sinkiang province of China*] (AD)
qq	Quaque [*Each*] [*Latin*] (AD)
qq	Quartos (AD)
qq	Quelques [*Some*] [*French*] (AD)
QQ	Que Que [*Rhodesia*] (AD)
qq	Questionable Questionnaire (AD)
qq	Quintales [*Quintals*] [*Spanish*] (AD)
qq	Quoque [*Every*] [*Latin*] (AD)
qqd	Quantum Quatra Die [*Every Fourth Day*] [*Latin*] (AD)
qqf	Quelquefois [*Sometimes*] [*French*] (AD)
qqh	Quantum Quatra Hora [*Every Four Hours*] [*Latin*] (AD)
qq hor	Quaque Hora [*Every Hour*] [*Latin*] (AD)
qqma	Quality Qualified Military Availability (AD)
qqpr	Quantitative and Qualitative Personnel Requirements (AD)
qqv	Quae Vide [*Which See*] [*Latin*] (AD)
q/qy	Question/Query (AD)
QR	Air Satellite [*ICAO designator*] (AD)
qr	Qualifications Record (AD)
qr	Quantum Rectus [*Quantity is Correct*] [*Latin*] (AD)
qr	Quarter (AD)
QR	Queensland Railways [*Australia*] (AD)
qr	Quick Reaction (AD)
qr	Quick Receipt (AD)
QR	Quick Response (AD)
QR	Quintana Roo (AD)
qr	Quire (AD)
qra	Quality Reliability Assurance (AD)
QRA	Queensland Rifle Association [*Australia*] (AD)
qra	Quick Reaction Alert (AD)
QRB	Quarterly Review of Biology [*A publication*] (BRI)
qrbm	Quasi-Random Band Model (AD)
QRC	Queensland Rubber Co. [*Australia*] (AD)
qrc	Quick Reaction Capability (AD)
qrcg	Quasi-Random Code Generator (AD)
QRCUP	Quebec Region Canadian University Press (AD)
qrg	Quick Response Graphic (AD)
qrga	Quadrupole Residual Gas Analyzer (AD)
qri	Qualitative Requirements Information (AD)
qric	Quick Reaction Installation Capability (AD)
QRL	Queensland Research League [*Australia*] (AD)
Qrmr	Quartermaster (AD)
QRO	Quality Review Organization (AD)
Qro.	Queretaro (AD)
qro	Quick Reaction Operation (AD)
Q Roo	Quintana Roo (AD)
QRPA	Quartermaster Radiation Planning Agency (AD)
qrs	Quarters (AD)
qrt	Quarter (AD)
qrtg	Quartering (AD)
qrtly	Quarterly (AD)
qrtmstr	Quartermaster (AD)
QRTR	Quarter-Plate (VRA)
QRV	Qualified Real-Estate Valuer (AD)
qrv	Quick-Release Valve (AD)
QRX	Queensland Railfast Express [*Australia*] (AD)
qry	Quality and Reliability Year (AD)
QS	Cal Sierra [*ICAO designator*] (AD)
qs	Quadrophonic Stereo (AD)
qs	Quantum Sufficit [*As Much as Suffices*] [*Latin*] (AD)
QS	Quarternote Society (AD)
qs	Quarter Section (AD)
QS	Quecksilbersaeule [*Mercury Column*] [*German*] (AD)
QS	Queensland Society [*Australia*] (AD)
QS	Queueing System (AD)
QSA	Queensland Shopkeepers Association [*Australia*] (AD)
qsam	Queued Sequential Access Method (AD)
qs & l	Quarters, Subsistence, and Laundry (AD)
qsbg	Quasi-Stellar Blue Galaxies (AD)
qsbo	Quasi-Stellar Blue Objects (AD)
QSC	Quebec Securities Commission [*Canada*] (AD)
qse	Qualified Scientists and Engineers (AD)
qsf	Quasi-Static Field (AD)
QSF	Queensland Soccer Federation [*Australia*] (AD)
qsg	Quasi-Stellar Galaxy (AD)
qsi	Quality Salary Increase (AD)
qsic	Quality Standard Inspection Criteria (AD)
QSJM	Queen's Silver Jubilee Medal [*British*] (AD)
QSL	Queensland State Library [*Australia*] (AD)
qsm	Quadruple-Screw Motorship (AD)
qsm	Quarter-Square Multipliers (AD)
qsm	Queen's Service Medal [*British*] (AD)
QSM	Queen's Service Medal [*British*] (AD)
QSM	South Molle Islands [*Queensland*] [*Airport symbol*] (AD)
QSMO	Quaker State Motor Oils (AD)
qso	Quasibiennial Stratospheric Oscillation (AD)
qso	Quasistellar Object (AD)
QSO	Quebec Symphony Orchestra [*Canada*] (AD)
QSO	Queensland Symphony Orchestra [*Australia*] (AD)
QSO	Queen's Service Order [*British*] (AD)
qsp	Quality Search Procedure (AD)
QSPP	Quebec Society for the Protection of Plants [*Canada*] (AD)
QSR	Quartier de Securite Renforcee [*Maximum Security Prison*] [*French*] (AD)

qsr	Quick-Strike Reconnaissance (AD)
qsra	Quiet Short-Haul Research Aircraft (AD)
QSRIG	Quantity Surveyors Research and Information Group (AD)
qsrs	Quasi-Stellar Radio Sources (AD)
QSS	Quadruple-Screw Ship (AD)
qss	Quasi-Stellar Source (AD)
qssa	Quasi-Stationary-State Approximation (AD)
QSSCT	Queensland Society of Sugar Cane Technologists [Australia] (AD)
qssp	Quasi-Solid-State Panel (AD)
QST	Quebec Standard Test [Canada] (AD)
qstn	Question (AD)
qstnr	Questionnaire (AD)
qstol	Quiet-and-Short Takeoff and Landing (AD)
qsts	Quadruple-Screw Turbine Steamship (AD)
Q-switch	Quantum Switch (AD)
qsy	Quiet Sun Year (AD)
QT	Quality Test (AD)
qt	Quality Test (AD)
qt	Quantity (AD)
qt	Quarry Tile (AD)
qt	Quart (AD)
qt	Quarter (AD)
qt	Quick Test (AD)
qt	Quiet (AD)
QT	Vaengir [ICAO designator] (AD)
qta	Quadrant Transformer Assembly (AD)
QTAC	Queensland Tertiary Admissions Centre [Australia] (AD)
qtam	Queued Telecommunication Access Method (AD)
qtaux	Quintaux [Quintals] [French] (AD)
qtb	Quarry-Tile Base (AD)
QTB	Queensland Timber Board [Australia] (AD)
QTB	Queensland Trotting Board [Australia] (AD)
QTC	Quebec Teaching Congress [Canada] (AD)
QTC	Queensland Turf Club [Australia] (AD)
qtd	Quartered (AD)
qte	Quote (AD)
qted	Quick Text Editor (AD)
qted	Quoted (AD)
qtf	Quarry-Tile Floor (AD)
QTF	Quebec Teachers' Federation [Canada] (AD)
qtfl	Quatrefoil (VRA)
qtg	Quoting (AD)
QTIB	Quebec Tourist Information Bureau [Canada] (AD)
QTIP	Qualified Terminable Interest Property Trust [Investment term] (DFIT)
QTLC	Queensland Trades and Labor Council [Australia] (AD)
qtly	Quarterly (AD)
QTM	Quechon Tribal Museum [Yuma, Arizona] (AD)
qtn	Quotation (AD)
qto	Quarto (AD)
qtol	Quiet Takeoff and Landing (AD)
qtp	Quantum Theory of Paramagnetism (AD)
QTR	Quality Technical Report (AD)
QTR	Quality Technical Requirement (AD)
qtr	Quarry-Tile Roof (AD)
qtr	Quarter (AD)
qts	Quarts (AD)
qts	Quick Turn Stock (AD)
QTTC	Queensland Tourist and Travel Corp. [Australia] (AD)
qtte	Quartette (AD)
QTU	Queensland Teachers Union [Australia] (AD)
qty	Quantity (AD)
qtydesreq	Quantity Desired or Requested (AD)
qtz	Quartz (AD)
qtze	Quartzose (AD)
qtzic	Quartzitic (AD)
qtzt	Quartzite (AD)
qu	Quart (AD)
qu	Quarter (AD)
qu	Quarterly (AD)
qu	Quasi [As It Were] [Latin] (AD)
Qu	Queen (AD)
QU	Queen's College [Cambridge, Oxford] (AD)
qu	Query (AD)
qu	Question (AD)
QU	Uganda Airlines [ICAO designator] (AD)
qua	Quadrate (AD)
quaal	Quaalude (AD)
quack	Quacksalver (AD)
quacks	Quacksalvers (AD)
quackupunc	Quackupuncture (AD)
quad	Quaalude (AD)
quad	Quadrangle (AD)
quad	Quadrant (AD)
quad	Quadrat (AD)
quad	Quadruplet (AD)
Qu-AD	Quality-Assurance Department (AD)
Qu-AD	Quality-Assurance Division (AD)
quad c	Quadripod Cane (AD)
quadplex	Quadriplex (AD)
quadrap	Quadraphonic (AD)
quadrip	Quadriplegia (AD)
quadro	Quadroon (AD)
quadrup	Quadruped (AD)
quadrupl	Quadruplicato [Four Times as Much] [Latin] (AD)
quag	Quagmire (AD)

Quaker	Quaker Oats (AD)
Quaker	Quaker Press (AD)
qual	Qualification (AD)
qual	Qualify (AD)
qual	Quality (AD)
qual anal	Qualitative Analysis (AD)
quals	Qualifying Examinations (AD)
quals	Qualifying Tests (AD)
quam	Quadrature-Amplitude Modulation (AD)
Quandary	Quandary Peak [Colorado] (AD)
quango	Quasi-Autonomous Non-Governmental Organization (AD)
quant	Quantity (AD)
quant	Quantum (AD)
quantras	Question Analysis Transformation and Search [Data processing] (AD)
quant suff	Quantum Sufficit [Sufficient Quantity] [Latin] (AD)
quaops	Quarantine Operations (AD)
Quaq	Quaquero [Quaker] [Spanish] (AD)
quar	Quarantine (AD)
quar pars	Quarta Pars [One-Fourth Part] [Latin] (AD)
quarpel	Quartermaster Water-Repellent [Military] (AD)
quarr	Quarry (AD)
quart	Quarter Gallon (AD)
Quart	Quarterly (AD)
quart	Quarterly (AD)
quart	Quartet (AD)
Quart Ital	Quartetto Italiano [Italian Quartet] [Italian] (AD)
quartzite	Granular Quartz Rock (AD)
quasar	Quasi-Stellar Radio (AD)
quaser	Quantum Amplification by Stimulated-Emission of Radiation (AD)
Quash	Quashey (AD)
Quat	Quaternary (AD)
quat	Quaternary (AD)
quat	Quattuor [Four] [Latin] (AD)
QUD	Queen's University of Dublin (AD)
Que	Quebec [Canada] (DD)
QUE	Quebecair (AD)
Que	Quebecois (AD)
Que	Quechua (AD)
Que	Quenia [Kenya] [Portuguese] (AD)
Queensl	Queensland (AD)
Queens Q	Queen's Quarterly [A publication] (BRI)
Quen	Quentin (AD)
Quent	San Quentin [California State Prison] (AD)
Quer	Queretaro (AD)
ques	Question (AD)
quest	Quality Electrical System Test (AD)
QUEST	Queens Educational and Social Team (AD)
quest	Questioned (AD)
questal	Quiet, Experimental, Short-Takeoff-and-Landing [NASA] (AD)
questar	Quantitative Utility Evaluation Suggesting Targets for the Allocations of Resources (AD)
quester	Quick and Efficient System to Enhance Retrieval (AD)
questn	Questionnaire (AD)
qufyd	Qualified (AD)
QUI	Quirindi [New South Wales] [Airport symbol] (AD)
QUIC	Question and Information Connection [St. Louis Public Library] (AD)
Quich	Quichua (AD)
quicha	Quantitative Inhalation Challenge Apparatus [Medicine] (AD)
QUICK	Queens University Interpretative Code (AD)
quico	Quality Improvement through Cost Optimization (AD)
quiktran	Quick Fortran [Computer science] (AD)
Quill & Q	Quill & Quire [A publication] (BRI)
Quilmas	San Quilmas (AD)
quilwk	Quillwork (VRA)
quim	Quimica [Chemistry] [Spanish] (AD)
Quimigal	Quimica de Portugal (AD)
Quin	Quincy (AD)
Quin	Quinten (AD)
quin	Quintet (AD)
Quin	Quintilianus (AD)
Quin	Quintilius (AD)
Quin	Quintillian (AD)
Quin	Quintino (AD)
Quin	Quintius (AD)
quin	Quintuplet (AD)
quins	Quintuplets (AD)
Quint	Quintilian (AD)
quint	Quintuplicate (AD)
quint	Quintus [Fifth] [Latin] (AD)
quintupl	Quintuplicate (AD)
quis	Quisling [World War II] (AD)
quix	Quixote (AD)
QUL	Queen's University Library (AD)
QUN	Qutdligssat [Greenland] [Airport symbol] (AD)
quod	Quodlibet [As You Please] [Latin] (AD)
Quoddy	Passamaquoddy Bay (AD)
quok	Quokka (AD)
Quon Pt	Quonset Point [Rhode Island] (AD)
quor	Quorom [Of Which] [Latin] (AD)
quor	Quorum (AD)
quot	Quotation (AD)
quot	Quotidie [Daily] [Latin] (AD)
quotid	Quotidie [Every Day] [Latin] (AD)
qup	Quantity per Unit Pack (AD)

QUP .... Quincemil [*Peru*] [*Airport symbol*] (AD)
Qur .... Quran [*Koran*] [*Malay*] (AD)
qv .... Quality Verification (AD)
q-v .... Q-Value (AD)
QVM .... Queen Victoria Museum [*Launceston, Tasmania*] (AD)
QVM .... Que Viva Mexico [*Long Live Mexico*] [*Spanish*] (AD)
QVS .... Quality Verification Surveillance (AD)
qvt .... Quality Verification Test (AD)
QW .... Air Turks and Caicos [*ICAO designator*] (AD)
qw .... Quarter Wave (AD)
qwa .... Quarter-Wave Antenna (AD)
qwd .... Quarterly World Day (AD)
q-wedge ...... Quartz Wedge (AD)
QWGCD .... Quadripartite Working Group for Combat Development [*American, Australian, British, and Canadian armies*] (AD)
qwl .... Quality of Working Life (AD)

qwl .... Quick Weight Loss (AD)
qwot .... Quarter-Wave Optical Thickness (AD)
qwp .... Quarter-Wave Plate (AD)
QX .... Century Airlines [*ICAO designator*] (AD)
QX .... Horizon Air [*ICAO designator*] (AD)
qx .... Quintaux [*Hundred-Weights*] [*French*] (AD)
QY .... Aero Virgin Islands [*ICAO designator*] (AD)
qy .... Quantum Yield (AD)
Qy .... Quay (AD)
qy .... Query (AD)
QYC .... Quincy Yacht Club (AD)
QYO .... Queensland Youth Orchestra [*Australia*] (AD)
qz .... Quartz (AD)
Qz .... Quartz (AD)
QZ .... Zambia Airways [*ICAO designator*] (AD)
QZS .... Quebec Zoological Society [*Canada*] (AD)

By Acronym

R
By Acronym

R .... Declared or Paid in the Preceding 12 Months Plus Stock Dividend [*Investment term*] (DFIT)
R .... Option Not Traded [*Investment term*] (DFIT)
RA .... Resident Assistant
RA .... Reviews in Anthropology [*A publication*] (BRI)
RA .... Royal Academy [*British*] (AIE)
RA .... Royal Nepal Airlines [*ICAO designator*] (AD)
RAE .... Research Assessment Exercise [*Higher Education Funding Council*] (AIE)
RAH .... Reviews in American History [*A publication*] (BRI)
RALPH .... Rapidly Adapting Lateral Position Handler
RAM .... RADAR-Absorbent Material [*Aviation*]
RAMP .... Raising Achievements in Mathematics Project (AIE)
RAMS .... Regional Atmospheric Modeling System
R&D .... Research and Development (DFIT)
R&R Bk N ... Reference & Research Book News [*A publication*] (BRI)
RANTES ...... Regulated-upon-Activation, Normal T Expressed and Secreted [*Immunology*]
Rapport .... Rapport: The Modern Guide to Books, Music & More [*A publication*] (BRI)
RASS .... ROSAT [*Roentgen Satellite*] All Sky Survey
RAU .... Rangpur [*Bangladesh*] [*Airport symbol*] (AD)
RAV .... Repackaged Asset Vehicle
RAYS .... Risk and Youth Smoking [*Project*] (AIE)
RBA .... Reserve Bank of Australia
RBC .... Royal British-Colonial Society of Artists, London [*1886*] (NGC)
RBDS .... Radio Broadcast Data System
RBDS .... Radio Broadcasting Data System
RBF .... Raba Raba [*New Guinea*] [*Airport symbol*] (AD)
RBG .... Roseburg [*Oregon*] [*Airport symbol*] (AD)
RBL .... Red Bluff [*California*] [*Airport symbol*] (AD)
rblt .... Rebuilt (VRA)
RBML .... Rare Books & Manuscript Librarianship [*American Library Association*]
RBO .... Robore [*Bolivia*] [*Airport symbol*] (AD)
rbr .... Rubber (VRA)
rby .... Ruby (VRA)
RC .... Reconstructed Communism Party [*Italy*]
RCC .... Residential Colleges Committee (AIE)
RCD .... Rabbit Calicivirus Disease
RCF .... Review of Contemporary Fiction [*A publication*] (BRI)
RCH .... Residential Children's Home (AIE)
RCN .... Residential Communications Network [*Telecommunications service*]
RCS .... Rochester [*England*] [*Airport symbol*] (AD)
RCVTP .... Reserve Component Virtual Training Program [*Army*] (RDA)
RD .... Aviona [*ICAO designator*] (AD)
Rd .... Road (DD)
RDC .... Reading Development Continuum (AIE)
RDS .... Rio Grande do Sul [*Brazil*] [*Airport symbol*] (AD)
RDU .... Regional Development Unit [*Manpower Services Commission*] (AIE)
rdwd .... Redwood (VRA)
rdymd .... Readymade (VRA)
RE .... Aer Arann Teo [*ICAO designator*] (AD)
RE .... Royal Society of Painter-Etchers and Engravers, London [*1880*] (NGC)
REA .... Retirement Equity Act of 1984 (WYGK)
Readings .... Readings: A Journal of Reviews and Commentary in Mental Health [*A publication*] (BRI)
REC .... Religious Education Centre (AIE)
recon .... Reconstruction (VRA)
RED .... Refunding Escrow Deposit [*Finance*] (DFIT)
REDS .... Retrovirus Epidemiology Donor Study [*Medicine*]
Ref Bk R ..... Reference Book Review [*A publication*] (BRI)
refty .... Refectory (VRA)
reg .... Region (DD)
REGE .... Regular Eight [*Motion picture*] (VRA)
regl .... Regional (DD)
REH .... Rehoboth Beach [*Delaware*] [*Airport symbol*] (AD)
REIT .... Real Estate Investment Trust [*Pooled funds that invest in income-producing residential and commerical properties*]
REITS .... Racial Equality in Training Schemes (AIE)
rel .... Relation (DD)
rel .... Relief (VRA)
Rel Ed .... Religious Education [*A publication*] (BRI)
relig .... Religion (VRA)
reliq .... Reliquary (VRA)

Rel St .... Religious Studies [*A publication*] (BRI)
Rel St Rev ... Religious Studies Review [*A publication*] (BRI)
Renais .... Renaissance (VRA)
Ren & Ref ... Renaissance and Reformation [*A publication*] (BRI)
Ren Q .... Renaissance Quarterly [*A publication*] (BRI)
REP .... Siem Reap [*Cambodia*] [*Airport symbol*] (AD)
repl .... Replica (VRA)
Repo .... Repurchase Agreement [*Finance*] (DFIT)
reprd .... Reproduction (VRA)
repres .... Representation (VRA)
repu .... Repousse (VRA)
RER .... Potrerillos [*Chile*] [*Airport symbol*] (AD)
res .... Resin (VRA)
Res .... Resources (DD)
RES .... Review of English Studies [*A publication*] (BRI)
Res & Exp ... Research and Exploration [*A publication*] (BRI)
resco .... Resin-Coated (VRA)
ResEdit ...... Resource Editor [*Computer science*] (DOM)
rest .... Restored (VRA)
RET .... Registered Engineering Technologist (DD)
ret .... Retired (DD)
RETO .... Retouched (VRA)
Rev .... Reverend (DD)
rev .... Reverse (VRA)
REX .... Rolodex Electronic Express
rf .... Roof (VRA)
RF .... Rossair [*ICAO designator*] (AD)
RF .... Travelair Goteborg [*ICAO designator*] (AD)
RFA .... Regional Financial Associates Inc.
RFEA .... Regional Further Education Adviser (AIE)
RFH .... Rio Mayo [*Argentina*] [*Airport symbol*] (AD)
RFIC .... Radio Frequency Integrated Circuit
RFT .... Request for Technology (DOM)
RFW .... Robinhood [*Queensland*] [*Airport symbol*] (AD)
RFX .... Roxborough [*Queensland*] [*Airport symbol*] (AD)
RGB monitor ... Red, Green, Blue Monitor
Rgcy .... Regency (VRA)
RGN .... Rangoon [*Burma*] [*Airport symbol*] (AD)
RGO .... Rosella Plains [*Queensland*] [*Airport symbol*] (AD)
RGR .... Rio Grande [*Brazil*] [*Airport symbol*] (AD)
RGS .... Regulators of G-Protein Signalling [*Biochemistry*]
RGT .... Rengat [*Sumatra, Indonesia*] [*Airport symbol*] (AD)
RH .... Regal Bahamas International Airlines [*ICAO designator*] (AD)
RHD .... Rio Hondo [*Argentina*] [*Airport symbol*] (AD)
RHE .... Rheims [*France*] [*Airport symbol*] (AD)
RHL .... Roy Hill [*Western Australia*] [*Airport symbol*] (AD)
RI .... Eastern Airlines [*ICAO designator*] (AD)
RI .... Royal Institute of Painters in Water-Colours, London [*1831*] (NGC)
RIBA .... Recombinant Immunoblot Assay [*Medicine*]
RIBA .... Royal Institute of British Architects, London [*1834*] (NGC)
RIBMESC ... Resources Information Bank on Multicultural Education (AIE)
ribnwk .... Ribbonwork (VRA)
rib vlt .... Ribbed Vault (VRA)
RICO .... Racketeer Influenced and Corrupt Organization Act (DFIT)
RIPEM .... Riordan's Internet Privacy Enhanced Mail [*Computer science*]
RISE .... Research and Information State Education Trust (AIE)
RISO .... Rocket Impacts on Stratospheric Ozone [*Air Force*]
RIY .... Riyan Mukalla [*South Arabia (Yemen)*] [*Airport symbol*] (AD)
RJH .... Rajshahi [*Bangladesh*] [*Airport symbol*] (AD)
RKT .... Ras-al-Khaima [*Trucial Oman*] [*Airport symbol*] (AD)
RL .... Aerolineas Nicaraguenses [*ICAO designator*] (AD)
RL .... Crown International Airlines [*ICAO designator*] (AD)
RLDU .... Resources for Learning Development Unit (AIE)
RLV .... Recordable LASER Videodisc [*Optical Disc Corp.*] (DOM)
RM .... Review of Metaphysics [*A publication*] (BRI)
rm .... Room (VRA)
Rm .... Room (DD)
RM .... Wings West [*ICAO designator*] (AD)
RMC .... Regional Management Centre (AIE)
RMI .... Remote Method Invocation [*Computer science*] (DOM)
RMI .... Rimini [*Italy*] [*Airport symbol*] (AD)
RMP .... Resistance Management Plans [*To prevent insect adaptation to toxins*]
RMR .... Rocky Mountain Review of Language & Literature [*A publication*] (BRI)
rms .... Root Mean Squared (DOM)

Rmsq	Romanesque (VRA)
RMT	Rocky Mount [*North Carolina*] [*Airport symbol*] (AD)
RN	Royal Air International [*ICAO designator*] (AD)
rndr	Rendering (VRA)
rnfd	Reinforced (VRA)
ROCAP	Regional Office for Central America and Panama
RocksMiner	Rocks & Minerals [*A publication*] (BRI)
ROEAP	Regional Office for Education, Asia and Pacific [*UNESCO*] (AIE)
ROF	Rose Hall [*Guyana*] [*Airport symbol*] (AD)
ROI	Royal Institute of Oil Painters, London [*1883*] (NGC)
ROLFE	Review of Law in Further Education (AIE)
Rom	Romania (VRA)
ROSEBUD	Rare Object Searches with Bolometers Underground [*Astrophysics*]
ROSPA	Royal Society for the Prevention of Accidents [*British*] (AIE)
roswd	Rosewood (VRA)
Roundup M	Roundup Magazine [*A publication*] (BRI)
RP	Precision Airlines [*ICAO designator*] (AD)
RP	Review of Politics [*A publication*] (BRI)
RPE	Record of Personal Experience (AIE)
rplx	Rhoplex (VRA)
RPO	Retail Postal Outlet (DD)
RQ	Maldives International Airlines [*ICAO designator*] (AD)
RR	Review for Religious [*A publication*] (BRI)
RR	Royal Air Force [*ICAO designator*] (AD)
RRA	Revenue Reconciliation Act of 1990 (WYGK)
RRAS	Routing and Remote Access Service [*Computer science*]
RRK	Rourkela [*India*] [*Airport symbol*] (AD)
RROSP	Race Relations and Overseas Students Panel (AIE)
RRP	Resource Referral Program (WYGK)
RR sta	Railroad Station (VRA)
RS	Aeropesca [*ICAO designator*] (AD)
RSA	Royal Scottish Academy, Edinburgh [*1826*] (NGC)
RSAC	Recreational Software Advisory Council
RSAM	Royal Scottish Academy of Music and Drama (AIE)
RSC	Respiratory Symptoms Complex [*Medicine*]
RSG	Revenue Support Grant (AIE)
RSK	Ransiki [*West Irian, Indonesia*] [*Airport symbol*] (AD)
RSO	Remanso [*Brazil*] [*Airport symbol*] (AD)
RSR	Reference Services Review [*A publication*] (BRI)
rstrau	Restaurant (VRA)
RSU	Rio Sucio [*Colombia*] [*Airport symbol*] (AD)
RSV	Respiratory Syncytial Virus [*Medicine*]
RSVP	Resource Reservation Protocol [*Videoconferencing*]
RSW	Residential Social Worker (AIE)
RT	Norving [*ICAO designator*] (AD)
RT	Reading Teacher [*A publication*] (BRI)
rt	Right (VRA)
rte	Route (DD)
RTF	Rutherford [*New Jersey*] [*Airport symbol*] (AD)
RTFM	Read the Fine Manual [*Computer science*] (DOM)
RTI	Remnant Tumor Index [*Surgery*]
RTTC	Redstone Technical Test Center [*Army*] (RDA)
RU	Britt Airways [*ICAO designator*] (AD)
rub	Rubbing (VRA)
Rum	Rumania (VRA)
RUMINT	Rumor Intelligence
RUP	Rupsi [*India*] [*Airport symbol*] (AD)
Rus	Russia (VRA)
RUSA	Reference and User Services Association [*Formerly, RASD*]
Russ Rev	Russian Review [*A publication*] (BRI)
rustc	Rustication (VRA)
RUY	Ruinas de Copan [*Honduras*] [*Airport symbol*] (AD)
RVC	River Cess [*Liberia*] [*Airport symbol*] (AD)
RVK	Rorvik [*Norway*] [*Airport symbol*] (AD)
rvl	Revival (VRA)
RVQ	Review of Vocational Qualifications (AIE)
RW	Republic [*ICAO designator*] (AD)
rwhi	Rawhide (VRA)
RWJF	Robert Wood Johnson Foundation
RWL	Rawlins [*Wyoming*] [*Airport symbol*] (AD)
RWS	Royal Society of Painters in Water-Colours, London [*1804*] (NGC)
RX	British Independent Airways [*ICAO designator*] (AD)
RX	Capitol Air Service [*ICAO designator*] (AD)
RXA	Raudha [*South Arabia*] [*Airport symbol*] (AD)
RY	Air Rwanda [*ICAO designator*] (AD)
RY	Perkiomen Airways [*ICAO designator*] (AD)
RYK	Rahimyar Kahn [*Pakistan*] [*Airport symbol*] (AD)
RZ	Arabia [*ICAO designator*] (AD)
RZB	Roseberth [*Queensland*] [*Airport symbol*] (AD)
RZR	Ramsar [*Iran*] [*Airport symbol*] (AD)
RZY	Rezayeh [*Iran*] [*Airport symbol*] (AD)

S
By Acronym

S .... No Option Offered [*Investment term*] (DFIT)
S .... San (VRA)
S .... Sankt (VRA)
S .... Santa (VRA)
S .... Santo (VRA)
S .... Signed (DFIT)
S .... South (VRA)
S .... Southern (VRA)
SA .... Scientific American [*A publication*] (BRI)
SA .... Species-Area [*Ecology*]
SAARD's ...... Slow-Acting Antirheumatic Drugs [*Medicine*]
SAAVQ .... Societe des Artistes en Arts Visuels du Quebec [*1980, founded 1966 as SAPQ, CPQ from 1978, CAPQ from 1982*] [*Canada*] (NGC)
SABEU .... Scottish Adult Basic Education Unit (AIE)
SAC .... Sacramento [*California*] [*Airport symbol*] (AD)
SACO .... Subject Authority Cooperative Program [*American Library Association*]
SACRE .... Standing Advisory Council for Religious Education (AIE)
SAD .... Safford [*Arizona*] [*Airport symbol*] (AD)
SADL .... Significant Activities of Daily Living (WYGK)
SAEMA .... Scottish Association for Educational Management and Administration (AIE)
SAF .... Societe des Artistes Francais, Paris [*1880*] [*French*] (NGC)
S Afr .... South Africa (VRA)
SAF-TE .... SCSI Accessed Fault-Tolerant Enclosures [*Computer science*]
SAIL .... Staged Assessment in Learning (AIE)
SAJ .... Sirajgang [*Bangladesh*] [*Airport symbol*] (AD)
Salm .... Salmagundi [*A publication*] (BRI)
SALPA .... Special Adult Learning Programmes Association (AIE)
SALTIRE ...... Scottish Academic Live Television Interconnect and Research Environment (AIE)
SAM .... Saba [*Netherlands Antilles*] [*Airport symbol*] (AD)
S Am .... South America (VRA)
SAN .... Satellite Access Nodes
sanct .... Sanctuary (VRA)
s&d .... Signed & Dated (VRA)
S&L .... Sale and Leaseback (DFIT)
S&L .... Savings and Loan (DFIT)
S&P .... Standard & Poor's (DFIT)
S&S .... Science & Society [*A publication*] (BRI)
sandst .... Sandstone (VRA)
S&T .... Sky & Telescope [*A publication*] (BRI)
sangu .... Sanguine (VRA)
SAP .... Secondary Audio Program
SAP .... Societe des Arts Plastiques de la Province de Quebec, Quebec City [*1955*] [*Canada*] (NGC)
SAP .... Society of Analytical Psychology (AIE)
SAPQ .... Societe des Artistes Professionnels du Quebec [*1966, CPQ from 1978, SAAVQ from 1980, CAPQ from 1982*] [*Canada*] (NGC)
SAQ .... South Atlantic Quarterly [*A publication*] (BRI)
SAR .... Special Administrative Region [*Hong Kong*]
SAR .... Synthetic Aperture RADAR
S Arab .... Saudi Arabia (VRA)
sarc .... Sarcophagi (VRA)
sarc .... Sarcophagus (VRA)
Sard .... Sardinia (VRA)
SARGE .... Surveillance and Reconnaissance Ground Equipment
SARSS/OSC... Standard Army Retail Supply System/Objective Supply Capability (RDA)
Sask .... Saskatchewan [*Canada*] (DD)
sat .... Satin (VRA)
SATEFL .... Scottish Association for the Teaching of English as a Foreign Language (AIE)
SATIS .... Science and Technology in Society (AIE)
satwd .... Satinwood (VRA)
SAVI .... Science Activities for the Visually Impaired (AIE)
SAW .... Surface Acoustic Wave [*Engineering*]
sawdu .... Sawdust (VRA)
SB .... Air Caledonie International [*ICAO designator*] (AD)
SB .... Science Books & Films [*A publication*] (BRI)
SB .... Sound Blaster [*Computer science*] (DOM)
SBB .... Santa Barbara-Barinas [*Venezuela*] [*Airport symbol*] (AD)
SBCL .... SmithKline Beecham Clinical Laboratories
SBFM .... Small Business Financial Manager [*Microsoft*] [*Computer science*]
SBIC .... Small Business Investment Corp. (DFIT)

SBIR/STTR ... Small Business Innovation Research/Small Business Technology Transfer [*Army*] (RDA)
SBJ .... Simla [*India*] [*Airport symbol*] (AD)
SBMP .... Safety Base Motion Picture (VRA)
SBQ .... Sao Borja [*Brazil*] [*Airport symbol*] (AD)
SBR .... Santa Barbara [*Monagas, Venezuela*] [*Airport symbol*] (AD)
SBS .... Save British Science [*An association*] (AIE)
SBS .... Smart Business Supersite [*Internet resource*] [*Computer science*]
SBT .... San Bernardino [*California*] [*Airport symbol*] (AD)
SC .... Cruzeiro do Sul [*ICAO designator*] (AD)
SCA .... Santa Catalina [*Colombia*] [*Airport symbol*] (AD)
SCA .... Society of Canadian Artists, Montreal [*1868-72*] (NGC)
SCAGES ...... Standing Conference of Associations for Guidance in Education Settings (AIE)
SCAMP .... Schools Computers Administration and Management Project (AIE)
SCC .... Stamford [*Connecticut*] [*Airport symbol*] (AD)
SCCML........ Scottish Central Committee on Modern Languages (AIE)
SCD .... Sulaco [*Honduras*] [*Airport symbol*] (AD)
SCDC .... Schools Computer Development Centre (AIE)
SCE .... Slope-Clearing Events [*Geology*]
SCE .... Software Capability Evaluation (RDA)
SCED .... Standing Conference on Education Development (AIE)
SCEO .... Scottish Centre for Education Overseas (AIE)
sch .... School (VRA)
Sch Arts ...... School Arts [*A publication*] (BRI)
Sch Lib .... School Librarian [*A publication*] (BRI)
schm .... Schematic (VRA)
schst .... Schist (VRA)
Sci .... Science [*A publication*] (BRI)
SCIA............ Society of Chief Inspectors and Advisers [*British*] (AIE)
SCINSET ...... Scottish Colleges In-Service Education of Teachers (AIE)
SCIP .... Stanford Computer Industry Project
SCIPHE .... Sparkman Centre for International Public Health Education (AIE)
SciTech........ SciTech Book News [*A publication*] (BRI)
scl .... Scroll (VRA)
SCM .... Skill Centre Manager (AIE)
SCMP.......... Scottish Computers in Schools Project (AIE)
SCMS.......... Serial Copy Master System (DOM)
SCOL .... Scottish Committee on Open Learning (AIE)
SCOPE .... Second Chance Opportunities and Education for Women (AIE)
Scot .... Scotland (VRA)
SCOTCAT ..... Scottish Credit Accumulation and Transfer (AIE)
SCOTTSU ..... Scottish Open Tech Training Support Unit (AIE)
SCOTVIC ..... Standing Conference of Principals of Tertiary and Sixth Form Colleges [*British*] (AIE)
SCOYO .... Standing Conference of Youth Organisations (AIE)
SCPDCIHE .... Standing Conference of Principals and Directors of Colleges and Institutes of Higher Education (AIE)
SCRA .... Specialized Carriers & Rigging Association
script .... Scripture (VRA)
scrn .... Screen (VRA)
scrnpr .... Screenprint (VRA)
SCSP .... Schools Cultural Studies Project (AIE)
SCT .... Special Committee on Trade
SCUDD........ Standing Conference of University Drama Departments (AIE)
SCUGA........ Schools, Curriculum, Unusual, Geography, and Alumni [*University admisssion rating system*]
sculp .... Sculpture (VRA)
Sculpt R ...... Sculpture Review [*A publication*] (BRI)
Scyt .... Scythia (VRA)
SD .... Sudan Airways [*ICAO designator*] (AD)
SDA .... Studies in the Decorative Arts [*A publication*] (BRI)
SDAF .... Special Development Assistance Fund
SDCP .... Slug Discharge Control Plan [*Pollution prevention*]
SDD .... Sa da Bandeira [*Angola*] [*Airport symbol*] (AD)
SDD .... Spin-Dependent Delocalization [*Physical chemistry*]
SDF............. Software Development Framework (RDA)
SDG .... Sao Domingos [*Brazil*] [*Airport symbol*] (AD)
SDMS .... Staff Development Management System (AIE)
SDO .... Singlet Delta Oxygen
SDR .... Single Drug Resistance
SDR .... Special Drawing Rights [*Investment term*] (DFIT)
SDS .... Serondela [*Botswana*] [*Airport symbol*] (AD)
SDS .... Side Detection System [*Delco*] (RDA)
SDSL .... Site-Directed Spin Labeling [*Physical chemistry*]
SDT............. Sandy Point [*Great Abaco Island, Bahamas*] [*Airport symbol*] (AD)

SDW	Sandwip [*Bangladesh*] [*Airport symbol*] (AD)
SDX	Storage Data Acceleration [*Computer science*]
sdy	Study (VRA)
SE	Secondary Education (AIE)
SE	Social Education [*A publication*] (BRI)
SE	Southeast Skyways [*ICAO designator*] (AD)
SE	Wings of Alaska [*ICAO designator*] (AD)
SEA	Self-Extracting Archive [*Computer science*] (DOM)
SEAC	Southern Examining Accreditation Council (AIE)
SeaFront	Sea Frontiers [*A publication*] (BRI)
Sea H	Sea History [*A publication*] (BRI)
SEANWFZ	Southeast Asian Nuclear Weapons Free Zone
SEASEE	Southeast Asia Association on Seismology and Earthquake Engineering
sec	Secretary (DD)
SEC	Social Education Centre (AIE)
SEC	Space Environment Center
sect	Section (VRA)
sec-treas	Secretary-Treasurer (DD)
SEDA	Staff and Educational Development Association (AIE)
SEFIC	Spoken English for Industry and Commerce (AIE)
SELANE	Secure Local-Area Network [*Computer science*]
SELB	Southern Education and Library Board [*Northern Ireland*] (AIE)
Sen	Senator (DFIT)
SEN	Southend [*Scotland*] [*Airport symbol*] (AD)
SEN	Special Educational Needs (AIE)
SENJIT	Special Educational Needs Joint Initiative for Training (AIE)
SEP	Saturday Evening Post [*A publication*] (BRI)
sep	Sepia (VRA)
SEP	Simplified Employee Pension Plan (DFIT)
SEPACS	Sheltered Employment Procurement and Consultancy Service (AIE)
SEPPA	Single Employer Pension Plan Amendments Act of 1986 (WYGK)
SEPSU	Science and Engineering Policy Studies Unit (AIE)
SEq	Spatial Equalization
seri	Serigraph (VRA)
SERM	Selective Estrogen-Receptor Modulator [*Medicine*]
SERP	Supplemental Executive Retirement Plan [*Human resources*] (WYGK)
Ser R	Serials Review [*A publication*] (BRI)
SES	Selma [*Alabama*] [*Airport symbol*] (AD)
SESM	Strategies and Errors in Secondary Mathematics [*Project*] (AIE)
SET	San Esteban [*Honduras*] [*Airport symbol*] (AD)
SET	Secure Electronic Transactions [*Computer science*]
SET	Stock Exchange of Thailand [*Thailand*]
SEU	Seronera [*Tanzania*] [*Airport symbol*] (AD)
Sev Cent N	Seventeenth-Century News [*A publication*] (BRI)
SEWAC	South East Wales Access Consortium (AIE)
Sew R	Sewanee Review [*A publication*] (BRI)
SF	Scruse Air [*ICAO designator*] (AD)
SF	Social Forces [*A publication*] (BRI)
SFB	Segmented Filamentous Bacteria
SF Chr	Science Fiction Chronicle [*A publication*] (BRI)
SFK	Safia [*Papua*] [*Airport symbol*] (AD)
sfm	Sfumato (VRA)
SFNG	Safety Based Negative (VRA)
SFP	Sherbrooke Forest Park [*Victoria, Australia*] [*Airport symbol*] (AD)
SFR	San Francisco Review [*A publication*] (BRI)
SFRB	San Francisco Review of Books [*A publication*] (BRI)
SFS	School Focused Secondment (AIE)
SFS	Science-Fiction Studies [*A publication*] (BRI)
SFS	Sharm es-Sheikh [*Israel*] [*Airport symbol*] (AD)
sft	Soffit (VRA)
SFT	Submerged Floating Tunnell
SFTE	Space Full Time Equivalent (AIE)
SFU	Surfdale [*Waiheke Island, New Zealand*] [*Airport symbol*] (AD)
SFX	San Felix [*Venezuela*] [*Airport symbol*] (AD)
SFZ	Pawtucket-Woonsocket [*Rhode Island*] [*Airport symbol*] (AD)
SG	Atlantis [*ICAO designator*] (AD)
SGA	Society of Graphic Art, Toronto [*1912, founded c.1903 as GAC, CSGA from 1923*] [*Canada*] (NGC)
SGC	Starburst Giant Cells [*Cytology*]
SGG	Simanggang [*Malaysia*] [*Airport symbol*] (AD)
SGH	Springfield [*Ohio*] [*Airport symbol*] (AD)
SGI	Silicon Graphics Incorporated [*Computer science*]
SGN	Saigon [*South Vietnam*] [*Airport symbol*] (AD)
SGPT	Gelatin Silver Print (VRA)
SGPT	Silver Gelatin Print (VRA)
sgrf	Sgraffito (VRA)
SGZ	Singora [*Thailand*] [*Airport symbol*] (AD)
Shakes Q	Shakespeare Quarterly [*A publication*] (BRI)
SHARE	Schoolboys Harness Aid for the Relief of the Elderly (AIE)
SHB	Shark Bay [*Western Australia*] [*Airport symbol*] (AD)
Shen	Shenandoah [*A publication*] (BRI)
shl	Shell (VRA)
SHP	Schools History Project (AIE)
sht	Sheet (VRA)
SHU	Shute Harbour [*Queensland*] [*Airport symbol*] (AD)
SI	Air Sierra [*ICAO designator*] (AD)
si	Silver (VRA)
SIA	Sian [*China*] [*Airport symbol*] (AD)
SIAM Rev	SIAM Review [*A publication*] (BRI)
Si & So	Sight and Sound [*A publication*] (BRI)
SIAP	System for Improved Acoustic Performance
Sib	Siberia (VRA)
SIBP	Self-Insured Benefits Plan [*Human resources*] (WYGK)
SIC	San Antonio do Ica [*Brazil*] [*Airport symbol*] (AD)

Sic	Sicily (VRA)
SICA	Securities Industry Committee on Arbitration (DFIT)
SICCI	Schools Information Centre on the Chemical Industry (AIE)
SID	Ilha do Sal [*Cape Verde Islands*] [*Airport symbol*] (AD)
SIF	Source Image Format (DOM)
SIF	Standard Image Format [*Computer science*]
SIG	Self-Insurance Group (WYGK)
Signs	Signs: Journal of Women in Culture and Society [*A publication*] (BRI)
SII	Sidi Ifni [*Morocco*] [*Airport symbol*] (AD)
SII	Soldier-Information Interface (RDA)
SIL	Sao Hill [*Tanzania*] [*Airport symbol*] (AD)
SILO	Schools Industry Liaison Officer (AIE)
SILPT	Silhouette Print (VRA)
sim	Simulated (VRA)
SIMS	Schools Information Management System (AIE)
SIO	Smithtown [*Tasmania*] [*Airport symbol*] (AD)
SIP	Support for Innovation Project (AIE)
sipt	Silverpoint (VRA)
SIQ	Singkep Island [*Indonesia*] [*Airport symbol*] (AD)
SIRRA	Sleep-Induction/Rapid Reawakening System [*Military*] (RDA)
SIS	Society for Italian Studies (AIE)
SISU	Schools In-Service Unit [*University of Birmingham*] [*British*] (AIE)
SIW	Samaria [*Papua*] [*Airport symbol*] (AD)
Six Ct J	Sixteenth Century Journal [*A publication*] (BRI)
SIXT	Sixth-Plate (VRA)
SJ	Stewart Island [*ICAO designator*] (AD)
SJA	San Juan de Arama [*Colombia*] [*Airport symbol*] (AD)
SJAL	School Journal Association of London [*British*] (AIE)
SJB	San Joaquin [*Bolivia*] [*Airport symbol*] (AD)
SJH	St. Johns [*Antigua, Leeward Islands, West Indies*] [*Airport symbol*] (AD)
SJP	San Juan [*Peru*] [*Airport symbol*] (AD)
SJQ	Sesheke [*Zambia*] [*Airport symbol*] (AD)
SJR	San Juan de Uraba [*Colombia*] [*Airport symbol*] (AD)
SJS	San Jose [*Bolivia*] [*Airport symbol*] (AD)
SJV	San Javier [*Bolivia*] [*Airport symbol*] (AD)
sk	Sketch (VRA)
SKG	Salonika [*Greece*] [*Airport symbol*] (AD)
SKI	Skilda [*Algeria*] [*Airport symbol*] (AD)
SKIA	Secure Key-Issuing Authority [*Computer science*]
SKR	Skogar [*Iceland*] [*Airport symbol*] (AD)
skyscr	Skyscraper (VRA)
SL	Rio-Sul [*ICAO designator*] (AD)
SL	Special Libraries [*A publication*] (BRI)
SLA	School Leaving Age (AIE)
sla	Slate (VRA)
Slav R	Slavic Review [*A publication*] (BRI)
SLD	Severe Learning Difficulties (AIE)
SLDRAM	Sync-link DRAM [*Display Random Access Memory*] [*Computer science*]
SLF	Sulayel [*Saudi Arabia*] [*Airport symbol*] (AD)
SLIP	Single Line Internet Protocol [*Telecommunications*] (DOM)
SLIPP	Second Language Learning in the Primary Classroom (AIE)
S Liv	Southern Living [*A publication*] (BRI)
SLJ	School Library Journal [*A publication*] (BRI)
SLK	Lake Placid-Saranac Lake [*New York*] [*Airport symbol*] (AD)
slk	Silk (VRA)
slksc	Silkscreen (VRA)
SLMQ	School Library Media Quarterly [*American Library Association*]
SLO	Santa Ana [*Columbia*] [*Airport symbol*] (AD)
SLP	San Luis Potosi [*Mexico*] [*Airport symbol*] (AD)
SLPT	Salted Paper Print (VRA)
sltgz	Saltglaze (VRA)
SLV	Sao Paulo de Olivenca [*Brazil*] [*Airport symbol*] (AD)
SLV	Sport-Luxury Vehicle
SLW	Saltillo [*Mexico*] [*Airport symbol*] (AD)
sm	Small (VRA)
SMA	Self-Managed Account (WYGK)
SMAO	Society of Management Accountants of Ontario [*Canada*] (DD)
SMB	Cerro Sombrero [*Chile*] [*Airport symbol*] (AD)
Sm Bus Rep	Small Business Reports [*A publication*] (BRI)
SMC	Senior Management Committee (AIE)
SMED	Single Minute Exchange of Die [*Manufacturing*]
SMHMO	Staff Model Health Maintenance Organization [*Insurance*] (WYGK)
Smith	Smithsonian [*A publication*] (BRI)
SMJ	Santa Margherita [*Italy*] [*Airport symbol*] (AD)
SMO	Santa Monica [*California*] [*Airport symbol*] (AD)
SMP	Simple Management Protocol [*Computer science*] (DOM)
Sm Pr	Small Press [*A publication*] (BRI)
Sm Pr R	Small Press Review [*A publication*] (BRI)
SMS	Smithsonian Institution's Marine Station
SMT	Senior Management Team (AIE)
SMX	Server Macro Expansion [*Computer science*]
SN	Saturday Night [*A publication*] (BRI)
SNA	Laguna Beach-Santa Ana [*California*] [*Airport symbol*] (AD)
SNAG	Sensitive New-Age Guy
SNAP	Special Needs Action Programme [*Education*] (AIE)
SNBA	Societe Nationale des Beaux-Arts, Paris [*1890*] [*French*] (NGC)
SND	Seno [*Laos*] [*Airport symbol*] (AD)
sndlwd	Sandalwood (VRA)
SNF	San Felipe [*Venezuela*] [*Airport symbol*] (AD)
sngl	Senegal (VRA)
SNIOS	Special Needs in the Ordinary School (AIE)
SNK	Snyder [*Texas*] [*Airport symbol*] (AD)
SNL	Sand Creek [*Guyana*] [*Airport symbol*] (AD)

SNM............	San Ignacio de Moxos [*Bolivia*] [*Airport symbol*] (AD)
SNP............	Single Nucleotide Polymorphism [*Genetics*]
SNP............	Soluble Nonreactive Phosphorus [*Marine science*]
snpa............	Sinopia (VRA)
SNS............	Salinas [*California*] [*Airport symbol*] (AD)
SNST............	Special Needs Support Team [*Education*] (AIE)
SNU............	Santa Clara [*Cuba*] [*Airport symbol*] (AD)
SO............	Austrian Air [*ICAO designator*] (AD)
SOA............	Soc Trang [*South Vietnam*] [*Airport symbol*] (AD)
soapst............	Soapstone (VRA)
SOB............	Sobral [*Brazil*] [*Airport symbol*] (AD)
Soc............	Society [*A publication*] (BRI)
Soc............	Sociology (DD)
SoCCS............	Study of Cataloguing Computer Software (AIE)
Socio R............	Sociological Review [*A publication*] (BRI)
SocSc............	Social Science (DD)
SocSciComR...	Social Science Computer Review [*A publication*] (BRI)
Soc Ser R....	Social Service Review [*A publication*] (BRI)
Soc W............	Social Work [*A publication*] (BRI)
SODA............	Salmonella Outbreak Detection Algorithm [*Medicine*]
SOED............	Scottish Office Education Department (AIE)
SOHO............	Solar Heliospheric Observatory
SOLAS............	Safety of Life at Sea [*An international agreement requiring operators of cruise ships to meet certain standards of construction and fire safety*]
Soltr............	Solutrean (VRA)
SOP............	Southern Pines [*North Carolina*] [*Airport symbol*] (AD)
South CR....	South Carolina Review [*A publication*] (BRI)
South Cul....	Southern Cultures [*A publication*] (BRI)
South HR....	Southern Humanities Review [*A publication*] (BRI)
South R......	Southern Review [*A publication*] (BRI)
Spa............	Spain (VRA)
SPACE............	Satellite Project for Adult and Continuing Education (AIE)
SPARC............	Scalar Processor Architecture Reduced-Instruction-Set Computer (DOM)
SPC............	Software Publishing Corp.
SPD............	Social Democratic Party [*Germany*] [*Political party*]
SPE............	Sepulot [*Malaysia*] [*Airport symbol*] (AD)
SPEB............	Streptococcal Pyrogenic Exotoxin B [*Immunochemistry*]
Spec............	Spectator [*A publication*] (BRI)
SPEC............	Streptococcal Pyrogenic Exotoxin C [*Immunochemistry*]
Specu............	Speculum [*A publication*] (BRI)
SPF............	Spearfish [*South Dakota*] [*Airport symbol*] (AD)
SPGJ............	Stomach-Partitioning Gastrojejunostomy [*Surgery*]
SPIR............	School Performance Information Regulations (AIE)
SPIRE............	Spatial Paradigm for Information Retrieval and Exploration [*Computer science*]
SPL............	San Pedro de Jagua [*Colombia*] [*Airport symbol*] (AD)
SPMG............	Scottish Primary Mathematics Group (AIE)
SPOD............	Sexual and Personal Relationships of the Disabled (AIE)
SPORT............	Soldier Portable On-System Repair Tool [*Military*]
SPP............	Serpa [*Portugal*] [*Airport symbol*] (AD)
SPPC............	Self-Pumped Phase Conjugator [*Optics*]
SPQ............	Student Progress Questionnaire (AIE)
spr............	Spruce (VRA)
SPRC............	Star Petroleum Refinery Complex [*Thailand*]
SPRITE............	Sheffield People's Resource for Information Technology [*British*] (AIE)
SPS............	Sheltered Placement Scheme (AIE)
SPX............	San Pedro [*Colombia*] [*Airport symbol*] (AD)
spy............	Spray (VRA)
SQ............	Singapore Airlines [*ICAO designator*] (AD)
sq............	Square (VRA)
Sq............	Square (DD)
SQA............	Simple, Quick & Affordable [*Office furniture*]
SQA............	Society for Quality Assurance
SQM............	Strategic Quality Management (AIE)
sr............	Senior (DD)
Sr............	Senior (DFIT)
SRA............	Santo Rosa [*Brazil*] [*Airport symbol*] (AD)
SREB............	Southern Regional Examinations Board [*Education*] (AIE)
srph............	Seraph (VRA)
SRR............	Sorreisa [*Norway*] [*Airport symbol*] (AD)
SRS............	San Marcos [*Colombia*] [*Airport symbol*] (AD)
SRS............	Skeletal Repair System [*Medicine*]
SS............	Social Studies [*A publication*] (BRI)
SS............	South Coast Airlines [*ICAO designator*] (AD)
ss............	Stainless Steel (VRA)
SS............	Suburban Service (DD)
SSA............	Streptococcal Superantigen [*Immunochemistry*]
SSC............	Secretarial Studies Certificate (AIE)
SSCFP............	Senior Service College Fellowship Program [*Army*] (RDA)
SSCVYO............	Scottish Standing Conference of Voluntary Youth Organisations (AIE)
SSE............	Site Server [*Microsoft Corp.*] [*Computer science*]
SSF............	Studies in Short Fiction [*A publication*] (BRI)
SSG............	Santa Isabel [*Spanish Guinea*] [*Airport symbol*] (AD)
SSI............	Brunswick [*Georgia*] [*Airport symbol*] (AD)
SSIRT............	Support Staff Interests Round Table [*American Library Association*]
SSN............	Auburn [*New York*] [*Airport symbol*] (AD)
SSO............	Second Surgical Opinion [*Insurance*] (WYGK)
SSPQ............	Science Studies' Perception Questionnaire (AIE)
SSQ............	Social Science Quarterly [*A publication*] (BRI)
SSRU............	Scottish Schools Rugby Union (AIE)
SSST............	Simulated Social Skills Training (AIE)
SSU............	Study Skills Unit (AIE)

SSY............	Sao Salvador [*Angola*] [*Airport symbol*] (AD)
SSZ............	Santos [*Brazil*] [*Airport symbol*] (AD)
ST............	Belize Airways [*ICAO designator*] (AD)
St............	Saint (DD)
st............	Stone (VRA)
st............	Street (VRA)
St............	Street (DD)
sta............	Station (VRA)
STAF............	Science Teachers' Authoring Facility (AIE)
STAF............	Simulation/Test Acceptance Facility [*Army*] (RDA)
Stand............	Stand Magazine [*A publication*] (BRI)
START............	Small Tight Aspect Ratio Tokamak [*Plasma physics*]
Stats............	Statistics (DD)
STC............	Short Training Courses (AIE)
STC............	Synaptic Transporter Current [*Neurochemistry*]
STD............	Santo Domingo [*Venezuela*] [*Airport symbol*] (AD)
stdgls............	Stained Glass (VRA)
steat............	Steatite (VRA)
STED............	Science Technology and Education Division [*British Council*] (AIE)
STEP............	Special Temporary Employment Programme (AIE)
ster............	Stereo (VRA)
STER............	Stereoview (VRA)
Stereo............	Stereo Review [*A publication*] (BRI)
STF............	Setif [*Algeria*] [*Airport symbol*] (AD)
STG............	Santiago [*Brazil*] [*Airport symbol*] (AD)
STGT............	Stargardt Disease [*Medicine*]
sti............	Stich (VRA)
STI............	Systems Technology Inc.
STILE............	Students' and Teachers' Integrated Learning Environment (AIE)
STIMSUP............	Stimulant to Sustain Performance (RDA)
STJ............	St. Joseph [*Missouri*] [*Airport symbol*] (AD)
stk............	Stock (VRA)
stl............	Steel (VRA)
STM............	Signature-Tagged Transposon Method [*Genetics*]
Stn............	Station (DD)
stncl............	Stencil (VRA)
S/TOP............	Selective Tubal Occlusion Procedure [*Medicine*]
STOP-H............	Swedish Trial in Old Patients with Hypertension
STORE............	Student's Own Record of Education (AIE)
STOW-SKID...	Synthetic Theater of War-Systems Engineering, Integration, and Demonstration [*Military*] (RDA)
STP............	Secure Transfer Protocol [*Computer science*] (DOM)
stret............	Stretcher (VRA)
strg............	String (VRA)
strgcr............	Stringcourse (VRA)
stri si............	Sterling Silver (VRA)
strm............	Store Room (VRA)
stu............	Stucco (VRA)
STV............	Staverton [*England*] [*Airport symbol*] (AD)
stwr............	Stoneware (VRA)
sty............	Stylus (VRA)
SUAC............	Scottish Universities Accommodation Consortium (AIE)
SUB............	Subaddressing [*Telecommunications*] (DOM)
succ............	Succursale (DD)
SUI............	Sukhumi [*USSR*] [*Airport symbol*] (AD)
SUM............	San Juan de Cesar [*Colombia*] [*Airport symbol*] (AD)
Sumat............	Sumatra (VRA)
SUMER............	Solar Ultraviolet Measurements of Emitted Radiation [*Instrumentation*]
sumpt............	Sumptuary (VRA)
SUMS............	Southern Universities' Management Services (AIE)
SUPE............	Super Eight [*Motion picture*] (VRA)
SUPS............	Services to User Populations Section [*Disbanded by the Board at the Midwinter meeting*]
supt............	Superintendent (DD)
supvr............	Supervisor (DD)
SUR............	Starcke [*Queensland*] [*Airport symbol*] (AD)
sur............	Surface (VRA)
Surface DJ...	Surface Design Journal [*A publication*] (BRI)
SUS............	Surkhet [*Nepal*] [*Airport symbol*] (AD)
SUSF............	Scottish Universities Sports Federation (AIE)
SV............	Saudi Arabian Airlines [*ICAO designator*] (AD)
SVN............	Saravena [*Colombia*] [*Airport symbol*] (AD)
SVQ............	Scottish Vocational Qualification (AIE)
SVT............	Special Vehicle Team [*Automotive engineering*]
SW............	Namib Air [*ICAO designator*] (AD)
SWATH............	Small Waterplane Area Twin Hull
Swe............	Sweden (VRA)
SWExB............	South Western Examinations Board [*Education*] (AIE)
SWFSC............	Southwest Fisheries Science Center [*San Diego, CA*]
SWH............	Swan Hill [*Victoria, Australia*] [*Airport symbol*] (AD)
Switz............	Switzerland (VRA)
SWL............	Spanish Wells [*Bahamas*] [*Airport symbol*] (AD)
SWOE............	Smart Weapons Operability Enhancement (RDA)
SWP............	Swakopmund [*South-West Africa*] [*Airport symbol*] (AD)
SWQ............	Sumbawa [*Indonesia*] [*Airport symbol*] (AD)
SWR............	Southwest Review [*A publication*] (BRI)
SWW............	Sweetwater [*Texas*] [*Airport symbol*] (AD)
Swzld............	Swaziland (VRA)
SX............	Christman Air System [*ICAO designator*] (AD)
SX70............	SX-70 (VRA)
SXC............	Santa Catalina Island [*California*] [*Airport symbol*] (AD)
SXM............	Sint Maarten [*Netherlands Antilles*] [*Airport symbol*] (AD)
SXU............	Soddu [*Ethiopia*] [*Airport symbol*] (AD)
SY............	Air Alsace [*ICAO designator*] (AD)

SYC.............. Sanday [*Scotland*] [*Airport symbol*] (AD)
SYI.............. Shelbyville [*Tennessee*] [*Airport symbol*] (AD)
SYMGR........ Sympalmograph (VRA)
synt............. Synthetic (VRA)
Syr.............. Syria (VRA)
SZ................ China Southwest Airlines [*ICAO designator*] (AD)

SZ................ ProAir Services [*ICAO designator*] (AD)
sz................ Size (VRA)
SZA............ Santo Antonio do Zaire [*Angola*] [*Airport symbol*] (AD)
SZB............ Santa Barbara [*Honduras*] [*Airport symbol*] (AD)
SZI.............. Soroti [*Uganda*] [*Airport symbol*] (AD)
SZU............. Segou [*Mali*] [*Airport symbol*] (AD)

T

By Acronym

TA .... Teacher Assessment (AIE)
TA .... Trade Acceptance [*Investment term*] (DFIT)
TA .... Transportation Act of 1989 (WYGK)
TAA .... Total Antioxidant Activity [*Chemistry*]
TAAS .... Texas Assessment of Academic Skills
TAC .... Technical and Agricultural College (AIE)
TACT .... TransAct Technologies
TAIU .... Training Agency Intelligence Unit (AIE)
Taiw .... Taiwan (VRA)
TAJ .... Taracua [*Brazil*] [*Airport symbol*] (AD)
T&C .... Technology and Culture [*A publication*] (BRI)
TANF .... Temporary Assistance to Needy Families [*An association*]
TAO .... Tropical Array Ocean
tap .... Tapestry (VRA)
TAP .... Training Access Point (AIE)
TAR .... Tape Archive [*Computer science*] (DOM)
TAR .... Taranto [*Italy*] [*Airport symbol*] (AD)
TAR .... Transformation-Associated Recombination [*Genetics*]
TARFS .... Three Axis Rotational Flight Simulator [*Military*] (RDA)
TARGET ...... Thames Action and Resources Group for Education and Training
               [*British*] (AIE)
tarp .... Tarpaulin (VRA)
TASL .... Toronto Art Students' League [*1886-1903*] [*Canada*] (NGC)
TASP .... Texas Academic Skills Program
TASR .... Tactical Automated Situation Receiver [*Military*]
TAU .... Tauramena [*Colombia*] [*Airport symbol*] (AD)
TAW .... Train America's Workforce [*An association*] (WYGK)
tax .... Taxation (DD)
TB .... Tejas Airlines [*ICAO designator*] (AD)
tb .... Tomb (VRA)
TB .... Trump Shuttle [*ICAO designator*] (AD)
TBAVF .... Translocated Basilic Vein Arteriovenous Fistula [*Surgery*]
TBB .... Tuy Hoa [*South Vietnam*] [*Airport symbol*] (AD)
TBF .... Teachers' Benevolent Fund (AIE)
TBL .... Tableland [*Western Australia*] [*Airport symbol*] (AD)
tbnle .... Tabernacle (VRA)
TBP .... Target Benefit Plan [*Human resources*] (WYGK)
TC .... Air Tanzania [*ICAO designator*] (AD)
TC .... Teachers' Centre (AIE)
TCI .... Santa Cruz de Tenerife [*Canary Islands*] [*Airport symbol*] (AD)
TCI .... TCI: The Business of Entertainment Technology and Design
               [*A publication*] (BRI)
TCM .... Traditional Chinese Medicine
TCP/IP .... Transmission Control Protocol/Internet Protocol [*Computer science*]
               (DOM)
TCR .... Teacher Contact Ratio (AIE)
TCR .... Teachers College Record [*A publication*] (BRI)
TCS .... Teaching Company Scheme (AIE)
TD .... Tansavio [*ICAO designator*] (AD)
TD .... Thanatophoric Dysplasia [*Lethal dwarfism*]
TDA .... Trinidad [*Colombia*] [*Airport symbol*] (AD)
TDLB .... Training and Development Lead Body (AIE)
TDM .... Palmyra [*Syria*] [*Airport symbol*] (AD)
TDM .... Time-Division Multiplexor [*Computer science*] (DOM)
TDR .... TDR: The Drama Review [*A publication*] (BRI)
TDUR .... Therapeutic Drug Utilization Review [*Insurance*] (WYGK)
TEA .... Tela [*Honduras*] [*Airport symbol*] (AD)
TEAC .... Transition Education Advisory Committee (AIE)
Teach Mus... Teaching Music [*A publication*] (BRI)
TEAME .... Teacher Educators and Advisers in Media Education (AIE)
TEAMS .... Texas Educational Assessment of Minimum Skills
TEB .... Teterboro [*New Jersey*] [*Airport symbol*] (AD)
tech .... Technology (DD)
Tec R .... Technology Review [*A publication*] (BRI)
TEE .... Tyee [*Alaska*] [*Airport symbol*] (AD)
TEEM .... Technology through Electricity, Electronics, and Microelectronics
               (AIE)
TEG .... Tenkodogo [*Upper Volta*] [*Airport symbol*] (AD)
TEI .... Technical Education Institute (AIE)
telecommun... Telecommunications (DD)
temp .... Distemper (VRA)
temp .... [*Egg*] Tempera (VRA)
TEMS .... Teacher Examiner Mark Sheet (AIE)
TEMS .... Tornado Electronic Messaging System [*Computer science*]
TEN .... Total Entertainment Network [*Online gaming service*]
tepid .... Tepidarium (VRA)

ter .... Terracotta (VRA)
TERA .... Tax Equity and Responsibility Act of 1982 (WYGK)
TERC .... Tertiary Education Research Centre [*British*] (AIE)
Terr .... Terrace (DD)
terr .... Terrace (VRA)
TES .... Tessenei [*Ethiopia*] [*Airport symbol*] (AD)
tes .... Tessera (VRA)
TES .... Times Educational Supplement [*A publication*] (BRI)
TES .... Tropospheric Emission Sensor
TESLA .... Technical Standards for Library Automation
TESS .... Times Educational Supplement Scotland (AIE)
TEU .... Turret Electronics Unit [*Military*] (RDA)
text .... Texture (VRA)
TEXT .... Trans-European Exchange and Transfer Consortium (AIE)
TF .... Veeneal [*ICAO designator*] (AD)
TFR .... Tarbes [*France*] [*Airport symbol*] (AD)
TFY .... Tarfaya [*Morocco*] [*Airport symbol*] (AD)
TG .... Thai Airways [*ICAO designator*] (AD)
TGN .... Tarragona [*Spain*] [*Airport symbol*] (AD)
TGS .... Tuxtla Gutierrez [*Mexico*] [*Airport symbol*] (AD)
TGX .... Taguatinga [*Brazil*] [*Airport symbol*] (AD)
TGY .... Punta Gorda [*British Honduras*] [*Airport symbol*] (AD)
TH .... Thai Airways [*ICAO designator*] (AD)
THA .... Tullahoma [*Tennessee*] [*Airport symbol*] (AD)
tHcy .... Total Homocysteine [*Clinical chemistry*]
Theat J .... Theatre Journal [*A publication*] (BRI)
Theol St ...... Theological Studies [*A publication*] (BRI)
THES .... Times Higher Education Supplement (AIE)
THG .... Thangool [*Queensland*] [*Airport symbol*] (AD)
THJ .... Theodore [*Queensland*] [*Airport symbol*] (AD)
THK .... Thakhek [*Laos*] [*Airport symbol*] (AD)
THP .... Thermal Hysteresis Proteins [*Biochemistry*]
thrd .... Thread (VRA)
THRIVE .... Tower Hamlets Reading Initiative via Exploration [*British*] (AIE)
thry .... Theory (VRA)
THS .... Theatre History Studies [*A publication*] (BRI)
thtr .... Theatre (VRA)
THY .... Thylungra [*Queensland*] [*Airport symbol*] (AD)
TI .... Texas International Airlines [*ICAO designator*] (AD)
Tib .... Tibet (VRA)
TIE .... Telescopes in Education
TIES .... The International English School (AIE)
TIIAP .... Telecommunications and Information Infrastructure Assistance
               Program [*Department of Commerce*]
TIIP .... Terrain-Intelligence Integration Prototype [*Army*] (RDA)
TIJ .... Tijuana [*Mexico*] [*Airport symbol*] (AD)
tik .... Ticking (VRA)
TIPS .... Treasury's Inflation Protection Securities
TIR .... Tiree Island [*Scotland*] [*Airport symbol*] (AD)
tis .... Tissue (VRA)
TIS .... Transaction Information Systems
TIS .... Travel to Interview Scheme (AIE)
TIW .... Tacoma [*Washington*] [*Airport symbol*] (AD)
TIX .... Titusville [*Florida*] [*Airport symbol*] (AD)
TJ .... Oceanair [*ICAO designator*] (AD)
TJI .... Trujillo [*Honduras*] [*Airport symbol*] (AD)
TK .... Turk Hava Yollari [*ICAO designator*] (AD)
TKC .... Tiko [*Cameroon*] [*Airport symbol*] (AD)
TKD .... Takoradi [*Ghana*] [*Airport symbol*] (AD)
TKG .... Telukbetung [*Sumatra, Indonesia*] [*Airport symbol*] (AD)
TKI .... Turks Islands [*West Indies*] [*Airport symbol*] (AD)
TKL .... Tak [*Thailand*] [*Airport symbol*] (AD)
TKR .... Thakurgaon [*Bangladesh*] [*Airport symbol*] (AD)
TKY .... Turkey Creek [*Western Australia*] [*Airport symbol*] (AD)
TL .... Trans Mediterranean [*ICAO designator*] (AD)
TLB .... Tortola [*British Virgin Islands*] [*Airport symbol*] (AD)
TLG .... Tres Lagoas [*Brazil*] [*Airport symbol*] (AD)
TLL .... Teachers' Labour League [*British*] (AIE)
TLP .... Talpa [*New Mexico*] [*Airport symbol*] (AD)
tlp .... Tulip (VRA)
TLR .... Talgarno [*Western Australia*] [*Airport symbol*] (AD)
TLS .... Teaching and Learning Support (AIE)
TLS .... Times Literary Supplement [*A publication*] (BRI)
TLW .... Talasea [*New Britain, New Guinea*] [*Airport symbol*] (AD)
TMA .... Treasury Management Association
TMA .... Truck Manufacturers Association

TMC .... The Maintenance Council
TMCXD .... Transverse Magnetic Circular X-Ray Dichroism [*Physics*]
TMD .... Timbedra [*Mauritania*] [*Airport symbol*] (AD)
TMK .... To My Knowledge [*Computer science*] (DOM)
TMM .... Times Mirror Magazines [*A publication*]
TMMPS .... Tris(methoxy)mercaptopropylsilane [*Organic chemistry*]
tmpl .... Temple (VRA)
TMQ .... Tambao [*Upper Volta*] [*Airport symbol*] (AD)
TMT .... Temora [*New South Wales*] [*Airport symbol*] (AD)
TMX .... Timimoun [*Algeria*] [*Airport symbol*] (AD)
TMZ .... Termez [*USSR*] [*Airport symbol*] (AD)
tn .... Toned (VRA)
TN .... Trans-Australia Airlines [*ICAO designator*] (AD)
TNA .... Training Needs Analysis (AIE)
TNC .... Threaded-Neill-Concelman (DOM)
TNC .... Total Nonstructural Carbohydrates
TND .... Trinidad [*Cuba*] [*Airport symbol*] (AD)
TNQ .... Tongo [*Sierra Leone*] [*Airport symbol*] (AD)
TNR .... Tananarive [*Malagasy*] [*Airport symbol*] (AD)
TNS .... Toensberg [*Norway*] [*Airport symbol*] (AD)
tnt .... Tint (VRA)
TNUSA .... Ted Nugent United Sportsmen of America
TO .... Alkan Air Ltd. [*ICAO designator*] (AD)
TOA .... Tromsoe [*Norway*] [*Airport symbol*] (AD)
TOC .... Training Occupational Classification (AIE)
TOD .... Target-Organ Damage [*Medicine*]
TOMP .... Toxic Organic Management Plan [*Pollution prevention*]
TOPMIS .... Total Officer Personnel Management [*Army*] (RDA)
TOPrS .... Trust Originated Preferred Securities [*Finance*]
TOQ .... Tocopilla [*Chile*] [*Airport symbol*] (AD)
tort .... Tortoise (VRA)
TOU .... Touraine [*South Vietnam*] [*Airport symbol*] (AD)
TOW .... Tororo [*Uganda*] [*Airport symbol*] (AD)
towd .... Toward (VRA)
town ha .... Town Hall (VRA)
TOX .... Tocantina [*Goias, Brazil*] [*Airport symbol*] (AD)
TP .... Terminal Portability [*Telecommunications*] (DOM)
TPA .... Thermal Polyaspartate [*Organic chemistry*]
TP-AGB .... Thermally Pulsing, Asymptotic Giant Branch [*Astronomy*]
TPG .... Taiping [*China*] [*Airport symbol*] (AD)
TPH .... Tonopah [*Nevada*] [*Airport symbol*] (AD)
TPI .... Training Place in Industry (AIE)
TPR .... Threepenny Review [*A publication*] (BRI)
TPS .... Tiered Premium System [*Insurance*] (WYGK)
TPU .... Taputuquara [*Brazil*] [*Airport symbol*] (AD)
TPY .... Tocantinopolis [*Brazil*] [*Airport symbol*] (AD)
tpyt .... Triptych (VRA)
TQ .... Las Vegas Airlines [*ICAO designator*] (AD)
TQV .... St. Moritz [*Switzerland*] [*Airport symbol*] (AD)
TR .... Royal Air [*ICAO designator*] (AD)
tr .... Traces (VRA)
TR .... Transbrasil [*ICAO designator*] (AD)
trab .... Trabeated (VRA)
trac .... Tracery (VRA)
TRACE .... Training and Approaches to Careers Education [*Project*] (AIE)
trans .... Transparency (VRA)
trans .... Transportation (DD)
transf .... Transfer (VRA)
transl .... Translucent (VRA)
TranslRev .... Translation Review [*A publication*] (BRI)
TranslRevS... Translation Review Supplement [*A publication*] (BRI)
transp .... Transportation (VRA)
trap .... Trapping (VRA)
Trav .... Travel-Holiday [*A publication*] (BRI)
TRAVIS .... Travel Industry School (AIE)
treas .... Treasurer (DD)
treas .... Treasury (DD)
TrEAT .... Trial for Early Alcohol Treatment
TRF .... Tissue Respiratory Factors [*Medicine*]
Trib Bks .... Tribune Books [*A publication*] (BRI)

TRICE .... Textile Care and Rental Industry Council for Education (AIE)
tricl .... Triclinium (VRA)
trifr .... Triforium (VRA)
trim arh .... Triumphal Arch (VRA)
TR-LSC .... Time-Resolved Liquid Scintillation Counting [*Instrumentation*]
TRQ .... Tarauaca [*Brazil*] [*Airport symbol*] (AD)
TRR .... Trincomalee [*Ceylon*] [*Airport symbol*] (AD)
trsp .... Transept (VRA)
TRT .... Tiaret [*Algeria*] [*Airport symbol*] (AD)
trum .... Trumeau (VRA)
TRUST .... Terminal Repeller Unconstrained Subenergy Tunneling [*An algorithm for global optimization*]
trvtn .... Travertine (VRA)
TRY .... Treviso [*Italy*] [*Airport symbol*] (AD)
TRZ .... Trichinopoly [*India*] [*Airport symbol*] (AD)
TS .... Samoa Air [*ICAO designator*] (AD)
TSAS .... Training Standards Advisory Service (AIE)
TSATA .... TCI Satellite Entertainment
TSC .... Tuberous Sclerosis Complex [*Medicine*]
TSH .... Transfer Scheme Handbook (AIE)
TSN .... Tientsin [*China*] [*Airport symbol*] (AD)
TSO .... Training for Skill Ownership (AIE)
TSR .... TeleService Resources
TSS .... Tebessa [*Algeria*] [*Airport symbol*] (AD)
tsse .... Terrasse (DD)
TSTWCS ...... Temporary Short-Time Working Compensation Scheme (AIE)
TSWL .... Tulsa Studies in Women's Literature [*A publication*] (BRI)
TT .... Caroline Islands (VRA)
TT .... Marshall Islands (VRA)
TT .... Royal West [*ICAO designator*] (AD)
TT .... Theology Today [*A publication*] (BRI)
TTC .... Taltal [*Chile*] [*Airport symbol*] (AD)
TTD .... Palm Island [*Windward Islands, West Indies*] [*Airport symbol*] (AD)
TTG .... Tartagal [*Argentina*] [*Airport symbol*] (AD)
TTM .... Tablon de Tamara [*Colombia*] [*Airport symbol*] (AD)
TTTA .... Training Technology Transfer Act of 1984 (WYGK)
TTWA .... Travel to Work Area (AIE)
TTYP .... Tintype (VRA)
TUB .... Tubarao [*Brazil*] [*Airport symbol*] (AD)
tub .... Tubing (VRA)
tub .... Tubular (VRA)
Tun .... Tunisia (VRA)
TUQ .... Tougan [*Upper Volta*] [*Airport symbol*] (AD)
TURC .... Trades Union Research Centre (AIE)
Turk .... Turkey (VRA)
turq .... Turqoise (VRA)
TUX .... Tuxpan [*Mexico*] [*Airport symbol*] (AD)
TV .... Haiti Trans Air [*ICAO designator*] (AD)
TV .... Transamerica [*ICAO designator*] (AD)
TVD .... Total Virus Defense [*McAfee*] [*Computer science*]
TVEI(P) .... Technical and Vocational Education Initiative: Pilot (AIE)
TV Q .... Television Quarterly [*A publication*] (BRI)
TWAIN .... Technology Without an Interesting Name [*Computer science*]
TWL .... Transition to Working Life [*Project*] (AIE)
Twp .... Township (DD)
TWR .... Third World Resources [*A publication*] (BRI)
twr .... Tower (VRA)
TWVRP .... Tactical Wheeled Vehicles Remanufacture Program [*Army*] (RDA)
TX .... Transportes Aereos Nacionales [*ICAO designator*] (AD)
TXA .... Texeira [*Portugal*] [*Airport symbol*] (AD)
TXG .... Taichung [*Formosa*] [*Airport symbol*] (AD)
TXM .... Teminabuan [*West Irian, Indonesia*] [*Airport symbol*] (AD)
TXR .... Tanbar [*Queensland*] [*Airport symbol*] (AD)
txtl .... Textile (VRA)
TY .... Air Caledonie [*ICAO designator*] (AD)
TYA .... Yalova [*Turkey*] [*Airport symbol*] (AD)
TYB .... Tibooburra [*New South Wales*] [*Airport symbol*] (AD)
tymp .... Tympanium (VRA)
typogr .... Typography (VRA)
TZ .... American Trans Air [*ICAO designator*] (AD)
TZG .... Waha Leaf [*British Honduras*] [*Airport symbol*] (AD)

U
By Acronym

U .... Upstage (WDMC)
UBC .... United Bowhunters of Connecticut
UBG .... Limon [Honduras] [Airport symbol] (AD)
UBK .... Port Augusta [South Australia] [Airport symbol] (AD)
UBS .... Columbus [Mississippi] [Airport symbol] (AD)
UBS .... Unit-Based Scheme (AIE)
uc .... Up Center (WDMC)
UC .... Urban Contemporary (WDMC)
UCA .... Rome-Utica [New York] [Airport symbol] (AD)
UCB .... University College Buckingham [British] (AIE)
UCET........... Universities Council for the Education of Teachers (AIE)
UCN .... Buchanan [Liberia] [Airport symbol] (AD)
UCTLIG .... Universities and Colleges Teaching, Learning, and Information Group [Universities and Colleges Information Systems Association] (AIE)
UD .... Georgian Bay [ICAO designator] (AD)
UD .... lloyd Your Trans-Australian Airline [ICAO designator] (AD)
UDD .... Cuddapan [Queensland] [Airport symbol] (AD)
UDE .... University Department of Education (AIE)
UDLP .... United Defense Limited Partnership (RDA)
UDs .... Undeliverables [Fundraising]
UDTV .... Ultra-High Definition Television (DOM)
UE .... Air La [ICAO designator] (AD)
UE .... United Air [ICAO designator] (AD)
UED .... Ultrafast Electron Diffraction [Physics]
UES .... Unified Energy System [Russia]
UETP........... University-Enterprise Training Partnership [European Community] (AIE)
UF .... Sydaero [ICAO designator] (AD)
Ugan .... Uganda (VRA)
UGB .... Urban Growth Boundary
UH .... Austin Airways [ICAO designator] (AD)
UI .... Flugfelag Nordurlands [Northlands Air] [ICAO designator] (AD)
UI................ Understanding Industry (AIE)
UIAS .... Unified Information Access System
UIH .... Qui Nhon [South Vietnam] [Airport symbol] (AD)
UJ .... Air Sedona [ICAO designator] (AD)
UKERNA....... United Kingdom Education and Research Networking Association (AIE)
UKI............. Ukiah [California] [Airport symbol] (AD)
UKR .... Mukeiras [South Arabia] [Airport symbol] (AD)
UL .... Air Lanka [ICAO designator] (AD)
ULEAC .... University of London and East Anglia Consortium [British] (AIE)
ULISC .... University Library and Information Services Committee [Committee of Vice Chancellors and Principals] [British] (AIE)
ULP............. Unfair Labor Practices (WYGK)
UM.............. Air Zimbabwe [ICAO designator] (AD)
UM.............. Utilization Management (WYGK)
UMI............. University Microfilms, Inc. (WDMC)
UMK............ Umanak [Greenland] [Airport symbol] (AD)
UMU .... Umuarama [Brazil] [Airport symbol] (AD)
UMW .... Mumbwa [Zambia] [Airport symbol] (AD)
UN .... East Coast Airlines [ICAO designator] (AD)
unb .... Unbound (WDMC)
Unbd.......... Unbound (WDMC)
UNC .... Unguia [Colombia] [Airport symbol] (AD)
UNCHR .... United Nations Commission on Human Rights
UNCSTD....... United Nations Conference on Science and Technology Education for Development (AIE)

Under Nat... Underwater Naturalist [A publication] (BRI)
undglz.......... Underglaze (VRA)
UNE .... Unst [Shetland Islands, Scotland] [Airport symbol] (AD)
UN/EAT........ United Nations Electoral Assistance Team
UNEP GC .... United Nations Environment Program Governing Council
unglz.......... Unglazed (VRA)
UNI .... Uniao da Vitoria [Brazil] [Airport symbol] (AD)
unid .... Unidentified (VRA)
uniq .... Unique (VRA)
univ .... University (VRA)
Univ Bkmn... University Bookman [A publication] (BRI)
unk............ Unknown (VRA)
UNSTAC....... United Nations Science and Technology Advisory Committee (AIE)
unsz c......... Unsized Canvas (VRA)
unt .... Untitled (VRA)
untemp .... Untempered (VRA)
UO .... Direct Air [ICAO designator] (AD)
UON .... Muong Sai [Laos] [Airport symbol] (AD)
UP............... Bahamas Air [ICAO designator] (AD)
UP............... Unified Programme [Education] (AIE)
UPA .... Upala [Costa Rica] [Airport symbol] (AD)
UPA .... Urban Programme Authority [Education] (AIE)
UPC .... Universal Product Code
uphol .... Upholstry (VRA)
UPORVC ..... Upper Peninsula Off Road Vehicle Committee [Michigan]
UPSA .... Upper Peninsula Sportsmen's Alliance
UPV .... Upernavik [Greenland] [Airport symbol] (AD)
UQ .... Suburban Airlines [ICAO designator] (AD)
UR .... British International Helicopters [ICAO designator] (AD)
UR .... Empire Airlines [ICAO designator] (AD)
Urban Ed ... Urban Education [A publication] (BRI)
URBED .... Urban and Economic Development Ltd. (AIE)
URF .... Urfa [Turkey] [Airport symbol] (AD)
Uru .... Uruguay (VRA)
US.............. Luminosity (WDMC)
US.............. USair Express [ICAO designator] (AD)
USAFISA...... US Army Force Integration Staff Agency (RDA)
US EPA .... United States Environmental Protection Agency
USI............. Union of Students in Ireland (AIE)
USO .... United States Outfitters
UT.............. Using Television (WDMC)
UTA .... Umtali [Zimbabwe] [Airport symbol] (AD)
UTI............. Uttaradit [Thailand] [Airport symbol] (AD)
UTL............. Utila Island [Honduras] [Airport symbol] (AD)
Utne R .... Utne Reader [A publication] (BRI)
utnsl .... Utensil (VRA)
UTU .... Ulster Teacher's Union [Ireland] (AIE)
UTW........... Queenstown [South Africa] [Airport symbol] (AD)
UU .... Reunion Air [ICAO designator] (AD)
UUP .... Uaupes [Brazil] [Airport symbol] (AD)
UUS .... User-to-User Signaling [Telecommunications] (DOM)
uv .... Ultraviolet (VRA)
UV.............. Universal Airways [ICAO designator] (AD)
UW............. Perimeter Airlines [ICAO designator] (AD)
UW............. Underwriter (DFIT)
UWHAT....... Understanding without Heavy Acronym Training (AIE)
UX .... Air Illinois [ICAO designator] (AD)
UY.............. Cameroon Airlines [ICAO designator] (AD)
UZ .... Air Resorts Airlines [ICAO designator] (AD)
UZ .... Nefertiti [ICAO designator] (AD)

V
By Acronym

v .... High Frequency (WDMC)
v .... Verb (WDMC)
v .... Verse (WDMC)
v .... Version (WDMC)
v .... Verso (WDMC)
v .... Versus (WDMC)
v .... Vertical (WDMC)
v .... Very (WDMC)
v .... Video (VRA)
v .... Voice (WDMC)
v .... Volume (WDMC)
v .... Vowel (WDMC)
VA .... [Department of] Veterans Affairs
VACSSS .... Veterans Affairs Cooperative Study of Systemic Sepsis
VAE .... Ciudad de Valles [Mexico] [Airport symbol] (AD)
VAG .... Vagar [Faeroe Islands] [Airport symbol] (AD)
VAIO .... Video Audio Integrated Operation [Computer science]
VALS .... Values and Lifestyles Program (WDMC)
van pt .... Vanishing Point (VRA)
VAP .... Ventilator-Associated Pneumonia [Medicine]
VAR .... Value-Added Reseller
var .... Varnish (VRA)
VARI .... Vacuum-Assisted Resin Infusion (RDA)
vari .... Various (VRA)
Vat .... Vatican (VRA)
VAT .... Vatomandry [Malagasy] [Airport symbol] (AD)
VAT .... Vertically Anchored Tire
VAV .... Vaxjo [Sweden] [Airport symbol] (AD)
VAX/VMS .... Virtual Address Extension/Virtual Memory System [Computer science] (DOM)
VB .... Birmingham European Airways [ICAO designator] (AD)
VB .... Westair Commuter Airlines [ICAO designator] (AD)
VBN .... Vrnjacka Banja [Yugoslavia] [Airport symbol] (AD)
VBNC .... Viable but Not Culturable [Microbiology]
v-chr .... Vice-Chair of the Board (DD)
VCO .... Volunteer Conservation Officers
VCOT .... Virtual Community of Tomorrow [Internet resource] [Computer science]
VCTV .... Viewer Controlled Television (WDMC)
VCW .... Victoria West [South Africa] [Airport symbol] (AD)
vd .... Various Dates (WDMC)
V disc .... Victory Disc [Music] (WDMC)
VDO .... Vadso [Norway] [Airport symbol] (AD)
VDP .... Valle de la Pascua [Venezuela] [Airport symbol] (AD)
VDP .... Video Datagram Protocol [Computer science]
VDR .... Videodisk Recorder (WDMC)
VDR .... Villa Dolores [Argentina] [Airport symbol] (AD)
VDS .... Volunteer Development Scotland (AIE)
VEI .... Visual Exposure Indicator [Advanced photo system]
vel .... Velvet (VRA)
VEM .... Voice E-Mail Messages [Computer science]
Venez .... Venezuela (VRA)
vent .... Ventriloquist (WDMC)
ver .... Version (VRA)
verfx .... Verifax (VRA)
vert .... Vertical (WDMC)
ves .... Vessel (VRA)
VEVRA .... Vietnam Era Veterans Readjustment and Assistance Act of 1974 (WYGK)
VF .... British Air Ferries [ICAO designator] (AD)
VF .... Golden West [ICAO designator] (AD)
VF .... Vanity Fair [A publication] (WDMC)
VG .... City Flug [ICAO designator] (AD)
vgnt .... Vignette (VRA)
VGR .... Virgin Gorda [British Virgin Islands] [Airport symbol] (AD)
VH .... Air Burkina [ICAO designator] (AD)
VH .... Air Volta [ICAO designator] (AD)
VH1 .... Video Hits One [Cable programming service] (WDMC)
VHSB .... Virtual Home Space Builder
VHY .... Vichy [France] [Airport symbol] (AD)
VI .... In Bankruptcy or Receivership [Investment term] (DFIT)
VI .... St. Croix Island (VRA)
VI .... St. John Island (VRA)
VI .... St. Thomas Island (VRA)
VI .... Vieques Airlink [ICAO designator] (AD)
VIC .... Vicenza [Italy] [Airport symbol] (AD)

VICE .... Virus Instructional Code Emulator [Computer science]
VIL .... Villa Cisneros [Spanish Sahara] [Airport symbol] (AD)
VIQ .... Violetvale [Queensland] [Airport symbol] (AD)
VIS .... Video Information System [Tandy Corp.] (DOM)
viz .... Vizmo (WDMC)
viz-code ..... Visual Time Code (WDMC)
VJ .... Trans-Colorado [ICAO designator] (AD)
VJB .... Vila de Joao Belo [Mozambique] [Airport symbol] (AD)
VK .... Air Tungaru [ICAO designator] (AD)
VKS .... Vicksburg [Mississippi] [Airport symbol] (AD)
VL .... Mid-South Commuter Airlines [ICAO designator] (AD)
VLDP .... Volunteer Leadership Development Program [Canada]
VLK .... Viqueque [Timor] [Airport symbol] (AD)
vlm .... Vellum (VRA)
VLPO .... Ventrolateral Preoptic
VLR .... Vallenar [Chile] [Airport symbol] (AD)
VLS .... Village Voice Literary Supplement [A publication] (BRI)
vlt .... Vault (VRA)
VM .... Ocean Airways [ICAO designator] (AD)
VMF .... Variable Message Formats (RDA)
VN .... Hang Khong Vietnam [ICAO designator] (AD)
vn .... Vinyl (VRA)
VNR .... Vanrook [Queensland] [Airport symbol] (AD)
vnr .... Veneer (VRA)
VNT .... Virus Neutralization Test [Analytical biochemistry]
VNX .... Vilanculos [Mozambique] [Airport symbol] (AD)
VO .... Tyrolean Airways [ICAO designator] (AD)
VOC .... Certificate of Vocational Preparation (AIE)
VOL .... Volos [Greece] [Airport symbol] (AD)
vol .... Volume (VRA)
volc .... Volcanic (VRA)
VOT .... Voice Output Terminal [Computer science] (WDMC)
VOYA .... Voice of Youth Advocates [A publication] (BRI)
v-p .... Vice-President (DD)
VPA .... Silver Plains [Queensland] [Airport symbol] (AD)
VPP .... Virtual Pivot Point [Suspension] [Tandem bike]
VPP .... Vocational Preparation Programme (AIE)
VPPPA .... Voluntary Protection Programs Participants' Association
VPS .... Eglin Air Force Base [Florida] [Airport symbol] (AD)
VPY .... Vila Pery [Mozambique] [Airport symbol] (AD)
VQ .... Oxley Airlines [ICAO designator] (AD)
VQR .... Virginia Quarterly Review [A publication] (BRI)
VR .... Transportes Aereos de Cabo Verde [ICAO designator] (AD)
VRBA .... Veterans' Readjustment Benefits Act of 1966 (WYGK)
VRT .... Video Round Table [American Library Association]
VRZ .... Voronezh [USSR] [Airport symbol] (AD)
vs .... Versus (WDMC)
VS .... Very Special [Age of the Cognac]
VS .... Victorian Studies [A publication] (BRI)
VS .... Virgin Atlantic Airways [ICAO designator] (AD)
VS .... Voluntary School (AIE)
VSC .... VirusScan Configuration [Computer science]
VSO .... Phuoc Long [Vietnam] [Airport symbol] (AD)
VSOP .... Very Long Baseline Interferometry [Used in a space orbiting project]
vsrs .... Voussoirs (VRA)
vstib .... Vestibule (VRA)
vstmt .... Vestment (VRA)
v-supt .... Vice-Superintendent (DD)
VT .... Air Polynesie [ICAO designator] (AD)
VT .... Vertical Tab [Computer science] (DOM)
VTE .... Venous Thromboembolism [Medicine]
VTL .... Vittel [France] [Airport symbol] (AD)
Vtnm .... Vietnam (VRA)
vtp .... Videotape (VRA)
VU .... Air Ivoire [ICAO designator] (AD)
VUI .... Video User Interface [Computer science] (DOM)
VV .... Semo Aviation [ICAO designator] (AD)
vv .... Vice Versa (WDMC)
VV .... Village Voice [A publication] (BRI)
VVC .... Variable Valve Control [Automotive]
VVEJ .... Venus-Venus-Earth-Jupiter [Trajectory]
VVO .... Vladivostok [USSR] [Airport symbol] (AD)
VVT .... Variable Valve Timing [Automotive]
VW .... Ama-Flyg [ICAO designator] (AD)
vw .... View (VRA)
VX .... Aces [ICAO designator] (AD)

VXC............ Vila Cabral [*Mozambique*] [*Airport symbol*] (AD)
VY............... Coral Air [*ICAO designator*] (AD)
vy............... Various Years (WDMC)
VZ............... Aquatic Airlines [*ICAO designator*] (AD)

W

By Acronym

w .... Wardrobe (WDMC)
w .... Watt (WDMC)
w .... Week (WDMC)
w .... Weekly (WDMC)
w .... Weight (WDMC)
w .... White (VRA)
w .... Wide (WDMC)
w .... Width (WDMC)
w .... Wife (WDMC)
w .... With (WDMC)
w/ .... With (VRA)
WA .... Wagner Act of 1935 (WYGK)
wa .... Wash (VRA)
WA .... Wide Angle (WDMC)
WAA .... Water Authorities Association (AIE)
WAAC .... Women's Art Association of Canada [1887, Lyceum Club and Women's Art Association from 1930] (NGC)
WAB .... Wabag [New Guinea] [Airport symbol] (AD)
WAC .... Work Assessment Course (AIE)
WAE .... Aoulef [Algeria] [Airport symbol] (AD)
waf .... With All Faults (WDMC)
wal .... Walnut (VRA)
WAL .... Western American Literature [A publication] (BRI)
WALRUS .... Water and Land Resource Utilization Simulation
WAN .... Waverney [Queensland] [Airport symbol] (AD)
W & F .... Work and Flop (WDMC)
W&I .... World & I [A publication] (BRI)
W&M Q .... William and Mary Quarterly [A publication] (BRI)
W&T .... Work and Turn (WDMC)
WAP .... Alto Palena [Chile] [Airport symbol] (AD)
wapa .... Wall Paper (VRA)
WARP .... Wind Amplified Rotor Platform
WARP .... Wind Amplifier Rotor Platform
Wash DC .... Washington, D.C. (VRA)
Wash M .... Washington Monthly [A publication] (BRI)
WATC .... Women's Air Training Corps
WBA .... Washington Bay [Alaska] [Airport symbol] (AD)
WBG .... Wichabai [Guyana] [Airport symbol] (AD)
WBL .... Work Based Learning (AIE)
WBT .... Windows-Based Terminal [Computer science]
wc .... Watercolor (VRA)
WC .... Wien Air Alaska [ICAO designator] (AD)
WCA .... Castro [Chile] [Airport symbol] (AD)
WCDT .... Westminster Centre for Design and Technology [British] (AIE)
WCH .... Chaiten [Chile] [Airport symbol] (AD)
WCJ .... Caleta Josefina [Chile] [Airport symbol] (AD)
WCO .... Coolullah [Australia] [Airport symbol] (AD)
wc/pa .... Watercolor on Paper (VRA)
WD .... Ward Air [ICAO designator] (AD)
wd .... Wide (VRA)
wd .... Width (VRA)
wd .... Wood (VRA)
WDA .... Wadi Ain [South Arabia] [Airport symbol] (AD)
wdbl .... Woodblock (VRA)
wdct .... Woodcut (VRA)
WE .... Votec [ICAO designator] (AD)
WEAP .... Women's Economic Agenda Project [An association]
web .... Web (VRA)
WEBS .... World Equity Benchmark Shares [Investment term]
WEDG .... Women's Education Group (AIE)
WEH .... Walter and Eliza Hall Institute of Medical Research [Australia]
WEN .... Papa Westray [Orkney Islands, Scotland] [Airport symbol] (AD)
WER .... Whole Earth Review [A publication] (BRI)
WF .... Wideros Flyveselskap [ICAO designator] (AD)
wf .... Wrong Font [Publishing] (WDMC)
WGARCR .... Working Group against Racism in Children's Resources (AIE)
WGM .... Wilmington [California] [Airport symbol] (AD)
WGU .... Western Governors University
WGWC .... Working Group on Waterborne Cryptosporidiosis [Medicine]
WH .... China Northwest Airlines [ICAO designator] (AD)
WH .... Southeastern Commuter Airlines [ICAO designator] (AD)
wh .... White (WDMC)
WHA .... Wadi Halfa [Sudan] [Airport symbol] (AD)
wha .... Whale (VRA)
WHA .... Work Hours Act of 1962 (WYGK)
WHAM .... Wisconsin H-Alpha Mapper [Astrophysics]

WHOOPS ..... Washington Public Power Supply System (DFIT)
WHQ .... Western Historical Quarterly [A publication] (BRI)
WHR .... Western Humanities Review [A publication] (BRI)
WHS .... Women's Health Study
WHYFU .... Why Have You Forsaken Us? [Fundraising]
WI .... Swift-Aire Lines [ICAO designator] (AD)
wi .... Wire (VRA)
WIAC .... Women's International Art Club, London [1899] (NGC)
WIHS .... Women's Interagency HIV [Human Immuno Deficiency Virus] Study [Medicine]
WIIFM .... What's in It for Me? [Fundraising]
Wil Q .... Wilson Quarterly [A publication] (BRI)
Win 95 .... Windows 95 [Computer science] (WDMC)
W Ind .... West Indies (VRA)
WinHEC .... Windows Hardware Engineering Conference
WIR .... Work Injury Reports [Human Resources] (WYGK)
WIS .... Central [Wisconsin] [Airport symbol] (AD)
WISE .... Wardens in the South East (AIE)
WISE .... Whistle-Blowers Integrity in Science and Education [An association]
WISH .... Women's Interview Study of Health
WJ .... Labrador Airways [ICAO designator] (AD)
WJ .... Torontair [ICAO designator] (AD)
WJC .... Western Journalism Center
wk .... Week (WDMC)
WK .... Westkuestenflug [ICAO designator] (AD)
WKB .... Warracknabeal [Victoria, Australia] [Airport symbol] (AD)
WKI .... Wankie [Zimbabwe] [Airport symbol] (AD)
WKM .... Wankie Game Reserve [Zimbabwe] [Airport symbol] (AD)
WKP .... Wrotham Park [Queensland] [Airport symbol] (AD)
wkr .... Wicker (VRA)
WL .... Bursa Hava Yollari [ICAO designator] (AD)
wl .... Wool (VRA)
WLB .... Wilson Library Bulletin [A publication] (BRI)
wld .... Welded (VRA)
WLG .... Work Learning Guide (AIE)
wlkwy .... Walkway (VRA)
wlrs .... Walrus (VRA)
WLT .... World Literature Today [A publication] (BRI)
WMF .... Windows Metafile Format [Computer science]
WMG .... Working Mathematics Group (AIE)
WMP .... Mampikony [Malagasy] [Airport symbol] (AD)
WMV .... Madirovalo [Malagasy] [Airport symbol] (AD)
WN .... Southwest Airlines [ICAO designator] (AD)
wndw .... Window (VRA)
wnsct .... Wainscot (VRA)
WNY .... Burnie-Wynward [Tasmania] [Airport symbol] (AD)
w/o .... Week Of (WDMC)
WO .... World Airways [ICAO designator] (AD)
WOC .... Work and Occupations [A publication] (BRI)
WOICE .... World Catalog of International Chemical Equipment [A publication]
WOLVES ...... Wireless Operationally Linked Electronic and Video Exploration System
WOMBAT .... Waves on Magnetised Beams and Turbulence
WOMEN .... Women's Organization for Mentoring, Education and Networking Unlimited, Inc.
Wom R Bks .. Women's Review of Books [A publication] (BRI)
WON .... Wondoola [Queensland] [Airport symbol] (AD)
WOQ .... Wooroona [Queensland] [Airport symbol] (AD)
WORD .... Wechsler Objective Reading Dimensions [Test]
WorldV .... WorldViews: A Quarterly Review of Resources for Education and Action [A publication] (BRI)
WORM .... Write-Once, Read-Many [Computer science]
WP .... Aloha Islandair [ICAO designator] (AD)
WP .... Princeville Airways [ICAO designator] (AD)
WP .... Work Preparation (AIE)
WP .... World Politics [A publication] (BRI)
WPA .... Puerto Aysen [Chile] [Airport symbol] (AD)
WPA .... Whistleblower Protection Act of 1989 (WYGK)
WPCTS .... When Push Comes to Shove
wpm .... Words per Minute (WDMC)
WPR .... Porvenir [Chile] [Airport symbol] (AD)
WPS .... Worldwide Port System [Army] (RDA)
WPU .... Puerto Williams [Chile] [Airport symbol] (AD)
WQ .... Wings Airways [ICAO designator] (AD)
wr .... Ware (VRA)
WR .... Wheeler Flying Service [ICAO designator] (AD)

WRET.......... Work-Related Education and Training (AIE)
wrhs............ Warehouse (VRA)
WRN .... Women Returners Network (AIE)
wrt .... Wrought (VRA)
WS............. Northern Wings [*ICAO designator*] (AD)
WSA.......... Williams-Steiger Act of 1970 (WYGK)
W Sam .... Western Samoa (VRA)
WSC.......... Water Studies Centre [*Australia*] [*Chisholm Institute of Technology*]
WSJ............ Wall Street Journal [*A publication*] (DFIT)
WSJ............ Wall Street Journal (Eastern Edition) [*A publication*] (BRI)
WSJ-MW ..... Wall Street Journal (Midwest Edition) [*A publication*] (BRI)
WSL........... Water Science Laboratories Proprietary Ltd. [*Australia*]
WSLBRUC.... WS and LB Robinson University College [*Australia*]
WSP........... Waspam [*Nicaragua*] [*Airport symbol*] (AD)
WSR .... Wasior [*West Irian, Indonesia*] [*Airport symbol*] (AD)
WSU .... Weighted Student Unit
WT............. Nigeria Airways [*ICAO designator*] (AD)
W/Tax......... Withholding Tax (DFIT)
WTD........... West End [*Grand Bahama Island, Bahamas*] [*Airport symbol*] (AD)
WTFU.......... Women Teachers' Franchise Union (AIE)
WTMA......... Wool Textile Manufacturers of Australia
WTN........... Worldwide Television News Corp. (WDMC)
wtr .... Water (VRA)

WTTS.......... Weak-Lined T Tauri Stars [*Astronomy*]
WU............. Netherlines [*ICAO designator*] (AD)
WU............. Rhine Air [*ICAO designator*] (AD)
WUT........... Woman Using Television (WDMC)
WUT........... Women Using Television (WDMC)
WV............. Midwest Aviation [*ICAO designator*] (AD)
wv.............. Weave (VRA)
wv.............. Woven (VRA)
WVA........... Alexandria [*Virginia*] [*Airport symbol*] (AD)
WVBA .... West Virginia Bowhunters Association
WVV........... Volovan [*Malagasy*] [*Airport symbol*] (AD)
WW .... Scottish European Airways [*ICAO designator*] (AD)
WW .... Trans-West [*ICAO designator*] (AD)
WWD .... Women's Wear Daily [*A publication*] (WDMC)
wwk .... Westwork (VRA)
WWW .... World Wide Wait [*Computer science*]
WX .... Ansett Airlines of New South Wales [*ICAO designator*] (AD)
wx............. Wax (VRA)
WX............ Weather Report (WDMC)
WY .... Indiana Airways [*ICAO designator*] (AD)
WYC.......... Yes Bay [*Alaska*] [*Airport symbol*] (AD)
WYD .... Wyandotte [*Queensland*] [*Airport symbol*] (AD)
WZ............. Berlin European [*ICAO designator*] (AD)
WZ............. Trans Western Airlines of Utah [*ICAO designator*] (AD)

X-Y-Z
By Acronym

XAR .... Extended Attribute Record [*Computer science*] (DOM)
XAY .... Xapuri [*Brazil*] [*Airport symbol*] (AD)
xbld .... Extrabold [*Type*] (WDMC)
XC .... Caribbean Air Transport [*ICAO designator*] (AD)
XE .... South Central [*ICAO designator*] (AD)
XF .... Cobden Airways [*ICAO designator*] (AD)
XG .... Air North [*ICAO designator*] (AD)
XGA .... Extended Graphics Adapter [*Computer science*] (DOM)
Xian .... Christian (VRA)
XIE .... Xieng Khouang [*Laos*] [*Airport symbol*] (AD)
XIQ .... Xique-Xique [*Brazil*] [*Airport symbol*] (AD)
XJ .... Mesaba Aviation [*ICAO designator*] (AD)
XL .... Extra Long (WDMC)
XLS .... Extra-Long Shot (WDMC)
XMC .... Malacoota [*New South Wales, Australia*] [*Airport symbol*] (AD)
XMM .... Mamaia [*Romania*] [*Airport symbol*] (AD)
XMT .... Transmit (WDMC)
XNG .... Quang Ngai [*Vietnam*] [*Airport symbol*] (AD)
XO .... Rio Airways [*ICAO designator*] (AD)
XOGP .... Xograph (VRA)
XP .... Avior [*ICAO designator*] (AD)
XQ .... Caribbean International [*ICAO designator*] (AD)
XS .... Across Shoulder (WDMC)
xsect .... Cross Section (VRA)
XT .... Executive Transportation [*ICAO designator*] (AD)
XTG .... Thargomindah [*Queensland*] [*Airport symbol*] (AD)
XTN .... Qatn [*South Arabia*] [*Airport symbol*] (AD)
XTO .... Taroom [*Queensland*] [*Airport symbol*] (AD)
XTR .... Tara [*Queensland*] [*Airport symbol*] (AD)
XU .... Trans Mo Airlines [*ICAO designator*] (AD)
XV .... Mississippi Valley Airways [*ICAO designator*] (AD)
XW .... Walker's Cay Air Terminal [*ICAO designator*] (AD)
XX .... Valdez Airlines [*ICAO designator*] (AD)
XY .... Munz Northern [*ICAO designator*] (AD)
XZ .... Air Tasmania [*ICAO designator*] (AD)
Y .... Ex-Dividend and Sales in Full [*Investment term*] (DFIT)
y .... Year (WDMC)
Y2Y .... Yellowstone to Canada's Yukon Territory
ya .... Yarn (VRA)
YAC .... Yacuiba [*Bolivia*] [*Airport symbol*] (AD)
Yacht .... Yachting [*A publication*] (BRI)
Yahoo .... Yet Another Hierarchically Officious Oracle [*World Wide Web*] (DOM)
YAL .... Youth Affairs Lobby (AIE)
YALSA .... Young Adult Library Services Association [*American Library Association*]
YB .... Hyannis Aviation [*ICAO designator*] (AD)
YB .... Your Business [*A publication*]
YC .... Alaska Aeronautical Industries [*ICAO designator*] (AD)
YD .... Ama Air Express [*ICAO designator*] (AD)
YDA .... Dawson City [*Yukon*] [*Airport symbol*] (AD)
YE .... Grand Canyon Airlines [*ICAO designator*] (AD)
YE .... Pearson Aircraft [*ICAO designator*] (AD)
YE .... Youth Enterprise (AIE)
yel .... Yellow (VRA)
YETI .... Youth Education and Training Innovators (AIE)
YF .... Youth Female [*International Bowhunting Organization*] [*Class Equipment*]
YGR .... Magdalen Island [*Quebec*] [*Airport symbol*] (AD)
ygr .... Younger (VRA)
YGT .... Thunder Bay [*Ontario*] [*Airport symbol*] (AD)
YH .... Trans New York [*ICAO designator*] (AD)
YHCFE .... Yorkshire and Humberside Council for Further and Higher Education [*British*] (AIE)
YI .... Intercity [*ICAO designator*] (AD)
YIL .... Yahoo Internet Life [*Computer science*]
YIP .... Youth Initiative Project (AIE)
YJ .... Commodore [*ICAO designator*] (AD)
YK .... Cyprus Turkish Airways [*ICAO designator*] (AD)
YL .... Long Island Airlines [*ICAO designator*] (AD)
YL .... Montauk Caribbbean Airways and Ocean Reef Airways [*ICAO designator*] (AD)
YLE .... Yule Island [*New Guinea*] [*Airport symbol*] (AD)
YLJ .... Yale Law Journal [*A publication*] (BRI)
YM .... Mountain Home Air Service [*ICAO designator*] (AD)
YMCK .... Yellow, Magenta, Cyan, Black (WDMC)

YMF .... Youth Male Fingers [*International Bowhunting Organization*] [*Class Equipment*]
YML .... Murray Bay [*Quebec*] [*Airport symbol*] (AD)
YMR .... Youth Male Release [*International Bowhunting Organization*] [*Class equipment*]
YMV .... Manicouagan [*Quebec*] [*Airport symbol*] (AD)
YN .... Nor-East Commuter Airlines [*ICAO designator*] (AD)
YND .... Yandina [*Solomon Islands*] [*Airport symbol*] (AD)
YNK .... Gagnon [*Quebec*] [*Airport symbol*] (AD)
YNPA .... Young National Party of Australia [*Political party*]
YO .... Heli-Air-Monaco [*ICAO designator*] (AD)
YOR .... Yoro [*Honduras*] [*Airport symbol*] (AD)
YOY .... Young-of-the-Year [*Conservation*]
YP .... Pagas Airlines [*ICAO designator*] (AD)
YP .... Young Person (AIE)
YQ .... Lakeland [*ICAO designator*] (AD)
YQJ .... Porquis Junction [*Ontario*] [*Airport symbol*] (AD)
YR .... Scenic Airlines [*ICAO designator*] (AD)
YR .... Yale Review [*A publication*] (BRI)
YRF .... Ross Bay [*Newfoundland*] [*Airport symbol*] (AD)
YRQ .... Trois Rivieres [*Quebec*] [*Airport symbol*] (AD)
YRX .... Rimouski [*Quebec*] [*Airport symbol*] (AD)
YS .... San Juan Airlines [*ICAO designator*] (AD)
YSU .... Summerside [*Prince Edward Island*] [*Airport symbol*] (AD)
YT .... Sky West [*ICAO designator*] (AD)
YT .... Youth Training (AIE)
YTP .... Youth Training Programme [*British*] (AIE)
YU .... Aerolineas Dominicanas [*ICAO designator*] (AD)
yuc .... Yucca (VRA)
Yugo .... Yugoslavia (VRA)
YV .... Mesa Aviation [*ICAO designator*] (AD)
YW .... Stateswest Airlines [*ICAO designator*] (AD)
YWH .... Whalehead [*Quebec*] [*Airport symbol*] (AD)
YWU .... Youth Work Unit [*National Youth Bureau*] (AIE)
YX .... Midwest Express Airlines [*ICAO designator*] (AD)
YX .... Societe Aeronautique Jurassienne [*ICAO designator*] (AD)
YYN .... Swift Current [*Saskatchewan*] [*Airport symbol*] (AD)
YZ .... Linhas Aereas da Guine-Bissau [*ICAO designator*] (AD)
z .... Zero (WDMC)
z .... Zone (WDMC)
ZA .... Alpine Aviation [*ICAO designator*] (AD)
ZAK .... Zero Administration Kit [*Computer science*]
ZAL .... Valdivia [*Chile*] [*Airport symbol*] (AD)
Zam .... Zambia (VRA)
ZAN .... Zanderij [*Surinam*] [*Airport symbol*] (AD)
Zanz .... Zanzibar (VRA)
ZAP .... Zaporozhe [*USSR*] [*Airport symbol*] (AD)
ZAP .... Zip Code Attachment Program [*Computer science*] (WDMC)
ZAR .... Zaria [*Nigeria*] [*Airport symbol*] (AD)
ZAW .... Zero Administration for Windows [*Microsoft Corp.*] [*Computer science*]
ZAW .... Zero Administration Initiative for Windows [*Microsoft Corp.*] [*Computer science*]
ZB .... Air Vectors [*ICAO designator*] (AD)
ZBA .... Zero Based Analysis
ZBO .... Bowen [*Queensland*] [*Airport symbol*] (AD)
ZBY .... Sayaboury [*Laos*] [*Airport symbol*] (AD)
ZC .... Royal Swazi National Airways [*ICAO designator*] (AD)
ZCO .... Temuco [*Chile*] [*Airport symbol*] (AD)
ZD .... Ross Aviation [*ICAO designator*] (AD)
ZDK .... Zonguldak [*Turkey*] [*Airport symbol*] (AD)
ZE .... Air Caribe International [*ICAO designator*] (AD)
ZE .... Pacific National [*ICAO designator*] (AD)
ZED .... Pakatoa [*New Zealand*] [*Airport symbol*] (AD)
ZF .... Berlin U.S.A. [*ICAO designator*] (AD)
ZG .... Silver State [*ICAO designator*] (AD)
ZGL .... South Galway [*Queensland*] [*Airport symbol*] (AD)
ZGM .... Ngoma [*Zambia*] [*Airport symbol*] (AD)
ZH .... Royal Hawaiian Airways [*ICAO designator*] (AD)
ZHM .... Shamshernagar [*Bangladesh*] [*Airport symbol*] (AD)
ZI .... Lucas Air Transport [*ICAO designator*] (AD)
zi .... Zinc (VRA)
ZIC .... Victoria [*Chile*] [*Airport symbol*] (AD)
zig .... Ziggurat (VRA)
ZK .... Great Lakes Aviation [*ICAO designator*] (AD)
ZK .... Shavano Air [*ICAO designator*] (AD)

ZKL .... Steenkool [*West Irian, Indonesia*] [*Airport symbol*] (AD)
ZKM .... Sette Cama [*Gabon*] [*Airport symbol*] (AD)
ZL .... Hazelton Air Services [*ICAO designator*] (AD)
ZLG .... La Guera [*Morocco*] [*Airport symbol*] (AD)
ZM .... Trans-Central [*ICAO designator*] (AD)
ZMD .... Sao Madureira [*Brazil*] [*Airport symbol*] (AD)
zmphm........ Zoomorphism (VRA)
ZN .... Tennessee Airways [*ICAO designator*] (AD)
ZNG .... New Glasgow [*Nova Scotia*] [*Airport symbol*] (AD)
ZO .... Trans-California [*ICAO designator*] (AD)
ZOM............ Zomba [*Malawi*] [*Airport symbol*] (AD)
ZON .... Queenstown [*New Zealand*] [*Airport symbol*] (AD)
ZOO .... Zero on Originality (WDMC)
ZOPFAN ...... Zone of Peace, Freedom and Neutrality [*ASEAN*]
ZOS............. Osorno [*Chile*] [*Airport symbol*] (AD)
ZP .... Virgin Air [*ICAO designator*] (AD)

ZQ................ Ansett New Zealand [*ICAO designator*] (AD)
ZQC............. Zero Quality Control
ZR .... Star Airways [*ICAO designator*] (AD)
ZS .... Hispaniola Airways [*ICAO designator*] (AD)
ZSM............ Zoologische Staatssammlung Muenchen
ZTK .... Stokmarknes [*Norway*] [*Airport symbol*] (AD)
ZU .... Zia Airlines [*ICAO designator*] (AD)
ZUD .... Ancud [*Chile*] [*Airport symbol*] (AD)
ZUL .... Silfi [*Saudi Arabia*] [*Airport symbol*] (AD)
ZV .... Air Midwest [*ICAO designator*] (AD)
ZVG............. Springvale [*Queensland*] [*Airport symbol*] (AD)
ZVK............. Savannakhet [*Laos*] [*Airport symbol*] (AD)
ZW .... Air Wisconsin [*ICAO designator*] (AD)
ZX .... Air West Airlines [*ICAO designator*] (AD)
ZY .... Air Pennsylvania [*ICAO designator*] (AD)
ZZU .... Mzuzu [*Malawi*] [*Airport symbol*] (AD)
ZZV .... Zanesville [*Ohio*] [*Airport symbol*] (AD)

Numerics
By Meaning

7th Army Training Command (RDA) 7ATC

A
By Meaning

AB Bookman's Weekly [*A publication*] (BRI) .... AB
ABA Journal [*A publication*] (BRI) .... ABA Jour
Ababa [*Ethiopia*] [*Airport symbol*] (AD) .... ABA
Abalone (VRA) .... abal
Abau [*Papua*] [*Airport symbol*] (AD) .... ABW
Abbottabad [*Pakistan*] [*Airport symbol*] (AD) .... AOT
Abecher [*Chad*] [*Airport symbol*] (AD) .... AEH
Aberdeen University Research and Industrial Services (AIE) .... AURIS
Abou Deia [*Chad*] [*Airport symbol*] (AD) .... AOD
Absolute Total and Complete Camouflage [*Hunting*] .... ATACC
Abstract Windowing Toolkit [*Computer science*] .... AWT
Aburra (VRA) .... abu
Academic Individual Advanced Development [*Military*] (RDA) .... AIAD
Academic Library Book Review [*A publication*] (BRI) .... ALBR
Academic Staff Training and Development Programme [*British*] (AIE) .... ASTDP
Academic Strategic Alliances Program .... ASAP
Academician of the National Academy of Design, New York [*1825*] (NGC) .... NA
Academy (VRA) .... acad
Academy Board (VRA) .... acad bd
Acanthus (VRA) .... acant
Accelerated Graphics Port [*Computer science*] .... AGP
Access to Information and Reading Service (AIE) .... AIRS
Access to Information on Multicultural Educational Resources (AIE) .... AIMER
Access to Learning for Adults (AIE) .... ALFA
Accident Officers Association (AIE) .... AOA
Account Balance Pension (WYGK) .... ABP
Accounting (DD) .... acctg
Accounting Review [*A publication*] (BRI) .... AR
Accreditation of Prior Achievement [*Education*] (AIE) .... APA
Accreditation of Prior Learning (AIE) .... APL
Accredited Center [*Youth Training Scheme*] [*British*] (AIE) .... AC
Accredited in Public Relations [*Canadian Public Relations Society, Inc.*] (DD) .... APR
Accredited Leasing Officer [*Canada*] (DD) .... ALO
Accredited Training Centre [*Education*] [*British*] (AIE) .... ATC
Aces [*ICAO designator*] (AD) VX
Acetate (VRA) .... acet
Achaete-Scute Homologue [*Genetics*] .... ASH
Acoustic Thermometry of Ocean Climate .... ATOC
Acoustic-Daylight, Ambient-Noise Imaging System .... ADONIS
Acquisition Career Field [*Army*] (RDA) .... ACF
Acquisition Career Management Advocate [*Army*] (RDA) .... ACMA
Acropolis (VRA) .... acrpl
Across Shoulder (WDMC) .... XS
Acroteria (VRA) .... acrt
Acrylic on Canvas (VRA) .... ac/c
Active (VRA) .... act
Active Streaming Format [*Computer science*] .... ASF
Active Universal Joints .... AUJ
Activities Integrating Math and Science .... AIMS
Activities of Daily Living (WYGK) .... ADL
Actuarial Science (DD) .... ActSc
Acute Flaccid Paralysis [*Medicine*] .... AFP
Ada [*Oklahoma*] [*Airport symbol*] (AD) .... ADH
Adaptation to Premises and Equipment Scheme [*Education*] (AIE) .... APE
Adapter Fault Tolerance [*Intel*] [*Computer science*] .... AFT
Addictions Community Centres for Education, Prevention, Treatment, and Research [*British*] (AIE) .... ACCEPT
Add-On Conference Call [*Telecommunications*] (DOM) .... CONF
Administrateur Agree [*Canada*] (DD) .... AdmA
Administration (DD) .... admin
Administrative, Business, and Commercial (AIE) .... ABC
Administrative, Business, and Commercial Training Group (AIE) .... ABCTG
Administrative, Professional, Technical, and Clerical Grades [*Education*] (AIE) .... APT&C
Administrative Science (DD) .... AdminSc
Adobe (VRA) .... adb
Adolescence [*A publication*] (BRI) .... Adoles
Adoptive Bit Rate Encoding [*Computer science*] .... ABRE
Adult Education Institute (AIE) .... AEI
Adult Education Quarterly [*A publication*] (BRI) .... AE
Adult Employment Training Programme [*British*] (AIE) .... ATP
Adult Language Use Survey (AIE) .... ALUS
Adult Learning [*A publication*] (BRI) .... Adult L
Adult Literacy Support Services Fund (AIE) .... ALSSF
Adult Training Strategy (AIE) .... ATS

Adult Unemployed Project [*Department of Education and Science*] [*British*] (AIE) .... AUP
Advance Airlines [*ICAO designator*] (AD) .... DR
Advanced Basic Input/Output System [*Computer science*] (DOM) .... ABIOS
Advanced Certificate of Education (AIE) .... ACE
Advanced Certified Fund Raising Executive [*National Society of Fund Raising Executives*] .... ACFRE
Advanced Collaborative Filtering [*Firefly Network*] [*Computer science*] .... ACF
Advanced Digital Television Service .... ACATS
Advanced Graphics Port [*Intel*] [*Computer science*] .... AGP
Advanced Materials at Tuskegee University (RDA) .... CEAM-TU
Advanced Mobile-Phone System .... AMPS
Advanced Natural Gas Vehicle .... ANGV
Advanced Photo System .... APS
Advanced Product Evaluation Laboratory .... APEL
Advanced Reproductive Technology [*Medicine*] .... ART
Advanced Vehicle Technologies [*Military*] (RDA) .... AVT
Advanced Wave Effects [*Sound synthesis*] (DOM) .... AWE
Advanced-Level Examination [*Education*] (AIE) .... A
Advection-Dominated Accretion Flow [*Planetary science*] .... ADAF
Advertisement (VRA) .... advt
Advertising (DD) .... advtg
Advice of Charge [*Telecommunications*] (DOM) .... AOC
Advisory (DD) .... adv
Advisory Committee for Teacher Education in the Mid-South (AIE) .... ACTEMS
Advisory Committee for the Research and Development Department [*British Library*] (AIE) .... ACORDD
Advisory Committee for the Supply and Education of Teachers, Further Education Sub-Committee (AIE) .... ACSET(FE)
Advisory Committee for Vocational Training (AIE) .... ACVT
Advisory Committee on Immunization Practices .... ACIP
Advisory Council on Education and Training (AIE) .... ACET
Advisory Defense Committee .... ADC
Advocates for Library Outreach [*Office for Literacy and Outreach*] [*American Library Association*] .... AFLO
Aedicula (VRA) .... aed
Aer Arann Teo [*ICAO designator*] (AD) .... RE
Aerial Common Sensor [*Military*] (RDA) .... ACS
Aerial View (VRA) .... arl vw
Aero Peru [*ICAO designator*] (AD) .... PL
Aero Transporti Italiani [*ICAO designator*] (AD) .... BM
Aero Virgin Islands [*ICAO designator*] (AD) .... QY
Aeroamerica [*ICAO designator*] (AD) .... EO
Aerobic Dive Limit [*Psysiology*] .... ADL
Aero-Chaco [*ICAO designator*] (AD) .... CQ
Aerolinea Federal Argentina [*ICAO designator*] (AD) .... CQ
Aerolineas Dominicanas [*ICAO designator*] (AD) .... YU
Aerolineas Nicaraguenses [*ICAO designator*] (AD) .... RL
Aeronautics (DD) .... Aero
Aeropelican Intercity Commuter Air Services [*ICAO designator*] (AD) .... PO
Aeropesca [*ICAO designator*] (AD) .... RS
Aeroquetzal [*ICAO designator*] (AD) .... AW
Aerosol Time-of-Flight Mass Spectrometer .... ATOFMS
Afghanistan (VRA) .... Afgh
Africa (VRA) .... Afr
Africa Report [*A publication*] (BRI) .... Afr Rep
Africa Today [*A publication*] (BRI) .... Africa T
African American Review [*A publication*] (BRI) .... Afr Am R
African Curriculum Organisation (AIE) .... ACO
African-American English [*A dialect*] .... AAE
Afro-Caribbean Educational Resource Project (AIE) .... ACER
After (VRA) .... aft
Afyon [*Turkey*] [*Airport symbol*] (AD) .... AFY
Agate (VRA) .... ag
Agateware (VRA) .... agwr
Age Weighted Pupil Unit [*Education*] (AIE) .... AWPU
Aggregate (VRA) .... agr
Aggregated School Budget (AIE) .... ASB
Agree en Relations Publiques [*Canada*] (DD) .... ARP
Agreed Syllabus Conference [*Education*] (AIE) .... ASC
Agri [*Turkey*] [*Airport symbol*] (AD) .... AGZ
Agricultural (DD) .... Agr
Agricultural Engineering (DD) .... AgrEng
Agricultural Librarians in Colleges and Universities (AIE) .... ALCU
Agriculture (DD) .... Agr
Agrinion [*Greece*] [*Airport symbol*] (AD) .... AGQ

Aharonov-Bohm [*Physics*] ... AB
Aids to Communication in Education (AIE) ... ACE
Air Algerie [*ICAO designator*] (AD) ... AH
Air Alpes [*ICAO designator*] (AD) ... LP
Air Alsace [*ICAO designator*] (AD) ... SY
Air America [*ICAO designator*] (AD) ... GM
Air & Space/Smithsonian [*A publication*] (BRI) ... A & S Sm
Air Anglia [*ICAO designator*] (AD) ... AQ
Air Aruba [*ICAO designator*] (AD) ... FQ
Air Atlantic Airlines [*ICAO designator*] (AD) ... OX
Air Atlantique [*ICAO designator*] (AD) ... ES
Air Atlantique [*ICAO designator*] (AD) ... KL
Air Botswana [*ICAO designator*] (AD) ... BP
Air Bremen [*ICAO designator*] (AD) ... HR
Air Bridge Carriers [*ICAO designator*] (AD) ... AG
Air Burkina [*ICAO designator*] (AD) ... VH
Air Burundi [*ICAO designator*] (AD) ... PB
Air BVI [*ICAO designator*] (AD) ... BL
Air Caledonie [*ICAO designator*] (AD) ... TY
Air Caledonie International [*ICAO designator*] (AD) ... SB
Air California [*Air carrier designation symbol*] (AD) ... OC
Air Caravane [*ICAO designator*] (AD) ... EN
Air Caribe [*ICAO designator*] (AD) ... QA
Air Caribe International [*ICAO designator*] (AD) ... ZE
Air Carolina [*ICAO designator*] (AD) ... FN
Air Central [*ICAO designator*] (AD) ... HV
Air Chico [*ICAO designator*] (AD) ... FZ
Air Comores [*ICAO designator*] (AD) ... OR
Air Djibouti [*ICAO designator*] (AD) ... DJ
Air Ecosse [*ICAO designator*] (AD) ... EC
Air Europe [*ICAO designator*] (AD) ... AE
Air Gabon [*ICAO designator*] (AD) ... GN
Air Great Lakes [*ICAO designator*] (AD) ... BB
Air Guadeloupe [*ICAO designator*] (AD) ... OG
Air Guinee [*ICAO designator*] (AD) ... GI
Air Guyane [*ICAO designator*] (AD) ... KJ
Air Hawaii [*ICAO designator*] (AD) ... HP
Air Illinois [*ICAO designator*] (AD) ... UX
Air India [*ICAO designator*] (AD) ... AI
Air Intelligence Agency [*Air Force*] ... AIA
Air Inter [*ICAO designator*] (AD) ... IT
Air Inter Gabon [*ICAO designator*] (AD) ... GB
Air Ivoire [*ICAO designator*] (AD) ... VU
Air Kentucky [*ICAO designator*] (AD) ... KN
Air La [*ICAO designator*] (AD) ... UE
Air Lanka [*ICAO designator*] (AD) ... UL
Air Liberia [*ICAO designator*] (AD) ... NL
Air Lingus [*ICAO designator*] (AD) ... EI
Air Link [*ICAO designator*] (AD) ... FF
Air Littoral [*ICAO designator*] (AD) ... FU
Air Madagascar [*ICAO designator*] (AD) ... MD
Air Mahe [*ICAO designator*] (AD) ... HM
Air Malawi [*ICAO designator*] (AD) ... QM
Air Mali [*ICAO designator*] (AD) ... MY
Air Malta [*ICAO designator*] (AD) ... KM
Air Martinique (Satair) [*ICAO designator*] (AD) ... BT
Air Mauritius [*ICAO designator*] (AD) ... MK
Air Melanesiae [*ICAO designator*] (AD) ... HB
Air Midwest [*ICAO designator*] (AD) ... ZV
Air Mongol [*ICAO designator*] (AD) ... OM
Air Nauru [*ICAO designator*] (AD) ... ON
Air Nebraska [*ICAO designator*] (AD) ... DF
Air Nevada [*ICAO designator*] (AD) ... LW
Air New England [*ICAO designator*] (AD) ... NE
Air Niugini [*Air New Guinea*] [*ICAO designator*] (AD) ... PX
Air Nordic Sweden [*ICAO designator*] (AD) ... EO
Air North [*ICAO designator*] (AD) ... GD
Air North [*ICAO designator*] (AD) ... NO
Air North [*ICAO designator*] (AD) ... XG
Air Pacific [*ICAO designator*] (AD) ... AIRPAC
Air Pacific [*ICAO designator*] (AD) ... FJ
Air Panama Internacional [*ICAO designator*] (AD) ... OP
Air Paris [*ICAO designator*] (AD) ... IO
Air Pennsylvania [*ICAO designator*] (AD) ... ZY
Air Polynesie [*ICAO designator*] (AD) ... VT
Air Rarotonga [*ICAO designator*] (AD) ... GZ
Air Reserve Wing [*Canada*] (DD) ... ARW
Air Resorts Airlines [*ICAO designator*] (AD) ... UZ
Air Rwanda [*ICAO designator*] (AD) ... RY
Air Satellite [*ICAO designator*] (AD) ... QR
Air Sedona [*ICAO designator*] (AD) ... UJ
Air Senegal [*ICAO designator*] (AD) ... DS
Air Sierra [*ICAO designator*] (AD) ... SI
Air St. Pierre [*ICAO designator*] (AD) ... PJ
Air Tanzania [*ICAO designator*] (AD) ... TC
Air Tasmania [*ICAO designator*] (AD) ... XZ
Air Tchad [*ICAO designator*] (AD) ... HT
Air Texana [*ICAO designator*] (AD) ... OJ
Air Toronto [*ICAO designator*] (AD) ... CS
Air Trails [*ICAO designator*] (AD) ... NN
Air Tungaru [*ICAO designator*] (AD) ... VK
Air Turks and Caicos [*ICAO designator*] (AD) ... QW
Air Vectors [*ICAO designator*] (AD) ... ZB
Air Virginia [*ICAO designator*] (AD) ... CE
Air Volta [*ICAO designator*] (AD) ... VH
Air West Airlines [*ICAO designator*] (AD) ... ZX
Air Wisconsin [*ICAO designator*] (AD) ... ZW
Air Zimbabwe [*ICAO designator*] (AD) ... UM
Airborne Lidar Bathymetry Technical Center of Expertise [*US Army Corps of Engineers*] ... ALBTCX
Airborne Standoff Minefield Detection System [*Military*] (RDA) ... ASTAMIDS
Airbrush (VRA) ... airbr
Airlines of Tasmania [*ICAO designator*] (AD) ... IP
Airport (VRA) ... airpt
Airways International [*ICAO designator*] (AD) ... HO
AJR: American Journalism Review [*A publication*] (BRI) ... AJR
Akhisar [*Turkey*] [*Airport symbol*] (AD) ... AKH
Akjoujt [*Mauritania*] [*Airport symbol*] (AD) ... AJJ
Akyab [*Burma*] [*Airport symbol*] (AD) ... AKY
Al Bayda [*Libya*] [*Airport symbol*] (AD) ... LAQ
Al Ghaydah [*Aden*] [*Airport symbol*] (AD) ... AAY
Alamo Commuter Airlines [*ICAO designator*] (AD) ... JZ
Alaska Aeronautical Industries [*ICAO designator*] (AD) ... YC
Alaska Airlines [*ICAO designator*] (AD) ... Alaska
Albania (VRA) ... Alb
Albany-Corvallis [*Oregon*] [*Airport symbol*] (AD) ... CVO
Albenga [*Italy*] [*Airport symbol*] (AD) ... ALL
Alberta [*Canada*] (DD) ... Alta
Alberta Association of Architects [*1906*] [*Canada*] (NGC) ... AAA
Alberta Medal [*Canada*] (DD) ... AM
Alberta Society of Artists [*1931*] [*Canada*] (NGC) ... ASA
[*Secretary of State Madeleine*] **Albright,** [*National-Security Adviser Sandy*] **Berger,** [*and Defense Secretary William*] **Cohen** [*A troika known in Washington*] ... ABC
Album (VRA) ... alb
Albumen (VRA) ... ALPT
Albury [*New South Wales*] [*Airport symbol*] (AD) ... ABX
Alchemy (VRA) ... alch
Alderney [*United Kingdom*] [*Airport symbol*] (AD) ... ACI
Aleg [*Mauritania*] [*Airport symbol*] (AD) ... LEG
Alenquer [*Brazil*] [*Airport symbol*] (AD) ... AQR
Alexandria [*Virginia*] [*Airport symbol*] (AD) ... WVA
Algeria (VRA) ... Alg
Alisarda [*ICAO designator*] (AD) ... IG
Alkan Air Ltd. [*ICAO designator*] (AD) ... TO
All Faiths for One Race (AIE) ... AFFOR
All Island Air [*ICAO designator*] (AD) ... AJ
All London Parents' Action Group [*British*] (AIE) ... ALPAG
All London Teachers Against Racism and Fascism [*British*] (AIE) ... ALTARF
All Nippon [*ICAO designator*] (AD) ... NH
All Source Analysis System/Software [*Military*] (RDA) ... ASAS/SFT
Allegheny Airlines [*ICAO designator*] (AD) ... AL
Allegory (VRA) ... alleg
Alliance of State Aftermarket Associations ... ASAAA
Alloy (VRA) ... aly
Aloha Airlines [*ICAO designator*] (AD) ... AQ
Aloha Islandair [*ICAO designator*] (AD) ... WP
Along [*India*] [*Airport symbol*] (AD) ... IXV
Alpha Proton X-Ray Spectrometer ... APXS
Alpine Aviation [*ICAO designator*] (AD) ... ZA
Altarpiece (VRA) ... altpc
Alternate (VRA) ... alt
Alternative Curriculum Strategies [*Education*] (AIE) ... ACS
Alternative Dispute Resolution (WYGK) ... ADR
Alternative Learning Program for High School Age ... ALPHA
Alternative Lengthening of Telomeres [*Genetics*] ... ALT
Alternative Press Review [*A publication*] (BRI) ... Alt Pr R
Alternative Technologies and Approaches [*Military*] (RDA) ... ATA
Alto Palena [*Chile*] [*Airport symbol*] (AD) ... WAP
Alto Parnaiba [*Brazil*] [*Airport symbol*] (AD) ... APY
Altoona-Martinsburg [*Pennsylvania*] [*Airport symbol*] (AD) ... AOO
Aluminum (VRA) ... alum
Alyemda Democratic Yemen [*ICAO designator*] (AD) ... DY
Ama Air Express [*ICAO designator*] (AD) ... YD
Ama-Flyg [*ICAO designator*] (AD) ... VW
Amalfi [*Colombia*] [*Airport symbol*] (AD) ... AFI
Amapa [*Brazil*] [*Airport symbol*] (AD) ... APA
Amber (VRA) ... amb
Ambrotype (VRA) ... ATYP
Ambulatory (VRA) ... ambul
Ambulatory Care Utilization Review [*Insurance*] (WYGK) ... ACUR
Amerasia Journal [*A publication*] (BRI) ... Amerasia J
America [*A publication*] (BRI) ... Am
America (VRA) ... Amer
America West Airlines [*ICAO designator*] (AD) ... HP
AmericaIntelligent Transportation Society of America [*Formerly, IVHS America*] ... ITS
American Academy of Political and Social Science. Annals [*A publication*] (BRI) ... AAPSS-A
American Anthropologist [*A publication*] (BRI) ... A Anth
American Antiquity [*A publication*] (BRI) ... Am Ant
American Archivist Quarterly [*A publication*] (BRI) ... A Arch
American Artist [*A publication*] (BRI) ... A Art
American Association of Fund-Raising Counsel, Inc. ... AAFRC
American Automobile Manufacturers Association ... AAMA
American Book Review [*A publication*] (BRI) ... ABR
American Center for Immuno-Biology and Metabolism ... ACIBM
American Craft [*A publication*] (BRI) ... Am Craft
American Ethnologist [*A publication*] (BRI) ... Am Ethnol
American Forests [*A publication*] (BRI) ... AF

American Genealogist [*A publication*] (BRI) ... Am Geneal
American Heritage [*A publication*] (BRI) ... AH
American Historical Review [*A publication*] (BRI) ... AHR
American History [*A publication*] (BRI) ... Am Hist
American Indian Culture and Research Journal [*A publication*] (BRI) ... Am Ind CRJ
American Institute of Architects, Washington, D.C. [*1867*] (NGC) ... AIA
American Journal of Archaeology [*A publication*] (BRI) ... AJA
American Journal of Education [*A publication*] (BRI) ... AJE
American Journal of Philology [*A publication*] (BRI) ... AJP
American Journal of Psychiatry [*A publication*] (BRI) ... AJPsych
American Journal of Psychology [*A publication*] (BRI) ... A J Psy
American Journal of Sociology [*A publication*] (BRI) ... AJS
American Journal on Mental Retardation [*A publication*] (BRI) ... AJMR
American Libraries [*A publication*] (BRI) ... A Lib
American Literature [*A publication*] (BRI) ... AL
American Music [*A publication*] (BRI) ... Am M
American Music Teacher [*A publication*] (BRI) ... Am MT
American Philatelist [*A publication*] (BRI) ... Am Phil
American Poetry Review [*A publication*] (BRI) ... APR
American Political Science Review [*A publication*] (BRI) ... APSR
American Professional Society on the Abuse of Children ... Apsac
American Quarterly [*A publication*] (BRI) ... Am Q
American Reference Books Annual [*A publication*] (BRI) ... ARBA
American Scholar [*A publication*] (BRI) ... AS
American Scientist [*A publication*] (BRI) ... Am Sci
American Spectator [*A publication*] (BRI) ... Am Spect
American Sportfishing Association ... ASA
American Studies International [*A publication*] (BRI) ... ASInt
American Theatre [*A publication*] (BRI) ... Am Theat
American Trans Air [*ICAO designator*] (AD) ... TZ
American University of Paris ... AUP
American Veterinary Lyme Disease Society ... AVLDS
American Visions [*A publication*] (BRI) ... Am Vis
American Water Color Society, New York [*1878, founded 1866 as American Society of Painters in Water Colors*] (NGC) ... AWCS
Americas: A Quarterly Review of Inter-American Cultural History [*A publication*] (BRI) ... Ams
Americas Review: A Review of Hispanic Literature and Art of the USA [*A publication*] (BRI) ... Amer R
Aminocyclopropanecarboxylicacid Oxidase [*An enzyme*] ... ACCO
Aminoethylaminopropylsilane ... AEPS
Ammunition Resupply Projectile [*Military*] (RDA) ... ARP
Amparafaravola [*Malagasy*] [*Airport symbol*] (AD) ... AMF
Ampenan [*Indonesia*] [*Airport symbol*] (AD) ... AMI
Amphitheater (VRA) ... ampth
Am-Timan [*Chad*] [*Airport symbol*] (AD) ... AMC
Analog Science Fiction and Fact [*A publication*] (BRI) ... Analog
Analog-to-Digital Converter [*Computer science*] (DOM) ... A/D converter
Anapolis [*Brazil*] [*Airport symbol*] (AD) ... APS
Ancient (VRA) ... anc
Ancient Egypt Research Associates ... AERA
Ancud [*Chile*] [*Airport symbol*] (AD) ... ZUD
Andean Group ... AG
Andorra (VRA) ... And
Andradina [*Brazil*] [*Airport symbol*] (AD) ... ARD
Angle Neovascularization [*Opthalmology*] ... ANV
Angolia (VRA) ... Ang
Anguilla [*Leeward Islands*] [*Airport symbol*] (AD) ... AXA
Anhydrous Hydrogen Fluoride [*Inorganic chemistry*] ... AHF
Animal Medicinal Drug Use Clarification Act of 1994 ... AMDUCA
Anisotropic Hypernetted Chain [*Chemical physics*] ... AHNC
Annotated Card Program ... AC
Annual Capital Grant [*Education*] (AIE) ... ACG
Annual Curriculum Review [*Education*] (AIE) ... ACR
Annual Rate Plus Stock Dividend [*Investment term*] (DFIT) ... B
Anodized Aluminum (VRA) ... anod alum
Anonymous (VRA) ... anon
Another Chicago Magazine [*A publication*] (BRI) ... ACM
ANQ: A Quarterly Journal of Short Articles, Notes, and Reviews [*A publication*] (BRI) ... ANQ:QJ
Ansett Airlines of Australia [*ICAO designator*] (AD) ... AN
Ansett Airlines of New South Wales [*ICAO designator*] (AD) ... WX
Ansett Airlines of South Australia [*ICAO designator*] (AD) ... GJ
Ansett New Zealand [*ICAO designator*] (AD) ... ZQ
Antarctica (VRA) ... Antar
Anthranilate Synthase [*An enzyme*] ... AS
Anthropology (DD) ... Anthro
Anthropology (VRA) ... anthrop
Anti Racist Teacher Education Network (AIE) ... ARTEN
Anti-Corruption Agency ... ACA
Antigen Detection Test [*Clinical chemistry*] ... ADT
Anti-Injunction Act of 1932 (WYGK) ... AIA
Antilles (VRA) ... L Anti
Antioch Review [*A publication*] (BRI) ... Ant R
Antiquaries Journal [*A publication*] (BRI) ... Antiq J
Antique (VRA) ... antq
Antiques & Collecting Magazine [*A publication*] (BRI) ... Ant & CM
Anti-Virus Emergency Response Team [*McAfee*] [*Computer science*] ... AVERT
Antler (VRA) ... atlr
Antonio Enes [*Mozambique*] [*Airport symbol*] (AD) ... ANO
Anuradhapura [*Ceylon*] [*Airport symbol*] (AD) ... ADP
Aoulef [*Algeria*] [*Airport symbol*] (AD) ... WAE
Apache Attack Helicopter [*Military*] (RDA) ... AAH
Apartment (VRA) ... apt
Apocalypse (VRA) ... apcys
Apocrypha (VRA) ... apocph
Apollo [*A publication*] (BRI) ... Apo
Apollo Airlines [*ICAO designator*] (AD) ... ID
Apoptosis-Inducing Factor [*Biochemistry*] ... AIF
Apoptosis-Inducing Factor [*Cytology*] ... AIF
Apostle (VRA) ... ap
Apple Programmers and Developers Association (DOM) ... APDA
Applicant Tracking System [*Human resources*] (WYGK) ... ATS
Application [*Computer science*] ... app
Applied (VRA) ... appl
Applied Mineral Sciences (DD) ... AppMinSci
Applique (VRA) ... apliq
Appraisal: Science Books for Young People [*A publication*] (BRI) ... ASBYP
Apprenticeship Program (DD) ... AP
Approved Training Organisation [*Manpower Services Commission*] (AIE) ... ATO
Approximate (VRA) ... appx
Aquatic Airlines [*ICAO designator*] (AD) ... VZ
Aquatint (VRA) ... aqut
Aqueduct (VRA) ... aqdt
Aquidauana [*Brazil*] [*Airport symbol*] (AD) ... AQU
Arabesque (VRA) ... arbsq
Arabia (VRA) ... Arab
Arabia [*ICAO designator*] (AD) ... RZ
Araguacema [*Brazil*] [*Airport symbol*] (AD) ... AGX
Arba Mintch [*Ethiopia*] [*Airport symbol*] (AD) ... AMH
Arcata-Eureka [*California*] [*Airport symbol*] (AD) ... ACV
Arch (VRA) ... arh
Archaeology (VRA) ... archeo
Architect (VRA) ... archt
Architectural Barriers Act of 1968 (WYGK) ... ABA
Architectural Institute of British Columbia [*1914*] [*Canada*] (NGC) ... AIBC
Architecture (VRA) ... arch
Architrave (VRA) ... archtr
Archival Research Catalog ... ARC
Archivaria [*A publication*] (BRI) ... Archiv
Archive (VRA) ... archv
Archivolt (VRA) ... arvlt
Arctic Goose Habitat Working Group ... AGHWG
Are You There? [*Computer science*] (DOM) ... ENQ?
Arena Magazine [*A publication*] (BRI) ... Arena
Argentina (VRA) ... Arg
Argillite (VRA) ... argil
Ariana Afghan Airlines [*ICAO designator*] (AD) ... FG
Arizona-Nogales [*Mexico*] [*Airport symbol*] (AD) ... NOG
Arkansas County Quality Deer Association ... ACQDA
Arkia-Israel Inland Airlines [*ICAO designator*] (AD) ... IZ
Armature (VRA) ... armt
Armchair Detective [*A publication*] (BRI) ... Arm Det
Armed Forces and Society [*A publication*] (BRI) ... Arm F & S
Armed Forces Librarians Round Table [*American Library Association*] ... AFLRT
Armenia (VRA) ... Arm
Armored Systems Integration [*Army*] (RDA) ... ASI
Arms & Armor (VRA) ... ar/arm
Armstrong Aldren Collins [*Lunar mineral named after three astronauts*] ... ARMALCOLITE
Army Interoperability Network (RDA) ... AIN
Army Modernization Plan (RDA) ... AMP
Army Research Consortium (RDA) ... ARC
Army System Engineering Office (RDA) ... ASEO
Army Tactical Missile System Block II (RDA) ... ATACMS BLK II
Army Tactical Missile System-Brilliant Anti-Armor Submunition (RDA) ... ATACMS-BAT
Army Technical Architecture [*Military*] ... ATA
Arona [*New Guinea*] [*Airport symbol*] (AD) ... AON
Arricaccato (VRA) ... arric
Art Bulletin [*A publication*] (BRI) ... Art Bull
Art Direction [*A publication*] (BRI) ... Art Dir
Art Directors Club of Montreal [*1950*] [*Canada*] (NGC) ... ADCM
Art Directors Club of Toronto [*1947*] [*Canada*] (NGC) ... ADCT
Art in America [*A publication*] (BRI) ... Art Am
Art Journal [*A publication*] (BRI) ... Art J
Artificial (VRA) ... artif
Artist's Collection (VRA) ... artist coll
ARTnews [*A publication*] (BRI) ... Art N
Arts and Letters Club, Toronto [*1908*] [*Canada*] (NGC) ... ALCT
Arts Education for a Multicultural Society (AIE) ... AEMS
Arts Management Training Initiative, Scotland (AIE) ... AMTIS
Arua [*Uganda*] [*Airport symbol*] (AD) ... AAU
Arusha [*Tanzania*] [*Airport symbol*] (AD) ... ARY
Arylhydrocarbon-Receptor Nuclear Translocator [*Genetics*] ... ARNT
Asbestos (VRA) ... asb
Asheville-Henderson [*North Carolina*] [*Airport symbol*] (AD) ... AVL
Asia (VRA) ... As
Asia Minor (VRA) ... As Min
Asmara [*Ethiopia*] [*Airport symbol*] (AD) ... ASM
Aspects of Gymnastics and Independent Learning Experience (AIE) ... AGILE
Aspen Airways [*ICAO designator*] (AD) ... AP
Assemblage (VRA) ... asmblg
Assessment and Training for Employment (AIE) ... ATE
Assessment of the Provision of Part Time Training [*Education*] (AIE) ... APPT
Assistant (DD) ... asst
Assisted Places Scheme (AIE) ... APS
Assistive Listening Device (WYGK) ... ALD
Assiut [*Egypt*] [*Airport symbol*] (AD) ... ATZ

Associate Fellow of the Canadian Aeronautic and Space Institute (DD) ... AFCASI
Associate in Customer Service [*Canada*] (DD) ... ACS
Associate in Risk Management [*Canada*] (DD) ... ARM
Associate Insurance Broker (DD) ... AIB
Associate of the Canadian Bankers Association (DD) ... ACBA
Associate of the Corporation of Insurance Brokers [*Canada*] (DD) ... ACIB
Associate of the Institute of Canadian Bankers (DD) ... AICB
Associate of the Institute of Electrical Engineers of Canada (DD) ... AIEE
Associate of the National Academy of Design, New York (NGC) ... ANA
Associate of the Royal Canadian Academy of Arts (NGC) ... ARCA
Associated Airlines [*ICAO designator*] (AD) ... CV
Associated Press Television ... APTV
Associated Water Colour Painters, Toronto [*1912*] [*Canada*] (NGC) ... AWCP
Associates (VRA) ... assoc
Association (DD) ... Assn
Association des Artistes Non Figuratifs de Montreal [*1956-61*] [*Canada*] (NGC) ... AANFM
Association des Arts Plastiques, Montreal [*1955*] [*Canada*] (NGC) ... AAP
Association des Graveurs du Quebec [*1971, CGQ from 1978, CQE from 1984*] [*Canada*] (NGC) ... AGQ
Association des Sculpteurs du Quebec [*1961, CSQ from 1978*] [*Canada*] (NGC) ... ASQ
Association Europea de Profesores de Espanol (AIE) ... AEPE
Association for Adult Education (AIE) ... AAE
Association for Colleges (AIE) ... AFC
Association for Computer Assisted Learning (AIE) ... ACAL
Association for Computers and Information Technology in Teaching (AIE) ... ACITT
Association for Healthcare Philanthropy ... AHP
Association for Maintained Girls' Schools (AIE) ... AMGS
Association for Student Counsellors (AIE) ... ASC
Association for the Advancement of Teacher Education in Music (AIE) ... AATEM
Association for the Study of Primary Education (AIE) ... ASPE
Association Internationale des Etudiants en Sciences Economiques et Commerciales (AIE) ... AIESEC
Association of American Geographers Annals [*A publication*] (BRI) ... AAAGA
Association of Canadian Alumni Administrators ... ACAA
Association of Directors of Education (AIE) ... ADE
Association of Fund Raising Professionals of British Columbia [*Canada*] ... AFRP BC
Association of Geography Teachers of Ireland (AIE) ... AGTI
Association of Heads of Polytechnic Student Services [*British*] (AIE) ... AHOPSS
Association of Hispanists of Great Britain and Ireland (AIE) ... ABH
Association of Information Technology Professionals ... AITP
Association of Inspectors, Advisers, and Consultants for Religious Education (AIE) ... AREIAC
Association of Lecturers in Scottish Central Institutions (AIE) ... ALSCI
Association of Management and Business Education (AIE) ... AMBE
Association of Online Professionals ... AOP
Association of Principals, Wardens, and Advisers of University Women Students [*British*] (AIE) ... APWA
Association of Professional Engineers, Geologists, and Geophysicists of Alberta [*Canada*] (DD) ... APEGGA
Association of Professional, Executive, Clerical, and Computer Staff (AIE) ... APEX
Association of Professors of Modern Languages in Technological Universities (AIE) ... APMLTU
Association of Representatives of Old Pupils' Societies (AIE) ... AROPS
Association of Special Libraries and Information Bureaux [*Association for Information Management*] [*British*] (AIE) ... ASLIB
Association of Teachers and Lecturers (AIE) ... ATL
Association of Teachers in Colleges and Departments of Education (AIE) ... ATCODE
Association of Teachers in Sixth Form and Tertiary Colleges [*British*] (AIE) ... ATVIC
Association of Teachers of French (AIE) ... ATF
Association of Waste Hazardous Materials Transporters ... AWHMT
Association of Young Computer Enthusiasts (AIE) ... AYCF
Assurances Generales de France ... AGF
Astronautics (DD) ... Astro
Astronomy [*A publication*] (BRI) ... Astron
Astrophysics Data System ... ADS
AT&T Global Information Solutions [*Computer science*] ... AT&T GIS
Atharan Hazari [*Pakistan*] [*Airport symbol*] (AD) ... ARH
Ati [*Chad*] [*Airport symbol*] (AD) ... ATV
ATI Multimedia Channel [*Computer science*] ... AMC
Atlantic Books Today [*A publication*] (BRI) ... Atl BT
Atlantic Monthly [*A publication*] (BRI) ... Atl
Atlantic Southeast [*ICAO designator*] (AD) ... EV
Atlantis [*ICAO designator*] (AD) ... SG
Atlantis Airlines [*ICAO designator*] (AD) ... MP
Atmosphere (VRA) ... atmos
Atomicity, Consistency, Isolation, and Durability Test (DOM) ... ACID test
Atom-Probe Field-Ion Microscopy ... APFIM
Attached Resource Computer Network ... ARCnet
Attainment Target (AIE) ... AT
Attention Dial Tone [*Computer science*] (DOM) ... ATDT
Attributed (VRA) ... attr
Auburn [*New York*] [*Airport symbol*] (AD) ... SSN
Auburn-Lewiston [*Maine*] [*Airport symbol*] (AD) ... LEW
Auction Preferred Stock [*Investment term*] (DFIT) ... APS
Audio Engineering Society/European Broadcast Union (DOM) ... AES/EBU
Audio Enhanced Computer Aided Learning (AIE) ... AECAL
Audio Video Interleave [*Computer science*] ... AVI
Audio-Video Interleaved [*Computer science*] ... AVI
Auditorium (VRA) ... audit
Audubon [*A publication*] (BRI) ... Aud
Augmentor of Liver Regeneration [*Biochemistry*] ... ALR
Augusta Airways [*ICAO designator*] (AD) ... BH
Augustus Downs [*Queensland*] [*Airport symbol*] (AD) ... AUD
Aurignacian (VRA) ... Aurig
Aurigny Air Services [*ICAO designator*] (AD) ... GR
Austin [*Minnesota*] [*Airport symbol*] (AD) ... AUM
Austin Airways [*ICAO designator*] (AD) ... UH
Austral Lineas Aereas [*ICAO designator*] (AD) ... AU
Australia (VRA) ... Austr
Australian Book Review [*A publication*] (BRI) ... Aust Bk R
Australian Nuclear Science and Technology Organisation ... ANSTO
Austria (VRA) ... Aust
Austrian Air [*ICAO designator*] (AD) ... SO
Austrian Airlines [*ICAO designator*] (AD) ... OS
Authentic (VRA) ... authn
Author (VRA) ... auth
Authorized Validating Agency (AIE) ... AVA
Autochrome (VRA) ... ATCH
Autologous Peripheral Blood Stem Cell Transplantation [*Medicine*] ... ABSCT
Automated Bond System [*Investment term*] (DFIT) ... ABS
Automated Endoscopic System for Optimal Positioning [*Medicine*] ... AESOP
Automated Flow Technology ... AFT
Automated Interactive Microscope ... AIM
Automated Tracking and Monitoring System ... ATAMS
Automated Weather Information Processing System ... AWIPS
Automatic Document Request (AIE) ... ADRS
Automatic Landing Flight Experiment [*Japan*] ... ALFLEX
Automatic Request [*Computer science*] (DOM) ... ARQ
Automotive Performance Execution and Layout ... APEAL
Autonomous Benthic Explorer [*Oceanography*] ... ABE
Autonomous Lagrangian Circulation Explorer [*Oceanography*] ... ALACE
Autonomous Precision Approach and Landing System [*Lockheed-Martin's radical landing-guidance system*] ... APALS
Autoroute (DD) ... aut
Auxaire-Bretagne [*ICAO designator*] (AD) ... BS
Auxin Response Factor [*Biochemistry*] ... ARF
Avalon Bay [*Santa Catalina, California*] [*Airport symbol*] (AD) ... AVX
Avant-Garde (VRA) ... av-gd
Avenue (DD) ... av
Avenue (DD) ... Ave
Avenue (VRA) ... ave
Average Oxidation State [*Physical chemistry*] ... AOS
Average Student Hours [*Education*] (AIE) ... ASH
Average Unit of Council Funding [*Higher Education Funding Council*] (AIE) ... AUCF
Avianca [*ICAO designator*] (AD) ... AV
Aviateca [*ICAO designator*] (AD) ... GU
Aviation Services [*ICAO designator*] (AD) ... ML
Aviona [*ICAO designator*] (AD) ... RD
Avior [*ICAO designator*] (AD) ... XP
Avis Rent a Car ... ARAC
Avisco [*ICAO designator*] (AD) ... AO
Axonometric (VRA) ... axon
Aydin [*Turkey*] [*Airport symbol*] (AD) ... ADN
Azores (VRA) ... Azo

B
By Meaning

Baccalaureat en Administration des Affaires [*Canada*] (DD) .... BAA
Baccalaureat en Ingenerie [*Canada*] (DD) .... Bing
Baccalaureat en Loisirs [*Canada*] (DD) .... BL
Baccalaureat en Sciences Administratives [*Canada*] (DD) .... BAS
Baccalaureat en Sciences Administratives [*Canada*] (DD) .... BSA
Bachelor in Law (DD) .... BL
Bachelor in Surgery (DD) .... BCh
Bachelor in Surgery (DD) .... BChir
Bachelor of Actuarial Sciences (DD) .... BActSci
Bachelor of Arts/Bachelor of Management Combines (DD) .... BA/BMgmt
Bachelor of Arts/Bachelor of Science Combined (DD) .... BA/BS
Bachelor of Arts in Pedagogy (DD) .... BAPed
Bachelor of Chemical Engineering (DD) .... BChemEng
Bachelor of Commercial Science (DD) .... BScComm
Bachelor of Computer Management (DD) .... BCM
Bachelor of Engineering Science (DD) .... BE
Bachelor of Industrial Relations (DD) .... BIR
Bachelor of Laws (DD) .... LLB
Bachelor of Management (DD) .... BMgmt
Bachelor of Management Arts (DD) .... BMA
Bachelor of Pharmacy (DD) .... BPh
Bachelor of Recreation Education (DD) .... BRE
Bachelor of Science [*Academic degree*] (AIE) .... BSc
Bachelor of Science, Engineering (DD) .... BScE
Bachelor of Science in Agriculture (DD) .... BAS
Bachelor of Science in Engineering (DD) .... BE
Bachelor of Science in Engineering (DD) .... BSc(Eng)
Bachelor of Surgery (DD) .... ChB
Background (VRA) .... bkgr
Background Natural Sound .... BGNS
Bactrian (VRA) .... Bactr
Bahamas (VRA) .... Baha
Bahamas Air [*ICAO designator*] (AD) .... UP
Bahawalpur [*Pakistan*] [*Airport symbol*] (AD) ..... BWP
Bahrain (VRA) .... Bahr
Baiyer River [*New Guinea*] [*Airport symbol*] (AD) ..... BYV
Bakhtar Afghan Airlines [*ICAO designator*] (AD) .... BJ
Balanced Extravehicular Training Aircraft [*NASA*] .... BETA
Baldachino (VRA) .... baldc
Balikesir [*Turkey*] [*Airport symbol*] (AD) .... BZI
Balkan [*ICAO designator*] (AD) .... LZ
Balsa Wood (VRA) .... bal wd
Balsas [*Brazil*] [*Airport symbol*] (AD) .... BSS
Balustrade (VRA) .... balstr
Ban Houei Sai [*Laos*] [*Airport symbol*] (AD) ...... OUI
Banda Atjeh [*Indonesia*] [*Airport symbol*] (AD) ... BTJ
Bangladesh Biman [*ICAO designator*] (AD) .... BG
Bangladesh Nationalist Party [*Political party*] .... BNP
Bangledesh [*E. Pakistan*] (VRA) .... Bangl
Bank of Ireland Asset Management .... BIAM
Bankair [*ICAO designator*] (AD) .... JA
Baptist (VRA) .... bapt
Bar Harbor Airlines [*ICAO designator*] (AD) .... QO
Barbados (VRA) .... Barb
Barisal [*Bangladesh*] [*Airport symbol*] (AD) ...... BZL
Bark (VRA) .... brk
Barkcloth (VRA) .... brkcth
Baroque (VRA) .... Barq
Barrel Vault (VRA) .... bar vlt
Barrel-Launched Adaptive Munitions .... BLAM
Bartlesville [*Oklahoma*] [*Airport symbol*] (AD) ... BVO
BAS Airlines [*ICAO designator*] (AD) .... GS
Bas Relief (VRA) .... barlf
Basalt (VRA) .... bst
Basic Spline (DOM) .... B-spline
Basilica (VRA) .... basl
Basket (VRA) .... bskt
Basra [*Iraq*] [*Airport symbol*] (AD) .... BSR
Basswood (VRA) .... baswd
Bata [*Spanish Guinea*] [*Airport symbol*] (AD) ..... BSG
Bath & Body Works .... BBW
Bath University Computing Services [*British*] (AIE) ..... BUCS
Bathroom (VRA) .... bathrm
Bathurst [*Gambia*] [*Airport symbol*] (AD) .... BTH
Batik (VRA) .... btk
Batse Coordinates Distribution Network .... BACODINE

Batticaloa [*Ceylon*] [*Airport symbol*] (AD) .... BTC
Bay City-Midland-Saginaw [*Michigan*] [*Airport symbol*] (AD) .... MBS
BC (VRA) .... BC
Be Seein' You [*Computer science*] (DOM) .... BCNU
Beads (VRA) .... bea
Beadwork (VRA) .... beawk
Bearskin Lake [*ICAO designator*] (AD) .... JV
Beauvais [*France*] [*Airport symbol*] (AD) .... BVA
Beaver [*A publication*] (BRI) .... Beav
Bed Nucleus of the Stria Terminalis [*Brain anatomy*] ..... BNST
Bedroom (VRA) .... bedrm
Beech (VRA) .... becwd
Beef Island [*British Virgin Islands*] [*Airport symbol*] (AD) .... EIS
Before (VRA) .... bef
Before Rotary Cutting [*Quilting*] .... BRC
Beginning (VRA) .... beg
Behavior-Based Incentive Compensation [*Human resources*] (WYGK) .... BBIC
Behaviour Modification Information Test (AIE) .... BMIT
Bela Vista [*Brazil*] [*Airport symbol*] (AD) .... BVS
Belgium (VRA) .... Belg
Belize Airways [*ICAO designator*] (AD) .... ST
Bell [*Computer science*] (DOM) .... BEL
Bell-Air [*ICAO designator*] (AD) LL
Bellefonte-Clearfield-Philipsburg [*Pennsylvania*] [*Airport symbol*] (AD) .... PSB
Belles Lettres [*A publication*] (BRI) .... Belles Let
Bend Over, Here It Comes Again [*Business term*] .... BOHICA
Beni Abbes [*Algeria*] [*Airport symbol*] (AD) ...... KBA
Bentwood (VRA) .... bntwd
Berlin European [*ICAO designator*] (AD) .... WZ
Berlin U.S.A. [*ICAO designator*] (AD) .... ZF
Betoota [*Queensland*] [*Airport symbol*] (AD) ...... BTX
Between (VRA) .... bet
Bevel (VRA) .... bev
Biblical Theology Bulletin [*A publication*] (BRI) .... BTB
Bibliographic Cooperative Program [*American Library Association*] .... BIBCO
Bibliographical Society of America Papers [*A publication*] (BRI) .... BSA-P
Bibliotheque (VRA) .... bibl
Bichromate (VRA) .... BICH
Bi-Directional Line-Switched Rings .... BLSR
Big Sky Airlines [*ICAO designator*] (AD) .... GQ
Big Spring [*Texas*] [*Airport symbol*] (AD) .... HCA
Billboard (VRA) .... bilbd
Binary Term [*Computer science*] .... byte
Binder (VRA) .... bndr
Biochemistry (DD) .... Biochem
Biogenic Carbon [*Chemistry*] .... BC
Biography: An Interdisciplinary Quarterly [*A publication*] (BRI) .... Biography
Biology (DD) .... Bio
Biology, Chemistry, Physics (DD) .... BCP
Biomedical Engineering (DD) .... BiomedEng
BioScience [*A publication*] (BRI) .... BioSci
Birao [*Central African Republic*] [*Airport symbol*] (AD) .... IRO
Birch (VRA) .... bir
Bird Investigation, Review, and Deterrent [*NASA*] .... BIRD
Birmingham European Airways [*ICAO designator*] (AD) .... VB
Birthdate (DD) .... b
Bistre (VRA) .... bist
Bit-Block Transfers [*Computer science*] .... blts
Bit-Mapped Graphics [*Computer science*] .... BMP
Black (VRA) .... b
Black & White (VRA) .... b&w
Black Enterprise [*A publication*] (BRI) .... B Ent
Black Scholar [*A publication*] (BRI) .... Bl S
Blacks in Media Broadcasting Organization .... BIMBO
Blackware (VRA) .... bwr
Blagden Management Training Programme [*British*] (AIE) .... BMTP
Blended Wing Body [*Megaplane*] .... BWB
Blind Bronchial Sampling [*Clinical chemistry*] ..... BBS
Blind Persons Technical Officer [*British*] (AIE) .... BPTO
Block (VRA) .... blk
Block Copolymer [*Organic chemistry*] .... BCP
Block Print (VRA) .... blkpr
Bloodstone (VRA) .... bldst
Bloomsbury Review [*A publication*] (BRI) .... Bloom Rev
Blue (VRA) .... bl
Blue Water Bridge Authority .... BWBA

Board (VRA) ... bd
Board of Education (AIE) ... BOE
Board Room (VRA) ... bdrm
Boarding Schools Association (AIE) ... BSA
Boat Owners Association of the United States ... BOATS
Bobo Dioulass [*Volta*] [*Airport symbol*] (AD) ... BOY
Bodhisattva (VRA) ... bodh
Bodycolor (VRA) ... bdyco
Bokhara (VRA) ... Bokh
Bol [*Chad*] [*Airport symbol*] (AD) ... OTC
Bolivia (VRA) ... Bol
Bolzano [*Italy*] [*Airport symbol*] (AD) ... BZO
Bond Enabling Annual Retirement Savings (DFIT) ... BEARS
Book (VRA) ... bk
Book Collector [*A publication*] (BRI) ... BC
Book of Moroni (AD) ... Moro
Book of Mosiah (AD) ... Mos
Book of Omni (AD) ... Om
Book Report [*A publication*] (BRI) ... B Rpt
Book World [*A publication*] (BRI) ... BW
Bookbird [*A publication*] (BRI) ... Bkbird
Booklist [*A publication*] (BRI) ... BL
Books & Culture [*A publication*] (BRI) ... Bks & Cult
Books for Keeps [*A publication*] (BRI) ... Bks Keeps
Books for Your Children [*A publication*] (BRI) ... BFYC
Books in Canada [*A publication*] (BRI) ... BIC
Books in English (AIE) ... BIE
Books Magazine [*A publication*] (BRI) ... Books
Bookwatch [*A publication*] (BRI) ... BWatch
Boots Contract Manufacturing ... BCM
Bora-Bora [*Society Islands*] [*Airport symbol*] (AD) ... BOB
Born (VRA) ... b
Borobudur (VRA) ... Boro
Bossangoa [*Central African Republic*] [*Airport symbol*] (AD) ... BSN
Boston Exchange Automated Communication Order-Routing Network (DFIT) ... BEACON
Boston Review [*A publication*] (BRI) ... Boston R
Botswana (VRA) ... Botsw
Bottega (VRA) ... btga
Bottom (VRA) ... bot
Bouar [*Central African Republic*] [*Airport symbol*] (AD) ... BOP
Bougair [*ICAO designator*] (AD) ... JX
Boulevard (VRA) ... blvd
Boulevard (DD) ... Blvd
Boulevard (DD) ... boul
Bouraq Indonesia Airlines [*ICAO designator*] (AD) ... BO
Bousso [*Chad*] [*Airport symbol*] (AD) ... OUT
Boutilimit [*Mauritania*] [*Airport symbol*] (AD) ... OTL
Bowen [*Queensland*] [*Airport symbol*] (AD) ... ZBO
Bowling Green [*Kentucky*] [*Airport symbol*] (AD) ... BWG
Box (VRA) ... bx
Boxwood (VRA) ... bxwd
Bozzetto (VRA) ... boz
Braathens SAFE Airtransport [*ICAO designator*] (AD) ... BU
Bradford [*England*] [*Airport symbol*] (AD) ... BRF
Bradford Action on Teacher Shortages (AIE) ... BATS
Bradford Community Learning and Education Resource (AIE) ... BE CLEAR
Bradley Desktop Trainer [*Military*] ... BDT
Brasileia [*Brazil*] [*Airport symbol*] (AD) ... BZY
Brass (VRA) ... bs
Brattleboro, Vermont-Keene, New Hampshire [*Airport symbol*] (AD) ... EEN
Brazed (VRA) ... braz
Brazil (VRA) ... Braz
Breit-Wigner-Fano [*Spectra interference*] ... BWF
Breviary (VRA) ... brev
Brick (VRA) ... bri
Brigade Operations Display and After Action Review System [*Army*] (RDA) ... BODAS
Brighton [*England*] [*Airport symbol*] (AD) ... BSH
Briquettes (VRA) ... briq
Britain (VRA) ... Brit
British Action for Children's Television (AIE) ... BAC
British Air Ferries [*ICAO designator*] (AD) ... VF
British and Foreign Schools Society (AIE) ... BFSS
British Association for Construction Heads (AIE) ... BACH
British Association of Lecturers in English for Academic Purposes (AIE) ... BALEAP
British Association of Teachers of the Deaf (AIE) ... BATD
British Caledonian Airways [*ICAO designator*] (AD) ... BCAL
British Columbia Society of Artists [*1949-68, founded 1908 as BCSFA*] [*Canada*] (NGC) ... BCSA
British Columbia Society of Fine Arts [*1908, BCSA from 1949*] [*Canada*] (NGC) ... BCSFA
British Comparative Education Society (AIE) ... BCES
British Computer Society Schools Committee (AIE) ... BCSSC
British Council Undergraduate Fellowship Scheme (AIE) ... BRUFS
British Educational Contractors Group (AIE) ... BECG
British Educational Furniture Manufacturers Council (AIE) ... BEFMC
British Educational Suppliers Association (AIE) ... BESA
British Humanities Research Board (AIE) ... BHRB
British Independent Airways [*ICAO designator*] (AD) ... RX
British Institute of Professional Photography (AIE) ... BIPP
British Interactive Broadcasting ... BIB
British International Helicopters [*ICAO designator*] (AD) ... UR
British Island Airways [*ICAO designator*] (AD) ... IV
British Library Information Skills (AIE) ... BLIS
British Library Research and Development Division (AIE) ... BLRDD
British Midland Airways [*ICAO designator*] (AD) ... BD
British Quality Awards Scheme (AIE) ... BOAS
British Science and Technology in Education (AIE) ... BSTF
British Technology Index (AIE) ... BTI
British Universities Transatlantic Exchange Committee (AIE) ... BUTEC
Britt Airways [*ICAO designator*] (AD) ... RU
Brittany Air International [*ICAO designator*] (AD) ... DB
Broadcasting Support Services (AIE) ... BSS
Brocade (VRA) ... brcd
Broker-Dealer (DFIT) ... BD
Bromoil Print (VRA) ... BRPT
Bronze (VRA) ... bz
Brown (VRA) ... brn
Brunei Town [*Brunei*] [*Airport symbol*] (AD) ... BTN
Brunett Downs [*Northern Territory, Australia*] [*Airport symbol*] (AD) ... BTD
Brunswick [*Georgia*] [*Airport symbol*] (AD) ... SSI
Brush (VRA) ... bru
Bruzual [*Venezuela*] [*Airport symbol*] (AD) ... BRZ
Bryan [*Texas*] [*Airport symbol*] (AD) ... CFD
Brymon Airways [*ICAO designator*] (AD) ... BC
Buchanan [*Liberia*] [*Airport symbol*] (AD) ... UCN
Buckskin (VRA) ... bcksk
Budget Analysis and Review Committee [*American Library Association*] ... BARC
Buenaventura [*Colombia*] [*Airport symbol*] (AD) ... BUN
Builder (VRA) ... bldr
Building (DD) ... bldg
Building Research Energy Conservation Support Unit (AIE) ... BRESCU
Buildings for College and University Libraries Committee [*Library Administration and Management Association*] [*American Library Association*] ... BCUL
Build-to-Order [*Compaq Computer Corp.*] [*Computer science*] ... BTO
Bulgaria (VRA) ... Bulg
Bulletin of the Atomic Scientists [*A publication*] (BRI) ... BAS
Bulolo [*New Guinea*] [*Airport symbol*] (AD) ... BUL
Bunia [*Zaire*] [*Airport symbol*] (AD) ... BUX
Burgas [*Bulgaria*] [*Airport symbol*] (AD) ... BOJ
Burl (VRA) ... br
Burlap (VRA) ... bur
Burley-Rupert [*Idaho*] [*Airport symbol*] (AD) ... BYI
Burlington Air Express [*ICAO designator*] (AD) ... BAX
Burlington Magazine [*A publication*] (BRI) ... BM
Burnie-Wynward [*Tasmania*] [*Airport symbol*] (AD) ... WNY
Burnished (VRA) ... burn
Burnthills [*ICAO designator*] (AD) ... KB
Bursa Hava Yollari [*ICAO designator*] (AD) ... WL
Burundi (VRA) ... Buru
Bush Pilots Airways [*ICAO designator*] (AD) ... QN
Bushire [*Iran*] [*Airport symbol*] (AD) ... BUZ
Business (DD) ... bus
Business and Society [*A publication*] (BRI) ... Bus Soc
Business and Technology Education Council National Certificate (AIE) ... BTECNC
Business Book Review [*A publication*] (BRI) ... Bus Bk R
Business Education Council General Award (AIE) ... BGen
Business Express [*ICAO designator*] (AD) ... HQ
Business History Review [*A publication*] (BRI) ... BHR
Business Improvement Services (AIE) ... BIS
Business Intelligence ... BI
Business Jets [*ICAO designator*] (AD) ... BQ
Business Library Review [*A publication*] (BRI) ... BusLR
Business Management (DD) ... BusMgmt
Business Professionals of America ... BPOA
Business Studies (DD) ... BusStudies
Business Week [*A publication*] (BRI) ... Bus W
Business Week [*A publication*] ... BW
Butare [*Rwanda*] [*Airport symbol*] (AD) ... BQR
Buttress (VRA) ... butr
BWIA International [*ICAO designator*] (AD) ... BW
Byzantine (VRA) ... Byz

C
By Meaning

Cabarien [*Cuba*] [*Airport symbol*] (AD) .... CBN
Cabinet Card (VRA) .... CABN
Cable Systems International .... CSI
Cabochon (VRA) .... cabo
Cachoeira do Sul [*Brazil*] [*Airport symbol*] (AD) .... CCQ
Cadmium, Zinc, and Telluride .... CZT
Caicara de Orinoco [*Venezuela*] [*Airport symbol*] (AD) .... CXA
Cairo [*Illinois*] [*Airport symbol*] (AD) .... CIR
Cajazeiras [*Brazil*] [*Airport symbol*] (AD) .... CJZ
Cal Sierra [*ICAO designator*] (AD) .... QS
Calais [*France*] [*Airport symbol*] (AD) .... CQF
Calculator-Aware Number [*Project*] (AIE) .... CAN
Caldarium (VRA) .... caldm
Calendar (VRA) .... cal
Caleta Josefina [*Chile*] [*Airport symbol*] (AD) .... WCJ
Calibration Validation Unit [*Instrumentation*] .... CVU
Call Deflection [*Telecommunications*] (DOM) .... CD
Call Forwarding Busy [*Telecommunications*] (DOM) .... CFB
Call Forwarding No Reply [*Telecommunications*] (DOM) .... CFNR
Call Forwarding Unconditional [*Telecommunications*] (DOM) .... CFU
Call Hold [*Telecommunications*] (DOM) .... HOLD
Calligraphy (VRA) .... calig
Calling Line Identification Presentation [*Telecommunications*] (DOM) .... CLIP
Calling Line Identification Restriction [*Telecommunications*] (DOM) .... CLIR
Calitype (VRA) .... calit
Calls Underwritten by Swanbrook [*Investment term*] (DFIT) .... CUBS
Call-Waiting Identification [*Telecommunications service*] ..... CWID
Calm Air International [*ICAO designator*] (AD) .... MO
Calotype (VRA) .... CALOT
Cambodia (VRA) .... Camb
Cambridge International Dictionary of English [*A publication*] ..... CIDE
Cambridge Optical Aperture Synthesis Telescope .... Coast
Cambridge, Oxford & Southern Secondary Examinations Council [*British*]
  (AIE) .... COSSEC
Cambridge Training and Development [*British*] (AIE) .... CTAD
Cambridge University Department of Education [*British*] (AIE) .... CUDE
Cambridgeshire College of Arts and Technology [*British*] (AIE) .... CCAT
Cameo (VRA) .... cmo
Camera (VRA) .... cam
Camera Obscura (VRA) .... cam obs
Cameroon Airlines [*ICAO designator*] (AD) .... UY
Cammooweal [*Queensland*] [*Airport symbol*] (AD) .... CML
Campaign Against Secret Records on Schoolchildren (AIE) ..... CASROS
Campaign for State-Supported Alternative Schools (AIE) ...... CSSAS
Campanile (VRA) .... cmpnl
Campbellpore [*Pakistan*] [*Airport symbol*] (AD) .... CWP
Campeche [*Mexico*] [*Airport symbol*] (AD) .... CPE
Canada (VRA) .... Can
Canadian (DD) .... Cdn
Canadian Accredited Insurance Broker (DD) .... CAIB
Canadian Advertising Rates and Data .... CARD
Canadian Art Club, Toronto [*1907-15*] (NGC) .... CAC
Canadian Association of Education Development Officers .... CAEDO
Canadian Association of Gift Planners .... CAGP
Canadian Book Review Annual [*A publication*] (BRI) .... CBRA
Canadian Children's Literature [*A publication*] (BRI) ...... Can CL
Canadian Council for the Advancement of Education .... CCAE
Canadian Efficiency Decoration [*Military*] (DD) .... ED
Canadian Forum [*A publication*] (BRI) .... CF
Canadian Geographic [*A publication*] (BRI) .... CG
Canadian Group of Painters [*1933-69*] (NGC) .... CGP
Canadian Historical Review [*A publication*] (BRI) .... Can Hist R
Canadian Insolvency Practitioner (DD) .... CIP
Canadian Literature [*A publication*] (BRI) .... Can Lit
Canadian Pacific Airlines [*ICAO designator*] (AD) .... CP Air
Canadian Philosophical Reviews [*A publication*] (BRI) .... CPR
Canadian Public Relations Society .... CPRS
Canadian Risk Manager (DD) .... CRM
Canadian Society for Education through Art [*1951*] (NGC) .... CSEA
Canadian Society of Applied Art [*1905, founded 1903 as Society of Arts and
  Crafts of Canada*] (NGC) .... CSAP
Canadian Society of Association Executives .... CSAE
Canadian Society of Fund Raising Executives .... CSFRE
Canadian Society of Graphic Art [*1923-76, founded c.1903 as GAC, SGA
  from 1912*] (NGC) .... CSGA
Canadian Society of Painters in Water Colour [*1925*] (NGC) .... CSPWC

Canadian Society of Petroleum Geologists (DD) .... CSPG
Canadian Transportation Equipment Association .... CTEA
Canadian Trucking Association .... CTA
Cananea [*Mexico*] [*Airport symbol*] (AD) .... CNA
Cancer Genetics Studies Consortium .... CGSC
Cancer Genome Anatomy Project [*A Cooperative database*] ..... CGAP
Cannes [*France*] [*Airport symbol*] (AD) .... CEQ
Canton [*China*] [*Airport symbol*] (AD) .... CAN
Canton Island [*Phoenix Islands*] [*Airport symbol*] (AD) .... CIS
Canutama [*Brazil*] [*Airport symbol*] (AD) .... CUJ
Canvas (VRA) c
Cape St. Jacques [*South Vietnam*] [*Airport symbol*] (AD) .... CSJ
Capital (VRA) .... cap
Capital Airlines [*ICAO designator*] (AD) .... BZ
Capitol Air Service [*ICAO designator*] (AD) .... RX
Capitol International Airways [*ICAO designator*] (AD) CL
Capri [*Italy*] [*Airport symbol*] (AD) .... PRJ
Captain (DD) .... Capt
Capture-Mark-Recapture [*Demography*] .... CMR
Carauari [*Brazil*] [*Airport symbol*] (AD) .... CAF
Caravelas [*Brazil*] [*Airport symbol*] (AD) .... CRV
Carbon-Fibre Electrode .... CFE
Carbonprint (VRA) .... CBPT
Carborondum (VRA) .... carbor
Card (VRA) .... cd
Card Stock (VRA) .... cdst
Cardboard (VRA) .... cdbd
Career Development (WYGK) .... CD
Careers and Occupational Information Unit (AIE) .... COIU
Careers Education and Guidance (AIE) .... CEG
Careers Guidance Observed (AIE) .... CARGO
Careers Literature and Information Prescription Service (AIE) ..... CLIPS
Careers Office Management and Public Appraisal System (AIE) ..... COMPAS
Careers Service Branch [*Department of Employment*] [*British*] (AIE) .... CSB
Caribbean Air Transport [*ICAO designator*] (AD) XC
Caribbean Airways [*ICAO designator*] (AD) .... IQ
Caribbean International [*ICAO designator*] (AD) .... XQ
Carl Karcher Enterprises .... CKE
Carmen de Patagones [*Argentina*] [*Airport symbol*] (AD) .... CPG
Carnarvon [*Western Australia*] [*Airport symbol*] (AD) ...... CVQ
Carnelian (VRA) .... carnl
Carnot [*Central African Republic*] [*Airport symbol*] (AD) .... CRF
Carolina [*Brazil*] [*Airport symbol*] (AD) .... CLN
Carolina Quarterly [*A publication*] (BRI) .... CQ
Caroline Islands (VRA) .... TT
Carpet (VRA) .... cpt
Carrasco [*Montevideo, Uruguay*] [*Airport symbol*] (AD) .... CSO
Carre (DD) .... car
Carried Forward [*Finance*] (DFIT) .... CF
Carte-de-Visite (VRA) .... CDVT
Carthage (VRA) .... Carth
Cartoon (VRA) .... crtn
Cartouche (VRA) .... crtch
Carved (VRA) .... crv
Caryatid (VRA) .... crytd
Cascade Airways [*ICAO designator*] (AD) .... CZ
Cascading Style Sheets [*Computer science*] .... CSS
Case Management Organization (WYGK) .... CMO
Case Postale (DD) .... CP
Casein (VRA) .... cas
Cash Index Participation [*Investment term*] (DFIT) .... CIP
Cashmere (VRA) .... cashm
Casigua [*Venezuela*] [*Airport symbol*] (AD) .... CUV
Cast (VRA) .... cst
Cast Arrested Repeating Persons [*Fictitious fishing term*] ... CARP
Castro [*Chile*] [*Airport symbol*] (AD) .... WCA
Cat Fancy [*A publication*] (BRI) .... Cat Fan
Cat Island [*Bahamas*] [*Airport symbol*] (AD) .... CAT
Catacomb (VRA) .... ctmb
Catalina Airlines [*ICAO designator*] (AD) .... KG
Catalog (VRA) .... cat
Cataloging Management Team [*American Library Association*] ... CMT
Catalogues on Microfiche (AIE) .... COM
Catalysed Signal Amplification [*Analytical biochemistry*] .... CSA
Cathay Pacific Airways [*ICAO designator*] (AD) CX
Cathedral (VRA) .... cath

89

Catholic Historical Review [*A publication*] (BRI) .... CHR
Catholic Library World [*A publication*] (BRI) .... CLW
Catholic World [*A publication*] (BRI) .... Cath W
Catskill Airways [*ICAO designator*] (AD) .... KF
Caxias [*Brazil*] [*Airport symbol*] (AD) .... CXS
Caxias do Sul [*Brazil*] [*Airport symbol*] (AD) .... CXJ
Cayman Airways [*ICAO designator*] (AD) .... KX
Cayo Mambi [*Cuba*] [*Airport symbol*] (AD) .... CMV
Ceiling (VRA) .... ceil
Celadon (VRA) .... cel
Cellophane (VRA) .... celph
Cellular and Molecular Life Sciences [*A publication*] [*Formerly Experientia*] .... CMLS
Celotex (VRA) .... celtx
Cement (VRA) .... cem
Cemetery (VRA) .... cemet
Center for Acquisition Education, Training, and Research [*Military*] (RDA) .... CAETR
Center for Aquatic Plant Research and Technology [*Army*] .... CAPRT
Center for Children's Books. Bulletin [*A publication*] (BRI) .... CCB-B
Center for Development Studies .... CDS
Center for Evaluative Clinical Sciences .... CECS
Center for Optics Manufacturing (RDA) .... COM
Centers for Disease Control and Prevention .... CDC
Central (VRA) .... cntr
Central [*Wisconsin*] [*Airport symbol*] (AD) .... WIS
Central African Republic (VRA) .... Cent Afr Rep
Central American (VRA) .... Cent Am
Central European History [*A publication*] (BRI) .... CEH
Central Health Services Council (AIE) .... CHSC
Central Institution [*Scotland*] (AIE) CI
Central Pay Office (AIE) .... CPO
Centre d'Etudes et de Recherches sur les Qualifications (AIE) .... CEREQ
Centre Europeen des Parents de l'Ecole Publique (AIE) .... CEPEP
Centre for Alcohol and Road Safety Education [*British*] (AIE) .... CARSE
Centre for Educational Development, Appraisal and Research [*University of Warwick*] [*British*] (AIE) .... CEDAR
Centre for Environmental Education [*British*] (AIE) .... CCE
Centre for Higher Education Policy Studies [*British*] (AIE) .... CHEPS
Centre for Information on Language Teaching and Research [*British*] (AIE) .... CILT
Centre for Learning and Development [*British*] (AIE) .... CLD
Centre for Research and Education on Gender [*University of London*] [*British*] (AIE) .... CREG
Centre for Science and Mathematics Education [*British*] (AIE) .... CSME
Century (VRA) c
Century Airlines [*ICAO designator*] (AD) .... QX
Ceramics (VRA) .... cer
Ceramics Industry Training Organisation [*British*] (AIE) .... CITO
Ceramics Monthly [*A publication*] (BRI) .... Ceram Mo
Cerebral Venous Sinus Thrombosis [*Medicine*] .... CVST
Cerro Sombrero [*Chile*] [*Airport symbol*] (AD) .... SMB
Certificant, Canadian Board of Occupational Medicine (DD) .... CCBOM
Certificate (DD) .... Cert
Certificate for Automobile Receivables [*Investment term*] (DFIT) .... CAR
Certificate for Vocational Preparation Tutors (AIE) .... CVPT
Certificate in Business Administration [*Academic degree*] (AIE) .... CBA
Certificate in Health Services Management [*Academic degree*] (AIE) .... CertHSM
Certificate in Human Resources Management (DD) .... CHRM
Certificate of Office Studies [*Academic degree*] (AIE) .... COS
Certificate of Origin [*Investment term*] (DFIT) .... CO
Certificate of Pre-Vocational Education [*Academic degree*] (AIE) .... CPVE
Certificate of Proficiency in English [*Cambridge*] [*British*] (AIE) .... CPE
Certificate of the College of Family Physicians of Canada (DD) .... CCFP
Certificate of Vocational Preparation (AIE) .... VOC
Certificates for Amortizing Revolving Debts [*Finance*] (DFIT) .... CARDS
Certified Arbitrator [*Canada*] (DD) .... CArb
Certified Associate of the Institute of Bankers [*Canada*] (DD) .... CAIB
Certified Building Society Executive [*Canada*] (DD) .... CBSE
Certified Business Solutions .... CBS
Certified Data Processor (DD) .... CDP
Certified Financial Consultant [*Canada*] (DD) .... CHFC
Certified Fraud Examiner [*Canada*] (DD) .... CFE
Certified Human Resources Professional [*Canada*] (DD) .... CHRP
Certified Management Accountant (DD) .... CMA
Certified Manufacturing Engineer (DD) .... CMgE
Certified Market Technician (DD) .... CMT
Certified Member of AHP [*Association of Healthcare Philanthropy*] .... CAHP
Certified Professional Insurance Women's Association [*Canada*] (DD) .... CPIW
Certified Professional Purchaser [*Canada*] (DD) .... CPP
Certified Psychologist [*Canada*] (DD) .... CPsych
Ceylon (VRA) .... Ceyl
Chabua [*India*] [*Airport symbol*] (AD) .... CHU
Chair of the Board (DD) .... chr
Chaiten [*Chile*] [*Airport symbol*] (AD) .... WCH
Chaitya (VRA) .... chya
Chalcedony (VRA) .... chldy
Chalk (VRA) .... ck
Chalk's International Airline [*ICAO designator*] (AD) .... BK
Chalna [*Bangladesh*] [*Airport symbol*] (AD) .... CHL
Chamber (VRA) .... chbr
Champleve (VRA) .... champ
Chanaral [*Chile*] [*Airport symbol*] (AD) .... CNR
Chandpur [*Bangladesh*] [*Airport symbol*] (AD) .... CDP
Change [*A publication*] (BRI) .... Cng
Changing Men [*A publication*] (BRI) .... Cha Men
Changing Role of the Secondary Head [*Project*] (AIE) .... CROSH
Channel Definition Format [*Microsoft Corp.*] [*Computer science*] .... CDF
Channel Flying [*ICAO designator*] (AD) .... IH
Chaparral [*Colombia*] [*Airport symbol*] (AD) .... CPL
Chaparral Airlines [*ICAO designator*] (AD) .... FC
Chapel (VRA) .... cpl
Chapter (VRA) .... chpt
Chapter House (VRA) .... chpt hs
Characters per Second [*Computer science*] .... cps
Charcoal (VRA) .... chl
Charge Exchange Excitations [*Physics*] .... CXE
Charitable Lead Trust .... CLT
Charitable Remainder Trust .... CRT
Charleston [*West Virginia*] [*Airport symbol*] (AD) .... CHW
Charlotte-Mecklenburg School District .... CMS
Charterair [*ICAO designator*] (AD) .... HO
Chartered Administrator (DD) .... CAdm
Chartered Business Valuator [*Canada*] (DD) .... CBV
Chartered Colorist (DD) .... CCol
Chartered Financial Counselor (DFIT) .... CFC
Chartered Investment Counsellor [*Canada*] (DD) CIC
Chartered Loss Adjuster (DD) .... CLA
Chasing (VRA) .... cha
Chasuble (VRA) .... chsbl
Chelsea [*A publication*] (BRI) .... Chel
Cheltenham-Gloucester [*England*] [*Airport symbol*] (AD) .... GLO
Chemical and Biological Defense Command [*Army*] (RDA) .... CBDCOM
Chemical/Biological Incident Response Force [*Marine Corps*] .... CBIRF
Chemical Demilitarization [*Military*] (RDA) .... CHEM DEMIL
Chemical/Petroleum Engineering (DD) .... Chem/PetEng
Chemical Stockpile Disposal [*Military*] (RDA) .... CSD
Chemical Stockpile Emergency Preparedness [*Military*] (RDA) .... CSEP
Chemin (DD) .... ch
Chemistry (DD) .... Chem
Chemogram (VRA) .... CHGR
Chengchow [*China*] [*Airport symbol*] (AD) .... CGO
Cherry (VRA) .... che
Cheshire Achievement of Scientific Skills in Schools [*British*] (AIE) .... CHASSIS
Cheshire Experiment in Educational Software [*British*] (AIE) .... CHEESE
Chester [*England*] [*Airport symbol*] (AD) .... CEG
Chestnut (VRA) .... chstnt
Chevalier (DD) .... Chev
Chevet (VRA) .... chvt
Cheyenne Mountain Upgrade .... CMU
Chiaroscuro (VRA) .... chiaro
Chicago-Argonne Resonant Ionization Spectrometer for Microanalysis [*Astronomy*] .... CHARISMA
Chief Education Officer (AIE) .... CEO
Child Care Resource and Referral Program (WYGK) .... CCR&R
Child Health Services Research .... CHSR
Childhood Education [*A publication*] (BRI) .... CE
Children Today [*A publication*] (BRI) .... CT
Children's Book News [*A publication*] (BRI) .... Ch Bk News
Children's Book Review Service [*A publication*] (BRI) .... CBRS
Children's Bookwatch [*A publication*] (BRI) .... Ch BWatch
Children's Literature [*A publication*] (BRI) .... Child Lit
Children's Literature Association Quarterly [*A publication*] (BRI) .... ChLAQ
Children's Literature in Education [*A publication*] (BRI) .... Ch Lit Ed
Chile Chico [*Chile*] [*Airport symbol*] (AD) .... CCH
China Airlines [*ICAO designator*] (AD) CI
China Container Holdings .... CCHL
China Eastern Airlines [*ICAO designator*] (AD) .... MU
China Education and Research Network [*Computer science*] .... CERnet
China National Cereals Oils & Foodstuffs Import & Export Corp. .... COFCO
China Northwest Airlines [*ICAO designator*] (AD) .... WH
China Review International [*A publication*] (BRI) .... Ch Rev Int
China Southwest Airlines [*ICAO designator*] (AD) .... SZ
Chinoiserie (VRA) .... Chino
Chippewa-Ottawa Treaty Fishery Management Authority .... COTFMA
Chita [*USSR*] [*Airport symbol*] (AD) .... CHT
Chitipa [*Malawi*] [*Airport symbol*] (AD) CII
Chlorite (VRA) .... chlr
Chlorobromide Print Process (VRA) .... CHBR
Choir Screen (VRA) .... chr scrn
Choroidal Neovascularization [*Opthalmology*] .... CNV
Christian (VRA) .... Xian
Christian Century [*A publication*] (BRI) CC
Christian Democratic Union [*Germany*] [*Political party*] .... CDU
Christian Science Monitor [*A publication*] (BRI) .... CSM
Christianity Today [*A publication*] (BRI) .... Ch Today
Christman Air System [*ICAO designator*] (AD) .... SX
Chrome (VRA) .... chr
Chromolithograph (VRA) .... chlith
Chronicle of Higher Education [*A publication*] (BRI) .... CHE
Chungking [*China*] [*Airport symbol*] (AD) .... CKG
Church (VRA) .... ch
Church History [*A publication*] (BRI) .... CH
Cibachrome (VRA) .... CIBCH
Ciborium (VRA) .... cibr
Cimber Air [*ICAO designator*] (AD) .... QI
Circle (DD) .... Cir
Circuit (DD) .... Circt
Circular Polarization Ratio [*Physics*] .... CPR
Citizens United for Bear .... CUB

City and Guilds of London Institute [*British*] (AIE) .... CGLI
City Express [*ICAO designator*] (AD) .... OU
City Flug [*ICAO designator*] (AD) .... VG
Ciudad de Valles [*Mexico*] [*Airport symbol*] (AD) .... VAE
Ciudad Mante [*Mexico*] [*Airport symbol*] (AD) .... MMC
Civilian Acquisition Position List [*Army*] (RDA) .... CAPL
Claimants and Unemployed Workers' Union (AIE) .... CUWU
Class Music Teaching (AIE) .... CMT
Classical and Modern Literature [*A publication*] (BRI) .... CML
Classical Journal [*A publication*] (BRI) .... CJ
Classical Outlook [*A publication*] (BRI) .... Class Out
Classical Review [*A publication*] (BRI) .... Class R
Classical T Tauri Stars [*Astronomy*] .... CTTS
Classical World [*A publication*] (BRI) .... CW
Clay (VRA) cl
Clear [*Alaska*] [*Airport symbol*] (AD) .... CLF
Clearwater-St. Petersburg [*Florida*] [*Airport symbol*] (AD) .... PIE
Cleidocranial Dysplasia [*Medicine*] .... CCD
Clerestory (VRA) .... clst
Cliche Verre (VRA) .... CLVR
Clinical Academic Staff Salaries Committee [*Committee of Vice Chancellors and Principals*] (AIE) .... CASSC
Clinical Dementia Rating .... CDR
Clio: A Journal of Literature, History and the Philosophy of History [*A publication*] (BRI) .... Clio
Cloisonne (VRA) .... clois
Cloister (VRA) .... clstr
Closed Circuit Television (AIE) .... CCTV
Closed-Fist Injury .... CFI
Closing Agreement Program (WYGK) .... CAP
Clostridium Difficile-Associated Diarrhea [*Medicine*] .... CDAD
Cloth (VRA) .... cth
Clothing and Allied Products Industry Training Board (AIE) .... CAPITB
Clubair [*ICAO designator*] (AD) .... CG
Cluny [*Queensland*] [*Airport symbol*] (AD) .... CZY
CM: A Reviewing Journal of Canadian Materials for Young People [*A publication*] (BRI) .... Can Mat
Coalition United for Bear .... CUB
Coari [*Brazil*] [*Airport symbol*] (AD) .... CZA
Coastal Air Transport [*ICAO designator*] (AD) .... DQ
Coastal Airways [*ICAO designator*] (AD) .... PN
Coastal Plains Commuter [*ICAO designator*] (AD) .... KA
Coat Protein .... COP
Cobden Airways [*ICAO designator*] (AD) .... XF
Co-Chair of the Board (DD) .... cochr
Cochise Airlines [*ICAO designator*] (AD) .... DP
Cocos Island [*Keeling Islands, Australia*] [*Airport symbol*] (AD) .... CCK
Coddair Air East [*ICAO designator*] (AD) .... JJ
Codex (VRA) .... cod
Codices (VRA) .... cod
Co-Educational (AIE) .... CoEd
Cognitive Abilities Screening Instrument .... CASI
Cognitive Acceleration through Science Education (AIE) .... CASE
Cognitive Acceleration through Science Education Project (AIE) .... CASEP
Cognitive Failure Questionnaire [*Education*] (AIE) .... CFQ
Colgan Airways [*ICAO designator*] (AD) .... CJ
Collaboration (VRA) .... colab
Collaborative Authoring Production and Transmission of Interactive Video for Education (AIE) .... CAPTIVE
Collaborative Forecasting and Replenishment [*Computer science*] .... CFAR
Collage (VRA) .... col
Collateralized Bond Obligation [*Investment term*] (DFIT) .... CBO
Collect on Delivery (DFIT) .... COD
Collection (VRA) .... coll
Collective-Electronic Oscillator [*Physics*] .... CEO
College (VRA) .... clg
College & Research Libraries [*A publication*] (BRI) .... CRL
College and University [*A publication*] (BRI) .... C & U
College Composition and Communication [*A publication*] (BRI) .... Col Comp
College Employers Links Project (AIE) .... CELP
College Literature [*A publication*] (BRI) .... Col Lit
College of Agriculture and Forestry (AIE) .... CAF
College of Art and Technology (AIE) .... CAT
College of Commerce (AIE) CC
College of Commerce and Technology (AIE) .... CCT
College of Further and Higher Education (AIE) .... CFHE
College of Further Education (AIE) .... CFE
College of Technology and Art (AIE) .... CTA
Colleges, Institutes, and Schools in Education (AIE) .... CISE
Collodion Glass Negative (VRA) .... CGNG
Collodion Print (VRA) .... CLPT
Collotype (VRA) .... COLTY
Colomb Bechar [*Algeria*] [*Airport symbol*] (AD) .... CBH
Colonel (DD) .... Col
Colonia Sarmiento [*Argentina*] [*Airport symbol*] (AD) .... OLN
Colonnade (VRA) .... colnd
Colony (VRA) .... colo
Color (VRA) .... clr
Color Prints [*Not tinted*] (VRA) .... CLRP
Columbia International Affairs Online [*Computer science*] .... Ciao
Columbia Journalism Review [*A publication*] (BRI) .... CJR
Columbia Law Review [*A publication*] (BRI) .... CLR
Columbus [*Mississippi*] [*Airport symbol*] (AD) .... UBS
Column (VRA) .... clm
Comair [*ICAO designator*] (AD) .... OH

Comanche Crew Support System [*Army*] (RDA) .... CCSS
Combat Vehicle Signature Management Plan [*Army*] (RDA) .... CVSMP
Combika [*Sao Paulo, Brazil*] [*Airport symbol*] (AD) .... CUK
Combination (VRA) .... comb
Combined Cooling Performance Factor .... CCPF
Combined Heating Performance Factor .... CHPF
Combined Higher Education Software Team (AIE) .... CHEST
Come-All-Ye [*A publication*] (BRI) .... CAY
Comilla [*Bangladesh*] [*Airport symbol*] (AD) .... CLA
Comiso [*Italy*] [*Airport symbol*] (AD) .... CIY
Command Airways [*ICAO designator*] (AD) .... CT
Command Airways [*ICAO designator*] (AD) .... DD
Commander and Staff Visualization Research Tool [*Army*] (RDA) .... CoVRT
Commander of the Order of Military Merit [*Canada*] (DD) .... CMM
Commander's Integrated Display [*Military*] (RDA) .... CID
Commemorative Bucks of Michigan .... CBM
Commentary [*A publication*] (BRI) .... Comt
Commerce Clearing House (DFIT) .... CCH
Commercial Financial Services Inc. .... CFS
Commission (DD) .... comm
Commission on Preservation and Access .... CPA
Commissioner (DD) .... commr
Committee for Exchange with Non-English Speaking Countries (AIE) .... CENESC
Committee for Research into Teacher Education (AIE) .... CRITE
Committee for the Employment of Disabled People (AIE) .... CEDP
Committee of 200 [*An association*] C200
Committee of Heads of Drama Departments in Scotland (AIE) .... CHDDS
Committee of Professors in Operational Research (AIE) .... COPIOR
Committee of Scottish Higher Education Principals (AIE) .... COSHEP
Committee on Education [*American Library Association*] .... COE
Committee on Legislation [*American Library Association*] .... COL
Committee on Principals and Directors of Central Institutions (AIE) .... COPADOCI
Committee on Restrictions Against Disabled People (AIE) .... CORAD
Committee on Special Educational Needs [*Scotland*] (AIE) .... COSPEN
Committee on the Training of University Teachers (AIE) .... CTUT
Commodore [*ICAO designator*] (AD) .... YJ
Common Object Request Broker Architecture [*Computer science*] .... CORBA
Common Procedural Terminology [*Human resources*] (WYGK) .... CPT
Common User Access Architecture [*Computer science*] (DOM) .... CUA Architecture
Commonweal [*A publication*] (BRI) .... Comw
Commonwealth Council for Educational Administration [*British*] (AIE) .... CCEA
Communication Connect Time Monitor [*Computer science*] .... CCTM
Communication Studies (AIE) .... CS
Communications (DD) .... commun
Communications Decency Act .... CDA
Communications Management Systems [*Military*] (RDA) .... COMM MGT SYS
Communications Satellite Corp. (DFIT) .... COMSAT
Communicative Use of English as a Foreign Language (AIE) .... CUEFL
Communist University of London [*England*] (AIE) .... CUL
Community and Youth Service Association (AIE) .... CYSA
Community Anti-Drug Coalitions of America .... CADCA
Community Development Trust .... CDT
Community Enterprise Trust (AIE) .... CET
Community Language in the Secondary Curriculum [*Project*] (AIE) .... CLSC
Community Skills Unit (AIE) .... CSU
Community-Acquired Pneumonia .... CAP
Compact Disc-Interactive [*Computer science*] .... CD-I
Compact Disc-Write Once [*Computer science*] (DOM) .... CD-WO
Compagnie Aerienne du Languedoc [*ICAO designator*] (AD) .... FQ
Companhia Vale do Rio Doce .... CVRD
Compania [*Company*] [*Spanish*] (DFIT) .... Cia
Companion of the Distinguished Service Order [*Canada*] (DD) .... DSO
Companion of the Order of Canada (DD) CC
Company (DD) .... Co
Comparative Drama [*A publication*] (BRI) .... Comp Dr
Comparative Library Organization Committee [*American Library Association*] .... CLOC
Comparative Literature [*A publication*] (BRI) .... Comp L
Comparative Literature Studies [*A publication*] (BRI) .... CLS
Comparison (VRA) .... comp
Competence-Based Qualification [*Education*] (AIE) .... CBQ
Competency Based Teaching (AIE) .... CBT
Competitive Development Group [*Army*] (RDA) .... CDG
Complete Affinity Server Enclosure [*Computer science*] .... CASE
Completed (VRA) .... compl
Completely in-the-Canal [*Audiology*] CIC
Completion of Calls to Busy Subscriber [*Telecommunications*] (DOM) .... CCBS
Component Management Interface [*Computer science*] .... CMI
Composite Educational Abilites Scale (AIE) .... CEAS
Composition (VRA) .... comps
Composition Board (VRA) .... compbd
Compound (VRA) .... compd
Compound Muscle Action Potential [*Neurophysiology*] .... CMAP
Compound-Specific Radiocarbon Analyses .... CSRA
CompScript .... CPRX
Comptroller (DD) .... compt
CompuServe Information Service .... CompuServe
Computer (DD) .... Comp
Computer (VRA) .... compr
Computer Aided Learning in Mathematics (AIE) .... CALM
Computer Assisted Careers Guidance System (AIE) .... CACGS
Computer Assisted Instruction (AIE) .... CAI
Computer Assisted Language Teaching (AIE) .... CALT
Computer Assisted Learning (AIE) .... CAL

Computer Assisted Virtual Environment ... CAVE
Computer Based English Language Testing (AIE) ... CBELT
Computer Engineering (DD) ... CompEng
Computer Enhanced Language Instruction Archive (AIE) ... CELIA
Computer Industry Coalition for Advanced Television Service ... CICATS
Computer Literacy and Studies in Schools (AIE) ... CLASS
Computer Science (DD) ... CompSc
Computer-Assisted Job Evaluation [*Human resources*] (WYGK) ... CAJE
Computerised Information Retrieval in Schools [*Project*] (AIE) ... CIRIS
Computers and Adult Basic Education [*Liverpool Institute of Higher Education*] [*British*] (AIE) ... CABE
Computers and the Humanities [*A publication*] (BRI) ... Compt & H
Computers in Teaching Initiative (AIE) ... CTI
Computers in Teaching Initiative Support Service (AIE) ... CTISS
Computers in the Curriculum [*Education*] (AIE) ... CIC
Computers in Training as a Resource (AIE) ... CITAR
Conceptual (VRA) ... concep
Concession (DD) ... Conc
Concord [*New Hampshire*] [*Airport symbol*] (AD) ... CON
Concorde out, Concorde Home ... COCH
Concorde out, Tourist Class Home ... COTCH
Concrete (VRA) ... concr
Condamine [*Queensland*] [*Airport symbol*] (AD) ... ONM
Condominium (VRA) ... condo
Conductive Education Association (AIE) ... CEA
Confederation of Art and Design Associations (AIE) ... CADA
Confederation of Institute Directors (AIE) ... CID
Conference of Scottish Centrally Funded Colleges (AIE) ... CSCFC
Conference on Fair Use ... CONFU
Conference on University Purchasing (AIE) ... COUP
Conference Permanente des Recteurs, Presidents et Vice Chancellors (AIE) ... CRE
Confidential Measurement-Based Self-Evaluation [*Project*] (AIE) ... COMBSE
Configuration and Administration ... C & A
Confined Disposal Facilities ... CDF
Congenital Generalized Hypertrichosis [*Werewolf syndrome*] [*Medicine*] ... CGH
Congestion Mitigation & Air Quality [*An association*] ... CMAQ
Conjunction (VRA) ... conj
Connair [*ICAO designator*] (AD) ... CK
Connectair [*ICAO designator*] (AD) ... AX
Connective-Tissue Growth Factor [*Biochemistry*] ... CTGF
Consecrated (VRA) ... consr
Conseil de la Gravure du Quebec [*1978, founded 1971 as AGQ, CQE from 1984*] [*Canada*] (NGC) ... CGQ
Conseil de la Peinture du Quebec [*1978, founded 1966 as SAPQ, SAVVQ from 1980, CAPQ from 1982*] [*Canada*] (NGC) ... CPQ
Conseil de la Reine [*Canada*] (DD) ... CR
Conseil de la Sculpture du Quebec [*1978, founded 1961 as ASQ*] [*Canada*] (NGC) ... CSQ
Conseil des Artistes Peintres du Quebec [*1982, founded 1966 as SAPQ*] [*Canada*] (NGC) ... CAPQ
Conseil National de l'Ordre des Medecins [*France*] ... CNOM
Conseil Quebecois de l'Estampe [*1984, founded 1971 as AGQ, CGQ from 1978*] [*Canada*] (NGC) ... CQE
Conservative Collegiate Forum (AIE) ... CCF
Consiglio Nazionale Scienza Tecnologia [*Italy*] ... CNST
Consolidated (DD) ... consol
Consortium for Advanced Residential Buildings ... CARB
Consortium for Assessment and Testing in Schools (AIE) ... CATS
Consortium of Academic Libraries in Manchester [*British*] (AIE) ... CALIM
Consortium to Establish a Registry for Alzheimer's Disease ... CERAD
Conspecific Sperm Precedence [*Entomology*] ... CSP
Constitutive Transport Element [*Biochemistry*] ... CTE
Construction (DD) ... const
Construction (VRA) ... constr
Construction Engineering (DD) ... ConstEng
Construction Equipment and Materials Handling Equipment [*Military*] (RDA) ... CE/MHE
Construction Management (DD) ... ConstMgmt
Consultancy and Research Unit [*Department of Information Studies, University of Sheffield*] [*British*] (AIE) ... CRU
Consulting (DD) ... cons
Consulting Committee on Educational Matters (AIE) ... CCEM
Contact a Family Computer Assisted Learning (AIE) ... CAFCAL
Contact Print (VRA) ... CONPR
Conte (VRA) ... cnte
Conte Crayon (VRA) ... cnte
Contemporary (VRA) ... cont
Contemporary Education [*A publication*] (BRI) ... Cont Ed
Contemporary Pacific [*A publication*] (BRI) ... Cont Pac
Contemporary Psychology [*A publication*] (BRI) ... CP
Contemporary Review [*A publication*] (BRI) ... CR
Contemporary Sociology [*A publication*] (BRI) ... CS
Continental Airlines [*ICAO designator*] (AD) ... CO
Contingency Contracting Officers [*Military*] (RDA) ... CCO
Contingency Remoting System [*Military*] (RDA) ... CRS
Continuing Education for Senior Citizens ... CESC
Continuing Education Standing Committee (AIE) ... CESC
Continuing-Care Retirement Communities ... CCRC
Continuous Acquisition and Life-Cycle Support [*Military*] (RDA) ... CALS
Continuous Hormones as Replacement Therapy [*Medicine*] ... CHART
Contract Student Numbers (AIE) ... CSN
Contrapposto (VRA) ... cntrps
Contrast Media-Induced Acute Renal Insufficiency [*Medicine*] ... CM-ARI
Control Panel Device [*Computer science*] (DOM) ... CDEV
Control Program for Microcomputers (DOM) ... CP/M
Control Program for Microprocessors [*Computer science*] ... CP/M
Controller (DD) ... cont
Convertible Adjustable Preferred Stock [*Investment term*] (DFIT) ... CAPS
Convertible Security [*Investment term*] (DFIT) ... CV
Cooch Behar [*India*] [*Airport symbol*] (AD) ... COH
Cook Islandair [*ICAO designator*] (AD) ... KH
Cook Islands International [*ICAO designator*] (AD) ... KC
Coolah [*New South Wales*] [*Airport symbol*] (AD) ... CLH
Coolangatta [*Queensland*] [*Airport symbol*] (AD) ... OOL
Coolullah [*Australia*] [*Airport symbol*] (AD) ... WCO
Cooperative Alliance for Refuge Enhancement ... CARE
Cooperative Cardiovascular Project ... CCP
Cooperative Threat Reduction [*Military*] (RDA) ... CTR
Copaipo [*Chile*] [*Airport symbol*] (AD) ... CPO
Copper (VRA) ... cu
Copperplate (VRA) ... cuplt
Coptic (VRA) ... Copt
Copyright Licensing Organisation [*British*] (AIE) ... CLO
Coral Air [*ICAO designator*] (AD) ... VY
Cordillo Downs [*South Australia*] [*Airport symbol*] (AD) ... ODL
Corinthian (VRA) ... Corin
Corner (VRA) ... crnr
Cornhusks (VRA) ... crnhs
Corning-Elmira [*New York*] [*Airport symbol*] (AD) ... ELM
Corowa [*New South Wales*] [*Airport symbol*] (AD) ... COW
Corozal [*Colombia*] [*Airport symbol*] (AD) ... CZU
Corporate (VRA) ... corp
Corporate-Owned Life Insurance (WYGK) ... COLI
Corporation (DD) ... Corp
Corporation for Laser Optics Research ... COLOR
Corporation of Certified Secretaries (AIE) ... CCS
Corps Eligible [*Army*] (RDA) ... CE
Corps Surface-to-Air Missile/Medium Extended Air Defense System [*Military*] (RDA) ... CSAM/MEADS
Correlation Metric Construction [*Analysis of chemical reaction*] ... CMC
Corresponding (VRA) ... corr
Corsica (VRA) ... Cors
Corten Steel (VRA) ... crtnstl
Cortina d'Ampezzo [*Italy*] [*Airport symbol*] (AD) ... CDF
Cost and Freight (DFIT) ... C&F
Cost Plus Fixed Fee [*Investment term*] (DFIT) ... CPFF
Costa Rica (VRA) ... C Rica
Costume (VRA) ... cstu
Cotonou [*Dahomey*] [*Airport symbol*] (AD) ... COO
Cotton (VRA) ... cot
Coulomb Blockade [*Physics*] ... CB
Council for Disabled Children (AIE) ... CDC
Council for Education and Training in Youth and Community Work (AIE) ... CETYCW
Council for Industry and Higher Education (AIE) ... CIHE
Council for Management Education and Development (AIE) ... CMED
Council for Tertiary Education in Scotland (AIE) ... CTES
Council for the Accreditation of Teacher Education (AIE) ... CATE
Council for the Advancement and Support of Education ... CASE
Council for University Classics Departments (AIE) ... CUCD
Council for Voluntary Youth Service (AIE) ... CVYS
Council of Indian Nations ... CIN
Council of Local Education Authorities/School Teacher Committee (AIE) ... CLEA/ST
Council of Principals (AIE) ... CP
Council of Subject Teaching Associations (AIE) ... COSTA
Council of Subject Teaching Associations (AIE) ... CSTA
Counselling and Career Development Organisation [*British*] (AIE) ... CCDO
Counterflow Virtual Impactor [*Instrumentation*] ... CVI
Counternarcotics Command Management System [*Army*] (RDA) ... CN/CMS
Country (VRA) ... ctry
Countrywide [*ICAO designator*] (AD) ... MB
County (VRA) ... co
County Links Access to Information about Resources and Expertise [*Education*] (AIE) ... CLAIRE
Course Approval and Monitoring Form [*Inner London Education Authority*] [*British*] (AIE) ... CAMF
Course Record Book [*Education*] (AIE) ... CRB
Court (DD) ... Crt
Court (VRA) ... ct
Courthouse (VRA) ... cths
Courtyard (VRA) ... ctyd
Cover (VRA) ... bv
Covered (VRA) ... bv
Coyhaique [*Chile*] [*Airport symbol*] (AD) ... GXQ
Crackle (VRA) ... ckcl
Crateus [*Brazil*] [*Airport symbol*] (AD) ... CTH
Crato [*Brazil*] [*Airport symbol*] (AD) ... CQQ
Crayon (VRA) ... cray
Creamware (VRA) ... crmwr
Creative and Performing Arts ... CAPA
Creative Incentive Coalition ... CIC
Crenellation (VRA) ... crnltn
Crescent (DD) ... Cres
Cressent [*A publication*] (BRI) ... Cres
Criminal Justice and Behavior [*A publication*] (BRI) ... Crim J & B
Cristalandia [*Brazil*] [*Airport symbol*] (AD) ... CLZ
Criteria of Teacher Selection [*Project*] (AIE) ... CATS
Critical Dimension Scanning Electron Microscopes ... CD-SEM

Critical Quarterly [*A publication*] (BRI) .... Crit Q
Critical Review [*A publication*] (BRI) .... Crit R
Critical Technical Parameters (RDA) .... CTP
Criticism [*A publication*] (BRI) .... Critm
Critique [*A publication*] (BRI) .... Critiq
Croissant (DD) .... crois
Cro-Magnon (VRA) .... CrMg
Cromwell [*New Zealand*] [*Airport symbol*] (AD) .... CWE
Cross Section (VRA) .... xsect
Crossair [*ICAO designator*] (AD) LX
Crossing (VRA) .... crsg
Crotone [*Italy*] [*Airport symbol*] (AD) .... CTW
Crown Aviation [*ICAO designator*] (AD) CC
Crown International Airlines [*ICAO designator*] (AD) .... RL
Crusader Armaments [*Army*] (RDA) .... CR ARM
Crusader Mobility [*Army*] (RDA) .... CR MOB
Crusader Munitions/Resupply [*Army*] (RDA) .... CR MUN/RES
Cruzeiro do Sul [*ICAO designator*] (AD) .... SC
Cryogenic Dark Matter Search [*Astrophysics*] .... CDMS
Cryogenic Rare Event Search with Superconducting Thermometers
  [*Astrophysics*] .... CRESST
Crystal (VRA) .... crys
Cubana Airlines [*ICAO designator*] (AD) .... CU
Cubicle (VRA) .... cub
Cucui [*Brazil*] [*Airport symbol*] (AD) .... CBZ
Cuddapan [*Queensland*] [*Airport symbol*] (AD) .... UDD

Cultural Action Committee .... CAC
Cumberland Airlines [*ICAO designator*] (AD) .... NQ
Cumulative Volcano Amplitude [*Volcanology*] .... CVA
Cuneiform (VRA) .... cunif
curity Organization] [*French*] (AD) ....
  Organisation Ibero-Americaine de Securite Sociale [Iberian-American Social Se
Current History [*A publication*] (BRI) .... Cu H
Curriculum Analysis Taxonomy [*Education*] (AIE) .... CAT
Curriculum and Resource Information Service (AIE) .... CRIS
Curriculum Association (AIE) .... CA
Curriculum Council for Wales (AIE) .... CCW
Curriculum Led Institutional Development (AIE) .... CLID
Curriculum Review [*A publication*] (BRI) .... Cur R
Customer/Field Support Elements (RDA) .... C/FSE
Customized Multimedia Connection .... CMC
Customized Networking Platform .... CNP
Cyanoacrylate Tissue Adhesive [*Medicine*] .... CTA
Cyanotype (VRA) .... CTYP
Cyclic-Nucleotide-Binding [*Neurobiology*] .... CNB
Cylindrical (VRA) .... cyl
Cypress (VRA) .... cyp
Cyprus (VRA) .... Cyp
Cyprus Airways [*ICAO designator*] (AD) .... CY
Cyprus Turkish Airways [*ICAO designator*] (AD) .... YK
Cytotoxic Necrotizing Factor [*Immunology*] .... CNF
Czechoslovak Airlines [*ICAO designator*] (AD) .... OK

By Meaning

D

By Meaning

Dabajuro [*Venezuela*] [*Airport symbol*] (AD) .... DJV
Dads Advising Dads .... DADS
Dadu [*Pakistan*] [*Airport symbol*] (AD) .... DDU
Daguerreotype (VRA) .... DTYP
Dahomy (VRA) .... Dah
Dajarra [*Queensland*] [*Airport symbol*] (AD) .... DJR
Dakota Indian Foundation .... DIF
Dalat [*South Vietnam*] [*Airport symbol*] (AD) .... DLI
Dalbandin [*Pakistan*] [*Airport symbol*] (AD) .... DWP
d'Albertis [*Australia*] [*Airport symbol*] (AD) .... DLB
Dalhousie Review [*A publication*] (BRI) .... Dal R
[*The*] Dalles [*Oregon*] [*Airport symbol*] (AD) .... DLS
Daly Waters [*Northern Territory, Australia*] [*Airport symbol*] (AD) .... DYW
Damask (VRA) .... dmsk
Danair [*ICAO designator*] (AD) .... DX
Dan-Air Services [*ICAO designator*] (AD) .... DA
Danang [*South Vietnam*] [*Airport symbol*] (AD) .... DAD
Dance Magazine [*A publication*] (BRI) .... Dance
Dance Research Journal [*A publication*] (BRI) .... Dance RJ
Dance Teachers' Association (AIE) .... DTA
Danghila [*Ethiopia*] [*Airport symbol*] (AD) .... DNG
Daniel, Mann, Johnson, & Mendenhall [*A major contributor to architecture in Jakarta, Sidney, Manila, and Seoul*] .... DMJM
Darien Airlines [*ICAO designator*] (AD) .... DG
Dark (VRA) .... dk
Dartmoor Prison [*Devon, England*] (AD) .... Moor
Daru [*Sierra Leone*] [*Airport symbol*] (AD) .... DSL
Data Capture Unit (AIE) .... DCU
Data Communication Channel (DOM) .... DCC
Data Communications Equipment (DOM) .... DCE
Data Exchange File [*Computer science*] .... DXF
Data Interchange Standards Association .... DISA
Data Processing Officer (AIE) .... DPO
Dathina [*Yemen*] [*Airport symbol*] (AD) .... DAH
Davenport Downs [*Queensland*] [*Airport symbol*] (AD) .... DVP
Dawson City [*Yukon*] [*Airport symbol*] (AD) .... YDA
Daydream Island [*Queensland*] [*Airport symbol*] (AD) .... DEQ
Days in Vitro [*Cell culture*] .... DIV
Dealt in Flat [*Investment term*] (DFIT) .... F
Deauville [*France*] [*Airport symbol*] (AD) .... DOL
Deboyne [*Louisiade Archipelago, Papua*] [*Airport symbol*] (AD) .... DOY
Debra Markos [*Ethiopia*] [*Airport symbol*] (AD) .... DBM
Debra Tabor [*Ethiopia*] [*Airport symbol*] (AD) .... DBT
Debris (VRA) .... dbrs
Decatur [*ICAO designator*] (AD) .... DK
Declared or Paid after Stock Dividend or Split-Up [*Investment term*] (DFIT) .... H
Declared or Paid in the Preceding 12 Months [*Investment term*] (DFIT) .... E
Declared or Paid in the Preceding 12 Months Plus Stock Dividend [*Investment term*] (DFIT) .... R
Declared or Paid This Year on a Cumulative Issue with Dividends in Arrears [*Investment term*] (DFIT) .... K
Decorative (VRA) .... dec
Dedicated (VRA) .... ded
Dedication and Everlasting Love to Animals [*An association*] .... DELTA
Dedougu [*Upper Volta*] [*Airport symbol*] (AD) .... DGU
Dedza [*Malawi*] [*Airport symbol*] (AD) .... DDZ
Deep Inelastic Scattering [*Particle physics*] .... DIS
Defense Acquisition Pilot Program [*Army*] (RDA) .... DAPP
Defense Acquisition Scholarship Program [*DoD*] (RDA) .... DASP
Defense Airborne Reconnaissance Office .... DARO
Defense Information Infrastructure [*Military*] .... DII
Defense Research and Engineering Network [*DoD*] .... DREN
Defined Benefit Plan [*Human resources*] (WYGK) .... DBP
Defined Contribution Plan [*Insurance*] (WYGK) .... DCP
Delftware (VRA) .... delfwr
Delhi [*India*] [*Airport symbol*] (AD) .... NDH
Delivery Order (DFIT) .... D/O
Dell SCSI Array [*Computer science*] .... DSA
Delta Air [*ICAO designator*] (AD) .... DI
Delta Channel [*Used for communicating between the phone company switch and an ISDN adapter*] [*Computer science*] .... D-channel
Dementia with Lewy Bodies [*Nerve cell pathology*] .... DLB
Denmark (VRA) .... Den
Dental Capitation Plan [*Insurance*] (WYGK) .... DCP
Dental Care Plan [*Insurance*] (WYGK) .... DCP
Dental Preferred Provider Organization [*Insurance*] (WYGK) .... DPPO

Department (DD) .... dept
Department of Continuing Education (AIE) .... DCE
Department of Disarmament and Arms Regulation [*United Nations*] .... DDAR
Department of Economic, Administrative, and Policy Studies (AIE) .... DEAPSIE
Department of Education .... DoEd
Department of Energy .... DoE
Department of Health (AIE) .... DoH
Department of the Interior .... DoI
Departmental Staff Records (AIE) .... DSR
Dependent Care Assistance Plan [*Insurance*] (WYGK) .... DCAP
Dependent Care Program [*Insurance*] (WYGK) .... DCP
Dependent Coverage Waiver [*Insurance*] (WYGK) .... DCW
Dependent-Care Reimbursement [*Insurance*] (WYGK) .... DCR
Depicting (VRA) .... depict
Deployable Universal Combat Earthmover (RDA) .... DEUCE
Deposit Administration Arrangement (WYGK) .... DAA
Depth (VRA) .... dp
Deputy Director for Acquisition Career Management [*Army*] (RDA) .... DDACM
Derby [*England*] [*Airport symbol*] (AD) .... DXY
Dermonecrotic Toxin [*Immunology*] .... DNT
Descriptive Cataloging of Rare Books [*American Library Association*] .... DCRB
Desert Pacific [*ICAO designator*] (AD) .... NP
Design (VRA) .... des
Design Accreditation and Certification Advisers (AIE) .... DACA
Design and Art Technician Education Council (AIE) .... DATEC
Design and Technology Association (AIE) .... DATA
Design and Technology in Education (AIE) .... DESTECH
Designated Disabled Persons Liaison Officer (AIE) .... DDPLO
Designated Mechanic Examiners .... DME
Desktop Management Suite [*Computer science*] .... DMS
Desktop Security Suite [*McAfee Associates, Inc.*] [*Computer science*] .... DSS
Destination Digital Media Computers [*Computer science*] .... DMC
Destroyed (VRA) .... destr
Detached (VRA) .... detch
Detached Youth Worker (AIE) .... DYW
Detail (VRA) .... det
Deterministic Microgrinding [*Optics manufacturing*] (RDA) .... DMG
Detrended Correspondence Analysis [*Mathematics*] .... DCA
Detroit [*Michigan*] [*Airport symbol*] (AD) .... DTT
Developing Anti-Sexist Innovations (AIE) .... DASI
Development (DD) .... devel
Development Alternatives, Inc. .... DAI
Development Assessment and Instruction for Success in the Early Years [*Education*] (AIE) .... DAISEY
Development of Learning and Teaching in the Arts (AIE) .... DELTA
Development Unit Executive Group [*Scotland*] (AIE) .... DUEG
Devis Directeurs Nationaux [*Canada*] (DD) .... DDN
Dhala [*Aden*] [*Airport symbol*] (AD) .... DHL
Dhoxaton [*Greece*] [*Airport symbol*] (AD) .... DXT
Diagnosis-Related Group [*Insurance*] (WYGK) .... DRG
Diagram (VRA) .... diag
Dialogue: Canadian Philosophical Review [*A publication*] (BRI) .... Dialogue
Dial-Up Networking [*Microsoft Windows 95*] [*Computer science*] .... DUN
Dial-Up Wide Area Network Gaming Operation [*Computer science*] .... Dwango
Diamantina [*Brazil*] [*Airport symbol*] (AD) .... DMT
Diamantina Lakes [*Queensland*] [*Airport symbol*] (AD) .... DYM
Diameter (VRA) .... dia
Diamond (VRA) .... dmd
Diapaga [*Upper Volta*] [*Airport symbol*] (AD) .... DIP
Didactic (VRA) .... did
Died (VRA) .... d
Dietary Reference Intakes .... DRI
Difference of Gaussians [*Image processing*] .... DOG
Different (VRA) .... dif
Differential Fluorescence Induction [*Analytic biochemistry*] .... DFI
Diffuse Ionized Gas [*Astrophysics*] .... DIG
Diffuse-Reflectance Ultraviolet-Visible [*Spectra*] .... DRUV
Digest of Middle East Studies [*A publication*] (BRI) .... DOMES
Digital Audio Radio Service .... DARS
Digital Audio Visual Council (DOM) .... DAVIC
Digital Dataphone Service [*Telecommunications*] (DOM) .... DDS
Digital Disk Recorder (DOM) .... DDR
Digital Future Coalition .... DFC
Digital Light Processing .... DLP
Digital Signal Processors [*Computer science*] .... DSPS
Digital Signature Initiative [*Computer science*] .... DSig

Digital Television Network .... DTN
Digital Versatile Disc .... DVD
Digital Versatile Disk .... DVD
Digital Video Cassette (DOM) .... DVC
Digitally Archived Library Images .... DALI
Dihydronicotinamide Adenine Dinucleotide (AD) .... NADH
Dihydronicotinamide Adenine Dinucleotide Phosphate (AD) ..... NADPH
Dihydronicotinamide Adenine Dinucleotide Phosphate (AD) ..... nadph
Dihydroxy Benoxazin One [Organic chemistry] .... DIBOA
Diisopropyl Carbodiimide [Organic chemistry] .... DIPC
Dijon [France] [Airport symbol] (AD) .... DIJ
Dili [Zaire] [Airport symbol] (AD) .... DIC
Dilly [Portuguese Timor] [Airport symbol] (AD) .... DIL
Dimension (VRA) .... dim
Dimethylamino Pyridiniumtoluenesulfonic Acid [Organic chemistry] .... DPTS
Dioleoyl Trimethylammonium Propane [Organic chemistry] .... DOTAP
Dioleoylphosphatidylserine [Biochemistry] .... DOPS
Diploma (DD) .... Dip
Diploma de Droit Notarial [Canada] (DD) .... DDN
Diploma in Urology (DD) .... DU
Diploma of the Imperial College of Science, Technology, and Medicine
    [Canada] (DD) .... DIC
Diplome d'Etudes Superieures [Canada] (DD) .... DES
Diplome en Droit Civil (DD) .... DipDN
Diplome en Sciences Administratives (DD) .... DSA
Diptych (VRA) .... dpty
Direct Air [ICAO designator] (AD) .... UO
Direct Instructional Systems to Arithmetic and Reading (AIE) ..... DISTAR
Direct Radiative Forcing [Atmospheric science] .... DRF
Direct Satellite System .... DSS
Directly Observed Treatment Short-Course [Therapy regime] .... DOTS
Director (DD) .... dir
Director General for Vocational Training (AIE) .... DGVT
Directory Number [Computer science] .... DN
Directory of Independent Training and Tutorial Organisations (AIE) .... DITTO
Direct-Recording Electronic [Technology] .... DRE
Disability Case Management [Insurance] (WYGK) .... DCM
Discovery Airlines [ICAO designator] (AD) .... DH
Discrete Variation Method .... DVM
Discrete Wavelet Transformation (DOM) .... DWT
Discussion Group on Information Technology in Library and Information
    Studies Schools (AIE) .... DIGITALIS
Dismounted Infantry Battle Space Battle Lab [Army] (RDA) .... DIBBL
Dispersion (VRA) .... disp
Disseminated Cryptococcus Neoformans Infection [Medicine] .... DCI
Dissent [A publication] (BRI) .... Dis
Distant (VRA) .... dist
Distemper (VRA) .... temp
Distribute (VRA) .... distrb
Distributed Component Object Model [Computer science] .... DCOM
Distributed Real-Time Groove Network [Computer science] .... DRGN
Distribution-Abundance [Ecology] .... DA
District (VRA) .... distr
Diversion (DD) .... divers
Dividends and Earnings in Canadian Dollars [Investment term] (DFIT) .... G
Division (DD) .... div
Division of Drug Marketing, Advertising, and Communications [Food and
    Drug Administration] .... DDMAC
Division of Quality Enhancement (AIE) .... DQF
Divisional Inspector [Education] (AIE) .... DI
Djajapura [West Irian, Indonesia] [Airport symbol] (AD) .... DJJ
Djakarta [Java, Indonesia] [Airport symbol] (AD) .... JKT
Djambala [Congo] [Airport symbol] (AD) .... DJM
Djambi [Indonesia] [Airport symbol] (AD) .... DJB
DLT Deutsche Regional [ICAO designator] (AD) .... DW
Docteur d'Universite [Doctor of the University] [Canada] (DD) .... DU
Docteur es Sciences Agricole [Doctor of Agricultural Sciences] (DD) .... DSA
Docteur es Sciences Economiques (DD) .... DesScEco
Doctor (DD) .... Dr

Doctor of Agricultural Sciences (DD) .... DSA
Doctor of Divinity (DD) .... DD
Doctor of Economic Science (DD) .... DESc
Doctor of Education (AIE) .... DEd
Doctor of Environmental Studies (DD) .... DES
Doctor of European Law (DD) .... DEurL
Doctor of Humane Letters (DD) .... LHD
Doctor of Jurisprudence (DD) .... JD
Doctor of Laws (DD) .... LLD
Doctor of Literature (DD) .... LHD
Doctor of Medicine and Master of Surgery (DD) .... MDCM
Doctor of Natural Science (AD) .... Nat ScD
Doctor of the Humanities (DD) .... LHD
Doctorat en Medecin Veterinaire (DD) .... DMV
Doctorat Honoris Causa [Canada] (DD) .... DHC
Doctorate of Military Science (DD) .... DMil Sc
Documents against Acceptance [Investment term] (DFIT) .... DA
Documents against Payment (DFIT) .... DP
Documents to the People [Government Documents Round Table] [American
    Library Association] .... DTTP
DodecylMaltoside [Organic chemistry] .... DM
Dodollo [Ethiopia] [Airport symbol] (AD) .... DDL
Dog Fancy [A publication] (BRI) .... Dog Fan
Dolphin Morbillivirus .... DMV
Dominica [Leeward Islands] [Airport symbol] (AD) .... DOM
Dominican Republic (VRA) .... Dom Rep
Dominicana de Aviacion [ICAO designator] (AD) .... DO
Door (VRA) .... dr
Dori [Upper Volta] [Airport symbol] (AD) .... DOR
Dormitory (VRA) .... dorm
Dorsolateral Prefrontal Cortex [Brain anatomy] .... DLPFC
Double (VRA) .... dbl
Double Homology [Biochemistry] .... DH
Double-Declining-Balance Depreciation Method [Finance] (DFIT) .... DDB
Double-Exposure Prevention [Advanced photo system] .... DEP
Douglas Airways [ICAO designator] (AD) .... DZ
Dover [Delaware] [Airport symbol] (AD) .... DOV
Downbeat [A publication] (BRI) .... Dbt
Downeast Airlines [ICAO designator] (AD) .... DE
Dr. & Mrs. (VRA) .... D/M
Drama [Greece] [Airport symbol] (AD) .... DRM
Drawing (VRA) .... dwg
Dredging Operations and Environmental Research [US Army Corps of
    Engineers] .... DOER
Drive (DD) .... Dr
Drivers Integrated Display [Military] (RDA) .... DID
Driver's Vision Enhancer [Military] .... DVE
Drop-In Skills Centre [British] (AIE) .... DISC
Drug-Free Workplace Act of 1988 (WYGK) .... DFWA
Dry Powder Inhaler [Pharmacy] .... DPI
Drypoint (VRA) .... dryp
Dual Employed With Kids (DFIT) .... DEWKS
Dual Energy X-Ray Absorptiometry [Painless bone mass test] [Medicine] ...... DXA
Dual In-Line Memory Module [Computer science] (DOM) .... DIMM
Dual In-Line Package Switch [Electronics] (DOM) .... DIP switch
Dual-Income, No Kids (DFIT) .... DINKS
Dubai [Trucial Oman] [Airport symbol] (AD) .... DXB
Dubbo [New South Wales] [Airport symbol] (AD) .... DBO
Duck (VRA) .... dc
Duisburg [Germany] [Airport symbol] (AD) .... DUI
Duluth [Minnesota-Superior, Wisconsin] [Airport symbol] (AD) .... DLH
Dumpu [New Guinea] [Airport symbol] (AD) .... DPU
Duotone (VRA) .... DUTN
Duplicate (VRA) .... dup
Dwelling (VRA) .... dwl
Dye Transfer Print (VRA) .... DYTRPT
Dynamic Bandwidth Allocation [Computer science] .... DBA
Dynamic HTML [HyperText Markup Language] [Computer science] .... dHTML
Dynamic Modelling System (AIE) .... DMS

E
By Meaning

E Magazine [*A publication*] (BRI) .... E Mag
Eagle Air [*ICAO designator*] (AD) .... IS
Eagle Aviation [*ICAO designator*] (AD) .... EX
Eagle Commuter Airlines [*ICAO designator*] (AD) .... EE
Early (VRA) .... ea
Early Childhood Education Journal [*A publication*] (BRI) .... ECEJ
Early to Mid-Holocene Transition .... EMHT
Earnings before Interest, Taxes, Depreciation, and Amortization [*Investment term*] (DFIT) .... EBITA
Earthenware (VRA) .... erthwr
Earthwork (VRA) .... erthwk
East Anglian Examinations Board (AIE) .... EAEB
East Anglian Regional Advisory Council for Further Education (AIE) .... EARAC
East Coast Airlines [*ICAO designator*] (AD) .... UN
East Hampton Air [*ICAO designator*] (AD) .... IN
East Midland Regional Advisory Committee on Special Education [*British*] (AIE) .... EMRACSE
East Midlands Education Union [*British*] (AIE) .... EMEU
Eastern Airlines [*ICAO designator*] (AD) .... RI
Eastern Group of Painters, Montreal [*1938*] [*Canada*] (NGC) .... EGP
Eastern Region Teacher Education Consortium (AIE) .... ERTEC
Eastern Upper Peninsula [*Michigan*] .... EUP
Eastman Kodak Inst. Print Film (VRA) .... EKIP
Easton [*Maryland*] [*Airport symbol*] (AD) .... ESN
East-West Airlines [*ICAO designator*] (AD) .... EW
Ebolowa [*Cameroon*] [*Airport symbol*] (AD) .... EBW
Ebonized (VRA) .... ebn
Ebony (VRA) .... ebn
Ecclesiastical (VRA) .... eccles
Ecology and Evolutionary Biology [*A discipline division*] .... EEB
Economic Awareness Teacher Training (AIE) .... EcATT
Economic Dislocation and Worker Adjustment Assistance Act of 1988 (WYGK) .... EDWAAA
Economic Geography [*A publication*] (BRI) .... EG
Economic Journal [*A publication*] (BRI) .... Econ J
Economics (DD) .... Econ
Economist [*A publication*] (BRI) .... Econ
Ecosystem Processes and Effects Branch [*Army*] .... EPEB
Ecuador (VRA) .... Ecu
Ecumenical Review [*A publication*] (BRI) .... ER
Edition (VRA) .... ed
Education (DD) .... Ed
Education (VRA) .... educ
Education Association (AIE) .... EA
Education Excellence Partnership .... EEP
Education for All Handicapped Children Act (AIE) .... EHA
Education for Enterprise Network (AIE) .... EEN
Education in Personal Relationships (AIE) .... EPR
Education in Science (AIE) .... EIS
Education Law Advisers Service (AIE) .... ELAS
Education Learning Services (AIE) .... ELS
Education Network for Environment and Development (AIE) .... ENED
Education Reform Act [*1988*] (AIE) .... ERA
Education Research Branch (AIE) .... ERB
Education Service Advisory Committee (AIE) .... ESAC
Education Service of the Plastics Industry (AIE) .... ESPI
Education Support Staff (AIE) .... ESS
Education Technology and Equipment Manufacturing Association (AIE) .... ETEMA
Educational Advice Service Project (AIE) .... EASP
Educational Broadcasting Services Trust (AIE) .... EBST
Educational Counselling Service [*British Council*] (AIE) .... ECS
Educational Forum [*A publication*] (BRI) .... Ed F
Educational Grants Advisory Service (AIE) .... EGAS
Educational Insights .... EI
Educational Leadership [*A publication*] (BRI) .... EL
Educational Priority Indices (AIE) .... EPI
Educational Studies [*A publication*] (BRI) .... ES
Educational Technology and Language Learning (AIE) .... ETLL
Educational Theory [*A publication*] (BRI) .... Ed Theory
Educational Workers' International (AIE) .... EWI
Educators of Library Media Specialists Section [*American Association of School Librarians*] [*American Library Association*] .... ELMSS
Effigy (VRA) .... efg
Eglin Air Force Base [*Florida*] [*Airport symbol*] (AD) .... VPS
Egypt (VRA) .... Egy
Egyptair [*ICAO designator*] (AD) .... MS
Eighteenth-Century Studies [*A publication*] (BRI) .... Eight-C St
Eilat [*Israel*] [*Airport symbol*] (AD) .... EIT
EJA/Newport [*ICAO designator*] (AD) .... NF
Ektachrome (VRA) .... EKT
El Aaiun [*Morocco*] [*Airport symbol*] (AD) .... EUN
El Adem [*Libya*] [*Airport symbol*] (AD) .... ELE
El Al Israel Airlines [*ICAO designator*] (AD) .... LY
El Arish [*Egypt*] [*Airport symbol*] (AD) .... EAH
El Dorado [*Venezuela*] [*Airport symbol*] (AD) .... EOR
El Golea [*Algeria*] [*Airport symbol*] (AD) .... ELG
El Qahira [*Cairo*] [*Egyptian Arabic*] (AD) .... Qahira
El Salvador (VRA) .... E Sal
Elder (VRA) .... eld
Elective Repeat Cesarean Section [*Obstetrics*] .... ERCS
Electrical Engineering (DD) .... EEng
Electrical Supply Industry Training Committee (AIE) .... ESITC
Electrohydrodynamic Convection [*Physics*] .... EHC
Electrolytic-in-Process-Dressing [*Optics manufacturing*] (RDA) .... ELID
Electromagnetic Dent Removal [*Aviation*] .... EDR
Electronic (VRA) .... elctr
Electronic Access Project .... EAP
Electronic Access to Medieval Manuscripts .... EAMM
Electronic Actuation System .... EAS
Electronic Check Presentment [*Finance*] .... ECP
[*The*] **Electronic Communications Privacy Act** .... ECPH
Electronic Document Delivery: Integrated Solutions [*Project*] (AIE) .... EDDIS
Electronic Engineering (DD) .... ElEng
Electronic Mail [*Computer science*] .... e-mail
Electro-Optic/Infrared (RDA) .... EO/IR
Electroplate (VRA) .... elctrpl
Electrostatic Print (VRA) .... ELSTPT
Element (VRA) .... elem
Elevation (VRA) .... elv
Elizabeth City [*North Carolina*] [*Airport symbol*] (AD) .... ECG
Elmwood (VRA) .... elmwd
Elvis Presley Enterprises .... EPE
Embossed (VRA) .... embs
Embrasure (VRA) .... embrs
Embroidery (VRA) .... embr
Emerald (VRA) .... emrl
Emerald Airlines [*ICAO designator*] (AD) .... OD
Emergency Advisory Committee for Political Defense .... EACPD
Emergency Librarian [*A publication*] (BRI) .... Emerg Lib
Emerging and Reemerging Infectious Diseases [*Medicine*] .... ERID
Emerging Company Marketplace (DFIT) .... ECM
Emirates Airlines [*ICAO designator*] (AD) .... EX
Emotional and Behavioural Difficulties (AIE) .... EBD
Emperor (VRA) .... emp
Empire Airlines [*ICAO designator*] (AD) .... EM
Empire Airlines [*ICAO designator*] (AD) .... UR
Employee Development and Assistance Programme (AIE) .... EDAP
Employee Educational Assistance Act of 1978 (WYGK) .... EEAA
Employee Home Ownership Plan [*Human resources*] (WYGK) .... EHOP
Employee Involvement [*Human resources*] (WYGK) .... EI
Employers' Perceptions of Colleges (AIE) .... EPOC
Employment and Enterprise Group (AIE) .... EEG
Employment Market Research Unit (AIE) .... EMRU
Employment Rehabilitation Divisional Manager (AIE) .... ERDM
Employment Relations Resource Centre [*British*] (AIE) .... ERRC
Emulsion (VRA) .... eml
En Nahud [*Sudan*] [*Airport symbol*] (AD) .... NUD
Enamel (VRA) .... enl
Encaustic (VRA) .... enc
End-of-File Mark [*Computer science*] .... EOF mark
End-of-Treatment Response [*Medicine*] .... ETR
Endogenous Retrovirus .... ERV
Endolymphatic Sac Tumors [*Oncology*] .... ELST
Endoscopic Ultrasonography [*Medicine*] .... EUS
Energy Journal [*A publication*] (BRI) .... En Jnl
Energy Saving Trust (AIE) .... EST
Energy Sciences Network [*Department of Energy*] .... ESnet
Engineering (DD) .... eng
Engineering & Business (DD) .... Eng&Bus
Engineering Careers Information Service (AIE) .... ECIS
Engineering Science (DD) .... EngSc

Engineering Technology (DD) .... EngTech
England (VRA) .... Eng
English (DD) .... Engl
English & American Literature Section [Association of College and Research
 Libraries] [American Library Association] .... EALS
English for Occupational Purposes (AIE) .... EOP
English Historical Review [A publication] (BRI) .... EHR
English Journal [A publication] (BRI) .... EJ
English Literature in Transition 1880-1920 [A publication] (BRI) .... ELT
English Teachers in University Departments of Education (AIE) .... ETUDE
Engraving (VRA) .... engr
Enhanced Cubic Grain [Photography] .... ECB
Enhanced Data Output Dynamic Access Random [Computer
 science] .... EDO DRAM
Enhanced Integral Drive Electronics (DOM) .... EIDE
Enhanced Land Warrior [Military] (RDA) .... ELW
Enhanced Metafile [Computer science] .... EMF
Enlargement (VRA) .... enlgmnt
Enniskillen [Northern Ireland] [Airport symbol] (AD) ...... ENK
Enrichment Science and Technology for Exceptionally Able and Motivated
 Pupils (AIE) .... ESTEAM
Ensemble (VRA) .... ensb
Entablature (VRA) .... entbl
Enterprise Airlines [ICAO designator] (AD) .... BE
Enterprise and Deregulation Unit (AIE) .... EDU
Enterprise Development Programme [University of Glasgow] (AIE) .... EDP
Enterprise Learning through Information Technology [University of
 Durham] (AIE) .... ELITE
Entertainment Software Rating Board .... ESRB
Entertainment Weekly [A publication] (BRI) .... Ent W
Entrance (VRA) .... entr
Environment [A publication] (BRI) .... Env
Environment (VRA) .... envir
Environment, Conservation, and Hunting Outreach [An association] .... ECHO
Environmental (DD) .... envirl
Environmental Laboratory Advisory Board [Environmental Protection
 Agency] .... ELAB
Environmental Processes and Effects Division [Army] ...... EPED
Environmental Resources Management .... ERM
Environmental Science Education (AIE) .... ESE
Epicatechin Gallate [Biochemistry] .... ECG
Epigallocatechin [Biochemistry] .... EGC
Epileptic (AIE) .... EP
Equine Morbillivirus .... EMV
Equipment (DD) .... equip
Erigavo [Somalia] [Airport symbol] (AD) .... ERA
Eromanga [New Hebrides] [Airport symbol] (AD) .... ERG
Error Correction and Control .... ECC
Erzincan [Turkey] [Airport symbol] (AD) .... ERC
Especially (VRA) .... esp
Esplanade (DD) .... Espl
Essays on Canadian Writing [A publication] (BRI) .... Essays CW
Established (VRA) .... est
Establishing Multimedia Authoring Skills in Higher Education (AIE) ...... EMASHE
Estonia (VRA) .... Esto
Etching (VRA) .... etch
Ethiopia (VRA) .... Eth
Ethiopian Airlines [ICAO designator] (AD) .... ET
Etruria (VRA) .... Etru
Eureka Aero Industries [ICAO designator] (AD) .... IK

Europe (VRA) .... Eur
Europe Aero Service [ICAO designator] (AD) .... EY
European Association of Users of Satellites in Training and Education
 Programmes (AIE) .... EUROSTEP
European Bone Marrow Transplantation .... EBMT
European Bureau of Library Information and Documentation
 Associations (AIE) .... EBLIDA
European Community Youth Exchange Bureau (AIE) .... ECYEB
European Council on Refugees and Exiles .... ECRE
European Information Centre (AIE) .... EIC
European Institute of Education and Social Policy (AIE) .... EIESP
European Laboratory for Particle Physics .... CERN
European Learning Technology Association (AIE) .... ELTA
European Parent Association (AIE) .... EPA
European Unified Research on Educational Development (AIE) .... EURED
European University Institute [Florence, Italy] (AIE) .... EUI
Evaluation Agree [Canada] .... EA
Evaluation of Testing in Schools Project (AIE) .... ETSP
Evangelist (VRA) .... evang
Event Verification System [Technology that encripts time and location on
 video recordings] .... EVS
Event-Related Optical Signal [Imaging science] .... EROS
Evergreen Helicopters of Alaska [ICAO designator] (AD) .... OT
Every Member Canvas [Fundraising] .... EMC
Every Member Visit [Fundraising] .... EMV
Examining and Validating Body (AIE) .... EVB
Example (VRA) .... ex
Exceptional Cancer Patients [Therapy program] .... ECaP
Exceptional Children [A publication] (BRI) .... Ex Child
Exchangeable Body Sodium (AD) .... Na
Ex-Dividend and Sales in Full [Investment term] (DFIT) .... Y
Exec Express [ICAO designator] (AD) .... AD
Executive (DD) .... exec
Executive Management Program (DD) .... EMP
Executive Master's of Business Administration (RDA) ..... ExMBA
Executive Master's of Science in Science and Technology
 Commercialization (RDA) .... ExMSE
Executive Transportation [ICAO designator] (AD) .... XT
Exhibit (VRA) .... exh
Exodus Online Services [Computer science] .... EOS
Explicit Call Transfer [Telecommunications] (DOM) .... ECT
Exploration (DD) .... explor
Exposition (VRA) .... expo
Exposure (VRA) .... exp
Express Air [ICAO designator] (AD) .... FX
Express Airways [ICAO designator] (AD) .... CH
Expressway (DD) .... Expy
Extended Attribute Record [Computer science] (DOM) .... XAR
Extended Care Facility (WYGK) .... ECF
Extended Graphics Adapter [Computer science] (DOM) .... XGA
Extended Task Analysis Procedure [Education] (AIE) .... ETAP
Extended-Height-to-Diameter [Aviation] .... EHD
Extension (VRA) .... extns
Exterior (VRA) .... ext
Extra Long (WDMC) XL
Extrabold [Type] (WDMC) .... xbld
Extra-Long Shot (WDMC) .... XLS
Extra-Mural (AIE) .... EM
Extrapolation [A publication] (BRI) .... Ext
Eyesafe LASER Rangefinder (RDA) .... ELRF

F
By Meaning

Fabric (VRA) .... fab
Fabrication and Architecture of Single-Electron Memories [*Computer Science*] .... FASEM
Fabricators and Manufacturers Association .... FMA
Facade (VRA) .... fac
Face-to-Face [*Fundraising*] F2F
Factory (VRA) .... fact
Faculty Review Group [*Education*] (AIE) .... FRG
Fagurholsmyri [*Iceland*] [*Airport symbol*] (AD) .... FAG
Faience (VRA) .... fai
Failure Analysis and Associates (RDA) .... FaAA
Falcon Airlines [*ICAO designator*] (AD) .... AB
Fall River-New Bedford [*Massachusetts*] [*Airport symbol*] (AD) ...... EWB
Familial Pure Depressive Disease .... FPDD
Familial Uveal Melanoma [*Oncology*] .... FUM
Families in Society [*A publication*] (BRI) .... Fam in Soc
Family and Medical Leave Act of 1993 (WYGK) .... FMLA
Family Care Program [*Insurance*] (WYGK) .... FCP
Family Education Network [*Computer science*] .... FEN
Family Radio Service .... FRS
Family Relations [*A publication*] (BRI) .... Fam Relat
Family Support Act of 1988 (WYGK) .... FSA
Fanfare [*A publication*] (BRI) .... FF
Far Eastern Air Transport [*ICAO designator*] (AD) .... EF
Far Eastern Economic Review [*A publication*] (BRI) .... FEER
Far Infrared and Submillimeter Space Telescope [*Proposed European*] ...... FIRST
Far Infrared Space Telescope .... FIRST
Faridpur [*Bangladesh*] [*Airport symbol*] (AD) .... FDP
Farnesyltransferase [*An enzyme*] .... FTase
Fascimile (VRA) .... fasc
Faucett [*ICAO designator*] (AD) .... CF
Fault Detection and Isolation Subsystem (RDA) .... FDIS
Favrile Glass (VRA) .... fvrl gls
Faya Largeau [*Chad*] [*Airport symbol*] (AD) .... FYA
Feathers (VRA) .... fthrs
Federal Defense Laboratory Diversification Program (RDA) .... FDLDP
Federal Probation [*A publication*] (BRI) .... Fed Prob
Federation of Fly Fishers .... FFF
Federation of Ontario Naturalists [*Canada*] .... FON
Federation of Professional Officers Association (AIE) .... FPOA
Federation of the Association of College Lecturers in Scotland (AIE) ...... FACLS
Fellow Association for Healthcare Philanthropy .... FAHP
Fellow of Business Administration (DD) .... FBA
Fellow of Commercial Actuaries (DD) .... FCommA
Fellow of the Administration Association (DD) .... FAdmA
Fellow of the American College of Trial Lawyers (DD) .... FACTL
Fellow of the Association of Certified Accountants (DD) .... FCCA
Fellow of the Canadian Academy of Engineering (DD) .... FCAE
Fellow of the Canadian Certified General Accountants Association (DD) ...... FCGA
Fellow of the Canadian College of Physicians (DD) .... FCCP
Fellow of the Canadian Credit Union Institute (DD) .... FCCUI
Fellow of the Canadian Institute of Chemistry (DD) .... FCIC
Fellow of the Canadian Securities Institute (DD) .... FCSI
Fellow of the Canadian Society of Civil Engineers (DD) .... FCSCE
Fellow of the Casualty Actuarial Science (DD) .... FCAS
Fellow of the Chartered Institute of Bankers (DD) .... FCIB
Fellow of the Chartered Institute of Marketing (DD) .... FCIM
Fellow of the College of Family Physicians (DD) .... FCFP
Fellow of the College of Physicians (DD) .... FCP
Fellow of the English Association of Accountants and Auditors (DD) .... FEAA
Fellow of the English Association of Corporate Secretaries (DD) .... FEAS
Fellow of the Guild of Industrial, Commercial, & Institutional Accounts (DD) ...... FICIA
Fellow of the Hotel and Catering International Management Association (DD) ...... FHIMA
Fellow of the Institute of Canadian Bankers (DD) .... FICB
Fellow of the Institute of Certified Administrative Managers (DD) .... FCAM
Fellow of the Institute of Certified Management Consultants (DD) .... FCMC
Fellow of the Institute of Chartered Secretaries and Administrators (DD) ...... FCIS
Fellow of the Institute of Management (DD) .... FIMgt
Fellow of the Institute of Management Consultants (DD) .... FMC
Fellow of the Institute of Materials (DD) .... FIM
Fellow of the Institute of Physics (DD) .... FInstP
Fellow of the Institution of Electrical Engineers (DD) .... FIEE

Fellow of the International Institute of Arts and Letters, Zurich [*1931*] (NGC) .... FIAL
Fellow of the Life Management Institute (DD) .... FLMI
Fellow of the Ontario Hostelry Institute [*Canada*] (DD) .... FHI
Fellow of the Ontario Teachers' Federation [*Canada*] (DD) .... FOTF
Fellow of the Real Estate Institute (DD) .... FRI
Fellow of the Royal Canadian Geographical Society (DD) .... FRCGS
Fellow of the Royal College of Medicine [*Canada*] (DD) .... FRCM
Fellow of the Royal College of Physicians of Canada (DD) .... FRCPC
Fellow of the Royal College of Surgeons of Canada (DD) .... FRCSC
Fellow of the Royal Institute of Chartered Surveyors [*Canada*] (DD) .... FRICS
Fellow of the Royal Society of Arts, London [*1909, founded 1754 as Society of Arts*] (NGC) .... FRSA
Fellow of the Royal Society of London [*1660*] (NGC) .... FRS
Fellow of the Society of Accountants and Auditors (DD) .... FSAA
Fellow of the Society of Management Accountants of Canada (DD) .... FCMA
Fellow of the Society of Management Accountants of Canada (DD) .... FSMAC
Fellow of the Surveyors' Institution (DD) .... FSI
Fellow of Trust Institute (DD) .... FTI
Felt (VRA) .... flt
Female (DD) .... f
Female Bowhunter Fingers [*International Bowhunting Organization*] [*Class equipment*] .... FBF
Female Seniors [*International Bowhunting Organization*] [*Class Equipment*] ..... FSR
Femtosecond Photoelectron Spectroscopy .... FPES
Fenestration (VRA) .... fnstr
Feng Yang-Pyongyang [*North Korea*] [*Airport symbol*] (AD) .... FNJ
Ferndale Internet Experiment [*Computer science*] .... FIX
Fetal Protection Policy [*Insurance*] (WYGK) .... FPP
Fez [*Morocco*] [*Airport symbol*] (AD) .... FEZ
Fiber (VRA) .... fbr
Fiberboard (VRA) .... fibd
Fiberglass (VRA) .... fibgl
Fiber-Optic Digital Device Interface [*Computer science*] .... FDDI
Fibroblast Growth-Factor Receptor [*Biochemistry*] .... FGFR
Fiction International [*A publication*] (BRI) .... Fic Int
Field Emission Display .... FED
Field Ordering Officer [*Army*] (RDA) .... FOO
Figure (VRA) .... fig
Fiji Air [*ICAO designator*] (AD) .... PC
Film Comment [*A publication*] (BRI) .... FC
Film Criticism [*A publication*] (BRI) .... Film Cr
Film Quarterly [*A publication*] (BRI) .... FQ
Films in Review [*A publication*] (BRI) .... FIR
Filmstrip (VRA) .... fs
Finance (DD) .... fin
Financial (DD) .... finl
Financial Accounting Standards Board .... FASB
Financial and Accounting Services Branch (AIE) .... FASB
Financial Executives Institute of Canada (DD) .... FEI
Financial Management .... FinlMgmt
Financial Services Technical Consortium .... FSTC
Fine Gardening [*A publication*] (BRI) .... Fine Gard
Fine Homebuilding [*A publication*] (BRI) .... FHB
Fingerprint Identification Unit [*Sony Corp.*] .... FIU
Finish (VRA) .... fin
Finished (VRA) .... fin
Finland (VRA) .... Finl
Finnair [*ICAO designator*] (AD) .... AY
Finnsnes [*Norway*] [*Airport symbol*] (AD) .... FNE
Fire Control Electronics Unit [*Military*] (RDA) .... FCEU
Firecracker Alternative Book [*Award Program*] .... FAB
Fired (VRA) .... frd
First Air [*ICAO designator*] (AD) .... HF
First Certificate in English [*Cambridge University*] [*British*] (AIE) ...... FCE
Firwood (VRA) .... firwd
Fitchburg [*Massachusetts*] [*Airport symbol*] (AD) .... FIT
Fixative (VRA) .... fxt
Fixed Time Printing Mode [*Photography*] .... FTPM
Fixed-Payment Mortgage (DFIT) .... FPM
Flamboyant (VRA) .... flamby
Flamenco Airlines [*ICAO designator*] (AD) .... FK
Flanders (VRA) .... Fland
Flandre Air [*ICAO designator*] (AD) IX
Flannel (VRA) .... flan
Flashlamp-Pumped Dye LASER .... FPDL

Flat-Panel Display [*Instrumentation*] .... FPD
Flemish (VRA) .... Flem
Flexible Benefits Program [*Human resources*] (WYGK) .... FBP
Flocked (VRA) .... flok
Floor (DD) .... fl
Floor (VRA) .... flr
Floppy Drive High Density [*Computer science*] .... FDHD
Floriano [*Brazil*] [*Airport symbol*] (AD) .... FLB
Florida Airlines and Air South [*ICAO designator*] (AD) .... FE
Florida Commuter [*ICAO designator*] (AD) .... PG
Flourescent (VRA) .... flour
Flourescent Discharge Tube [*Technology*] .... FDT
Flourished (VRA) .... fl
Flugfelag Nordurlands [*Northlands Air*] [*ICAO designator*] (AD) .... UI
Flugfelag-Icelandair [*ICAO designator*] (AD) .... FI
Fluorescent Discharge Tube [*Panasonic*] .... FDT
Flying [*A publication*] (BRI) .... Fly
Flying Buttress (VRA) .... fly butr
Flying Infrared Signature Technology Aircraft [*Air Force*] .... FISTA II
Flying Needle [*A publication*] (BRI) .... Fly Needle
Foam (VRA) .... fm
Focused Appendix Computed Tomography [*Medicine*] .... FACT
Foggia [*Italy*] [*Airport symbol*] (AD) .... FOG
Folklore [*A publication*] (BRI) .... Folkl
Follicle-Associated Epithelium [*Immunology*] .... FAE
Fonte Boa [*Brazil*] [*Airport symbol*] (AD) .... FBA
Food Science (DD) .... FoodSc
Forces Mobile Command [*Canada*] (DD) .... FMC
Foreground (VRA) .... forgr
Foreign Affairs [*A publication*] (BRI) .... For Aff
Foreign Language Use in Northern Commerce and Industry (AIE) .... FLUNCI
Foreign Languages at Work (AIE) .... FLAW
Foreign Languages for Lower Attaining Pupils [*Project*] (AIE) .... FLLAP
Foreign Service (DD) .... ForServ
Foreshorten (VRA) .... foresh
Forestry Training Council (AIE) .... FTC
Forged (VRA) .... forg
Forli [*Italy*] [*Airport symbol*] (AD) .... FRL
Form (VRA) .... form
Form/Genre .... f/g
Forte Princip [*Brazil*] [*Airport symbol*] (AD) .... FDB
Fortification (VRA) .... ft
Forum Europeen de l'Orientation Academique (AIE) .... FEDORA
Forum for the Advancement of Educational Therapy (AIE) .... FAET
Forward Logistical Element [*Military*] .... FLE
Forward Sortation Area [*Mailing technique*] .... FSA
Fossil (VRA) .... fsl
Foumban [*Cameroon*] [*Airport symbol*] (AD) .... FOM
Found Object (VRA) .... fndobj
Foundation (VRA) .... fdtn
Foundation for Education Business Partnerships (AIE) .... FEBP
Foundation for Information Technology in Local Government (AIE) .... FITLOG

Foundations of Communication and Language (AIE) .... FOCAL
Fountain (VRA) .... fount
Four by Five Inches (VRA) .... FRFV
Four Stroke-Direct Injection [*Engine*] (RDA) 4SDI
Fox Glacier [*New Zealand*] [*Airport symbol*] (AD) .... FGL
Fragment (VRA) .... frag
Frame (VRA) .... fra
Frames Per Second [*Electronics*] .... fps
France (VRA) .... Fr
Frankfurt [*Kentucky*] [*Airport symbol*] (AD) .... FFT
Frederick A. Praeger (AD) .... Praeger
Frederick Post Drafting Equipment (AD) .... POST
Free-Floating Thrombus [*Medicine*] .... FFT
Freephone Supplementary Service [*Telecommunications*] (DOM) .... FPH
Freeway (DD) .... Fwy
Freeze-Fracture Transmission Electron Microscopy .... FF-TEM
Frejus [*France*] [*Airport symbol*] (AD) .... FRJ
French Review [*A publication*] (BRI) .... FR
French Somaliland (VRA) .... Fr Soma
Fresco (VRA) .... frsc
Fria [*Guinea*] [*Airport symbol*] (AD) .... FIG
Friend of a Friend .... FOAF
Friends Involved in Sportfishing Heritage .... FISH
Friends of Libraries USA [*American Library Association*] .... FOLUSA
Frieze (VRA) .... frz
Frisia Luftverkehr [*ICAO designator*] (AD) .... FV
From (VRA) .... fr
Front (VRA) .... fnt
Frontispiece (VRA) .... fntpc
Fruitwood (VRA) .... frutwd
Ft. Derik [*Mauritania*] [*Airport symbol*] (AD) .... FGD
Ft. Johnson [*Malawi*] [*Airport symbol*] (AD) .... FJO
Ft. Rousset [*Congo*] [*Airport symbol*] (AD) .... FTX
Funafuti Atoll [*Ellice Islands*] [*Airport symbol*] (AD) .... FUN
Functional Acquisition Specialist [*Army*] (RDA) .... FAS
Functional Feeding Groups [*Ecology*] .... FFG
Functionalized Monolayers on Mesoporous Supports [*Organic chemistry*] .... FMMS
Fundacion [*Colombia*] [*Airport symbol*] (AD) .... FDA
Furniture (VRA) .... furn
Furniture and Fixtures (DFIT) .... F&F
Further and Adult Council for Art and Design Education (AIE) .... FACADE
Further Education Information Service (AIE) .... FEIS
Further Education Marketing Unit (AIE) .... FEMU
Further Education Revenue Account Survey (AIE) .... FERAS
Further Education Staff College (AIE) .... FESC
Further Education Work Experience Co-Ordinator (AIE) .... FEWEC
Fuse (VRA) .... fus
Futaleufu [*Chile*] [*Airport symbol*] (AD) .... FFU
Futurism (VRA) .... futr
Futurist [*A publication*] (BRI) .... Fut
Fuze Engineering Standardization Working Group [*Military*] (RDA) .... FESWG

G
By Meaning

Gach Saran [*Iran*] [*Airport symbol*] (AD) .... GAS
Gadolinium Aluminium Perovskite [*Inorganic chemistry*] .... GAP
Gage .... GA
Gagnoa [*Ivory Coast*] [*Airport symbol*] (AD) .... GGQ
Gagnon [*Quebec*] [*Airport symbol*] (AD) .... YNK
Gainesville [*Georgia*] [*Airport symbol*] (AD) .... GVL
Gal Oya [*Ceylon*] [*Airport symbol*] (AD) .... GOY
Galatians [*New Testament book*] .... Ga
Galileo [*NASA*] .... GLL
Gallery (VRA) .... gall
Gallium Arsenide [*Phosphide Semiconductor*] .... GAASD
Galvanized (VRA) .... galv
Gambia Air Shuttle [*ICAO designator*] (AD) .... GO
Gamboma [*Congo*] [*Airport symbol*] (AD) .... GMM
Game Oriented Activities for Learning (AIE) .... GOAL
Gap Filler/Reporting Post .... GFRP
Garbage: The Independent Environmental Quarterly [*A publication*] (BRI) .... Garbage
Garden (VRA) .... gard
Gardens (DD) .... Gdns
Garment (VRA) .... grmt
Garuda Indonesian Airways [*ICAO designator*] (AD) .... GA
Gas Anti-Solvent [*Chemical engineering*] .... GAS
Gas Chromatography and Mass Spectroscopy .... GCMS
Gas Gathering Data File [*Phillips Petroleum*] .... GGDF
Gas-Phase Electron Diffraction [*Physics*] .... GED
Gateway (VRA) .... gtwy
Gateway to Care .... GTC
Gateway to Educational Materials .... GEM
GC Optronics, Inc. .... GCO
Gedaref [*Sudan*] [*Airport symbol*] (AD) .... GSU
Geelong Air Travel [*ICAO designator*] (AD) .... FK
Geinsheim Staging Activity .... GSA
Gelatin (VRA) .... gel
Gelatin Glass Negative (VRA) .... GGNG
Gelatin Silver Print (VRA) .... SGPT
Gem State Airlines [*ICAO designator*] (AD) .... GG
General (VRA) .... gen
General American Life Insurance Co. .... GALIC
General Areas of Competence [*Education*] (AIE) .... GAC
General Delivery (DD) .... GD
General Dynamics Astronautics .... GDA
General Dynamics, Convair .... GDC
General Electric Telemetering and Control .... GETAC
General Estimating Equation [*Mathematics*] .... GEE
General Headquarters Exercise .... GHQS
General Obligation Bonds [*Finance*] .... GOB
General Officer Steering Group .... GOSG
General Receptor for Phosphoinositide [*Biochemistry*] .... GRP
General School Budget (AIE) .... GSB
General Secretariat .... GS
General Technical Services, Inc. .... GTS
Generalized Hadamand Matrix .... GH-MATRIX
Generations [*A publication*] (BRI) .... Generation
Genetic Resources Action International [*Spain*] .... GRAIN
Genetics Institute, Inc. .... GI
Geographical [*A publication*] (BRI) .... Geog
Geographical Association Package Exchange (AIE) .... GAPE
Geographical Journal [*A publication*] (BRI) .... GJ
Geography (DD) .... Geog
Geological Science (DD) .... GeolSci
Geology (DD) .... Geol
Geomagnetic Electrorinetograph .... GER
Geophysics (DD) .... Geoph
Georgetown [*Delaware*] [*Airport symbol*] (AD) .... GED
Georgetown [*Guyana*] [*Airport symbol*] (AD) .... GRG
Georgia Hospital Computer Group .... GHCP
Georgia Review [*A publication*] (BRI) .... Ga R
Georgian Bay [*ICAO designator*] (AD) .... UD
Georgians for Preservation Action [*An association*] .... GPA
Geostatistical Environmental Assessment Software [*US Environmental Protection Agency*] .... GEO-EAS
Geriatric-Care Manager .... GCM
German Army Material Office .... GAMO
German Army Office .... GAO
German Association for Applied Mathematics and Mechanics .... GAMM
German Quarterly [*A publication*] (BRI) .... Ger Q
Germany (VRA) .... Ger
Gerstmann-Straussler-Sheinker [*Disease*] .... GSS
Gesellschaft Fuer Biochemie Und Molekularbiologie [*Germany*] .... GBM
Gesso (VRA) .... ges
Get a Life .... GAL
Ghana Airways [*ICAO designator*] (AD) .... GH
Ghanzi [*Botswana*] [*Airport symbol*] (AD) .... GNZ
Ghinnir [*Ethiopia*] [*Airport symbol*] (AD) .... GNN
Ghuraf [*South Arabia*] [*Airport symbol*] (AD) .... GFX
Giant Gaseous Protoplanet [*Planetary science*] .... GGPP
Gilbues [*Brazil*] [*Airport symbol*] (AD) .... GLB
Gilding (VRA) .... glt
Gilgit [*Pakistan*] [*Airport symbol*] (AD) .... GIL
Gilt (VRA) .... glt
Girls' Education in Mathematics, Science, and Technology (AIE) .... GEMSAT
Gissel Bargaining Order [*Labor relations*] (WYGK) .... GBO
Gladewater-Kilgore-Longview [*Texas*] [*Airport symbol*] (AD) .... GGG
Glasgow College of Technology (AIE) .... GCT
Glass (VRA) .... gls
Glass Training Ltd. (AIE) .... GTL
Glassine (VRA) .... glsn
Glaze (VRA) .... glz
Glazed (VRA) .... glz
Glens Falls [*New York*] [*Airport symbol*] (AD) .... GFL
Glitter (VRA) .... glit
Global Command and Control System .... GCCS
Global Data Management System .... GDMS
Global Distribution Systems .... GDS
Global Exchange, Inc. .... GXI
Global Positioning System/Inertial Navigation System [*Air Force*] .... GPS/INS
Global Roaming Internet Connection [*Computer science*] .... GRIC
Global Simulation Control Center .... GSCC
Gloss (VRA) .... glo
Glutamate Receptor Interacting Protein [*Neurochemistry*] .... GRIP
Glyph (VRA) .... gly
Glypotootheca (VRA) .... glypto
Goba [*Ehtiopia*] [*Airport symbol*] (AD) .... GOB
Gold (VRA) .... go
Gold Leaf (VRA) .... go lf
Golden West [*ICAO designator*] (AD) .... VF
Golden West Airlines [*ICAO designator*] (AD) .... GW
Goose Management Unit .... GMU
Gore [*New Zealand*] [*Airport symbol*] (AD) .... GOE
Gothic (VRA) .... Goth
Gouache (VRA) .... gou
Gould Belt [*Galactic science*] .... GB
Governesses Benevolent Institute [*British*] (AIE) .... GBI
Government (VRA) .... gov
Government (DD) .... govt
Government Computer News .... GCN
Government Concept of Operations (RDA) .... GCO
Government Furnished Repair Parts .... GFRP
Government Information Subcommittee [*American Library Association*] .... GIS
Government of Tunisia .... GOT
Governor (DD) .... gov
GPC [*General Purpose Computer*] **Memory** .... G-MEM
G-Protein-Coupled Receptor [*Biochemistry*] .... GPCR
GPS [*Global Positioning System*] **Guidance Package** .... GGP
Graded Assessment in Design and Technology (AIE) .... GADT
Graded Assessment in Science Project (AIE) .... GASP
Graded Levels of Achievement in Foreign Language Learning (AIE) .... GLAFLI
Graduate Diploma (DD) .... GDip
Graduate Diploma in Public Accountancy (DD) .... GDPA
Graduate Diploma in Public Accounting (DD) .... GDPA
Graduate Division of Applied Mathematics .... GDAM
Graduate Employment and Training Survey (AIE) .... GET
Graduate Search by Computer after Personal Evaluation (AIE) .... GRADSCOPE
Graduated Payment Mortgage (DFIT) .... Jeep
Graft-Versus Host Disease [*Immunology*] .... GvHD
Graft-Versus-Leukemia [*Medicine*] .... GvL
Grahamstown [*South Africa*] [*Airport symbol*] (AD) .... GHO
Grajau [*Brazil*] [*Airport symbol*] (AD) .... GRU
Grand Canyon Airlines [*ICAO designator*] (AD) .... YE
Grand Cross, St. Lazarus of Jerusalem (DD) .... GCLJ
Grand Officier de l'Ordre National du Quebec [*Canada*] (DD) .... GOONQ

Grand Traverse Area Sportfishing Association [*Michigan*] .... GTASFA
Grand Traverse Bay Watershed Initiative .... GTBWI
Grand Unified Force .... GUF
Granite (VRA) .... gran
Grant Maintained School (AIE) .... GMS
Grant Opportunities for Academic Liaison with Industry [*National Science
   Foundation*] .... GOALI
Granular Quartz Rock (AD) .... quartzite
Granulation (VRA) .... grnln
Granville [*France*] [*Airport symbol*] (AD) .... GFR
Graphic Art Club, Toronto [*c.1903, SGA from 1912, CSGA from 1923*]
   [*Canada*] (NGC) .... GAC
Graphic Standards Management Board .... GSMB
Graphics (VRA) .... gra
Graphite (VRA) .... grph
Grass Roots Art and Community Effort [*Vermont*] .... GRACE
Gravdal [*Norway*] [*Airport symbol*] (AD) .... GVD
GRAvity PipE no. 4 [*Computer science*] GRAPE-4
Gravure (VRA) .... grv
Great Barrier Island [*New Zealand*] [*Airport symbol*] (AD) .... GTR
Great Education Reform Act [*1988*] (AIE) .... GERIACT
Great Inagua Island [*Bahamas*] [*Airport symbol*] (AD) .... IGA
Great Lakes Airlines [*ICAO designator*] (AD) .... GX
Great Lakes Aviation [*ICAO designator*] (AD) .... ZK
Great Plains Coliseum [*Lawton, OK*] .... GPC
Great Planes Area Vocational Technical School [*Oklahoma*] .... GPAVTS
Great Sierra [*ICAO designator*] (AD) .... LT
Greater London Training Board [*British*] (AIE) .... GLTB
Greater Orlando Area Legal Services [*Florida*] .... GOALS
Greater Southwest [*Ft. Worth and Dallas, Texas*] [*Airport symbol*] (AD) .... GSW
Greece (VRA) .... Gre
Green (VRA) .... grn
Green Bay Aviation [*ICAO designator*] (AD) .... HE
Green Hills Aviation [*ICAO designator*] (AD) .... NG
Greenfield [*Massachusetts*] [*Airport symbol*] (AD) .... ORE
Greenland (VRA) .... Grld
Greenwood [*Mississippi*] [*Airport symbol*] (AD) .... GNL
Grisaille (VRA) .... gris
Gronlandsfly [*ICAO designator*] (AD) .... GL
Gross Criminal Product .... GCP

Grosse Ile Nature and Land Conservancy .... GINLC
Grosseto [*Italy*] [*Airport symbol*] (AD) .... GRS
Ground (VRA) .... grd
Ground Master Measurements List .... GMML
Ground Standoff Minefield Detection System [*Military*] (RDA) .... GSTAMIDS
Ground Vehicular LASER Locator Designator [*Military*] .... G/VLL-D
Ground-Based Common Sensor .... GBCS
Grounds (DD) .... Grnds
Group (VRA) .... gp
Group (DD) .... grp
Group of Pictures [*Computer science*] .... GOP
Group Practice Health Maintenance Organization [*Insurance*] (WYGK) ..... GPHMO
Group Relations Training Association (AIE) .... GRTA
Group Universal Life Policy [*Insurance*] (DFIT) .... GULP
Growth at the Right Price .... GARP
Guajara Mirim [*Brazil*] [*Airport symbol*] (AD) .... GJM
Guam [*Marianas*] [*Airport symbol*] (AD) .... GUM
Guaranteed Overnight Delivery .... GOD
Guarapuava [*Brazil*] [*Airport symbol*] (AD) .... GPP
Guardian Weekly [*A publication*] (BRI) .... GW
Guatemala (VRA) .... Guat
Guernsey Airlines [*ICAO designator*] (AD) .... GE
Guidance and Learner Autonomy [*Project*] (AIE) .... GALA
Guided Aerial Rocket .... GAR
Guided Parafoil Aerial Delivery System .... GPADS
Guidelines for Review and Internal Development in Schools (AIE) .... GRIDS
Guinea (VRA) .... Guin
Guiratinga [*Brazil*] [*Airport symbol*] (AD) .... GUZ
Gujrat [*Pakistan*] [*Airport symbol*] (AD) .... GRT
Gulf Air [*ICAO designator*] (AD) .... GF
Gulf Universities Research Corp. .... GURC
Gull Air [*ICAO designator*] (AD) .... JI
Gulu [*Uganda*] [*Airport symbol*] (AD) .... GUU
Gum Print [*Gum bichromates*] (VRA) .... GMPT
Gun Laying RADAR .... GL RADAR
Gunner's Control and Display Panel [*Military*] (RDA) .... GCDP
Gunshot Residue [*Forensics*] .... GSR
Gusau [*Nigeria*] [*Airport symbol*] (AD) .... GSA
Guyana Airways [*ICAO designator*] (AD) .... GY
Gymnasium (VRA) .... gym

H
By Meaning

Hackers on Planet Earth [*An association*] .... HOPE
Hadag Air Seebaederflug [*ICAO designator*] (AD) .... GP
Hadley Centre Climate Model .... HCCM
[*The*] Hague [*Netherlands*] [*Airport symbol*] (AD) ...... HAG
Hair (VRA) .... hr
Hairdressing Training Board (AIE) .... HTB
Haiti Air International [*ICAO designator*] (AD) .... HC
Haiti Trans Air [*ICAO designator*] (AD) .... TV
Halden Reactor Project [*Norway*] .... HPR
Haldwani [*India*] [*Airport symbol*] (AD) .... HWN
Half-plate (VRA) .... HALF
Half-timber (VRA) .... halftmb
Halftone (VRA) .... HLFTN
Hall Effect Transducer .... HET
Hall-Effect Imaging [*Medical imaging*] .... HEI
Hamadan [*Iran*] [*Airport symbol*] (AD) .... HDM
Hamburg Airlines [*ICAO designator*] (AD) .... HX
Hamilton Technology, Inc. .... HTI
Hammel Green and Abrahamson, Inc. [*A national leader in innovative design*] .... HGA
Hammered (VRA) .... ham
Hammond's Air Service [*ICAO designator*] (AD) .... EM
Hancock-Houghton [*Michigan*] [*Airport symbol*] (AD) .. CMX
Hand Carry .... HC
Hand Colored (VRA) .... HDCOL
Hand, Foot, and Mouth [*Disease*] .... HFM
Handheld PC [*Personal Computer*] .... HPC
Handheld Standoff Minefield Detection System [*Military*] (RDA) .. HSTAMIDS
Handmade .... handmd
Handover .... H/O
Handscroll (VRA) .... handscr
Hands-on Turret Trainer [*Military*] .... HOTT
Hang Khong Vietnam [*ICAO designator*] (AD) .... VN
Hangchow [*China*] [*Airport symbol*] (AD) .... HGH
Hanging (VRA) .... hng
Hanging Scroll (VRA) .... hngscr
Hanscom Electronic Request [*for Proposals*] Bulletin Board [*Air Force*] .... HERBB
Harbor Airlines [*ICAO designator*] (AD) .... HG
Hardboard (VRA) .... hardbd
Hardware (VRA) .... hdwe
Hardware Emulation [*Computer science*] .... HEL
Hardware Emulation Layer [*Computer science*] .... HEL
Harnosand [*Sweden*] [*Airport symbol*] (AD) .... HSD
Harper's Magazine [*A publication*] (BRI) .... HM
Harrisburg-New Cumberland [*Pennsylvania*] [*Airport symbol*] (AD) .. HAR
Harstad [*Norway*] [*Airport symbol*] (AD) .... HRD
Harvard Business Review [*A publication*] (BRI) .... Har Bus R
Harvard Educational Review [*A publication*] (BRI) ...... HER
Harvard Gay & Lesbian Review [*A publication*] (BRI) .. H G & L Rev
Harvard Journal of Asiatic Studies [*A publication*] (BRI) .. HJAS
Harvard Law Review [*A publication*] (BRI) .... HLR
Harvard Pilgrim Health Care .... HPHC
Hastings Center Report [*A publication*] (BRI) .... Hast Cen R
Hatia [*Bangladesh*] [*Airport symbol*] (AD) .... HAE
Hattiesburg [*Mississippi*] [*Airport symbol*] (AD) .... HBG
Haura [*South Arabia (Yemen)*] [*Airport symbol*] (AD) .. HRA
Hautes Etudes Commerciales (DD) .... HEC
Havasu Airlines [*ICAO designator*] (AD) .... HW
Haverfordwest [*Wales*] [*Airport symbol*] (AD) .... HFW
Hawaii Imaging Fabry-Perot Interferometer .... HIFI
Hazardous Waste Management Association .... HWMA
Hazelton Air Services [*ICAO designator*] (AD) .... ZL
Head Masters' Association (AIE) .... HMA
Head of Faculty [*Education*] (AIE) .... HOF
Headway Corporate Resources .... HDWY
Health and Safety Technology Management (AIE) ...... HASTAM
[*United States*] Health Care Financing Administration .. HCFA
Health Care Purchasing Organization [*Insurance*] (WYGK) .. HPO
Health Maintenance Organization Acts of 1973 and 1988 (WYGK) .. HMOA
Health Online Service [*Computer science*] [*Medicine*] .. HOS
Heart and Estrogen/Progestin Replacement Study [*Medicine*] .. HERS
Heartsong Review [*A publication*] (BRI) .... Heartsong R
Heating Seasonal Performance Factor .... HSPF
Heavy (VRA) .... hv
Heavy Equipment Maintenance .... HEM
Height (VRA) .... ht

Heightened (VRA) .... htnd
Heights (DD) .... Hts
Held For [*Investment term*] (DFIT) .... H/F
Held for Perishable Tools .... HFPT
Held for Tool Liaison .... HFTL
Heli-Air-Monaco [*ICAO designator*] (AD) .... YO
Heliotype [*Modified collotype*] (VRA) .... HTYP
Hemin Storage .... HMS
Henebery Aviation [*ICAO designator*] (AD) .... HZ
Heraldry (VRA) .... her
Hercegnovi [*Yugoslavia*] [*Airport symbol*] (AD) .... HNO
Heussler Air Service [*ICAO designator*] (AD) .... HQ
Hickory (VRA) .... hick
Hidden Broad-Line Region [*Spectra*] .... HBLR
Hidrotic Ectodermal Dysplasia [*Dermatology*] .... HED
Hieroglyph (VRA) .... hiergl
High Air Pollution Potential .... HAAP
High Arcal Learning Objectives (AIE) .... HALO
High Circle Fatique .... HCF
High Energy Transient Explorer .... HETE
High Frequency (WDMC) v
High Interest Tracks .... HIT
High Mobility Trailer .... HMT
High Pressure Chamber .... HIPC
High Salinity Shelf Water [*Oceanography*] .... HSSW
High School Magazine [*A publication*] (BRI) .... H Sch M
High Technology National Training (AIE) .... HTNT
High-Data-Rate Digital Subscriber Line [*Telecommunications*] (DOM) .. HDSL
Higher Certificate [*Academic degree*] (AIE) .... HC
Higher Diploma in Education [*Academic degree*] (AIE) .. HDipEd
Higher Education Action Research Team (AIE) .... HEART
Higher Education Authority [*Ireland*] (AIE) .... HEA
Higher Education Business Enterprises Ltd. (AIE) ...... HEBE
Higher Education Careers Service Unit (AIE) .... HECSU
Higher Education External Relations Association (AIE) .. HEERA
Higher Education Funding Council (AIE) .... HEFC
Higher Education Information Service (AIE) .... HEIS
Higher Education Learning Programmes Information Service (AIE) .. HELPIS
Higher Education Students Early Statistics (AIE) .... HESES
Higher Education Teachers of English (AIE) .... HETE
High-Gain Emissive Display [*Technology*] .... HGED
High-Grade Squamous Intraepithelial Lesions [*OCLC symbol*] .. HSIL
High-Intensity Discharge .... HID
Highlands (DD) .... Hghlds
High-Level Data Link Control [*Computer science*] (DOM) .. HLDLC
Highly Active Antiretroviral Therapy [*Medicine*] .... HAART
Highly Advanced Laboratory for Communications and Astronomy [*Japanese satellite*] .... HALCA
Highly Compensated Employee [*Human resources*] (WYGK) .. HCE
High-Mass X-Ray Binary [*Star system*] .... HMXB
High-Precision Parallax Collecting Satellite [*European Space Agency*] .. Hipparcos
Highway (DD) .... Hwy
Higuerote [*Venezuela*] [*Airport symbol*] (AD) .... HIU
Hill Monastic Manuscript Library [*Saint John's University, Collegeville, MN*] .. HMML
Hippo Valley [*Zimbabwe*] [*Airport symbol*] (AD) ...... HPO
Hispania [*A publication*] (BRI) .... Hisp
Hispanic American Historical Review [*A publication*] (BRI) .. HAHR
Hispaniola Airways [*ICAO designator*] (AD) .... ZS
Histone Deacetylase [*An enzyme*] .... HD
Historical Sources Collection Program .... HSCP
History (VRA) .... hist
History & Political Science (DD) .... Hist&PolSc
History and Theory [*A publication*] (BRI) .... Hist & T
History: Reviews of New Books [*A publication*] (BRI) .. HRNB
History Today [*A publication*] (BRI) .... HT
Hoechst Marion Roussel .... HMR
Hoffman Military Products Division .... HMPD
Hold .... HLD
Holddown .... HD
Holiday Airlines [*ICAO designator*] (AD) .... JO
Holland (DD) .... Holl
Hollandse Signaalapparaten [*Dutch*] .... HSA
Hologram (VRA) .... holgr
Home & Garden Television .... HGTV

Home Automated Living .... HAL
Home Plug and Play [*Technology*] .... HPnP
Home-on-Burn .... HOB
Home-School Liaison (AIE) .... HSL
Honda [*Colombia*] [*Airport symbol*] (AD) .... HDA
Honduras (VRA) .... Hond
Hong Kong [*British Crown Colony*] [*Airport symbol*] (AD) .... HKG
Hong Kong Interbank Offered Rate (DFIT) .... HIBOR
Honorable (DD) .... Hon
Honorary (DD) .... honry
Honorary Sergeant Major of the Corps [*Marine Corps*] .... HSGMOC
Honors (DD) .... Hons
Honours Bachelor of Arts in Business Administration (DD) .... HBA
Horizon Air [*ICAO designator*] (AD) .... QX
Horizons Technology, Inc. .... HTI
Horizontal Blanking Interval (DOM) .... HBI
Horizontal Tab [*Computer science*] (DOM) .... HT
Horn Book Guide [*A publication*] (BRI) .... HB Guide
Horn Book Magazine [*A publication*] (BRI) .... HB
Horticulture [*A publication*] (BRI) .... Hort
Hosana [*Ethiopia*] [*Airport symbol*] (AD) .... HOS
Hospital (VRA) .... hosp
Hospital Communication and Information System [*McDonnell Douglas
    Automation Co.*] .... HCIS
Hospital Financial Control [*McDonnell Douglas Automation Co.*] ...... HFC
Host Proximity Service [*Computer science*] .... HOPS
Hot Springs [*Virginia*] [*Airport symbol*] (AD) .... HSP
Hot Springs [*South Dakota*] [*Airport symbol*] (AD) .... HSR
Hotel and Catering Training Co. (AIE) .... HCTC
Hourly Earnings Rate .... HERATES
House (VRA) .... hs
Household Goods Carriers Bureau .... HHGCB
Hover out of Ground Effect .... HOGE
How You Test is What You Get [*Education*] (AIE) .... HYTIWYG
Howardite, Eucrite, Diogenite [*Meteorite composition*] .... HED
Howitzer Strap-On Trainer [*Military*] (RDA) .... HSOT

HR Magazine [*A publication*] (BRI) .... HR Mag
Hudson Review [*A publication*] (BRI) .... HR
Hue [*South Vietnam*] [*Airport symbol*] (AD) .... HUI
Hughes Air West [*ICAO designator*] (AD) .... Hughes
Hughes Network Systems .... HNS
Hull [*England*] [*Airport symbol*] (AD) .... HEU
Hull Electronics Unit [*Military*] (RDA) .... HEU
Hull-Turret Position Sensor [*Military*] (RDA) .... HTPS
Humaita [*Brazil*] [*Airport symbol*] (AD) .... HYT
Human Achaete-Scute Homologue [*Genetics*] .... haSH
Human Artificial Chromosome [*Genetics*] .... HAC
Human Engineering Program Plan .... HEPP
Human Events [*A publication*] (BRI) .... HE
Human Factors, Manpower, Personnel, and Training [*Military*] (RDA) .... HMPT
Human Genome Sciences .... HGS
Human Potential Research Project [*University of Surrey*] [*British*] (AIE) .... HPRP
Human Resource Development Staff .... HRDS
Human Resources [*Research*] and Development Program .... HRDP
Human Resources Information System (WYGK) .... HRIS
Human Resources Research Office [*George Washington University*] .... HumRRO
Humanist [*A publication*] (BRI) .... Hum
Hungary (VRA) .... Hung
Hungry Mind Review [*A publication*] (BRI) .... HMR
Hunting and Angling With Kids .... HAWK
Huntington Beach Development Engineering [*McDonnell Douglas Aircraft
    Corp.*] .... HBDE
Huntsville Association of Technical Societies .... HATS
Hurn [*England*] [*Airport symbol*] (AD) .... HUR
Hyannis Aviation [*ICAO designator*] (AD) .... YB
Hybrid Fiber-Coax [*Telecommunications*] .... HFC
Hydrolytic Kinetic Resolution .... HKR
Hydroxyl Radical (AD) .... OH
HyperMedia Management Protocol [*Computer science*] .... HMMP
Hyper-Media Management Schema [*Computer science*] .... HMMS
HyperMedia Object Manager [*Computer science*] .... HMOM
Hypostyle (VRA) .... hypst
Hypoxia-Inducible Factor [*Physiology*] .... HIF

I

By Meaning

Iberia Air Lines of Spain [*ICAO designator*] (AD) .... IB
Icabaru [*Venezuela*] [*Airport symbol*] (AD) .... ICA
Icana [*Brazil*] [*Airport symbol*] (AD) .... INA
Ice Sounding RADAR .... ISR
Iceland (VRA) .... Icel
Icon (VRA) .... icn
Iconostasis (VRA) .... iconst
Icy Grain Halo [*Model of comet structure*] .... IGH
Ideas in the Teaching of Mathematics and Science (AIE) .... ITeMS
Identified Camouflaged Objects [*Hunting*] .... ICO
IEEE Expert: Intelligent Systems and Their Applications [*A publication*]
  (BRI) .... IEEE Exp
Iguatu [*Brazil*] [*Airport symbol*] (AD) .... IGZ
Ikela [*Zaire*] [*Airport symbol*] (AD) .... IKL
Ilha do Sal [*Cape Verde Islands*] [*Airport symbol*] (AD) .... SID
Illegal Immigrant II
Illuminated (VRA) .... illum
Illuminated Manuscript (VRA) .... mss
Illustrated London News [*A publication*] (BRI) .... ILN
Illustration (VRA) .... illus
Illustrative Material (VRA) .... illus mat
Image Stabilization [*Technology from Canon*] .... IS
Image Synthesis Processor [*Computer science*] .... ISP
Immigration Act of 1990 (WYGK) .... IMAC 90
Immigration Restriction League .... IRL
Impasse (DD) .... imp
Impasto (VRA) .... impst
Imperial Airlines [*ICAO designator*] (AD) II
Implementing Primary Science Education (AIE) .... IPSE
Impressionism (VRA) .... Impr
Imprimatura (VRA) .... imprm
Improved Efficiency of Learning [*Project*] (AIE) .... IEL
In Bankruptcy or Receivership [*Investment term*] (DFIT) VI
In Vitro Expression Cloning [*Analytical biochemistry*] .... IVEC
Inanwatan [*West Irian, Indonesia*] [*Airport symbol*] (AD) .... INX
Inch (VRA) .... in
Inches (VRA) .... in
Inches per Second (DOM) .... ips
Incised (VRA) .... inc
Includes Extra [*Investment term*] (DFIT) .... A
Inclusion Body Myositis .... IBM
Incoherent Scatter RADAR [*Instrumentation*] .... ISR
Indefinite Delivery/Indefinite Quantity [*Military*] (RDA) .... IDIQ
Indeo Video Interactive [*Computer science*] IVI
Independence [*Kansas*] [*Airport symbol*] (AD) .... IDP
Independent Appeals Authority for School Examinations (AIE) .... IAASE
Independent Inspector (AIE) II
Independent Schools Association Inc. (AIE) .... ISAI
Independent Schools Joint Action Committee (AIE) .... ISJAC
Independent Schools Physical Education Conference (AIE) .... ISPEC
Independent Schools Section [*American Association of School Libraries*]
  [*American Library Association*] .... ISS
Independent Schools Working Group (AIE) .... ISWG
Independent Truck Owner-Operators Association .... ITOO
Index of Spouse Abuse .... ISA
India Ink (VRA) .... ind i
Indian Airlines [*ICAO designator*] (AD) IC
Indiana Airways [*ICAO designator*] (AD) .... WY
Individual Case Management (WYGK) .... ICM
Individual Learning Programme (AIE) .... ILP
Individually Carried Records [*Military*] .... ICR
Individuals .... idv
Indo-Pacific International [*ICAO designator*] (AD) .... JP
Indore [*India*] [*Airport symbol*] (AD) .... IDR
Industrial (DD) .... ind
Industrial Administration (DD) .... IndAdmin
Industrial and Labor Relations Review [*A publication*] (BRI) .... ILRR
Industrial and Occupational Knowledge (AIE) .... IOK
Industrial, Commercial, and Institutional Accountant (DD) .... ICIA
Industrial Engineering (DD) .... IndEng
Industrial Health (DD) .... IndHealth
Industrial Research and Development Advisory Committee [*European
  Union*] .... IRDAC
Industrial Society (AIE) .... IS
Industrial Training Service (AIE) .... ITS
Industry and Teacher Education Liaison (AIE) .... INDTEL

Industry Education Liaison (AIE) .... INDEL
Inertial Interchange True Polar Wander [*Geophysics*] .... IITPW
Infant Health and Development Program .... IHDP
Informant Questionnaire on Cognitive Decline in the Elderly .... IQCODE
Information (DD) .... info
Information Exchange [*Advanced photo system*] IX
Information Officers Working in Voluntary Organisations (AIE) .... INVOG
Information Retrieval & Library Automation [*A publication*] (BRI) ...... IRLA
Information Systems Committee [*Universities Funding Council*] (AIE) .... ISC
Information Systems Professional (DD) .... ISP
Information Technology Centre Consultancy Unit [*British*] (AIE) .... ITCCU
Information Warfare Squadron [*Air Force*] .... IWS
Infrared (VRA) .... infra
Infrared Brightness Temperature .... IRBT
Ingenieur (DD) .... ing
Inhambane [*Mozambique*] [*Airport symbol*] (AD) .... INH
Initial Public Offering [*Stock exchange term*] .... IPO
Initial Teacher Education and New Technology [*Project*] (AIE) .... INTENT
Initial Teacher Training (AIE) .... ITT
Initiative on Communication Arts for Children (AIE) .... ICAL
Ink (VRA) i
Inland Empire Airlines [*ICAO designator*] (AD) .... LQ
Inland Seas Education Association .... ISEA
Inlay (VRA) .... inl
Innamincka [*South Australia*] [*Airport symbol*] (AD) .... INM
Inner London Tertiary Education Board [*British*] (AIE) .... ILTEB
Inoffizielle Mitarbeiter [*Unofficial Collaborators*] [*German*] .... IM
Input/Output [*Computer science*] .... I/O
Inscription (VRA) .... inscr
In-Service Training and Education Panel (AIE) .... INSTEP
[*Office of the*] Inspector General .... IG
Inspectors Based in Schools [*British*] (AIE) .... IBIS
Installation (VRA) .... instl
Instant (VRA) .... ins
Instant Messaging [*Computer science*] .... IM
Institute for Academic Technology .... IAT
Institute for Continuing Education (AIE) .... ICE
Institute for the Integration of Latin America .... IILA
Institute of Chartered Accountants of Scotland (AIE) .... ICAS
Institute of Chartered Secretaries and Administrators (AIE) .... ICSA
Institute of Donations and Public Affairs Research [*Canada*] .... IDPAR
Institute of Legal Executives (AIE) .... ILEx
Institute of Local Government [*University of Birmingham*] [*British*]
  (AIE) .... INLOGOV
Institute of Medicine .... IoM
Institute of Practitioners in Work Study, Organisation, and Management
  (AIE) .... IPWSOM
Institution (VRA) .... inst
Institutional Management in Higher Education (AIE) .... IMHE
Instruction Section [*Association of College and Research Libraries*] [*American
  Library Association*] .... IS
Instructional Systems Design (DOM) .... ISD
Instructor [*A publication*] (BRI) .... Inst
Instrument (VRA) .... instr
Instrumented Sensor Technologies .... IST
Insurance Services Group .... ISG
Intaglio (VRA) .... intg
Intarsia (VRA) .... intr
Integrated Booking System [*Army*] (RDA) .... IBS
Integrated Building and Construction Solutions .... IBACOS
Integrated Learning System (AIE) .... ILS
Integrated Mathematics Project (AIE) .... IMP
Integrated Product and Process Development Team [*Military*] (RDA) ...... IPPDT
Integrated Sachs-Wolfe [*Effect in cosmic microwave background*] .... ISW
Integrating Graduate Education and Research Training [*National Science
  Foundation*] .... IGERT
Intel Mobile Module [*Computer science*] .... MMO
Intel Smart Video Recorder III ISVR3
Intelligent Agent .... IA
Intelligent Concept Extraction [*Technology*] [*Computer science*] ...... ICE
Intensified Charge-Coupled Device [*Electronics*] .... ICCD
Interactive Careers Guidance System (AIE) .... ICGS
Interactive Digital Electronic Appliance [*Computer science*] .... IDEA
Interactive Learning International Corp. .... ILINC
Interactive Profiles [*Computer science*] .... I/Pro
Interactive Software Engineering .... ISE

Interactive SQL [*Computer science*] .... ISQL
Interactive Video in Education [*National Interactive Video Centre*] (AIE) .... IVIE
Interactive Voice System [*Electronics*] .... IVS
Inter-American Committee for Science and Technology .... IACST
Inter-American Committee of Presidential Representatives .... IACPR
Inter-American Council for Education, Science, and Culture .... IACESC
Inter-American Cultural Council ICC
Inter-American Statistical Institute .... IASI
Inter-American Statistical Teaching Center .... IASC
Inter-American System .... IAS
Inter-American Telecommunications Commission .... IATC
Interchromatin Granular Cluster [*Cytology*] .... IGS
Intercity [*ICAO designator*] (AD) .... YI
Interdisciplinary Enquiry [*Education*] (AIE) .... IDE
Inter-Disciplinary Studies [*Education*] (AIE) .... IDS
Interferometric Synthetic Aperture RADAR (RDA) .... IFSAR
Interflug [*ICAO designator*] (AD) .... IF
Intergovernmental Forum on Chemical Safety .... IFCS
Interior (VRA) .... int
Interlibrary Cooperation & Networking [*Association of Specialized and
    Cooperative Library Agencies*] [*American Library Association*] .... ICAN
Intermarket Surveillance Information System (DFIT) .... ISIS
Inter-media (VRA) .... intr-md
Intermodal Association of North America .... IANA
International (VRA) .... intl
International Affairs (DD) .... IntlAffairs
International Air Bahama [*ICAO designator*] (AD) .... IW
International Association for Rural Development (AIE) .... IARD
International Association for Rural Development Overseas (AIE) .... AIDR
International Bowhunting Organization .... IBO
International Brotherhood of Teamsters [*Union*] .... IBT
International Bulletin of Bibliography on Education [*A publication*] (AIE) ..... BIBE
International Center for Cooperation in BioInformatics [*UNESCO*] .... ICCB
International Comfort Products .... ICP
International Congress on Mathematical Education (AIE) .... ICME
International Federation of Reproductive Rights Organisations (AIE) .... IFRRO
International Freelance Photographers Organization .... IFPO
International Garment Processors .... IGP
International General Certificate of Secondary Education (AIE) .... IGCSE
International Group for the Advancement of Physics Teaching (AIE) ...... GIREP
International Journal of Impotence Research [*A publication*] .... IJIR
International Labour Review [*A publication*] (BRI) .... ILR
International Merchant Purchases Authorization Care [*Visa*] (RDA) .... IMPAC
International Multimedia Teleconferencing Consortium .... IMTC
International Organisation for Science and Technology Education
    (AIE) .... IOSTE
International Philosophical Quarterly [*A publication*] (BRI) .... IPQ
International Society for Individualized Instruction (AIE) .... ISII
International Standing Conference for the History of Education (AIE) ...... ISCHE
International Stock Exchange of the United Kingdom and the Republic of
    Ireland (DFIT) .... ISE
International Survey Research Corp. .... ISRC
International Symposium on Fluorine Chemistry .... ISFC
International Youth Year [*1985*] (AIE) .... IYY
Internet Content Provider [*Computer science*] .... ICP
Internet Department of Motor Vehicles .... I-DMV
Internet Entertainment Group, Inc. .... IEG
Internet Inter-ORG [*Object Request Broker*] **Protocol** [*Computer science*] .... IIOP
Internet Network Information Center [*Computer science*] .... InterNIC

Internet Printing System [*Computer science*] .... IPS
Internet Server API [*All-Purpose Interface*] [*Microsoft and Process Software
    Corp.*] [*Computer science*] .... ISAPI
Internet Services API [*Computer science*] .... ISAPI
Internet3D Space Builder .... ISB
Interpretation: A Journal of Bible and Theology [*A publication*] (BRI) .... Intpr
Interrupt Request Line [*Computer science*] .... IRQ
Interstate Truckers Association .... ITA
Inter-University Software Committee [*Inter-University Committee on
    Computing*] (AIE) .... IUSC
Intracytoplasmic Sperm Injection .... ICSI
Intramolecular Charge Transfer [*Physical chemistry*] .... ICT
Intravascular Ultrasound [*Medicine*] .... IVUS
Intuit Services Corp. .... ISC
Inventory Update Rule [*Environmental Protection Agency*] .... IUR
Inverse Kinematics [*Computer science*] .... IK
Investigative Group International .... IGI
Investment (DD) .... invest
Ion-Channel Switch [*Biochemistry*] .... ICS
Iowa Airlines and Horizon Airways [*ICAO designator*] (AD) .... BF
Iowa Airways [*ICAO designator*] (AD) .... JT
Iowa City [*Iowa*] [*Airport symbol*] (AD) .... IOW
Ipora [*Brazil*] [*Airport symbol*] (AD) .... IPO
Ipswich [*England*] [*Airport symbol*] (AD) .... IPW
Iran Air [*ICAO designator*] (AD) .... IR
Iran National Airlines [*ICAO designator*] (AD) .... IR
Ireland (VRA) .... Ire
Iris Neovascularization [*Opthalmology*] .... INV
Irish Association for Curriculum Development (AIE) .... IACD
Irish Joint Fiction Reserve Scheme (AIE) .... IJFRS
Irish Literary Supplement [*A publication*] (BRI) .... ILS
Iron (VRA) .... fe
Iron Range [*Queensland*] [*Airport symbol*] (AD) .... IRG
Iron Regulatory Protein [*Biochemistry*] .... IRP
Ironwood (VRA) .... fewd
Irridescent (VRA) .... irid
Ischemia Research and Education Foundation .... IREF
Iskenderon [*Turkey*] [*Airport symbol*] (AD) .... ISK
Island Air [*ICAO designator*] (AD) IL
Island Arts and Crafts Club, Victoria [*1910, IACS from 1922*] (NGC) .... IACC
Island Arts and Crafts Society, Victoria [*1922, founded 1910 as IACC*]
    (NGC) .... IACS
Isle des Pins [*New Caledonia*] [*Airport symbol*] (AD) .... ILP
Isles of Scilly Skybus [*ICAO designator*] (AD) .... FW
Isoform of Nitric Oxide Synthase [*An enzyme*] .... INOS
Isometric (VRA) .... iso
Israel (VRA) .... Isr
Istituto di Fisica Cosmica [*Italy*] .... IFC
Itacoatiara [*Brazil*] [*Airport symbol*] (AD) .... ITA
Itajai [*Brazil*] [*Airport symbol*] (AD) .... ITJ
Italy (VRA) .... It
Itambacuri [*Brazil*] [*Airport symbol*] (AD) .... IBU
Itapetinga [*Brazil*] [*Airport symbol*] (AD) .... ITI
Itaqui [*Brazil*] [*Airport symbol*] (AD) .... ITQ
Itavia [*ICAO designator*] (AD) .... IH
IUBS Commission on Biological Education (AIE) .... IUBS-CBE
Ivory (VRA) iv
Ivory Coast (VRA) .... Iv Co
Iwakuni [*Japan*] [*Airport symbol*] (AD) .... IWA
Ixtepec [*Mexico*] [*Airport symbol*] (AD) .... IZT

J
By Meaning

Jackson [*Michigan*] [*Airport symbol*] (AD) .... JNX
Jacksonville [*Illinois*] [*Airport symbol*] (AD) .... JAE
Jacobean (VRA) .... Jacbn
Jade (VRA) .... ja
Jadeite (VRA) .... jadt
Jaffa [*Israel*] [*Airport symbol*] (AD) .... JFA
Jaffna [*Ceylon*] [*Airport symbol*] (AD) .... JAF
Jaicos [*Brazil*] [*Airport symbol*] (AD) .... JCS
Jamaica (VRA) .... Jama
Jamaire [*ICAO designator*] (AD) .... IM
Jamshedpur [*India*] [*Airport symbol*] (AD) .... IXW
Januaria [*Brazil*] [*Airport symbol*] (AD) .... JNA
Japan (VRA) .... Jap
Jasper (VRA) .... jsp
Jasper National Park [*Alberta*] [*Airport symbol*] (AD) .... JNP
Jatai [*Brazil*] [*Airport symbol*] (AD) .... JTI
Java Virtual Machine [*Computer science*] .... JVM
JavaSoft Java Archive [*Computer science*] .... JAR
Jersey European [*ICAO designator*] (AD) .... JY
Jersey European Airways [*ICAO designator*] (AD) .... JV
Jesolo [*Italy*] [*Airport symbol*] (AD) .... JLO
Jet Express [*ICAO designator*] (AD) .... JI
Jewelry (VRA) .... jlry
Jewish Social Studies [*A publication*] (BRI) .... JSS
Jinja [*Uganda*] [*Airport symbol*] (AD) .... JIN
Jipijapa [*Ecuador*] [*Airport symbol*] (AD) .... JIP
Joacaba [*Brazil*] [*Airport symbol*] (AD) .... JCB
Job Creation Programme [*Manpower Services Commission*] (AIE) .... JCP
Job Ideas and Information Generator - Computer Assisted Learning
    (AIE) .... JIIG-CAL
Job Rehearsal Scheme (AIE) .... JRS
Joint Academic Services Providers to Education and Research
    (AIE) .... JASPER
Joint Ad Hoc Working Group on Shipping [*ASEAN*] .... JAHWGS
Joint Collection Management Tools [*Army*] (RDA) .... JCMT
Joint Efficiency Study (AIE) .... JES
Joint Lightweight 155mm Howitzer (RDA) JLW-155
Joint National Council (AIE) .... JNC
Joint Steering Committee for Revision of AACR [*Anglo-American Cataloging Rules*] .... JSCAACR
Joint Strike Fighter .... JSF
Joint Tactical Terminal/Common Integrated Broadcast System Module
    [*Military*] (RDA) .... JTT/CIBSM
Joint Training Scheme (AIE) .... JTS
Jordan (VRA) .... Jor
Journal of Academic Librarianship [*A publication*] (BRI) .... JAL
Journal of Accountancy [*A publication*] (BRI) .... J Account
Journal of Adolescent & Adult Literacy [*A publication*] (BRI) .... JAAL
Journal of Aesthetic Education [*A publication*] (BRI) .... J Aes Ed
Journal of Aesthetics and Art Criticism [*A publication*] (BRI) ...... JAAC
Journal of American Culture [*A publication*] (BRI) .... J Am Cult
Journal of American Folklore [*A publication*] (BRI) .... JAF
Journal of American History [*A publication*] (BRI) .... JAH
Journal of American Studies [*A publication*] (BRI) .... J Am St
Journal of Arts Management, Law & Society [*A publication*] (BRI) .... JAML

Journal of Asian Studies [*A publication*] (BRI) .... JAS
Journal of Biblical Literature [*A publication*] (BRI) .... JBL
Journal of Biological Inorganic Chemistry [*A publication*] ...... JBIC
Journal of Black Studies [*A publication*] (BRI) .... J Bl St
Journal of Broadcasting and Electronic Media [*A publication*] (BRI) ..... J Broadcst
Journal of Career Planning and Employment [*A publication*] (BRI) ..... J Car P & E
Journal of Chemical Education [*A publication*] (BRI) .... J Chem Ed
Journal of Church and State [*A publication*] (BRI) .... J Ch St
Journal of Clinical Psychiatry [*A publication*] (BRI) .... J ClinPsyc
Journal of Communication [*A publication*] (BRI) .... JC
Journal of Consumer Affairs [*A publication*] (BRI) .... J Con A
Journal of Economic History [*A publication*] (BRI) .... JEH
Journal of Economic Literature [*A publication*] (BRI) .... JEL
Journal of Education [*A publication*] (BRI) .... JE
Journal of English and Germanic Philology [*A publication*] (BRI) .... JEGP
Journal of Film & Video [*A publication*] (BRI) .... J Film & Vid
Journal of Government Information [*A publication*] (BRI) ...... J Gov Info
Journal of Higher Education [*A publication*] (BRI) .... J Hi E
Journal of Historical Geography [*A publication*] (BRI) ...... J Hist G
Journal of Homosexuality [*A publication*] (BRI) .... J Homosex
Journal of Interdisciplinary History [*A publication*] (BRI) .... JIH
Journal of International Business Studies [*A publication*] (BRI) .... JIB
Journal of Marketing [*A publication*] (BRI) .... JM
Journal of Marriage and the Family [*A publication*] (BRI) .... JMF
Journal of Military History [*A publication*] (BRI) .... J Mil H
Journal of Modern History [*A publication*] (BRI) .... JMH
Journal of Molecular Medicine [*A publication*] .... JMM
Journal of Multicultural Social Work [*A publication*] (BRI) ...... JMSW
Journal of Negro Education [*A publication*] (BRI) .... JNE
Journal of Parapsychology [*A publication*] (BRI) .... JP
Journal of Peace Research [*A publication*] (BRI) .... JPR
Journal of Philosophy [*A publication*] (BRI) .... J Phil
Journal of Political Economy [*A publication*] (BRI) .... JPE
Journal of Politics [*A publication*] (BRI) .... J Pol
Journal of Popular Culture [*A publication*] (BRI) .... JPC
Journal of Popular Film and Television [*A publication*] (BRI) .... J Pop F&TV
Journal of Rehabilitation Research and Development [*A publication*]
    (BRI) .... J Rehab RD
Journal of Religion [*A publication*] (BRI) .... JR
Journal of Social History [*A publication*] (BRI) .... J Soc H
Journal of Southern History [*A publication*] (BRI) .... JSH
Journal of Teacher Education [*A publication*] (BRI) ...... J Teach Ed
Journal of the American Academy of Religion [*A publication*] (BRI) .... JAAR
Journal of the History of Ideas [*A publication*] (BRI) .... JHI
Journal of Urban History [*A publication*] (BRI) .... J Urban H
Journal of Youth Services in Libraries [*American Library Association*] .... JOYS
Journalism (DD) .... Journ
Journalism & Mass Communication Quarterly [*A publication*] (BRI) ...... JMCQ
Journalism Quarterly [*A publication*] (BRI) .... JQ
Juan-les-Pins [*France*] [*Airport symbol*] (AD) .... JLP
Judgement Purchase Corp. .... JPC
Julienhaab [*Greenland*] [*Airport symbol*] (AD) .... JJU
Jundah [*Queensland*] [*Airport symbol*] (AD) .... JUN
Junior (DD) .... Jr
Junior Bookshelf [*A publication*] (BRI) .... JB
Juris Utrisuque Doctor (DD) .... JUD

K
By Meaning

Kabalo [Zaire] [Airport symbol] (AD) .... KBO
Kaele [Cameroon] [Airport symbol] (AD) .... KLE
Kaiapit [New Guinea] [Airport symbol] (AD) .... KIA
Kailashahar [India] [Airport symbol] (AD) .... IXH
Kainantu [New Guinea] [Airport symbol] (AD) .... KIU
Kai's Power Tools [Computer science] KPT3
Kakemono (VRA) .... kakm
Kalima [Zaire] [Airport symbol] (AD) .... KLY
Kalitype (VRA) .... KATYP
Kamalpur [India] [Airport symbol] (AD) .... IXQ
Kamaran Island [South Arabia (Yemen)] [Airport symbol] (AD) .... KAM
Kamishli [Syria] [Airport symbol] (AD) .... KAC
Kampala [Uganda] [Airport symbol] (AD) .... KLA
Kandla [India] [Airport symbol] (AD) .... IXY
Kankan [Guinea] [Airport symbol] (AD) .... KNN
Kaolack [Senegal] [Airport symbol] (AD) .... KLC
Kar-Air [ICAO designator] (AD) .... KR
Kars [Turkey] [Airport symbol] (AD) .... KAR
Kashmir (VRA) .... Kash
Kasongo [Zaire] [Airport symbol] (AD) .... KGO
Kastamonu [Turkey] [Airport symbol] (AD) .... KXU
Katherine [Northern Territory, Australia] [Airport symbol] (AD) .... KTR
Kauhava [Finland] [Airport symbol] (AD) .... KAU
Kavieng [New Ireland] [Airport symbol] (AD) .... KVG
Kawasaki Automatic Power-Drive System [Kawasaki Motors Corp.] ..... KAPS
Kawau Island [New Zealand] [Airport symbol] (AD) .... KWU
Kayseri [Turkey] [Airport symbol] (AD) .... KYZ
Keflavik [Iceland] [Airport symbol] (AD) .... KEF
Kendell Airlines [ICAO designator] (AD) .... KD
Kent Mathematics Project [British] (AIE) .... KMP
Kentucky Education Reform Act .... KERA
Kenya (VRA) .... Ken
Kenya Airways [ICAO designator] (AD) .... KQ
Kenyon Review [A publication] (BRI) .... Ken R
Kerang [Victoria, Australia] [Airport symbol] (AD) .... KRA
Kermanshah [Iran] [Airport symbol] (AD) .... KSH
Key Airlines [ICAO designator] (AD) .... FS
Key Stage [Of National Curriculum] [British] (AIE) .... KS
Keystone (VRA) .... kyst
Keywords and Learning (AIE) .... KAL
Khapalu [Pakistan] [Airport symbol] (AD) .... KPU
Khasm el Girba [Sudan] [Airport symbol] (AD) .... GBU
Kherson [USSR] [Airport symbol] (AD) .... KHE
Khowai [India] [Airport symbol] (AD) .... IXN
Khulna [Bangladesh] [Airport symbol] (AD) .... KHL
Khuzdar [Pakistan] [Airport symbol] (AD) .... KZR
Kids' Clubs Network (AIE) .... KCN
Killer-Cell Inhibitory Receptor [Immunology] .... KIR
Kilobits per Second [Computer science] .... Kbps
Kilobytes per Second [Computer science] (DOM) .... KBps
Kilowatt (DFIT) .... KW

Kilowatt-Hour (DFIT) .... KWH
Kinetic (VRA) .... kin
King Salmon-Naknek [Alaska] [Airport symbol] (AD) .... AKN
Kiplinger's Personal Finance Magazine [A publication] (BRI) .... Kiplinger
Kirkjubaejar [Iceland] [Airport symbol] (AD) .... KBK
Kirkuk [Iraq] [Airport symbol] (AD) .... KIK
Kirkus Review [A publication] (BRI) .... KR
Kissidougou [Guinea] [Airport symbol] (AD) .... KSI
Kitale [Kenya] [Airport symbol] (AD) .... KTL
Kliatt Young Adult Paperback Book Guide [A publication] (BRI) .... Kliatt
Knapsack (AD) .... nap
Knight Commander of the Order of St. Lazarus of Jerusalem (DD) ..... KCLJ
Knight of the Holy Sepulchre of Jerusalem (DD) .... KHS
Knight of the Legion of Honour (DD) .... KLH
Knight of the Military and Hospitalier Order of St. Lazarus (DD) .... KLJ
Knight of the Order of St. John of Jerusalem (DD) .... KStJ
Knight of the Sovereign and Military Order of Malta (DD) .... KM
Knight-Ridder .... KR
Knight-Ridder Information Inc. .... KRII
Know Your Customer [Investment term] (DFIT) .... KYC
Knowledge and Distributed Intelligence .... KDI
Knowledge Information Skills and Curriculum [Project] (AIE) .... KISC
Known (VRA) .... kn
Koala Bear Park [Adelaide] [Airport symbol] (AD) .... KBP
Kodachrome (VRA) .... KODCH
Kodalith (VRA) .... kdlth
Kodiak [Alaska] [Airport symbol] (AD) .... NHB
Kokonao [West Irian, Indonesia] [Airport symbol] (AD) .... KOX
Kolda [Senegal] [Airport symbol] (AD) .... KDA
Kolwezi [Zaire] [Airport symbol] (AD) .... KWZ
Kongo Boumba [Gabon] [Airport symbol] (AD) .... GKO
Kongoussi [Upper Volta] [Airport symbol] (AD) .... ONU
Kontum [South Vietnam] [Airport symbol] (AD) .... KON
Konya [Turkey] [Airport symbol] (AD) .... KYA
Korea (VRA) .... Kor
Korean Air Lines [ICAO designator] (AD) .... KE
Korean Airways [ICAO designator] (AD) .... JS
Koronadal [Mindanao, Philippines] [Airport symbol] (AD) .... KDL
Kosti [Sudan] [Airport symbol] (AD) .... KST
Kotabaru [West Irian, Indonesia] [Airport symbol] (AD) .... KBU
Kratie [Cambodia] [Airport symbol] (AD) .... KTI
Kuiper Belt Objects [Planetary science] .... KBO
Kulu [India] [Airport symbol] (AD) .... KUU
Kulusuk Island [Greenland] [Airport symbol] (AD) .... KUS
Kushan (VRA) .... Kush
Kushtia [Bangladesh] [Airport symbol] (AD) .... KHS
Kutahya [Turkey] [Airport symbol] (AD) .... KUT
Kutaisi [USSR] [Airport symbol] (AD) .... KTU
Kuwait (VRA) .... Kuw
Kuwait Airways [ICAO designator] (AD) .... KU
Kweiyang [China] [Airport symbol] (AD) .... KWE

L
By Meaning

La Baule [*France*] [*Airport symbol*] (AD) .... LBY
La Cumbre [*Argentina*] [*Airport symbol*] (AD) .... LCM
La Gloria [*Colombia*] [*Airport symbol*] (AD) .... LGL
La Guaira [*Venzuela*] [*Airport symbol*] (AD) .... LAG
La Guera [*Morocco*] [*Airport symbol*] (AD) .... ZLG
La Junta [*Colorado*] [*Airport symbol*] (AD) .... LHX
La Serena [*Chile*] [*Airport symbol*] (AD) .... LSC
LAB Flying Service [*ICAO designator*] (AD) .... JF
Labe [*Guinea*] [*Airport symbol*] (AD) .... LEK
Labrador Airways [*ICAO designator*] (AD) .... WJ
Labrea [*Brazil*] [*Airport symbol*] (AD) .... LBR
Lacquer (VRA) .... lac
Laghouat [*Algeria*] [*Airport symbol*] (AD) .... LOO
Laguna Beach-Santa Ana [*California*] [*Airport symbol*] (AD) .... SNA
Lagunillas [*Venezuela*] [*Airport symbol*] (AD) .... LGY
Lai [*Chad*] [*Airport symbol*] (AD) .... LTC
Lajes [*Brazil*] [*Airport symbol*] (AD) .... LJZ
Lake Placid-Saranac Lake [*New York*] [*Airport symbol*] (AD) .... SLK
Lake State Airways [*ICAO designator*] (AD) .... NT
Lake Superior State University [*Michigan*] .... LSSU
Lakeland [*Florida*] [*Airport symbol*] (AD) .... LAL
Lakeland [*ICAO designator*] (AD) .... YQ
Laker Airways [*ICAO designator*] (AD) .... GK
Lalmonirhat [*Bangladesh*] [*Airport symbol*] (AD) .... LLJ
Lambda Book Report [*A publication*] (BRI) .... Lam Bk Rpt
Laminated (VRA) .... lam
LanClient Control Manager [*Computer science*] .... LCCM
Land O'Lakes [*Wisconsin*] [*Airport symbol*] (AD) .... LNL
Land Surface Parmeterization [*Environmental science*] .... LSP
LANDesk Client Manager Technology [*Intel*] [*Computer science*] .... LDCM
Landscape (VRA) .... ldscp
Language Arts [*A publication*] (BRI) .... LA
Language in Society [*A publication*] (BRI) .... Lang Soc
Language Information Network Coordination [*Education*] (AIE) .... LINC
Language of Functions and Graphs (AIE) .... LEG
Lantern Slide (VRA) .... LTRN
Lanthanum/Calcium/Manganese/Oxygen [*Inorganic chemistry*] .... LCMO
Laparoscopic Ultrasonography [*Medicine*] .... LUS
Lapis Lazuli (VRA) ll
Laredo [*Texas*] [*Airport symbol*] (AD) .... LOI
Larkana [*Pakistan*] [*Airport symbol*] (AD) .... LKW
Las Vegas Airlines [*ICAO designator*] (AD) .... TQ
Laser (VRA) .... lsr
LASER-Engineered Net Shaping .... LENS
Last Cast Syndrome [*Fictitious fishing malady*] .... LCS
Last Year but Not This [*Fundraising*] .... LYBNT
Late (VRA) .... la
Late Pleistocene Origins [*Ecology*] .... LPO
Lateral (VRA) .... lat
Latex (VRA) .... ltx
Latin American Antiquity [*A publication*] (BRI) .... LA Ant
Latvia (VRA) .... Latv
Law Quarterly Review [*A publication*] (BRI) .... Law Q Rev
Lawrence [*Massachusetts*] [*Airport symbol*] (AD) .... LWM
Layout (VRA) .... lyot
Leaf (VRA) .... lf
Learning Systems and Access Branch [*Education*] (AIE) .... LSAB
Learning Technology Dissemination Initiative (AIE) .... LTDI
Least Widely Used and Least Taught Languages (AIE) .... LWULT
Leather (VRA) .... lea
Lebanon (VRA) .... Leb
Lectionary (VRA) .... lectn
Leeds University Institute of Education [*British*] (AIE) .... LUIE
Left (VRA) .... lft
Legacy: A Journal of American Women Writers [*A publication*] (BRI) .... Legacy
Legend (VRA) .... lgd
Lekythos (VRA) .... lekyt
Lengeh [*Iran*] [*Airport symbol*] (AD) .... LNH
Length (VRA) .... lgth
Lentigo Maligna [*Oncology*] .... LM
Lesotho Airways [*ICAO designator*] (AD) .... QL
L'Esprit Createur [*A publication*] (BRI) .... L'Esprit
Lesser Antilles (VRA) .... L Anti
Less-than-Carload Lot (DFIT) LCL
Letaba Airways [*ICAO designator*] (AD) .... LK
Letter Carrier Depot (DD) .... LCD

Letter of Credit (DFIT) .... L/C
Letter of Intent (DFIT) .... L/I
Level (VRA) lvl
Lewisville Aquatic Ecosystem Research Facility [*Army*] .... LAERF
Liberia (VRA) .... Liber
Libraries & Culture [*A publication*] (BRI) .... Lib & Cult
Library [*A publication*] (BRI) .... Lib
Library (VRA) .... libr
Library Access and Sixth-Form Studies [*British*] (AIE) .... LASS
Library Advocacy Now [*American Library Association*] .... LAN
Library and Information Statistics Unit (AIE) .... LISU
Library Association Information Technology Group (AIE) .... LAITG
Library Association Record [*A publication*] (BRI) .... LAR
Library Fundraising Resource Center [*American Library Association*] .... LFRC
Library Information Plan (AIE) .... LIP
Library Journal [*A publication*] (BRI) .... LJ
Library Quarterly [*A publication*] (BRI) .... LQ
Library Resources & Technical Services [*Association for Library Collections and Technical Services*] [*American Library Association*] .... LRTS
Library Review [*A publication*] (BRI) .... LR
Library Service to Developmentally Disabled Persons Membership Activity Group [*Association of Specialized and Cooperative Library Agencies*] [*American Library Association*] .... LSSDDPMAG
Library Service to People with Visual or Physical Disabilities Forum [*Association of Specialized and Cooperative Library Agencies*] [*American Library Association*] .... LSPVPD
Library Service to the Developmentally Disabled Persons Forum [*Association of Specialized and Cooperative Library Agencies*] [*American Library Association*] .... LSSDPF
Library Talk [*A publication*] (BRI) .... LT
Library Technology Reports [*American Library Association*] .... LTR
Libyan Arab Airlines [*ICAO designator*] (AD) .... LN
Licence in Administration [*Canada*] (DD) .... LScAdmin
Licence in Economics [*Canada*] (DD) .... LScEco
Licence in the Science of Optometry [*Canada*] (DD) .... LScO
Licencie en Sciences Comptables [*Licentiate of Accounting*] (DD) .... LScCompt
License Economic Sciences [*Canada*] (DD) .... LEconSc
Licentiate in Accountancy (DD) .... LIA
Licentiate in Commercial Science (DD) .... LScC
Licentiate in Commercial Science (DD) .... LScComm
Licentiate in Religion (DD) .... LScRel
Licentiate in Science (DD) .... LSc
Licentiate in Social, Economic, & Political Sciences (DD) .... LSSE
Licentiate of the Medical College of Canada (DD) .... LMCC
Lieutenant of the Victorian Order [*Canada*] (DD) .... LVO
Life Size (VRA) .... lf sz
Light (VRA) .... lt
Lightning Protection System [*Boating*] .... LPS
Lightweight Directory Access Protocol [*Computer science*] .... LDAP
Limestone (VRA) .... lmst
Limewood (VRA) .... lmwd
Limited (DD) .... Ltd
Limon [*Honduras*] [*Airport symbol*] (AD) .... UBG
Lina-Congo [*ICAO designator*] (AD) .... GC
Lindenwood (VRA) .... lindwd
Line (VRA) .... ln
Line Feed [*Computer science*] (DOM) .... LF
Line Printer [*Computer science*] (DOM) .... LPT
Lineas Aereas Privadas Argentinas [*ICAO designator*] (AD) .... MJ
Linen (VRA) .... lin
Linguistic Minorities Project [*Education*] (AIE) .... LMP
Linhas Aereas da Guine-Bissau [*ICAO designator*] (AD) .... YZ
Linjeflyg [*ICAO designator*] (AD) .... LF
Link Access Procedure-D [*Telecommunications*] (DOM) .... LAPD
Linking Industry and School Education (AIE) .... LIASE
Linocut (VRA) .... lino
Linotronic [*Computer science*] .... Lino
Linseed Oil (VRA) .... lnsd
Liquidating Dividend [*Investment term*] (DFIT) C
Liquid-Crystal Displays [*Computer science*] .... LCDS
Liquitex (VRA) .... lqtx
List of Common Abbreviations in Training and Education (AIE) .... LOCATE
Literary Magazine Review [*A publication*] (BRI) .... LMR
Lithium Thallium Tartrate [*Inorganic chemistry*] .... LTT
Lithograph (VRA) .... litho
Lithuania (VRA) .... Lith

Liturgy (VRA) .... litg
Living Benefits Rider [*Insurance*] (WYGK) .... LBR
Livonia Career/Technical Center .... LC/TC
Lloyd Aereo Boliviano [*ICAO designator*] (AD) .... LB
lloyd Your Trans-Australian Airline [*ICAO designator*] (AD) .... UD
Llymphocryptovirus LCV
Loanda [*Brazil*] [*Airport symbol*] (AD) .... LOP
Lobatsi [*Botswana*] [*Airport symbol*] (AD) .... LOQ
Lobito [*Angola*] [*Airport symbol*] (AD) .... LOB
Local Application Numerical Control [*Sony Corp.*] (DOM) .... LANC
Local Authority Associations Group of Work Related Non-Advanced Further Education (AIE) .... LAAGOWRNAFE
Local Authority Catering Advisory Service (AIE) .... LACAS
Local Authority Financial Institution System (AIE) ...... LAFIS
Local Education Authorities and Schools Item Banking [*Project*] (AIE)..... LEASIB
Local Education Authorities Project for School Management Training (AIE) .... LEAP
Local Education Authority Training Grants Scheme (AIE) .... LEATGS
Local Employment Network (AIE) .... LEN
Local Government Management Board (AIE) .... LGMB
Local Labour Market Information/Intelligence [*British*] (AIE) .... LLMI
Local Multipoint Distribution Systems [*Broadcasting term*] .... LMDS
Local Pay Authority (AIE) .... LPA
Location (VRA) .... loc
Lock Haven [*Pennsylvania*] [*Airport symbol*] (AD) ...... LHV
Lodar [*South Arabia*] [*Airport symbol*] (AD) .... LDR
Lodz [*Poland*] [*Airport symbol*] (AD) .... LDZ
Loganair [*ICAO designator*] (AD) LC
Loggia (VRA) .... log
Logistics Anchor Desk [*Army*] (RDA) .... LAD
London Association for the Teaching of English [*British*] (AIE) .... LATE
London Chamber of Commerce Examinations Board [*British*] (AIE) .... LCCEB
London City Airways [*ICAO designator*] (AD) II
London East Training and Enterprise Council [*British*] (AIE) .... LETEC
London Montessori Centre [*British*] (AIE) .... LMC
London Regional Examining Board [*British*] (AIE) ..... LREB
London Review of Books [*A publication*] (BRI) .... Lon R Bks

London School of Polymer Technology [*British*] (AIE) .... LSPT
London's Central Criminal Court [*England*] (AD) .... Old Bailey
Long Akha [*Malaysia*] [*Airport symbol*] (AD) .... KLH
Long Island Airlines [*ICAO designator*] (AD) .... YL
Long Lama [*Malaysia*] [*Airport symbol*] (AD) .... LLM
Long Throw [*Speaker system*] .... LT
Long Time, No See [*Computer science*] (DOM) .... LTNS
Longitudinal (VRA) .... longit
Longman's Dictionary of Contemporary English [*A publication*] .... LDOCE
Long-Term Effects of Dredging Operations [*Coastal Engineering Research Center*] .... LEDO
Long-Term Equity Anticipation Securities [*Investment term*] (DFIT) .... LEAPS
Lorica [*Colombia*] [*Airport symbol*] (AD) .... LRI
Los Angeles Times Book Review [*A publication*] (BRI) .... LATBR
Loss of Mesodermal Competence [*Developmental biology*] .... LMC
Lost Wax (VRA) .... lstwx
Lovell-Powell [*Wyoming*] [*Airport symbol*] (AD) .... POY
Low Achievers Project [*Education*] (AIE) .... LAP
Low Attaining Pupils in Secondary Schools (AIE) ...... LAPS
Low Income Cut-Off [*Canada*] .... LICO
Lower (VRA) .... low
Lower-Extremity Amputation Protocol [*Orthopedics*] .... LEAP
Low-Temperature Magnetic Force Microscope .... LTMFM
Luang Prabang [*Laos*] [*Airport symbol*] (AD) .... LPQ
Lucas Air Transport [*ICAO designator*] (AD) .... ZI
Lufthansa German Airlines [*ICAO designator*] (AD) ..... LH
Lukulu [*Zambia*] [*Airport symbol*] (AD) .... LXU
Luluabourg [*Zaire*] [*Airport symbol*] (AD) .... LLB
Luminosity (WDMC) .... US
Lunette (VRA) .... lun
Luong Namtha [*Laos*] [*Airport symbol*] (AD) .... LXG
Lushoto [*Tanzania*] [*Airport symbol*] (AD) .... LUY
Lustre (VRA) .... lus
Luton College of Higher Education (AIE) .... LCHE
Luxembourg (VRA) .... Lux
Lyallpur [*Pakistan*] [*Airport symbol*] (AD) .... LYP
Lympne [*England*] [*Airport symbol*] (AD) .... LYM

M
By Meaning

Maart [*March*] [*Dutch*] (AD) .... Mrt
Maatschappij [*Company*] [*Dutch*] (AD) .... Mpy
Mac Knight Airlines [*ICAO designator*] (AD) .... MT
Macenta [*Guinea*] [*Airport symbol*] (AD) .... MCA
Machine Power Transmission Association (AD) .... MPTA
Machine Record (AD) .... mr
Machine Rifle (AD) .... mr
Machine Screw (AD) .... ms
Machine Steel (AD) .... ms
Machine-Oriented Language (AD) .... mol
Machine-Readable Data Files [*Computer science*] (AD) .... mrdf
Machine-Readable Passport (AD) .... mrp
Machinery Failure Prevention Technology (RDA) .... MFPT
Mackey International Airlines [*ICAO designator*] (AD) .... MI
Maclean's [*A publication*] (BRI) .... Mac
MacRobertson-Miller Airline Service [*ICAO designator*] (AD) ...... MV
Macro-Oriented Business Language [*Computer science*] (AD) ...... mobl
Macrophage Scavenger Receptor [*Immunology*] .... MSR
Madagascar [*Malagasy Republic*] (VRA) .... Madag
Madirovalo [*Malagasy*] [*Airport symbol*] (AD) .... WMV
Madjelis Permusiawaratan Rakat [*People's Deliberative Assembly*]
  [*Indonesia*] (AD) .... MPR Assembly]=>> Indonesia
Madonna [*Our Lady*] [*Italian*] (AD) .... Mona
Maestro (AD) .... Mro
Maestro GG1MasterGG2 [*Italian*] (AD) .... Mo
Magangue [*Colombia*] [*Airport symbol*] (AD) .... MGN
Magazine (VRA) .... mag
Magazine Antiques [*A publication*] (BRI) .... Mag Antiq
Magazine of Fantasy and Science Fiction [*A publication*] (BRI) ...... MFSF
Magazine of History [*A publication*] (BRI) .... M of Hist
Magazine Research, Inc. (AD) .... MRI
Magdalen Island [*Quebec*] [*Airport symbol*] (AD) .... YGR
Magdalenian (VRA) .... Magdl
Magical Blend [*A publication*] (BRI) .... Mag Bl
Magnesium (VRA) .... magns
Magnetic Particle Inspection (AD) .... mpi
Magnetic Porous Glass [*Materials science*] .... MPG
Magnetic Radiation Generator (AD) .... mrg
Magnetic Rectifier Control (AD) .... mrc
Magnetic Resonating (AD) .... MR
Magnetic Rubber Inspection (AD) .... mri
Magnetic-Resonance Imager (AD) .... mri
Magnetocrystalline Anisotropy [*Physics*] .... MCA
Magneto-Optical Disc (AD) .... mod
Magneto-Optical System (AD) .... MOS
Magnetoplasmadynamics (AD) .... mpd
Magnetorheological Finishing [*Optics manufacturing*] (RDA) ...... MRF
Magnum Airlines [*ICAO designator*] (AD) .... LE
Magnum Airlines [*ICAO designator*] (AD) .... MQ
Mahfid [*South Arabia*] [*Airport symbol*] (AD) .... MJZ
Mahogany (VRA) .... mah
Mail Order (AD) .... mo
Mail Payment (AD) .... mp
Mail Readership Measurement (AD) .... mrm
Main Port (AD) .... mnpo
Main Propulsion Test Article (AD) .... mpta
Main Switch (AD) .... ms
Maine Personnel and Guidance Association (AD) .... MPGA
Mainstream of American Thought (AD) .... moAt
Mainstream of Republican Thought (AD) .... moRt
Maintain (AD) .... mntn
Maintainability and Reliability (AD) .... m & r
Maintainability and Repairs (AD) .... m & r
Maintainability Program Requirements (AD) .... MPR
Maintainability Requirements Group (AD) .... MRG
Maintained (AD) .... mntnd
Maintaining (AD) .... mntng
Maintenance (AD) .... mntnc
Maintenance and Overhaul (AD) .... m & o
Maintenance and Service (AD) .... ms
Maintenance and Supply (AD) .... M & S
Maintenance Part (AD) .... mp
Maintenance, Repair, and Operating (AD) .... mro
Maintenance Replacement Factor (AD) .... mrf
Maintenance Requirements Task Analysis (AD) .... MRTA
Maintenance-Operations Support Set (AD) .... moss

Maintenance-to-Operation (AD) .... m/o
Maiquetia [*Venezuela*] [*Airport symbol*] (AD) .... MIQ
Maiquetia [*Venezuelan airport*] (AD) .... MQI
Maison [*House*] [*French*] (AD) .... mon
Maitrise en Fiscalite (DD) .... MFisc
Maitrise en Ingenierie [*Master of Engineering*] (DD) .... Ming
Maji [*Ethiopia*] [*Airport symbol*] (AD) .... MJI
Majma [*Saudi Arabia*] [*Airport symbol*] (AD) .... MJH
Majolica (VRA) .... maj
Major Subject (AD) .... ms
Majors Electronic Data Interchange Communications System [*Computer
  science*] .... MEDICS
Makabana [*Congo*] [*Airport symbol*] (AD) .... KMK
Makapuu Oceanic Center [*Hawaii*] (AD) .... MOC
Makassar [*Sulawesi, Indonesia*] [*Airport symbol*] (AD) .... MSR
Make or Buy (AD) .... mob
Maker (VRA) .... mkr
Makerere-University Zoology Museum [*Uganda*] .... MUZM
Makimono (VRA) .... makm
Malacoota [*New South Wales, Australia*] [*Airport symbol*] ...... XMC
Malagasy Republic (VRA) .... Madag
Malaria Research Centre [*India*] .... MRC
Malawi Nyika National Park (AD) .... MNNP
Malay National Party [*Political party*] (AD) .... MNP
Malayan Rubber Fund Board (AD) .... MRFB
Malaysia (VRA) .... Malay
Malaysian Airline System [*ICAO designator*] (AD) .... MH
Malaysian Peasants Front [*Political party*] (AD) .... MPF
Malaysian Refrigerator Co. (AD) .... MRCo
Malaysian Rubber Exchange and Licensing Board (AD) .... MRELB
Malaysian Rubber Research and Development Board (AD) ...... MRRDB
Malaysian University of Science and Technology .... MUST
Maldives International Airlines [*ICAO designator*] (AD) .... RQ
Male (DD) .... m
Male Bowhunter Aided [*International Bowhunting Organization*] [*Class
  equipment*] .... MBA
Male Oriental (AD) .... m/O
Male Pattern Baldness (AD) .... mpb
Male Pipe Thread (AD) .... mpt
Male Seniors [*International Bowhunting Organization*] [*Class equipment*] ...... MSR
Malheur National Wildlife Refuge [*Oregon*] (AD) .... MNWR
Malicious Call Identification [*Telecommunications*] (DOM) ...... MCID
Mall Airways [*ICAO designator*] (AD) .... FH
Malleable Research and Development Foundation (AD) .... MR&DF
Malone [*New York*] [*Airport symbol*] (AD) .... MAL
Mamaia [*Romania*] [*Airport symbol*] (AD) .... XMM
Mambone [*Mozambique*] [*Airport symbol*] (AD) .... MBM
Mampikony [*Malagasy*] [*Airport symbol*] (AD) .... WMP
Man Overboard and Breakdown Light (AD) .... mob lt
Mana Pools Game Reserve [*Rhodesia*] (AD) .... MPGR
Managed Care [*Insurance*] (WYGK) .... MC
Management (DD) .... mgmt
Management & Operation of Public Services Section [*Reference and User
  Services Association*] [*American Library Association*] ...... MOPSS
Management and Operation of User Services Section .... MOUSS
Management and Organisation in Secondary Schools (AIE) ...... MOSS
Management and Organization (AD) .... m & o
Management and Personnel Office (AIE) .... MPO
Management Development Adviser (AIE) .... MDA
Management Education Training and Development (AIE) ...... METD
Management Information Bases [*Compaq*] [*Computer science*] ...... MIBs
Management Review and Analysis Program (AD) .... MRAP
Management Verification Consortium (AIE) .... MVC
Manager (DD) .... mgr
Managing (DD) .... man
Manaus (AD) .... Mns
Manchester Metropolitan University [*British*] (AIE) .... MMU
Manchester Open College Federation [*British*] (AIE) ...... MOCF
Mandalay [*Burma*] [*Airport symbol*] (AD) .... MDL
Mandatory Retirement Age Law of 1978 (WYGK) .... MRAL
Mandorla (VRA) .... mandl
Manganese Oxide Mesoporous Structure [*Inorganic Chemistry*] ...... MOMS
Mangla [*Pakistan*] [*Airport symbol*] (AD) .... MWP
Manicore [*Brazil*] [*Airport symbol*] (AD) .... MRE
Manicouagan [*Quebec*] [*Airport symbol*] (AD) .... YMV
Manifesto (VRA) .... manif

Manifold Pressure (AD) ... mp
Manifold-Regulator Accumulator Charging (AD) ... mrac
Maniti Sugar [Stock exchange symbol] (AD) ... MNU
Manitoba [Canada] (DD) ... Man
Manitoba Association of Architects [1914] [Canada] (NGC) ... MAA
Manitoba Society of Artists [1925] [Canada] (NGC) ... MSA
Mankoya [Zambia] [Airport symbol] (AD) ... MNK
Mannan-Binding Lectin [Immunology] ... MBL
Manned Orbital Systems Concept (AD) ... mosc
Manned Reusable Payload (AD) ... mrp
Manned Reusable Product (AD) ... mrp
Manned Revolving Space Systems Simulator (AD) ... mrsss
Manner of Performance Rating (AD) ... mopr
Mannerism (VRA) ... Mnrsm
Mannlicher-Schoenauer (AD) ... M/S
Manportable Office System [Army] (RDA) ... MPOS
Manpower Intelligence and Planning Division (AIE) ... MIPD
Manpower-Planning Quota (AD) ... mpq
Mansa [Zambia] [Airport symbol] (AD) ... FZB
Manston [England] [Airport symbol] (AD) ... MSE
Manual Operation (AD) ... mo
Manually Operated Plotting Board (AD) ... mopb
Manufacture (DD) ... mfr
Manufacturing (DD) ... mfg
Manufacturing Other Charges (AD) ... moc
Manufacturing Plan Control Board (AD) ... MPCB
Manus Island [Bismarck Archipelago] [Airport symbol] (AD) ... MAS
Manuscript (VRA) ... ms
Manx Gaelic (AD) ... Mnx
Manzanillo (AD) ... Mnzlo
Mao [Chad] [Airport symbol] (AD) ... AMO
Maoist Reorganization Movement of the Party of the Proletariat [Political party] (AD) ... MRPP Political party
Maoist Revolutionary Communist Party [Political party] (AD) ... MRCP
Map Reading (AD) ... M/R
Map Reading (AD) ... m/r
Map Reference (AD) ... mr
Maquette (VRA) ... maq
Marble (VRA) ... marb
Marble Base (AD) ... mrb
Marble Floor (AD) ... mrf
Marbled Paper Sides (AD) ... mps
Marco Island Airways [ICAO designator] (AD) ... LS
Margaret (AD) ... Mog
Margin (AD) ... mrg
Margin of Safety (AD) ... ms
Marginal Credit (DFIT) ... MC
Marginal Physical Product (AD) ... mpp
Marginal Propensity to Consume (AD) ... mpc
Marginal Propensity to Invest (AD) ... mpi
Marginal Rate of Substitution (AD) ... mrs
Marginal Rate of Technical Substitution (AD) ... mrts
Marginal Revenue (AD) ... mr
Marginal Revenue Product (AD) ... mrp
Marginalia (AD) ... mrg
Mariana Islands (VRA) ... CM
Marianna [Florida] [Airport symbol] (AD) ... MAI
Marie-Galante Island [Guadeloupe] [Airport symbol] (AD) ... GJB
Marina di Massa [Italy] [Airport symbol] (AD) ... QMM
Marine and Allied Industries Training Association (AIE) ... MAITA
Marine and Ports Council of Australia (AD) ... MPCA
Marine Builders Training Trust (AIE) ... MBTT
Marine Corps Gazette [A publication] (BRI) ... Mar Crp G
Marine Office of America (AD) ... MOA
Marine Physician Assistant (AD) ... MPA
Marine Protein Concentrate (AD) ... mpc
Mariner-Like Elements [Genetics] ... MLE
Mariners [Seattle Baseball Team] (AD) ... Ms
Marion [Indiana] [Airport symbol] (AD) ... MZZ
Marion Downs [Queensland] [Airport symbol] (AD) ... MXD
Marion Power Shovel [Stock exchange symbol] (AD) ... MNV
Maritime (AD) ... mrtm
Maritime Patrol Aircraft (AD) ... mpa
Maritime Polar Air Mass (AD) ... mpam
Maritime Provinces Higher Education Commission (AD) ... MPHEC
Mark (VRA) ... mrk
Mark Russell (AD) ... MR
Marked (AD) ... mrkd
Marker (AD) ... mrkr
Market (VRA) ... mark
Market Opening Sector Specific (AD) ... MOSS
Market Research Corp. of America (AD) ... MRCA
Market Value Added ... MVA
Market Value Appraiser (DD) ... MVA
Marketing (DD) ... mktg
Marketing Organization (AD) ... MO
Marketing Services Group ... MSGI
Markets (AD) ... Mrkts
Marking (AD) ... mrkg
Marking and Stenciling (AD) ... m/s
Marlin-Rockwell Corp. (AD) ... MRC
Marquardt Corp. [Stock exchange symbol] (AD) ... MRQ
Marquetry (VRA) ... marq
Marromeu [Mozambique] [Airport symbol] (AD) ... MEU
Marrow Stromal Cell [Biochemistry] ... MSC
Mars Global Surveyor [NASA] ... MGS
Mars In-situ-utilization Sample Return [Computer science] ... MISR
Marsa Brega [Libya] [Airport symbol] (AD) ... LMQ
Marsabit National Park [Kenya] (AD) ... MNP
Marshall Islands (VRA) ... TT
Marshall's Air [ICAO designator] (AD) ... HS
Martin Luther King, Jr. ... MLK
Martinez (AD) ... Mrtnz
Martini & Rossi ... M&R
Martinique (AD) ... Mqe
Martinique (AD) ... Mrt
Martyrdom (VRA) ... mtydm
Marxist Progressive Labor Party [Political party] (AD) ... MPLP
Maryland Personnel and Guidance Association (AD) ... MPGA
Maryland Port Authority (AD) ... mpa
Maryland Probation, Patrol and Corrections Association (AD) ... MPPCA
Maryport (AD) ... Mpt
Marysville [California] [Airport symbol] (AD) ... MYV
Marzo [March] [Spanish] (AD) ... mrz
Mas o Menos [More or Less] [Spanish] (AD) ... m/ o m/
Maschinenpistole [Submachine Gun] [German] (AD) ... MP
Mascota [Mexico] [Airport symbol] (AD) ... MSX
Masjed Soleyman [Iran] [Airport symbol] (AD) ... MJX
Masling Commuter Services [ICAO designator] (AD) ... EK
Masonic Relief Association of the United States and Canada (AD) ... MRAUSCAN
Masonite (VRA) ... masn
Mason-Pfizer Virus [Medicine] (AD) ... M-P v
Masonry (VRA) ... mas
Masonry Opening (AD) ... mo
Mass Observation (AD) ... mo
Mass Radiography Unit (AD) ... mru
Mass Rapid Transit (AD) ... MRT
Mass Rapid Transit System (AD) ... MRTS
Mass Spectrometric (AD) ... ms
Massachusetts Organized Crime Control Council (AD) ... MOCCC
Massenya [Chad] [Airport symbol] (AD) ... MYC
Massio [Ethiopia] [Airport symbol] (AD) ... MZX
Massive Nuclear Retaliation (AD) ... mnr
Mastaba (VRA) ... mstb
Master (AD) ... Mr
Master (VRA) ... mstr
Master in Accounting Science (DD) ... MAccSc
Master in Commercial Science (DD) ... MCommSc
Master in Commercial Science (DD) ... MScComm
Master in Communication (DD) ... MCommun
Master in Regional Planning (DD) ... MRP
Master of Agricultural Science (DD) ... MASc
Master of Applied Science (DD) ... MScA
Master of Environmental Design (DD) ... MEDes
Master of Environmental Science (DD) ... MES
Master of Environmental Studies (DD) ... MEnv
Master of Health Services Administration (DD) ... MHSA
Master of International Management (DD) ... MIM
Master of Landscape Architecture [Canada] (DD) ... MLandArch
Master of Mining and Metallurgy (DD) ... MIMM
Master of Obstetrics and Gynecology (AD) ... MOG
Master of Pest Management (DD) ... MPM
Master of Physics (DD) ... MPhysics
Master of Science [Academic degree] (AIE) ... MSc
Master of Science in Commerce (DD) ... MSC
Master of Science in Commerce (DD) ... MScC
Master of Science in Economics (DD) ... MScEcon
Master of Science in Engineering (DD) ... MScE
Master of Surgery (DD) ... ChM
Master of Surgery (DD) ... CM
Master of the Fox Hunt (DD) ... MFH
Master of the Queen's Music [British] (AD) ... MQM
Master Operation Control (AD) ... moc
Master Oscillator Power Amplifier (AD) ... mopa
Master Oscillator (AD) ... mo
Master Oscillator-Power Amplifier RADAR (AD) ... mopar
Master Painters, Decorators, and Signwriters Association (AD) ... MPDSA
Master Pastry Cooks Association (AD) ... MPCA
Master Photographers Association (AD) ... MPA
Master Plan for Academic Computing (AD) ... MPAC
Master Plan for Computing Services (AD) ... MPCS
Master Plan for Data Processing and Information Systems (AD) ... MPDPIS
Master Plan Works Breakdown Structure (AD) ... MPWBS
Master Printers and Engravers Association of the United States (AD) ... MPEAUS
Master Retail Milk Vendors Association (AD) ... MRMVA
Master Retailers Association (AD) ... MRA
Master Switch (AD) ... ms
Mastic Point [Andros Islands, Bahamas] [Airport symbol] (AD) ... MSK
Mastuj [Pakistan] [Airport symbol] (AD) ... MJP
Mastung [Pakistan] [Airport symbol] (AD) ... MAU
Matched and Lost [Investment term] (DFIT) ... M&L
Matched Set (AD) ... ms
Matching Alcoholism Treatments to Client Heterogeneity ... MATCH
Material (VRA) ... mat
Material Overhead (AD) ... moh
Material Process Instruction (AD) ... MPI
Material Receipt Discrepancy Notice (AD) ... MRDN
Material Receipt Voucher (AD) ... mrv
Material Recorder Notice (AD) ... MRN

Material Standard (AD) ...... MS
Materials and Processes (AD) ...... m & p
Materials Program Code (AD) ...... mpc
Materials Research and Standards (AD) ...... MR & S
Maternity and Surgical (AD) ...... M&S
Mates Receipt (AD) ...... M/R
Mathematical, Physical, and Engineering Science (AD) ...... MPES
Mathematical Programming Language [Computer science] (AD) ...... mpl
Mathematics (DD) ...... Math
Mathematics in Society Project (AIE) ...... MISP
Mathematics, Physics, Chemistry (AD) ...... mpc
Mathematics/Science/Computer ...... MSC
Mathematics Teacher [A publication] (BRI) ...... Math T
Mato Grosso [Brazil] [Airport symbol] (AD) ...... MGO
Matrix Glass [Geology] ...... MG
Matrix Information and Directory Services, Inc. ...... MIDS
Matrix Isolation and Electron Spin Resonance [Analytical chemistry] ...... MIESR
Mattamuskeet National Wildlife Refuge [North Carolina] (AD) ...... MNWR
Mature Motion Pictures (AD) ...... Ms
Matured Bonds [Investment term] (DFIT) ...... M
Maues [Brazil] [Airport symbol] (AD) ...... MBZ
Mauna Olu College [Maui] (AD) ...... MOC
Mauricio [Mauritius] [Spanish] (AD) ...... Mrc
Mauritania (VRA) ...... Maurti
Mauritius (AD) ...... Mrts
Maurituis Rupee [Monetary unit] (AD) ...... M rps
Mausoleum (VRA) ...... mauso
Max Planck Institute (AD) ...... MPI
Maximum Aggregate Student Number [Higher Education Funding Council] (AIE) ...... MASN
Maximum Observed Frequency (AD) ...... mof
Maximum Obtainable Irradiance (AD) ...... moi
Maximum Operating Hours (AD) ...... moh
Maximum Output Level (AD) ...... mol
Maximum Payload (AD) ...... m payl
Maximum Payload (AD) ...... mpl
Maximum Permissible Annual Dose (AD) ...... mpad
Maximum Permissible Annual Intake (AD) ...... mpai
Maximum Permissible Body Burden [of Radiation] (AD) ...... mpbb
Maximum Permissible Concentration (AD) ...... mpc
Maximum Permissible Concentration of Unidentified Radionuclides (AD) ...... mpcur
Maximum Permissible Dose (AD) ...... mpd
Maximum Permissible Exposure [to Radiation] (AD) ...... mpe
Maximum Permissible Language (AD) ...... mpl
Maximum Permissible Level (AD) ...... mpl
Maximum Point of Impulse (AD) ...... mpi
Maximum Recommended Daily Human Dose (AD) ...... mrdhd
Maximum Resolving Power (AD) ...... mrp
Maximum Retail Price (AD) ...... mrp
Maximum Stress (AD) ...... ms
Maya Airways [ICAO designator] (AD) ...... MW
Mayajigua [Cuba] [Airport symbol] (AD) ...... MJG
Mayo Research Foundation (AD) ...... MRF
Mayoko [Gabon] [Airport symbol] (AD) ...... MYZ
Mayor's Office of Manpower Resources (AD) ...... MOMR
Mbala [Zambia] [Airport symbol] (AD) ...... ACN
Mbout [Mauritania] [Airport symbol] (AD) ...... MBR
McCall's Needlework [A publication] (BRI) ...... McCall Nee
McGraw-Hill Learning Architecture ...... MHLA
McKinley Park [Alaska] [Airport symbol] (AD) ...... MPK
McNamara-O'Hara Service Contract Act of 1965 (WYGK) ...... MOSCA
Meal Ready to Eat (AD) ...... mre
Meals Rejected by Everyone ...... MRE
Mean Neap Rise (AD) ...... mnr
Mean Neap Tide (AD) ...... mnt
Mean Operating Time (AD) ...... mot
Mean Point of Impact (AD) ...... mpi
Mean Pressure Suction Head (AD) ...... mpsh
Mean Radial Error (AD) ...... mre
Mean Radiant Temperature (AD) ...... mrt
Mean Rise Interval (AD) ...... mri
Mean Square (AD) ...... ms
Measles-Containing Vaccine ...... MCV
Measure of Effectiveness (AD) ...... moe
Measurements of Pollution in the Troposphere ...... MOPITT
Meat Industry Training Organisation (AIE) ...... MITO
Meat Packing House (AD) ...... MPH
Meat Research Institute of New Zealand (AD) ...... MRINZ
Mechanical (DD) ...... mech
Mechanical Operability Test (AD) ...... mot
Mechanically Operated Inlet Valve (AD) ...... moiv
Mechanically Recovered Meat (AD) ...... mrm
Mechanization of Warehousing and Shipment Processing (AD) ...... mowasp
Mechlorethamine, Vincristine, Procarbazine, Prednisone [Medicine] (AD) ...... moop
Medal (VRA) ...... med
Medallion (VRA) ...... medln
Media (VRA) ...... medi
Media and Methods [A publication] (BRI) ...... Media M
Media Generated (VRA) ...... medi gen
Media Resources Officer (AIE) ...... MRO
Medical and Surgical (AD) ...... M&S
Medical Education Technologies, Inc. ...... METI
Medical Humanities Review [A publication] (BRI) ...... MHR

Medical Neuropsychiatric Research Unit (AD) ...... MNRU
Medical Officer in Command (AD) ...... MOIC
Medical Outpatient (AD) ...... mop
Medical Quality Assurance (AD) ...... MQA
Medical Quality Assurance Board (AD) ...... MQAB
Medical Records Index (AD) ...... MRI
Medical Records Library (AD) ...... MRL
Medical Reference Department (AD) ...... MRD
Medical Registration Council of Ireland (AD) ...... MRCI
Medical Rehabilitation Unit (AD) ...... MRU
Medical Research and Development Command [Army] (AD) ...... MR & DC
Medical Research Reactor (AD) ...... mrr
Medical Savings Account ...... MSA
Medical Service Agency (WYGK) ...... MSA
Medical Systems Integration Office [Army] (RDA) ...... MSIO
Medicare Carve-Out [Insurance] (WYGK) ...... MCO
Medicare Catastrophic Coverage Repeal Act of 1989 (WYGK) ...... MCCRA
Medicine and Surgery (AD) ...... M & S
Medicine in the Public Interest (AD) ...... MPI
Medieval (VRA) ...... mdvl
Medium Altitude Endurance (RDA) ...... MAE
Medium Observation Aircraft (AD) ...... moa
Medium Pressure (AD) ...... mp
Medium Pressure (AD) ...... mpress
Medium Range (AD) ...... mr
Medium Resolution Infrared (AD) ...... mrir
Medium Shot (AD) ...... ms
Medium Steel (AD) ...... ms
Medium-Power RADAR (AD) ...... mpr
Medium-Powered Radio Range (AD) ...... mra
Medium-Powered Radio Range (AD) ...... mrl
Medium-Processing Channel Black (AD) ...... mpc black
Medium-Range Air-to-Air Missile [Military] (AD) ...... mraam
Medium-Range Air-to-Surface Missile [Military] (AD) ...... mrasm
Medium-Range Applied Technology (AD) ...... mrat
Medium-Range Ballistic Missile [Military] (AD) ...... mrbm
Medium-Range Interceptor (AD) ...... mri
Medium-Range Surveillance Aircraft (AD) ...... mrsa
Medroxyprogesterone [Medicine] (AD) ...... MPA
Meersk Air [ICAO designator] (AD) ...... DM
Meester [Master] [Dutch] (AD) ...... mr
Meet Me Conference [Telecommunications] (DOM) ...... MMC
Meeting of Consultation of Ministers of Foreign Affairs ...... MCMFA
Meeting Point (AD) ...... mp
Mega Floating-Point Operations per Second [Computer science] ...... MFLOP
Megacycles per Second (AD) ...... mps
Megapascal (AD) ...... mpa
Megarad (AD) ...... mrad
Megaron (VRA) ...... meg
Meknes [Morocco] [Airport symbol] (AD) ...... MEK
Melfi [Chad] [Airport symbol] (AD) ...... MEF
Melt Inclusions [Geology] ...... MI
Melting Point (AD) ...... mp
Melting Point (AD) ...... mpt
Member (DD) ...... mbr
Member Canadian Institute of Mining and Metallurgy (DD) ...... MCIM
Member of Our Tribe (AD) ...... mot
Member of Parliament [British] (AD) ...... M o P
Member of the Architectural Institute of British Columbia [Canada] (DD) ...... MAIBC
Member of the Institute of Accredited Public Accountants [Canada] (DD) ...... APA
Member of the Institute of Management (DD) ...... MIM
Member of the Order of Merit [Canada] (DD) ...... OM
Member of the Order of Military Merit [Canada] (DD) ...... MMM
Member of the Police Force (AD) ...... mof
Member of the Royal College of Physicians of the United Kingdom [British] (AD) ...... MRCPUK British
Member of the Royal Household [British] (AD) ...... MRH
Member of the Royal Pharmaceutical Society [Canada] (DD) ...... MPPhS
Member of the Royal Pharmaceutical Society [Canada] (DD) ...... MRPhS
Member of the Royal Sanitary Association [British] (AD) ...... MR San Asn
Member of the Royal Society of Musicians of Great Britian (AD) ...... MRSMGB
Member of the Trust Companies Institute (DD) ...... MTCI
Member of the Trust Institute (DD) ...... MTI
Membrano Proliferative Glomerulonephritis [Medicine] (AD) ...... mpgn
Membre de l'Ordre des Chimistes du Quebec [Canada] (DD) ...... OCQ
Memorandum of Agreement (AD) ...... M o A
Memorandum of Understanding (AD) ...... MoU
Memorandum of Understanding (AD) ...... mou
Memorandum Purchase Order (AD) ...... MPO
Memorial (VRA) ...... memrl
Memory Controller Gate Array [Computer science] ...... MCGA
Memory Printout (AD) ...... mpo
Memory Quotient ...... MQ
Memory Quotient (AD) ...... mq
Memphis Power Boat Club [Tennessee] (AD) ...... MPBC
Memphis Public Library (AD) ...... MPL
Mendes (AD) ...... Ms
Men's Journal [A publication] (BRI) ...... Men's J
Men's Republican Club [Political party] (AD) ...... MRC
Menstruation Pill [Medicine] (AD) ...... M-pill
Mental Parents Union (AD) ...... MPU
Mentally Handicapped (AIE) ...... MH
Mentally Retarded (AD) ...... mr
Mentone [France] [Airport symbol] (AD) ...... MNE

Merced [*California*] [*Airport symbol*] (AD) .... MCE
Merced National Wildlife Refuge [*California*] (AD) .... MNWR
Merces [*Brazil*] [*Airport symbol*] (AD) .... MEZ
Merchandise (DD) .... mdse
Merchandise Ordering Processing System (AD) .... MOPS
Merchandising (DD) .... mdsg
Merpati Nusatnara Airlines [*ICAO designator*] (AD) .... MZ
Merrill Lynch Financial Advantage .... MLFA
Mersa Matruh [*Egypt*] [*Airport symbol*] (AD) .... MUH
Merseyside and North Wales Electricity Board [*British*] (AD) .... MNWEB
Meru National Park [*Equatorial Kenya*] (AD) .... MNP
Mervaerdiomsaetningsskat [*Value-Added Tax*] [*Danish*] (AD) .... moms
Mesa Aviation [*ICAO designator*] (AD) .... YV
Mesaba Aviation [*ICAO designator*] (AD) .... XJ
Meshed [*Iran*] [*Airport symbol*] (AD) .... MHD
Mesial Temporal Lobe Seizure [*Medicine*] .... MTLS
Mesial-Occlusal-Distal [*Dentistry*] (AD) .... m-o-d
Mesial-Occlusal-Distal [*Dentistry*] (AD) .... mods
Mesial-Occlusal-Distal-Buccal [*Dentistry*] (AD) .... m-o-d-b
Meso American (VRA) .... MesoAm
Mesolithic (VRA) .... Mesol
Mesopotamia (VRA) .... Mesop
Mesothorium (AD) .... Ms
Message Processing Language [*Computer science*] (AD) .... mpl
Messenger Transport Organizer [*Developmental biology*] .... METRO
Mesters Vig [*Greenland*] [*Airport symbol*] (AD) .... MRG
Meta Content File [*Netscape*] [*Computer science*] .... MCF
Metabolic Rate (AD) .... mr
Metal Oxide Film (AD) .... mof
Metal Rolling Door (AD) .... mrd
Metal Roof Deck (AD) .... mrd
Metal Shank (AD) .... m/s
Metallic Nitrogen-Oxide Semiconductor (AD) .... mnos
Metallo-Organic Liquid LASER (AD) .... moll
Metallurgical Engineering (DD) .... MetEng
Metallurgical Plantmakers Federation (AD) .... MPF
Metallurgical Quenching Dilatometry .... MQD
Metal-Nitride-Semiconductor (AD) .... mns
Metal-Oxide Semiconductor (AD) .... mos
Metal-Oxide Semiconductor Field-Effect Transistor (AD) .... mosfet
Metal-Oxide Semiconductor Transistor (AD) .... most
Metal-Oxide Semiconductor Transistor Logic (AD) .... mostl
Metal-Oxide Silicon (AD) .... mos
Metal-Oxide-Semiconductor Integrated Circuit (AD) .... mosic
Metalpoint (VRA) .... metpt
Metal-Point (AD) .... m-p
Metalwork (VRA) .... metwk
Metekel [*Ethiopia*] [*Airport symbol*] (AD) .... MXK
Meteorological Research Flight (AD) .... mr flight
Meteorological Research Institute (AD) .... MRI
Meters above Sea Level .... masl
Meters Per Minute (AD) .... mpm
Meters per Second (AD) .... mps
Meters per Second (AD) .... ms
Methane-Rich Gas (AD) .... mrg
Method of Operation (AD) .... mo
Methods Research Corp. (AD) .... MRC
Methyl Red (AD) .... mr
Methyl Red Voges-Proskauer [*Bacteriology*] (AD) .... mrV-P
Methylphenidate [*Central Nervous system stimulant*] .... MP
Metol-Quinol [*Medicine*] (AD) .... mq
Metol-Quinone [*Medicine*] (AD) .... MQ
Metol-Quinone [*Medicine*] (AD) .... mq
Metric System (AD) .... ms
Metric Units (DFIT) .... MTU
Metro Airlines [*ICAO designator*] (AD) .... HY
Metro Rating Area (AD) .... mra
Metroflight Airlines and Great Plains Airline [*ICAO designator*] (AD) .... FY
Metropolitan Architectural Consortium for Education (AIE) .... MACE
Metropolitan Opera Association (AD) .... MOA
Metropolitan Opera Auditions (AD) .... MOA
Metropolitan Park District (AD) .... MPD
Metropolitan Pensions Associations (AD) .... MPA
Metropolitan Police College (AD) .... MPC
Metropolitan Police Commissioner (AD) .... MPC
Metropolitan Police Department (AD) .... MPD
Metropolitan Police Laboratory (AD) .... MPL
Metropolitan Region Planning Authority (AD) .... MRPA
Mexicana de Aviacion [*ICAO designator*] (AD) .... MX
Mexico (VRA) .... Mex
Mezhdunarodnaya Organizacia Zhurnalistov [*International Organization of Journalists*] [*Russian*] (AD) .... MOZ [Journalists]=>> Russian
Mezzanine (VRA) .... mezn
Mezzo-Piano [*Moderately Soft*] [*Italian*] (AD) .... mp
Mezzotint (VRA) .... mez
MGM Grand Air [*ICAO designator*] (AD) .... MG
Mi Orden [*My Order*] [*Spanish*] (AD) .... m/o
Miami Philharmonic Orchestra (AD) .... MPO
Miami Public Library (AD) .... MPL
Michael Reese Hospital and Medical Center (AD) .... MRHMC
Michigan Airways [*ICAO designator*] (AD) .... QQ
Michigan Department of Transportation .... MDOT
Michigan Opportunities and Skills Training (AD) .... MOST
Michigan Personnel and Guidance Association (AD) .... MPGA
Michigan Quarterly Review [*A publication*] (BRI) .... MQR

Michigan Reformatory (AD) .... MR
Michigan State University of Agriculture and Applied Sciences (AD) .... MS
Michigan Travel System .... MITS
Michigan Travel Trade Information Service .... MITTINS
Michigan Wild Turkey Hunters Association .... MWTHA
Michigan Wildlife Habitat Foundation .... MWHF
Michigan Youth Hunter Education Challenge .... MYHEC
Microbiological Research Department (AD) .... MRD
Microcomputer Users in Education (AIE) .... MUE
Microcomputers in Mathematics Education (AIE) .... MIME
Microelectronics Application Programme (AIE) .... MAP
Microgravity Science Laboratory [*NASA*] .... MSL
Micromation Online Microfilmer [*Computer science*] .... mom
Micron's Millenia XKU [*Computer science*] .... MMX
Micro-Opto-Mechanical Systems .... MOMS
Microprocessing Programmable Terminal [*Computer science*] (AD) .... mpt
Microprocessor Unit (AD) .... mpu
Microseismic (AD) .... ms
Microsoft Active Accessibility [*Computer science*] .... MSAA
Microsoft Compact Disc Extension [*Computer science*] (DOM) .... MSCDEX
Microsoft Developer Network [*Computer science*] .... MSDN
Microsoft Tape Format [*Computer science*] .... MTF
Microtunneling Boring Machine (RDA) .... MTBM
Microwave Anisotropy Probe [*NASA*] .... MAP
Mid-America: An Historical Review [*A publication*] (BRI) .... Mid-Am
Mid-Blastula Transition [*Developmental biology*] .... MBT
Mid-Continent Petroleum [*Stock exchange symbol*] (AD) .... MPZ
Middle (VRA) .... mid
Middle East Airlines [*ICAO designator*] (AD) .... ME
Middle East Journal [*A publication*] (BRI) .... MEJ
Middle East Policy [*A publication*] (BRI) .... MEP
Middle East Quarterly [*A publication*] (BRI) .... MEQ
Middle of Month (AD) .... m-o-m
Middle of Target (AD) .... mot
Middle of the Road (AD) .... mor
Middle Persian (AD) .... MPers
Middle Right (AD) .... m/r
Middleground (VRA) .... mgrd
Middlesborough [*England*] [*Airport symbol*] (AD) .... MME
Midland Operational Research Society (AD) .... MORS
Midland Railway Company of Western Australia (AD) .... MRCWA
Midland Railway of Western Australia (AD) .... MRWA
Midland-Odessa Symphony and Chorale (AD) .... MOSC
Midlands Examining Group [*British*] (AIE) .... MEG
Midpoint (AD) .... mpt
Mid-Range Trajectory (AD) .... mrt
Mid-Roll Interchange [*Advanced photo system*] .... MRC
Mid-South Commuter Airlines [*ICAO designator*] (AD) VL
Midstate Airlines [*ICAO designator*] (AD) .... IU
Midwest Aviation [*ICAO designator*] (AD) .... WV
Midwest Express Airlines [*ICAO designator*] (AD) .... YX
Miele Mimbale [*Gabon*] [*Airport symbol*] (AD) .... GIM
Migrant and Seasonal Agricultural Worker Act of 1983 (WYGK) .... MSAWA
Mijnheer [*Mr.*] [*Dutch*] (AD) .... Mnr
Mikumi National Park [*Tanzania*] (AD) .... MNP
Mild Steel (AD) .... ms
Mildew-Resistant Thread (AD) .... mrt
Milepost (AD) .... mp
Miles of Relative Movement (AD) .... mrm
Miles Per Hour Per Second (AD) .... mphps
Miles per Tankful (AD) .... MPT
Miles per Tankful (AD) .... mpt
Milestone (AD) .... m/s
Milford Haven [*Wales*] [*Airport symbol*] (AD) .... ILF
Milgarra [*Queensland*] [*Airport symbol*] (AD) .... MQG
Military Acquisition Management Branch [*Army*] (RDA) .... MAMB
Military Advanced Technology Management Office (RDA) .... MATMO
Military Occupational Information (AD) .... moi
Military Occupational Specialty (AD) .... mos
Military Operations Area (AD) .... MOA
Military Operations Other than War (RDA) .... MOOTW
Military Order of the Loyal Legion of the USA (AD) .... MOLLUSA
Military Ordinary Mail (AD) .... mom
Military Pay Division (AD) .... MPD
Military Payment Certificate (AD) .... mpc
Military Police Force (AD) .... MPC
Military Railroad (AD) .... MR
Military Reform Institute (AD) .... MRI
Military Review [*A publication*] (BRI) .... Mil Rev
Military Review Team (AD) .... MRT
Military-Rated Thrust (AD) .... mrt
Milk of Magnesia (AD) .... mom
Milk Powder (AD) .... m/p
Milk-of-Magnesia in the Morning if No Bowel Movement by Evening [*Medicine*] (AD) .... m-o-m in am if no bm by pm Medicine
Mill Run (AD) .... mr
Mille Pasuum [*Thousand Paces*] [*Latin*] (AD) .... M
Milli (DFIT) .... M
Milligram (DFIT) .... MGM
Millimeter (DFIT) .... MM
Milliohms (AD) .... mohms
Million Pulses per Second (AD) .... mpps
Millions of Particles per Cubic Foot of Air (AD) .... mppcf
Milliosmol (AD) .... mosm
Millipascal Second (AD) .... mpas

Millirad (AD)	mrad
Milliroentgen (AD)	mR
Milliroentgen Equivalent Man (AD)	mrem
Milstrip Routing Identifier (AD)	mri
Milwaukee Public Library (AD)	MPL
Milwaukee Public Museum (AD)	MPM
Milwaukee Public Museum (AD)	MPS
Minaret (VRA)	mnrt
Mind/Body Medical Institute	MBMI
Mine Run (AD)	mr
Mineiros [Brazil] [Airport symbol] (AD)	MRX
Mineral (VRA)	mnrl
Mineral Rubber (AD)	mr
Mineral Wells [Texas] [Airport symbol] (AD)	MWL
Minerology (DD)	miner
Mines (AD)	Mns
Mines and Quarries (AD)	M&Q
Mingo National Wildlife Refuge [Missouri] (AD)	MNWR
Miniature (VRA)	minat
Miniature Precision Bearings (AD)	MPB
Miniature Quartz Incandescent Lamp (AD)	mqil
Miniature Quartz Lamp (AD)	mql
Miniature Sheet of Stamps (AD)	m/s
Minidoka National Wildlife Refuge [Idaho] (AD)	MNWR
Minimal Reproductive Unit (AD)	mru
Minimum (DFIT)	Min
Minimum (AD)	mnm
Minimum Obstruction Clearance Altitude (AD)	moca
Minimum Orbital Unmanned Satellite (AD)	MOUSE
Minimum Planning Chart (AD)	mpc
Minimum Quantity Yards per Color (AD)	mqyco
Minimum Quantity Yards per Design (AD)	mqyds
Minimum Reacting Dose (AD)	mrd
Minimum Reception Altitude (AD)	mra
Minimum Stress (AD)	ms
Minimum Temperature (AD)	mntmp
Mining (DD)	min
Mining Permit (AD)	MP
Minister of Labour [British] (AD)	M o L
Minister of Pensions [British] (AD)	M o P
Minister of Pensions [British] (AD)	M Pen
Minister of Power [British] (AD)	M o P
Minister of Production [British] (AD)	M o P
Minister of Reconstruction [British] (AD)	M of R
Minister of Transport [British] (AD)	M o T
Minister of War Transport [British] (AD)	M o WT
Minister of Works [British] (AD)	M o W
Minister Provincial (AD)	MP
Ministere de la Qualite de la Vie [Ministry of the Quality of Life] [France] (AD)	MQV Life]=>> France
Ministerio de Obras Publicas [Ministry of Public Works] [Spanish] (AD)	MOP
Ministerstwo Opieki Spolecznes [Ministry of Social Welfare] [Poland] (AD)	MOS Poland
Ministry of Agriculture [British] (AD)	MoA
Ministry of Commerce and Industry [British] (AD)	MOCI
Ministry of Defence [British] (AD)	M o D
Ministry of Economic Affairs [British] (AD)	MOEA
Ministry of Education [British] (AD)	MoE
[The] Ministry of Electronics Industry [China]	MEI
Ministry of Energy [British] (AD)	M o E
Ministry of Finance [British] (AD)	MoF
Ministry of Health [British] (AD)	M o H
Ministry of Housing and Local Government [British] (AD)	MOHLG
Ministry of Pensions [British] (AD)	M Pen
Ministry of Reconstruction [British] (AD)	M o R
Ministry of Recreation and Sport [British] (AD)	MRS
Ministry of Supply Inspection Department [British] (AD)	MOSID
Ministry of the Interior [British] (AD)	MoI
Ministry of Town and Country Planning [British] (AD)	M o TCP
Ministry of Transit and Communications [Philippines] (AD)	MOTC
Ministry of Works and Development [British] (AD)	MoWD
Minitrack Optical Tracking System (AD)	mots
Minj [New Guinea] [Airport symbol] (AD)	MZN
Minneapolis (AD)	Mpls
Minneapolis-Moline [Stock exchange symbol] (AD)	MPW
Minnesota and Ontario Paper [Stock exchange symbol] (AD)	MNT
Minnesota Occupational Information System (AD)	MOIS
Minnesota Orchestral Association (AD)	MOA
Minnesota Perception Diagnostic Test (AD)	MPDT
Minnesota Personnel and Guidance Association (AD)	MPGA
Minnesota Private College Council (AD)	MPCC
Minnesota Restitution Center (AD)	MRC
Minnesota Review [A publication] (BRI)	MR
Minorities in Medicine [Eastern Michigan University Macy Scholarship]	MIM
Minorities Research Group (AD)	MRG
Mint State (AD)	ms
Minute of Angle (AD)	moa
Miracema do Norte [Brazil] [Airport symbol] (AD)	MMX
Miravant [NASDAQ symbol]	MRVT
Miri [Malaysia] [Airport symbol] (AD)	LUT
Mirror (VRA)	mirr
Miscellaneous (DFIT)	Misc
Miscellaneous Proposal (AD)	MP
Miscellaneous Reference Tool (AD)	mrto
Misrair [ICAO designator] (AD)	MU

Missile on Internal Power [Military] (AD)	moip
Missile On Stand (AD)	mos
Missile Onloading Prism Fixture (AD)	mopf
Missile Operate Mode Simulator (AD)	moms
Missile Operations System (AD)	MOPS
Missile Optical Alignment (AD)	moa
Missile Out of Commission for Parts [Military] (AD)	mocp
Missile Power Control Panel (AD)	mpcp
Missile Power Monitor (AD)	mpm
Missile Purchase Description (AD)	mpd
Missile Recovery Vessel (AD)	MRV
Missile Re-Entry Vehicle (AD)	mrv
Missile-on-Aircraft Testing [Military] (AD)	moat
Missiles Made to Order [Military] (RDA)	MMTO
Missing Persons Unit (AD)	MPU
Mission Enhancement-Little Bird [Military] (RDA)	MELB
Mission for Outreach, Renewal, and Evangelism (AD)	MORE
Mission Operation Control Room (AD)	mocr
Mission Operations Computer (AD)	moc
Mission Readiness Tester (AD)	mrt
Mississippi River Bridge Authority (AD)	MRBA
Mississippi River Gulf Outflow (AD)	MRGO
Mississippi Valley Airways [ICAO designator] (AD)	XV
Mississiquoi National Wildlife Refuge [Vermont] (AD)	MNWR
Missouri Pacific Lines (AD)	MPL
Missouri Pacific - Texas & Pacific (AD)	MoPac
Missouri Personnel and Guidance Association (AD)	MPGA
Missouri Sexual Offender Program (AD)	MOSOP
Missourian (AD)	Mo
Missus (AD)	Mrs
Mistress (AD)	Mrs
Mitomycin C Resistance Protein A	MCRA
Mit-Out Sound (AD)	mos
Mitral Stenosis (AD)	ms
Mitsui Petrochemical Industries (AD)	MPI
Mixed Ionic and Electronic Conducting [Polymers]	MIEC
Mixed Media (VRA)	mm
Mixed Oxides (AD)	mox
Mixed Respiratory Vaccine [Medicine] (AD)	mrv
MLN (Modern Language Notes) [A publication] (BRI)	MLN
Mnemonic (AD)	mnm
Mobile (AD)	mob
Mobile, Alabama [Maritime abbreviation] (AD)	Mob
Mobile Bay, Alabama [Montego Bay, Jamaica] (AD)	Mo' Bay
Mobile Branch Librarian (AD)	Mobilarian
Mobile Command [Canada] (AD)	MOBCOM
Mobile Command (AD)	MoCom
Mobile Communications (AD)	mobcom
Mobile Data Acquisition System (AD)	MOBIDACS
Mobile Digital Computer (AD)	mobidic
Mobile Emergency Unit (AD)	mobeu
Mobile Laboratory (AD)	molab
Mobile LASER Satellite Tracking Station (AD)	moblas
Mobile Librarian (AD)	mob lib
Mobile Library (AD)	mobilary
Mobile Lunar Laboratory (AD)	MOLAB
Mobile Mine Assembly Unit (AD)	momau
Mobile Module [Computer science]	MMO
Mobile Noise Barge (AD)	monob
Mobile Printing Office (AD)	MPO
Mobile Quality Services (AD)	MQS
Mobile Quarantine Facility (AD)	mqf
Mobile Radio Unit (AD)	mru
Mobile Robot (AD)	mobot
Mobile Vulgus [Disorderly Group of People] [Latin] (AD)	mob
Mobility (AD)	mobil
Mobilizacion Republicana [Republican Mobilization] [Nicaragua] [Political party] (AD)	MR
Mobilization Table of Distribution and Allowances (AD)	MOBTA
Mocassin (AD)	moc
Mochaware (VRA)	mochwr
Mocimboa da Praia [Mozambique] [Airport symbol] (AD)	MZB
Model (AD)	mod
Model and Series (AD)	m & s
Model Penal Code (AD)	MPC
Model-Building Language (AD)	mobula
Modeling Paste (VRA)	mod pst
Moderate (AD)	mod
Moderate Learning Difficulties (AIE)	MLD
Moderate Room Rate Desired (AD)	modr
Moderato [Moderately] [Italian] (AD)	modo
Moderato [Moderately] [Italian] (AD)	modto
Modern (AD)	Mod
Modern (AD)	mod
Modern Age [A publication] (BRI)	MA
Modern Conveniences (AD)	mod cons
Modern English (AD)	ModE
Modern Fiction Studies [A publication] (BRI)	MFS
Modern Hebrew (AD)	ModHeb
Modern Language Journal [A publication] (BRI)	MLJ
Modern Language Review [A publication] (BRI)	MLR
Modern Languages (AIE)	ML
Modern Languages Working Group (AIE)	MLWG
Modern Library (AD)	Modern Lib
Modern Mobile Army (AD)	momar

Modern Philology [*A publication*] (BRI) ... MP
Modern Railroad Club (AD) ... MRC
Modern-Construction Houses (AD) ... mod-cons
Modernity Commercialized (AD) ... modcom
Modest Petrovich Mussorgsky [*1839-1881*] (AD) ... MPM
Modification (AD) ... mod
Modification (AD) ... modf
Modification and Repair Order and Acceptance Record (AD) ... MROAR
Modification, Inspection, and Repair as Necessary (AD) ... mod/iran
Modo Prescripto [*In the Manner Prescribed*] [*Latin*] (AD) ... mod pres
Modoc National Wildlife Refuge [*California*] (AD) ... MNWR
Modular (AD) ... mod
Modular Air-to-Surface Missile [*Military*] (AD) ... modasm
Modulate-Demodulate (AD) ... mod/demod
Modulating-Demodulating (AD) ... modem
Modulator-Demodulator (AD) ... moddem
Modulus of Rupture Test (AD) ... MRT
Mohammedan (AD) ... Moham
Mohanbari [*India*] [*Airport symbol*] (AD) ... MHO
Mohawk Carpet Mills [*Stock exchange symbol*] (AD) ... MOK
Mohorovicic Discontinuity [*Geology*] (AD) ... moho
Moises (AD) ... Mose
Moishe (AD) ... Moish
Mokpo (AD) ... Mok
Mold (VRA) ... mld
Moldavia (AD) ... Moldv
Molecular (AD) ... mol
Molecular (AD) ... mole
Molecular and Cellular Neuroscience [*A publication*] ... MCN
Molecular Cellular, and Developmental Biology [*A discipline division*] ... MCDB
Molecular Crystals and Liquid Crystals (AD) ... Mol Crys Liq Crys
Molecular Evolutionary Genetics Analysis [*Computer software*] ... MEGA
Molecular Orbital (AD) ... mo
Molecular Physics (AD) ... Mol Phys
Molecular Weight (AD) ... mol wt
Molecularized Computer (AD) ... molecom
Mole-Percent Metal (AD) ... mpm
Mollendo (AD) ... Mol
Mollienisia (AD) ... mollie
Mollis [*Soft*] [*Latin*] (AD) ... mol
Mollusca (AD) ... Mollus
Molten (AD) ... molt
Molybdenum (AD) ... moly
Mombo [*Tanzania*] [*Airport symbol*] (AD) ... MBN
Moment (AD) ... mo
Momentum [*Measurement*] ... H
Momma (AD) ... Mom
Monaco (AD) ... Mon
Monaco (VRA) ... Mona
Monaghan (AD) ... Monag
Monastery (AD) ... Mony
Monastic (AD) ... Monas
Monastir [*Tunisia*] [*Airport symbol*] (AD) ... MIR
Monclova [*Mexico*] [*Airport symbol*] (AD) ... LOV
Monday (AD) ... Mon
Monday through Saturday (AD) ... M-S
Monegasque (AD) ... Mon
Monetary (AD) ... mon
Money (AD) ... moy
Money Management Analytical Research Group ... MMAR
Money-Purchase Pension Plan [*Human resources*] (WYGK) ... MPPP
Mongo [*Chad*] [*Airport symbol*] (AD) ... MVO
Mongol (AD) ... Mon
Mongol (AD) ... Mong
Mongolia (VRA) ... Mongo
Mongolisch [*Mongolian*] [*German*] (AD) ... mong
Moniker (AD) ... monik
Monitor (AD) ... mntr
Monitor (AD) ... Mon
Monitor Out of Service (AD) ... monos
Monitor Printing Unit (AD) ... mpu
Monitor Station Reports (AD) ... moreps
Monitoring (AD) ... montrg
Monitoring Direction (AD) ... mon/dir
Monk Seal Morbillivirus ... MSMV
Monkey Bay [*Malawi*] [*Airport symbol*] (AD) ... ONB
Monkira [*Queensland*] [*Airport symbol*] (AD) ... ONR
Monmouthshire (AD) ... Mon
Monobasic (AD) ... monbas
Monochrome (VRA) ... monch
Monoclinic (AD) ... monocl
Monogram (AD) ... monog
Monograph (AD) ... monog
Monohydrogen (AD) ... mon-H
Monon Railroad (AD) ... Monod
Monon Railroad (AD) ... MR
Monongahela (AD) ... Mon
Monongahela River (AD) ... Mon River
Mononucleosis [*Medicine*] (AD) ... mono
Monophonic (AD) ... mono
Monopolization (AD) ... mnpzn
Monopolize (AD) ... mnpz
Monopolized (AD) ... mnpzd
Monopolizing (AD) ... mnpzg
Monopoly (AD) ... mono
Monopoly (AD) ... monpl
Monoprint (VRA) ... monpr
Monopropellant (AD) ... mono
Monopulse Resolution Improvement (AD) ... mri
Monorail (AD) ... mono
Monotonous (AD) ... monot
Monotype (AD) ... mono
Monotype (AD) ... monot
Monotype (VRA) ... montp
Monseigneur [*My Lord*] [*French*] (AD) ... Monsig
Monsieur [*Mister*] [*French*] (AD) ... Mons
Monsoon (AD) ... mon
Monsoon Current (AD) ... Mons Cur
Monsoon Experiment (AD) ... monex
Monstrosity (AD) ... monstro
Montag [*Monday*] [*German*] (AD) ... Mon
Montage (VRA) ... montg
Montana (AD) ... Mont
Montauk Caribbbean Airways and Ocean Reef Airways [*ICAO designator*] (AD) ... YL
Monte Alegre [*Brazil*] [*Airport symbol*] (AD) ... MTE
Monte Carlo (AD) ... Monte
Monte Caseros [*Argentina*] [*Airport symbol*] (AD) ... MCS
Montebianco (AD) ... Monte
Montefiore (AD) ... Monte
Monterey Bay Aquarium Research Institute [*California*] ... MBARI
Monterrey (AD) ... Mont
Monterrey [*Colombia*] [*Airport symbol*] (AD) ... MOY
Montevideo (AD) ... Mont
Montevideo (AD) ... Monte
Montezuma National Wildlife Refuge [*New York*] (AD) ... MNWR
Montgomery (AD) ... Mont
Montgomery (AD) ... Monte
Montgomery (AD) ... Monty
Montgomery [*Pakistan*] [*Airport symbol*] (AD) ... MYP
Montgomeryshire [*England*] (AD) ... Montgom
Month after Sight (AD) ... m/s
Monthly Labor Review [*A publication*] (BRI) ... M Lab R
Months (AD) ... mos
Months after Sight (AD) ... ms
Months Old (AD) ... m-o
Montmorency (AD) ... Monty
Montparnasse (AD) ... Montparno
Montpelier (AD) ... Mont
Montreal (AD) ... Mont
Montreal [*Canada*] (AD) ... Montr
Montreal Public Library [*Canada*] (AD) ... MPL
Montreal Star [*A publication*] (AD) ... Mont S
Montreux-Oberland-Bernois [*Railway*] [*Canada*] (AD) ... MOB
Monument (AD) ... Mon
Monument (AD) ... mon
Monument (VRA) ... mont
Moody's Investment Grade (DFIT) ... MIG-1
Mooraberrie [*Queensland*] [*Airport symbol*] (AD) ... OOR
Moore's Digest [*Legal term*] (AD) ... Moore's Dig
Moore's International Adjudications [*Legal term*] (AD) ... Moore's Adj
Moore's International Arbitrations [*Legal term*] (AD) ... Moore's Arb
Mooring (AD) ... mrng
Moosehorn National Wildlife Refuge [*Maine*] (AD) ... MNWR
Mop Rack (AD) ... mopr
Mopliert [*Furnished*] [*German*] (AD) ... mobl
Moral Fiber (AD) ... mor fib
Moral Majority (AD) ... Mor Maj
Morale, Recreation, and Welfare (AD) ... mrw
Moravia (AD) ... Morav
Morbihan (AD) ... Morb
Mordechai (AD) ... Mordy
Mordehai (AD) ... Mord
Mordehai (AD) ... Mordhy
More Dicto [*As Directed*] [*Latin*] (AD) ... mor dict
More Solito [*In the Usual Manner*] [*Latin*] (AD) ... mor sal
Morelia (AD) ... Mor
Morelos (AD) ... Mor
Morendo [*Dying Away*] [*Italian*] (AD) ... mor
Moreover (AD) ... mrov
Mores Island [*Bahamas*] [*Airport symbol*] (AD) ... MIX
Morgan Library (AD) ... Mor Lib
Morganatic Marriage (AD) ... morg mar
Morisco (AD) ... Mor
Mormon (AD) ... Morm
Morning (AD) ... morn
Morning (AD) ... mrng
Moroccan (AD) ... Mor
Moroccan (AD) ... Moroc
Moroccan National Tourist Office (AD) ... MNTO
Morocco (AD) ... mor
Morocco (VRA) ... Moro
Morphine (AD) ... morph
Morphology (AD) ... morph
Morphophysiological (AD) ... morphophysio
Morris-Oxford (AD) ... M-O
Morse Taper (AD) ... mor t
Mortal (AD) ... mort
Mortar (AD) ... mor
Mortar (AD) ... mort

Mortar Howitzer (AD) ... moritzer
Mortemart (AD) ... Mort
Mortgage (AD) ... mort
Mortgage (DD) ... mtge
Mortgage-Backed Security (DFIT) ... MBS
Mortician (AD) ... mort
Mortimer (AD) ... Mort
Morton (AD) ... Mort
Mosaic (VRA) ... mos
Mosca [*Moscow*] [*Italian*] (AD) ... Mos
Moscou [*Moscow*] [*French*] (AD) ... Mos
Moscovici (AD) ... Mosk
Moscow (AD) ... Mos
Moscow Basin (AD) ... Mosbas
Moscow Link (AD) ... Molink
Moscowitz (AD) ... Mosk
Moscu [*Moscow*] [*Spanish*] (AD) ... Mos
Moseley (AD) ... Mose
Mosen (AD) ... Mose
Moses (AD) ... Mose
Moshe (AD) ... Mos
Moshi [*Tanzania*] [*Airport symbol*] (AD) ... MSI
Moskau [*Moscow*] [*German*] (AD) ... Mos
Moskou [*Moscow*] [*Dutch*] (AD) ... Mos
Moskowitz (AD) ... Mosk
Moslem (AD) ... Mos
Moslem Meal (AD) ... Moml
Mosque (AD) ... Mq
Mossoro [*Brazil*] [*Airport symbol*] (AD) ... MSD
Most Probable Number (AD) ... mpn
Most Probable Position (AD) ... mpp
Most Recently Used [*Computer science*] ... MRU
Mostar [*Yugoslavia*] [*Airport symbol*] (AD) ... OMO
Mosul [*Iraq*] [*Airport symbol*] (AD) ... OSM
Mota [*Ethiopia*] [*Airport symbol*] (AD) ... OTA
Moth Eaten (AD) ... mo
Mother (AD) ... moth
Mother (AD) ... Mr
Mother Jones [*A publication*] (BRI) ... Moth Jones
Mother of Pearl (AD) ... mop
Mother Tongue and English Teaching (AIE) ... MOTET
Mother Tongue Project (AIE) ... MTP
Mother-in-Law (AD) ... moth-in-law
Mother-of-Pearl (VRA) ... moprl
Motion Picture (AD) ... mp
Motion Picture Distributors Association (AD) ... MPDA
Motion Picture Exhibitors Association (AD) ... MPEA
Motion Picture Experts Group ... MPEG
Motion-Picture Film (AD) ... mpf
Motivational Research (AD) ... mr
Motive Power and Rolling Stock (AD) ... mp & rs
Motor (AD) ... mot
Motor Camp (AD) ... mocamp
Motor Gasoline (AD) ... mogas
Motor Octane Number (AD) ... mon
Motor Operated (AD) ... mo
Motor Operated (AD) ... mot op
Motor Parts Stock (AD) ... mps
Motor Racing Club (AD) ... MRC
Motor Refrigerator Lighter (AD) ... mrl
Motor Repair Insurance (AD) ... MRI
Motorcycle Cross (AD) ... motorcross
Motorcycle Cross Country Race (AD) ... motocross
Motorized Pedals (AD) ... mopeds
Motorized Rifle Division [*Military*] (AD) ... MRD
Motorized Skateboard (AD) ... motoboard
Motorized-Vehicle Parade (AD) ... motorcade
Motormannes Riksforbund [*Motorists' Association*] [*Swedish*] (AD) ... MR
Motorskib [*Motorship*] [*Norwegian*] (AD) ... m/s
Moundou [*Chad*] [*Airport symbol*] (AD) ... MQQ
Mount Rainier National Park [*Washington*] (AD) ... MRNP
Mount Revelstoke National Park [*British Columbia*] (AD) ... MRNP
Mountain (VRA) ... mt
Mountain Home Air Service [*ICAO designator*] (AD) ... YM
Mountain Rescue Service (AD) ... MRS
Mountain West Airlines [*ICAO designator*] (AD) ... FX
Mounted (VRA) ... mtd
Moussoro [*Chad*] [*Airport symbol*] (AD) ... MXR
Movable (AD) ... mov
Movable Partition (AD) ... m part
Moved Out of Town (AD) ... moot
Movement Order (AD) ... movord
Movement Overseas Verification of Enlisted Members (AD) ... movem
Movement Report (AD) ... moverep
Movement Shorthand Society (AD) ... Move Short Soc
Movie (AD) ... movi
Movimento [*Movement*] [*Italian*] (AD) ... mov
Movimento Sem Terra [*Political party*] [*Brazil*] ... MST
Movimiento Patriotico Cuba Libre [*Free Cuba Patriotic Movement*] [*Political party*] (AD) ... MPCL Movement]=>> Political party
Movimiento Revolucionario de 13 de Noviembre [*Revolutionary Movement of 13 November*] [*Guatemala*] [*Political party*] (AD) ... MR-13 Movement of 13 NoGuatemala
Moving Call for Fire [*Military*] ... MCFF
Mozambique (AD) ... Moz
Mozambique (AD) ... Mozam
Mozambique [*Mozambique*] [*Airport symbol*] (AD) ... MZQ
Mozambique Current (AD) ... Moz Cur
Mozambique National Resistance [*Political party*] (AD) ... MNR
Mozzarella (AD) ... mozza
Mpanda [*Tanzania*] [*Airport symbol*] (AD) ... MPD
Mr. & Mrs. (VRA) ... M/M
Mt. Cook Airlines [*ICAO designator*] (AD) ... NM
Mud and Snow (AD) ... m & s
MUD [*Multi-User Dungeon*] **Object-Oriented** [*Computer science*] (DOM) ... MOO
Mud, Oil, Hooks, Slings [*Insurance*] (AD) ... mohs
Mud on Airstrip (AD) ... moa
Mukalla [*South Arabia*] [*Airport symbol*] (AD) ... MKX
Mukeiras [*South Arabia*] [*Airport symbol*] (AD) ... UKR
Mulege [*Mexico*] [*Airport symbol*] (AD) ... MVU
Multiangle LASER Light-Scattering [*Instrumentation*] ... MALLS
Multibank DRAM [*Computer science*] ... MDRAM
Multicast Backbone [*Computer science*] (DOM) ... M-bone
Multicenter Acute Stroke Trial-Europe [*Neurology*] ... MAST-E
Multicenter Study of Perioperative Ischemia ... McSPI
Multichannel Connection Protocol Based on the Point-to-Point Protocol [*Computer science*] ... Multilink PPP
Multicolor /Graphics Array [*Computer science*] ... MCGA
MultiCultural Review [*A publication*] (BRI) ... MultiCul R
Multidomain Polymer [*Biology*] ... MDP
Multifamily Residential Zone (AD) ... MR
Multilateral Initiative in Malaria ... MIM
Multi-Market Radio ... MMR
Multimedia Access Terminals [*Philips*] [*Electronics*] ... MAT
Multimedia Compact Disc ... MMCD
Multimedia Marketing Council (DOM) ... MMC
Multiphasic Personality Inventory (AD) ... mpi
Multiphoton Ionization (AD) ... mpi
Multiple Organ Dysfunction Syndrome [*Medicine*] ... MODS
Multiple Personality Disorder (AD) ... mpd
Multiple Product Announcement (AD) ... mpa
Multiple Protective Structure System (AD) ... MPSS
Multiple Pure Tone (AD) ... mpt
Multiple Quotient (AD) ... mq
Multiple Read/Write (AD) ... mr/w
Multiple Reading, Writing, Compiling (AD) ... mrwc
Multiple Rocket Launcher (AD) ... mrl
Multiple Sclerosis (AD) ... ms
Multiple Sclerosis Association of America ... MSAA
Multiple Starters (AD) ... ms
Multiple Subscriber Number [*Telecommunications*] (DOM) ... MSN
Multiple-Employer Welfare Association (WYGK) ... MEWA
Multiple-Orifice Valve (AD) ... mov
Multiple-Position Lock (AD) ... mpl
Multiplex (AD) ... mpx
Multiplex Fluorescence in Situ Hybridization ... MFISH
Multiplexor (AD) ... mpxr
Multiplex-Section, Shared-Protection Rings ... MS-SPRING
Multiplicity of Infection (AD) ... moi
Multiply (AD) ... mpy
Multipole (AD) ... mp
Multipower Transmission (AD) ... mpt
Multiprogramming System (AD) ... MPS
Multipunch Bar (AD) ... mp br
Multipunch Die (AD) ... mp di
Multipunch Plate (AD) ... mp pl
Multipurpose (AD) ... mp
Multipurpose Carrier (AD) ... mpc
Multi-Purpose Food (AD) ... mpf
Multi-Purpose Individual Munition/Short Range Assault Weapon [*Military*] (RDA) ... MPIM/SRAW
Multipurpose Meal (AD) ... mpm
Multipurpose Vehicle (AD) ... mpv
Multi-Racial Education Resources Centre [*British*] (AIE) ... MERC
Multirole Combat Aircraft (AD) ... mrca
Multispectral Opium Poppy Sensor System (AD) ... MOPSS
Multitier Distributed Application Services [*Computer science*] ... MIDAS
Multi-User Domain [*Computer science*] ... MUD
Multi-User Engineering Change Proposal Automated Review System (RDA) ... MEARS
Mumbwa [*Zambia*] [*Airport symbol*] (AD) ... UMW
Municipal Certificates of Accrual on Tax-Exempt Securities [*Investment term*] (DFIT) ... M-CATS
Municipal Utility District [*Investment term*] (DFIT) ... MUD
Munster (AD) ... Mnstr
Munz Northern [*ICAO designator*] (AD) ... XY
Muong Sai [*Laos*] [*Airport symbol*] (AD) ... UON
Muong Sing [*Laos*] [*Airport symbol*] (AD) ... MOJ
Mural (VRA) ... mur
Murchison Falls [*Uganda*] [*Airport symbol*] (AD) ... MUD
Murder Release Risk Assessment Scale (AD) ... MRRAS
Murray Bay [*Quebec*] [*Airport symbol*] (AD) ... YML
Muscat and Oran (AD) ... M & O
Muscle Strength (AD) ... ms
Musee (VRA) ... mus
Musee Oceanographique Monaco [*Monaco Oceanographic Museum*] [*France*] (AD) ... MOM France
Museen (VRA) ... mus
Museo (VRA) ... mus

Museo Nacional de Rio de Janeiro GG1National Museum of Rio de JaneiroGG2 [*Portugal*] (AD) .... MNRJ JaneiroGG2 Portugal
Museo Oceanografico de Rio Grande [*Oceanographic Museum of Rio Grande*] [*Brazil*] (AD) .... MORG Grande]=>> Brazil
Museum (VRA) .... mus
Museum of Modern Art [*New York*] (AD) .... MoMA
Museum of Photographic Arts [*San Diego*] (AD) .... MOPA
Museum of the Plains Indians (AD) .... MPI
Museum of Transport and Technology (AD) .... MOTAT
Museum Plantin Moretus [*Belgium*] (AD) .... MP-M
Mushandike National Park [*Rhodesia*] (AD) .... MNP
Music Educators Journal [*A publication*] (BRI) .... M Ed J
Music Masters and Mistresses Association (AIE) .... MMMA
Music Operators of New York (AD) .... MONY

Musical (VRA) .... musi
Musical Quarterly [*A publication*] (BRI) .... MQ
Muslim Education Co-Ordinating Council (AIE) .... MECC
Muslim Peoples Republican Party [*Political party*] (AD) .... MPRP
Muslim Teachers' Association (AIE) .... MTA
Muslin (VRA) .... musl
Must Have Reply Here by Tomorrow Morning (AD) ... mrytm
Mustered Out (AD) .... mo
Mustering-Out Pay (AD) .... mop
Mutarara [*Mozambique*] [*Airport symbol*] (AD) .... MUW
Mutual Permanent Building Society (AD) .... MPBS
Muzaffarpur [*India*] [*Airport symbol*] (AD) .... MZU
Myakka River State Park [*Florida*] (AD) .... MRSP
Mzimba [*Malawi*] [*Airport symbol*] (AD) .... MZY
Mzuzu [*Malawi*] [*Airport symbol*] (AD) .... ZZU

N
By Meaning

Na Priklad [*For Example*] [*Czech*] (AD) .... na pr
Nacala [*Mozambique*] [*Airport symbol*] (AD) .... MNC
N-Acetylneuraminic Acid (AD) .... nana
Nacional Financiera [*National Finance Coro.*] [*Spanish*] (AD) .... NAFINSA
Nacionalista [*Nationalist Party*] [*Spain*] [*Political party*] (AD) .... PN
Nadir (AD) .... nad
Nador [*Morocco*] [*Airport symbol*] (AD) .... NDR
Nagasaki [*Japan*] (AD) .... Nag
Nagasaki [*Japan*] (AD) .... Nagas
Nagoya [*Japan*] (AD) .... Nag
Nagpur, India (AD) .... Nagp
Nahichevan Autonomous Soviet Socialist Republic (AD) .... NASSR
[*The Book of*] Nahum (AD) .... Nah
Nairnshire, Scotland (AD) .... Nairns
Naklad [*Edition*] [*Polish*] (AD) .... nakl
Nakladatel [*Edition*] [*Czech*] (AD) .... nakl
Namakwaland Lugdiens [*ICAO designator*] (AD) .... NJ
Namib Air [*ICAO designator*] (AD) .... SW
Namibia (AD) .... Namib
Namligen [*Namely*] [*Swedish*] (AD) .... naml
Nancy (AD) .... Nan
Nanette (AD) .... Nan
Nanjing Institute of Geology and Paleontology [*China*] .... NIG&P
Nanking [*China*] (AD) .... Nan
Nantucket Airlines [*ICAO designator*] (AD) .... DV
Nanuque [*Brazil*] [*Airport symbol*] (AD) .... NNU
Na'or Halutsi Lohem [*Fighting Pioneer Youth*] [*Israel*] (AD) .... Nahal
Napalm (AD) .... nap
Napan [*West Irian, Indonesia*] [*Airport symbol*] (AD) .... NPA
Naphtha (AD) .... nap
Naphtha (AD) .... naph
Naphthene Palmitate (AD) .... napalm
Naphthyl (AD) .... naph
Napier's Bones [*First slide rule*] (AD) .... Nap's bones
Naples (AD) .... Nap
Napoleon (AD) .... Nap
Nappamerrie [*Queensland*] [*Airport symbol*] (AD) .... NMR
Narcotic (AD) .... narc
Narcotic (AD) .... narco
Narcotic (AD) .... narcot
Narcotic Traffic Dollars (AD) .... narcodollars
Narcotic-Addict Registration Card (AD) .... narcocard
Narcotics (AD) .... narcos
Narcotics (AD) .... narcs
Narcotics Agent (AD) .... narc
Narcotics Agents (AD) .... narcs
Narcotics and Dangerous Drugs Intelligence File (AD) .... NADDIS
Narcotics Anonymous [*An association*] (AD) .... Narconon
Narcotics Commission [*United Nations*] (AD) .... NARCO
Narcotics Hospital (AD) .... narcs
Narcotics Investigation (AD) .... Nar Inv
Narcotics Officer (AD) .... narco
Narcotics Officers (AD) .... narcs
Narcotics Police Officers (AD) .... narcos
Narcotics Test (AD) .... narcotest
Narcotics Traffick (AD) .... narco-traf
Narcotics Treatment Centers (AD) .... narcs
Naristillae [*Nasal Drops*] [*Latin*] (AD) .... narist
Narodna Republika Bulgaria [*Bulgarian People's Republic*] [*Political party*] (AD) .... Nar Rep Bul Political party
Narodni Divadlo [*National Theater*] [*Czechoslavakia*] (AD) .... Nar Div
Narodny Komissariat Vneshney Torgovli [*People's Commissariate of Foreign Trade*] [*Russian*] (AD) .... Narkomvneshtorg
Narragansett (AD) .... Nar
Narrow (AD) .... nar
Narthex (VRA) .... nhx
Nasal (AD) .... nas
Nashville [*Tennessee*] (AD) .... Nash
Nasionale Party [*National Party*] [*Political party*] (AD) .... Nas Par
Nasionale Pers [*National Press*] [*South Africa*] (AD) .... Nas Pers
Nassau, Bahamas (AD) .... Nass
Natal Museum (AD) .... Nat Mus
Natalia (AD) .... Nat
Natalie (AD) .... Nat
Natasha (AD) .... Nat
Natation (AD) .... natat

Natchez (AD) .... Natch
Nathalie (AD) .... Nat
Nathan (AD) .... Nat
Nathaniel (AD) .... Nat
Nathaniel (AD) .... Nathl
Nathaniel Bowditch (AD) .... Nath B
Nation (AD) .... nat
Nation [*A publication*] (BRI) .... Nat
National (AD) .... Nat
National (AD) .... nat
National (AD) .... natl
National (DD) .... ntL
National Aboriginal Sports Foundation (AD) .... NASF
National Abortion Foundation (AD) .... NAF
National Abstentionalist (AD) .... Nat Absten
National Academic Recognition Information Centre (AIE) .... NARIC
National Academy of Foreign Affairs (AD) .... NAFA
National Accreditation Council for Certification Bodies (AIE) .... NACCB
National Action Committee on the Status of Women [*Canada*] (AD) .... NACSW
National Action Plan on Breast Cancer .... NAPBC
National Acute Spinal Cord Injury Study .... NASCIS
National Ad Hoc Committee Against Censorship (AD) .... NAHCAC
National Administrative Expenses (AD) .... nae
National Advertising News Association (AD) .... NANA
National Advisory Committee on Women (AD) .... NACW
National Advisory Council for Youth Services (AIE) .... NACYS
National Advisory Council on the Training and Supply of Teachers (AD) .... NACTST
National Aero Manufacturing (AD) .... NAM
National Aerobic Fitness Award (AD) .... NAFA
National Aerometric Data Bank (AD) .... NADB
National Aeronautics and Space Administration Act (AD) .... NASAA
National Aeronautics and Space Administration - Cleveland, Ohio (AD) .... NASA-CO
National Aeronautics and Space Administration - Cocoa Beach, Florida (AD) .... NASA-CF Florida
National Aeronautics and Space Administration - Edwards, California (AD) .... NASA-EC California
National Aeronautics and Space Administration - Greenbelt, Maryland (AD) .... NASA-GM Maryland
National Aeronautics and Space Administration - Houston, Texas (AD) .... NASA-HT
National Aeronautics and Space Administration - Huntsville, Alabama (AD) .... NASA-HA Alabama
National Aeronautics and Space Administration - Langley Field, Virginia (AD) .... NASA-LV Virginia
National Aeronautics and Space Administration Large Space Telescope (AD) .... NASA LST Telescope
National Aeronautics and Space Administration - Moffett Field, California (AD) .... NASA-MC California
National Aeronautics and Space Administration - Santa Monica, California (AD) .... NASA-SC California
National Aeronautics and Space Administration Tracking Network (AD) .... NASCOM
National Aerospace Laboratory (AD) .... NAL
National Aerospace Plane (AD) .... NAP
National Aero-Space Plane (AD) .... NASP
National Affiliate of Printing Industries of America (AD) .... NAPIA
National Agricultural Society (AD) .... NAS
National Aid to Visually Handicapped (AD) .... NAVH
National Air and Space Museum Library [*Smithsonian Institute*] (AD) .... NASML
National Air Forwarding Division [*Institute of Freight Forwarders*] (AD) .... NAFD
National Air Quality Index (AD) .... NAQI
National Air Traffic Controllers (AD) .... NATC
National Aircraft Underwriters' Association (AD) .... NAUA
National Airlines (AD) .... NAL
National Alliance for Democracy [*Political party*] (AD) .... NAD
National Alliance of Financially-Responsible Local Governments (AD) .... NAFRLG
National Alliance of Postal Supervisors (AD) .... NAPS
National Alternative Fuel Test (AD) .... NAFT
National Alzheimer's Disease Autopsy and Brain Bank (AD) .... NADABB
National Alzheimer's Disease Foundation (AD) .... NADF
National Amalgamated Stevedores and Dockers (AD) .... NASD
National Anti-Drug Abuse Campaign (AD) .... NADAC
National Anti-Steel-Trap League (AD) .... NASTL

National Archives (AD) ... Nat Arc
National Archives and Records Service (AD) ... NARC
National Armed Forces Museum (AD) ... NAFM
National Art Education Archive (AIE) ... NAEA
National Assembly of National Voluntary Health and Social Welfare Organizations (AD) ... NANVH&SWO
National Assessment of Educational Progress (AD) ... NAEP
National Assessment of Juvenile Correction [*University of Michigan*] (AD) ... NAJC
National Asset Seizure and Forfeiture Office (AD) ... NASFO
National Association (AD) ... Nat Assn
National Association for Lesbian and Gay Gerontology (AD) ... NALGG
National Association for Road Safety Instruction in Schools (AD) ... NARSIS
National Association for Special Educational Needs (AIE) ... NASEN
National Association for Standing Advisory Councils for Religious Education (AIE) ... NASACRE
National Association for State-Enrolled Assistant Nurses (AD) ... NASAEN
National Association for Stock Car Advancement and Research (AD) ... NASCAR
National Association for Teaching English and other Community Languages to Adults [*Formerly, NATELSA*] (AIE) ... NATELCA
National Association for the Paralysed (AD) ... NAP
National Association for the Prevention of Rape by Castration (AD) ... NAPRC
National Association for the Prevention of Venereal Disease (AD) ... NAPVD
National Association for the Teaching of English (AD) ... NATE
National Association for Training the Disabled in Office Work (AD) ... NADOW
National Association of Advisers in Computer Education (AIE) ... NAACE
National Association of Careers Teachers (AD) ... NACT
National Association of Chief Education Social Workers (AIE) ... NACESW
National Association of Chiefs of Police (AD) ... NACP
National Association of College and University Business Office Associations (AD) ... NACUBO
National Association of College Wind and Percussion Instruments (AD) ... NACWPI
National Association of Conservative Graduates (AIE) ... NACG
National Association of Counsellors in Education (AIE) ... NACE
National Association of Cycle Trades (AD) ... NACT
National Association of Design and Fine Art Societies (AD) ... NADFAS
National Association of Drop Forgers and Stampers (AD) ... NADFS
National Association of Drug Addiction (AD) ... NADA
National Association of Educational Inspectors, Advisers, and Consultants (AIE) ... NAEIAC
National Association of Educational Programs [*Carnegie Foundation*] (AD) ... NAEP
National Association of Flower Arrangement Societies (AD) ... NAFAS
National Association of Foot Specialists (AD) ... NAFS
National Association of Foreign Student Advisors (AD) ... NAFSA
National Association of Forensic Sciences (AD) ... NAFS
National Association of Frozen Food Producers (AD) ... NAFFP
National Association of Furniture Warehousemen and Removers (AD) ... NAFWR
National Association of Grained Plate Makers (AD) ... NAGPM
National Association of Health Authorities in England and Wales (AIE) ... NAHA
National Association of Homebuilders (AD) ... NAH
National Association of Iron and Steel Stockholders (AD) ... NAISS
National Association of Jazz Education (AD) ... NAJE
National Association of Land Settlement Association Tenants (AD) ... NALSAT
National Association of Latino Elected and Appointed Officials (AD) ... NALEAO
National Association of Local Government Officers (AIE) ... NALGO
National Association of Marine Engine Builders (AD) ... NAMEB
National Association of Marine Engineers (AD) ... NAME
National Association of Married Priests (AD) ... NAMP
National Association of Metal Name Plate Manufacturers (AD) ... NAME
National Association of Motor Bus Operators (AD) ... NAMBO
National Association of Music Merchandisers (AD) ... NAMM
National Association of Outfitters (AD) ... NAO
National Association of Para-Legal Personnel (AD) ... NAPLP
National Association of Partners in Education ... NAPE
National Association of Performing Artists (AD) ... NAPO
National Association of Plumbing/Heating/Cooling Contractors (AD) ... NAPHC
National Association of Police Driving (AD) ... NAPD
National Association of Pretrial Service Agencies (AD) ... NAPSA
National Association of Purchasing Agents (AD) ... NAPO
National Association of Regimental Drummers (AD) ... NARD
National Association of Retail Furnishers (AD) ... NARF
National Association of Retail Grocers of Australia (AD) ... NARGA
National Association of Retail Merchants (AD) ... NARM
National Association of Retired Catholics (AD) ... NARC
National Association of Rope and Twine Merchants (AD) ... NARTM
National Association of School Superintendents (AD) ... NASS
National Association of Secondary School Principals. Bulletin [*A publication*] (BRI) ... NASSP-B
National Association of Security Dealers Automated Quotation System (AD) ... NASDAQS
National Association of Socialist Students' Organizations [*Political party*] (AD) ... NASSO
National Association of Specimen Hunters (AD) ... NASH
National Association of Sports Car Racing (AD) ... NASCAR
National Association of Stationary Engineers (AD) ... NASE
National Association of Theatrical and Kine Employees (AD) ... NATKE
National Association of Youth Training Agencies (AIE) ... NAYTA
National Astronomical Observatory of Japan ... NAOJ
National Atmospheric Research Institute (AD) ... NARI
National Audio Visual Aids Library (AIE) ... NAVAL
National Automated Highway System Consortium ... NAHSC
National Automated Transportation Association (AD) ... NATA
National Automatic Sprinkler and Fire Control Association (AD) ... NAS & FCA
National Automotive Service Co. (AD) ... NASCO
National Aviation Noise Abatement Council (AD) ... NANAC
National Bureau of Economic Research (AD) ... Nat Bur Econ Res
National Bureau of Standards Circular [*A publication*] (AD) ... Nat Bur Stand Circ
National Cancer Pain Coalition ... NCPC
National Center for Genome Resources ... NCGR
National Center for Health Services Research ... NCHSR
National Centre for Athletics Literature (AIE) ... NCAL
National Centre for School Biotechnology (AIE) ... NCSB
National Civic Review [*A publication*] (BRI) ... NCR
National Commission for Education (AIE) ... NCE
National Committee for the In-Service Training of Teachers [*Scotland*] (AIE) ... NCITT
National Communications (AD) ... natcom
National Conference of University Professors (AIE) ... NCUP
National Council for Educational Standards (AIE) ... NCES
National Council for Foundation Education in Art and Design (AIE) ... NCFEAD
National Council for Mother Tongue Teaching (AIE) ... NCMTT
National Curriculum [*Education*] (AIE) ... NC
National Democrats [*Political party*] (AD) ... Nat Dem
National Diploma [*Academic degree*] (AIE) ... ND
National Disaster Warning System (AD) ... NADWARN
National Distribution Guide [*Mailing technique*] ... NDG
National Enterprise Education Development and Information Service (AIE) ... NEEDIS
National Equivalence Information Centre (AIE) ... NEIC
National Federation (AD) ... Nat Fed
National Federation of Class Teachers (AIE) ... NFCT
National Festival of Music for Youth (AIE) ... NFMY
National Forum [*A publication*] (BRI) ... Nat For
National Fresh Water Fishing Hall of Fame ... NFWHF
National Gallery (AD) ... Nat Gal
National Genealogical Society Quarterly [*A publication*] (BRI) ... NGSQ
National Geographic Magazine [*A publication*] (AD) ... Nat Geog Mag
National Heritage Memorial Fund (AIE) ... NHMF
National Hiking and Ski Touring Association (AD) ... NAHSTA
National Hybrid Rice Research Center [*China*] ... NHRRC
National Industrial Language Training Centre (AIE) ... NILTC
National Information of Software and Services (AIE) ... NISS
National Institute for Nursing Research ... NINR
National Institute of Neurological Disorders and Stroke ... NINDS
National Joint Council (AIE) ... NJC
National Liberal (AD) ... Nat Lib
National Library of Canada (AD) ... Nat Lib
National Library of Canada (AD) ... NATLIBCAN
National Library of Ireland (AIE) ... NLI
National Library of New Zealand (AD) ... NATLIBNZ
National Longitudinal Study of Youth ... NLSY
National Low-Emission Vehicles ... NLEV
National Mapping (AD) ... NATMAP
National Missile Defense-Ground Based RADAR [*Army*] (RDA) ... NMD/GBR
National Monument (AD) ... Nat Mon
National Museum (AD) ... Nat Mus
National Observer [*A publication*] (AD) ... Nat Obs
National Open College Network (AIE) ... NOCN
National Oracy Project (AIE) ... NOP
National Organization on Disability ... NOD
National Parks [*A publication*] (BRI) ... NP
National Policy Forum ... NPF
National Primary Teacher Education Conference (AIE) ... NaPTEC
National Private Truck Council ... NPTC
National Proficiency Test Council (AIE) ... NPTC
National Propane Gas Association ... NPGA
National Public Domain Software Archive (AIE) ... NPDSA
National Record of Vocational Achievement (AIE) ... NROVA
National Registry of Myocardial Infarction ... NRMI
National Research and Manufacturing Co. (AD) ... NARMCO
National Review [*A publication*] (BRI) ... Nat R
National Science Foundation (AD) ... Nat Sci Fdn
National Secular Society (AD) ... Nat Sec Soc
National Semiconductor Inc. (AD) ... NATSEMI
National Small Shipments Traffic Council ... NASSTRAC
National Society's Religious Education Centre (AIE) ... NSREC
National Space Science Center [*British*] ... NSSC
National Spherical Torus Experiment [*Plasma physics*] ... NSTX
National Sporting Clays Association ... NSCA
National Steering Group (AIE) ... NSG
National Superannuation (AD) ... Nat Sup
National Tank Co. (AD) ... NATCO
National Tank Truck Carriers (AD) ... NATTC
National Telemarketing Fulfillment Center ... NTCF
National Telemarketing Fulfillment Center ... NTFC
National Television Standards Committee ... NTSC
National Union of Women Teachers (AIE) ... NUWT
National University (AD) ... Nat Uni
National Used Truck Association ... NUTA
National Vessel Traffic Information System (AD) ... NAVTIS
National Vulvodynia Association [*Disseminate information about vulvar pain and establish support networks across the country*] [*Medicine*] ... NVA
National Working Party of Youth Volunteer Organisers (AIE) ... NWPYVO
National Youth Development Officer (AIE) ... NYDO

Nationalen Genossenschaft fuer die Lagerung Radioaktiver Abfaelle [*National Cooperative Society for the Storage of Radioactive Wastes*] [*Germany*] (AD) ... NAGRA
Nationalist-Communist (AD) ... Nasakom
Nationalists (AD) ... Nats
Nationality (AD) ... nation
Nations Unies [*United Nations*] [*French*] (AD) ... Nat U
Natitingou [*Dahomey*] [*Airport symbol*] (AD) ... DNT
Native (AD) ... nat
Native American Studies (AD) ... NAS
Native American Teacher Education (AD) ... NATE
Native Peoples [*A publication*] (BRI) ... Nat Peop
Natividade [*Brazil*] [*Airport symbol*] (AD) ... NAV
Nativity (AD) ... Nativ
NATO [*North Atlantic Treaty Organization*] **Defense College** (AD) ... NaDefCo
NATO [*North Atlantic Treaty Organization*] **Multi-Role Combat Aircraft Development a** (AD) ... NAMMO Development a
Natrium [*Sodium*] [*Latin*] (AD) ... natr
Natsionalnyii [*National*] [*Russian*] (AD) ... Nats
Natural (AD) ... nat
Natural Asphalt Mineowners' and Manufacturers' Council (AD) ... NAMMC
Natural Axial-Resonant Frequency (AD) ... narf
Natural Color (AD) ... natcol
Natural History (AD) ... nat hist
Natural History [*A publication*] (BRI) ... NH
Natural Philosophy (AD) ... nat phil
Natural Protamine Hagadorn [*Insulin*] ... NPH
Natural Resources International ... NRI
Natural Resources Journal [*A publication*] (BRI) ... NRJ
Naturalism (VRA) ... Natlm
Naturalist (AD) ... nat
Naturalist (AD) ... natur
Naturalization (AD) ... nat
Naturally (AD) ... natch
Naturally (AD) ... naty
Nature (AD) ... nat
Natuurkunde [*Natural Science*] [*Dutch*] (AD) ... nat
Naugahide (AD) ... nauga
Nauru Island (AD) ... Nau
Nauruan (AD) ... Nau
Nautica [*Nautical*] [*Spanish*] (AD) ... nau
Nautical (AD) ... naut
Nautical Air Miles per Gallon (AD) ... nampg
Nautical Air Miles per Pound of Fuel (AD) ... namppf
Navaho (AD) ... Nav
Naval (AD) ... Nav
Naval (AD) ... nav
Naval Aeronautical Establishment [*Canada*] (AD) ... NAE
Naval Aerospace Recovery Facility (AD) ... NAVAERORECOVF
Naval Air Development Center (AD) ... NaDevCen
Naval Air Forces, Japan (AD) ... NAVFORJAP
Naval Air Forces, Korea (AD) ... NAVFORKOR
Naval Air Rework Facility (AD) ... NAVAIRREWORKF
Naval Air Station, Terminal Island (AD) ... NASTI
Naval Air Systems Command (AD) ... NASCom
Naval Air Test Station (AD) ... NATS
Naval Aircraft Establishment (AD) ... NAE
Naval Aircraft Inventory Log (AD) ... NAIL
Naval Aircraft Investigation Center (AD) ... NAIC
Naval and Mechanical Co. (AD) ... NAMCO
Naval Attache (AD) ... N Att
Naval Aviation Pilot (AD) ... nap
Naval Aviation Supply Depot (AD) ... NASD
Naval Avionics Facility (AD) ... NAFI
Naval Ballistic Missile (AD) ... navbm
Naval Base (AD) ... Nav Bs
Naval Bronze (AD) ... nav brz
Naval Cadet (AD) ... NavCad
Naval Deputy [*NATO*] (AD) ... Nav Dep
Naval Facilites (AD) ... NAVFEC
Naval Facilities Engineering Command (AD) ... NAVFECENGCOM
Naval Forces (AD) ... NAVFOR
Naval Forces Baltic Approaches [*NATO*] (AD) ... NAVBALTAP
Naval Forces Far East (AD) ... NAVFE
Naval Forces, Marianas (AD) ... NAVMAR
Naval Forces, Northern Norway [*NATO*] (AD) ... NAVNON
Naval Forces - Philippines (AD) ... NAVPHIL
Naval Forces, Scandinavian Approaches [*NATO*] (AD) ... NAVSCAP
Naval Forces, Southern Europe (AD) ... NAVSOUTH
Naval Inspection Certificate (AD) ... navicert
Naval Missile Center (AD) ... NavMisCen
Naval Oceanographic Officer (AD) ... NavOceanO
Naval Personnel (AD) ... NAVPERS
Naval Publications (AD) ... NAVPUB
Naval Research Electronic Computer (AD) ... narec
Naval Sea Support Center - Atlantic (AD) ... NAVSEACENTLANT
Naval Sea Support Center - Pacific (AD) ... NAVSEACENTPAC
Naval Ship Systems Command (AD) ... NAVSHIPCOM
Naval Shipyard (AD) ... NavShipyd
Naval Support Forces, Antarctica (AD) ... NAVSUPORANT
Naval Underwater Weapons Systems Engineering Center (AD) ... NAVUWSEC
Navarra (AD) ... Nav
Navarre (AD) ... Nav
Navassa Island (AD) ... Nav
Navassa Island (AD) ... Nav I
Navigable (AD) ... nav
Navigation (AD) ... nav
Navigation Action Cutout (AD) ... navaco
Navigation along the East Coast of Asia (AD) ... NavEast
Navigation Communication (AD) ... navcom
Navigation Countermeasures and Deception (AD) ... NavCm
Navigation Data Assimilation Center (AD) ... NAVDAC
Navigation Data Assimilation Computer (AD) ... navdac
Navigation Exercise (AD) ... navex
Navigation in Australian Waters (AD) ... NavAus
Navigation in the Eastern Atlantic and the Mediterranean (AD) ... NavEams
Navigation in the Indian Ocean (AD) ... NavInd
Navigation in the North Atlantic (AD) ... NavNorlant
Navigation in the North Pacific (AD) ... NavNoPac
Navigation in the South Atlantic (AD) ... NavSat
Navigation of the South Pacific (AD) ... NavSoPac
Navigation System Using Time and Ranging (AD) ... NAVSTAR
Navigation Tactical (AD) ... NAVTAC
Navigation Tactical (AD) ... navtac
Navigational Aids Inoperative for Parts (AD) ... naiop
Navigational Satellite (AD) ... navsat
Navy Ocean Surveillance System ... NOSS
Navy Officers Accounts Office (AD) ... NAOA
Navy Prototype Optical Interferometer ... NPOI
Navy Research and Development (AD) ... NARAD
Neanderthal (VRA) ... Ndthl
Near (VRA) ... nr
Near-Earth Asteroid Tracking ... NEAT
Necropolis (VRA) ... necrp
Nederlandsche Aluminium Maatschappij [*Netherlands Aluminum Co.*] (AD) ... NAM Co.]=>>
Nedezhda (AD) ... Nad
Need for Affiliation (AD) ... naff
Needlework (VRA) ... ndlwk
Nefertiti [*ICAO designator*] (AD) ... UZ
Negative (VRA) ... neg
Negative Acknowledge Character [*Computer science*] (AD) ... nak
Negative Acknowledgment (DOM) ... NAK
Negative Expected Value ... NEV
Negative Knowledge (AD) ... nak
Negative Print (VRA) ... NEGPT
Negative Return in Cartridge [*Advanced photo system*] ... NRIC
Neghelli [*Ethiopia*] [*Airport symbol*] (AD) ... EGL
Neighborhood Action Group (AD) ... NAG
Neighborhood Awareness Program (AD) ... NAP
Neighborhood Electric Vehicle ... NEV
Nejo [*Ethiopia*] [*Airport symbol*] (AD) ... EJO
Nekempt [*Ethiopia*] [*Airport symbol*] (AD) ... LKM
Nelson Aldrich Rockefeller (AD) ... NAR
Neolithic (VRA) ... Neol
Neon (VRA) ... ne
Nepal (VRA) ... Nep
Nephrite (VRA) ... neph
Net Annual Gain (AD) ... nag
Net Asset Value (AD) ... n/a/v
Net Asset Value (AD) ... NAVA
Net Assimilation Rate (AD) ... nar
Netherlands (VRA) ... Nethl
Netherlands-Australia Trade and Industrial Development Council (AD) ... NATIDC
Netherlines [*ICAO designator*] (AD) ... WU
Netscape Server API [*All-Purpose Interface*] [*Computer science*] ... NSAPI
NetWare Configuration File [*Computer science*] ... NCF
Network Access Machine [*Computer science*] (AD) ... nam
Network and Mixed Model Health Maintenance Organization [*Insurance*] (WYGK) ... NMMHMO
Network Basic Input/Output System [*Computer science*] (DOM) ... NetBIOS
Network Computer [*Computer science*] ... NC
Network Computer, Inc. ... NCI
Network for Informal Adult Learning (AIE) ... NIAL
Network Interface Card [*Computer science*] ... NIC
Network of European Teacher Education (AIE) ... NETE
Network Solutions, Inc. ... NSI
Networked Interactive Multimedia ... NIM
Networking Addressing Device [*Computer science*] (AD) ... nad
Neurogenic Muscle Weakness, Ataxia, and Retinitis Pigmentosa [*Medicine*] ... NARP
Neurologically Typical [*Psychology*] ... NT
Neuronal Thread Protein [*Biology*] ... NTP
Neutral Atom Space Engine (AD) ... nase
New Advocate [*A publication*] (BRI) ... New Ad
New Age Journal [*A publication*] (BRI) ... New Age
New Amsterdam Musical Association (AD) ... NAMA
New Armed Forces of the Philippines (AD) ... NAFP
New Attainment Target (AIE) ... NAT
New Auxiliary Boiler (AD) ... n aux b
New England Airlines [*ICAO designator*] (AD) ... EJ
New England Quarterly [*A publication*] (BRI) ... NEQ
New England Review [*A publication*] (BRI) ... New ER
New England Technical Services Librarians ... NETSL
New Experiences in Teaching [*Mathematics*] ... NExt
New Glasgow [*Nova Scotia*] [*Airport symbol*] (AD) ... ZNG
New Haven Airways [*ICAO designator*] (AD) ... NB
New Issue [*Investment term*] (DFIT) ... N
New Jersey Airways [*ICAO designator*] (AD) ... OY

New Large Airplane ... NLA
New Leader [*A publication*] (BRI) ... NL
New Learning Initiative (AIE) ... NLI
New Moon [*Queensland*] [*Airport symbol*] (AD) ... NCM
New Nickerie [*Surinam*] [*Airport symbol*] (AD) ... NNI
New Opportunities in Animal Health Sciences ... NOAHS
New Parent-Infant Network (AIE) ... NEWPIN
New Physics Project (AIE) ... NPP
New Republic [*A publication*] (BRI) ... New R
New Scientist [*A publication*] (BRI) ... New Sci
New Statesman [*A publication*] (BRI) ... NS
New Statesman & Society [*A publication*] (BRI) ... NS & S
New Technical and Vocational Education Initiative (AIE) ... NTVEI
New Technical Books [*A publication*] (BRI) ... New TB
New Technical Education Initiative (AIE) ... NTEI
New Technology Access Centre (AIE) ... NTAC
New Workers Scheme (AIE) ... NWS
New York Coffee, Sugar, and Cocoa Exchange (DFIT) ... NYCSCE
New York Cotton Exchange, Citrus Associates (DFIT) ... NYCTN,CA
New York Helicopter [*ICAO designator*] (AD) ... HD
New York Helicopter [*ICAO designator*] (AD) ... HQ
New York Magazine [*A publication*] (BRI) ... New York
New York Review of Books [*A publication*] (BRI) ... NYRB
New York Society for the Prevention of Cruelty to Children ... NYSPCC
New York Times Book Review [*A publication*] (BRI) ... NYTBR
New York Times (Late Edition) [*A publication*] (BRI) ... NYTLa
New York Water Color Club [*1890-1941*] (NGC) ... NYWCC
New Yorker [*A publication*] (BRI) ... NY
New Zealand (VRA) ... N Zea
New Zealand Air Charter [*ICAO designator*] (AD) ... NX
New Zealand-Australia Free Trade Agreement (AD) ... NAFTA
Newair [*ICAO designator*] (AD) ... NC
Newark [*New Jersey*] [*Airport symbol*] (AD) ... EWR
Newfoundland [*Canada*] (DD) ... Nfld
Newly Industrialized Countries (DFIT) ... NICS
Newport [*Vermont*] [*Airport symbol*] (AD) ... EFK
Newspaper (VRA) ... nwspa
Newsweek [*A publication*] (BRI) ... NW
Next Generation Internet [*A governmental research initiative*] ... NGI
Next Hop Resolution Protocol [*Computer science*] ... NHRP
Ngoma [*Zambia*] [*Airport symbol*] (AD) ... ZGM
N'Guigmi [*Niger*] [*Airport symbol*] (AD) ... GUG
Nhill [*Victoria, Australia*] [*Airport symbol*] (AD) ... ANH
Nicaragua (VRA) ... Nic
Nickel (VRA) ... ni
Nickel-Cadmium ... Ni-Cd
Nicosia [*Cyprus*] [*Airport symbol*] (AD) ... NIC
Nicotinamide Adenine Dinucleotide (AD) ... NAD/NADH
Nicotinamide Adenine Dinucleotide Phosphate (AD) ... nadp
Nicoya [*Costa Rica*] [*Airport symbol*] (AD) ... NCT
Niello (VRA) ... niel
Nielsen-Kellerman ... NK
Nigeria (VRA) ... Nigr
Nigeria Airways [*ICAO designator*] (AD) ... WT
Nigeria America Line (AD) ... NAL
Nigerian Agip Oil Co. (AD) ... NAOC
Night-Alarm Cutoff (AD) ... nacro
Nihon Aeroplane Manufacturing Co. (AD) ... NAMC
Nihon Kinkyori Airways [*ICAO designator*] (AD) ... EL
Nikolai Andreyvich Rimsky-Korsakov (AD) ... NARK
Nimes [*Frances*] [*Airport symbol*] (AD) ... FNI
Nincompoop (AD) ... poop
Nineteenth-Century Literature [*A publication*] (BRI) ... Nine-C Lit
Ninth-Plate (VRA) ... NINE
Nippon Advanced Ship Design (AD) ... NASD
Nippon Australian Relations Agreement (AD) ... NARA
Nisab [*South Arabia*] [*Airport symbol*] (AD) ... ISB
Nisi Aliter Notetur [*Unless It is Otherwise Noted*] [*Latin*] (AD) ... nan
Nissan Air Pollution System (AD) ... NAPS
Nitrate Motion Picture (VRA) ... NTMP
Nitrate Negative (VRA) ... NTNG
Nitrobenzylthioinosine [*Organic chemistry*] ... NBTI
Njdole [*Gabon*] [*Airport symbol*] (AD) ... KDJ
Njombe [*Tanzania*] [*Airport symbol*] (AD) ... JOM
Nkolo [*Zaire*] [*Airport symbol*] (AD) ... NKL
NLM-Dutch Airlines [*ICAO designator*] (AD) ... HN
No Action Indicated (AD) ... nai
No Added Salt (AD) ... n-a-s
No Address Instruction (AD) ... nai
No American Equivalent (AD) ... nAe
No Apparent Defect (AD) ... nad
No Apparent Rate (AD) ... nar
No Appreciable Difference (AD) ... nad
No Appreciable Disease (AD) ... nad
No Date (VRA) ... nd
No Option Offered [*Investment term*] (DFIT) ... S
No Qualified Bidders [*Investment term*] (DFIT) ... NQB
Noemfoor [*New Guinea*] [*Airport symbol*] (AD) ... FOO
Noise Abatement Office (AD) ... NAO
Noise Abatement Society (AD) ... N A S
Noise Abatement Society of Great Britain (AD) ... NAS-GB
Non-Adherent Peritoneal Cells (AD) ... napc
Non-Agency Purchase (AD) ... nap
Non-Aligned Movement (AD) ... nam
Nonappropriated Funds (AD) ... naf
Non-Contact Time (AIE) ... NCT
Nonhuman Primate ... NHP
Non-Orthogonal Analysis of Variance (AD) ... nanova
Nonpolychrome (VRA) ... nonpoly
Nonqualified Stock Options (WYGK) ... NQSO
Non-Stockpile Chemical Materiel [*Military*] (RDA) ... NSCM
Nonuniform Rational B-Spline [*A type of spline*] [*Computer science*] ... NURBS
Non-Volatile Field-Effect-Transistor [*Electronics*] ... NVFET
Noosa Air [*ICAO designator*] (AD) ... OF
Nordair [*ICAO designator*] (AD) ... ND
Nordeste-Lineas Aereas Regionais [*ICAO designator*] (AD) ... JH
Nordmaling [*Sweden*] [*Airport symbol*] (AD) ... OLG
Nor-East Commuter Airlines [*ICAO designator*] (AD) ... YN
Norges Automobil Fornund [*Norway Automobile Association*] (AD) ... NAF
Norgulf Lines (North Atlantic & Gulf) (AD) ... NA & G
Normal Allowed Time (AD) ... nat
North African Theater of Operations (AD) ... NATUSA
North America (AD) ... N Am
North American Land Sailing Association (AD) ... NALSA
North American Maritime Agencies (AD) ... NAMA
North American Movement (AD) ... NAM
North American Presentation Level Protocol Standard (DOM) ... NAPLPS
North American Regional Office (AD) ... NARO
North American Regional World Anti-Communist League (AD) ... NARWACL
North American Review [*A publication*] (BRI) ... NAR
North American Royalties (AD) ... NAR
North American Sailing Association (AD) ... NASA
North American Sporting Clays [*An association*] ... NASC
North American Survival and Homesteading Association (AD) ... NASHA
North Arizona University (AD) ... NAU
North Atlantic (AD) ... N Atl
North Atlantic Biocultural Organization [*A research cooperative*] ... NABO
North Atlantic Current (AD) ... N Atl Cur
North Atlantic Current [*Oceanography*] ... NAC
North Atlantic Institute for Defense Studies [*NATO*] (AD) ... NAIDS
North Atlantic Military Committee (AD) ... NAMilCom
North Australian Research Unit (AD) ... NARU
North Celestial Pole (AD) ... Pn
Northampton [*England*] [*Airport symbol*] (AD) ... ORM
Northern Agricultural Development Corp. (AD) ... NADC
Northern Australia Jockey Club (AD) ... NAJC
Northern Examinations and Assessment Board (AIE) ... NEAB
Northern Independent Steel Training Association (AIE) ... NISTA
Northern Ireland Council for Educational Research (AIE) ... NICER
Northern Ireland Further Education Guidance Service (AIE) ... NIFEGS
Northern Ireland Schools Examination Council (AIE) ... NISEC
Northern Telecom [*Canada*] ... Nortel
Northern Universities Joint Matriculation Board (AIE) ... NUJMB
Northern Wings [*ICAO designator*] (AD) ... WS
Northwest Alabama Junior College (AD) ... NAJC
Northwest Skyways [*ICAO designator*] (AD) ... BV
Northwest Territorial Airways [*ICAO designator*] (AD) ... NV
North-Wright Air Ltd. [*ICAO designator*] (AD) ... HW
Norving [*ICAO designator*] (AD) ... RT
Norway (VRA) ... Nor
Norwegian-American Historical Museum (AD) ... NAWH
Not Always Excused (AD) ... nae
Not at Present (AD) ... nap
Not on Active Duty [*Military*] (AD) ... nad
Notes (Music Library Association) [*A publication*] (BRI) ... Notes
Notes Payable [*Finance*] (DFIT) ... N/P
Nothing Abnormal Detected (AD) ... nad
Nothing Adverse Known (AD) ... nak
Notodden [*Norway*] [*Airport symbol*] (AD) ... NDE
Nottignham and Nottinghamshire Technical Information Service [*British*] (AD) ... NANTIS
Nouadhibou [*Mauritania*] [*Airport symbol*] (AD) ... PTE
Nova Freixo [*Mozambique*] [*Airport symbol*] (AD) ... FXO
Nova Lisboa [*Angola*] [*Airport symbol*] (AD) ... NOV
Nova Scotia Society of Artists [*1922-72*] [*Canada*] (NGC) ... NSSA
Novell Distributed Print Services [*Computer science*] ... NDPS
Novo Redondo [*Angola*] [*Airport symbol*] (AD) ... NDD
NT File System [*Computer science*] ... NTFS
Nuclear Age (AD) ... N-age
Nuclear Aircraft Research Facility (AD) ... NARF
Nuclear Armament (AD) ... N-arm
Nuclear Attack (AD) ... N-attack
Nuclear Weapons Accident Report Procedures (AD) ... NARP
Nuclear-Armed (AD) ... N-armed
Nucleotide Binding Site [*Genetics*] ... NBS
Nuernberger [*ICAO designator*] (AD) ... NS
Nueva Casas Grandes [*Mexico*] [*Airport symbol*] (AD) ... NCG
Nurses' Central Clearing House (AIE) ... NCCH
NWSA Journal [*A publication*] (BRI) ... NWSA Jnl
Nymphaeum (VRA) ... nymphm
Nzerekore [*Guinea*] [*Airport symbol*] (AD) ... NZE

O

By Meaning

O Estado de Sao Paulo [State of Sao Paulo] [Brazil] [A publication] (AD) ..... OESP
Oahu Education Association [Hawaii] (AD) .... OEA
Oahu Metropolitan Planning Organization [Hawaii] (AD) .... OMPO
Oak Bark Tanners' Association (AD) .... OBTA
Oakey [Queensland] [Airport symbol] (AD) .... OKY
Obedient (AD) .... obt
Oberkommando der Marine [Naval High Command] [Germany] (AD) .... OKM
Oberlin College (AD) .... OC
Oberste Herresleitung [Supreme Headquarters] [German] (AD) .... OHL
Oberwerk [Highest Organ Bank] [German] (AD) .... Obw
Obidos [Brazil] [Airport symbol] (AD) .... OBI
Obiedinennoye Gosudartsvennoye Politicheskoye Upravlenie [United State
   Political Administration] [Russian] (AD) .... OGPU
Obiit [He Died] [Latin] (AD) .... obt
Object (VRA) .... obj
Object Definition Language [Computer science] .... ODL
Oblate College (AD) .... OC
Obscura (VRA) .... obs
Obscure Glass (AD) .... ogl
Observable Evidence of Good Teaching (AD) .... oegt
Observation (AD) .... obsv
Observation Research and Classroom Learning Evaluation (AIE) .... ORACLE
Observation Window (AD) .... obw
Observatory (AD) .... obsv
Observer (AD) .... obsv
Observer Foreign News Service (AD) .... OFNS
Observer Group in El Salvador .... OGELS
Observer (London) [A publication] (BRI) .... Obs
Obsessive Compulsive Disorder [Medicine] (AD) .... ocd
Obstacle Clearance Surface (AD) .... ocs
Obstacle Planner Software (RDA) .... OPS
Obstetrical Conjugate [Medicine] (AD) .... oc
Obstruction (AD) .... obstr
Obstruction Light (AD) .... obstl
Obtained (AD) .... obtd
Obtaining Money by False Pretenses (AD) .... omfp
Obverse (AD) .... obv
Obvious (AD) .... obv
Obviously (AD) .... obvy
Ocarina (AD) .... oca
Occasion (AD) .... ocsn
Occasional (AD) .... occas
Occasional (AD) .... ocnl
Occasional (AD) .... ocsnl
Occasionally (AD) .... occ
Occasionally (AD) .... ocsnly
Occidental College (AD) .... OC
Occipital (AD) .... occip
Occipito-Dextra Anterior (AD) .... oda
Occipito-Dextra Posterior (AD) .... odp
Occipito-Dextra Transverse (AD) .... odt
Occipito-Laeva Anterior (AD) .... ola
Occipito-Laeva Posterior (AD) .... olp
Occipito-Laeva Transverse (AD) .... olt
Occlude (AD) .... occl
Occulting (AD) .... Occ
Occupation (AD) .... occ
Occupation (AD) .... occup
Occupational Health Administration (AD) .... OHA
Occupational Health Nursing Officer (AD) .... OHNO
Occupational Health Nursing Sister (AD) .... OHNS
Occupational Health-Safety-Programs Accreditation Commission
   (AD) .... OHSPAC
Occupational Preparation Scheme (AIE) .... OPS
Occupational Standards Council (AIE) .... OSC
Occupational Therapy (AD) .... occ th
Occupational Training (AIE) .... OT
Occupied (AD) .... occd
Ocean (AD) .... Oc
Ocean (AD) .... oc
Ocean Airways [ICAO designator] (AD) .... VM
Ocean Beach (AD) .... Ocn Bch
Ocean Bill of Lading (AD) .... oc b/l
Ocean Boarding Vessel (AD) .... obv
Ocean Cargo Line (AD) .... OCL
Ocean Container Zebrugge (AD) .... OCZ

Ocean Design Engineering Corp. (AD) .... ODEC
Ocean Drilling and Exploration Co. (AD) .... ODECO
Ocean Heat Convergence .... OHC
Ocean Heat Transport .... OHT
Ocean Hill-Brownsville (AD) .... OH-B
Ocean Industries Association (AD) .... OIA
Ocean Mining Administration (AD) .... OMA
Ocean View .... oc vu
Oceanair [ICAO designator] (AD) .... TJ
Ocean-Atmosphere General Circulation Model [Oceanography] .... OAGCM
Oceanografiska Institute [Oceanographic Institute] [Goeteborg, Sweden]
   (AD) .... Ocean Inst
Oceanographic Institute Wellington New Zealand (AD) .... OIW
Oceanography (AD) .... oceanog
Oceanologist (AD) .... oceano
Och Dylika [And the Like] [Swedish] (AD) .... od
Ochre (AD) .... och
Octagon (AD) .... oct
Octal (AD) .... oct
Octal Debugging Technique (AD) .... odt
Octane (AD) .... oct
Octane Blending Value (AD) .... obv
Octane Number (AD) .... on
Octans (AD) .... Oct
Octava Pars [Eighth Part] [Latin] (AD) .... oct pars
Octave (AD) .... oct
Octavius (AD) .... Oct
Octavo (AD) .... oct
Octet (AD) .... oct
October (AD) .... Oct
October League (AD) .... OL
Octrooi Protectie [Patent Protected] [Dutch] (AD) .... octr prot
Octuplicate (AD) .... octupl
Ocular Herpes [Medicine] (AD) .... OH
Ocular Hypertension Indicator (AD) .... ohi
Oculentum [Eye Ointment] [Latin] (AD) .... oculent
Oculis [To the Eyes] [Latin] (AD) .... ocul
Oculus Dexter [Right Eye] [Latin] (AD) .... od
Oculus Laevus [Left Eye] [Latin] (AD) .... ol
Odalisque (VRA) .... odlsq
Odense (AD) .... Odn
Odessa (AD) .... Oda
Odessa College (AD) .... OC
Odin (AD) .... Odn
Odometer (AD) .... odom
Odontology (AD) .... odont
Odor Control (AD) .... oc
Odor Detection Threshold (AD) .... odt
Odorless (AD) .... odorl
Odur [or] [German] (AD) .... od
Oenanthic (AD) .... oen
Oenanthyl (AD) .... oen
oenomancy (AD) .... oen
oenomel (AD) .... oen
oenometer (AD) .... oen
oenophilist (AD) .... oen
oenophobist (AD) .... oen
oenopoetic (AD) .... oen
Oersted (AD) .... oe
Oesophagus (AD) .... oesoph
Oesterreichische Computer Gesellscahft [Austrian Computer Society]
   [German] (AD) .... OCG
Oesterreichische Galerie [Austrian Gallery] (AD) .... OG
Oesterreichische Gesseleschaft fuer Informatik [Austrian Society for
   Information Processing] [German] (AD) .... OGI
Oesterreichischer Aero-Club [Austrian Aero Club] [German] (AD) ...... OEC
Oesterreichischer Gewerkschaftsbund [Austrian Trade Union Federation]
   [German] (AD) .... OGB
Off Frequency Rejection (AD) .... ofr
Off Our Backs [A publication] (BRI) .... OOB
Offaly (AD) .... Ofly
Offender-Based Transaction Statistics (AD) .... obts
Offensive (AD) .... offen
Offering (AD) .... offg
Offertories (AD) .... offer
Office (AD) .... ofc

Office (DD) ... off
Office and Industrial Records Management (AD) ... OIRM
Office Consultation (AD) ... OC
Office Contents Special Form [*Inventor*] (AD) ... ocsf
Office de Protection contre les Rayonnements Ionisants [*France*] ... OPRI
Office Equipment (AD) ... offeq
Office Equipment Manufacturers Association (AD) ... OEMA
Office Executives Association (AD) ... OEA
Office for Accreditation [*American Library Association*] ... OA
Office for Improvements in the Administration of Justice (AD) ... OIAJ
Office for Information Technology Policy [*American Library Association*] ... OITP
Office for Research (AD) ... OfR
Office for Research & Statistics [*American Library Association*] ... ORS
Office for Standards in Education (AIE) ... OFSTED
Office Francais d'Exportation de Materiel Aeronautique [*French Office for theExportation of Aeronautical Materiel*] (AD) ... OFEMA
Office Hours (AD) ... oh
Office Internationale de la Vigne et du Vin [*International Office of Vines and Wines*] [*French*] (AD) ... OIVV
Office Methods Research (AD) ... omr
Office of Aerospace Research [*Air Force*] (AD) ... OER
Office of Arid Land Studies [*University of Arizona*] (AD) ... OLAS
Office of Civil Aviation Security (AD) ... OCAS
Office of Communication and Research Utilization (AD) ... OCRU
Office of Community Services (AD) ... OComS
Office of Consumer Protection (AD) ... OCP
Office of Crime Prevention and Criminal Justice Research (AD) ... OCPCJR
Office of Criminal Justice Planning (AD) ... OCJP
Office of Cultural Presentations (AD) ... OCP
Office of Curriculum Frameworks and Textbooks (AD) ... OCFT
Office of Defender Services (AD) ... ODS
Office of Disaster Preparedness (AD) ... ODP
Office of Drug Abuse (AD) ... ODA
Office of Earthquakes, Volcanoes, and Engineering [*US Geological Survey*] (AD) ... OEVE
Office of Education and Training (AD) ... OET
Office of Emergency Planning (AD) ... OEP
Office of Employment Development Programs (AD) ... OEDP
Office of Environmental Affairs (AD) ... OEA
Office of Environmental Quality Control (AD) ... OEQC
Office of Exploratory Research and Problem Assessment [*National Science Foundation*] (AD) ... OERPA
Office of Fuels and Engergy (AD) ... OFE
Office of Graduate Studies and Research (AD) ... OGSR
Office of Home Care Services (AD) ... OHCS
Office of Humanities Communication (AD) ... OHC
Office of Industrial Associates (AD) ... OIA
Office of Inter-American Radio (AD) ... OIR
Office of International Criminal Justice (AD) ... OICJ
Office of International Economic Research (AD) ... OIER
Office of International Epizootics (AD) ... OIE
Office of International Public Health (AD) ... OIPH
Office of International Scientific Affairs (AD) ... OISA
Office of Interstate Land Sales Registration (AD) ... OILSR
Office of Invention and Innovation (AD) ... OII
Office of Juvenile Justice (AD) ... OJJ
Office of Labor Management Relations (AD) ... OLMR
Office of Law Enforcement and Planning (AD) ... OLEP
Office of Law Enforcement Assistance (AD) ... OLEA
Office of Legislative Liaison (AD) ... OLL
Office of Management and Finance (AD) ... OMF
Office of Maritime Affairs (AD) ... OMA
Office of Mental Health (AD) ... OMH
Office of Minerals Policy and Research Analysis (AD) ... OMPRA
Office of Recruitment-American Library Association (AD) ... OFR-ALA
Office of Technical Services (AD) ... OFTS
Office of the Chief Chemical Officer (AD) ... Oc C Cm O
Office of the Chief of Protocol [*US Department of State*] (AD) ... OCP
Office of the City Attorney (AD) ... OCA
Office of the Coordinator of Information (AD) ... OCI
Office of the County Recorder (AD) ... OCR
Office of the Director of Scientific Research (AD) ... ODSR
Office of the District Administrator (AD) ... ODA
Office of the District Attorney (AD) ... ODA
Office of the Federal Inspector (AD) ... OFI
Office of the Insurance Commissioner (AD) ... OIC
Office of the Secretary of the Air Force (AD) ... OFST
Office of Transportation Security (AD) ... OFTS
Office Publications (AD) ... Office Pubns
Officer (AD) ... Off
Officer Engineering Reserve (AD) ... OER
Officer in Charge (AD) ... OC
Officer in Training (AD) ... O i T
Officer of Merit, Order of St. Lazarus of Jerusalem (DD) ... OMLJ
Officer of the Order of Canada (DD) ... OC
Officer of the Order of Military Merit [*Canada*] (DD) ... OMM
Officer of the Order of the British Empire (NGC) ... OBE
Officer-Cadet (AD) ... O/Cdt
Officer-in-Charge (AD) ... O-i-C
Officer-in-Charge Police District (AD) ... OCPD
Officer-Like Qualities (AD) ... olq
Officer's Eyes Only (AD) ... oeo
Officer's Mess [*Military*] (AD) ... O-Mess
Officers Training School (AD) ... OFTS
Official (AD) ... ofcl
Official (AD) ... offic
Official (AD) ... ofl
Official Guide of the Railways [*A publication*] (AD) ... OGR
Official Hotel and Resort Guide [*A publication*] (AD) ... OHRG
Official Journal of the European Communities [*A publication*] (AD) ... OJEC
Offizierlager [*Officer's Prison Camp*] [*German*] (AD) ... Oflag
Off-Market Date (AD) ... omd
Off-Market Date Received (AD) ... omdr
Offset (VRA) ... ofst
Offset Doppler (AD) ... odop
Off-Street Parking (AD) ... off-st pkg
Oficial [*Official*] [*Spanish*] (AD) ... ofic
Oficina Central de Organizacion y Metodos [*Central Office of Organization and Methods*] [*Spain*] (AD) ... OCOM
Oficina Central de Personal [*Central Personnel Office*] [*Spain*] (AD) ... OCP
Oficina de Planificacion Nacional [*Office of National Planning*] [*Spain*] (AD) ... ODEPLAN
Oficina del Coordinador de las Naciones Unidas para la Ayuda en los Desastres [*Office of the Coordinator of the United Nations for Help in Disasters*] [*Spanish*] (AD) ... OCNAUD
Oficina Municipale de Planeamiento Urbano [*Municipal Office of Urban Planning*] [*Spain*] (AD) ... OMPU
Ogden [*Utah*] [*Airport symbol*] (AD) ... OGD
Ogden Nash (AD) ... ON
Ogdensburg (AD) ... Ogd
Oggetto [*Object*] [*Italian*] (AD) ... ogg
Oh Gee (AD) ... og
Oh, I See [*Computer science*] (DOM) ... OIC
Ohio College (AD) ... OC
Ohio College Association (AD) ... OCA
Ohio Correctional and Court Services Association (AD) ... OCCSA
Ohio Education Association (AD) ... OEA
Ohio Educational Library/Media Association (AD) ... OEL/MA
Ohio Federation of Teachers (AD) ... OFT
Ohio Foundation of Independent Colleges (AD) ... OFIC
Ohio Inspection Bureau (AD) ... OIB
Ohio Library Association (AD) ... OLA
Ohio Library Foundation (AD) ... OLF
Ohio Turnpike (AD) ... Ohio Turn
Ohio University Press (AD) ... Ohio U Pr
Ohm-Centimeter (AD) ... ohm-cm
Ohmmeter (AD) ... ohm
Ohne Jahr [*Without Year*] [*German*] (AD) ... oJ
Ohne Kosten [*Without Cost*] [*German*] (AD) ... ok
Ohne Pedale [*Without Pedals*] [*German*] (AD) ... oh Ped
Oiapoque [*Brazil*] [*Airport symbol*] (AD) ... OYK
Oil (VRA) ... o
Oil and Gas Development Corp. (AD) ... OGDC
Oil and Gas Journal [*A publication*] (AD) ... OGJ
Oil, Chemical, and Atomic Workers (AD) ... OCAW
Oil Circuit Breaker (AD) ... ocb
Oil Company of Australia (AD) ... OCA
Oil Content Monitor (AD) ... ocm
Oil Control Coordination Committee (AD) ... OCCC
Oil Drilling and Exploration (AD) ... ODE
Oil Engineering Apprentices Association (AD) ... OEAA
Oil Exporting Countries (AD) ... OEC
Oil Gland (AD) ... og
Oil Heat Institute (AD) ... OHI
Oil Import Appeals Board (AD) ... OIAB
Oil in Place (AD) ... oip
Oil Industry Commission (AD) ... OIC
Oil Industry Working Party (AD) ... OIWP
Oil Level (AD) ... ol
Oil on Board (VRA) ... o/bd
Oil on Burlap (VRA) ... o/bur
Oil on Canvas (VRA) ... o/c
Oil on Cardboard (VRA) ... o/cdbd
Oil on Panel (VRA) ... o/p
Oil on Paper (VRA) ... o/pa
Oil Ripoff (AD) ... oiloff
Oil Spill Response Plan [*Pollution prevention*] ... OSRP
Oil-Emulsion Mud (AD) ... oem
Oil-Extended Styrene-Butadiene Rubber (AD) ... oesbr
Oil-Immersed (AD) ... oi
Oilstick (VRA) ... ostk
Ointment (AD) ... oint
Okinawa (AD) ... Okin
Oklahoma (AD) ... Okla
Oklahoma City (AD) ... OklaC
Oklahoma City Community Foundation (AD) ... OCCF
Oklahoma City Public Library (AD) ... OCPL
Oklahoma Crime Commission (AD) ... OCC
Oklahoma Criminal Justice Association (AD) ... OCJA
Oklahoma Electronics (AD) ... Oktronics
Oklahoma Independent College Foundation (AD) ... OICF
Oklahoma Inspection Bureau (AD) ... OIB
Oklahoma Library Association (AD) ... OLA
Oklahomans for Indian Opportunity (AD) ... OIO
Okolona College (AD) ... OC
Oktober [*October*] [*GRM*] (AD) ... okt
Oktyab [*October*] [*Russian*] (AD) ... okt
Ola Kala [*All is Fine*] [*Greek*] (AD) ... ok
Olav Trygvason (AD) ... Olav Tryg
Old Bulgarian (AD) ... O Bul

By Meaning

Old Catalan (AD)	O Cat
Old Celtic (AD)	O Celt
Old Colony Historical Society (AD)	OCHS
Old Cornish (AD)	O Corn
Old Danish (AD)	ODa
Old Dominion College Technical Institute (AD)	ODCTI
Old Dominion Foundation (AD)	ODF
Old Established Forces (AD)	Oldfos
Old Face (AD)	of
Old Fashioned (AD)	old-fash
Old Folks Association (AD)	OFA
Old Frankish (AD)	O Frk
Old French (AD)	O Fr
Old Frisian (AD)	OFris
Old Gaelic (AD)	O Gael
Old Gaelic (AD)	OG
Old Girl (AD)	og
Old Irish (AD)	OIr
Old Italian (AD)	O It
Old Italian (AD)	OIt
Old Jamaica Rum (AD)	oJr
Old Maid's Day [June 4] (AD)	Old Maid's
Old Man (AD)	om
Old Measurement (AD)	om
Old Mission Beach Athletic Club (AD)	OMBAC
Old Repertory (AD)	old rep
Old Testament (AD)	Old Test
Older People with Active Lifestyles [Lifestyle classification]	OPALs
Older Workers Benefit Protection Act of 1990 (WYGK)	OWBPA
Oldsmobile (AD)	Olds
Olean [New York] [Airport symbol] (AD)	OLE
Oleoresin (AD)	ol res
Oleoresins (AD)	oleo
Olericulture (AD)	olericult
Oleum [Oil] [Latin] (AD)	ol
Olfactory Research Fund	ORF
Oligocene (AD)	Olig
Olivaceous (AD)	olv
Olive [Political party] (AD)	Ol
Olive (AD)	olv
Olive Brown (AD)	OlBr
Olive Green (AD)	OIG
Olive Oil (AD)	ol ol
Olive-Drab (AD)	od
Oliver (AD)	Oli
Olivera (AD)	Olive
Olivet College (AD)	OC
Olney Communication College (AD)	OCC
Olomouc [Czechoslovakia] [Airport symbol] (AD)	OLO
Olsen Line (AD)	OL
Olympia [Washington] [Airport symbol] (AD)	OLM
Olympia (AD)	Oly
Olympia (AD)	Olym
Olympic (AD)	Oly
Olympic College (AD)	OC
Olympic Media Information (AD)	OMI
Olympic National Park, Washington (AD)	Olympic
Omaha (AD)	Om
Omaha, Nebraska (AD)	Oma
Oman (AD)	Om
Omarbetad [Revised] [Swedish] (AD)	omarb
Ombudsman (AD)	Omb
Omdring [About] [Norwegian] (AD)	omkr
Omega House (AD)	OH
Omissions Expected (AD)	oe
Omni Bihora [Every Two Hours] [Latin] (AD)	omn bih
Omni Hora [Hourly] [Latin] (AD)	oh
Omni Mane [Every Morning] [Latin] (AD)	om
Omni Mane [Every Morning] [Latin] (AD)	omn man
Omni Nocte [Every Night] [Latin] (AD)	om
Omni Nocte [Every Night] [Latin] (AD)	omn noct
Omnibus Bidendis [Every Two Days] [Latin] (AD)	om bid
Omnicardiogram [Medicine] (AD)	ocg
Omnirange (AD)	omni
Omnivisual (AD)	omni
Omphaloskepsis (AD)	ompf
Omsk Hemorrhagic Fever (AD)	ohf
On Camera (AD)	oc
On Center (AD)	oc
On Company Service (AD)	ocs
On Demand (AD)	od
On Examination (AD)	o/e
On Ground (AD)	og
On Guard (AD)	og
On Hand (AD)	oh
On the Issues [A publication] (BRI)	OnIssues
Onboard Health Monitoring System (AD)	OHMS
One Day at a Time (AD)	odat
One Man, One Responsibility (AD)	omor
One Term In-Service Course (AIE)	OTIS
One-Day Event (AD)	ode
One-Day One-Trial System (AD)	ODOTS
One-Day Trials (AD)	odt
One-Function Diagram (AD)	ofd
One-Function Sketch (AD)	ofs

One-Man Pension Arrangement (AD)	ompa
On-Going Thing (AD)	ogt
On-Hudson (AD)	o-H
On-Line Communications Driver [Computer science] (AD)	ocd
On-Line Computer (AD)	olc
On-Line Computer System (AD)	OLCS
On-Line Cryptanalytic Aid Language [Computer science] (AD)	ocal
On-Line Debugging Technique [Computer science] (AD)	odt
On-Line Filing (AD)	olf
Online Information Search Service [Computer science] (AD)	OISS
Online Public Education Network	OPEN
On-Line Real Time [Computer science] (AD)	olrt
On-Line Scientific Computer (AD)	olsc
On-Line Teller Terminal [Computer science] (AD)	oltt
On-Line Validation [Computer science] (AD)	olv
Onmidirectional (AD)	omni
Onomastikon [Lexicon] [Greek] (AD)	on
Onondaga Community College (AD)	OCC
Onorevole [Honorable] [Italian] (AD)	On
On-Screen Manager [Computer science]	OSM
Onsdag [Wednesday] [Danish] (AD)	On
Onset and Course [Medicine] (AD)	o & c
Ontario [Oregon] [Airport symbol] (AD)	ONO
Ontario [Canada] (DD)	Ont
Ontario Association of Architects [1890] [Canada] (NGC)	OAA
Ontario College of Ophthalmology [Canada] (AD)	OCO
Ontario Community College Librarians [Canada] (AD)	OCCL
Ontario Confederation of University Facility Associations [Canada] (AD)	OCUFA
Ontario Council on University Affairs [Canada] (AD)	OCUA
Ontario Department of Health [Canada] (AD)	ODH
Ontario Federation of Construction Associations [Canada] (AD)	OFCA
Ontario Federation of Students [Canada] (AD)	OFS
Ontario Government Railway [Canada] (AD)	OGR
Ontario Health-Services Insurances Plan [Canada] (AD)	OHSIP
Ontario Hospital Insurance Plan [Canada] (AD)	OHIP
Ontario Humane Society [Canada] (AD)	OHS
Ontario Institute of Chartered Accountants [Canada] (DD)	OICA
Ontario Institute of Painters, Toronto [1958] [Canada] (NGC)	OIP
Ontario Labor Relations Board [Canada] (AD)	OLRB
Ontario Land Economist [Canada] (DD)	OLE
Ontario Land Surveyor [Canada] (DD)	OLS
Ontario Library Association [Canada] (AD)	OLA
Ontario Medical Association [Canada] (AD)	OMA
Ontario Medical Surgical Insurance Plan [Canada] (AD)	OMSIP
Ontario Motor League [Canada] (AD)	OML
Ontario Northland Railway [Canada] (AD)	ON
On-the-Job Injuries (AD)	oji
On-the-Job Training (AD)	ojt
Onyx (VRA)	onx
Onze Lieve Vrouw [Our Lady] [Dutch] (AD)	OLV
Opal Air [ICAO designator] (AD)	OB
Opalotype (VRA)	OPTYP
Open and Distance Learning (AIE)	ODL
Open Charter (AD)	oc
Open College (AIE)	OC
Open College Network (AIE)	OCN
Open Communications Architecture (AD)	OCA
Open Cover (AD)	o/c
Open Cup (AD)	oc
Open End (AD)	oe
Open Financial Connectivity [Microsoft Computer Software] [Computer Science]	OFC
Open Financial Exchange [Computer science]	OFX
Open Hearth (AD)	oh
Open Learning (AIE)	OL
Open Learning Programme (AIE)	OLP
Open Media Framework (DOM)	OMF
Open Network Environment [Netscape network] [Computer science]	ONE
Open Profiling Standard [Firefly Network] [Computer science]	OPS
Open Tech Training Support Unit (AIE)	OTTSU
Open Transport [Computer science]	OT
Open-Circuit Television (AD)	octv
Open-Circuit Voltage (AD)	ocv
Open-Close-Open (AD)	oco
Open-Door International [An association] (AD)	ODI
Open-Ended Health Maintenance Organization [Insurance] (WYGK)	OEHMO
Open-Ended Plan [Human resources] (WYGK)	OEP
Open-Ended System [Computer science]	OES
Open-Hearth Steel (AD)	ohs
Open-Joint (AD)	oj
Opera Company (AD)	OC
Opera Guilds International (AD)	OGI
Opera House (AD)	OH
Opera News [A publication] (BRI)	ON
Opera-Comique [Comic Opera] [French] (AD)	OC
Operating Ground Equipment Specification [Italian] (AD)	OGES
Operating License (AD)	ol
Operating Procedure for Ministers	OPM
Operation (DD)	oper
Operation and Maintenance (AD)	O & M
Operation Blessing International [An association]	OBI
Operational Capability Date (AD)	ocd
Operational Checkout Instruction (AD)	OCI
Operational Control Equipment (AD)	oce

Operational Conversion Unit (AD) ... ocu
Operational Deployment Force (AD) ... ODF
Operational Ground Equipment (AD) ... oge
Operational Ground-Support Equipment (AD) ... ogse
Operational Monitor (AD) ... om
Operations and Engineering (AD) ... o & e
Operations/Logistics (AD) ... o/l
Operative Bootmakers Union (AD) ... OBU
Operative Personenkontrolle [*Operational Person Control*] [*German*] ... OPK
Operator Control Language (AD) ... ocl
Operator Distance Dialing (AD) ... odd
Operator's License (AD) ... O-license
Opere Citato [*In the Work Cited*] [*Latin*] (AD) ... oc
Ophthalmodynamometry [*Ophthalmology*] (AD) ... odm
Opiate-Directed Behavior (AD) ... odb
Opportunities for Youth [*Canada*] (AD) ... OFY
Opsonic Index (AD) ... o/i
Opthalmology Medical Group (AD) ... OMG
Optical Character Definition [*Computer science*] (AD) ... ocd
Optical Character Reader [*Computer science*] (AD) ... ocr
Optical Character Recognition [*Computer science*] (AD) ... ocr
Optical Character Recognition Equipment [*Computer science*] (AD) ... ocre
Optical Character-Recognizing Intelligent Terminal [*Computer science*] (AD) ... ocrit
Optical Coating Evaluation Laboratory (AD) ... OCEL
Optical Communications Linkage (AD) ... ocl
Optical Component Testing and Evaluation (AD) ... octe
Optical Density (AD) ... od
Optical Distributors and Manufacturers Association (AD) ... ODMA
Optical Effects Module Electronic Controller and Processor (AD) ... oemcp
Optical Electron Microscope (AD) ... oem
Optical Fire Detector (AD) ... ofd
Optical Imaging Systems (RDA) ... OIS
Optical Immunoassay [*Clinical chemistry*] ... OIA
Optical Klystron (AD) ... ok
Optical Mark Page Reader (AD) ... ompr
Optical Mark Reader (AD) ... omr
Optical Mark Recognition (AD) ... omr
Optical Memory Disc Recorder (DOM) ... OMDR
Optical Prism Uniformity System ... OPUS
Optical Transient Detector ... OTD
Optical-Density Units (AD) ... od units
Optics Automation and Management (RDA) ... Opticam
Optimal Missile Engagement Guidance Algorithm (AD) ... OMEGA
Optimized Delivery Model [*Compaq*] [*Computer science*] ... ODM
Optimized Distribution Model [*Compaq Computer Corp.*] [*Computer science*] ... ODM
Optimum Earth-Reentry Corridor (AD) ... oerc
Optimum Life-Cycle Costing (AD) ... olcc
Option Growth Fund (AD) ... ogf
Option Not Traded [*Investment term*] (DFIT) ... R
Optional Educational Programs (AD) ... OEP
Optional Form (AD) ... of
Opto/Graphic (AD) ... O/G
Opto-Graphic (AD) ... o/g
Optometric Corp. (AD) ... OC
Or Less (AD) ... ol
Oral Contraceptive [*Medicine*] (AD) ... oc
Oral Hygiene Service (AD) ... OHS
Oral Mucosal Transudate [*Clinical chemistry*] ... OMT
Oran [*Argentina*] [*Airport symbol*] (AD) ... ORA
Orange County Community College (AD) ... OCCC
Orange Juice (AD) ... oj
Orange Walk [*British Honduras*] [*Airport symbol*] (AD) ... ORW
Orange-Green (AD) ... o-g
Orange-Green Stain (AD) ... o-g stain
Orbital Launched Balistic Missile (AD) ... olbm
Orbiter Liftoff Weight (AD) ... olow
Order (AD) ... odr
Order and Change Control (AD) ... o & cc
Order of Architects of Quebec [*1974, founded 1890 as PQAA*] [*Canada*] (NGC) ... OAQ
Order of British Columbia [*Canada*] (DD) ... OBC
Order of De Molay (AD) ... ODM
Order of Japan (DD) ... OJapan
Order of Ontario [*Canada*] (DD) ... OOnt
Order of the White Rose of Finland (DD) ... OWR
Order-Despatched (AD) ... odp
Orderly Marketing Arrangement (AD) ... oma
Ordinance Lieutenent-Commander (AD) ... O L Cr
Ordinance Map (AD) ... Om
Ordinary Levels [*of educational tests*] (AD) ... O-levels
Ordnance Engineer Overseer (AD) ... OEO
Ordre de Comptables Agrees du Quebec [*Canada*] (DD) ... OCAQ
Ordre des Ingenieurs du Quebec [*Canada*] (DD) ... OIQ
Ordre du Quebec [*Order of Quebec*] [*Canada*] (DD) ... OQ
Oregon, California, and Eastern Railroad (AD) ... OC & E
Oregon Caves National Monument (AD) ... OCNM
Oregon Coastal Conservation and Development Commission (AD) ... OCCDC
Oregon Corrections Association (AD) ... OCA
Oregon Department of Energy (AD) ... ODOE
Oregon Education Association (AD) ... OEA
Oregon Educational Broadcasting (AD) ... OEB
Oregon Independent College Foundation (AD) ... OICF
Oregon Insurance Rating Bureau (AD) ... OIRB
Orenstein & Koppel (AD) ... O & K
Organ of Consultation ... OC
Organe de Controle des Stupefiants [*Narcotic Drug Control Organization*] [*France*] (AD) ... OCS
Organic Brain Syndrome [*Medicine*] (AD) ... ob syn
Organic Hearing Disease [*Medicine*] (AD) ... ohd
Organic Heart Disease [*Medicine*] (AD) ... ohd
Organic Liquid-Moderator Reactor (AD) ... olmr
Organic Matter (AD) ... om
Organisation Clandestine de la Revolution Algerienne [*Secret Organization of the Algerian Revolution*] [*France*] (AD) ... OCRA
Organisation Europeene pour la Controle de la Qualite GG1European Quality-Control OrganizationGG2 [*France*] (AD) ... OECQ
Organisation Interafricaine du Cafe [*Inter-African Coffee Organization*] [*French*] (AD) ... O-I-C
Organisation Intergouvernementale [*Inter-Governmental Organization*] [*French*] (AD) ... OIG
Organisation Internationale de Police Criminelle [*International Criminal Police Organization*] [*French*] (AD) ... OIPC
Organisation Internationale Non-Gouvernementale [*Non-Governmental International Organization*] [*French*] (AD) ... OING
Organisation Internationale pour la Science et la Technique du Vide [*International Organization for Vacuum Science and Technology*] [*French*] (AD) ... OISTV
Organisation Juive de Combat [*Jewish Combat Organization*] [*French*] (AD) ... OJC
Organismo Coordinador de Operaciones Antisubversivas [*Coordinating Organism of Antisubversive Operations*] [*Uruguay*] (AD) ... OCOA
Organizacion de Estados Americanos [*Organization of American States*] [*Spain*] (AD) ... OES
Organizacion Interamericana de Cooperacion [*Inter-American Cooperation Organ ization*] [*Spanish*] (AD) ... OICI
Organizacion Internacional de la Aviacion Civil [*International Civil AviationOrganization*] [*Spanish*] (AD) ... OIAC
Organizacion Latin-Americana de Energia [*Latin American Energy Organization*] [*Spanish*] (AD) ... OLADE
Organizacion Latino-Americana de Solidaridad [*Latin American Solidarity Organization*] [*Spanish*] (AD) ... OLAS
Organizacion Maritima Internacional [*International Maritime Organization*] [*Spanish*] (AD) ... OMI
Organizacion para la Educacion la Ciencia, y la Cultura [*Organization for Education, Science, and Culture*] [*United Nations*] (AD) ... OECCNU
Organizacion para la Liberacion Palestina [*Palestinian Liberation Organization*] [*Spanish*] [*Political party*] (AD) ... OLP
Organization Conflict of Interest (AD) ... oci
Organization Development [*Human resources*] (WYGK) ... OD
Organization for European Research (AD) ... OER
Organization of American States Electoral Observation Mission ... OAS/EOM
Organization of American States-Observer Group in Nicaragua ... OAS-OGN
Organization of Central American Armies (AD) ... OCAA
Organization of European States (AD) ... OES
Organization of Historical Studies (AD) ... OHS
Organization of Latin American Petroleum Exporting Countries (AD) ... OLAPEC
Organization of Latin American Students (AD) ... OLAS
Organizational and Intermediate (AD) ... o & i
Organizational Behaviour (DD) ... OrgBehav
Organizational Development (AD) ... od
Organizational Effectiveness (AD) ... oe
Organizational Entity Code (AD) ... oec
Organizational Entity Identity (AD) ... oei
Organizational Leadership for Executives [*Military*] (RDA) ... OLE
Organizations Concerned about Rural Education (AD) ... OCRE
Organized Crime (AD) ... o/c
Organized Crime and Racketeering Strike Force (AD) ... OCRSF
Organized Crime Intelligence Bureau (AD) ... OCIB
Organized Crime-Control Commission [*California*] (AD) ... OCCC
Organizing Committee for a Fifth Estate (AD) ... OC-5
Organo Corale [*Choir Organ*] [*Latin*] (AD) ... OC
Organo Espressivo [*Swell Organ*] [*Italian*] (AD) ... oe
Organo-Metallic Polymer (AD) ... omp
Orgasmic Impairment (AD) ... o-i
Oribi Gorge Nature Reserve [*South Africa*] (AD) ... OGNR
Oriel College (AD) ... OC
Oriens & King [*ICAO designator*] (AD) ... KZ
Orient Mid-East Lines (AD) ... OMEL
Oriental Herb Association (AD) ... OHA
Oriental Institute (AD) ... OI
Oriental Institute Museum [*University of Chicago*] (AD) ... OIM
Orientos [*Queensland*] [*Airport symbol*] (AD) ... OXO
Origin (VRA) ... orig
Origin and Destination (AD) ... o & d
Original Design (AD) ... od
Original Equipment Manufacturer (AD) ... OEM
Original Equipment Manufacturer (AD) ... oem
Original Equipment Replacement (AD) ... oer
Original Gum (AD) ... og
Original Issue Discount (AD) ... oid
Original List Price (AD) ... olp
Original Meaning is the Only Meaning (AD) ... omiom
Originally Cultured Formulation (AD) ... ocf
Orinthine-Decarboxylase, Motility, Indole, Trytophandeaminase (AD) ... omit
Oriximina [*Brazil*] [*Airport symbol*] (AD) ... ORX
Orlando College (AD) ... OC
Ormara [*Pakistan*] [*Airport symbol*] (AD) ... ORP
Ormolu (VRA) ... orm

By Meaning

Ornament (VRA) .... ornam
Orthogonals (VRA) .... orthg
Orthomode Transducer (AD) .... omt
Oruro [Bolivia] [Airport symbol] (AD) .... ORU
Oslo [Norway] [Airport symbol] (AD) .... FBU
Oslo Kommune Tunnelbanekontoret [Oslo Subway System] (AD) .... OKT
Osorno [Chile] [Airport symbol] (AD) .... ZOS
Ossining Correctional Facility [Sing Sing] (AD) .... OCF
Osteopathic Educational Foundation (AD) .... OEF
Osteuropaeische Zeit [East European Time] [German] (AD) .... OEZ
Otago Daily Times [A publication] (AD) .... ODT
Otavi [South-West Africa] [Airport symbol] (AD) .... OTV
Otero College (AD) .... OC
Other (VRA) .... oth
Other Direct Costs (AD) .... odc
Other Large Phased-Array RADAR (AD) .... olpar
Other Side [A publication] (BRI) .... OS
Otherwise Known As (AD) .... oka
Otitis Externa (AD) .... o/e
Otjiwarongo [South-West Africa] [Airport symbol] (AD) .... OJW
Otonabee Airways [ICAO designator] (AD) .... OU
Ottawa Fundraisers Network [Ontario, Canada] .... OFN
Ottawa Fundraising Executives [Ontario, Canada] .... OFE
Ouadda [Central African Republic] [Airport symbol] (AD) .... ODA
Ouahigouya [Upper Volta] [Airport symbol] (AD) .... OUG
Ouanda Djalle [Central African Republic] [Airport symbol] (AD) ..... ODJ
Our Memo (AD) .... om
Out Home (AD) .... oh
Out of Line of Sight (AD) .... olos
Outboard Engine Cutoff (AD) .... oeco
Outboard Engine Cutoff (AD) .... oecu
Outdoor Education (AD) .... oe
Outer Continental Shelf Policy Committee [California] (AD) ...... OCSPC
Outer Dead Center (AD) .... odc
Outer Enamel Epithelium (AD) .... oee
Outer Hair Cells (AD) .... ohc
Outer Harbor Dock and Wharf (AD) .... OHD & W
Outer Keel (AD) .... ok
Outer Marker (AD) .... om
Outgoing (AD) .... o/g
Outler Continental Shelf (AD) .... ocs
Outlet Gas Temperature (AD) .... ogt
Outlet Guide Vane (AD) .... ogv
Outline (VRA) .... outl
Outlook (AD) .... o/l
Out-of-House Operation (AD) .... oho
Output Control Pulses (AD) .... ocp
Output per Man Shift (AD) .... oms
Output to Display Buffer [Computer science] (AD) .... odb
Outside Cable Rehabilitation II [Army] (RDA) .... OSCAR II
Outside Continental Limits of the United States (AD) .... OConUS
Outside Diameter (AD) .... od
Outside Diameter of Female Coupling (AD) .... odfc
Outside Diameter of Male Coupling (AD) .... odmc
Outside Dimension (AD) .... od
Outside Face (AD) .... of
Outside Helix Angle (AD) .... oha
Outside Mold Line (AD) .... oml
Outstanding Media Advertising by Restaurants (AD) .... OMARS
Oval Head (AD) .... oh
Ovarian Cholesterol Depletion [Medicine] (AD) .... ocd
Oven Dried (AD) .... od
Ovenstone Factor (AD) .... Of
Over (VRA) .... ov
Overall Manufacturers' Association (AD) .... OMA
Overcast (AD) .... ocst
Overcharge (AD) .... o/c
Overdose (AD) .... od

Overdraft Charge [Banking] (AD) .... oc
Overdrive (AD) .... od
Overhaul (AD) .... o/h
Overhaul Factor (AD) .... ohf
Overhaul Replacement Factor (AD) .... ohrf
Overhead (AD) .... oh
Overhead Cam (AD) .... ohc
Overhead Projection (AD) .... ohp
Overhead Valve (AD) .... ohv
Overheat (AD) .... oheat
Overheating Temperature (AD) .... oht
Overland Common Points (AD) .... ocp
Overload Relay (AD) .... olr
Overseas Branch Transfer (AD) .... OBT
Overseas Chinese (AD) .... OC
Overseas Chinese Banking Corp. (AD) .... OCBC
Overseas Civil Servants (AD) .... OCS
Overseas Container Line (AD) .... OCL
Overseas Container Line Unit (AD) .... OCLU
Overseas Container Lines and Associated Container Transport (AD) .... OCL/ACT
Overseas Containers Ltd. (AD) .... OCL
Overseas Containers of Australia, Ltd. (AD) .... OCAL
Overseas Courier Service (AD) .... OCS
Overseas Development Assistance (AD) .... ODA
Overseas Development Corp. (AD) .... ODC
Overseas Development Institute Ltd. (AD) .... ODIL
Overseas Duty Selection Date (AD) .... odsd
Overseas Economic Cooperation Fund (AD) .... OECF
Overseas Exchange Transactions (AD) .... OET
Overseas Finance and Trade Corp. (AD) .... OFTC
Overseas Fixed Telecommunications System (AD) .... OFTS
Overseas Food Corp. (AD) .... OFC
Overseas Hotel Corp. (AD) .... OHC
Overseas Investment Commission (AD) .... OIC
Overseas Investors Services (AD) .... OIS
Overseas Mineral Resource Development (AD) .... OMRD
Ovulation-Producing Hormone [Medicine] (AD) .... OIH
Owensboro [Kentucky] [Airport symbol] (AD) .... OWB
Own Doppler Nullifer (AD) .... odn
Own Name (AD) .... o/n
Owner President Management Program (DD) .... OPM
Owners, Landlords, and Tenants (AD) .... ol & t
Owning the Weather [Army] (RDA) .... OTW
Oxbow Falls (AD) .... OF
Oxenstierna Foundation (AD) .... OF
Oxford [England] [Airport symbol] (AD) .... OXF
Oxford Committee for Family Relief [British] (AD) .... OCFR
Oxford Companion to English Literature [A publication] (AD) ... OCEL
Oxford Companion to Music [A publication] (AD) .... OCM
Oxford Foundation (AD) .... OF
Oxford India Paper (AD) .... oip
Oxford University Dramatic Society [British] (AIE) .... OUDS
Oxfordshire Modern Languages Achievement Certificate [British] (AIE) .... OMLAC
Oxfordshire Project for the Training of Instructors and Supervisors [British] (AIE) .... OPTIS
Oxidation/Fermentation (AD) .... o/f
Oxide Dispersion Strengthened (AD) .... ods
Oxides (VRA) .... ox
Oxidizable Carbon Ratio (AD) .... OCR
Oxidized Metal Explosive (AD) .... mox
Oxidizer to Fuel Ratio (AD) .... o/f
Oxidizing Flame (AD) .... of
Oxley Airlines [ICAO designator] (AD) .... VQ
Oxy Metal Industries International (AD) .... OMII
Oxygen at High Pressure (AD) .... obp
Oxygen-Free High Conductivity (AD) .... ofhc
Oxygen-Free High-Carbon (AD) .... ofhc

P
By Meaning

Pacific Affairs [*A publication*] (BRI) ... Pac A
Pacific Historical Review [*A publication*] (BRI) ... PHR
Pacific Merchant Shipping Association (AD) ... PMSA
Pacific Micronesian Line (AD) ... PML
Pacific Molasses (AD) ... P/M
Pacific Motor Boat Club (AD) ... PMBC
Pacific Motor Tariff Bureau (AD) ... PMTB
Pacific Mountain Network Association (AD) ... PMNA
Pacific National [*ICAO designator*] (AD) ... ZE
Pacific National Exchange Vancouver [*Vancouver*] (AD) ... PNE
Pacific National Exhibition [*Vancouver*] (AD) ... PNE
Pacific Naval Laboratories (AD) ... PNL
Pacific Navigation Systems (AD) ... PNS
Pacific Northern [*Airline*] (AD) ... PN
Pacific Northern Airlines (AD) ... PNA
Pacific Northwest Booksellers Association (AD) ... PNBA
Pacific Northwest Division/Battelle Memorial Institute (AD) ... PNWD/BMI
Pacific Northwest International Trade Council (AD) ... PNITC
Pacific Oceanographic Group [*British Columbia*] (AD) ... POG
Pacific Passenger Services (AD) ... PPS
Pacific Petroleum (AD) ... PP
Pacific Power and Light (AD) ... PP&L
Pacific Studies [*A publication*] (BRI) ... Pac S
Packet-Switching Data Network [*Computer science*] (DOM) ... PSDN
Paducah [*Kentucky*] [*Airport symbol*] (AD) ... PUK
Pagas Airlines [*ICAO designator*] (AD) ... YP
Page (VRA) ... pg
Paged Memory-Management Unit (AD) ... pmmu
Page-Replacement Algorithm and Control Logic (AD) ... pracl
Pages Per Inch (AD) ... pp/in
Pages Per Inch (AD) ... ppi
Paget-Gorman Sign System (AIE) ... PGSS
Pahlavi [*Iran*] [*Airport symbol*] (AD) ... PHV
Paid Educational Leave (AIE) ... PEL
Paid on Delivery (AD) ... pod
Paid This Year, Dividend Omitted, Deferred, or No Action Taken at Last Dividend Meeting [*Investment term*] (DFIT) ... I
Pain Rehabilitation Center (AD) ... PRC
Paint (AD) ... pnt
Paint (VRA) ... pt
Painted (AD) ... pntd
Painted (VRA) ... ptd
Painted Metal (AD) ... pmet
Painter (AD) ... pntr
Painter (VRA) ... ptr
Painting (VRA) ... ptg
Paints and Oil (AD) ... p & o
Paintstick (VRA) ... ptst
Pair (AD) ... pr
Pak Lay [*Laos*] [*Airport symbol*] (AD) ... PKY
Pakatoa [*New Zealand*] [*Airport symbol*] (AD) ... ZED
Pakistan (VRA) ... Pak
Pakistan Minerals Development Corp. (AD) ... PMDC
Pakistan National Scientific and Technical Documentation Center (AD) ... PNSTDC
Pakistan Naval Ship (AD) ... PNS
Pakistan Press Association (AD) ... PPA
Pakse [*Laos*] [*Airport symbol*] (AD) ... PKZ
Pala [*Chad*] [*Airport symbol*] (AD) ... PLF
Palace (VRA) ... pala
Palazzo (VRA) ... pala
Palenque [*Mexico*] [*Airport symbol*] (AD) ... PGM
Paleolithic (VRA) ... Paleol
Palestine (VRA) ... Pale
Palestine Red Crescent (AD) ... PRC
Palette (VRA) ... pal
Palladium Print (VRA) ... PAPT
Palletizing Optimization Potential (AD) ... POP
Palm Island [*Queensland*] [*Airport symbol*] (AD) ... PCE
Palm Island [*Windward Islands, West Indies*] [*Airport symbol*] (AD) ... TTD
Palma de Mallorca Balearic Islands, Spain (AD) ... PMI
Palmar [*Costa Rica*] [*Airport symbol*] (AD) ... PMZ
Palmoplantar Keratoderma [*Dermatology*] ... PPK
Palmyra [*Syria*] [*Airport symbol*] (AD) ... TDM
Palomar Mountain Observatory (AD) ... pmo
Palpitation, Percussion, and Auscultation (AD) ... pp & a
Palpitation, Percussion, Auscultation (AD) ... ppa
Pamphlet (AD) ... pph
Pan American Sanitary Bureau ... PASB
Pan Pacific and Southeast Asia Women's Association (AD) ... PPSAWA
Panama (VRA) ... Pan
Panama Canal Zone [*Panama*] [*Airport symbol*] (AD) ... PCZ
Panamanian Public Force (AD) ... PPF
Panama-Red Marijuana (AD) ... Pr
Pan-American World Airways [*Stock exchange symbol*] (AD) ... PN
Panchromatic (VRA) ... panchr
Pandjang (AD) ... Pnd
Panel (VRA) ... p
Panel (AD) ... pnl
Panel Point (AD) ... pp
Panjim [*India*] [*Airport symbol*] (AD) ... PAG
Panna [*India*] [*Airport symbol*] (AD) ... PNA
Panno Type (VRA) ... PNTYP
Panorama (VRA) ... PANA
Pantnagar [*India*] [*Airport symbol*] (AD) ... PGH
Papa [*Father*] [*Latin*] (AD) ... Pp
Papa Westray [*Orkney Islands, Scotland*] [*Airport symbol*] (AD) ... WEN
Papeete, Society Islands [*Airport*] (AD) ... PPT
Paper (VRA) ... pa
Paper Negative (VRA) ... PRNG
Paper, Printing, and Binding (AD) ... pp&b
Paperboard (AD) ... pprbd
Papier Mache (VRA) ... pm
Papillon Airways [*ICAO designator*] (AD) ... HI
Pappaband [*Hard Cover*] [*German*] (AD) ... Ppb
Papua New Guinea Line (AD) ... PNGL
Papua Nueva Guinea [*Papua New Guinea*] [*Spanish*] (AD) ... PNG
Papyrus (VRA) ... pap
Paraburdoo [*Western Australia*] [*Airport symbol*] (AD) ... PAF
Parachute (AD) ... prcht
Parachutist (AD) ... prchst
Paradise Regained [*A publication*] (AD) ... PR
Paraffin, Olefin, Naphthene, Aromatic (AD) ... pona
Parallax and Refraction (AD) ... p & r
Parameters: US Army War College Quarterly [*A publication*] (BRI) ... Parameters
Paramethoxyamphetamine (AD) ... pma
Paramilitary (AD) ... pm
Paramilitary Specialists (AD) ... pm specialists
Parana (AD) ... Pr
Parana [*Brazil*] [*Airport symbol*] (AD) ... PXA
Paranagua [*Brazil*] [*Airport symbol*] (AD) ... PRU
Paranavai [*Brazil*] [*Airport symbol*] (AD) ... PVI
Paranoid Personality Disorder (AD) ... PPD
Parasympathetic Nervous System (AD) ... pns
Parc National de la Boucle de la Pendjari [*Penjari River Bend National Park*] [*French*] [*Dahamey*] (AD) ... PNBP
Parc National de la Boucle du Baoule [*Baoule River Bend National Park*] [*French*] [*Mali*] (AD) ... PNBB
Parcel Post (AD) ... pp
Parcel Post Insured (AD) ... ppi
Parcel Receipt (AD) ... pr
Parchment (VRA) ... parc
Parent Assisted Instruction in Reading and Spelling (AIE) ... PAIRS
Parental Alliance for Choice in Education (AIE) ... PACE
Parental Involvement in Education ... Apple PIE
Parental Involvement Project (AIE) ... PIP
Parents' Charter (AIE) ... PC
Parents, Children, and Teachers (AIE) ... PACT
Parents' Choice [*A publication*] (BRI) ... Par Ch
Parents Magazine [*A publication*] (BRI) ... Par
Parents of Large Families (AD) ... polf
Parents Opposed to Opting Out [*An association*] (AIE) ... POO
Pari-Cachoeira [*Brazil*] [*Airport symbol*] (AD) ... PCH
Parintins [*Brazil*] [*Airport symbol*] (AD) ... PIN
Parish Church (AD) ... Pr Ch
Park (VRA) ... pk
Park (DD) ... Pk
Park Ranger (AD) ... PR
Parkers Marsh Natural Area [*Virginia*] (AD) ... PMNA
Park-Neutral-Drive-Low-Reverse (AD) ... P-N-D-L-R
Parks & Recreation [*A publication*] (BRI) ... P&R
Parkway (DD) ... Pky

Parmelia (AD) ... pmla
Parnassus: Poetry in Review [*A publication*] (BRI) ... Parnassus
Parole Officer (AD) ... P/O
Paroxysmal Noctural Dyspnoea (AD) ... pnd
Paroxysmal Nocturnal Hemoglobinuria (AD) ... pnh
Parque Nacional Canaima [*Canaima National Park*] [*Venezuela*] (AD) ... PNC
Parque Nacional El Avila [*El Avila National Park*] [*Spanish*] (AD) ... PNEA
Parque Nacional Guatopo [*Guatopo National Park*] [*Venezuela*] [*Spanish*] (AD) ... PNG
Parque Nacional Henri Pittier [*Henri Pittier National Park*] [*Venezuela*] [*Spanish*] (AD) ... PNHP
Parque Nacional Iguazu [*Iguazu National Park*] [*Spanish*] (AD) ... PNI
Parque Nacional Ordesa [*Ordesa National Park*] [*Spanish*] (AD) ... PNO
Parque Nacional Sierra Nevada [*Sierra Nevada National Park*] [*Venezuela*] [*Spanish*] (AD) ... PNSN
Parque Nacional Tijuca [*Tijuca National Park*] [*Brazil*] [*Portuguese*] (AD) ... PNT
Parsimonious and Penurious (AD) ... p & p
Part Number (AD) ... P/N
Part Number (AD) ... pn
Part of (AD) ... p/o
Part Paid (AD) ... pp
Partai Muslimin Indonesia [*Indonesian Muslim Party*] [*Political party*] (AD) ... PMI
Partial (VRA) ... part
Partial Nuclear Test Ban Treaty (AD) ... PNTBT
Partial Reaction of Degeneration (AD) ... prd
Partially Hearing (AIE) ... PtHg
Partially Sighted (AIE) ... PS
Participative Management by Objectives (AD) ... pmbo
Particle Board (VRA) ... parti bd
Particulate Polycyclic Organic Matter (AD) ... ppom
Partido de la Revolucion Boliviana [*Bolivian Revolutionary Party*] [*Political party*] (AD) ... PRB
Partido Nacional [*National Party*] [*Spain*] [*Political party*] (AD) ... PN
Partido Proletario de Mexico [*Proletarian Party of Mexico*] [*Political party*] (AD) ... PPM
Partisan Review [*A publication*] (BRI) ... PR
Partition (AD) ... pn
Partner Violence Screen [*Health*] ... PVS
Parts Manufacturing Associates (AD) ... PMA
Parts per Billion (AD) ... ppb
Parts Per Hundred Parts of Mix (AD) ... pphpm
Parts Per Hundred Parts of Rubber (AD) ... pphr
Parts Per Million (AD) ... ppm
Pasighat [*India*] [*Airport symbol*] (AD) ... IXT
Paso Robles [*California*] [*Airport symbol*] (AD) ... PRB
Passage (DD) ... Pass
Passamaquoddy Bay (AD) ... Quoddy
Passive Activity Loss [*Investment term*] (DFIT) ... PAL
Passive Participle (AD) ... pp
Passive-Ranging Interferometer Sensor (AD) ... prais
Passport to Knowledge [*Children's computer program sponsored by NASA and NSF*] ... PTK
Past Medical History (AD) ... pmh
Past Participle (AD) ... pple
Paste (VRA) ... pst
Pasteboard (VRA) ... pstbd
Pastel (VRA) ... ps
Patent Office Library (AD) ... POL
Paterson [*New Jersey*] [*Airport symbol*] (AD) ... PNJ
Pathankot [*India*] [*Airport symbol*] (AD) ... IXP
Pathological Internet Use ... PIU
Patient-Operated Selected Mechanisms (AD) ... posm
Patients Protection Law Commission (AD) ... PPLC
Patina (VRA) ... pat
Pattern Makers Union (AD) ... PMU
Paul Revere Associated Yeoman (AD) ... PRAY
Pavilion (VRA) ... pavl
Pawtucket-Woonsocket [*Rhode Island*] [*Airport symbol*] (AD) ... SFZ
Pay for Skills [*Human resources*] (WYGK) ... PFS
Payable on Death (AD) ... pod
Pay-As-You-Go ... PAYG
Paymaster (AD) ... Pmr
Paymaster General (AD) ... PmG
Payment (AD) ... pmt
Payment Outstanding Suspense Accounts (AD) ... posa
Payment-in-Kind Securities [*Investment term*] (DFIT) ... PIK Securities
Payments and Progress (AD) ... p&p
Payola (AD) ... p-ola
Pay-on-Receipt (AD) ... p-o-r
Pay-Per-View (AD) ... ppv
Pay-Raise Commission (AD) ... PRC
Payroll (AD) ... P/R
Payroll (AD) ... pr
Payroll Audit (AD) ... pra
Payroll-Based Stock Option Plan [*Human resources*] (WYGK) ... PAYSOP
Peabody Museum (AD) ... PM
Peabody Museum of Archeology and Ethnology (AD) ... PMAE
Peabody Museum of Natural History (AD) ... PMNH
Peabody Museum of Salem (AD) ... PMS
Peace and Quiet (AD) ... p & q
Peace and Reconciliation Inter-Schools Movement (AIE) ... PRISM
Peace Officers Association of California (AD) ... POAC
Peace Officers Association of Georgia (AD) ... POAG
Peaceful Nuclear Explosion (AD) ... pne
Peak Program Meter (AD) ... ppm
Peanut-Butter Sandwich (AD) ... p-nut butter
Peanut-Butter Sandwich (AD) ... pnutbutsan
Peanut-Butter Sandwich (AD) ... pnutbutwich
Pear Tree Wood (VRA) ... pearwd
Pearl (VRA) ... prl
Pearson Aircraft [*ICAO designator*] (AD) ... YE
Peculiar (AD) ... pq
Pedestal (VRA) ... pdstl
Pediment (VRA) ... pedm
Pedro Afonso [*Brazil*] [*Airport symbol*] (AD) ... PAB
Peer Review Oversight Group [*National Institutes of Health*] ... PROG
Peking [*China*] [*Airport symbol*] (AD) ... PEK
Peking Review [*A publication*] (AD) ... PR
Pellagra Preventive (AD) ... pp
Pellagra-Preventive Factor (AD) ... P-P
Pellagra-Preventive Factor (AD) ... p-p factor
Pem Air [*ICAO designator*] (AD) ... PD
Pen (VRA) ... pe
Pen and Ink (VRA) ... pe/i
Penang (AD) ... Png
Pencil (VRA) ... pl
Pencillin (AD) ... pnc
Pend Oreille Valley Railroad (AD) ... POV
Pendant (VRA) ... pend
Pendentive (VRA) ... pndnt
Pending (AD) ... pndg
Penicillin-Nonsusceptible S. Pneumoniae [*Clinical chemistry*] ... PNSP
Penicillin-Resistant S. Pneumoniae [*Clinical chemistry*] ... PRSP
Peninsula Airways [*ICAO designator*] (AD) ... KS
Peninsular & Occidental Steamship Co. (AD) ... P & O
Pennsylvania Electric Association ... PEA
Pennsylvania Military Academy (AD) ... PMC
Pennsylvania New York Central Transportation Co. (AD) ... PNYCTC
Pennsylvania Personnel and Guidance Association (AD) ... PPGA
Pennsylvania Power and Light (AD) ... PP&L
Pennsylvania Prison Society (AD) ... PPS
Pennsylvania-Reading [*Seashore Lines*] (AD) ... P-R
Pennzoil Offshore Gas Operators (AD) ... POGO
Pensacola, Florida (AD) ... Pncla
Pension Portability Act of 1992 (WYGK) ... PPA
Pentagon (AD) ... Pnt
Pentagon Annex (AD) ... Pnt Anx
Pentateuch (VRA) ... pentu
Pentelic (VRA) ... Pentl
Penthouse (DD) ... PH
Penultimate Profit [*Investment term*] (DFIT) ... PPP
Penzance (AD) ... Pnz
People Express [*ICAO designator*] (AD) ... PE
People for Prison Alternatives [*An association*] (AD) ... PPA
People of the State of New York (AD) ... POSNY
People Persecuted by Pablo Escobar ... PEPES
People-Powered Vehicle (AD) ... ppv
Peoples Party of Pakistan [*Political party*] (AD) ... PPP
People's Republic of Benin (AD) ... PRB
Peoria and Pekin Union [*Railroad*] (AD) ... P & PU
Per Os [*By Mouth*] [*Latin*] (AD) ... po
Per Person (AD) ... pp
Per Person, Double Occupancy (AD) ... ppdo
Per Person, Single Occupancy (AD) ... ppso
Per Rectum [*By the Rectum*] [*Latin*] (AD) ... pr
Peralta Oaks Research Center (AD) ... PORC
Perambulator (AD) ... pram
Perceived Noise Decibels (AD) ... pndb
Percentage Quota System (AD) ... PQS
Percentile Rank (AD) ... pr
Perceptual Performance (AD) ... pp
Percussion Note (AD) ... pn
Performance (VRA) ... perf
Performance Monitor Unit (AD) ... pmu
Performance Share Plan [*Human resources*] (WYGK) ... PSP
Performance Support System [*Human resources*] (WYGK) ... PSS
Performance Technology [*Human resources*] (WYGK) ... PT
Performance-Based Measurement System [*Environmental Protection Agency*] ... PBMS
Performance-Measuring Equipment (AD) ... pme
Performing Arts Journal [*A publication*] (BRI) ... Per A J
Pergamino [*Parchment*] [*Spanish*] (AD) ... pno
Periadenitis Mucosa Necrotica Recurrens (AD) ... pmnr
Pericles, Prince of Tyre [*A publication*] (AD) ... PPT
Pericope (VRA) ... peric
Perigean Range (AD) ... Pn
Perimeter Airlines [*ICAO designator*] (AD) ... UW
Period (VRA) ... per
Periodic Motor Vehicle Inspection (AD) ... pmvi
Periodic Order Quantity (AD) ... poq
Periodical Publishers' Service Bureau (AD) ... PPSB
Peripheral Nervous System (AD) ... pns
Peripheral On-Line-Oriented Function [*Computer science*] (AD) ... poof
Peripheral Resistance (AD) ... pr
Peristyle (VRA) ... pstyl
Perkiomen Airways [*ICAO designator*] (AD) ... RY
Permanent Consultative Committee ... PCC
Permanent Council of the Organization of American States ... PCOAS
Permanent Executive Committee of the Inter-American Council for Education, Science, and Culture ... PECIACESC

Permanent Executive Committee of the Inter-American Economic and Social Council PECIAECOSOC
Permanent Magnet (AD) p-m
Permanent Manual System (AD) PMS
Permanent Mission of the United States of America to the Organization of American States (AD) PMUSAOAS
Permanent Party (AD) pp
Permanent Secretariat of the Central American Common Market PSCACM
Permanent-Equity Pension Plan [*Human resources*] (WYGK) PEPP
Permeability Quotient (AD) pq
Permeability Transition [*Biochemistry*] PT
Per-Member Payment (AD) pmp
Permuted on Subject Headings (AD) posh
Perpendicular (VRA) perp
Perpendicular Ocean Platform (AD) pop
Persia (VRA) Per
Persistent Occipito-Posterior (AD) pop
Persistent Organic Pollutant POP
Person of Opposite Sex Sharing Living Quarters (AD) poosslq
Person of the Opposite Sex in Same Living Quarters (AD) posslq
Persona Non Grata [*An Unacceptable Person*] [*Latin*] (AD) png
Personal Computer-Disk Operating System (DOM) PC-DOS
Personal Digital Assistant [*Computer science*] PDA
Personal Effectiveness Inventory (AIE) PEL
Personal Guidance Base (AIE) PGB
Personal Information Manager [*Computer science*] PIM
Personal Portable Shopper [*Computer science*] PPS
Personal Property Floater [*Insurance*] (AD) ppf
Personal Social and Moral Education (AIE) PSME
Personalised System of Induction (AIE) PSI
Personality and Personal Illness Questionnaire (AD) PPIQ
Personality, Matter, Energy, Space, Time (AD) pmest
Personality Quotient (AD) pq
Personnel (DD) pers
Personnel Management for Executives [*Military*] (RDA) PME
Personnel Pool of America [*An association*] (AD) PPA
Personnel Protection and Communication Services [*British*] (AD) PPCS
Personnel Psychology [*A publication*] (BRI) Per Psy
Personnel Qualification Standard (AD) PQS
Personnel Review Board (AD) PRB
Persons of the Opposite Sex Sharing Living Quarters (AD) potosslq
Persons on Board (AD) pob
Persons Using Television (WDMC) PUT
Perspective (VRA) persp
Perspectives on Political Science [*A publication*] (BRI) Pers PS
Persutuan Perpustakaan Malaysia [*Library Association of the Federation of Malaysia*] (AD) PPM
Persutuan Perpustakaan Singapura [*Library Association of Singapore*] (AD) PPS
Perth [*Scotland*] [*Airport symbol*] (AD) PSL
Pesticides Regulation Division (AD) PRD
Pet Population Control (AD) PPC
Petersen's Photographic Magazine [*A publication*] (BRI) Pet PM
Petroglyph (VRA) petrgly
Petroleos Mexicanos [*Spanish*] (AD) PM
Petroleum (DD) Pet
Petroleum Marketers Association of America PPMA
Petroleum, Oil, and Lubrication Installation Damage Report (AD) poldamr
Petroleum Production Division (AD) PPD
Petroleum Production Pioneers (AD) PPP
Petroleum-Oil-and-Lubricants (AD) pol
Petty Office First Class [*Military*] (AD) PO 1/C
Petty Office Second Class [*Military*] (AD) PO 2/C
Petty Office Third Class [*Military*] (AD) PO 3/C
Petty Officer on Watch [*Military*] (AD) POoW
Pewter (VRA) pew
Phan Thiet [*South Vietnam*] [*Airport symbol*] (AD) PHH
Pharmaceutical Research and Manufacturers of America PhRMA
Pharmacy (DD) Pharm
Phase Image of Poly(diethylsiloxane) [*Organic chemistry*] PDES
Phase Modulation (AD) p-m
Phenazine Methosulphate (AD) pms
Phenol-Hydroquinone [*Photography*] (AD) p-q
Phenylpropanolamine (AD) ppa
Phiala Prius Agitate [*Bottle Having First Been Shaken*] [*Latin*] (AD) ppa
Philadelphia Museum of Art (AD) PMA
Philadelphia Naval Shipyard (AD) PNS
Philadelphia Public Library (AD) PPL
Philadelphia Pulmonary Neoplasm Research Project (AD) PNRP
Philharmonic Orchestra of Florida (AD) POF
Philippine Airlines [*ICAO designator*] (AD) PR
Philippine National Bank (AD) PNB
Philippine National Line (AD) PNL
Philippine National Oil Co. (AD) PNOC
Philippines (VRA) Phil
Philippines News Agency (AD) PNA
Philippines Relief and Trade Rebilitation Administration (AD) PRATRA
Phillips Airlines [*ICAO designator*] (AD) PP
Philological Quarterly [*A publication*] (BRI) PQ
Philosophical Review [*A publication*] (BRI) Phil R
Philosophy (DD) Phil
Philosophy, Politics, and Economics (AD) ppe
Phoenix Public Library (AD) PPL
Phoolbagh [*India*] [*Airport symbol*] (AD) IPG
Photo Marketing Association (AD) PMA
Photo Mural (VRA) photmur
Photoengraving (VRA) PHENG
Photoetching (VRA) PHET
Photogenic (VRA) PHGNDWG
Photogram (VRA) PHGRM
Photograph (VRA) photo
Photographic Exercise (AD) podex
Photographic Micro-Image (AD) pmi
Photogravure (VRA) PGRV
Photolithographic (VRA) PHLITHO
Photomechanical (VRA) PTMC
Photomontage (VRA) photomon
Photomultiplier Tubes (AD) pmt
Photo-Optical Recorder Tracker (AD) port
Photo-Peak Analysis (AD) ppa
Photo-Processing Interpretation Facility (AD) ppif
Phuket [*Thailand*] [*Airport symbol*] (AD) PKC
Phuoc Long [*Vietnam*] [*Airport symbol*] (AD) VSO
Phuquoc [*South Vietnam*] [*Airport symbol*] (AD) PQC
Physical Medicine and Rehabilitation (AD) pm & r
Physical Mockup (AD) pmu
Physical Profile (AD) pp
Physical Properties (AD) pp
Physicians for the Prevention of Nuclear War (AD) PPNW
Physicians' Health Study PHS
Physics (DD) Phys
Physics Today [*A publication*] (BRI) Phys Today
Pianissimo [*Very Softly*]=>> [*Italian*] [*Music*] (AD) pmo
Pianistic and Orchestral Orgasm [*Music*] (AD) p & oo
Piano (AD) pno
Piano Nobile (VRA) pn nb
Piazza (VRA) pl
Picatinny Research Center [*Picatinny Arsenal*] (AD) PRC
Pickled and Oiled (AD) p & o
Pickpocket (AD) pp
Picos [*Brazil*] [*Airport symbol*] (AD) PIC
Pictograph (VRA) pictg
Picture Postcard (AD) ppc
Pictures Per Second (AD) pps
Piece (VRA) pc
Piedmont and Northern Railroad (AD) P & N
Piedmont National Wildlife Refuge [*Georgia*] (AD) PNWR
Piedras Negras [*Mexico*] [*Airport symbol*] (AD) PDS
Piena Pelle [*Full Leather*] [*Italian*] (AD) pp
Pietermaritzburg [*South Africa*] [*Airport symbol*] (AD) PTL
Pilaster (VRA) pil
Pilgrim Airlines [*ICAO designator*] (AD) PM
Pillars Bay [*Alaska*] [*Airport symbol*] (AD) PBY
Pilot Officer (AD) P/O
Pilot on Board (AD) pob
Pilot Overhaul Provisioning Review (AD) popr
Pilot Records of Achievement in Schools Evaluation (AIE) PRAISE
Pilotless Airplane (AD) P-plane
Pilot's Projected-Display Indicator (AD) ppdi
Pinar del Rio (AD) PR
Pinatype (VRA) PITYP
Pine (VRA) pn
Pine Manor Junior College (AD) PMJC
Pinedo (AD) Pndo
Pines (AD) Pnes
Pin-Grid Arrays PGA
Pinnacles National Monument [*California*] (AD) PNM
Pints Per Hundred Parts of Mix (AD) pphpm
Pinxit [*He or She Painted It*] [*Latin*] (AD) pnxt
Pioneer (AD) Pnr
Pioneer Airways [*ICAO designator*] (AD) JB
Pipeline (AD) ppl
Pirapora [*Brazil*] [*Airport symbol*] (AD) PPR
Pitch Mark (AD) pmk
Pittsburgh Naval Reactor (AD) PNR
Pittsburgh Opera Co. (AD) POC
Pittsburgh Public Library (AD) PPL
Pittsfield [*Massachusetts*] [*Airport symbol*] (AD) PSF
Piu Pianissimo [*Very Very Softly*] [*Italian*] [*Music*] (AD) ppp
Piu Piu Piu Pianissimo [*Very, Very, Very Softly*] [*Italian*] [*Music*] (AD) pppp
Place (DD) Pl
Place (VRA) pl
Place of Acceptance (AD) poa
Plain Old Telephone Service (AD) pots
Plain Paper Optimized Printing [*Canon*] [*Computer science*] P-POP
Plan Position Indicator (AD) ppi
Planeta Rica [*Colombia*] [*Airport symbol*] (AD) PLC
Plank-on-Edge Buoy (AD) poe buoy
Planned Amortization Class [*Investment term*] (DFIT) PAC
Planned Maintenance System for Surface Missile Ships (AD) PMSSMS
Planned Parenthood League (AD) PPL
Planning and Programming Guidance (AD) ppg
Planning, Management, Evaluation (AD) pme
Planning Management Information System (AD) PMIS
Planning, Measurements & Evaluation Section [*Public Library Association*] [*American Library Association*] PLMES
Planning Permission (AD) pp
Planning-Organization-Staffing-Directing-Coordinating-Reporting-Budgeting g (AD) posdcorb
Planning-Programming-Budgeting-Accounting System (AD) PPBAS

Plan-Paper Copier (AD) ... ppc
Plant Pest Control Division (AD) ... PPCD
Plant Quarantine Division (AD) ... PQD
Plant Quarantine Inspection House (AD) ... PQIH
Plant Variety Protection ... PVP
Plasma Osmotic Pressure (AD) ... pop
Plasma Prothrombin Conversion Accelerator (AD) ... ppca
Plasma Prothrombin Conversion Factor (AD) ... ppcf
Plasma Renin Activity [*Medicine*] (AD) ... pra
Plasmacytoma Repressor Factor [*Cytology*] ... PRF
Plaster (VRA) ... pla
Plaster of Paris (AD) ... pop
Plastic (VRA) ... plas
Plate (VRA) ... plat
Plate Number Coil (AD) ... pnc
Plate Printers, Die Stampers, and Engravers [*Union*] (AD) ... PPDSE
Platelet-Derived Growth Factor [*Medicine*] ... PDGF
Plateresque (VRA) ... Pltrsq
Platform for Internet Content Selection [*Computer science*] ... PICS
Platform for Internet Content Specification [*Computer science*] ... PICS
Platform Independent File Format [*Computer science*] ... PDF
Platform Position Unit (AD) ... ppu
Platinum [*Metal*] (VRA) ... platn
Platinum Print (VRA) ... PTPT
Platt National Park [*Oklahoma*] (AD) ... PNP
Platz (VRA) ... pl
Plaza (VRA) ... pl
Plaza (AD) ... Plz
Please Mind Your Own Business (AD) ... pmyob
Please Note (AD) ... pn
Please Omit Flowers (AD) ... pof
Pleiku [*South Vietnam*] [*Airport symbol*] (AD) ... PXU
Plettenberg Bay [*South Africa*] [*Airport symbol*] (AD) ... PBS
Pleuropneumonia-Like Organism (AD) ... pplo
Plexiglass (VRA) ... plexg
Plugged Telescoping Catheter [*Clinical chemistry*] ... PTC
Plumbeotype (VRA) ... PLTYP
Plumbers and Pipefitters [*Union*] (AD) ... PPF
Plumbing and Piping Industry Council (AD) ... PPIC
Plus or Minus (AD) ... porm
Plywood (VRA) ... ply
Pneumatic (AD) ... pneu
Pneumatic Scale Corp. [*Stock exchange symbol*] (AD) ... PNU
Pneumocconiosis [*Medicine*] (AD) ... pneumoccon
Pneumograph (AD) ... pneumog
Pneumonoultra-Microscopicsilicovolcanoconiosis [*Medicine*] (AD) ... pneumonoultra
Pneumothorax [*Medicine*] (AD) ... pnx
Po [*Upper Volta*] [*Airport symbol*] (AD) ... PUP
Poblacion [*Population*] [*Spanish*] (AD) ... pob
Pocket (AD) ... pock
Pocket Books (AD) ... Pocket Bks
Pocono Mountain Vacation Bureau (AD) ... PMVB
Poculum [*Cup*] (AD) ... pocul
Podiatrist (AD) ... podia
Podium (VRA) ... pdm
Poetical (AD) ... poet
Poetics Today [*A publication*] (BRI) ... Poetics T
Poetry (AD) ... po
Poetry [*A publication*] (BRI) ... Poet
Poetry Criticism (AD) ... poecrit
Pohang (AD) ... Poh
Poids Moliculaire [*Molecular Weight*] [*French*] (AD) ... pm
Point (DD) ... Pt
Point of Beginning (AD) ... pob
Point of Contact (AD) ... poc
Point of Maximum Impulse (AD) ... pmi
Point of No Return (AD) ... PN
Point of No Return (AD) ... pnr
Point of Presence [*Telecommunications*] (DOM) ... POP
Point of Sale (AD) ... pos
Point of tangency (AD) ... pot
Point Pelee National Park [*Ontario, Canada*] (AD) ... PPNP
PointCast Network [*Computer science*] ... PCN
Pointe Noire (AD) ... PNe
Point-of-Origin Device (AD) ... pod
Point-of-Purchase Advertising (AD) ... pop advertising
Point-of-Sale System (AD) ... P-O-S S
Point-of-Sale Terminal (AD) ... pos terminal
Point-of-Service [*Human resources*] (WYGK) ... POS
Point-of-Service System (AD) ... P-O-S S
Point-of-View (AD) ... p-o-v
Point-to-Point Tunneling Protocol [*Computer science*] ... PPTP
Poison (AD) ... pois
Poland (VRA) ... Pol
Polar (AD) ... pol
Polar Avia [*ICAO designator*] (AD) ... JW
Polar Beacon Experiments and Auroral Research (AD) ... Polar BEAR
Polar Maritime Air Colder than Underlying Surface (AD) ... mPk
Polaris Missile Facility, Atlantic (AD) ... POMFLANT
Polaris Missile Facility, Pacific (AD) ... POMPAC
Polarity (AD) ... po
Polarity (AD) ... polar
Polarization Angle (AD) ... polang
Polaroid (VRA) ... PLRD
Polaska Rzeczpospolita Ludowa [*Polish People's Republic*] (AD) ... Pol Rze Lud
Polemic (AD) ... polem
Polen [*Poland*] [*Norwegian*] (AD) ... Pol
Police College (AD) ... Pol Col
Police Commissaire [*Interpol*] [*British*] (AD) ... Pol Com
Police Commissioner (AD) ... Pol Com
Police Federation [*London*] (AD) ... Pol Fed
Police Foundation [*Washington, D.C.*] (AD) ... Pol Found
Police Officer Student Training (AD) ... POST
Police Officers (AD) ... POs
Police Officers Research Association (AD) ... PORA
Police Protective League (AD) ... PPL
Policy Proof of Interest (AD) ... ppi
Policy Studies Journal [*A publication*] (BRI) ... Pol Stud J
Poliomyelitis [*Medicine*] (AD) ... polio
Polish Ocean Lines (AD) ... POL
Polished (VRA) ... pol
Political (AD) ... polit
Political Action Committee ... PAC
Political Adviser (AD) ... Pol Ad
Political Adviser (AD) ... polad
Political Committee (AD) ... pol com
Political Critic (AD) ... polcrit
Political Economy (AD) ... pol econ
Political Plugola (AD) ... p-p-ola
Political Prisoners (AD) ... pols
Political Research Quarterly [*A publication*] (BRI) ... Pol Res Q
Political Science (AD) ... pol sci
Political Science (DD) ... PolSc
Political Science (AD) ... poly sci
Political Science Quarterly [*A publication*] (BRI) ... PSQ
Political Science Reviewer [*A publication*] (BRI) ... PSR
Political Warfare (AD) ... polwar
Political-Military Interdepartmental Group (AD) ... PMIG
Politicheskoe Byuro [*Political Bureau of the Central Committee*] [*Russian*] (AD) ... Politburo
Politician (AD) ... poli
Politician in the Penitentiary (AD) ... pol in the pen
Politicians (AD) ... pols
Polizia Ferroviaria [*Railroad Police*] [*Italian*] (AD) ... POLFER
Polizia Stradale [*Highway Police*] [*Italian*] (AD) ... POLSTRADA
Pollen Index (AD) ... pol ind
Pollution (AD) ... poll
Pollution-Monitoring Satellite (AD) ... pms
polnisch [*Polish*] [*German*] (AD) ... poln
Polonais [*Polish*] [*French*] (AD) ... Polon
Polskie Radio [*Polish Radio*] (AD) ... PR
Polybrominated-Biphenyl (AD) ... PPB
Polychrome (VRA) ... plyc
Polycyclic Aromatic Hydrocarbon ... PAH
Polycyclic Organic Matter (AD) ... pom
Polyester (VRA) ... plyes
Polyethylene (AD) ... poly
Polyethylene Bottle (AD) ... poly bot
Polygraph (AD) ... polyg
Polymer (VRA) ... plym
Polymer (AD) ... poly
Polymer Products Development Center (AD) ... PPDC
Polymerized Water (AD) ... polywater
Polymethylmethacrylate (AD) ... pmma
Polymorphonuclear Leukocyte (AD) ... pmnl
Polymorphonuclear Neutrophil (AD) ... pmn
Polymorphous (AD) ... polymorph
Polynesia (AD) ... Poly
Polynesia (VRA) ... Polyn
Polyoxyethylene (AD) ... poe
Polyoxymethylene (AD) ... pom
Polyphenylene Oxide (AD) ... ppo
Polyphenylquinoxaline (AD) ... ppq
Polyptic (VRA) ... plypt
Polysexual (AD) ... polysex
Polystyrene (VRA) ... plyst
Polysulphide Rubber Compound (AD) ... prc
Polytechnic (AIE) ... P
Polytechnic (AD) ... Poly
Polytechnic (AD) ... poly
Polytechnic Academic Registrars' Group (AIE) ... PARG
Polytechnic Personnel Officers Group (AIE) ... PPOG
Polytechnics and Colleges Computer Committee (AIE) ... PCCC
Polyurethane (VRA) ... plyur
Polyvinyl (VRA) ... plyvn
Polyvinyl (AD) ... poly
Pomeranian (AD) ... pom
Pomeridiano [*Afternoon*] [*Italian*] (AD) ... pom
Pomologic (AD) ... pomol
Pomological (AD) ... pom
Pomona [*California*] [*Airport symbol*] (AD) ... JPO
Pompano Airways [*ICAO designator*] (AD) ... MG
Pompey (AD) ... Pomp
Pom-Pom (AD) ... pom
Pondere [*By Weigh*] [*Latin*] (AD) ... pond
Pondoland (AD) ... Pondo
Pontevedra (AD) ... Pont
Pontiac (AD) ... Ponti
Pontifex Maximus [*Supreme Pontiff*] [*Latin*] (AD) ... Pont Max

Pontoon (AD)	pon
Pontoon Bridge (AD)	PonBrg
Pontoon Bridge (AD)	pont b
Pony and Zebra (AD)	pobra
Poodle Dog (AD)	pood
Poole (AD)	Poo
Poor Miserable Soul (AD)	pms
Popayan, Colombia (AD)	Popa
Poplar (VRA)	plr
Popliteal (AD)	pop
Popliteal (AD)	poplit
Popondetta [New Guinea] [Airport symbol] (AD)	PNG
Poppa (AD)	Pop
Poppet (AD)	pop
Popular (AD)	pop
Popular Art (AD)	pop art
Popular Concerts (AD)	pops
Popular Music (AD)	pop music
Popular Music and Society [A publication] (BRI)	PMS
Popular Psychiatry (AD)	pop psych
Popular Science [A publication] (AD)	Pop Sci
Population (AD)	pop
Population Explosion (AD)	popex
Porangatu [Brazil] [Airport symbol] (AD)	PGT
Porcelain (AD)	porc
Porch (VRA)	pch
Porifera (AD)	Por
Pork Sandwich (AD)	porksan
Pork Sandwich (AD)	porkwich
Pornofilm (AD)	porno
Pornographer (AD)	porno
Pornographic (AD)	porn
Pornographic Biography (AD)	pornobio
Pornographic Cassette (AD)	pornette
Pornographic Magazine (AD)	porno mag
Pornographic Magazines (AD)	pornzines
Pornographic Motion Picture (AD)	pornofilm
Pornographic Motion Picture Film (AD)	pornfilm
Pornographic Novel (AD)	pornovel
Pornographic Novelist (AD)	pornovelist
Pornographic Squad (AD)	Porn Squad
Porogi [Waterfall] [Russian] (AD)	Por
Porosity (AD)	por
Porphyry (VRA)	porph
Porquis Junction [Ontario] [Airport symbol] (AD)	YQJ
Port Adelaide [South Australia] (AD)	Port Ade
Port Alberni [Vancouver Island, British Columbia] (AD)	Port Ald
Port Alexander [Alaska] (AD)	Port Alex
Port Alexander [Alaska] [Airport symbol] (AD)	POX
Port Antonio [Jamaica] (AD)	Port Ant
Port Arthur (AD)	Port Art
Port Augusta [South Australia] [Airport symbol] (AD)	UBK
Port Chicago (AD)	Port Chi
Port Dalhousie [Ontario, Canada] (AD)	Port Dal
Port Elizabeth [South Africa] (AD)	Port Liz
Port Elizabeth [New Jersey] (AD)	Port Liz
Port Francqui [Zaire] [Airport symbol] (AD)	PFR
Port Huron [Michigan] [Airport symbol] (AD)	PHN
Port Jackson Sydney [Sydney, New South Wales, Australia] (AD)	Port Jack
Port Macquarie [New South Wales] [Airport symbol] (AD)	PTR
Port Moresby (AD)	P Mor
Port Nicholson (AD)	P Nic
Port Nicholson [Wellington, New Zealand] (AD)	Port Nick
Port of Baltimore (AD)	PoB
Port of Debarkation (AD)	pod
Port of Departure (AD)	pod
Port of Embarkation (DFIT)	POE
Port of Miami (AD)	PoM
Port of New Orleans (AD)	PNO
Port of Service (AD)	PoS
Port of Spain (AD)	PoS
Port of The Dalles (AD)	P o TD
Port Phillip (AD)	P Php
Port Phillip [Melbourne, Victoria, Australia] (AD)	Port Phil
Port Pirie (AD)	PPr
Port Richmond [Staten Island, New York] (AD)	Port Rich
Port Said [Egypt] [Airport symbol] (AD)	PSD
Port Side Out, Starboard Side Home [British slang] (AD)	posdsplt
Port Sudan (AD)	Port Sud
Port Swettenham [Malaysia] (AD)	Port Swett
Port Talbot [Wales] (AD)	Port Talb
Port Tewfik [Egypt] (AD)	Port Tew
Port Washington [Long Island, New York] (AD)	Port Wash
Port Wellen [Ontario, CAN] (AD)	Port Wel
Portable (VRA)	port
Portable Automated Remote Inspection System [Failure Analysis Associates] (RDA)	PARIS
Portable Computer Memory Card Industry Association (DOM)	PCMCIA
Portable Educational Tools Environment (AIE)	PETE
Portable Network Graphics [Computer science] (DOM)	PNG
Portable Operating Systems for Computer Environments (AD)	POSIX
Portable Outdoor Toilet (AD)	pot
Portable Toilet (AD)	portalet
Portable Water (AD)	pot w
Portal (VRA)	ptl

Portal-to-Portal Act of 1947 (WYGK)	PTPA
Portland (AD)	Por
Portland, Maine (AD)	P Me
Portland Motor Boat Club [Oregon] (AD)	PMBC
Portland Opera Association [Oregon] (AD)	POA
Portland Oregonian [A publication] (AD)	PO
Portland Public Docks (AD)	PPD
Portmadoc (AD)	Pmd
Porto Alfonso [Brazil] [Airport symbol] (AD)	PXX
Porto Amelia [Mozambique] [Airport symbol] (AD)	POL
Porto Murtinho [Brazil] [Airport symbol] (AD)	PMJ
Porto Nacional [Brazil] [Airport symbol] (AD)	PNB
Porto Seguro [Brazil] [Airport symbol] (AD)	ORO
Portrait (AD)	port
Portrait (VRA)	ptrt
Portsmouth [England] [Airport symbol] (AD)	PME
Portsmouth [New Hampshire] [Airport symbol] (AD)	PSM
Portugais [Portuguese] [French] (AD)	Portug
Portugal (AD)	Por
Portugal (VRA)	Port
Portugese Overseas Province (AD)	POP
Portugiesisch [Portuguese] [German] (AD)	port
Portuguese (AD)	Por
Portuguese China (AD)	Port Chi
Portuguese India (AD)	Port Ind
Portuguese Timor (AD)	Port Tim
Porvenir [Chile] [Airport symbol] (AD)	WPR
Poseidon Random-Access Memory (AD)	Pram
Poseidon Technical Information Bulletin [A publication] (AD)	POTIB
Position (AD)	pn
Position (AD)	pos
Position (AD)	posit
Position (AD)	posn
Positive (AD)	pos
Positive (AD)	posit
Positive Displacement (AD)	posdsplt
Positive Electron (AD)	positron
Positive Expected Value	PEV
Positive Matte Technique (AD)	pmt
Positive Mental Attitude (AD)	pma
Positive Negative Positive (AD)	pnp
Positive Noninterfering (AD)	pni
Positive on Negative (AD)	p-on-n
Positive Peer Culture (AD)	PPC
Positive Resistor (AD)	posistor
Positive-Negative Ambivalent Quotient (AD)	pnavq
Positive-Negative Positive-Negative (AD)	pnpn
Positive-Negative Pressure Respiration (AD)	pnpr
Positron (AD)	posit
Possession (AD)	poss
Possessive (AD)	posses
Possessive Pronoun (AD)	pos pron
Possibility (AD)	pos
Possibly (VRA)	posb
Post Aurem [Behind the Ear] [Latin] (AD)	post aur
Post Experience Vocational Education (AIE)	PEVE
Post Meridiem [After noon] [Latin] (AD)	pm
Post Mortem (AD)	pm
Post Mortem (AD)	post
Post Mortem (AD)	post-mort
Post Office (VRA)	post ofc
Post Office Advisory Council (AD)	POAC
Post Office Position Indicator [British] (AD)	popi
Post Office Radio Interference Station (AD)	PORIS
Post Office Research Station (AD)	PORS
Post Office Savings Department (AD)	POSD
Post Partum [Afterbirth] [Latin] (AD)	post part
Post Partum [Afterbirth] [Latin] (AD)	pp
Post Script: Essays in Film and the Humanities [A publication] (BRI)	Post Script
Postage (AD)	post
Postage Paid (AD)	pp
Postal Orders (AD)	POs
Postal Reorganization Act (AD)	PRA
Post-Augustan (AD)	post-Aug
Postcard (VRA)	PSCD
Poster (VRA)	post
Posterior [Spanish] (AD)	post
Posterior (AD)	poster
Posterior Diameter (AD)	post d
Postgraduate Medical Institute (AD)	Postgrad Med Inst
Posthumous (AD)	posth
Postlude (AD)	postl
Postmark (AD)	pmk
Postmaster General (AD)	PmG
Post-Menopausal Bleeding [Medicine] (AD)	pmb
Post-Menopausal Syndrome [Medicine] (AD)	pms
Post-Mortem Dumps (AD)	pmd
Postnasal Drip [Medicine] (AD)	pnd
Postoperative (AD)	p-o
Post-Operative (AD)	p-op
Post-Operative (AD)	post-op
Post-Partum Hemorrhage [Medicine] (AD)	pph
Post-Pill Galactorrheamenorrhea [Medicine] (AD)	ppga
Post-Polio Muscular Atrophy [Medicine] (AD)	ppma

Post-Polio Syndrome [*Medicine*] (AD) .... p-ps
Post-Qualification Education (AD) .... pqe
Post-Synchronization (AD) .... post-sync
Potash (AD) .... pot
Potash, Oil, and Wheat Country [*Saskatoon, Saskatchewan*] (AD) .... POW Country
Potassium Aluminum Sulfate (AD) .... potash alum
Potato Carrot Agar [*Culture Media*] .... PCA
Potatoes (AD) .... potats
Potato-Tomato (AD) .... pomato
Potential (AD) .... pot
Potential Host Institures List [*European Commission*] .... PHIL
Potentiometer (AD) .... pot
Potentiometers (AD) .... pots
Potosi [*Bolivia*] [*Airport symbol*] (AD) .... POI
Potrerillos [*Chile*] [*Airport symbol*] (AD) .... RER
Potrero [*Cattle Ranch*] [*Spanish*] (AD) .... potr
Pottery (AD) .... pott
Pottery (VRA) .... ptry
Poultry (AD) .... poul
Pounds Per Hour (AD) .... pph
Pounds Per Minute (AD) .... ppm
Pounds Per Second (AD) .... pps
Pour Prendre Conge [*To Take Leave*] [*French*] (AD) .... p p c
Powder (AD) .... powd
Power (AD) .... pow
Power Information Network [*Computer science*] .... PIN
Power of Attorney (AD) .... PoA
Power Oscillator (AD) .... po
Power Regulation and Control Unit (AD) .... prcu
Power-Operated (AD) .... po
Poznan (AD) .... Poz
Praca [*Plaza*] [*Portuguese*] (AD) .... Pr
Practical (AD) .... pract
Practical Nurse's Education (AD) .... pne
Practice (AD) .... prac
Practice (AD) .... pract
Practitioner (AD) .... pract
Prado [*Brazil*] [*Airport symbol*] (AD) .... PDO
Praenomen (AD) .... praen
Praeventivpille [*Dano-Norwegian*] [*Contraceptive pill*] (AD) .... p-pille
Pragmatic (AD) .... prag
Prairie (AD) .... Pr
Prairie Schooner [*A publication*] (BRI) .... PS
Prambanam (VRA) .... Pram
Prandium [*dinner*]=>> [*Latin*] (AD) .... prand
Prattsburgh Railroad (AD) .... PRAT
Preadmission Review (WYGK) .... PAR
Pre-Authorized Chequing [*Canada*] .... PAC
Precast (AD) .... prcst
Precio Maximo de Venta al Publico [*Maximum Price Charged the Public*] [*Spanish*] (AD) .... pmvp
Precious (VRA) .... prec
Precious Metal Plating (AD) .... pmp
Precipitate (AD) .... ppt
Precipitated (AD) .... pptd
Precipitation (AD) .... pptn
Precision Airlines [*ICAO designator*] (AD) .... RP
Precision Measuring Equipment Laboratory (AD) .... PMEL
Precision Mirror Calorimeter (AD) .... pmc
Predella (VRA) .... prdl
Preferred Stock [*Investment term*] (DFIT) .... PFD
Preferred-Provided Organization [*Insurance*] (AD) .... PPO
Pregnancy Discrimination Act of 1978 (WYGK) .... PDA
Pregnant Mare's Serum (AD) .... pms
Pregnant Mare's Serum Gonadotrophin (AD) .... pmsg
Preliminary (VRA) .... prelm
Preliminary Management Plan (AD) .... PMP
Pre-Marital Inventory (AD) .... PMI
Premature Nodal Contraction (AD) .... pnc
Pre-Menstrual Syndrome [*Medicine*] (AD) .... pms
Premenstrual Tension [*Medicine*] (AD) .... pmt
Premier Automobiles Ltd. [*India*] .... PAL
Premium (AD) .... pm
Premolar [*Dentistry*] (AD) .... pm
Pre-Oriented Yarn (AD) .... poy
Preparation for Overseas Movement (AD) .... pom
Preparation, Operation, Maintenance, Shipboard Electronics Equipment (AD) .... pomsee
Preparatory (VRA) .... prep
Prepared-on-Premises Flavor (AD) .... popf
Prepositioned Material Configured in Unit Sets (AD) .... pomcus
Prerefunded Municipal Note [*Investment term*] (DFIT) .... PRE-RE
Pre-Retirement Education (AIE) .... PRE
Presbyopia (AD) .... Pr
Presbyter [*Elder*] [*Latin*] (AD) .... Pr
Presbytery (VRA) .... presby
Prescription Drug Plan [*Insurance*] (WYGK) .... PDP
Prescription Drug User Fee Act .... PDUFA
Present Not for Duty (AD) .... pnfd
Present Participle (AD) .... ppr
Present Position (AD) .... pp
Present Position (AD) .... ppsn
Present Pupil (AIE) .... PP
Presentation (VRA) .... presen
Presentation Portfolio (VRA) .... PORT
Preservation & Reformatting Section [*Association for Library Collections and Technical Services*] [*American Library Association*] .... PARS
President (DD) .... pres
President of the Royal Architectural Institute of Canada (NGC) .... PRAIC
President of the Royal Canadian Academy of Arts (NGC) .... PRCA
Presidente Prudente [*Brazil*] [*Airport symbol*] (AD) .... PPB
Presidente Roque Saenz Pena [*Argentina*] [*Airport symbol*] (AD) .... PRQ
Presidential Medal of Freedom (AD) .... PMF
Presidential Studies Quarterly [*A publication*] (BRI) .... Pres SQ
President's Management Improvement Council (AD) .... PMIC
President's National Advisory Committee (AD) .... PNAC
President's National Crime Commission (AD) .... PNCC
President's Organization for Unemployment Relief (AD) .... POUR
Presov [*Czechoslovakia*] [*Airport symbol*] (AD) .... POV
Presquile National Wildlife Refuge [*Virginia*] (AD) .... PNWR
Press (AD) .... Pr
Press Control, Inc. .... PCI
Pressure-Modulated Radiometer (AD) .... pmr
Pressure-Proof (AD) .... pp
Preston [*Cuba*] [*Airport symbol*] (AD) .... PST
Prestwick [*Scotland*] [*Airport symbol*] (AD) .... PIK
Presynaptic Action Potential [*Neurochemistry*] .... pAP
Presystolic Murmur [*Medicine*] (AD) .... pm
Prevention of Blindness (AD) .... pob
Preventive Maintenance (AD) .... pm
Preventive Maintenance Contract (AD) .... pmc
Previous Menstrual Period [*Medicine*] (AD) .... pmp
Previous Orders (AD) .... po
Previous Question (AD) .... pq
Price Earnings Ratio [*Investment term*] (DFIT) .... PE
Priced (AD) .... prcd
Price-to-Book Value Ratio [*Investment term*] (DFIT) .... PBR
Primary Education (AIE) .... PE
Primary Initiatives in Mathematics Education (AIE) .... PRIME
Primary Language Record [*Education*] (AIE) .... PLR
Primary Mental Health Project (AD) .... PMHP
Primary Military Occupational Code (AD) .... PMOSC
Primary Optical Area (AD) .... poa
Primary Producers' Cooperative Society (AD) .... PPCS
Primary Producers Union (AD) .... PPU
Primary Protection System [*Computer science*] .... PPS
Primary School Staff Relations [*Project*] (AIE) .... PSSR
Primary School Teachers and Science [*Project*] (AIE) .... PSTS
Prime Mover (AD) .... p mvr
Prince (AD) .... Pr
Prince of Wales (AD) .... P o W
Princess Patricia's Canadian Light Infantry (AD) .... PPCLI
Princeton Aviation [*ICAO designator*] (AD) .... PN
Princeville Airways [*ICAO designator*] (AD) .... WP
Principal [*Principal*] [*Spanish*] (AD) .... pral
Principal and Interest [*Finance*] (DFIT) .... P&I
Principal Borehole (AD) .... prb
Principal Careers Officer (AIE) .... PCO
Principal Military Landing Officer (AD) .... PMLO
Principal Only (DFIT) .... PO
Principal Operating Component (AD) .... poc
Principle (VRA) .... prin
Print (VRA) .... pr
Print Alphanumerically (AD) .... pra
Print and Drawing Council of Canada [*1976*] (NGC) .... PDCC
Print Quality Improvement [*Advanced photo system*] .... PQI
Printed (VRA) .... prtd
Printed Matter Only (AD) .... pmo
Printed on Recycled Paoer (AD) .... PORP
Printed Paper Rate (AD) .... ppr
Printer Command Language [*Hewlett Packard*] [*Computer science*] .... PCL
Printer Dump (AD) .... prd
Printers' Managers and Overseers Association (AD) .... PM & OA
Printing, Packaging, and Allied Trades Research Association (AD) .... PPATRA
Prior Notice Required (AD) .... pnr
Prior Permission Only (AD) .... ppo
Prior Permission Required (AD) .... ppr
Priority Admission to Nursery Schools (AIE) .... PANS
Priority Area Children (AIE) .... PAC
Prismacolor (VRA) .... prsmc
Prison Officer's Club (AD) .... POC
Prison Service Establishment (AIE) .... PSE
Prisoner of War (AD) .... pow
Prisoner of Watergate (AD) .... P o W
Private (VRA) .... prv
Private (DD) .... Pvt
Private and Executive Secretary's Diploma (AIE) .... PESD
Private Collection (VRA) .... prv coll
Private Communications Technology [*Computer science*] .... PCT
Private Manual Branch Exchange (AD) .... pmbx
Private Manual Exchange (AD) .... pmx
Private Market Value [*Investment term*] (DFIT) .... PMV
Private Mortgage Insurance (AD) .... pmi
Private Parliamentary Secretary [*British*] (AD) .... pps
Private Property (AD) .... pp
Private Training College for the Disabled (AIE) .... PTCD
Privately Owned Conveyance (AD) .... poc
Privately Owned Vehicle (AD) .... pov
Privately Printed (AD) .... pp
Pro Female [*International Bowhunting Organization*] [*Class Equipment*] .... PF

Pro Male Fingers [*International Bowhunting Organization*] [*Class equipment*] ... PMF
Pro Male Release [*International Bowhunting Organization*] [*Class equipment*] ... PMR
Pro Ratione Aetatis [*In Proportion to Age*] [*Latin*] (AD) ... p rat aet
Pro Seniors [*International Bowhunting Organization*] [*Class Equipment*] ... PSR
ProAir Services [*ICAO designator*] (AD) ... SZ
Pro-Am Bowfishing Association ... PABA
Probability of Detection (AD) ... pod
Probable Maximum Flooding (AD) ... pmf
Probable Maximum Hurricane (AD) ... pmh
Probable Maximum Loss (AD) ... pml
Probably (VRA) ... prob
Probate and Matrimonial (AD) ... p&m
Probation and Rehabilitation of Airmen (AD) ... pra
Probation Officer (AD) ... P/O
Probing Lensing Anomalies Network [*Astronomy*] ... PLANET
Problem-Oriented Language (AD) ... pol
Process (AD) ... prcs
Process (VRA) ... proc
Process Monitoring and Control Systems (AD) ... pmcs
Processes of Science Test (AD) ... POST
Processing Routines Aided by Graphics for Manipulation of Arrays (AD) ... pragma
Process-Oriented Design (AD) ... pod
Processors-Memories-Switches (AD) ... p-m-s
Proctoscopy (AD) ... Pr
Proctosigmoidoscopy [*Medicine*] (AD) ... PR
Procurement Methods and Practices (AD) ... PMP
Procurement Problem Report (AD) ... PPR
Procurement Quality Assurance (AD) ... pqa
Produce Packaging Development Association (AD) ... PPDA
Product Management Information System (AD) ... PMIS
Product of Sums (AD) ... pos
Product Oriented Procedures Evaluation (AD) ... POPE
Production (DD) ... prod
Productive Man Work Unit (AD) ... pmu
Productivity Increases, Quality Control, Robotization, and Savings [*Japanese formula for economic success*] (AD) ... pqrs
Productivity, Reliability, Availability, and Maintainability (AD) ... pram
Producto Material Neto [*Net Material Product*] [*Spain*] (AD) ... pmn
Producto Nacional Bruto [*Gross National Product*] [*Spanish*] (AD) ... pnb
Produto National Bruto [*Gross National Product*] [*Portugal*] (AD) ... PNB
Professional Accounting System for Schools (AIE) ... PASS
Professional Administrator (DD) ... PAdm
Professional Agrologist (DD) ... PAg
Professional and Linguistic Assessment Board (AIE) ... PLAB
Professional and Statutory Board (AIE) ... PSB
Professional Associate of the Royal Institution of Chartered Surveyors [*Canada*] (DD) ... ARICS
Professional Classes Aid Council (AIE) ... PCAC
Professional Development Education [*Military*] (RDA) ... PDE
Professional Engineers Ontario [*Canada*] (DD) ... APEO
Professional Geologist (DD) ... PGeol
Professional Geophysicist (DD) ... PGeoph
Professional Land Economist [*Canada*] (DD) ... PLE
Professional Landman [*Canada*] (DD) ... PLand
Professional Manager (DD) ... PMgr
Professional Paper (AD) ... pp
Professional Photographers of America (AD) ... PPA
Professional Qualification Index (AD) ... pqi
Professional Walleye Trail ... PWT
Profile (VRA) ... prof
Profile of Nonverbal Sensitivity (AD) ... pons
Profile of Phonology (AIE) ... PROPH
Profit and Loss Statement [*Finance*] (DFIT) ... P&L
Profound and Multiple Learning Difficulties (AIE) ... PMLD
Profoundly Retarded Multiply Handicapped (AIE) ... PRMH
Program Calibration Area [*Computer science*] (DOM) ... PCA
Program Engineering Management Network [*Computer science*] (RDA) ... PEMN
Program Evaluation and Review Technique/Critical Path Method [*Computer science*] (DOM) ... PERT/CPM
Program for Cooperative Cataloging [*American Library Association*] ... PCC
Program for Management Development [*Harvard Business School*] (DD) ... PMD
Program Management Office for Armored Systems Integration [*Army*] (RDA) ... PM-ASI
Program Manager (AD) ... pm
Program of Technical Cooperation [*Organization of American States*] ... PTC
Program Opportunity Notification (AD) ... PON
Program Planning and Evaluation (AD) ... PP & E
Program Quality Review (AD) ... PQR
Program to Monitor Emerging Diseases ... ProMED
Programa Mundial de Alimentos [*World Food Program*] [*Spanish*] (AD) ... PMA
Programmed Operational Warshot Evaluation and Review (AD) ... power
Programs, Materials, Techniques (AD) ... pmt
Progressive [*A publication*] (BRI) ... Prog
Progressive Architecture [*A publication*] (BRI) ... Prog Arch
Progressive Massive Fibrosis [*Medicine*] (AD) ... pmf
Progressive Patient Care (AD) ... ppc
Progressive Retinal Atrophy [*Medicine*] (AD) ... pra
Project (VRA) ... proj
Project Engineering System ... PEGS
Project in Foreign Language Pedagogy (AIE) ... PIF
Project Management Body of Knowledge ... PMBOK
Project Management Committee (AD) ... PMC
Project Management Division/Batelle Memorial Institute (AD) ... PMD/BMI
Project Management Professional ... PMP
Project Manager for Night Vision/Reconnaissance Surveillance and Target Acquisition [*Military*] (RDA) ... PM NV/RSTA
Projected Map Display (AD) ... pmd
Projected Map Display Set (AD) ... pmds
Projector (VRA) ... projt
Proletarian Party of America [*Political party*] (AD) ... PPA
Prolyl Endopeptidase ... PEP
Promenade (DD) ... Pr
Promenade (DD) ... prom
Promissory Note (AD) ... pn
Promulgators of Public Toilets in Public Parks (AD) ... PPTPP
Proof (VRA) ... prf
Property (AD) ... ppty
Property (DD) ... prop
Prophenoloxidase ... proPO
Proportion (AD) ... ppn
Proposed Operating Plan and Budget (AD) ... popb
Proprietary (DD) ... Pty
Proprioceptive Neuromuscular Facilitation (AD) ... pnf
Propylaeum (VRA) ... prpylm
Pro-Rata Distribution (AD) ... prd
Prostitutes of Los Angeles [*An association*] (AD) ... POLA
Protective Multiple Earthing (AD) ... pme
Protective Packaging, Inc. (AD) ... PPI
Protein Kinase B [*An enzyme*] ... PKB
Provenance (VRA) ... prov
Providence Public Library (AD) ... PPL
Province of Quebec Association of Architects [*1890, OAQ from 1974*] [*Canada*] (NGC) ... PQAA
Provincetown-Boston Airline [*ICAO designator*] (AD) ... PT
Provincial Newspapers Association of Ireland (AD) ... PNAI
Provisional Legislative Council [*Hong Kong*] ... PLC
Psalter (VRA) ... pslt
Psychiatric Record (AD) ... PR
Psychiatry and Neurology (AD) ... p & n
Psychiatry-Neurology (AD) ... pn
Psychoactive Substance Use Disorder ... PSUD
Psychology (DD) ... Psych
Psychology Today [*A publication*] (BRI) ... PT
Psychoneuroimmunology (AD) ... pni
Public (DD) ... Pub
Public Administration Review [*A publication*] (BRI) ... PAR
Public Affairs Council for Education [*Canada*] ... PACE
Public Awareness Committee [*American Library Association*] ... PAC
Public Broadcasting System ... PBS
Public Lands Appreciation Day ... PLAD
Public Liability Company (DFIT) ... PLC
Public Offering Price (AD) ... POP
Public Oil Co. (AD) ... POC
Public Opinion Quarterly [*A publication*] (AD) ... POQ
Public Opinion Quarterly [*A publication*] (BRI) ... Pub Op Q
Public Opinion Research (AD) ... por
Public Policy for Public Libraries Section [*Public Library Association*] [*American Library Association*] ... PPPLS
Public Relations (AD) ... pr
Public Relations Club (AD) ... PRC
Public Relations Journal [*A publication*] (BRI) ... Pub Rel J
Publication of the Modern Language Association of America (AD) ... PMLA
Publicity Man (AD) ... pm
Publishers' Parcels Delivery Service (AD) ... PPDS
Publishers Weekly [*A publication*] (BRI) ... PW
Puerto Armuellas [*Panama*] [*Airport symbol*] (AD) ... AML
Puerto Aysen [*Chile*] [*Airport symbol*] (AD) ... WPA
Puerto Barrios [*Guatemala*] [*Airport symbol*] (AD) ... PBR
Puerto Cabezas [*Nicaragua*] [*Airport symbol*] (AD) ... PUZ
Puerto Lempira [*Honduras*] [*Airport symbol*] (AD) ... PRS
Puerto Lopez [*Colombia*] [*Airport symbol*] (AD) ... PRM
Puerto Maldonado [*Peru*] [*Airport symbol*] (AD) ... MDD
Puerto Paez [*Venezuela*] [*Airport symbol*] (AD) ... PPZ
Puerto Rican American Insurance Co. (AD) ... PRAICO
Puerto Rico [*Colombia*] [*Airport symbol*] (AD) ... PCC
Puerto Rico Association (AD) ... PRA
Puerto Williams [*Chile*] [*Airport symbol*] (AD) ... WPU
Pull and Push Plate (AD) ... p & pp
Pull Out of Hole (AD) ... poh
Pulletop Nature Reserve [*New South Wales*] (AD) ... PNR
Pulp and Paper Research Institute of Canada (AD) ... PPRICA
Pulpboard (VRA) ... pulpbd
Pulpwood (VRA) ... pulpwd
Pulse Mode Multiplex (AD) ... pmm
Pulse Modulation (AD) ... pm
Pulse Position Modulation (AD) ... ppm
Pulsed Neutron Interrogation (AD) ... pni
Pulses Per Hour (AD) ... pph
Pulses Per Second (AD) ... pps
Pumice (AD) ... pm
Punch (AD) ... pnch
Punch-On [*Computer science*] (AD) ... pn
Punctum Remotum [*Remote Point*] [*Latin*] (AD) ... pr
Pungo National Wildlife Refuge [*North Carolina*] (AD) ... PNWR
Punia [*Zaire*] [*Airport symbol*] (AD) ... PUN
Punishment Quarters (AD) ... pq
Punta Gorda [*British Honduras*] [*Airport symbol*] (AD) ... TGY

Purchase Price Control (AD) .... PPC
Purchased Part (AD) .... pp
Purchasing (DD) .... purch
Pure Mexican Cocaine (AD) .... pMc
Pure Peruvian Cocaine (AD) .... pPc
Purified Protein Derivative (AD) .... ppd
Purplish Pink (AD) .... pPk

Purplish Red (AD) .... pR
Push-Pull (AD) .... p-p
Putao [*Burma*] [*Airport symbol*] (AD) .... PUT
Pyramid (VRA) .... pyrm
Pyrenees-Orientales (AD) .... P-O
Pyrgos [*Greece*] [*Airport symbol*] (AD) .... PYR
Pyroxiline (VRA) .... pyrox

Q
By Meaning

Qara Qash [*Sinkiang province of China*] (AD) ..... QQ
Qara Qum [*Sinkiang province of China*] (AD) ..... QQ
Qatar (AD) ..... Qat
Qatar General Petroleum Organization (AD) ..... QGPO
Qatar Monetary Agency (AD) ..... QMA
Qatar Petroleum Co. (AD) ..... QPC
Qatn [*South Arabia*] [*Airport symbol*] (AD) ..... XTN
Quaalude (AD) ..... quaal
Quaalude (AD) ..... quad
Quacksalver (AD) ..... quack
Quacksalvers (AD) ..... quacks
Quackupuncture (AD) ..... quackupunc
Quad-Cities Nuclear Information Center (AD) ..... QCNIC
Quad-Phase Amplitude Modulation System (AD) ..... QAMS
Quad-Phase Shift Key [*Computer science*] (AD) ..... qpsk
Quadrangle (AD) ..... quad
Quadrant (AD) ..... qdrnt
Quadrant (AD) ..... quad
Quadrant Continuous Wave (AD) ..... qcw
Quadrant Electrometer (AD) ..... qem
Quadrant Elevation (AD) ..... qe
Quadrant Transformer Assembly (AD) ..... qta
Quadrantal Correction (AD) ..... QC
Quadraphonic (AD) ..... quadrap
Quadrat (AD) ..... quad
Quadrate (AD) ..... qua
Quadratic Performance Index (AD) ..... qpi
Quadratkilometer [*Square Kilometer*] [*German*] (AD) ..... qkm
Quadratmeter [*Square Meter*] [*German*] (AD) ..... qm
Quadrature Amplitude Modulation (AD) ..... qam
Quadrature Grid (AD) ..... qg
Quadrature-Amplitude Modulation (AD) ..... quam
Quadrennial Defense Review [*Army*] ..... QDR
Quadrillion (AD) ..... Q
Quadripartite Development Objective (AD) ..... qdo
Quadripartite Working Group for Combat Development [*American, Australian, British, and Canadian armies*] (AD) ..... QWGCD
Quadriplegia (AD) ..... quadrip
Quadriplex (AD) ..... quadplex
Quadripod Cane (AD) ..... quad c
Quadroon (AD) ..... quadro
Quadrophonic Stereo (AD) ..... qs
Quadruped (AD) ..... quadrup
Quadruple Expansion Engine (AD) ..... qee
Quadruple Flip-Flop (AD) ..... qff
Quadruple-Screw Motorship (AD) ..... qsm
Quadruple-Screw Ship (AD) ..... QSS
Quadruple-Screw Turbine Steamship (AD) ..... qsts
Quadruplet (AD) ..... quad
Quadruplicato [*Four Times as Much*] [*Latin*] (AD) ..... quadrupl
Quadrupole Residual Gas Analyzer (AD) ..... qrga
Quae Vide [*Which See*] [*Latin*] (AD) ..... qqv
Quagmire (AD) ..... quag
Quai [*Embankment*] [*French*] (AD) ..... Q
Quai d'Orsay (AD) ..... Qd'O
Quais-LASER-Intensity Interferometer (AD) ..... qlii
Quaker Action Group (AD) ..... QAG
Quaker Committee on Social Rehabilitation (AD) ..... QCSR
Quaker Line (AD) ..... Q
Quaker Oats (AD) ..... Quaker
Quaker Oats Foundation (AD) ..... QOF
Quaker Peace and Service (AD) ..... Q P & S
Quaker Press (AD) ..... Quaker
Quaker State Motor Oils (AD) ..... QSMO
Qualcosa [*Something*] [*Italian*] (AD) ..... qc
Qualification (AD) ..... qlfyn
Qualification (AD) ..... qual
Qualification Card (AD) ..... Q-card
Qualification Correlation Certification (AD) ..... qcc
Qualification Course (AD) ..... qc
Qualification Information and Test (AD) ..... qit
Qualifications Record (AD) ..... qr
Qualified (AD) ..... qufyd
Qualified Bidders (AD) ..... qb
Qualified for Deep Diving (AD) ..... qdd
Qualified for Mobilization Ashore Only (AD) ..... qmao
Qualified International Executive (AD) ..... QIE
Qualified Military Available (AD) ..... qma
Qualified Real-Estate Valuer (AD) ..... QRV
Qualified Scientists and Engineers (AD) ..... qse
Qualified Terminable Interest Property Trust [*Investment term*] (DFIT) ..... QTIP
Qualify (AD) ..... qlfy
Qualify (AD) ..... qual
Qualifying (AD) ..... qlfyg
Qualifying Examinations (AD) ..... quals
Qualifying Tests (AD) ..... quals
Qualitative Analysis (AD) ..... qual anal
Qualitative Equipment Requirements (AD) ..... qer
Qualitative Incentive Procurement Service (AD) ..... QIPS
Qualitative Material Objective (AD) ..... qmo
Qualitative Material Requirement (AD) ..... qmr
Qualitative Operational Requirement (AD) ..... qor
Qualitative Operational Requirements (AD) ..... qopri
Qualitative Point Average (AD) ..... qpa
Qualitative Requirements Information (AD) ..... qri
Quality (AD) ..... qlty
Quality (AD) ..... qual
Quality Acceptance (AD) ..... QA
Quality Achievement Factor (RDA) ..... QAF
Quality and Reliability Year (AD) ..... qry
Quality Answering System (AD) ..... QAS
Quality Assessment Division [*Higher Education Funding Council*] (AIE) ..... QAD
Quality Assurance (AD) ..... qa
Quality Assurance Board (AD) ..... QAB
Quality Assurance Bulletin (AD) ..... QAB
Quality Assurance Check (AD) ..... QAC
Quality Assurance Coding (AD) ..... QAC
Quality Assurance Data Summary (AD) ..... QADS
Quality Assurance Department (AD) ..... QAD
Quality Assurance Department Instruction (AD) ..... QADI
Quality Assurance Interface Coordination Group (AD) ..... QAICG
Quality Assurance Monitoring Information System (AD) ..... QAMIS
Quality Assurance Operating Procedure (AD) ..... QAOP
Quality Assurance Operation (AD) ..... qao
Quality Assurance Overview Contractor (AD) ..... QAOC
Quality Assurance Planning (AD) ..... QAP
Quality Assurance Report [*A publication*] (AD) ..... QAR
Quality Assurance System (AD) ..... QAS
Quality Assurance Systems Analysis Review (AD) ..... QASAR
Quality Assurance Test Procedure (AD) ..... QATP
Quality Basic-Oxygen Process (AD) ..... qbop
Quality Brands Associates of America (AD) ..... QBAA
Quality Completion Order (AD) ..... QCO
Quality Control (AD) ..... qc
Quality Control and Reliability (AD) ..... QC & R
Quality Control and Test (AD) ..... QC & T
Quality Control Bulletin (AD) ..... QCB
Quality Control Departmental Instruction (AD) ..... QCDI
Quality Control Engineering (AD) ..... QCE
Quality Control/Reliability (AD) ..... QC/R
Quality Control/Reliability (AD) ..... qcr
Quality Control Stop Order (AD) ..... QCSO
Quality Deer Management Association ..... QDMA
Quality Education for Minorities (AD) ..... QEM
Quality, Efficiency, Dependability (AD) ..... QED
Quality Electrical System Test (AD) ..... quest
Quality Engineering Operations (AD) ..... qeo
Quality Engineering Significant Control Points (AD) ..... qescp
Quality Factor (AD) ..... q
Quality Factor (AD) ..... qf
Quality Improvement (AD) ..... qi
Quality Improvement through Cost Optimization (AD) ..... quico
Quality in Education [*Project*] (AIE) ..... QET
Quality Indices (AD) ..... qi
Quality Inspection Criteria (AD) ..... qic
Quality International Hotels (AD) ..... QIH
Quality Material Approach (AD) ..... qma
Quality of Care Measurement [*Insurance*] (WYGK) ..... QCM
Quality of Life Index (AD) ..... qli
Quality of Working Life (AD) ..... qwl
Quality per End Item (AD) ..... qpei
Quality per Final Article (AD) ..... qfa

Quality per Next Assembly (AD) ... qna
Quality Performance Instruction Sheet (AD) ... QPIS
Quality Qualified Military Availability (AD) ... qqma
Quality Reliability Assurance (AD) ... qra
Quality Review Organization (AD) ... QRO
Quality Salary Increase (AD) ... qsi
Quality Search Procedure (AD) ... qsp
Quality Standard Inspection Criteria (AD) ... qsic
Quality Technical Report (AD) ... QTR
Quality Technical Requirement (AD) ... QTR
Quality Test (AD) ... QT
Quality Test (AD) ... qt
Quality Verification (AD) ... qv
Quality Verification Surveillance (AD) ... QVS
Quality Verification Test (AD) ... qvt
Quality-Assurance Department (AD) ... Qu-AD
Quality-Assurance Division (AD) ... Qu-AD
Quality-Assurance Field Operation (AD) ... qafo
Quality-Assurance Firing (AD) ... qaf
Quality-Assurance Liaison Division (AD) ... QALD
Quality-Control Data (AD) ... qcd
Quality-Control Information (AD) ... qci
Quality-Control Level (AD) ... qcl
Quality-Control Report (AD) ... QC Rept
Quality-Control Representative (AD) ... QC Rep
Quality-Control Standard (AD) ... QC Stand
Quanah, Acme & Pacific Railroad (AD) ... QA & P
Quandary Peak [*Colorado*] (AD) ... Quandary
Quang Duc [*South Vietnam*] [*Airport symbol*] (AD) ... HOO
Quang Ngai [*Vietnam*] [*Airport symbol*] (AD) ... XNG
Quanti-Pirquet (AD) ... q-P
Quantisizer (AD) ... qnt
Quantitative and Qualitative Personnel Requirements (AD) ... qqpr
Quantitative Assessment and Training Center (AD) ... QAT
Quantitative Command (AD) ... qc
Quantitative Decision System (AD) ... QDS
Quantitative Differential Thermal Analysis (AD) ... qdta
Quantitative Evaluative Device (AD) ... qed
Quantitative Flight Characteristics (AD) ... qfc
Quantitative Flight Characteristics Criteria (AD) ... qfcc
Quantitative Inhalation Challenge Apparatus [*Medicine*] (AD) ... quicha
Quantitative Leak Test (AD) ... qlt
Quantitative Physical Science (AD) ... qps
Quantitative Precipitation Forecast (AD) ... qpf
Quantitative Utility Evaluation Suggesting Targets for the Allocations of Resources (AD) ... questar
Quantity [*Microeconomics*] (AD) ... Q
Quantity (AD) ... qnty
Quantity (AD) ... qt
Quantity (AD) ... qty
Quantity (AD) ... quant
Quantity Desired or Requested (AD) ... qtydesreq
Quantity Discount Agreement (AD) ... qda
Quantity Not Sufficient (AD) ... qns
Quantity per Article (AD) ... qpa
Quantity per Assembly (AD) ... qpa
Quantity per Unit Pack (AD) ... qup
Quantity Progress Report (AD) ... QPR
Quantity Surveyors Research and Information Group (AD) ... QSRIG
Quantized Decision Detection (AD) ... qdd
Quantized Field Theory (AD) ... qft
Quantized Frequency Modulation (AD) ... qfm
Quantized Gate Video (AD) ... qgv
Quantock Marine Enterprises (AD) ... QME
Quantum (AD) ... quant
Quantum Amplification by Stimulated-Emission of Radiation (AD) ... quaser
Quantum Chromodynamics (AD) ... qcd
Quantum Counter (AD) ... qc
Quantum Electrodynamics (AD) ... qed
Quantum Electrodynamics Electron Volts (AD) ... qeev
Quantum Libet [*As Much as You Like*] [*Latin*] (AD) ... ql
Quantum Mechanics (AD) ... qm
Quantum Placet [*At Discretion*] [*Latin*] (AD) ... qp
Quantum Quatra Die [*Every Fourth Day*] [*Latin*] (AD) ... qqd
Quantum Quatra Hora [*Every Four Hours*] [*Latin*] (AD) ... qqh
Quantum Rectus [*Quantity is Correct*] [*Latin*] (AD) ... qr
Quantum Sufficit [*As Much as Suffices*] [*Latin*] (AD) ... qs
Quantum Sufficit [*Sufficient Quantity*] [*Latin*] (AD) ... quant suff
Quantum Switch (AD) ... Q-switch
Quantum Theory of Paramagnetism (AD) ... qtp
Quantum Yield (AD) ... qy
Quantum-Dot Cellular Automata [*Microelectronics*] ... QCA
Quaque [*Each*] [*Latin*] (AD) ... q
Quaque [*Each*] [*Latin*] (AD) ... qq
Quaque Hora [*Every Hour*] [*Latin*] (AD) ... qh
Quaque Hora [*Every Hour*] [*Latin*] (AD) ... qq hor
Quaque Mane [*Every Morning*] [*Latin*] (AD) ... qm
Quaque Nocte [*Every Night*] [*Latin*] (AD) ... qn
Quaquero [*Quaker*] [*Spanish*] (AD) ... Quaq
Quarantine (AD) ... Q
Quarantine (AD) ... quar
Quarantine Launch (AD) ... Q/L
Quarantine Maximum (AD) ... Q-max
Quarantine Officer in Charge [*Military*] (AD) ... QOIC
Quarantine Operations (AD) ... quaops
Quarrel (AD) ... ql
Quarry (AD) ... quarr
Quarry Products Training Council (AIE) ... QPTC
Quarry Tile (AD) ... qt
Quarry-Tile Base (AD) ... qtb
Quarry-Tile Floor (AD) ... qtf
Quarry-Tile Roof (AD) ... qtr
Quart (AD) ... q
Quart (AD) ... qt
Quart (AD) ... qu
Quarta Pars [*One-Fourth Part*] [*Latin*] (AD) ... quar pars
Quarter (AD) ... q
Quarter (AD) ... qr
Quarter (AD) ... qrt
Quarter (AD) ... qt
Quarter (AD) ... qtr
Quarter (AD) ... qu
Quarter Gallon (AD) ... quart
Quarter Ocean Net (AD) ... qon
Quarter Section (AD) ... qs
Quarter Wave (AD) ... qw
Quarterback (AD) ... qb
Quarterdeck (AD) ... qd
Quartered (AD) ... qtd
Quarter-Girth Measure (AD) ... qgm
Quartering (AD) ... qrtg
Quarterly (AD) ... qrtly
Quarterly (AD) ... qtly
Quarterly (AD) ... qu
Quarterly (AD) ... Quart
Quarterly (AD) ... quart
Quarterly Economic Review [*A publication*] (AD) ... QER
Quarterly Index [*A publication*] (AD) ... QI
Quarterly Journal of Speech [*A publication*] (BRI) ... QJS
Quarterly Journal of Studies in Alcohol [*A publication*] (AD) ... QJSA
Quarterly Review of Biology [*A publication*] (BRI) ... QRB
Quarterly World Day (AD) ... qwd
Quartermaster [*Military*] (AD) ... Qmr
Quartermaster (AD) ... Qrmr
Quartermaster (AD) ... qrtmstr
Quartermaster Fellows (AD) ... Q-fellows
Quartermaster Food and Container Institute (AD) ... QMFCI
Quartermaster Radiation Planning Agency (AD) ... QRPA
Quartermaster Research and Engineering [*Military*] (AD) ... QMR & E
Quartermaster Sergeant [*Military*] (AD) ... Qm Sgt
Quartermaster Water-Repellent [*Military*] (AD) ... quarpel
Quarternote Society (AD) ... QS
Quarter-Plate (VRA) ... QRTR
Quarters (AD) ... qrs
Quarters, Subsistence, and Laundry (AD) ... qs & l
Quarter-Square Multipliers (AD) ... qsm
Quarter-Wave Antenna (AD) ... qwa
Quarter-Wave Optical Thickness (AD) ... qwot
Quarter-Wave Plate (AD) ... qwp
Quartet (AD) ... quart
Quartette (AD) ... qtte
Quartetto Italiano [*Italian Quartet*] [*Italian*] (AD) ... Quart Ital
Quartier de Securite Renforcee [*Maximum Security Prison*] [*French*] (AD) ... QSR
Quartier General [*Headquarters*] [*French*] (AD) ... QG
Quartier Generale [*Headquarters*] [*Italian*] (AD) ... QG
Quartile (AD) ... q
Quartile Deviation (AD) ... qd
Quartile Variation [*Symbol*] (AD) ... Q
Quarto (AD) ... q
Quarto (AD) ... qto
Quartos (AD) ... qq
Quarts (AD) ... qts
Quartz (AD) ... qtz
Quartz (AD) ... Qz
Quartz (AD) ... qz
Quartz Aircraft Lamp (AD) ... qal
Quartz Aircraft Landing Lamp (AD) ... qall
Quartz Crystal (AD) ... qc
Quartz Crystal Unit (AD) ... qcu
Quartz Crystal Unit Set (AD) ... qcus
Quartz Fiber Electrometer (AD) ... qfe
Quartz Fiber Product (AD) ... qfp
Quartz Frequency Oscillator (AD) ... qfo
Quartz Helix (AD) ... qh
Quartz Incandescent Lamp (AD) ... qil
Quartz Insulation Part (AD) ... qip
Quartz Iodine Lamp (AD) ... qil
Quartz Landing Lamp (AD) ... qll
Quartz Metal Sealed Window (AD) ... qmsw
Quartz Metal Window (AD) ... qmw
Quartz Wedge (AD) ... q-wedge
Quartz-Crystal Filter (AD) ... qcf
Quartz-Crystal Frequency Oscillator (AD) ... qcfo
Quartz-Crystal Oscillator (AD) ... qco
Quartz-Halogen (AD) ... q-h
Quartz-Iodine Crystal (AD) ... qic
Quartzite (AD) ... qtzt
Quartzitic (AD) ... qtzic
Quartzose (AD) ... qtze
Quashey (AD) ... Quash

Quasi [*As It Were*] [*Latin*] (AD) .... qu
Quasi-Autonomous Non-Governmental Organization (AD) .... quango
Quasibiennial Stratospheric Oscillation (AD) .... qso
Quasi-Fermi Level (AD) .... qfl
Quasi-LASER Machine (AD) .... qlm
Quasi-LASER Sequential Machine (AD) .... qlsm
Quasi-Official Agencies (AD) .... QOA
Quasi-Random Band Model (AD) .... qrbm
Quasi-Random Code Generator (AD) .... qrcg
Quasi-Solid-State Panel (AD) .... qssp
Quasi-Static Field (AD) .... qsf
Quasi-Stationary-State Approximation (AD) .... qssa
Quasi-Stellar Blue Galaxies (AD) .... qsbg
Quasi-Stellar Blue Objects (AD) .... qsbo
Quasi-Stellar Galaxy (AD) .... qsg
Quasistellar Object (AD) .... qso
Quasi-Stellar Radio (AD) .... quasar
Quasi-Stellar Radio Sources (AD) .... qsrs
Quasi-Stellar Source (AD) .... qss
Quatar Fertilizer Co. (AD) .... QAFCO
Quater in Die [*Four Times a Day*] [*Latin*] (AD) .... qd
Quater in Die [*Four Times a Day*] [*Latin*] (AD) .... qid
Quaternary (AD) .... Quat
Quaternary (AD) .... quat
Quaternary Alluvium (AD) .... qal
Quaternary Ammonium Compound (AD) .... qac
Quatrefoil (VRA) .... qtfl
Quattuor [*Four*] [*Latin*] (AD) .... quat
Quay (AD) .... Qy
Que Besa su Mano [*Who Kisses Your Hand*] [*Spanish*] (AD) .... QBSM
Que Besa sus Pies [*Who Kisses Your Feet*] [*Spanish*] (AD) .... QBSP
Que Que [*Rhodesia*] (AD) .... QQ
Que Viva Mexico [*Long Live Mexico*] [*Spanish*] (AD) .... QVM
Quebec (AD) .... Q
Quebec (AD) .... Qbc
Quebec (AD) .... QE
Quebec [*Canada*] (DD) .... Que
Quebec and Ontario [*Canada*] (AD) .... Q & O
Quebec Central Railway [*Canada*] (AD) .... QC Ry
Quebec Central Railway Co. [*Canada*] (AD) .... QCRC
Quebec City (AD) .... QC
Quebec Land Surveyor [*Canada*] (DD) .... QLS
Quebec North Shore and Labrador Railway [*Canada*] (AD) .... QNS & L
Quebec Order of Dentists [*Canada*] (AD) .... QOD
Quebec Police Force [*Canada*] (AD) .... QPF
Quebec Provincial Police [*Canada*] (AD) .... QPP
Quebec Region Canadian University Press (AD) .... QRCUP
Quebec Securities Commission [*Canada*] (AD) .... QSC
Quebec Society for the Protection of Plants [*Canada*] (AD) .... QSPP
Quebec Standard Test [*Canada*] (AD) .... QST
Quebec Symphony Orchestra [*Canada*] (AD) .... QSO
Quebec Teachers' Federation [*Canada*] (AD) .... QTF
Quebec Teaching Congress [*Canada*] (AD) .... QTC
Quebec Tourist Information Bureau [*Canada*] (AD) .... QTIB
Quebec Zoological Society [*Canada*] (AD) .... QZS
Quebecair (AD) .... QBA
Quebecair (AD) .... QUE
Quebecois (AD) .... Que
Quechan Indian Reservation (AD) .... QIR
Quechon Tribal Museum [*Yuma, Arizona*] (AD) .... QTM
Quechua (AD) .... Que
Quecksilbersaeule [*Mercury Column*] [*German*] (AD) .... QS
Queen (AD) .... Qn
Queen (AD) .... Qu
Queen Alexandra's Royal Air Force Nursing Service [*British*] (AD) .... QARAFNS
Queen Alexandra's Royal Army Nursing Service [*British*] (AD) .... QARANC
Queen Charlotte Islands (AD) .... QC Isl
Queen Elizabeth Chemical Center [*British*] (AD) .... QECC
Queen Elizabeth National Park [*Uganda*] (AD) .... QENP
Queen Elizabeth Park (AD) .... QEP
Queen Elizabeth Planetarium (AD) .... QEP
Queen Elizabeth Theatre [*Vancouver*] (AD) .... QET
Queen Elizabeth's Foundation for the Disabled [*British*] (AD) .... QEFD
Queen Emma Summer Palace (AD) .... QESP
Queen Post (AD) .... qp
Queen Victoria Museum [*Launceston, Tasmania*] (AD) .... QVM
Queens (AD) .... Qns
Queen's Award to Industry [*British*] (AD) .... QAI
Queen's Bench Reports [*A publication*] (AD) .... QBRs
Queen's Bureau of Investigation [*British*] (AD) .... QBI
Queen's College (AD) .... Qns Coll
Queen's College [*Cambridge, Oxford*] (AD) .... QU
Queens College Press [*Australia*] (AD) .... QCP
Queen's Commendation for Brave Conduct [*British*] (AD) .... QCBC
Queens' Council Member of Parliament [*British*] (AD) .... QCMP
Queens County (AD) .... Q Co
Queens Educational and Social Team (AD) .... QUEST
Queen's Fire Services Medal [*British*] (AD) .... QFSM
Queen's Hall (AD) .... QH
Queen's Honorary Veterinarian [*British*] (AD) .... QHV
Queens Museum (AD) .... QM
Queens Park (AD) .... Qns Pk
Queen's Park Football Club (AD) .... QPFC
Queen's Polar Medal [*British*] (AD) .... QPM
Queen's Printer [*British*] (AD) .... QP
Queens Public Library (AD) .... QPL
Queen's Quarterly [*A publication*] (BRI) .... Queens Q
Queen's Service Medal [*British*] (AD) .... QSM
Queen's Service Medal [*British*] (AD) .... qsm
Queen's Service Order [*British*] (AD) .... QSO
Queen's Silver Jubilee Medal [*British*] (AD) .... QSJM
Queens University Interpretative Code (AD) .... QUICK
Queen's University Library (AD) .... QUL
Queen's University of Dublin (AD) .... QUD
Queensboro Bridge [*New York City*] (AD) .... QB
Queensland [*Airline code*] (AD) .... QL
Queensland (AD) .... Qld
Queensland (AD) .... Qnsd
Queensland (AD) .... Queensl
Queensland Airlines Proprietary Ltd. [*Australia*] (AD) .... QAPL
Queensland Alumina Ltd. [*Australia*] (AD) .... QAL
Queensland Amateur Gymnastic Association [*Australia*] (AD) .... QAGA
Queensland Amateur Swimming Association [*Australia*] (AD) .... QASA
Queensland Amateur Wrestling Association [*Australia*] (AD) .... QAWA
Queensland Ambulance Transport Brigade [*Australia*] (AD) .... QATB
Queensland Association of Personnel Services [*Australia*] (AD) .... QAPS
Queensland Australian Football League (AD) .... QAFL
Queensland Book Depot [*Australia*] (AD) .... QBD
Queensland Bowling Association [*Australia*] (AD) .... QBA
Queensland Butter Board [*Australia*] (AD) .... QBB
Queensland Cane-Growers Council [*Australia*] (AD) .... QCGC
Queensland Cleaning Contractors Association [*Australia*] (AD) .... QCCA
Queensland Coal Associates [*Australia*] (AD) .... QCA
Queensland Coal Mining [*Australia*] (AD) .... QCM
Queensland Colliery Employees Union [*Australia*] (AD) .... QCEU
Queensland Confederation of Industry [*Australia*] (AD) .... QCI
Queensland Conservation Council [*Australia*] (AD) .... QCC
Queensland Cooperative Milling Association [*Australia*] (AD) .... QCMA
Queensland Country Women's Association [*Australia*] (AD) .... QCWA
Queensland Cricket Association [*Australia*] (AD) .... QCA
Queensland Croquet Association (AD) .... QCA
Queensland Dairymens Organisation [*Australia*] (AD) .... QDO
Queensland Employers Federation [*Australia*] (AD) .... QEF
Queensland Environmental Program [*Australia*] (AD) .... QEP
Queensland Fisheries Research Institute [*Australia*] (AD) .... QFRI
Queensland Fisheries Service [*Australia*] (AD) .... QFS
Queensland Government Tourist Bureau [*Australia*] (AD) .... QGTB
Queensland Grain Growers Association [*Australia*] (AD) .... QGGA
Queensland Institute for Educational Research [*Australia*] (AD) .... QIER
Queensland Institute of Architects [*Australia*] (AD) .... QIA
Queensland Institute of Medical Research [*Australia*] (AD) .... QIMR
Queensland Institute of Public Affairs [*Australia*] (AD) .... QIPA
Queensland Institute of Technology [*Australia*] (AD) .... QIT
Queensland Insurance [*Australia*] (AD) .... QI
Queensland Law Society [*Australia*] (AD) .... QLS
Queensland Lawn Tennis Association [*Australia*] (AD) .... QLTA
Queensland Library Promotion Council [*Australia*] (AD) .... QLPC
Queensland Light Opera Co. [*Australia*] (AD) .... QLOC
Queensland Littoral Society [*Australia*] (AD) .... QLS
Queensland Local Government Association [*Australia*] (AD) .... QLGA
Queensland Master Builders Association [*Australia*] (AD) .... QMBA
Queensland Master Painters Association [*Australia*] (AD) .... QMPA
Queensland Motor Industry Association [*Australia*] (AD) .... QMIA
Queensland Police Academy [*Australia*] (AD) .... QPA
Queensland Polynesian Association [*Australia*] (AD) .... QPA
Queensland Professional Fishermens League [*Australia*] (AD) .... QPFL
Queensland Railfast Express [*Australia*] (AD) .... QRX
Queensland Railways [*Australia*] (AD) .... QR
Queensland Research League [*Australia*] (AD) .... QRL
Queensland Rifle Association [*Australia*] (AD) .... QRA
Queensland Rubber Co. [*Australia*] (AD) .... QRC
Queensland Shopkeepers Association [*Australia*] (AD) .... QSA
Queensland Soccer Federation [*Australia*] (AD) .... QSF
Queensland Society [*Australia*] (AD) .... QS
Queensland Society of Sugar Cane Technologists [*Australia*] (AD) .... QSSCT
Queensland State Library [*Australia*] (AD) .... QSL
Queensland Symphony Orchestra [*Australia*] (AD) .... QSO
Queensland Teachers Union [*Australia*] (AD) .... QTU
Queensland Tertiary Admissions Centre [*Australia*] (AD) .... QTAC
Queensland Timber Board [*Australia*] (AD) .... QTB
Queensland Tourist and Travel Corp. [*Australia*] (AD) .... QTTC
Queensland Trades and Labor Council [*Australia*] (AD) .... QTLC
Queensland Trotting Board [*Australia*] (AD) .... QTB
Queensland Turf Club [*Australia*] (AD) .... QTC
Queensland Youth Orchestra [*Australia*] (AD) .... QYO
Queens-Midtown Tunnel (AD) .... QMT
Queenstown [*South Africa*] [*Airport symbol*] (AD) .... UTW
Queenstown [*New Zealand*] [*Airport symbol*] (AD) .... ZQN
Queer (AD) .... q
Queer Fellows (AD) .... Q-fellows
Quelquefois [*Sometimes*] [*French*] (AD) .... qqf
Quelques [*Some*] [*French*] (AD) .... qq
Quench (AD) .... q
Quench Frequency (AD) .... qf
Quenched and Tempered (AD) .... q & t
Quenia [*Kenya*] [*Portuguese*] (AD) .... Que
Quensk [*Language of the Quains*] (AD) .... Qndk
Quentin (AD) .... Quen
Queretaro (AD) .... Qro
Queretaro (AD) .... Quer

Query (AD)	qu
Query (AD)	qy
Query Fever (AD)	Q fever
Query Language (AD)	ql
Query Message (AD)	qm
Query, Update Entry, Search, Time Sharing [*Computer science*] (AD)	QESTS
Question (AD)	q
Question (AD)	qn
Question (AD)	qstn
Question (AD)	qu
Question (AD)	ques
Question Analysis Transformation and Search [*Data processing*] (AD)	quantras
Question and Information Connection [*St. Louis Public Library*] (AD)	QUIC
Question/Query (AD)	q/qy
Questionable Corrective Task (AD)	qct
Questionable Questionnaire (AD)	qq
Questioned (AD)	quest
Questioned Document (AD)	qd
Questionnaire (AD)	qstnr
Questionnaire (AD)	questn
Questions of Procedure for Ministers	QPM
Quetico Provincial Park [*Ontario, Canada*] (AD)	QPP
Queue Control Block [*Data processing*] (AD)	qcb
Queue Jump (AD)	qjump
Queued Access Method (AD)	qam
Queued Indexed Access Memory [*Computer science*] (AD)	qiam
Queued Sequential Access Method (AD)	qsam
Queued Telecommunication Access Method (AD)	qtam
Queued-Indexed Sequential-Access Method [*Computer science*] (AD)	qisam
Queueing Matrix Evaluation (AD)	qme
Queueing System (AD)	QS
Quezon City [*Philippines*] (AD)	Q City
Quezon City (AD)	QC
Quezon Memorial Park [*Philippines*] (AD)	QMP
Quezon National Park [*Philippines*] (AD)	QNP
Qui Nhon [*South Vietnam*] [*Airport symbol*] (AD)	UIH
Quichua (AD)	Quich
Quick (AD)	q
Quick (AD)	qk
Quick and Dirty (AD)	q & d
Quick and Efficient System to Enhance Retrieval (AD)	quester
Quick Assembly (AD)	qa
Quick Attach-Detach-Kit (AD)	qadk
Quick Break (AD)	qb
Quick Change (AD)	q/c
Quick Changeover [*Manufacturing*]	QCO
Quick Connect (AD)	qc
Quick Delivery (AD)	qd
Quick Detachable [*Weapon*] (AD)	qd
Quick Detachable Communication (AD)	qdc
Quick Disconnect Valve (AD)	qdv
Quick Engine Change (AD)	qec
Quick Engine-Change Unit (AD)	qecu
Quick Estimate (AD)	qe
Quick Exhaust Valve (AD)	qev
Quick Flashing (AD)	Qk Fl
Quick Fortran [*Computer science*] (AD)	quiktran
Quick Freeze (AD)	qf
Quick Law Systems (AD)	QLS
Quick Loading System (AD)	QLS
Quick Look (AD)	ql
Quick Make-and-Break (AD)	qmb
Quick Mechanical Disconnect Kit (AD)	qmdk
Quick on System (AD)	QOS
Quick Opening (AD)	qo
Quick Process (AD)	qp
Quick Reaction (AD)	qr
Quick Reaction Alert (AD)	qra
Quick Reaction Capability (AD)	qrc
Quick Reaction Installation Capability (AD)	qric
Quick Reaction Operation (AD)	qro
Quick Receipt (AD)	qr
Quick Response (AD)	QR
Quick Response Graphic (AD)	qrg
Quick Test (AD)	qt
Quick Text Editor (AD)	qted
Quick Turn Stock (AD)	qts
Quick Weight Loss (AD)	qwl
Quick-Access Recording (AD)	qar
Quick-Acting (AD)	qa
Quick-Acting Scuttle (AD)	qas
Quick-Attach Kit (AD)	qak
Quick-Attach-Detach (AD)	qad
Quick-Change Real Time (AD)	qcrt
Quick-Change Response (AD)	qcr
Quick-Change Unit (AD)	qcu
Quick-Connect Coupling (AD)	qcc
Quick-Connect Handle (AD)	qch
Quick-Connect Kit (AD)	qck
Quick-Connect Valve Coupler (AD)	qcvc
Quick-Connects Bulkhead Mounting (AD)	qcbm
Quick-Disconnect (AD)	q-d
Quick-Disconnect Cap (AD)	qdc
Quick-Disconnect Circular Connection (AD)	qdcc

Quick-Disconnect Handle (AD)	qdh
Quick-Disconnect Kit (AD)	qdk
Quick-Disconnect Nipple (AD)	qdn
Quick-Disconnect Pivot (AD)	qdp
Quick-Disconnect Series (AD)	qds
Quick-Disconnect Swivel (AD)	qds
Quick-Exhaust Air Valve (AD)	qeav
Quick-Fix Interference-Reduction Capability (AD)	qfirc
Quick-Look Intermediate Tape (AD)	qlit
Quickly (AD)	qkly
Quick-Make Quick-Break (AD)	qmqb
Quick-Opening Device (AD)	qod
Quick-Reaction Dome (AD)	qed
Quick-Release Valve (AD)	qrv
Quick-Strike Reconnaissance (AD)	qsr
Quiescent Aerial (AD)	qa
Quiescent Carrier Telephony (AD)	qct
Quiet (AD)	qt
Quiet Automatic Gain Control (AD)	qagc
Quiet Automatic Volume Control (AD)	qavc
Quiet Cab (AD)	Q-cab
Quiet, Experimental, Short-Takeoff-and-Landing [*NASA*] (AD)	questal
Quiet Extended Life (AD)	qel
Quiet Propulsion Lift Technology (AD)	qplt
Quiet Short-Haul Research Aircraft (AD)	qsra
Quiet Sun Year (AD)	qsy
Quiet Takeoff and Landing (AD)	qtol
Quiet-and-Short Takeoff and Landing (AD)	qstol
Quilate [*Carat*] [*Portuguese*]	ql
Quill & Quire [*A publication*] (BRI)	Quill & Q
Quillwork (VRA)	quilwk
Quimica [*Chemistry*] [*Spanish*]	quim
Quimica de Portugal (AD)	Quimigal
Quincemil [*Peru*] [*Airport symbol*] (AD)	QUP
Quincy (AD)	Qcy
Quincy (AD)	Quin
Quincy College (AD)	QC
Quincy Division/General Dynamics (AD)	QD/GD
Quincy Junior College (AD)	QJC
Quincy Yacht Club (AD)	QYC
Quinine, Atebrin, Plasmoquine [*Medicine*] (AD)	qap
Quinnipiac College (AD)	QC
Quint-A (AD)	Q-A
Quintal (AD)	q
Quintal [*Hundred-weight*] [*Spanish*] (AD)	Q1
Quintal [*Hundred-weight*] [*French*] (AD)	qal
Quintal (AD)	ql
Quintal Metrico [*Metric Quintal*] [*Spain*] (AD)	qm
Quintales [*Quintals*] [*Spanish*] (AD)	qq
Quintana Roo (AD)	Q Roo
Quintana Roo (AD)	QR
Quintaux [*Quintals*] [*French*] (AD)	qtaux
Quintaux [*Hundred-Weights*] [*French*] (AD)	qx
Quinten (AD)	Quin
Quintet (AD)	qnt
Quintet (AD)	quin
Quintilian (AD)	Quint
Quintilianus (AD)	Quin
Quintilius (AD)	Quin
Quintillian (AD)	Quin
Quintino (AD)	Quin
Quintius (AD)	Quin
Quintuplet (AD)	quin
Quintuplets (AD)	quins
Quintuplicate (AD)	quint
Quintuplicate (AD)	quintupl
Quintus [*Fifth*] [*Latin*] (AD)	quint
Quintus Tullius Cicero (AD)	Q Cic
Quire (AD)	q
Quire (AD)	qr
Quirindi [*New South Wales*] [*Airport symbol*] (AD)	QUI
Quisling [*World War II*] (AD)	quis
Quit Claim (AD)	qc
Quit-Claim Deed (AD)	qcd
Quite Bloody Impossible [*Slang*] (AD)	qbi
Quivira National Wildlife Refuge [*Kansas*] (AD)	QNWR
Quixote (AD)	quix
Qunatitative Immuno-Electrophoresis (AD)	qie
Quo Modo [*In What Manner*] [*Latin*] (AD)	qm
Quod Erat Demonstrandum [*That Which Was to Be Proved*] [*Latin*] (AD)	qed
Quod Erat Faciendum [*That Which Was to Be Done*] [*Latin*] (AD)	qef
Quod Erat Inveniendum [*That Which Was to Be Discovered*] [*Latin*] (AD)	qei
Quod Est [*Which Is*] [*Latin*] (AD)	qe
Quodlibet [*As You Please*] [*Latin*] (AD)	quod
Quokka (AD)	quok
Quonset Point [*Rhode Island*] (AD)	Quon Pt
Quoque [*Every*] [*Latin*] (AD)	qq
Quorom [*Of Which*] [*Latin*] (AD)	quor
Quorum (AD)	quor
Quotation (AD)	qtn
Quotation (AD)	qotn
Quotation (AD)	qtn
Quotation (AD)	quot
Quote (AD)	qot
Quote (AD)	qte

Quoted (AD) .... qted
Quotidie [*Daily*] [*Latin*] (AD) .... quot
Quotidie [*Every Day*] [*Latin*] (AD) .... quotid
Quoting (AD) .... qtg
Quran [*Koran*] [*Malay*] (AD) .... Qur
Qutdligssat [*Greenland*] [*Airport symbol*] (AD) .... QUN
Q-Value (AD) .... q-v

R
By Meaning

Raba Raba [*New Guinea*] [*Airport symbol*] (AD) .... RBF
Rabbit Calicivirus Disease .... RCD
Race Relations and Overseas Students Panel (AIE) .... RROSP
Racial Equality in Training Schemes (AIE) .... REITS
Racketeer Influenced and Corrupt Organization Act (DFIT) .... RICO
RADAR-Absorbent Material [*Aviation*] .... RAM
Radio Broadcast Data System .... RBDS
Radio Broadcasting Data System .... RBDS
Radio Frequency Integrated Circuit .... RFIC
Rahimyar Kahn [*Pakistan*] [*Airport symbol*] (AD) .... RYK
Railroad Station (VRA) .... RR sta
Raising Achievements in Mathematics Project (AIE) .... RAMP
Rajshahi [*Bangladesh*] [*Airport symbol*] (AD) .... RJH
Ramsar [*Iran*] [*Airport symbol*] (AD) .... RZR
Rangoon [*Burma*] [*Airport symbol*] (AD) .... RGN
Rangpur [*Bangladesh*] [*Airport symbol*] (AD) .... RAU
Ransiki [*West Irian, Indonesia*] [*Airport symbol*] (AD) .... RSK
Rapidair [*ICAO designator*] (AD) .... MC
Rapidly Adapting Lateral Position Handler .... RALPH
Rapport: The Modern Guide to Books, Music & More [*A publication*]
   (BRI) .... Rapport
Rare Books & Manuscript Librarianship [*American Library Association*] ...... RBML
Rare Object Searches with Bolometers Underground [*Astrophysics*] .... ROSEBUD
Ras-al-Khaima [*Trucial Oman*] [*Airport symbol*] (AD) .... RKT
Raudha [*South Arabia*] [*Airport symbol*] (AD) .... RXA
Rawhide (VRA) .... rwhi
Rawlins [*Wyoming*] [*Airport symbol*] (AD) .... RWL
Read the Fine Manual [*Computer science*] (DOM) .... RTFM
Reading Development Continuum (AIE) .... RDC
Reading Teacher [*A publication*] (BRI) .... RT
Readings: A Journal of Reviews and Commentary in Mental Health
   [*A publication*] (BRI) .... Readings
Readymade (VRA) .... rdymd
Real Estate Investment Trust [*Pooled funds that invest in income-producing
   residential and commerical properties*] .... REIT
Rebuilt (VRA) .... rblt
Recombinant Immunoblot Assay [*Medicine*] .... RIBA
Reconstructed Communism Party [*Italy*] .... RC
Reconstruction (VRA) .... recon
Record of Personal Experience (AIE) .... RPE
Recordable LASER Videodisc [*Optical Disc Corp.*] (DOM) .... RLV
Recreational Software Advisory Council .... RSAC
Red Bluff [*California*] [*Airport symbol*] (AD) .... RBL
Red Carpet Flying Service [*ICAO designator*] (AD) .... MF
Red, Green, Blue Monitor .... RGB monitor
Redstone Technical Test Center [*Army*] (RDA) .... RTTC
Redwood (VRA) .... rdwd
Refectory (VRA) .... refty
Reference & Research Book News [*A publication*] (BRI) .... R&R Bk N
Reference and User Services Association [*Formerly, RASD*] .... RUSA
Reference Book Review [*A publication*] (BRI) .... Ref Bk R
Reference Services Review [*A publication*] (BRI) .... RSR
Refunding Escrow Deposit [*Finance*] (DFIT) .... RED
Regal Bahamas International Airlines [*ICAO designator*] (AD) .... RH
Regency (VRA) .... Rgcy
Region (DD) .... reg
Regional (DD) .... regl
Regional Atmospheric Modeling System .... RAMS
Regional Development Unit [*Manpower Services Commission*] (AIE) .... RDU
Regional Financial Associates Inc. .... RFA
Regional Further Education Adviser (AIE) .... RFEA
Regional Management Centre (AIE) .... RMC
Regional Office for Central America and Panama .... ROCAP
Regional Office for Education, Asia and Pacific [*UNESCO*] (AIE) .... ROEAP
Registered Engineering Technologist (DD) .... RET
Registered Professional Engineer (DD) .... PEng
Regular Eight [*Motion picture*] (VRA) .... REGE
Regulated-upon-Activation, Normal T Expressed and Secreted
   [*Immunology*] .... RANTES
Regulators of G-Protein Signalling [*Biochemistry*] .... RGS
Rehoboth Beach [*Delaware*] [*Airport symbol*] (AD) .... REH
Reinforced (VRA) .... rnfd
Relation (DD) .... rel
Relief (VRA) .... rel
Religion (VRA) .... relig
Religious Education [*A publication*] (BRI) .... Rel Ed

Religious Education Centre (AIE) .... REC
Religious Studies [*A publication*] (BRI) .... Rel St
Religious Studies Review [*A publication*] (BRI) .... Rel St Rev
Reliquary (VRA) .... reliq
Remanso [*Brazil*] [*Airport symbol*] (AD) .... RSO
Remnant Tumor Index [*Surgery*] .... RTI
Remote Method Invocation [*Computer science*] (DOM) .... RMI
Renaissance (VRA) .... Renais
Renaissance and Reformation [*A publication*] (BRI) .... Ren & Ref
Renaissance Quarterly [*A publication*] (BRI) .... Ren Q
Rendering (VRA) .... rndr
Rengat [*Sumatra, Indonesia*] [*Airport symbol*] (AD) .... RGT
Repackaged Asset Vehicle .... RAV
Replica (VRA) .... repl
Repousse (VRA) .... repu
Representation (VRA) .... repres
Reproduction (VRA) .... reprd
Republic [*ICAO designator*] (AD) .... RW
Repurchase Agreement [*Finance*] (DFIT) .... Repo
Request for Technology (DOM) .... RFT
Research and Development (DFIT) .... R&D
Research and Exploration [*A publication*] (BRI) .... Res & Exp
Research and Information State Education Trust (AIE) .... RISE
Research Assessment Exercise [*Higher Education Funding Council*] (AIE) .... RAE
Reserve Bank of Australia .... RBA
Reserve Component Virtual Training Program [*Army*] (RDA) .... RCVTP
Resident Assistant .... RA
Residential Children's Home (AIE) .... RCH
Residential Colleges Committee (AIE) .... RCC
Residential Communications Network [*Telecommunications service*] .... RCN
Residential Social Worker (AIE) .... RSW
Resin (VRA) .... res
Resin-Coated (VRA) .... resco
Resistance Management Plans [*To prevent insect adaptation to toxins*] .... RMP
Resource Editor [*Computer science*] (DOM) .... ResEdit
Resource Referral Program (WYGK) .... RRP
Resource Reservation Protocol [*Videoconferencing*] .... RSVP
Resources (DD) .... Res
Resources for Learning Development Unit (AIE) .... RLDU
Resources Information Bank on Multicultural Education (AIE) ...... RIBMESC
Respiratory Symptoms Complex [*Medicine*] .... RSC
Respiratory Syncytial Virus [*Medicine*] .... RSV
Restaurant (VRA) .... rstrau
Restored (VRA) .... rest
Retail Postal Outlet (DD) .... RPO
Retired (DD) .... ret
Retirement Equity Act of 1984 (WYGK) .... REA
Retouched (VRA) .... RETO
Retrovirus Epidemiology Donor Study [*Medicine*] .... REDS
Reunion Air [*ICAO designator*] (AD) .... UU
Revenue Reconciliation Act of 1990 (WYGK) .... RRA
Revenue Support Grant (AIE) .... RSG
Reverend (DD) .... Rev
Reverse (VRA) .... rev
Review for Religious [*A publication*] (BRI) .... RR
Review of Contemporary Fiction [*A publication*] (BRI) .... RCF
Review of English Studies [*A publication*] (BRI) .... RES
Review of Law in Further Education (AIE) .... ROLFE
Review of Metaphysics [*A publication*] (BRI) .... RM
Review of Politics [*A publication*] (BRI) .... RP
Review of Vocational Qualifications (AIE) .... RVQ
Reviews in American History [*A publication*] (BRI) .... RAH
Reviews in Anthropology [*A publication*] (BRI) .... RA
Revival (VRA) .... rvl
Rezayeh [*Iran*] [*Airport symbol*] (AD) .... RZY
Rheims [*France*] [*Airport symbol*] (AD) .... RHE
Rhine Air [*ICAO designator*] (AD) .... WU
Rhoplex (VRA) .... rplx
Ribbed Vault (VRA) .... rib vlt
Ribbonwork (VRA) .... ribnwk
Right (VRA) .... rt
Rimini [*Italy*] [*Airport symbol*] (AD) .... RMI
Rimouski [*Quebec*] [*Airport symbol*] (AD) .... YRX
Rio Airways [*ICAO designator*] (AD) .... XO
Rio Grande [*Brazil*] [*Airport symbol*] (AD) .... RGR
Rio Grande do Sul [*Brazil*] [*Airport symbol*] (AD) .... RDS

Rio Hondo [*Argentina*] [*Airport symbol*] (AD) .... RHD
Rio Mayo [*Argentina*] [*Airport symbol*] (AD) .... RFH
Rio Sucio [*Colombia*] [*Airport symbol*] (AD) .... RSU
Riordan's Internet Privacy Enhanced Mail [*Computer science*] .... RIPEM
Rio-Sul [*ICAO designator*] (AD) .... SL
Risk and Youth Smoking [*Project*] (AIE) .... RAYS
River Cess [*Liberia*] [*Airport symbol*] (AD) .... RVC
Riyan Mukalla [*South Arabia (Yemen)*)] [*Airport symbol*] (AD) .... RIY
Road (DD) .... Rd
Robert Wood Johnson Foundation .... RWJF
Robinhood [*Queensland*] [*Airport symbol*] (AD) .... RFW
Robore [*Bolivia*] [*Airport symbol*] (AD) .... RBO
Rochester [*England*] [*Airport symbol*] (AD) .... RCS
Rocket Impacts on Stratospheric Ozone [*Air Force*] .... RISO
Rocks & Minerals [*A publication*] (BRI) .... RocksMiner
Rocky Mount [*North Carolina*] [*Airport symbol*] (AD) .... RMT
Rocky Mountain Airways [*ICAO designator*] (AD) .... JC
Rocky Mountain Review of Language & Literature [*A publication*] (BRI) ...... RMR
Roederer Aviation [*ICAO designator*] (AD) .... EG
Roland Air [*ICAO designator*] (AD) .... DU
Rolodex Electronic Express .... REX
Romanesque (VRA) .... Rmsq
Romania (VRA) .... Rom
Romanian Merchant Marine (AD) .... NAVROM
Rome-Utica [*New York*] [*Airport symbol*] (AD) .... UCA
Roof (VRA) .... rf
Room (VRA) .... rm
Room (DD) .... Rm
Root Mean Squared (DOM) .... rms
Rorvik [*Norway*] [*Airport symbol*] (AD) .... RVK
ROSAT [*Roentgen Satellite*] **All Sky Survey** .... RASS
Rose Hall [*Guyana*] [*Airport symbol*] (AD) .... ROF
Roseberth [*Queensland*] [*Airport symbol*] (AD) .... RZB
Roseburg [*Oregon*] [*Airport symbol*] (AD) .... RBG
Rosella Plains [*Queensland*] [*Airport symbol*] (AD) .... RGO
Rosewood (VRA) .... roswd
Rosh-Pina [*Israel*] [*Airport symbol*] (AD) .... MYH
Ross Aviation [*ICAO designator*] (AD) .... ZD
Ross Bay [*Newfoundland*] [*Airport symbol*] (AD) .... YRF

Rossair [*ICAO designator*] (AD) .... RF
Roundup Magazine [*A publication*] (BRI) .... Roundup M
Rourkela [*India*] [*Airport symbol*] (AD) .... RRK
Route (DD) .... rte
Routing and Remote Access Service [*Computer science*] .... RRAS
Roxborough [*Queensland*] [*Airport symbol*] (AD) .... RFX
Roy Hill [*Western Australia*] [*Airport symbol*] (AD) .... RHL
Royal Academy [*British*] (AIE) .... RA
Royal Air [*ICAO designator*] (AD) .... TR
Royal Air Force [*ICAO designator*] (AD) .... RR
Royal Air International [*ICAO designator*] (AD) .... RN
Royal Air Maroc [*ICAO designator*] (AD) .... AT
Royal American [*ICAO designator*] (AD) .... JW
Royal British-Colonial Society of Artists, London [*1886*] (NGC) .... RBC
Royal Brunei Airlines [*ICAO designator*] (AD) .... BI
Royal Hawaiian Airways [*ICAO designator*] (AD) .... ZH
Royal Institute of British Architects, London [*1834*] (NGC) .... RIBA
Royal Institute of Oil Painters, London [*1883*] (NGC) .... ROI
Royal Institute of Painters in Water-Colours, London [*1831*] (NGC) .... RI
Royal Nepal Airlines [*ICAO designator*] (AD) .... RA
Royal Scottish Academy, Edinburgh [*1826*] (NGC) .... RSA
Royal Scottish Academy of Music and Drama (AIE) .... RSAM
Royal Society for the Prevention of Accidents [*British*] (AIE) .... ROSPA
Royal Society of Painter-Etchers and Engravers, London [*1880*] (NGC) .... RE
Royal Society of Painters in Water-Colours, London [*1804*] (NGC) .... RWS
Royal Swazi National Airways [*ICAO designator*] (AD) .... ZC
Royal West [*ICAO designator*] (AD) .... TT
Royale Airlines [*ICAO designator*] (AD) .... OQ
Rubber (VRA) .... rbr
Rubbing (VRA) .... rub
Ruby (VRA) .... rby
Ruinas de Copan [*Honduras*] [*Airport symbol*] (AD) .... RUY
Rumania (VRA) .... Rum
Rumor Intelligence .... RUMINT
Rupsi [*India*] [*Airport symbol*] (AD) .... RUP
Russia (VRA) .... Rus
Russian Review [*A publication*] (BRI) .... Russ Rev
Rustication (VRA) .... rustc
Rutherford [*New Jersey*] [*Airport symbol*] (AD) .... RTF

S
By Meaning

Sa da Bandiera [*Angola*] [*Airport symbol*] (AD) .... SDD
Saba [*Netherlands Antilles*] [*Airport symbol*] (AD) .... SAM
Sacramento [*California*] [*Airport symbol*] (AD) .... SAC
Safair [*ICAO designator*] (AD) .... KP
Safety Base Motion Picture (VRA) .... SBMP
Safety Based Negative (VRA) .... SFNG
Safety of Life at Sea [*An international agreement requiring operators of cruise ships to meet certain standards of construction and fire safety*] .... SOLAS
Safford [*Arizona*] [*Airport symbol*] (AD) .... SAD
Safia [*Papua*] [*Airport symbol*] (AD) .... SFK
Saigon [*South Vietnam*] [*Airport symbol*] (AD) .... SGN
Saint (DD) .... St
Sale and Leaseback (DFIT) .... S&L
Salima [*Malawi*] [*Airport symbol*] (AD) .... AIM
Salinas [*California*] [*Airport symbol*] (AD) .... SNS
Salmagundi [*A publication*] (BRI) .... Salm
Salmonella Outbreak Detection Algorithm [*Medicine*] .... SODA
Salonika [*Greece*] [*Airport symbol*] (AD) .... SKG
Salted Paper Print (VRA) .... SLPT
Saltglaze (VRA) .... sltgz
Saltillo [*Mexico*] [*Airport symbol*] (AD) .... SLW
Sam Neua [*Laos*] [*Airport symbol*] (AD) .... KSN
Samaria [*Papua*] [*Airport symbol*] (AD) .... SIW
Samoa Air [*ICAO designator*] (AD) .... TS
Samoan [*ICAO designator*] (AD) .... OE
San (VRA) .... S
San Antonio do Ica [*Brazil*] [*Airport symbol*] (AD) .... SIC
San Bernardino [*California*] [*Airport symbol*] (AD) .... SBT
San Esteban [*Honduras*] [*Airport symbol*] (AD) .... SET
San Felipe [*Venezuela*] [*Airport symbol*] (AD) .... SNF
San Felix [*Venezuela*] [*Airport symbol*] (AD) .... SFX
San Francisco Review [*A publication*] (BRI) .... SFR
San Francisco Review of Books [*A publication*] (BRI) .... SFRB
San Ignacio de Moxos [*Bolivia*] [*Airport symbol*] (AD) .... SNM
San Javier [*Bolivia*] [*Airport symbol*] (AD) .... SJV
San Joaquin [*Bolivia*] [*Airport symbol*] (AD) .... SJB
San Jose [*Bolivia*] [*Airport symbol*] (AD) .... SJS
San Juan [*Peru*] [*Airport symbol*] (AD) .... SJP
San Juan Airlines [*ICAO designator*] (AD) .... YS
San Juan de Arama [*Colombia*] [*Airport symbol*] (AD) .... SJA
San Juan de Cesar [*Colombia*] [*Airport symbol*] (AD) .... SUM
San Juan de Uraba [*Colombia*] [*Airport symbol*] (AD) .... SJR
San Luis Potosi [*Mexico*] [*Airport symbol*] (AD) .... SLP
San Marcos [*Colombia*] [*Airport symbol*] (AD) .... SRS
San Pedro [*Colombia*] [*Airport symbol*] (AD) .... SPX
San Pedro de Jagua [*Colombia*] [*Airport symbol*] (AD) .... SPL
San Quentin [*California State Prison*] (AD) .... Quent
San Quentin Prison (AD) .... Q
San Quilmas (AD) .... Quilmas
Sanandaj [*Iran*] [*Airport symbol*] (AD) .... KNT
Sanctuary (VRA) .... sanct
Sand Creek [*Guyana*] [*Airport symbol*] (AD) .... SNL
Sandalwood (VRA) .... sndlwd
Sanday [*Scotland*] [*Airport symbol*] (AD) .... SYC
Sandstone (VRA) .... sandst
Sandwip [*Bangladesh*] [*Airport symbol*] (AD) .... SDW
Sandy Point [*Great Abaco Island, Bahamas*] [*Airport symbol*] (AD) .... SDT
Sanguine (VRA) .... sangu
Sankt (VRA) .... S
Santa (VRA) .... S
Santa Ana [*Columbia*] [*Airport symbol*] (AD) .... SLO
Santa Barbara [*Monagas, Venezuela*] [*Airport symbol*] (AD) .... SBR
Santa Barbara [*Honduras*] [*Airport symbol*] (AD) .... SZB
Santa Barbara-Barinas [*Venezuela*] [*Airport symbol*] (AD) .... SBB
Santa Catalina [*Colombia*] [*Airport symbol*] (AD) .... SCA
Santa Catalina Island [*California*] [*Airport symbol*] (AD) .... SXC
Santa Clara [*Cuba*] [*Airport symbol*] (AD) .... SNU
Santa Cruz de Tenerife [*Canary Islands*] [*Airport symbol*] (AD) .... TCI
Santa Isabel [*Spanish Guinea*] [*Airport symbol*] (AD) .... SSG
Santa Margherita [*Italy*] [*Airport symbol*] (AD) .... SMJ
Santa Monica [*California*] [*Airport symbol*] (AD) .... SMO
Santa Vitoria [*Brazil*] [*Airport symbol*] (AD) .... CTQ
Santiago [*Brazil*] [*Airport symbol*] (AD) .... STG
Santo (VRA) .... S
Santo Antonio do Zaire [*Angola*] [*Airport symbol*] (AD) .... SZA
Santo Domingo [*Venezuela*] [*Airport symbol*] (AD) .... STD
Santo Rosa [*Brazil*] [*Airport symbol*] (AD) .... SRA
Santos [*Brazil*] [*Airport symbol*] (AD) .... SSZ
Sao Borja [*Brazil*] [*Airport symbol*] (AD) .... SBQ
Sao Domingos [*Brazil*] [*Airport symbol*] (AD) .... SDG
Sao Hill [*Tanzania*] [*Airport symbol*] (AD) .... SIL
Sao Madureira [*Brazil*] [*Airport symbol*] (AD) .... ZMD
Sao Paulo de Olivenca [*Brazil*] [*Airport symbol*] (AD) .... SLV
Sao Salvador [*Angola*] [*Airport symbol*] (AD) .... SSY
Saravena [*Colombia*] [*Airport symbol*] (AD) .... SVN
Sarcophagi (VRA) .... sarc
Sarcophagus (VRA) .... sarc
Sardinia (VRA) .... Sard
Sargodha [*Pakistan*] [*Airport symbol*] (AD) .... GDH
Saskatchewan [*Canada*] (DD) .... Sask
Satellite Access Nodes .... SAN
Satellite Project for Adult and Continuing Education (AIE) .... SPACE
Satin (VRA) .... sat
Satinwood (VRA) .... satwd
Saturday Evening Post [*A publication*] (BRI) .... SEP
Saturday Night [*A publication*] (BRI) .... SN
Saudi Arabia (VRA) .... S Arab
Saudi Arabian Airlines [*ICAO designator*] (AD) .... SV
Savannakhet [*Laos*] [*Airport symbol*] (AD) .... ZVK
Save British Science [*An association*] (AIE) .... SBS
Savings and Loan (DFIT) .... S&L
Sawdust (VRA) .... sawdu
Sayaboury [*Laos*] [*Airport symbol*] (AD) .... ZBY
Scalar Processor Architecture Reduced-Instruction-Set Computer (DOM) .... SPARC
Scenic Airlines [*ICAO designator*] (AD) .... YR
Schematic (VRA) .... schm
Schist (VRA) .... schst
School (VRA) .... sch
School Arts [*A publication*] (BRI) .... Sch Arts
School Focused Secondment (AIE) .... SFS
School Journal Association of London [*British*] (AIE) .... SJAL
School Leaving Age (AIE) .... SLA
School Librarian [*A publication*] (BRI) .... Sch Lib
School Library Journal [*A publication*] (BRI) .... SLJ
School Library Media Quarterly [*American Library Association*] .... SLMQ
School Performance Information Regulations (AIE) .... SPIR
Schoolboys Harness Aid for the Relief of the Elderly (AIE) .... SHARE
Schools Computer Development Centre (AIE) .... SCDC
Schools Computers Administration and Management Project (AIE) .... SCAMP
Schools Cultural Studies Project (AIE) .... SCSP
Schools, Curriculum, Unusual, Geography, and Alumni [*University admisssion rating system*] .... SCUGA
Schools History Project (AIE) .... SHP
Schools Industry Liaison Officer (AIE) .... SILO
Schools Information Centre on the Chemical Industry (AIE) .... SICCI
Schools Information Management System (AIE) .... SIMS
Schools In-Service Unit [*University of Birmingham*] [*British*] (AIE) .... SISU
Science [*A publication*] (BRI) .... Sci
Science Activities for the Visually Impaired (AIE) .... SAVI
Science and Engineering Policy Studies Unit (AIE) .... SEPSU
Science & Society [*A publication*] (BRI) .... S&S
Science and Technology in Society (AIE) .... SATIS
Science Books & Films [*A publication*] (BRI) .... SB
Science Fiction Chronicle [*A publication*] (BRI) .... SF Chr
Science Studies' Perception Questionnaire (AIE) .... SSPQ
Science Teachers' Authoring Facility (AIE) .... STAF
Science Technology and Education Division [*British Council*] (AIE) .... STED
Science-Fiction Studies [*A publication*] (BRI) .... SFS
Scientific American [*A publication*] (BRI) .... SA
SciTech Book News [*A publication*] (BRI) .... SciTech
Scotland (VRA) .... Scot
Scottish Academic Live Television Interconnect and Research Environment (AIE) .... SALTIRE
Scottish Adult Basic Education Unit (AIE) .... SABEU
Scottish Association for Educational Management and Administration (AIE) .... SAEMA
Scottish Association for the Teaching of English as a Foreign Language (AIE) .... SATEFL
Scottish Central Committee on Modern Languages (AIE) .... SCCML
Scottish Centre for Education Overseas (AIE) .... SCEO
Scottish Colleges In-Service Education of Teachers (AIE) .... SCINSET

Scottish Committee on Open Learning (AIE) .... SCOL
Scottish Computers in Schools Project (AIE) .... SCMP
Scottish Credit Accumulation and Transfer (AIE) ...... SCOTCAT
Scottish European Airways [ICAO designator] (AD) ..... WW
Scottish Office Education Department (AIE) .... SOED
Scottish Open Tech Training Support Unit (AIE) .... SCOTTSU
Scottish Primary Mathematics Group (AIE) .... SPMG
Scottish Schools Rugby Union (AIE) .... SSRU
Scottish Standing Conference of Voluntary Youth Organisations
  (AIE) .... SSCVYO
Scottish Universities Accommodation Consortium (AIE) . SUAC
Scottish Universities Sports Federation (AIE) .... SUSF
Scottish Vocational Qualification (AIE) .... SVQ
Scranton-Wilkes-Barre [Pennsylvania] [Airport symbol] (AD) . AVP
Screen (VRA) .... scrn
Screenprint (VRA) .... scrnpr
Scripture (VRA) .... script
Scroll (VRA) .... scl
Scruse Air [ICAO designator] (AD) .... SF
SCSI Accessed Fault-Tolerant Enclosures [Computer science] .. SAF-TE
Sculpture (VRA) .... sculp
Sculpture Review [A publication] (BRI) .... Sculpt R
Scythia (VRA) .... Scyt
Sea Frontiers [A publication] (BRI) .... SeaFront
Sea History [A publication] (BRI) .... Sea H
Second Chance Opportunities and Education for Women (AIE) .. SCOPE
Second Language Learning in the Primary Classroom (AIE) .... SLIPP
Second Surgical Opinion [Insurance] (WYGK) .... SSO
Secondary Audio Program .... SAP
Secondary Education (AIE) .... SE
Secretarial Studies Certificate (AIE) .... SSC
Secretary (DD) .... sec
Secretary-Treasurer (DD) .... sec-treas
Section (VRA) .... sect
Secure Electronic Transactions [Computer science] ... SET
Secure Key-Issuing Authority [Computer science] ..... SKIA
Secure Local-Area Network [Computer science] .... SELANE
Secure Transfer Protocol [Computer science] (DOM) ... STP
Securities Industry Committee on Arbitration (DFIT) .. SICA
See You Later [Computer science] (DOM) CUL8R
Segmented Filamentous Bacteria .... SFB
Segou [Mali] [Airport symbol] (AD) .... SZU
Selective Estrogen-Receptor Modulator [Medicine] .... SERM
Selective Tubal Occlusion Procedure [Medicine] ...... S/TOP
Self-Extracting Archive [Computer science] (DOM) .... SEA
Self-Insurance Group (WYGK) .... SIG
Self-Insured Benefits Plan [Human resources] (WYGK) . SIBP
Self-Managed Account (WYGK) .... SMA
Self-Pumped Phase Conjugator [Optics] .... SPPC
Selma [Alabama] [Airport symbol] (AD) .... SES
Sematan [Sarawak, Malaysia] [Airport symbol] (AD) ... BSE
Semo Aviation [ICAO designator] (AD) VV
Sena Maduereira [Brazil] [Airport symbol] (AD) ...... MAQ
Senator (DFIT) .... Sen
Senegal (VRA) .... sngl
Senior (DFIT) .... Sr
Senior (DD) .... sr
Senior Management Committee (AIE) .... SMC
Senior Management Team (AIE) .... SMT
Senior Service College Fellowship Program [Army] (RDA) .. SSCFP
Seno [Laos] [Airport symbol] (AD) .... SND
Sensitive New-Age Guy .... SNAG
Sepia (VRA) .... sep
Sepulot [Malaysia] [Airport symbol] (AD) .... SPE
Seraph (VRA) .... srph
Serial Copy Master System (DOM) .... SCMS
Serials Review [A publication] (BRI) .... Ser R
Serigraph (VRA) .... seri
Serondela [Botswana] [Airport symbol] (AD) .... SDS
Seronera [Tanzania] [Airport symbol] (AD) .... SEU
Serpa [Portugal] [Airport symbol] (AD) .... SPP
Server Macro Expansion [Computer science] .... SMX
Services to User Populations Section [Disbanded by the Board at the
  Midwinter meeting] .... SUPS
Sesheke [Zambia] [Airport symbol] (AD) .... SJQ
Setif [Algeria] [Airport symbol] (AD) .... STF
Sette Cama [Gabon] [Airport symbol] (AD) .... ZKM
Seventeenth-Century News [A publication] (BRI) ...... Sev Cent N
Severe Learning Difficulties (AIE) .... SLD
Sewanee Review [A publication] (BRI) .... Sew R
Sexual and Personal Relationships of the Disabled (AIE) .. SPOD
Sfumato (VRA) .... sfm
Sgraffito (VRA) .... sgrf
Shakespeare Quarterly [A publication] (BRI) .... Shakes Q
Shamshernagar [Bangladesh] [Airport symbol] (AD) .... ZHM
Shark Bay [Western Australia] [Airport symbol] (AD) . SHB
Sharm es-Sheikh [Israel] [Airport symbol] (AD) ...... SFS
Shavano Air [ICAO designator] (AD) .... ZK
Sheet (VRA) .... sht
Sheffield People's Resource for Information Technology [British]
  (AIE) .... SPRITE
Shelbyville [Tennessee] [Airport symbol] (AD) .... SYI
Shell (VRA) .... shl
Sheltered Employment Procurement and Consultancy Service (AIE) .. SEPACS
Sheltered Placement Scheme (AIE) .... SPS

Shenandoah [A publication] (BRI) .... Shen
Sherbrooke Forest Park [Victoria, Australia] [Airport symbol] (AD) .. SFP
Short Training Courses .... STC
Shute Harbour [Queensland] [Airport symbol] (AD) .... SHU
SIAM Review [A publication] (BRI) .... SIAM Rev
Sian [China] [Airport symbol] (AD) .... SIA
Siberia (VRA) .... Sib
Sicily (VRA) .... Sic
Side Detection System [Delco] (RDA) .... SDS
Sidi Ifni [Morocco] [Airport symbol] (AD) .... SII
Siem Reap [Cambodia] [Airport symbol] (AD) .... REP
Sierra Leone Airways [ICAO designator] (AD) .... LJ
Sight and Sound [A publication] (BRI) .... Si & So
Signature-Tagged Transposon Method [Genetics] .... STM
Signed (DFIT) .... S
Signed & Dated (VRA) .... s&d
Significant Activities of Daily Living (WYGK) .... SADL
Signs: Journal of Women in Culture and Society [A publication] (BRI) .. Signs
Siguiri [Guinea] [Airport symbol] (AD) .... GII
Silfi [Saudi Arabia] [Airport symbol] (AD) .... ZUL
Silhouette Print (VRA) .... SILPT
Silicon Graphics Incorporated [Computer science] .... SGI
Silk (VRA) .... slk
Silkscreen (VRA) .... slksc
Silver (VRA) .... si
Silver Gelatin Print (VRA) .... SGPT
Silver Plains [Queensland] [Airport symbol] (AD) .... VPA
Silver State [ICAO designator] (AD) .... ZG
Silverpoint (VRA) .... sipt
Simanggang [Malaysia] [Airport symbol] (AD) .... SGG
Simla [India] [Airport symbol] (AD) .... SBJ
Simmons [ICAO designator] (AD) .... FP
Simmons Airlines [ICAO designator] (AD) .... MQ
Simple Management Protocol [Computer science] (DOM) . SMP
Simple, Quick & Affordable [Office furniture] .... SQA
Simplified Employee Pension Plan (DFIT) .... SEP
Simulated (VRA) .... sim
Simulated Social Skills Training (AIE) .... SSST
Simulation/Test Acceptance Facility [Army] (RDA) .... STAF
Singapore Airlines [ICAO designator] (AD) .... SQ
Singkep Island [Indonesia] [Airport symbol] (AD) .... SIQ
Single Drug Resistance .... SDR
Single Employer Pension Plan Amendments Act of 1986 (WYGK) .. SEPPA
Single Line Internet Protocol [Telecommunications] (DOM) .. SLIP
Single Minute Exchange of Die [Manufacturing] .... SMED
Single Nucleotide Polymorphism [Genetics] .... SNP
Singlet Delta Oxygen .... SDO
Singora [Thailand] [Airport symbol] (AD) .... SGZ
Sinopia (VRA) .... snpa
Sint Maarten [Netherlands Antilles] [Airport symbol] (AD) .. SXM
Sirajgang [Bangladesh] [Airport symbol] (AD) .... SAJ
Site Server [Microsoft Corp.] [Computer science] .... SSE
Site-Directed Spin Labeling [Physical chemistry] .... SDSL
Sixteenth Century Journal [A publication] (BRI) ..... Six Ct J
Sixth-Plate (VRA) .... SIXT
Size (VRA) .... sz
Skardu [Pakistan] [Airport symbol] (AD) .... KDU
Skeletal Repair System [Medicine] .... SRS
Sketch (VRA) .... sk
Skilda [Algeria] [Airport symbol] (AD) .... SKI
Skill Centre Manager (AIE) .... SCM
Skogar [Iceland] [Airport symbol] (AD) .... SKR
Sky & Telescope [A publication] (BRI) .... S&T
Sky West [ICAO designator] (AD) .... YT
Skyfreighters [ICAO designator] (AD) .... BZ
Skyscraper (VRA) .... skyscr
Skystream Airlines [ICAO designator] (AD) .... DN
Slate (VRA) .... sla
Slavic Review [A publication] (BRI) .... Slav R
Sleep-Induction/Rapid Reawakening System [Military] (RDA) .. SIRRA
Slope-Clearing Events [Geology] .... SCE
Slow-Acting Antirheumatic Drugs [Medicine] .... SAARD's
Slug Discharge Control Plan [Pollution prevention] .. SDCP
Small (VRA) .... sm
Small Business Financial Manager [Microsoft] [Computer science] .. SBFM
Small Business Innovation Research/Small Business Technology Transfer
  [Army] (RDA) .... SBIR/STTR
Small Business Investment Corp. (DFIT) .... SBIC
Small Business Reports [A publication] (BRI) .... Sm Bus Rep
Small Press [A publication] (BRI) .... Sm Pr
Small Press Review [A publication] (BRI) .... Sm Pr R
Small Tight Aspect Ratio Tokamak [Plasma physics] ... START
Small Waterplane Area Twin Hull .... SWATH
Smart Business Supersite [Internet resource] [Computer science] .. SBS
Smart Weapons Operability Enhancement (RDA) .... SWOE
SmithKline Beecham Clinical Laboratories .... SBCL
Smithsonian [A publication] (BRI) .... Smith
Smithsonian Institution's Marine Station .... SMS
Smithtown [Tasmania] [Airport symbol] (AD) .... SIO
Snyder [Texas] [Airport symbol] (AD) .... SNK
Soapstone (VRA) .... soapst
Sobral [Brazil] [Airport symbol] (AD) .... SOB
Soc Trang [South Vietnam] [Airport symbol] (AD) ..... SOA
Social Democratic Party [Germany] [Political party] . SPD
Social Education [A publication] (BRI) .... SE

Social Education Centre (AIE) ... SEC
Social Forces [*A publication*] (BRI) ... SF
Social Science (DD) ... SocSc
Social Science Computer Review [*A publication*] (BRI) ... SocSciComR
Social Science Quarterly [*A publication*] (BRI) ... SSQ
Social Service Review [*A publication*] (BRI) ... Soc Ser R
Social Studies [*A publication*] (BRI) ... SS
Social Work [*A publication*] (BRI) ... Soc W
Sociedad Aeronautica Medellin [*ICAO designator*] (AD) ... MM
Societe Aeronautique Jurassienne [*ICAO designator*] (AD) ... YX
Societe des Artistes en Arts Visuels du Quebec [*1980, founded 1966 as SAPQ, CPQ from 1978, CAPQ from 1982*] [*Canada*] (NGC) ... SAAVQ
Societe des Artistes Francais, Paris [*1880*] [*French*] (NGC) ... SAF
Societe des Artistes Professionnels du Quebec [*1966, CPQ from 1978, SAAVQ from 1980, CAPQ from 1982*] [*Canada*] (NGC) ... SAPQ
Societe des Arts Plastiques de la Province de Quebec, Quebec City [*1955*] [*Canada*] (NGC) ... SAP
Societe Nationale des Beaux-Arts, Paris [*1890*] [*French*] (NGC) ... SNBA
Society [*A publication*] (BRI) ... Soc
Society for Italian Studies (AIE) ... SIS
Society for Quality Assurance ... SQA
Society of Analytical Psychology (AIE) ... SAP
Society of Canadian Artists, Montreal [*1868-72*] (NGC) ... SCA
Society of Canadian Painter-Etchers and Engravers [*1916-76*] (NGC) ... CPE
Society of Chief Inspectors and Advisers [*British*] (AIE) ... SCIA
Society of Graphic Art, Toronto [*1912, founded c.1903 as GAC, CSGA from 1923*] [*Canada*] (NGC) ... SGA
Society of Management Accountants of Ontario [*Canada*] (DD) ... SMAO
Sociological Review [*A publication*] (BRI) ... Socio R
Sociology (DD) ... Soc
Soddu [*Ethiopia*] [*Airport symbol*] (AD) ... SXU
Sodium Hydroxide (AD) ... NaOH
Soffit (VRA) ... sft
Software Capability Evaluation (RDA) ... SCE
Software Development Framework (RDA) ... SDF
Software Publishing Corp. ... SPC
Solar Heliospheric Observatory ... SOHO
Solar Ultraviolet Measurements of Emitted Radiation [*Instrumentation*] ... SUMER
Soldier Portable On-System Repair Tool [*Military*] ... SPORT
Soldier-Information Interface (RDA) ... SII
Solomon Islands Airways [*ICAO designator*] (AD) ... IE
Soluble Nonreactive Phosphorus [*Marine science*] ... SNP
Solutrean (VRA) ... Soltr
Somali Airlines [*ICAO designator*] (AD) ... HH
Soroti [*Uganda*] [*Airport symbol*] (AD) ... SZI
Sorreisa [*Norway*] [*Airport symbol*] (AD) ... SRR
Sound Blaster [*Computer science*] (DOM) ... SB
Source Image Format (DOM) ... SIF
South (VRA) ... S
South Africa (VRA) ... S Afr
South America (VRA) ... S Am
South Atlantic Quarterly [*A publication*] (BRI) ... SAQ
South Carolina Review [*A publication*] (BRI) ... South CR
South Central [*ICAO designator*] (AD) ... XE
South Coast Airlines [*ICAO designator*] (AD) ... SS
South East Wales Access Consortium (AIE) ... SEWAC
South Galway [*Queensland*] [*Airport symbol*] (AD) ... ZGL
South Molle Islands [*Queensland*] [*Airport symbol*] (AD) ... QSM
South Pacific Airlines of New Zealand (AD) ... PQ
South Pacific Island Airways [*ICAO designator*] (AD) ... HK
South Western Examinations Board [*Education*] (AIE) ... SWExB
Southeast Asia Association on Seismology and Earthquake Engineering ... SEASEE
Southeast Asian Nuclear Weapons Free Zone ... SEANWFZ
Southeast Skyways [*ICAO designator*] (AD) ... SE
Southeastern Commuter Airlines [*ICAO designator*] (AD) ... WH
Southend [*Scotland*] [*Airport symbol*] (AD) ... SEN
Southern (VRA) ... S
Southern Cultures [*A publication*] (BRI) ... South Cul
Southern Education and Library Board [*Northern Ireland*] (AIE) ... SELB
Southern Examining Accreditation Council (AIE) ... SEAC
Southern Humanities Review [*A publication*] (BRI) ... South HR
Southern Living [*A publication*] (BRI) ... S Liv
Southern Nevada [*ICAO designator*] (AD) ... FO
Southern Pines [*North Carolina*] [*Airport symbol*] (AD) ... SOP
Southern Regional Examinations Board [*Education*] (AIE) ... SREB
Southern Review [*A publication*] (BRI) ... South R
Southern Universities' Management Services (AIE) ... SUMS
Southwest Airlines [*ICAO designator*] (AD) ... NU
Southwest Airlines [*ICAO designator*] (AD) ... WN
Southwest Fisheries Science Center [*San Diego, CA*] ... SWFSC
Southwest Review [*A publication*] (BRI) ... SWR
Space Environment Center ... SEC
Space Full Time Equivalent (AIE) ... SFTE
Spain (VRA) ... Spa
Spanish Wells [*Bahamas*] [*Airport symbol*] (AD) ... SWL
Sparkman Centre for International Public Health Education (AIE) ... SCIPHE
Spatial Equalization ... SEq
Spatial Paradigm for Information Retrieval and Exploration [*Computer science*] ... SPIRE
Spearfish [*South Dakota*] [*Airport symbol*] (AD) ... SPF
Special Administrative Region [*Hong Kong*] ... SAR
Special Adult Learning Programmes Association (AIE) ... SALPA
Special Committee on Trade ... SCT
Special Development Assistance Fund ... SDAF
Special Drawing Rights [*Investment term*] (DFIT) ... SDR
Special Educational Needs (AIE) ... SEN
Special Educational Needs Joint Initiative for Training (AIE) ... SENJIT
Special Libraries [*A publication*] (BRI) ... SL
Special Needs Action Programme [*Education*] (AIE) ... SNAP
Special Needs in the Ordinary School (AIE) ... SNIOS
Special Needs Support Team [*Education*] (AIE) ... SNST
Special Temporary Employment Programme (AIE) ... STEP
Special Vehicle Team [*Automotive engineering*] ... SVT
Specialized Carriers & Rigging Association ... SCRA
Species-Area [*Ecology*] ... SA
Spectator [*A publication*] (BRI) ... Spec
Speculum [*A publication*] (BRI) ... Specu
Spikenard (AD) ... nard
Spin-Dependent Delocalization [*Physical chemistry*] ... SDD
Spoken English for Industry and Commerce (AIE) ... SEFIC
Sport-Luxury Vehicle ... SLV
Spray (VRA) ... spy
Springfield [*Ohio*] [*Airport symbol*] (AD) ... SGH
Springvale [*Queensland*] [*Airport symbol*] (AD) ... ZVG
Spruce (VRA) ... spr
Square (VRA) ... sq
Square (DD) ... Sq
St. Andrews Airways [*ICAO designator*] (AD) ... CW
St. Barthelemy [*Leeward Islands, West Indies*] [*Airport symbol*] (AD) ... BTO
St. Croix Island (VRA) ... VI
St. Helens [*Tasmania*] [*Airport symbol*] (AD) ... HLS
St. John Island (VRA) ... VI
St. Johns [*Antigua, Leeward Islands, West Indies*] [*Airport symbol*] (AD) ... SJH
St. Joseph [*Missouri*] [*Airport symbol*] (AD) ... STJ
St. Moritz [*Switzerland*] [*Airport symbol*] (AD) ... TQV
St. Thomas Island (VRA) ... VI
Staff and Educational Development Association (AIE) ... SEDA
Staff Development Management System (AIE) ... SDMS
Staff Model Health Maintenance Organization [*Insurance*] (WYGK) ... SMHMO
Staged Assessment in Learning (AIE) ... SAIL
Stained Glass (VRA) ... stdgls
Stainless Steel (VRA) ... ss
Stamford [*Connecticut*] [*Airport symbol*] (AD) ... SCC
Stand Magazine [*A publication*] (BRI) ... Stand
Standard & Poor's (DFIT) ... S&P
Standard & Poor's 100 Stock Index (DFIT) ... OEX
Standard Army Retail Supply System/Objective Supply Capability (RDA) ... SARSS/OSC
Standard Image Format [*Computer science*] ... SIF
Standing Advisory Council for Religious Education (AIE) ... SACRE
Standing Conference of Associations for Guidance in Education Settings (AIE) ... SCAGES
Standing Conference of Principals and Directors of Colleges and Institutes of Higher Education (AIE) ... SCPDCIHE
Standing Conference of Principals of Tertiary and Sixth Form Colleges [*British*] (AIE) ... SCOTVIC
Standing Conference of University Drama Departments (AIE) ... SCUDD
Standing Conference of Youth Organisations (AIE) ... SCOYO
Standing Conference on Education Development (AIE) ... SCED
Stanford Computer Industry Project ... SCIP
Star [*Mauritania*] [*Airport symbol*] (AD) ... ATR
Star Airways [*ICAO designator*] (AD) ... ZR
Star Petroleum Refinery Complex [*Thailand*] ... SPRC
Starburst Giant Cells [*Cytology*] ... SGC
Starcke [*Queensland*] [*Airport symbol*] (AD) ... SUR
Stargardt Disease [*Medicine*] ... STGT
Stateswest Airlines [*ICAO designator*] (AD) ... YW
Station (VRA) ... sta
Station (DD) ... Stn
Statistics (DD) ... Stats
Staverton [*England*] [*Airport symbol*] (AD) ... STV
Steatite (VRA) ... steat
Steel (VRA) ... stl
Steenkool [*West Irian, Indonesia*] [*Airport symbol*] (AD) ... ZKL
Stencil (VRA) ... stncl
Stereo (VRA) ... ster
Stereo Review [*A publication*] (BRI) ... Stereo
Stereoview (VRA) ... STER
Sterling Silver (VRA) ... strl si
Stewart Island [*ICAO designator*] (AD) ... SJ
Stich (VRA) ... sti
Stimulant to Sustain Performance (RDA) ... STIMSUP
Stock (VRA) ... stk
Stock Exchange of Thailand [*Thailand*] ... SET
Stokmarknes [*Norway*] [*Airport symbol*] (AD) ... ZTK
Stomach-Partitioning Gastrojejunostomy [*Surgery*] ... SPGJ
Stone (VRA) ... st
Stoneware (VRA) ... stwr
Storage Data Acceleration [*Computer science*] ... SDX
Store Room (VRA) ... strm
Strategic Quality Management (AIE) ... SQM
Strategies and Errors in Secondary Mathematics [*Project*] (AIE) ... SESM
Street (VRA) ... st
Street (DD) ... St
Streptococcal Pyrogenic Exotoxin B [*Immunochemistry*] ... SPEB
Streptococcal Pyrogenic Exotoxin C [*Immunochemistry*] ... SPEC
Streptococcal Superantigen [*Immunochemistry*] ... SSA
Stretcher (VRA) ... stret
String (VRA) ... strg

Stringcourse (VRA) .... strgcr
Stucco (VRA) .... stu
Student Progress Questionnaire (AIE) .... SPQ
Students' and Teachers' Integrated Learning Environment (AIE) .... STILE
Student's Own Record of Education (AIE) .... STORE
Studies in Short Fiction [*A publication*] (BRI) .... SSF
Studies in the Decorative Arts [*A publication*] (BRI) .... SDA
Study (VRA) .... sdy
Study of Cataloguing Computer Software (AIE) .... SoCCS
Study Skills Unit (AIE) .... SSU
Stylus (VRA) .... sty
Subaddressing [*Telecommunications*] (DOM) .... SUB
Subject Authority Cooperative Program [*American Library Association*] .... SACO
Submerged Floating Tunnell .... SFT
Suburban Airlines [*ICAO designator*] (AD) .... UQ
Suburban Service (DD) .... SS
Succursale (DD) .... succ
Sudan Airways [*ICAO designator*] (AD) .... SD
Sukhumi [*USSR*] [*Airport symbol*] (AD) .... SUI
Sukkertoppen [*Greenland*] [*Airport symbol*] (AD) .... JSU
Sulaco [*Honduras*] [*Airport symbol*] (AD) .... SCD
Sulayel [*Saudi Arabia*] [*Airport symbol*] (AD) .... SLF
Sumatra (VRA) .... Sumat
Sumbawa [*Indonesia*] [*Airport symbol*] (AD) .... SWQ
Summerside [*Prince Edward Island*] [*Airport symbol*] (AD) .... YSU
Sumptuary (VRA) .... sumpt
Sun West [*ICAO designator*] (AD) .... KY
Sun World [*ICAO designator*] (AD) .... JK
Sun-Air of Scandinavia [*ICAO designator*] (AD) .... EZ
Sunaire Lines [*ICAO designator*] (AD) .... OO
Sunbird [*ICAO designator*] (AD) .... ED
Sunbird [*ICAO designator*] (AD) .... QP
Super Eight [*Motion picture*] (VRA) .... SUPE
Superintendent (DD) .... supt

Supervisor (DD) .... supvr
Supplemental Executive Retirement Plan [*Human resources*] (WYGK) .... SERP
Support for Innovation Project (AIE) .... SIP
Support Staff Interests Round Table [*American Library Association*] .... SSIRT
Surface (VRA) .... sur
Surface Acoustic Wave [*Engineering*] .... SAW
Surface Design Journal [*A publication*] (BRI) .... Surface DJ
Surfdale [*Waiheke Island, New Zealand*] [*Airport symbol*] (AD) .... SFU
Surinam Airways [*ICAO designator*] (AD) .... PY
Surkhet [*Nepal*] [*Airport symbol*] (AD) .... SUS
Surveillance and Reconnaissance Ground Equipment .... SARGE
Susquehanna [*ICAO designator*] (AD) .... FR
Swakopmund [*South-West Africa*] [*Airport symbol*] (AD) .... SWP
Swan Hill [*Victoria, Australia*] [*Airport symbol*] (AD) .... SWH
Swaziland (VRA) .... Swzld
Swedair [*ICAO designator*] (AD) .... JG
Sweden (VRA) .... Swe
Swedish Trial in Old Patients with Hypertension .... STOP-H
Sweetwater [*Texas*] [*Airport symbol*] (AD) .... SWW
Swift Current [*Saskatchewan*] [*Airport symbol*] (AD) .... YYN
Swift-Aire Lines [*ICAO designator*] (AD) .... WI
Switzerland (VRA) .... Switz
SX-70 (VRA) SX70
Sydaero [*ICAO designator*] (AD) .... UF
Sympalmograph (VRA) .... SYMGR
Synaptic Transporter Current [*Neurochemistry*] .... STC
Sync-link DRAM [*Display Random Access Memory*] [*Computer science*].... SLDRAM
Synthetic (VRA) .... synt
Synthetic Aperture RADAR .... SAR
Synthetic Theater of War-Systems Engineering, Integration, and Demonstration [*Military*] (RDA) .... STOW-SKID
Syria (VRA) .... Syr
System for Improved Acoustic Performance .... SIAP
Systems Technology Inc. .... STI

T

By Meaning

TAAG-Angola Airlines [*ICAO designator*] (AD) .... DT
Tabernacle (VRA) .... tbnle
Tableland [*Western Australia*] [*Airport symbol*] (AD) .... TBL
Tablon de Tamara [*Colombia*] [*Airport symbol*] (AD) .... TTM
Tacoma [*Washington*] [*Airport symbol*] (AD) .... TIW
Tactical Automated Situation Receiver [*Military*] .... TASR
Tactical Wheeled Vehicles Remanufacture Program [*Army*] (RDA) .... TWVRP
Taguatinga [*Brazil*] [*Airport symbol*] (AD) .... TGX
Taichung [*Formosa*] [*Airport symbol*] (AD) .... TXG
Taiping [*China*] [*Airport symbol*] (AD) .... TPG
Taiwan (VRA) .... Taiw
Tak [*Thailand*] [*Airport symbol*] (AD) .... TKL
Takoradi [*Ghana*] [*Airport symbol*] (AD) .... TKD
Talair [*ICAO designator*] (AD) .... GV
Talasea [*New Britain, New Guinea*] [*Airport symbol*] (AD) .... TLW
Talgarno [*Western Australia*] [*Airport symbol*] (AD) .... TLR
Talpa [*New Mexico*] [*Airport symbol*] (AD) .... TLP
Taltal [*Chile*] [*Airport symbol*] (AD) .... TTC
Tambao [*Upper Volta*] [*Airport symbol*] (AD) .... TMQ
Tananarive [*Malagasy*] [*Airport symbol*] (AD) .... TNR
Tanbar [*Queensland*] [*Airport symbol*] (AD) .... TXR
Tansavio [*ICAO designator*] (AD) .... TD
Tape Archive [*Computer science*] (DOM) .... TAR
Tapestry (VRA) .... tap
Taputuquara [*Brazil*] [*Airport symbol*] (AD) .... TPU
Tara [*Queensland*] [*Airport symbol*] (AD) .... XTR
Taracua [*Brazil*] [*Airport symbol*] (AD) .... TAJ
Taranto [*Italy*] [*Airport symbol*] (AD) .... TAR
Tarauaca [*Brazil*] [*Airport symbol*] (AD) .... TRQ
Tarbes [*France*] [*Airport symbol*] (AD) .... TFR
Tarfaya [*Morocco*] [*Airport symbol*] (AD) .... TFY
Target Benefit Plan [*Human resources*] (WYGK) .... TBP
Target-Organ Damage [*Medicine*] .... TOD
Taroom [*Queensland*] [*Airport symbol*] (AD) .... XTO
Tarpaulin (VRA) .... tarp
Tarragona [*Spain*] [*Airport symbol*] (AD) .... TGN
Tartagal [*Argentina*] [*Airport symbol*] (AD) .... TTG
Tauramena [*Colombia*] [*Airport symbol*] (AD) .... TAU
Tax Equity and Responsibility Act of 1982 (WYGK) .... TERA
Taxation (DD) .... tax
TCI Satellite Entertainment .... TSATA
TCI: The Business of Entertainment Technology and Design
[*A publication*] (BRI) .... TCI
TDR: The Drama Review [*A publication*] (BRI) .... TDR
Teacher Assessment (AIE) .... TA
Teacher Contact Ratio (AIE) .... TCR
Teacher Educators and Advisers in Media Education (AIE) .... TEAME
Teacher Examiner Mark Sheet (AIE) .... TEMS
Teachers' Benevolent Fund (AIE) .... TBF
Teachers' Centre (AIE) .... TC
Teachers College Record [*A publication*] (BRI) .... TCR
Teachers' Labour League [*British*] (AIE) .... TLL
Teaching and Learning Support (AIE) .... TLS
Teaching Company Scheme (AIE) .... TCS
Teaching Music [*A publication*] (BRI) .... Teach Mus
Tebessa [*Algeria*] [*Airport symbol*] (AD) .... TSS
Technical and Agricultural College (AIE) .... TAC
Technical and Vocational Education Initiative: Pilot (AIE) .... TVEI(P)
Technical Education Institute (AIE) .... TEI
Technical Standards for Library Automation .... TESLA
Technology (DD) .... tech
Technology and Culture [*A publication*] (BRI) .... T&C
Technology Review [*A publication*] (BRI) .... Tec R
Technology through Electricity, Electronics, and Microelectronics
(AIE) .... TEEM
Technology Without an Interesting Name [*Computer science*] .... TWAIN
Ted Nugent United Sportsmen of America .... TNUSA
Tejas Airlines [*ICAO designator*] (AD) .... TB
Tela [*Honduras*] [*Airport symbol*] (AD) .... TEA
Telecommunications (DD) .... telecommun
Telecommunications and Information Infrastructure Assistance Program
[*Department of Commerce*] .... TIIAP
Telescopes in Education .... TIE
TeleService Resources .... TSR
Television Quarterly [*A publication*] (BRI) .... TV Q
Telukbetung [*Sumatra, Indonesia*] [*Airport symbol*] (AD) .... TKG

Teminabuan [*West Irian, Indonesia*] [*Airport symbol*] (AD) .... TXM
Temora [*New South Wales*] [*Airport symbol*] (AD) .... TMT
[*Egg*] Tempera (VRA) .... temp
Temple (VRA) .... tmpl
Temporary Assistance to Needy Families [*An association*] .... TANF
Temporary Short-Time Working Compensation Scheme (AIE) .... TSTWCS
Temsco Airlines [*ICAO designator*] (AD) .... KN
Temuco [*Chile*] [*Airport symbol*] (AD) .... ZCO
Tenkodogo [*Upper Volta*] [*Airport symbol*] (AD) .... TEG
Tennessee Airways [*ICAO designator*] (AD) .... ZN
Tepidarium (VRA) .... tepid
Termez [*USSR*] [*Airport symbol*] (AD) .... TMZ
Terminal Portability [*Telecommunications*] (DOM) .... TP
Terminal Repeller Unconstrained Subenergy Tunneling [*An algorithm for
global optimization*] .... TRUST
Terrace (VRA) .... terr
Terrace (DD) .... Terr
Terracotta (VRA) .... ter
Terrain-Intelligence Integration Prototype [*Army*] (RDA) .... TIIP
Terrasse (DD) .... tsse
Tertiary Education Research Centre [*British*] (AIE) .... TERC
Tessenei [*Ethiopia*] [*Airport symbol*] (AD) .... TES
Tessera (VRA) .... tes
Teterboro [*New Jersey*] [*Airport symbol*] (AD) .... TEB
Texas Academic Skills Program .... TASP
Texas Assessment of Academic Skills .... TAAS
Texas Educational Assessment of Minimum Skills .... TEAMS
Texas International Airlines [*ICAO designator*] (AD) .... TI
Texeira [*Portugal*] [*Airport symbol*] (AD) .... TXA
Textile (VRA) .... txtl
Textile Care and Rental Industry Council for Education (AIE) .... TRICE
Texture (VRA) .... text
Thai Airways [*ICAO designator*] (AD) .... TG
Thai Airways [*ICAO designator*] (AD) .... TH
Thakhek [*Laos*] [*Airport symbol*] (AD) .... THK
Thakurgaon [*Bangladesh*] [*Airport symbol*] (AD) .... TKR
Thames Action and Resources Group for Education and Training [*British*]
(AIE) .... TARGET
Thanatophoric Dysplasia [*Lethal dwarfism*] .... TD
Thangool [*Queensland*] [*Airport symbol*] (AD) .... THG
Thargomindah [*Queensland*] [*Airport symbol*] (AD) .... XTG
The International English School (AIE) .... TIES
The Maintenance Council .... TMC
Theatre (VRA) .... thtr
Theatre History Studies [*A publication*] (BRI) .... THS
Theatre Journal [*A publication*] (BRI) .... Theat J
Theodore [*Queensland*] [*Airport symbol*] (AD) .... THJ
Theological Studies [*A publication*] (BRI) .... Theol St
Theology Today [*A publication*] (BRI) .... TT
Theory (VRA) .... thry
Therapeutic Drug Utilization Review [*Insurance*] (WYGK) .... TDUR
Thermal Hysteresis Proteins [*Biochemistry*] .... THP
Thermal Polyaspartate [*Organic chemistry*] .... TPA
Thermally Pulsing, Asymptotic Giant Branch [*Astronomy*] .... TP-AGB
Theron Airways [*ICAO designator*] (AD) .... LU
Thira [*Greece*] [*Airport symbol*] (AD) .... JTR
Third World Resources [*A publication*] (BRI) .... TWR
Thread (VRA) .... thrd
Threaded-Neill-Concelman (DOM) .... TNC
Three Axis Rotational Flight Simulator [*Military*] (RDA) .... TARFS
Three-Dimensional Geometry File [*Computer science*] (DOM) 3-DGF
Three-Dimensional Laminate 3DL
Three-Party Service [*Telecommunications*] (DOM) 3PTY
Threepenny Review [*A publication*] (BRI) .... TPR
Thunder Bay [*Ontario*] [*Airport symbol*] (AD) .... YGT
Thylungra [*Queensland*] [*Airport symbol*] (AD) .... THY
Tiaret [*Algeria*] [*Airport symbol*] (AD) .... TRT
Tibet (VRA) .... Tib
Tibooburra [*New South Wales*] [*Airport symbol*] (AD) .... TYB
Ticking (VRA) .... tik
Tientsin [*China*] [*Airport symbol*] (AD) .... TSN
Tiered Premium System [*Insurance*] (WYGK) .... TPS
Tijuana [*Mexico*] [*Airport symbol*] (AD) .... TIJ
Tiko [*Cameroon*] [*Airport symbol*] (AD) .... TKC
Timbedra [*Mauritania*] [*Airport symbol*] (AD) .... TMD
Time-Division Multiplexor [*Computer science*] (DOM) .... TDM

Time-Resolved Liquid Scintillation Counting [*Instrumentation*] .... TR-LSC
Times Educational Supplement [*A publication*] (BRI) .... TES
Times Educational Supplement Scotland (AIE) .... TESS
Times Higher Education Supplement (AIE) .... THES
Times Literary Supplement [*A publication*] (BRI) .... TLS
Times Mirror Magazines [*A publication*] .... TMM
Timimoun [*Algeria*] [*Airport symbol*] (AD) .... TMX
Tint (VRA) .... tnt
Tintype (VRA) .... TTYP
Tiree Island [*Scotland*] [*Airport symbol*] (AD) .... TIR
Tissue (VRA) .... tis
Tissue Respiratory Factors [*Medicine*] .... TRF
Titusville [*Florida*] [*Airport symbol*] (AD) .... TIX
To My Knowledge [*Computer science*] (DOM) .... TMK
Toa Domestic Airlines [*ICAO designator*] (AD) .... JD
Tocantina [*Goias, Brazil*] [*Airport symbol*] (AD) .... TOX
Tocantinopolis [*Brazil*] [*Airport symbol*] (AD) .... TPY
Tocopilla [*Chile*] [*Airport symbol*] (AD) .... TOQ
Toensberg [*Norway*] [*Airport symbol*] (AD) .... TNS
Tomb (VRA) .... tb
Toned (VRA) .... tn
Tonga Air Service [*ICAO designator*] (AD) .... DH
Tongo [*Sierra Leone*] [*Airport symbol*] (AD) .... TNQ
Tonopah [*Nevada*] [*Airport symbol*] (AD) .... TPH
Tornado Electronic Messaging System [*Computer science*] .... TEMS
Torontair [*ICAO designator*] (AD) .... WJ
Toronto Art Students' League [*1886-1903*] [*Canada*] (NGC) .... TASL
Tororo [*Uganda*] [*Airport symbol*] (AD) .... TOW
Tortoise (VRA) .... tort
Tortola [*British Virgin Islands*] [*Airport symbol*] (AD) .... TLB
Total Antioxidant Activity [*Chemistry*] .... TAA
Total Entertainment Network [*Online gaming service*] .... TEN
Total Homocysteine [*Clinical chemistry*] .... tHcy
Total Nonstructural Carbohydrates .... TNC
Total Officer Personnel Management [*Army*] (RDA) .... TOPMIS
Total Virus Defense [*McAfee*] [*Computer science*] .... TVD
Tougan [*Upper Volta*] [*Airport symbol*] (AD) .... TUQ
Touraine [*South Vietnam*] [*Airport symbol*] (AD) .... TOU
Touraine Air Transport [*ICAO designator*] (AD) .... IJ
Toward (VRA) .... towd
Tower (VRA) .... twr
Tower Hamlets Reading Initiative via Exploration [*British*] (AIE) .... THRIVE
Town Hall (VRA) .... town ha
Township (DD) .... Twp
Toxic Organic Management Plan [*Pollution prevention*] .... TOMP
Trabeated (VRA) .... trab
Tracery (VRA) .... trac
Traces (VRA) .... tr
Trade Acceptance [*Investment term*] (DFIT) .... TA
Trades Union Research Centre (AIE) .... TURC
Traditional Chinese Medicine .... TCM
Train America's Workforce [*An association*] (WYGK) .... TAW
Training Access Point (AIE) .... TAP
Training Agency Intelligence Unit (AIE) .... TAIU
Training and Approaches to Careers Education [*Project*] (AIE) .... TRACE
Training and Development Lead Body (AIE) .... TDLB
Training for Skill Ownership (AIE) .... TSO
Training Needs Analysis (AIE) .... TNA
Training Occupational Classification (AIE) .... TOC
Training Place in Industry (AIE) .... TPI
Training Standards Advisory Service (AIE) .... TSAS
Training Technology Transfer Act of 1984 (WYGK) .... TTTA
Trans Catalina Airlines [*ICAO designator*] (AD) .... DC
Trans Mediterranean [*ICAO designator*] (AD) .... TL
Trans Mo Airlines [*ICAO designator*] (AD) .... XU
Trans Mountain Airlines [*ICAO designator*] (AD) .... OW
Trans New York [*ICAO designator*] (AD) .... YH
Trans Pennsylvania Airlines [*ICAO designator*] (AD) .... PF
Trans Western Airlines of Utah [*ICAO designator*] (AD) .... WZ
TransAct Technologies .... TACT
Transaction Information Systems .... TIS
Transamerica [*ICAO designator*] (AD) .... TV
Trans-Australia Airlines [*ICAO designator*] (AD) .... TN
Transbrasil [*ICAO designator*] (AD) .... TR
Trans-California [*ICAO designator*] (AD) .... ZO
Trans-Central [*ICAO designator*] (AD) .... ZM
Trans-Colorado [*ICAO designator*] (AD) .... VJ
Transept (VRA) .... trsp
Trans-European Exchange and Transfer Consortium (AIE) .... TEXT
Transfer (VRA) .... transf

Transfer Scheme Handbook (AIE) .... TSH
Transformation-Associated Recombination [*Genetics*] .... TAR
Transition Education Advisory Committee (AIE) .... TEAC
Transition to Working Life [*Project*] (AIE) .... TWL
Trans-Jamaican Airlines [*ICAO designator*] (AD) .... JQ
Transkei Airways [*ICAO designator*] (AD) .... KV
Translation Review [*A publication*] .... TranslRev
Translation Review Supplement [*A publication*] (BRI) .... TranslRevS
Translocated Basilic Vein Arteriovenous Fistula [*Surgery*] .... TBAVF
Translucent (VRA) .... transl
Transmission Control Protocol/Internet Protocol [*Computer science*]
     (DOM) .... TCP/IP
Transmit (WDMC) .... XMT
Transparency (VRA) .... trans
Transportation (DD) .... trans
Transportation (VRA) .... transp
Transportation Act of 1989 (WYGK) .... TA
Transportes Aereos de Cabo Verde [*ICAO designator*] (AD) .... VR
Transportes Aereos Nacionales [*ICAO designator*] (AD) .... TX
Trans-Provincial Airlines [*ICAO designator*] (AD) .... CD
Transverse Magnetic Circular X-Ray Dichroism [*Physics*] .... TMCXD
Trans-West [*ICAO designator*] (AD) .... WW
Trapping (VRA) .... trap
Travel Industry School (AIE) .... TRAVIS
Travel to Interview Scheme (AIE) .... TIS
Travel to Work Area (AIE) .... TTWA
Travelair Goteborg [*ICAO designator*] (AD) .... RF
Travel-Holiday [*A publication*] (BRI) .... Trav
Travertine (VRA) .... trvtn
Treasurer (DD) .... treas
Treasury (VRA) .... treas
Treasury Management Association .... TMA
Treasury's Inflation Protection Securities .... TIPS
Tres Lagoas [*Brazil*] [*Airport symbol*] (AD) .... TLG
Treviso [*Italy*] [*Airport symbol*] (AD) .... TRY
Trial for Early Alcohol Treatment .... TrEAT
Tribune Books [*A publication*] (BRI) .... Trib Bks
Trichinopoly [*India*] [*Airport symbol*] (AD) .... TRZ
Triclinium (VRA) .... tricl
Triforium (VRA) .... trifr
Trincomalee [*Ceylon*] [*Airport symbol*] (AD) .... TRR
Trinidad [*Colombia*] [*Airport symbol*] (AD) .... TDA
Trinidad [*Cuba*] [*Airport symbol*] (AD) .... TND
Trinidad and Tobago Air Services [*ICAO designator*] (AD) .... HU
Triptych (VRA) .... tpyt
Tris(methoxy)mercaptopropylsilane [*Organic chemistry*] .... TMMPS
Triumphal Arch (VRA) .... trim arh
Trois Rivieres [*Quebec*] [*Airport symbol*] (AD) .... YRQ
Tromsoe [*Norway*] [*Airport symbol*] (AD) .... TOA
Tropic Air [*ICAO designator*] (AD) .... CN
Tropic Air Services [*ICAO designator*] (AD) .... EP
Tropical Array Ocean .... TAO
Tropospheric Emission Sensor .... TES
Truck Manufacturers Association .... TMA
Trujillo [*Honduras*] [*Airport symbol*] (AD) .... TJI
Trumeau (VRA) .... trum
Trump Shuttle [*ICAO designator*] (AD) .... TB
Trust Originated Preferred Securities [*Finance*] .... TOPrS
Tubarao [*Brazil*] [*Airport symbol*] (AD) .... TUB
Tuberous Sclerosis Complex [*Medicine*] .... TSC
Tubing (VRA) .... tub
Tubular (VRA) .... tub
Tulip (VRA) .... tlp
Tullahoma [*Tennessee*] [*Airport symbol*] (AD) .... THA
Tulsa Studies in Women's Literature [*A publication*] (BRI) .... TSWL
Tunisia (VRA) .... Tun
Turk Hava Yollari [*ICAO designator*] (AD) .... TK
Turkey (VRA) .... Turk
Turkey Creek [*Western Australia*] [*Airport symbol*] (AD) .... TKY
Turks Islands [*West Indies*] [*Airport symbol*] (AD) .... TKI
Turqoise (VRA) .... turq
Turret Electronics Unit [*Military*] (RDA) .... TEU
Turtle Airways [*ICAO designator*] (AD) .... KT
Tuxpan [*Mexico*] [*Airport symbol*] (AD) .... TUX
Tuxtla Gutierrez [*Mexico*] [*Airport symbol*] (AD) .... TGS
Tuy Hoa [*South Vietnam*] [*Airport symbol*] (AD) .... TBB
Tyee [*Alaska*] [*Airport symbol*] (AD) .... TEE
Tympanium (VRA) .... tymp
Typography (VRA) .... typogr
Tyrolean Airways [*ICAO designator*] (AD) .... VO

U
By Meaning

Uaupes [*Brazil*] [*Airport symbol*] (AD) .... UUP
Uganda (VRA) .... Ugan
Uganda Airlines [*ICAO designator*] (AD) .... QU
Ukiah [*California*] [*Airport symbol*] (AD) .... UKI
Ulster Teacher's Union [*Ireland*] (AIE) .... UTU
Ultrafast Electron Diffraction [*Physics*] .... UED
Ultra-High Definition Television (DOM) .... UDTV
Ultraviolet (VRA) .... uv
Umanak [*Greenland*] [*Airport symbol*] (AD) .... UMK
Umtali [*Zimbabwe*] [*Airport symbol*] (AD) .... UTA
Umuarama [*Brazil*] [*Airport symbol*] (AD) .... UMU
Unbound (WDMC) .... unb
Unbound (WDMC) .... Unbd
Undeliverables [*Fundraising*] .... UDs
Underglaze (VRA) .... undglz
Understanding Industry (AIE) .... UI
Understanding without Heavy Acronym Training (AIE) .... UWHAT
Underwater Naturalist [*A publication*] (BRI) .... Under Nat
Underwriter (DFIT) .... UW
Unfair Labor Practices (WYGK) .... ULP
Unglazed (VRA) .... unglz
Unguia [*Colombia*] [*Airport symbol*] (AD) .... UNC
Uniao da Vitoria [*Brazil*] [*Airport symbol*] (AD) .... UNI
Unidentified (VRA) .... unid
Unified Energy System [*Russia*] .... UES
Unified Information Access System .... UIAS
Unified Programme [*Education*] (AIE) .... UP
Union of Students in Ireland (AIE) .... USI
Unique (VRA) .... uniq
Unit-Based Scheme (AIE) .... UBS
United Air [*ICAO designator*] (AD) .... UE
United Bowhunters of Connecticut .... UBC
United Defense Limited Partnership (RDA) .... UDLP
United Kingdom Airlines [*ICAO designator*] (AD) .... Air UK
United Kingdom Education and Research Networking Association
    (AIE) .... UKERNA
United Nations Commission on Human Rights .... UNCHR
United Nations Conference on Science and Technology Education for
    Development (AIE) .... UNCSTD
United Nations Electoral Assistance Team .... UN/EAT
United Nations Environment Program Governing Council .... UNEP GC
United Nations Science and Technology Advisory Committee (AIE) ...... UNSTAC
United States Environmental Protection Agency .... US EPA

United States Outfitters .... USO
Universal Airways [*ICAO designator*] (AD) .... UV
Universal Product Code .... UPC
Universities and Colleges Teaching, Learning, and Information Group
    [*Universities and Colleges Information Systems Association*] (AIE) .... UCTLIG
Universities Council for the Education of Teachers (AIE) .... UCET
University (VRA) .... univ
University Bookman [*A publication*] (BRI) .... Univ Bkmn
University College Buckingham [*British*] (AIE) .... UCB
University Department of Education (AIE) .... UDE
University Library and Information Services Committee [*Committee of Vice
    Chancellors and Principals*] [*British*] (AIE) .... ULISC
University Microfilms, Inc. (WDMC) .... UMI
University of London and East Anglia Consortium [*British*] (AIE) .... ULEAC
University-Enterprise Training Partnership [*European Community*] (AIE) ..... UETP
Unknown (VRA) .... unk
Unsized Canvas (VRA) .... unsz c
Unst [*Shetland Islands, Scotland*] [*Airport symbol*] (AD) .... UNE
Untempered (VRA) .... untemp
Untitled (VRA) .... unt
Up Center (WDMC) .... uc
Upala [*Costa Rica*] [*Airport symbol*] (AD) .... UPA
Updated (VRA) .... nd
Upernavik [*Greenland*] [*Airport symbol*] (AD) .... UPV
Upholstry (VRA) .... uphol
Upper Peninsula Off Road Vehicle Committee [*Michigan*] .... UPORVC
Upper Peninsula Sportsmen's Alliance .... UPSA
Upstage (WDMC) .... U
Urban and Economic Development Ltd. (AIE) .... URBED
Urban Contemporary (WDMC) .... UC
Urban Education [*A publication*] (BRI) .... Urban Ed
Urban Growth Boundary .... UGB
Urban Programme Authority [*Education*] (AIE) .... UPA
Urfa [*Turkey*] [*Airport symbol*] (AD) .... URF
Uruguay (VRA) .... Uru
US Army Force Integration Staff Agency (RDA) .... USAFISA
USair Express [*ICAO designator*] (AD) .... US
User-to-User Signaling [*Telecommunications*] (DOM) .... UUS
Using Television (WDMC) .... UT
Utensil (VRA) .... utnsl
Utila Island [*Honduras*] [*Airport symbol*] (AD) .... UTL
Utilization Management (WYGK) .... UM
Utne Reader [*A publication*] (BRI) .... Utne R
Uttaradit [*Thailand*] [*Airport symbol*] (AD) .... UTI

V

By Meaning

Vacuum-Assisted Resin Infusion (RDA) .... VARI
Vadso [Norway] [Airport symbol] (AD) .... VDO
Vaengir [ICAO designator] (AD) .... QT
Vagar [Faeroe Islands] [Airport symbol] (AD) .... VAG
Valdez Airlines [ICAO designator] (AD) XX
Valdivia [Chile] [Airport symbol] (AD) .... ZAL
Valetta [Malta] [Airport symbol] (AD) .... MLA
Valle de la Pascua [Venezuela] [Airport symbol] (AD) .... VDP
Vallenar [Chile] [Airport symbol] (AD) .... VLR
Value-Added Reseller .... VAR
Values and Lifestyles Program (WDMC) .... VALS
Vanishing Point (VRA) .... van pt
Vanity Fair [A publication] (WDMC) .... VF
Vanrook [Queensland] [Airport symbol] (AD) .... VNR
Variable Message Formats (RDA) .... VMF
Variable Valve Control [Automotive] VVC
Variable Valve Timing [Automotive] .... VVT
Various (VRA) .... vari
Various Dates (WDMC) .... vd
Various Years (WDMC) .... vy
Varnish (VRA) .... var
Vatican (VRA) .... Vat
Vatomandry [Malagasy] [Airport symbol] (AD) .... VAT
Vault (VRA) .... vlt
Vaxjo [Sweden] [Airport symbol] (AD) .... VAV
Veeneal [ICAO designator] (AD) .... TF
Vellum (VRA) .... vlm
Velvet (VRA) .... vel
Veneer (VRA) .... vnr
Venezuela (VRA) .... Venez
Venous Thromboembolism [Medicine] .... VTE
Ventilator-Associated Pneumonia [Medicine] .... VAP
Ventriloquist (WDMC) .... vent
Ventrolateral Preoptic .... VLPO
Venus-Venus-Earth-Jupiter [Trajectory] .... VVEJ
Verb (WDMC) v
Verifax (VRA) .... verfx
Verse (WDMC) v
Version (WDMC) v
Version (VRA) .... ver
Verso (WDMC) v
Versus (WDMC) v
Versus (WDMC) .... vs
Vertical (WDMC) v
Vertical (WDMC) .... vert
Vertical Tab [Computer science] (DOM) .... VT
Vertically Anchored Tire .... VAT
Very (WDMC) v
Very Long Baseline Interferometry [Used in a space orbiting project] .... VSOP
Very Special [Age of the Cognac] .... VS
Vessel (VRA) .... ves
Vestibule (VRA) .... vstib
Vestment (VRA) .... vstmt
[Department of] Veterans Affairs .... VA
Veterans Affairs Cooperative Study of Systemic Sepsis .... VACSSS
Veterans' Readjustment Benefits Act of 1966 (WYGK) .... VRBA
Viable but Not Culturable [Microbiology] .... VBNC
Vice Versa (WDMC) vv
Vice-Chair of the Board (DD) .... v-chr
Vicenza [Italy] [Airport symbol] (AD) VIC
Vice-President (DD) .... v-p
Vice-Superintendent (DD) .... v-supt
Vichy [France] [Airport symbol] (AD) .... VHY
Vicksburg [Mississippi] [Airport symbol] (AD) .... VKS
Victoria [Chile] [Airport symbol] (AD) .... ZIC
Victoria West [South Africa] [Airport symbol] (AD) .... VCW
Victorian Studies [A publication] (BRI) .... VS

Victory Disc [Music] (WDMC) .... V disc
Video (VRA) v
Video Audio Integrated Operation [Computer science] .... VAIO
Video Datagram Protocol [Computer science] .... VDP
Video Hits One [Cable programming service] (WDMC) VH1
Video Information System [Tandy Corp.] (DOM) .... VIS
Video Round Table [American Library Association] .... VRT
Video User Interface [Computer science] (DOM) .... VUI
Videodisk Recorder (WDMC) .... VDR
Videotape (VRA) .... vtp
Vieques Airlink [ICAO designator] (AD) VI
Vietnam (VRA) .... Vtnm
Vietnam Era Veterans Readjustment and Assistance Act of 1974
    (WYGK) .... VEVRA
Vietnam Prisoners of War [An association] (AD) .... NAMPMW
View (VRA) .... vw
Viewer Controlled Television (WDMC) .... VCTV
Vignette (VRA) .... vgnt
Vila Cabral [Mozambique] [Airport symbol] (AD) VXC
Vila de Joao Belo [Mozambique] [Airport symbol] (AD) .... VJB
Vila Pery [Mozambique] [Airport symbol] (AD) .... VPY
Vilanculos [Mozambique] [Airport symbol] (AD) .... VNX
Vilhena [Brazil] [Airport symbol] (AD) .... BVH
Villa Cisneros [Spanish Sahara] [Airport symbol] (AD) VIL
Villa Dolores [Argentina] [Airport symbol] (AD) .... VDR
Village Voice [A publication] (BRI) VV
Village Voice Literary Supplement [A publication] (BRI) .... VLS
Vinyl (VRA) .... vn
Violetvale [Queensland] [Airport symbol] (AD) .... VIQ
Viqueque [Timor] [Airport symbol] (AD) .... VLK
Virgin Air [ICAO designator] (AD) .... ZP
Virgin Atlantic Airways [ICAO designator] (AD) .... VS
Virgin Gorda [British Virgin Islands] [Airport symbol] (AD) .... VGR
Virginia Quarterly Review [A publication] (BRI) .... VQR
Virtual Address Extension/Virtual Memory System [Computer science]
    (DOM) .... VAX/VMS
Virtual Community of Tomorrow [Internet resource] [Computer science] ...... VCOT
Virtual Home Space Builder .... VHSB
Virtual Pivot Point [Suspension] [Tandem bike] .... VPP
Virus Instructional Code Emulator [Computer science] .... VICE
Virus Neutralization Test [Analytical biochemistry] .... VNT
VirusScan Configuration [Computer science] .... VSC
Visual Exposure Indicator [Advanced photo system] .... VEI
Visual Time Code (WDMC) .... viz-code
Vittel [France] [Airport symbol] (AD) .... VTL
Vizmo (WDMC) .... viz
Vladivostok [USSR] [Airport symbol] (AD) .... VVO
Vocational Preparation Programme (AIE) .... VPP
Voice (WDMC) v
Voice E-Mail Messages [Computer science] .... VEM
Voice of Youth Advocates [A publication] (BRI) .... VOYA
Voice Output Terminal [Computer science] (WDMC) .... VOT
Volcanic (VRA) .... volc
Volos [Greece] [Airport symbol] (AD) .... VOL
Volovan [Malagasy] [Airport symbol] (AD) .... WVV
Volume (WDMC) .... vol
Volume (VRA) .... vol
Voluntary Protection Programs Participants' Association .... VPPPA
Voluntary School (AIE) .... VS
Volunteer Conservation Officers .... VCO
Volunteer Development Scotland (AIE) .... VDS
Volunteer Leadership Development Program [Canada] .... VLDP
Voronezh [USSR] [Airport symbol] (AD) .... VRZ
Votec [ICAO designator] (AD) .... WE
Voussoirs (VRA) .... vsrs
Vowel (WDMC) v
Vrnjacka Banja [Yugoslavia] [Airport symbol] (AD) .... VBN

W
By Meaning

Wabag [*New Guinea*] [*Airport symbol*] (AD) .... WAB
Wad Medani [*Sudan*] [*Airport symbol*] (AD) .... DNI
Wadi Ain [*South Arabia*] [*Airport symbol*] (AD) .... WDA
Wadi Halfa [*Sudan*] [*Airport symbol*] (AD) .... WHA
Wagner Act of 1935 (WYGK) .... WA
Waha Leaf [*British Honduras*] [*Airport symbol*] (AD) .... TZG
Wainscot (VRA) .... wnsct
Wake [*Wake Island, Pacific Ocean*] [*Airport symbol*] (AD) .... AWK
Walker's Cay Air Terminal [*ICAO designator*] (AD) .... XW
Walkway (VRA) .... wlkwy
Wall Paper (VRA) .... wapa
Wall Street Journal [*A publication*] (DFIT) .... WSJ
Wall Street Journal (Eastern Edition) [*A publication*] (BRI) .... WSJ
Wall Street Journal (Midwest Edition) [*A publication*] (BRI) .... WSJ-MW
Walnut (VRA) .... wal
Walrus (VRA) .... wlrs
Walter and Eliza Hall Institute of Medical Research [*Australia*] .... WEH
Wankie [*Zimbabwe*] [*Airport symbol*] (AD) .... WKI
Wankie Game Reserve [*Zimbabwe*] [*Airport symbol*] (AD) .... WKM
Ward Air [*ICAO designator*] (AD) .... WD
Wardens in the South East (AIE) .... WISE
Wardrobe (WDMC) .... w
Ware (VRA) .... wr
Warehouse (VRA) .... wrhs
Warracknabeal [*Victoria, Australia*] [*Airport symbol*] (AD) .... WKB
Wash (VRA) .... wa
Washington Bay [*Alaska*] [*Airport symbol*] (AD) .... WBA
Washington, D.C. (VRA) .... Wash DC
Washington Monthly [*A publication*] (BRI) .... Wash M
Washington Public Power Supply System (DFIT) .... WHOOPS
Wasior [*West Irian, Indonesia*] [*Airport symbol*] (AD) .... WSR
Waspam [*Nicaragua*] [*Airport symbol*] (AD) .... WSP
Water (VRA) .... wtr
Water and Land Resource Utilization Simulation .... WALRUS
Water Authorities Association (AIE) .... WAA
Water Science Laboratories Proprietary Ltd. [*Australia*] .... WSL
Water Studies Centre [*Australia*] [*Chisholm Institute of Technology*] .... WSC
Waterbury [*Connecticut*] [*Airport symbol*] (AD) .... OXC
Watercolor (VRA) .... wc
Watercolor on Paper (VRA) .... wc/pa
Watt (WDMC) .... w
Waverney [*Queensland*] [*Airport symbol*] (AD) .... WAN
Waves on Magnetised Beams and Turbulence .... WOMBAT
Wax (VRA) .... wx
Weak-Lined T Tauri Stars [*Astronomy*] .... WTTS
Weather Report (WDMC) .... WX
Weave (VRA) .... wv
Web (VRA) .... web
Wechsler Objective Reading Dimensions [*Test*] .... WORD
Week (WDMC) .... w
Week (WDMC) .... wk
Week Of (WDMC) .... w/o
Weekly (WDMC) .... w
Weight (WDMC) .... w
Weighted Student Unit .... WSU
Welded (VRA) .... wld
West African Airways [*ICAO designator*] (AD) .... QH
West End [*Grand Bahama Island, Bahamas*] [*Airport symbol*] (AD) .... WTD
West Indies (VRA) .... W Ind
West Virginia Bowhunters Association .... WVBA
Westair Commuter Airlines [*ICAO designator*] (AD) .... VB
Western Airlines [*ICAO designator*] (AD) .... MB
Western American Literature [*A publication*] (BRI) .... WAL
Western Governors University .... WGU
Western Historical Quarterly [*A publication*] (BRI) .... WHQ
Western Humanities Review [*A publication*] (BRI) .... WHR
Western Journalism Center .... WJC
Western Samoa (VRA) .... W Sam
Westkuestenflug [*ICAO designator*] (AD) .... WK
Westminster Centre for Design and Technology [*British*] (AIE) .... WCDT
Westwork (VRA) .... wwk
Whale (VRA) .... wha
Whalehead [*Quebec*] [*Airport symbol*] (AD) .... YWH
What's in It for Me? [*Fundraising*] .... WIIFM
Wheeler Flying Service [*ICAO designator*] (AD) .... WR
Wheeling [*West Virginia*] [*Airport symbol*] (AD) .... HLG

When Push Comes to Shove .... WPCTS
Whistleblower Protection Act of 1989 (WYGK) .... WPA
Whistle-Blowers Integrity in Science and Education [*An association*] .... WISE
White (VRA) .... w
White (WDMC) .... wh
Whole Earth Review [*A publication*] (BRI) .... WER
Why Have You Forsaken Us? [*Fundraising*] .... WHYFU
Wichabai [*Guyana*] [*Airport symbol*] (AD) .... WBG
Wicker (VRA) .... wkr
Wide (WDMC) .... w
Wide (VRA) .... wd
Wide Angle (WDMC) .... WA
Wideros Flyveselskap [*ICAO designator*] (AD) .... WF
Width (WDMC) .... w
Width (VRA) .... wd
Wien Air Alaska [*ICAO designator*] (AD) .... WC
Wife (WDMC) .... w
William and Mary Quarterly [*A publication*] (BRI) .... W&M Q
Williams-Steiger Act of 1970 (WYGK) .... WSA
Wilmington [*California*] [*Airport symbol*] (AD) .... WGM
Wilson Library Bulletin [*A publication*] (BRI) .... WLB
Wilson Quarterly [*A publication*] (BRI) .... Wil Q
Wind Amplified Rotor Platform .... WARP
Wind Amplifier Rotor Platform .... WARP
Window (VRA) .... wndw
Windows 95 [*Computer science*] (WDMC) .... Win 95
Windows Hardware Engineering Conference .... WinHEC
Windows Metafile Format [*Computer science*] .... WMF
Windows-Based Terminal [*Computer science*] .... WBT
Wings Airways [*ICAO designator*] (AD) .... WQ
Wings of Alaska [*ICAO designator*] (AD) .... SE
Wings West [*ICAO designator*] (AD) .... RM
Winona [*Minnesota*] [*Airport symbol*] (AD) .... ONA
Winston-Salem [*North Carolina*] [*Airport symbol*] (AD) .... INT
Wire (VRA) .... wi
Wireless Operationally Linked Electronic and Video Exploration System .... WOLVES
Wiscair [*ICAO designator*] (AD) .... FD
Wisconsin H-Alpha Mapper [*Astrophysics*] .... WHAM
With (VRA) .... w/
With (WDMC) .... w
With All Faults (WDMC) .... waf
Withholding Tax (DFIT) .... W/Tax
Wittenoom Gorge [*Western Australia*] [*Airport symbol*] (AD) .... ITT
Woman Using Television (WDMC) .... WUT
Women Returners Network (AIE) .... WRN
Women Teachers' Franchise Union (AIE) .... WTFU
Women Using Television (WDMC) .... WUT
Women's Air Training Corps .... WATC
Women's Art Association of Canada [*1887, Lyceum Club and Women's Art Association from 1930*] (NGC) .... WAAC
Women's Economic Agenda Project [*An association*] .... WEAP
Women's Education Group (AIE) .... WEDG
Women's Health Study .... WHS
Women's Interagency HIV [*Human Immuno Deficiency Virus*] Study [*Medicine*] .... WIHS
Women's International Art Club, London [*1899*] (NGC) .... WIAC
Women's Interview Study of Health .... WISH
Women's Organization for Mentoring, Education and Networking Unlimited, Inc. .... WOMEN
Women's Review of Books [*A publication*] (BRI) .... Wom R Bks
Women's Wear Daily [*A publication*] (WDMC) .... WWD
Wondoola [*Queensland*] [*Airport symbol*] (AD) .... WON
Wood (VRA) .... wd
Woodblock (VRA) .... wdbl
Woodcut (VRA) .... wdct
Wool (VRA) .... wl
Wool Textile Manufacturers of Australia .... WTMA
Wooroona [*Queensland*] [*Airport symbol*] (AD) .... WOQ
Words per Minute (WDMC) .... wpm
Work and Flop (WDMC) .... W & F
Work and Occupations [*A publication*] (BRI) .... WOC
Work and Turn (WDMC) .... W&T
Work Assessment Course (AIE) .... WAC
Work Based Learning (AIE) .... WBL
Work Hours Act of 1962 (WYGK) .... WHA

Work Injury Reports [*Human Resources*] (WYGK) .... WIR
Work Learning Guide (AIE) .... WLG
Work Preparation (AIE) .... WP
Working Group against Racism in Children's Resources (AIE) .... WGARCR
Working Group on Waterborne Cryptosporidiosis [*Medicine*] .... WGWC
Working Mathematics Group (AIE) .... WMG
Work-Related Education and Training (AIE) .... WRET
World Airways [*ICAO designator*] (AD) .... WO
World & I [*A publication*] (BRI) .... W&I
World Association of Commercial and Special Vehicle Editors .... ACE
World Catalog of International Chemical Equipment [*A publication*] .... WOICE
World Equity Benchmark Shares [*Investment term*] .... WEBS
World Literature Today [*A publication*] (BRI) .... WLT

World Politics [*A publication*] (BRI) .... WP
World Wide Wait [*Computer science*] .... WWW
WorldViews: A Quarterly Review of Resources for Education and Action
    [*A publication*] (BRI) .... WorldV
Worldwide Port System [*Army*] (RDA) .... WPS
Worldwide Television News Corp. (WDMC) .... WTN
Woven (VRA) .... wv
Write-Once, Read-Many [*Computer science*] .... WORM
Wrong Font [*Publishing*] (WDMC) .... wf
Wrotham Park [*Queensland*] [*Airport symbol*] (AD) .... WKP
Wrought (VRA) .... wrt
WS and LB Robinson University College [*Australia*] .... WSLBRUC
Wyandotte [*Queensland*] [*Airport symbol*] (AD) .... WYD

X-Y-Z
By Meaning

Xapuri [*Brazil*] [*Airport symbol*] (AD) .... XAY
Xieng Khouang [*Laos*] [*Airport symbol*] (AD) .... XIE
Xique-Xique [*Brazil*] [*Airport symbol*] (AD) .... XIQ
Xograph (VRA) .... XOGP
Yachting [*A publication*] (BRI) .... Yacht
Yacuiba [*Bolivia*] [*Airport symbol*] (AD) .... YAC
Yahoo Internet Life [*Computer science*] .... YIL
Yale Law Journal [*A publication*] (BRI) .... YLJ
Yale Review [*A publication*] (BRI) .... YR
Yalova [*Turkey*] [*Airport symbol*] (AD) .... TYA
Yandina [*Solomon Islands*] [*Airport symbol*] (AD) .... YND
Yarn (VRA) .... ya
Year (WDMC) .... y
Yellow (VRA) .... yel
Yellow, Magenta, Cyan, Black (WDMC) .... YMCK
Yellowstone to Canada's Yukon Territory Y2Y
Yemen Airways [*ICAO designator*] (AD) .... IY
Yes Bay [*Alaska*] [*Airport symbol*] (AD) .... WYC
Yet Another Hierarchically Officious Oracle [*World Wide Web*] (DOM) .... Yahoo
Yorkshire and Humberside Council for Further and Higher Education
   [*British*] (AIE) .... YHCFE
Yoro [*Honduras*] [*Airport symbol*] (AD) .... YOR
Yosemite Airlines [*ICAO designator*] (AD) .... JE
Young Adult Library Services Association [*American Library
   Association*] .... YALSA
Young National Party of Australia [*Political party*] .... YNPA
Young Person (AIE) .... YP
Younger (VRA) .... ygr
Young-of-the-Year [*Conservation*] .... YOY
Your Business [*A publication*] .... YB
Youth Affairs Lobby (AIE) .... YAL
Youth Education and Training Innovators (AIE) .... YETI
Youth Enterprise (AIE) .... YE
Youth Female [*International Bowhunting Organization*] [*Class Equipment*] .... YF
Youth Initiative Project (AIE) .... YIP

Youth Male Fingers [*International Bowhunting Organization*] [*Class
   Equipment*] .... YMF
Youth Male Release [*International Bowhunting Organization*] [*Class
   equipment*] .... YMR
Youth Training (AIE) .... YT
Youth Training Programme [*British*] (AIE) .... YTP
Youth Work Unit [*National Youth Bureau*] (AIE) .... YWU
Yucca (VRA) .... yuc
Yugoslav Airlines [*ICAO designator*] (AD) .... JU
Yugoslavia (VRA) .... Yugo
Yule Island [*New Guinea*] [*Airport symbol*] (AD) .... YLE
Zambia (VRA) .... Zam
Zambia Airways [*ICAO designator*] (AD) .... QZ
Zanderij [*Surinam*] [*Airport symbol*] (AD) .... ZAN
Zanesville [*Ohio*] [*Airport symbol*] (AD) .... ZZV
Zanzibar (VRA) .... Zanz
Zaporozhe [*USSR*] [*Airport symbol*] (AD) .... ZAP
Zaria [*Nigeria*] [*Airport symbol*] (AD) .... ZAR
Zero (WDMC) .... z
Zero Administration for Windows [*Microsoft Corp.*] [*Computer science*] .... ZAW
Zero Administration Initiative for Windows [*Microsoft Corp.*] [*Computer
   science*] .... ZAW
Zero Administration Kit [*Computer science*] .... ZAK
Zero Based Analysis .... ZBA
Zero on Originality (WDMC) .... ZOO
Zero Quality Control .... ZQC
Zia Airlines [*ICAO designator*] (AD) .... ZU
Ziggurat (VRA) .... zig
Zinc (VRA) .... zi
Zip Code Attachment Program [*Computer science*] (WDMC) .... ZAP
Zomba [*Malawi*] [*Airport symbol*] (AD) .... ZOM
Zone (WDMC) .... z
Zone of Peace, Freedom and Neutrality [*ASEAN*] .... ZOPFAN
Zonguldak [*Turkey*] [*Airport symbol*] (AD) .... ZDK
Zoologische Staatssammlung Muenchen .... ZSM
Zoomorphism (VRA) .... zmphm